# Macroeconomic Theory

**STEPHEN McCAFFERTY**

*The Ohio State University*

1817

**HARPER & ROW, PUBLISHERS, New York**

Grand Rapids, Philadelphia, St. Louis, San Francisco,
London, Singapore, Sydney, Tokyo

Sponsoring Editor: John Greenman
Project Editor: David Nickol
Art Direction: Heather A. Ziegler
Cover Coordinator: Mary Archondes
Cover Design: Heather A. Ziegler
Production: Beth Maglione

**Macroeconomic Theory**

**Library of Congress Cataloging-in-Publication Data**

McCafferty, Stephen.
   Macroeconomic theory / Stephen McCafferty.
      p.    cm.
   Includes bibliographical references.
   ISBN 0-06-044324-3
    1. Macroeconomics.  I. Title.
HB172.5.M365  1990                       89-19932
339—dc20                             CIP

89  90  91  92  9  8  7  6  5  4  3  2  1

# Contents

# PART TWO

## Dynamic, Deterministic Macroeconomic Models    127

# PART THREE

## Stochastic Macroeconomics Models and Recent Topics in Macroeconomic Theory    321

# Preface

The book offers first-year Ph.D. students and mathematically well prepared masters students in economics an introduction to graduate-level macroeconomic theory. The primary goal of the text is to provide students whose backgrounds end with intermediate undergraduate macroeconomics the necessary foundation for more advanced course work and the ability to follow current developments in the field as presented in major scholarly economics journals. Alternatively, this text can also serve the needs of advanced undergraduate students who have some background in calculus and are seriously entertaining the possibility of graduate study in economics.

Motivation for this project grew out of experience teaching macroeconomics to first-year graduate students in economics and related disciplines at The Ohio State University from 1978 through 1989. Dissatisfaction with a large gap in the levels of presentation between undergraduate texts and more advanced graduate-level texts led me to abandon the practice of assigning a primary textbook in favor of providing students with an extensive set of class notes as their principal source of reading material, supplemented with assigned readings of journal articles and selected portions of several undergraduate- and graduate-level textbooks. Those class notes are the direct antecedent of this textbook.

Economics is a discipline in which undergraduate courses are taught from a perspective of primarily verbal, intuitive arguments, supplemented with a light use of graphs and algebra. Graduate-level training, however, is articulated with a heavily technical orientation. My experience in teaching beginning-level graduate students is that many of them find this transition to be a very difficult one to master. It is my hope that this book will provide an easier introduction to the world of modern, professional macroeconomic analysis.

## SCOPE AND STRUCTURE OF THE BOOK

Macroeconomics is a particularly difficult branch of economics to study, because there is no basic, universally accepted paradigm. Older-style models posited what were hoped to be reasonable behavioral relationships and studied the market equilibrium consequences of such assumptions. More recent work in macroeconomics builds models up from the constrained optimizing behavior of economic agents, with explicit market interactions playing a secondary role in the analysis. Unfortunately, the older and more recent models are not always closely comparable, and recently constructed alternative models are often built on considerably different economic landscapes. It is my hope that the present text adequately spans both macroeconomic models of differing vintages and recent macroeconomic models that cover differing terrains.

The plan of study of this text centers on differing modeling styles and differing analytical tools. Part One of this text analyzes static, deterministic models. Although such models can be presented as being entirely ad hoc in nature, and were often originally presented in such an ad hoc manner, appendixes to Chapters 1 and 2 demonstrate that such models also emerge as the solutions to some specific, yet simple, dynamic optimization problems.

Chapter 1 carefully lays out the basic macroeconomic building blocks, and Chapter 2 then presents a comprehensive analysis of simultaneous equilibrium in product and financial markets. This analysis follows the classical tradition of price flexibility and full contemporaneous information on the part of all economic agents. The underlying philosophy of presentation is that students can only appreciate the economic problems inherent in slowly adjusting prices and expectations if they have first mastered the equilibrium properties of the classical model, since it is toward this equilibrium that most such disequilibrium models adjust over time.

Chapter 3 then presents the standard fixed-price Keynesian model. This model is presented as a particular limiting form of the classical model of Chapter 2 in order to highlight important similarities and differences. Analysis in this chapter makes clear the importance of the issue of price flexibility for the study of macroeconomic policy effects.

Part Two of this book studies dynamic, deterministic macroeconomic models. Chapter 4 presents a self-contained introduction to dynamic macroeconomic model building. This chapter permits students whose primary mathematical training ends with differential and integral calculus to successfully handle the basic dynamic models presented in later chapters and encountered elsewhere in the macroeconomics literature. Emphasis here is on the application of second order, linear, constant coefficient differential equation models to economic analysis.

Chapter 5 reintroduces the labor market, first analyzing the possibilities of intertemporal substitution and incomplete information in the labor-supply function, and then showing how these considerations affect the workings of the classical macroeconomic model. Chapter 5 also presents a simple dynamic analysis of wage- and price-level expectation adjustment. This model offers a rich menu of possible wage-employment dynamics and also allows study of instantaneous wage and expectation adjustment as natural special cases.

Chapters 6 and 7 consider the effects of inflation on financial, goods, and labor markets. The analysis of these chapters stresses how the flows of additional money and bonds already introduced in Chapter 2 generate inflation over time and the restrictions the government budget constraint places on the growth of these government liabilities over time. Emphasis here is on inflation as a steady-state result of such growth over time in the stocks of government liabilities. Chapter 6 analyzes the effects of such inflation on nominal and real interest rates, and Chapter 7 discusses unemployment, inflation, and the Phillips Curve, both in the context of search theoretic labor market models and in the context of disequilibrium analyses of the labor market.

Chapter 8 introduces the effects of capital accumulation over time. The basic premise of this analysis is that economic growth is not an obscure separate topic of economics but rather that capital accumulation is simply a generally overlooked by-product of the functioning of most standard macroeconomic models. This perspective permits a natural discussion of the effects of government fiscal and inflation policies on the equilibrium capital intensity. Chapter 9 then concludes the study of dynamic models with an explicitly dynamic treatment of international trade and finance.

Chapter 10 introduces the student to the stochastic models that dominate Part Three of the text. Topics here include the use of difference equations, the signal extraction problem, and an introduction to rationally formed expectations. Chapter 11 then presents an analysis of policymaking under uncertainty. While Chapter 11 highlights models that pose the idea of activist government policy in its best light, the analysis of Chapter 12 highlights the policy ineffectiveness proposition that holds in many classically oriented stochastic macromodels. Chapter 12 also introduces strategic aspects of monetary policy, and addresses the time-inconsistency problem.

Chapters 13 through 16 attempt to summarize some of the more important recent topics in macroeconomic theory. Chapter 13 emphasizes the potential role of labor contracts as a way for employers to provide their employees with insurance against adverse movements in relative prices, and then discusses how costly contracting, while solving the problem of wage-setting in the face of short-run conditions of bilateral monopoly, simultaneously exposes the contracting parties to possibilities of ex post inefficiencies. Finally, Chapter 13 discusses the scope for government policy rules to help mitigate the effects of these inefficiencies.

Chapter 14 presents an analysis of equilibrium stochastic monetary models. In such models, confusion between real and nominal disturbances has the potential of generating economic inefficiencies. However, monetary policy is generally only able to exacerbate the informational difficulties that lead to such inefficiencies in these types of models.

Chapters 15 and 16 present some important recent topics of research of the classical and Keynesian schools of thought in macroeconomics. Chapter 15 analyzes real business-cycle models that hope to explain many features of typical patterns of macroeconomic fluctuations, as the result of stochastic shifts in the aggregate production function. Chapter 16 first discusses efficiency wage models that hope to generate Keynesian-style unemployment as an equilibrium outcome. Chapter 16 then discusses monopolistically competitive macroeconomic models in which firms' optimizing responses to seemingly inconsequential price-changing costs can lead to large-scale aggregate level inefficiencies.

## ACKNOWLEDGMENTS

Many individuals have contributed to the development of this textbook. Richard Cantor and Robert Driskill have worked closely with me in the presentation of this material to graduate students at The Ohio State University throughout the years. Colleagues Stephen Cecchetti and Pok-sang Lam provided me with some important help in digesting and expositing the material presented in Chapters 15 and 16. Roger Craine and Case Sprenkle read early partial versions, and Christopher Ellis, John Haltiwanger, Peter Howitt, and Thomas Potiowsky all read various versions of the manuscript in its entirety. They all provided many excellent suggestions for improvement. Jeanette White typed much of the original material that appears in this book, when it was in its early, "class notes" stage. Finally, and most importantly, an entire generation of graduate students at Ohio State has had the patience to allow me to work toward what I hope is a much smoother and more comprehensible version of the material in this book.

*Stephen McCafferty*

# PART ONE

## STATIC, DETERMINISTIC MACROECONOMIC MODELS

# Chapter **1**

## **Introduction**

Macroeconomics is the study of the measurement and analysis of broadly constructed aggregate indices of economic performance. These indices include measures of total economywide production and employment and measures of the average prices paid for the goods and services produced.

This chapter examines the ways in which these macroeconomic measures are constructed and gives a broad overview of a strategy for analyzing macroeconomic problems and issues. Section 1.1 provides an introduction to some of the more important questions macroeconomists seek to answer. These basic questions reappear again and again in the course of our study. Section 1.1 also defines several key macroeconomic indicators and explains how they are measured. Finally, Section 1.1 introduces the reader to the general modeling strategy employed throughout the text.

Section 1.2 shifts attention to the specific details of macroeconomic modeling. In this section, we introduce the reader to the strategy of aggregating commodities into composite commodities and aggregating agents across sectors into representative households, firms, and government. Section 1.2 then postulates behavioral relationships for these representative agents that attempt to capture these agents' interactions in the markets for goods, labor services, earning assets, and money.

These behavioral relationships postulated in Section 1.2 are not, however, derived from rigorous microeconomic foundations. This admittedly ad hoc modeling strategy reflects an attempt to provide as much intuition as possible for those readers with a minimum level of technical expertise. A much more formal, mathematical treatment of representative firm and representative household behavior is presented in appendixes to this chapter.

## 1.1 BASIC CONCEPTS AND DEFINITIONS

In macroeconomics, we study production and exchange in a small number of interrelated, highly aggregated markets. In each market, interest focuses first on measuring the average quantity of the good produced in that market, the average absolute price of products sold in that market, and the average price of that good relative to the prices of goods transacted in other markets. Once we have carefully identified the nature of the variables we are interested in, attention then shifts to attempts to explain movements in these variables over time and attempts to predict how these variables might respond to policy actions and other changes in the economic environment.

### Macroeconomic Questions

Our primary macroeconomic concern is the aggregate level of production or output of goods and services. The most well-known such measure of production or output is gross national product, a measure defined in some detail below. Movements in this broad output measure are thought to be closely related to movements in the levels of employment of factors of production, chiefly labor and capital. Macroeconomists are therefore also interested in the levels of employment and unemployment of workers, labor force participation, capital formation, and capital utilization and how these measures move over time.

Broad price indexes like the consumer price index, the producer price index, and the implicit gross national product deflator attempt to measure the average prices of various components of gross national product. An important part of the study of macroeconomics is concerned with explaining changes in the level of product prices and the rate of change in these prices over time, or the rate of price inflation.

Another important topic of concern to macroeconomists is the analysis of credit markets. Here interest centers on how the volume of transactions in credit markets interacts with the levels of activity in other sectors of the economy. An important part of this study focuses on theories of the determination of interest rates and the prices of earning assets like stocks and bonds.

Increasingly over time, macroeconomists have come to be interested in the volume of international transactions. Such transactions are summarized in the levels of imports and exports of goods and services, the balance of trade and the balance of payments, and the rates of exchange between national currencies.

Finally, much of macroeconomics is concerned with how actions taken by the government affect the level and composition of economic activity. Specific attention attaches to the levels of government spending, taxation, budget surpluses and deficits, and government issuance of money and debt instruments.

A major goal of macroeconomics is to provide a thoroughly convincing and logically consistent explanation of an empirical phenomenon referred to as the ''business cycle.'' Business cycle analysis is concerned with a series of stylized facts about interrelationships among economic time series. In particular, the conventional wisdom is in agreement on the existence of strong positive correlations between measures of output, production, employment, consumption, investment, prices, real wages, and the money supply. Furthermore, there is also evidence of serial correlation in most of these time series. While many of our theories provide explanations of many aspects of these comovements taken individually, most such explanations are in conflict with one or more of the other co-movements we observe.

Other important questions for study include the effects of monetization of exchange and potential sources of aggregate market failures that preclude the realization of Pareto-optimal allocations. Since the medium that circulates as money is typically a liability of government, we also consider government liability management behavior, government issue of interest-bearing debt, and whether the structure of government liabilities affects the allocation of resources. Potential sources of market failure include the possibility that the price system may fail to exhaust all mutually beneficial exchanges and that agents may lack complete information about their opportunities for advantageous transactions. Another important topic of consideration is the optimal intertemporal allocation of resources and the related decision to divert current production to provide additional future productive capacity.

A final topic that unifies all of the other concerns about the macroeconomy is the question of the appropriate conduct of macroeconomic policy. If we judge macroeconomic performance to be less than ideal, does this observation necessarily imply that government actions are likely to improve such performance in any way? If government policy can be beneficial, what sorts of policies are optimal? Finally, is it possible that such government macroeconomic policy may be totally ineffective or perhaps even counterproductive? Such policy questions remain a prominent feature of most of the discussions in later chapters.

## Macroeconomic Measurements: Income and Product Accounting

Our interest in macroeconomics focuses primarily on analysis of the current level of production of a composite good that provides utility for households and may be used as an input in future production. Gross national product (GNP) is the nominal or dollar value of production of this composite good per unit of time. The study of national income accounting provides useful classifications of components of the level of production of this composite good.

Product accounting classifies components of production by measuring the levels of production going to different groups of final purchasers. In a closed economy, these purchasers include households, business firms, and the government. We identify household spending as consumption and business firm spending as investment. We therefore have

$$
\begin{aligned}
\text{GNP} &= C + I + G \\
&= \text{consumption} + \text{investment} + \text{government spending} \\
&= \text{household spending} + \text{business firm spending} \\
&\quad + \text{government spending}.
\end{aligned}
\tag{1.1.1}
$$

By definition, income of all economic agents must exactly exhaust total production. Since business firms and the government are simply agents of households, all income ultimately accrues to households. Income received by households may be spent on final output (consumption) or paid to the government (taxes). Savings is defined as that part of total income left over from consumption and payment of taxes. Income accounting classifies total output by the way in which households allocate the income they receive from the production of output. We therefore define

$$\text{GNP} = C + S + T$$
$$= \text{consumption} + \text{saving} + \text{taxes}.$$

(1.1.2)

In addition to the usefulness these classifications present to statisticians, they provide a natural starting point for economic analysis. Product accounting suggests a disaggregation of economic agents into households, business firms, and government units. Income accounting suggests a natural focus on household consumption behavior. Study of households' intertemporal allocation of income and the implications of this choice process for the consumption-saving decision is a prominent feature of macroeconomic analysis.

The way we define the components of income and product accounts ensures that

$$C + I + G = C + S + T$$

(1.1.3)

or

$$I + G = S + T.$$

(1.1.4)

In the absence of government, this relationship is the familiar investment-savings identity, $I = S$. This relationship holds as an identity because actual investment and savings are simply two names we give to the same concept. Savings is that part of income households do not spend on consumption. Investment includes firm expenditures on new productive capacity and additions to inventory. Because investment includes all additions to inventory, whether planned by business or not, investment includes all production not bought by households. Therefore, in the absence of government, actual investment and savings both measure current production not purchased by households.

## Macroeconomic Measurements: Prices and Inflation

Gross national product accounts measure nominal or dollar amounts. We are more interested in actual physical quantities. Since output, $y$, times price, $P$, equals the dollar amount, we have

$$\text{GNP} = yP.$$

(1.1.5)

We therefore need to deflate nominal magnitudes by a price index to get measures of real magnitudes. We define real values of GNP, consumption, investment, and government spending as follows:

$$y = \text{gnp} = \frac{\text{GNP}}{P} = \frac{C}{P} + \frac{I}{P} + \frac{G}{P}$$
$$= c + i + g.$$

(1.1.6)

We denote real quantities by lowercase letters. To measure the price of aggregate gross national product, we use a composite index, the GNP deflator. This index is the ratio of nominal to real gross national product:

$$P \equiv \frac{\text{GNP}}{\text{gnp}}.$$

(1.1.7)

Much of our analysis centers on theories of the determination of the magnitude of this composite index. Furthermore, in addition to our interest in the level of prices, we also have a great deal of interest in the rate of change in prices over time. In particular, the rate of inflation measures the percentage rate of change in the price level per unit of time. That is, denoting the rate of inflation as $\pi$, we have

$$\pi \equiv \frac{1}{P}\frac{dP}{dt}. \tag{1.1.8}$$

Study of factors influencing the determination of the rate of inflation is a central topic of Chapter 6.

## Macroeconomic Methods

When analyzing anything as large and complex as an entire industrialized economy, it is necessary to abstract from most of the important institutional details of production and exchange. We hope to represent or simulate the behavior of the more important aspects of the workings of such economies by studying the behavior of model economies. These model economies are designed to be optimal simplifications of reality. We try to closely portray the end results of market interactions rather than trying to closely mimic the processes in which these outcomes occur.

Such models are the tools of the trade in macroeconomics. They can generally be presented in several equivalent representations. Such representations include diagrams, mathematical models, and verbal descriptions. Most of our analyses are conducted by means of mathematical modeling. However, we gain significant added insight by providing graphical analyses and intuitive verbal descriptions as complementary methods of analysis. As long as our modeling is done carefully and correctly, all three tools of analysis give consistent answers to economic problems.

In these models, we attempt to simulate the effects of exogenous disturbances on the economic variables that are of interest to us. These exogenous disturbances include changes in policy settings and changes in the economic environment, such as changes in tastes and technology. Our fundamental aim is to present models as mappings between sets of assumptions and sets of conclusions in the form of specific effects of disturbances on economic variables.

Our hope is that the models we study help us to understand interrelationships between different groups of markets and different groups of economic agents. We also hope to shed light on historical patterns of relationships between different observable economic time series. We finally hope to be able to generate recommendations for the effective conduct of macroeconomic policy.

The principal component parts of our economic models include identities and definitions, hypothesized behavioral relationships, and equilibrium conditions. Identities and definitions are mechanical relationships among the economic variables in our models that always hold independent of any particular set of assumptions we may wish to employ about agents' behavior. Behavioral assumptions are the links we hypothesize between agents' actions in the markets they participate in and the relative prices and other constraints they may face. Such behavioral relationships include our specifications of supplies and demands in the markets we choose to study. Finally, equilibrium conditions allow us to find those values of prices and other economic variables consistent with the coordination of agent behavior implied by market interaction of agents' behavioral relationships. Frequently, but not exclusively, such interaction is in the form of market-clearing conditions imposed by competitive market forces.

The variables we use to quantify economic magnitudes in our models consist of exogenous and endogenous variables and constants and parameters. Exogenous variables are those magnitudes we take as given from outside the realm of our model. Endogenous variables are those magnitudes whose behavior our models are designed to explain. Constants and parameters are those parts of the economic landscape whose values are taken as given—that is, their determination is not considered part of the problem at hand. Basic types of constants and parameters include technical parameters, behavioral parameters, and institutional constants and parameters.

Technical parameters include parameters of production functions or parameters of the transaction technology. Behavioral parameters include those elements underlying the characteristics of supply and demand. These elements could include coefficients in utility functions, discount rates, or measures of risk aversion. Institutional constants or parameters might include legally fixed magnitudes like reserve requirements or tax rates.

The basic problem in macroeconomic modeling is to relate the time paths of the endogenous variables to the time paths of the exogenous variables and the parameters of the problem at hand. The solution of these reduced-form equations is the goal of our analytical efforts.

While the main focus of macroeconomics, as distinct from microeconomics, is the determination of broad aggregate economic magnitudes, we always need remember that economics is a unified discipline with a unified approach to analyzing problems. We therefore identify economic behavior as much as possible with the constrained optimization of economic agents. We also highlight the key roles of tastes and factor endowments and the importance of production and exchange technologies.

Although there is a longstanding tradition in macroeconomics of placing primary emphasis on analyses of aggregate output and price levels, there is also a renewed interest in the more classical orientation toward analyses of the determination of relative prices. Classical economic theory suggests that equilibrium levels of production and exchange are optimal agent responses to relative price signals. In the one-good models we study, we must also remember that the aggregate price level is not the relative price of anything. In such one-good economies, the fundamental relative price ratios are the terms of trade between goods delivered at different points in time. We therefore put renewed interest in analyses of the determination of such intertemporal relative price ratios.

## 1.2 REPRESENTATIVE AGENTS AND COMPOSITE COMMODITIES

As suggested by the terminology of national income accounting, we disaggregate the economy into households, business firms, and governments and use these same sectoral distinctions in analyzing economic behavior. We postulate a large number of identical or representative households and another large number of representative firms. All government economic activities are aggregated into a single governmental entity.

Each set of firms and households behaves in a competitive manner. We also assume that all households have identical tastes and endowments. All firms have identical production functions and identical predetermined amounts of physical capital. These assumptions allow us to treat the firm sector as one single aggregate firm and the household sector as one single aggregate household. Behavior of the government is treated as exogenous.

In addition to our aggregation of agents into sectors, we also aggregate economic goods into composite commodities. We may then characterize general equilibrium in our model economy by specifying market-clearing conditions that equalize the supplies and demands of the representative agents in each of the composite commodity markets. The remainder of this section first characterizes the individual composite commodity markets and then specifies assumptions about how firms, households, and the government behave in each of those markets. Since the remainder of this section introduces a substantial amount of notation, the reader should be aware that all of the notation in Chapter 1 is summarized in Appendix 1.A.

## Markets in Composite Commodities

In macroeconomics, we emphasize market interactions. The study of macroeconomics is the analysis of solutions to general equilibrium problems. In order to keep things tractable, we need to limit ourselves to a small number of composite commodities. The traditional choices are

1. labor services,
2. goods,
3. earning assets, and
4. money.

Labor services are inputs into the production process organized by firms. These labor services are owned by households who sell them to firms. Labor services are measured in hours worked per unit of time. We denote employment of labor services by $\ell$. We denote the nominal wage rate paid to workers per unit of time by $W$.

Goods are produced by firms. The single good can be consumed by households, used by firms to augment their stock of capital, or bought by the government to be distributed as public goods. While the assumption of such a multipurpose good is clearly unrealistic, it greatly simplifies the analysis. Without this sort of assumption macroeconomics becomes intractable. Production of the composite good is measured in goods produced per unit of time and is denoted by $y$. The nominal price of a unit of output is denoted by $P$.

Earning assets are a composite for all financial claims that earn a return. Earning assets are distinct from money, which earns no explicit interest. To simplify matters, we assume that there are only two types of earning assets: bonds, issued by the government, and equities, issued by firms. We therefore explicitly ignore the possibility of debt finance by firms.

Government bonds are perpetuities paying $1 per year. These bonds are sold by the government to households in exchange for money. Denote the price of a bond by $P_b$. The rate of return on bonds, $r_b$, is the discount factor that equates the price of a bond with the present value of its stream of interest payments. We assume that interest payments to holders of government bonds are made in the form of a continuous stream. We therefore find that

$$P_b = \int_0^\infty (\$1)e^{-r_b t} \, dt = \frac{\$1}{r_b} = \text{nominal bond price.} \tag{1.2.1}$$

The real value of a bond is its price deflated by the aggregate price level (the price of goods). We therefore find that

$$\text{Value of one bond in units of goods} = \frac{1}{r_b P}. \tag{1.2.2}$$

If there are $B$ bonds outstanding, then the real value of the aggregate bond supply is given by $B/r_b P$.

Equities are issued by firms to finance the purchase of new capital. Since we assume that all previous acquisitions of capital were also equity financed, equity holders are the sole owners of the firms and have claim to all firm profits. We further assume that all such profits are paid out in a continuous stream to equity holders as dividends as soon as these profits are realized—that is, we ignore the possibility of retained earnings.

Denote the nominal price of a unit of equity as $P_e$. Nominal dividend payments to equity holders are given by $P\Pi$, where $\Pi$ denotes the real value of firm profits. The return on equity, $r_e$, is the discount rate that, when applied to expected dividends, equates the present value of future dividends per share with the price of an equity claim. If we further assume that all economic agents expect current real profits and current prices to remain constant over time into the indefinite future, then we have

$$P_e = \int_0^\infty \frac{P\Pi}{E} e^{-r_e t} \, dt = \frac{P\Pi}{r_e E} \tag{1.2.3}$$

where $E$ denotes the number of equities outstanding. The real value of an equity is therefore given by

$$\text{Value of one unit of equity in terms of goods} = \frac{P_e}{P} = \frac{\Pi}{r_e E} \tag{1.2.4}$$

If there are $E$ equities outstanding, the real value of total equity will be $\Pi/r_e$.

Assume that labor and capital are the only factors of production and that the representative firm owns all capital. Real profits $\Pi$ must therefore satisfy

$$P\Pi = Py - W\ell. \tag{1.2.5}$$

If we further assume that the labor market is competitive, that the representative firm's employment of labor equates the marginal product of labor with the real wage, and that the production function is linearly homogeneous, then we obtain

$$\Pi = y - \frac{W}{P}\ell = \frac{\partial \Phi}{\partial K} K \equiv RK, \tag{1.2.6}$$

where $K$ denotes the capital stock, and production is governed by the relationship $y = \Phi(\ell, K)$. The symbol $R$ denotes the marginal product of capital, $\partial \Phi/\partial K$.

The total nominal value of equity is now given by

$$P_e E = \frac{P\Pi}{r_e} = \frac{PRK}{r_e}.$$

(1.2.7)

The real value of equity is therefore

$$\frac{P_e E}{P} = \frac{\Pi}{r_e} = \frac{RK}{r_e}.$$

(1.2.8)

We have already noted that new goods may be used to augment the stock of capital. Therefore, at current prices, the replacement value of the capital stock is $PK$. Tobin (1969) emphasizes the importance of the ratio of the current market value of the capital stock (the market value of all equity) to the replacement cost of the capital stock. This ratio, which is often referred to as Tobin's $q$, is equal to $R/r_e$. Subsequent analysis demonstrates that investment spending is likely to be positively related to this ratio.

In most of what follows we assume that bonds and equities are viewed as perfect substitutes. We therefore abstract from default risk and the risk of dividend variability. In such an integrated earning asset market competitive forces equate the returns on equities and bonds. We therefore have

$$r = \text{rate of return on earning assets} = r_b = r_e.$$

(1.2.9)

We also refer to $r$ as the rate of interest.

Money is used in transactions. Money is issued by the government and earns no explicit interest. Denote the quantity of money in circulation as $M$, measured in dollars. The real value of the money supply in purchasing power over goods is given by $M/P$.

## Firm Behavior

Firms own all of the capital goods and employ labor services to produce and sell output. Firms also distribute all profits to equity holders and sell new equity to finance current investment spending. Furthermore, such investment spending is the only way that firms can change the amount of capital that they own; that is, we explicitly rule out the possibility of a market in existing capital goods. Therefore, at any point in time, firms make contingency plans for the entire future time paths of employment of labor and ownership of capital. Although a formal, dynamic analysis of this decision problem is deferred until Appendix 1.B, the present section studies the representative firm's problem in a more intuitive, less technical manner.

In the absence of depreciation we require that the flow increase in nominal equity equals the nominal flow level of investment spending,

$$P_e \, dE = P \, dK,$$

(1.2.10)

where $K$ denotes the capital stock of the representative firm. Denote the level of desired real investment, which is the desired rate of change in the capital stock, by $i^d$. Denote the nominal value of new equity issued by the representative firm per unit of time by $P_e(dE/dt)$. Denote the real flow supply of new equity issued by the representative firm by

$\dot{e}^s$. The representative firm's finance constraint therefore requires that

$$i^d = \dot{e}^s. \tag{1.2.11}$$

Let us now examine the representative firm's investment decision in some detail. Our analysis of the investment process follows closely that of Jorgenson (1963). In the absence of adjustment costs, the representative firm employs labor, purchases capital, and sells equity shares to maximize the market value of existing equity. With the number of outstanding shares predetermined, this amounts to maximizing the price of an existing share. Recall that share prices are given by

$$P_e = \frac{P}{E} \int_0^\infty \left[ \Phi(\ell, K) - \frac{W}{P}\ell \right] e^{-r_e t} \, dt \tag{1.2.12}$$

Because the representative firm expects $r_e$ to be constant and because, in the absence of adjustment costs, the optimal paths of $\ell$ and $K$ are constant over time, this equation can be rewritten as

$$P_e = \frac{P}{r_e E} \left[ \Phi(\ell, K) - \frac{W}{P}\ell \right]. \tag{1.2.13}$$

We further assume that the representative firm is a price taker with respect to $P$, $W/P$, and $r_e$. The first-order conditions for the representative firm's maximization problem are therefore given by

$$\frac{dP_e}{d\ell} = \frac{P}{r_e E} \left[ \frac{\partial \Phi}{\partial \ell} - \frac{W}{P} \right] = 0, \tag{1.2.14}$$

$$\frac{dP_e}{dK} = \frac{P}{r_e E} \frac{\partial \Phi}{\partial K} - \frac{P[\Phi(\ell, K) - (W/P)\ell]}{r_e E^2} \frac{dE}{dK} = 0. \tag{1.2.15}$$

The first of these conditions generates the standard labor demand curve. Additional labor is employed until the marginal product of labor equals the real wage. Recalling the firm's finance constraint, $dE/dK = P/P_e$, the second of these conditions can be rewritten as

$$\frac{\partial \Phi}{\partial K} = \frac{[\Phi(\ell, K) - (W/P)\ell]}{E} \frac{P}{P_e}. \tag{1.2.16}$$

Recalling that the representative firm's profits, $\Pi = \Phi - (W/P)\ell$, are given by $RK$, we obtain

$$\frac{\partial \Phi}{\partial K} = \frac{PRK}{P_e E}. \tag{1.2.17}$$

However, we have already shown that

$$r_e = \frac{PRK}{P_e E}. \tag{1.2.18}$$

Therefore, the optimal value of the capital stock, $K^*$, equates the marginal product of capital with the rate of return on capital:

$$R = \frac{\partial \Phi}{\partial K} = r_e. \tag{1.2.19}$$

The determination of the optimal capital stock is depicted in Figure 1.1.

To get some additional intuitive insight into the meaning of the first-order condition $R = r_e$, let us consider what happens when the representative firm issues new equity and uses the proceeds to buy new capital. Because the equity market is competitive, new equity can only be sold if the new shareholders are promised a percentage return on that holding equal to $r_e$. Therefore, one unit of goods worth of new equity costs the firm a perpetual flow of $r_e$ units of goods per unit of time. The proceeds of the sale of the equity is then used by the firm to buy one new unit of production, which is then installed as one additional unit of capital. However, the net return per unit of time to the firm from installing the new unit of capital is just equal to the marginal product of capital, $R$. Therefore, if $R > r_e$, the new shareholders can be paid their required return, and existing shareholders get to split the difference between $R$ and $r_e$. As long as $R > r_e$, it is therefore in the interest of the firm's existing shareholders for the firm to expand its holdings of new capital goods.

Alternatively, we can also look at the investment decision from the point of view of the cost of new capital goods versus the market value of existing capital goods. The cost of a new unit of capital is simply equal to the cost of a new unit of output, $P$. To calculate the market value of an existing unit of capital, divide the market value of all equity shares, $P_eE$, by the total quantity of existing capital, $K$. We therefore obtain

$$\frac{P_eE}{K} = \frac{PRK}{r_eE} \frac{E}{K} = \frac{PR}{r_e}. \tag{1.2.20}$$

Rearranging the above equation, we see that the difference between the market value of an existing unit of capital and the market price of a new unit of capital is equal to $(P/r_e)(R - r_e)$. As long as $R > r_e$, the purchase of a new unit of capital results in a capital gain for the firm. Therefore, to maximize its market value, the representative firm should expand its holdings of $K$ as long as $R > r_e$.

At first blush, it would appear that $R \neq r_e$ results in the emergence of riskless profit

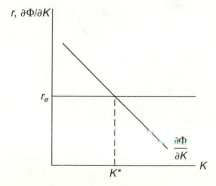

Figure 1.1

opportunities, which should be eliminated by the activities of arbitrageurs. However, such arbitrage is only possible if there is an active market in used-capital goods, a possibility we have ruled out by assumption. If such a used-capital market existed, then $R = r_e$ would emerge as a market-clearing condition in the used-capital market. Interestingly, the workings of macroeconomic models with such used-capital markets turn out to be qualitatively quite different from the workings of more standard macroeconomic models.[1]

In the absence of adjustment costs, the representative firm immediately adopts a value of $K$ that equates $R$ with $r_e$, and therefore $i^d$ cannot be defined. We instead adopt the usual convention that it is costly to quickly adjust the stock of capital and so investment only gradually eliminates differences between $R$ and $r_e$. In particular, we assume that[2]

$$i^d = \dot{e}^s = \xi_k(R - r_e), \qquad \xi_k > 0, \quad \text{a constant.} \tag{1.2.21}$$

The representative firm therefore adopts a positive level of net investment as long as $R > r_e$. This investment process implies the eventual elimination of any gap between $R$ and $r_e$ when the representative firm's stock of capital is equal to $K^*$.

Suppressing the existing capital stock, $K$, and the marginal product of capital, $R$, as arguments of the investment demand function and recalling that with a unified financial market the return on capital equals the rate of interest $r$, we obtain

$$i^d = i^d(r), \qquad \frac{\partial i^d}{\partial r} < 0, \tag{1.2.22}$$

$$\dot{e}^s = \dot{e}^s(r), \qquad \frac{\partial \dot{e}^s}{\partial r} < 0. \tag{1.2.23}$$

The firm finance constraint again requires that[3]

$$\frac{\partial i^d}{\partial r} = \frac{\partial \dot{e}^s}{\partial r}. \tag{1.2.24}$$

We assume that the capital stock owned by the representative firm is predetermined and equals $\overline{K} = K(0)$. We also assume that the time frame of analysis is sufficiently short so that investment leads to insignificant changes in the capital stock. We have already shown that firm behavior implies a labor demand schedule of the form

$$\ell^d = \ell^d\left(\frac{W}{P}\right), \qquad \frac{\partial \ell^d}{\partial(W/P)} = \frac{1}{\partial^2\Phi/\partial\ell^2} < 0. \tag{1.2.25}$$

With output uniquely related to employment, this labor demand schedule implies an

---

[1]For more insight into this issue, see Sargent (1987, Ch. 3).

[2]This presentation of the relationship between ''adjustment costs'' and investment behavior is, like much of the literature in this area, admittedly ad hoc. For the more technically oriented reader, Appendix 1.B presents a more formal derivation of an investment demand function identical in form to that postulated here. Hayashi (1982) also presents a very nice exposition of how such an investment function can be derived in an explicitly intertemporal optimization framework. The classic works in this area are Lucas (1967) and Gould (1968).

[3]Empirical support for investment demand functions of this form is summarized by Jorgenson (1971) and Abel (1980).

output supply schedule of the form

$$y^s = \Phi\left[\ell^d\left(\frac{W}{P}\right), \overline{K}\right] = y^s\left(\frac{W}{P}\right), \qquad \frac{\partial y^s}{\partial(W/P)} < 0. \tag{1.2.26}$$

## Household Behavior

Households sell labor services to firms and receive wage income in exchange for their labor services. Households also receive interest income from holdings of government-issued bonds and dividend income from holdings of firm-issued equities. Households dispose of this income by paying taxes to the government, buying consumption goods, and acquiring additional money, government bonds, and equities.

The representative household's maximization problem therefore involves selecting optimal current levels of labor supply $\ell^s$, consumption demand $c^d$, desired real rate of accumulation of additional money balances $\dot{m}^d$, and desired real rate of accumulation of additional earning assets $\dot{f}^d$. The representative household also has the related problem of allocating its total current real wealth across real money balances $M/P$, real holdings of government bonds $B/rP$, and real holdings of firm equities $RK/r$.

Rigorous analysis of the representative household's problem properly views all of these decisions as interdependent. A unified presentation of the simultaneous determination of optimal time paths of $\ell^s$, $c^d$, $\dot{m}^d$, and $\dot{f}^d$ is presented in Appendix 1.C. However, a considerable amount of insight into the trade-offs faced by the household may be obtained by viewing each of the choices as if they were made in isolation.

Let us first consider the labor-leisure choice. Assume that the representative household faces a single-period decision problem. Denote nonlabor real income by $a$. Assume that the household can sell all the labor services $\ell$ it wants in the market at the given nominal wage $W$. Assume that the household can buy all of the consumption good $c$ that it wants at the given nominal price $P$. The representative household's budget constraint is therefore given by

$$Pa + W\ell - Pc = 0. \tag{1.2.27}$$

We next assume that the representative household seeks to maximize the concave single-period utility function

$$U = U(c, \ell). \tag{1.2.28}$$

The household therefore maximizes the Lagrangian

$$\mathscr{L} = U(c, \ell) + \lambda\left(a + \frac{W}{P}\ell - c\right). \tag{1.2.29}$$

First-order conditions for this maximization are given by

$$\frac{\partial \mathscr{L}}{\partial c} = U_1 - \lambda = 0, \tag{1.2.30}$$

$$\frac{\partial \mathscr{L}}{\partial \ell} = U_2 + \frac{W}{P}\lambda = 0, \tag{1.2.31}$$

$$\frac{\partial \mathcal{L}}{\partial \lambda} = a + \frac{W}{P}\ell - c = 0.$$

(1.2.32)

Combining the first two of these first-order conditions, we find that the optimal labor-leisure choice requires that

$$-\frac{U_2(c, \ell)}{U_1(c, \ell)} = \frac{W}{P}.$$

(1.2.33)

The household therefore equates the ratio of the marginal utilities of leisure and consumption to the real wage rate $W/P$. Solution for the optimal amount of labor services $\ell$ is equivalent to specifying the labor supply function $\ell^s$. In this simple example, the labor supply function is given by

$$\ell^s = \ell^s\left(\frac{W}{P}, a\right).$$

(1.2.34)

In the most general case, the signs of the effects of changes in both $W/P$ and $a$ on labor supply are theoretically ambiguous. For most of the analysis, we are particularly interested in the effects of changes in the real wage $W/P$ on the level of labor supply. However, a higher real wage induces both a substitution effect favoring increased work effort and an income effect favoring reduced work effort.

In many applications throughout the text we consider the special case of the "no-wealth-effects" utility function:

$$U(c, \ell) = U[c - h(\ell)], \qquad h' > 0, \qquad h'' > 0.$$

(1.2.35)

This form of the utility function places considerable limitations on the extent of substitutability between $c$ and $\ell$. However, in this more restricted case, it is straightforward to demonstrate that

$$\ell^s = \ell^s\left(\frac{W}{P}\right), \qquad \frac{\partial \ell^s}{\partial (W/P)} > 0.$$

(1.2.36)

In this case, a higher real wage unambiguously increases labor supply. Furthermore, the level of labor supply is independent of the amount of nonlabor income $a$. In most applications, we adopt this simple form for the labor supply function.

We next consider the representative household's intertemporal consumption-saving decision. Assume that the household lives for two discrete time periods. Further assume that the household's optimal labor supply choice results in levels of real disposable income equal to $z_1$ in the first period and $z_2$ in the second period. Let us finally assume that the household can borrow and lend in unlimited amounts at the prevailing rate of interest, $r$.

Denote the representative household's objection function by

$$V = U(c_1) + \frac{U(c_2)}{1 + \beta},$$

(1.2.37)

where $U$ is a concave, single-period utility function, $c_1$ and $c_2$ denote first- and second-period consumption, respectively, and $\beta$ is the subjective rate of discount applied to future utility levels.

Resources available to the household for second-period consumption include second-period disposable income $z_2$ plus savings carried forward from the first period, $z_1 - c_1$, and accrued interest on that savings, $r(z_1 - c_1)$. The intertemporal budget constraint is therefore given by

$$c_2 = z_2 + (1 + r)(z_1 - c_1) \tag{1.2.38}$$

or

$$c_1 + \frac{c_2}{1 + r} = z_1 + \frac{z_2}{1 + r}. \tag{1.2.39}$$

The second equation above expresses the budget constraint in an easily interpretable form. The representative household's budget constraint requires that the present value of consumption equal the present value of disposable income.

Optimal behavior by the representative household therefore requires that $c_1$ and $c_2$ be chosen to maximize the Lagrangian

$$\mathscr{L} = U(c_1) + \frac{U(c_2)}{1 + \beta} + \lambda\left(z_1 + \frac{z_2}{1 + r} - c_1 - \frac{c_2}{1 + r}\right). \tag{1.2.40}$$

First-order conditions for this maximization are given by

$$\frac{\partial \mathscr{L}}{\partial c_1} = U'(c_1) - \lambda = 0, \tag{1.2.41}$$

$$\frac{\partial \mathscr{L}}{\partial c_2} = \frac{U'(c_2)}{1 + \beta} - \frac{\lambda}{1 + r} = 0, \tag{1.2.42}$$

$$\frac{\partial \mathscr{L}}{\partial \lambda} = z_1 + \frac{z_2}{1 + r} - c_1 - \frac{c_2}{1 + r} = 0. \tag{1.2.43}$$

Combining the first two first-order conditions, we find that

$$\frac{U'(c_1)}{U'(c_2)} = \frac{1 + r}{1 + \beta}. \tag{1.2.44}$$

Therefore, the ratio of marginal utility in the first period to marginal utility in the second period must equal 1 plus the interest rate divided by 1 plus the discount rate.

A number of interesting implications can be gleaned from this representation of the first-order conditions. First of all, note that since $U'' < 0$, if the rate of interest exceeds the rate of discount, then second-period consumption is unambiguously higher than first-period consumption. Alternatively, if the rate of discount exceeds the rate of interest, then first-period consumption is unambiguously higher than second-period consumption. Also note that these results are independent of the relative magnitudes of $z_1$ and $z_2$. A corollary of these results concerns the behavior of first-period savings, $z_1 - c_1$. Suppose that real disposable income is constant across time; that is, suppose $z_1 = z_2 = z$. In this case savings $z_1 - c_1$ is positive when $r > \beta$ and negative when $r < \beta$.

One particularly simple special case is that in which $U(c) = \ln(c)$. In this case, we can derive the following closed-form expressions for $c_1$ and $c_2$:

$$c_1 = \frac{1 + \beta}{2 + \beta}\left(z_1 + \frac{z_2}{1 + r}\right), \tag{1.2.45}$$

$$c_2 = \frac{1 + r}{1 + \beta}\left(z_1 + \frac{z_2}{1 + r}\right). \tag{1.2.46}$$

In this special case, it is straightforward to demonstrate that $dc_1/dr$ is negative. That is, an increase in the rate of interest lowers first-period consumption and therefore raises savings. However, in the more general case, an increase in the interest rate includes a substitution effect inducing higher first-period savings and an income effect inducing higher first-period consumption.

Throughout much of the analysis, we adopt the assumption of static expectations about future income levels. In the present setup, such an assumption amounts to an assumption that $z_1 = z_2 = z$. For this case, first-period consumption is given by

$$c_1 = 1 - \frac{r - \beta}{(1 + r)(2 + \beta)}z. \tag{1.2.47}$$

For most of what follows, we take an interpretation of the above with $r > \beta$ so that $c_1 < z$. We also assume that the effect of changes in the rate of interest on the level of current consumption are negligible so that $dc/dr \approx 0$. We therefore generally adopt a first-period or current-consumption function of the form

$$c^d = c^d(z), \qquad 0 < \frac{\partial c^d}{\partial z} < 1. \tag{1.2.48}$$

In the basic form of the macroeconomic model of Chapters 1 and 2, real disposable income includes aggregate output $y$ plus the real value of interest on government bonds $B/P$ minus taxes $\tau$. Consumption is therefore given by[4]

$$c^d = c^d\left(y + \frac{B}{P} - \tau\right). \tag{1.2.49}$$

The representative household's participation in labor and commodity markets presented above has been in the setting of a pure barter economy. That is, we have abstracted from the use of money in facilitating transactions. We now turn our attention to monetized exchange and derive the representative household's demand for money.

Important early contributions to the theory of the demand for money for transaction purposes are due to Baumol (1952) and Tobin (1956). These analyses view the household's portfolio problem as one of balancing two competing factors. As noted above, one factor is that earning assets pay interest while money does not. However, money is required to make transactions, and therefore brokerage costs may be incurred any time

---

[4]This form of the consumption function is similar in spirit to that suggested by Friedman (1957). Note, however, that this form requires that agents expect that the levels of income and taxation will be constant into the indefinite future.

earning assets must be sold to finance a transaction. Higher average holdings of money help minimize on such transaction costs, but higher money holdings also involve greater foregone earnings of interest.

In order to get some intuition on the nature of this trade-off, we now consider a highly simplified model of household transaction activity along the lines of Baumol (1952) and Tobin (1956). Assume that gross real income per unit of time is given by $y$ and that expenditures per unit of time are also given by $y$. We therefore abstract from saving behavior. Further assume that income is received in the form of earning assets but expenditures must be made in cash.

In order to finance expenditures, the representative household must periodically liquidate some earning assets for cash. We assume that each such transaction incurs a real cost equal to $\gamma_0$ independent of the size of the transaction. Such transaction costs might include the time cost of a trip to the "bank" to sell the earning asset or a brokerage fee paid to an agent to handle the transaction. The lumpy nature of such costs guarantee that such transactions should only be undertaken at discrete time intervals.

Denote the number of transactions in the financial market per unit of time by $1/\phi$. Therefore, a separate sale of earning assets occurs at intervals of time equal to $\phi$. While financial market transactions occur at discrete intervals, goods market transactions are assumed to occur continuously at the rate $y$ per unit of time.

This assumed transaction technology results in a pattern of money holding presented in Figure 1.2. Immediately after a financial transaction, money holding is at its peak. Money is spent continuously over time so that money holdings fall in a linear fashion. As noted above, holding money is costly because money, unlike earning assets, pays no interest. Therefore, it pays for the representative household to exactly exhaust its holdings of money just at the time it makes its next financial transaction. Each fresh injection of cash is exactly depleted in $\phi$ units of time if the size of the sale of assets is exactly equal to $\phi y$.

The average level of real money balances held by the representative household in this example is given by $\frac{1}{2}\phi y$. We denote this average holding of real money balances by $m = M/P$. Recall that we began the discussion of optimal money management with the

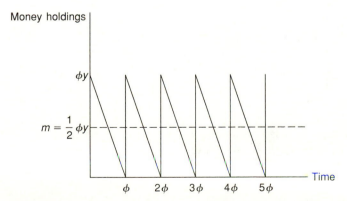

**Figure 1.2**

introduction of the brokerage fee $\gamma_0$. If the representative household chooses to make $1/\phi$ financial transactions per unit of time, then total transaction costs per unit of time are given by

$$\gamma = \frac{\gamma_0}{\phi}. \tag{1.2.50}$$

However, given the relationship $m = \frac{1}{2}\phi y$, we can also express total transaction costs as

$$\gamma = \frac{\gamma_0 y}{2m}. \tag{1.2.51}$$

The representative household's problem involves choosing the optimal frequency $1/\phi^*$ of transactions in the earning asset market. Alternatively, the representative household's problem can be cast in terms of the selection of the optimal average level of real money balances $m^*$. Suppose that the representative household has total real wealth $\Omega$, which must be allocated across real earning assets $f$ and real money balances $m$. If the average level of money balances is equal to $m$, then gross interest income on wealth is given by

$$r(\Omega - m) = rf. \tag{1.2.52}$$

Net income from the representative household's portfolio equals gross interest income minus transaction costs. The representative household therefore seeks to choose $m$ (and therefore $\phi$) to maximize $rf - \gamma$. Since the wealth constraint is given by $\Omega = m + f$, the representative household maximizes the Lagrangian expression

$$\mathcal{L} = rf - \frac{\gamma_0 y}{2m} + \lambda(\Omega - f - m). \tag{1.2.53}$$

First-order conditions are given by

$$\frac{\partial \mathcal{L}}{\partial f} = r - \lambda = 0, \tag{1.2.54}$$

$$\frac{\partial \mathcal{L}}{\partial m} = \frac{\gamma_0 y}{2m^2} - \lambda = 0, \tag{1.2.55}$$

$$\frac{\partial \mathcal{L}}{\partial \lambda} = \Omega - f - m = 0. \tag{1.2.56}$$

Optimal money management therefore requires that

$$m^* = \left(\frac{\gamma_0 y}{2r}\right)^{1/2}. \tag{1.2.57}$$

This example is based upon one particularly simple pattern of income and expenditures. However, the general nature of the problem is likely to be quite similar for other, more complex transaction patterns. In a more general setting, we might anticipate transaction cost technologies of the form

$$\gamma = \gamma(m, y), \qquad \frac{\partial \gamma}{\partial m} < 0, \qquad \frac{\partial^2 \gamma}{\partial m^2} > 0, \qquad \frac{\partial \gamma}{\partial y} > 0, \qquad \frac{\partial^2 \gamma}{\partial y \, \partial m} < 0. \tag{1.2.58}$$

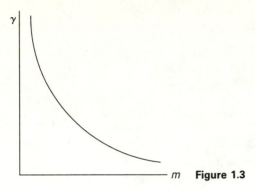

**Figure 1.3**

A typical $\gamma$ function is depicted in Figure 1.3. Optimal money holding in this more general setting solves

$$r = -\frac{\partial \gamma(m^*, y)}{\partial m}.$$  (1.2.59)

Inverting this first-order condition, we obtain a specification for desired real money balances given by

$$\left(\frac{M}{P}\right)^d = m^* = \left(\frac{M}{P}\right)^d(y, r), \qquad \frac{\partial (M/P)^d}{\partial y} > 0, \qquad \frac{\partial (M/P)^d}{\partial r} < 0.$$  (1.2.60)

An alternative to this transaction-technology-based derivation of the money demand function is based on money's role as an alternative store of value to the holding of earning assets. Tobin (1958) postulates that the rate of return on holding money, while on average less than the rate of return on holding earning assets, is nevertheless more certain than the rate of return on holding earning assets. This difference in riskiness may arise because government bonds and equities are subject to market price variability, while money is not. One consequence of this difference in riskiness is that risk-averse economic agents may wish to include some money in an optimally structured portfolio.

While the portfolio approach to the demand for money views the money demand process in a very different light, the resulting implications for household behavior are very similar. The portfolio approach shares with the transaction approach the property that the optimal stock of real money balances is inversely related to the rate of return on earning assets (the rate of interest). The only principal difference between the two approaches is that the portfolio approach suggests using wealth as a scaling variable, while the transactions approach suggests using income as a scaling variable. In most of the analysis, we continue to use income as the scaling variable, as described above. However, in Chapter 2 we introduce a model in which the demand for money depends both on income and on wealth, as suggested by the portfolio approach.

Both the transaction approach and the portfolio approach to the demand for money views the demand for money as the determination of an optimal *stock* of real money balances. However, the representative household's budget is given by

$$z = \frac{W}{P} \ell^s + RK + \frac{B}{P} - \tau = c^d + \dot{f}^d + \dot{m}^d,$$  (1.2.61)

where

$$\frac{W}{P}\ell^s = \text{real wage income}$$

$$RK = \text{real dividend income}$$

$$\frac{B}{P} = \text{real interest income}$$

$$\tau = \text{real tax payments}$$
$$c^d = \text{real consumption demand}$$
$$\dot{f}^d = \text{real rate of accumulation of earning assets}$$
$$\dot{m}^d = \text{real rate of accumulation of money balances}$$

Furthermore, since the aggregate production function is linearly homogeneous and as long as markets clear, the representative household's budget constraint may also be written as

$$z = y + \frac{B}{P} - \tau = c^d + \dot{f}^d + \dot{m}^d \qquad (1.2.62)$$

since

$$y = \frac{W}{P}\ell^s + RK.$$

Note that all of the components of this budget constraint are measured as *flows*. That is, they are all measured in units of real goods per unit of time. We therefore need to convert the stock demand for real money balances into a flow demand for real additional money balances $\dot{m}^d$. The partial-adjustment view of portfolio management offers a natural way of bridging the inherent inconsistencies in the two approaches.

The partial-adjustment approach to money demand argues that if the actual quantity of real money balances differs from the desired quantity of real money balances, the discrepancy will only gradually be eliminated.[5] If agents only gradually adjust their actual holdings of real money balances to their desired holdings of real money balances, then we might expect the representative household's desired real rate of accumulation of money balances to be given by

$$\dot{m}^d = \xi_m \left[ \left( \frac{M}{P} \right)^d (y, r) - \frac{M}{P} \right], \qquad \xi_m > 0, \quad \text{a constant}, \qquad (1.2.63)$$

where $M/P$ denotes actual real money balances and $(M/P)^d$ denotes desired real money

---

[5]This theoretical argument has long been recognized by monetary economists and is well explained by Laidler (1982, Ch. 2; 1984). A formal model of this type of behavior is included in the analysis of Appendix 1.C. Empirical results consistent with the implied lag structure in money demand regressions are summarized by Judd and Scadding (1982).

balances.[6] We can now rewrite the representative household's desired real rate of accumulation of money balances as

$$\dot{m}^d = \dot{m}^d\left(y, r, \frac{M}{P}\right) \tag{1.2.64}$$

where

$$\frac{\partial \dot{m}^d}{\partial y} > 0, \qquad \frac{\partial \dot{m}^d}{\partial r} < 0, \qquad \frac{\partial \dot{m}^d}{\partial (M/P)} < 0. \tag{1.2.65}$$

Having specified the representative household's demand for goods and the representative household's desired real rate of accumulation of money balances, the representative household's demand for additional earning assets is determined by the representative household's budget constraint. In particular,

$$\dot{f}^d = z - c^d(z) - \dot{m}^d\left(y, r, \frac{M}{P}\right). \tag{1.2.66}$$

The flow demand for additional earning assets is therefore given implicitly as

$$\dot{f}^d = \dot{f}^d\left(z, y, r, \frac{M}{P}\right). \tag{1.2.67}$$

The representative household's budget constraint implies the following restrictions on the partial derivatives of $\dot{f}^d$:

$$\frac{\partial \dot{f}^d}{\partial z} = 1 - \frac{\partial c^d}{\partial z} > 0, \tag{1.2.68}$$

$$\frac{\partial \dot{f}^d}{\partial y} = -\frac{\partial \dot{m}^d}{\partial y} < 0, \tag{1.2.69}$$

$$\frac{\partial \dot{f}^d}{\partial r} = -\frac{\partial \dot{m}^d}{\partial r} > 0, \tag{1.2.70}$$

$$\frac{\partial \dot{f}^d}{\partial (M/P)} = -\frac{\partial \dot{m}^d}{\partial (M/P)} > 0. \tag{1.2.71}$$

Recall from the definition of a partial derivative that $\partial \dot{f}^d / \partial y$ is measured holding all variables other than $y$ (including $z$) constant. This partial derivative measures the effect of a change in $y$ solely as a transactions measure on earning asset demand. We can measure the *total* effect of a change in $y$ on $\dot{f}^d$ by recalling that $z = y + B/P - \tau$ and setting

---

[6]For examples of the use of this assumption in macroeconomic models, see Archibald and Lipsey (1958) and Barro and Grossman (1976, Ch. 4). Carr and Darby (1981) and Santomero and Seater (1981) attribute behavior similar to that postulated here as optimal agent response to unanticipated disturbances. While their analyses suggest gradual adjustment of nominal rather than real money balances, this distinction is less crucial in the present, static analysis in which all variables, including the level of prices, are constant at their market-clearing values.

$dB = dP = d\tau = 0$. We therefore find that

$$\frac{d\dot{f}^d}{dy} = 1 - \frac{\partial c^d}{\partial z} - \frac{\partial \dot{m}^d}{\partial y} \gtreqqless 0. \tag{1.2.72}$$

## Labor Market Equilibrium

The analyses of Chapters 1–3 highlight the role of financial markets and their interrelationships with the goods market. Current interest in the details of the labor market is secondary. Therefore, while our current analysis of labor market activity is admittedly rather sketchy, the analyses of the labor market in Chapters 5 and 7 should restore a more appropriate balance in coverage. We now assume that the real wage rate adjusts to equate the supply of labor $\ell^s(W/P)$ and the demand for labor $\ell^d(W/P)$ at the equilibrium real wage rate $(W/P)^*$. Denote the resulting equilibrium level of employment as $\ell^*$. Labor supply, labor demand, and the equilibrium values $(W/P)^*$ and $\ell^*$ are depicted in Figure 1.4.

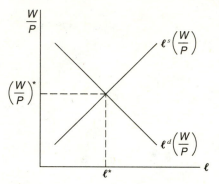

**Figure 1.4**

With the level of employment and the real wage determined solely in the labor market, output supply is simply given by

$$y^s = \Phi(\ell^*, \overline{K}) = y^*. \tag{1.2.73}$$

For the rest of the analysis of Chapters 1 and 2, the level of output supply is therefore viewed as an exogenous variable determined in a separate labor market. Furthermore, we assume that the real wage and therefore the optimal value of labor supply are expected to remain constant over time.

## Government Behavior

The government purchases goods and services at a real rate, $g$, and distributes them to households as public goods. The government also collects lump-sum taxes from households at a real rate, $\tau$, and makes nominal interest payments equal to $B$ to holders of government bonds. Finally, the government issues new money and bonds, which are acquired by households.

Denote the rate of expansion of the nominal money supply as $dM/dt$. Denote the nominal value of the flow of additional government bonds as

$$P_b \frac{dB}{dt} = \frac{1}{r} \frac{dB}{dt}.$$

Government spending on goods and services plus interest payments on existing debt not financed through tax collections must be financed either through money creation or through the sale of additional government bonds. The government's budget constraint is therefore given by

$$P\left(g + \frac{B}{P} - \tau\right) = \frac{dM}{dt} + \frac{1}{r} \frac{dB}{dt}. \tag{1.2.74}$$

If we now denote the real supply of additional money balances as

$$\dot{m}^s \equiv \frac{1}{P} \frac{dM}{dt}$$

and the real supply of additional government bonds as

$$\dot{b}^s \equiv \frac{1}{rP} \frac{dB}{dt},$$

the government budget constraint may be rewritten in the alternate form

$$g + \frac{B}{P} - \tau = \dot{m}^s + \dot{b}^s. \tag{1.2.75}$$

In order to get experience working with the model in its simplest form, we begin our analysis of Chapter 2 with the case in which there are no existing bonds and the government sells no new bonds. That is, we assume that

$$\dot{b}^s = B = 0. \tag{1.2.76}$$

The government has three remaining policy instruments: government spending $g$, taxes $\tau$, and money creation $\dot{m}^s$. However, only two of these may be controlled independently due to the government budget constraint, $g - \tau = \dot{m}^s$. As we shall see, the reintroduction of government bonds is fairly simple once the basic model has been mastered.

## Some Reservations About Static, Deterministic Macroeconomic Modeling

This chapter introduces a considerable amount of material on representative agent behavior in aggregate markets. Chapters 2 and 3 present a considerable amount of material on market interactions arising from such behavior. However, before the reader gets too much further involved in the mechanics of analyses of this type, a few words of caution are in order about the relative merits and potentially debilitating deficiencies of the models studied in these early chapters.

A most basic difficulty with this modelling strategy is that market equilibrium is an entirely timeless phenomenon. Much of the microeconomic foundations of the analysis developed in this chapter works on the presumption of a continuum of time—that is, households and firms choose indefinite time functions for their supplies and demands in markets even though there is in fact only one instant of time in which the markets meet and equilibrium prices are determined. Actions taken in the present therefore have no future implications even though agents act as if such actions do have important future implications.

A related criticism applies to the method of comparative statics as applied to such models and the implicit and explicit shortcomings of the models' treatment of expectations. In these models, agents expect with certainty that the future values of all economic variables will be exactly equal to the current values of these economic variables. Furthermore, any change in an exogenous or endogenous economic variable, while always unanticipated, is nevertheless expected to be entirely permanent. Agents are therefore routinely confronted with disturbances they confidently believed were blatantly impossible, yet these same agents react not with incredulity, but rather as if such an event were perfectly normal. Furthermore, even when such disturbances do not occur, we are often confronted with situations in which the economic status quo, which agents firmly believe in, is clearly an inconsistent economic outcome.

Many of the shortcomings of these models can be significantly remedied by allowing the models to be formally dynamic in nature and by carefully modeling agents' access to information in an explicitly stochastic environment. Results of much of this more ambitious methodology are summarized in later chapters. One may wonder, however, whether the study of such simple, static deterministic models is a useful pursuit.

An affirmative answer to this question is justified on a number of grounds. First, for all of these models' technical simplicity vis-à-vis more carefully specified models, the implications of the analyses of these more simple models are not terribly different in many respects from the implications of those more rigorously specified models. Furthermore, where differences do emerge, they are more easily highlighted after intuition is firmly grasped in the context of more basic models. Second, such models are an important part of the legacy of the history of thought in macroeconomics. It is very difficult to understand some of the earlier contributions in the field without an appreciation of how these models work. Third, results generated in such simple models often permeate the thoughts of economic policymakers and their economic advisors. Finally, such models continue to be the bread and butter of undergraduate training in macroeconomics.

# APPENDIX A: Summary of Notation

## Income Variables

$y$ = total factor payments received by households

$\tau$ = real value of taxes collected by government

$z$ = disposable income, $\equiv y + B/P - \tau$

## Goods Market

$y$ = real output produced and sold, $= c + i + g$

$c$ = goods purchased by households

$i$ = goods purchased by firms

$g$ = goods purchased by the government

$y^d$ = real aggregate goods demand, $= c^d + i^d + g$

$c^d$ = goods demanded by households

$i^d$ = goods demanded by firms

$g$ = goods demanded by government

$y^s$ = real aggregate goods supply, $\equiv \Phi[\ell^d, \overline{K}]$

$y^*$ = equilibrium goods supply

$\overline{K}$ = predetermined stock of capital

$P$ = aggregate goods price

## Labor Market

$\ell$ = employment of labor services

$\ell^d$ = labor demand

$\ell^s$ = labor supply

$\ell^*$ = equilibrium level of employment

$W$ = nominal wage rate

$w$ = real wage rate, $\equiv W/P$

## Money Market

$M$ = nominal money stock

$m$ = actual stock of real money balances, $\equiv M/P$

$(M/P)^d$ = desired stock of real money balances

$\dot{m}$ = real additional money balances

$\dot{m}^d$ = real demand for additional money balances

$\dot{m}^s$ = real supply of additional money balances, $\equiv (1/P)(dM/dt)$

## Earning Asset Market

$B$ = number of government-issued bonds

$P_b$ = price of a government-issued bond

$r_b$ = rate of return on a government-issued bond

$E$ = number of equities issued by firms

$P_e$ = price of an equity

$r_e$ = rate of return on an equity

$K$ = stock of capital

$R$ = marginal product of capital

$F$ = nominal stock of earning assets, $= P_b B + P_e E = B/r + PRK/r$

$\dot{f}^d$ = real demand for additional earning assets

$\dot{f}^s$ = real supply of additional earning assets, $= \dot{b}^s + \dot{e}^s$

$\dot{b}^s$ = real supply of additional government bonds, $\equiv (P_b/P)(dB/dt) \equiv (dB/dt)/r_b P$

$\dot{e}^s$ = real supply of additional equities, $\equiv (P_e/P)(dE/dt) \equiv dK/dt \equiv i$

$r$ = rate of interest, $= r_b = r_e$

# APPENDIX B: The Representative Firm's Intertemporal Choice Problem

This appendix presents a formal, dynamic analysis of the representative firm's choice problem. In order to derive an investment demand schedule instead of a capital demand schedule, we now explicitly allow for capital stock adjustment costs. In particular, assume that such costs are given by

$$C(\dot{K}) = \frac{\alpha}{2}(\dot{K})^2, \quad \text{where } \alpha > 0, \quad \text{a constant.} \tag{1.B.1}$$

As in our earlier analysis, we assume that the representative firm expects that the interest rate $r$, the price level $P$, and the wage rate $W$ will be constant into the indefinite future. The representative firm seeks to choose time paths for $\ell(t)$ and $K(t)$ that maximize the price of an existing share of equity. However, we must now subtract from the firm's cash flow over time expenditures on new capital, $P\dot{K}(t)$, plus expenditures on adjustment costs, $PC[\dot{K}(t)]$.

The representative firm's problem is therefore given by

$$\max_{\ell(t),\, u(t)} \frac{1}{E} \int_0^\infty \left\{ P\Phi(\ell(t), K(t)) - W\ell(t) - Pu(t) - P\frac{\alpha}{2}[u(t)]^2 \right\} e^{-rt}\, dt \tag{1.B.2}$$

subject to

$$\dot{K}(t) = i = u. \tag{1.B.3}$$

This problem is a straightforward application of the maximum principle.[7] Dividing through by the constant price level $P$ and recalling the definition $w = W/P$, the present-value Hamiltonian for this problem is given by

$$H^* = \Phi(\ell(t), K(t)) - w\ell(t) - u(t) - \frac{\alpha}{2}[u(t)]^2 + \lambda u. \tag{1.B.4}$$

First-order conditions for this maximization are given by

$$\frac{\partial H^*}{\partial \ell} = \frac{\partial \Phi(\ell, K)}{\partial \ell} - w = 0, \tag{1.B.5}$$

$$\frac{\partial H^*}{\partial u} = -(1 + \alpha u) + \lambda = 0, \tag{1.B.6}$$

$$\dot{\lambda} = -\frac{\partial H^*}{\partial K} + r\lambda = -\frac{\partial \Phi(\ell, K)}{\partial K} + r\lambda. \tag{1.B.7}$$

The first of these first-order conditions (1.B.5) generates the standard labor demand schedule

$$\ell^d = \ell^d(w, K(0)), \qquad \frac{\partial \ell^d}{\partial w} < 0, \qquad \frac{\partial \ell^d}{\partial K(0)} > 0. \tag{1.B.8}$$

Since the initial stock of capital is fixed by the requirement that $dK/dt$ be finite, current labor demand depends only on the current real wage and not on the current rate of interest.

Differentiating the second first-order condition (1.B.6) with respect to time, combining the resulting expression with equation (1.B.7), and recalling the definition $u = \dot{K}$, we obtain the follow-

---

[7]See Intriligator (1971, Ch. 14). A much more detailed treatment of a similar although slightly more complicated problem is deferred until Chapter 8.

ing second-order differential equation:

$$\ddot{K} - r\dot{K} + \frac{1}{\alpha}\left(\frac{\partial\Phi}{\partial K} - r\right) = 0.$$ (1.B.9)

The steady-state solution to this differential equation is given by $K = K^*$, where $K^*$ solves

$$r = \frac{\partial\Phi(\ell^d(w, K^*), K^*)}{\partial K}.$$ (1.B.10)

This value of $K^*$ is identical to that derived in Section 1.2. In general, we find that

$$K^* = K^*(w, r).$$ (1.B.11)

In order to get a closed-form solution for $K(t)$, we next assume that $\Phi$ is approximately quadratic in $K$, so that

$$\frac{\partial\Phi}{\partial K} = \frac{\partial\Phi(\ell^d(w, K^*), K^*)}{\partial K} + \frac{\partial^2\Phi}{\partial K^2}(K - K^*) = r + \frac{\partial^2\Phi}{\partial K^2}(K - K^*).$$ (1.B.12)

Plugging equation (1.B.12) into equation (1.B.9), we obtain the linear, second-order, constant-coefficient differential equation

$$\ddot{K} - r\dot{K} + \frac{1}{\alpha}\frac{\partial^2\Phi}{\partial K^2}K = \frac{1}{\alpha}\frac{\partial^2\Phi}{\partial K^2}K^*.$$ (1.B.13)

The characteristic roots of this differential equation are given by

$$s_i = \frac{1}{2}\left[r \pm \left(r^2 - \frac{4}{\alpha}\frac{\partial^2\Phi}{\partial K^2}\right)^{1/2}\right].$$ (1.B.14)

Only one of these two roots is negative. Therefore, the only stable solution for $K(t)$ is given by

$$K(t) = K^* + [K(0) - K^*]e^{s_1 t},$$ (1.B.15)

where

$$s_1 = \frac{1}{2}\left[r - \left(r^2 - \frac{4}{\alpha}\frac{\partial^2\Phi}{\partial K^2}\right)^{1/2}\right] < 0.$$ (1.B.16)

Differentiating expression (1.B.15) with respect to time, we obtain the following expression for the time path of investment:

$$i = u = \frac{dK}{dt} = -s_1[K^* - K(0)]e^{s_1 t}.$$ (1.B.17)

Evaluating this expression at $t = 0$ and recalling that

$$K^* - K(0) = -\left(\frac{\partial^2\Phi}{\partial K^2}\right)^{-1}\left(\frac{\partial\Phi}{\partial K} - r\right),$$ (1.B.18)

we obtain the current investment demand schedule

$$i^d = \xi_k\left[\frac{\partial\Phi[\ell^d(w, K(0)), K(0)]}{\partial K} - r\right] = \xi_k(R - r),$$ (1.B.19)

where

$$\xi_k \equiv s_1\left(\frac{\partial^2\Phi}{\partial K^2}\right)^{-1} > 0.$$

This form of the investment demand schedule is identical to that postulated in Section 1.2.

# APPENDIX C: The Representative Household's Intertemporal Choice Problem

This appendix presents a formal analysis of the representative household's optimal intertemporal consumption demand, labor supply, and money demand problem. Assume that the representative household's preferences are summarized by the instantaneous concave utility function, $U = U(c, \ell)$. Further assume that the interest rate $r$, price level $P$, wage rate $W$, and real level of taxation $\tau$ are expected to remain constant over time.

The transaction cost technology is summarized by a rate of loss in real income equal to

$$\gamma = \gamma(m, y), \quad \text{where } m \equiv \frac{M}{P}, \tag{1.C.1}$$

just as in Section 1.2. However, in order to introduce the possibility of adjustment costs, we assume an additional loss in real income given by

$$C(\dot{m}) = \frac{\eta}{2}(\dot{m})^2, \quad \text{with } \eta > 0, \quad \text{a constant.} \tag{1.C.2}$$

The evolution of the nominal value of the representative household's nonmonetary wealth is therefore characterized by

$$\frac{dF}{dt} = W\ell(t) + rF(t) - P\left\{ c(t) + \tau + \gamma(m(t), y) + \frac{\eta}{2}[\dot{m}(t)]^2 + \dot{m}(t) \right\}, \tag{1.C.3}$$

where

$$F \equiv \frac{B}{P} + \frac{P\Pi}{r} = \text{nominal value of government bonds} \atop + \text{ nominal value of equities.} \tag{1.C.4}$$

That is, the nominal value of earning assets is augmented by nominal wage income plus nominal interest and dividend income minus nominal tax payments minus the nominal value of transaction costs minus the rate of accumulation of additional nominal money balances.

Since wages and prices are expected to remain constant over time, the evolution of real interest-bearing wealth, $f \equiv F/P$, takes the relatively simple form

$$\frac{df}{dt} = rf(t) + w\ell(t) - c(t) - \tau - \gamma(m(t), y) - \frac{\eta}{2}[u(t)]^2 - u(t), \tag{1.C.5}$$

where $u(t) \equiv \dot{m}(t)$ and $w \equiv W/P$, the real wage rate.

We now assume that the representative household maximizes the discounted present value of $U(t)$ over its lifetime:

$$V = \int_0^N U(c(t), \ell(t))e^{-\beta t} \, dt \tag{1.C.6}$$

subject to

$$\dot{m} = u \tag{1.C.7}$$

$$\dot{f} = rf(t) + w\ell(t) - c(t) - \tau - \gamma(m(t), y) - \frac{\eta}{2}[u(t)]^2 - u(t), \tag{1.C.8}$$

where $N$ is the amount of time remaining until the approach of the planning horizon and $\beta$ is the subjective rate of time preference. Maximization of $V$ subject to the asset accumulation equation above is a relatively straightforward example of the maximum principle.[8]

In this problem, the control variables are $c(t)$, $\ell(t)$, and $u(t)$. The state variables are $f(t)$ and $m(t)$. The present-value Hamiltonian is given by

$$H^* = U(c(t), \ell(t)) + \lambda_1 u + \lambda_2 \left[ rf + w\ell - c - \tau - \gamma(m, y) - \frac{\eta}{2}(u)^2 - u \right]. \tag{1.C.9}$$

Necessary conditions for this maximization are given by

$$\frac{\partial H^*}{\partial c} = \frac{\partial U(c, \ell)}{\partial c} - \lambda_2 = 0, \tag{1.C.10}$$

$$\frac{\partial H^*}{\partial \ell} = \frac{\partial U(c, \ell)}{\partial \ell} + w\lambda_2 = 0, \tag{1.C.11}$$

$$\frac{\partial H^*}{\partial u} = \lambda_1 - (1 + \eta u)\lambda_2 = 0, \tag{1.C.12}$$

$$\dot{\lambda}_1 = -\frac{\partial H^*}{\partial m} + \beta\lambda_1 = \frac{\partial \gamma}{\partial m}\lambda_2 + \beta\lambda_1 \tag{1.C.13}$$

$$\dot{\lambda}_2 = -\frac{\partial H^*}{\partial f} + \beta\lambda_2 = (\beta - r)\lambda_2 \Rightarrow \lambda_2 = \lambda_2(0)e^{-(r-\beta)t}. \tag{1.C.14}$$

The first two of these conditions may be combined to yield

$$w = \frac{W}{P} = -\frac{\partial U(c(t), \ell(t))/\partial \ell(t)}{\partial U(c(t), \ell(t))/\partial c(t)}. \tag{1.C.15}$$

This condition states that the representative household should, at each instant of time, equate the marginal rate of substitution between goods and leisure with the real wage rate. If we further assume that the instantaneous utility function is of the form

$$U = U[c - h(\ell)], \qquad h' > 0, \qquad h'' > 0, \tag{1.C.16}$$

the so-called no-wealth-effects utility function, then we obtain

$$w = \frac{W}{P} = h'(\ell^s). \tag{1.C.17}$$

In this case, current labor supply at any point in time depends only on the current (as opposed to the past or future) real wage independent of nonwage income, wealth, taxes, or anything else. We therefore generate the result that

$$\ell^s = \ell^s(w), \qquad \frac{\partial \ell^s}{\partial w} = \frac{1}{h''} > 0. \tag{1.C.18}$$

For the remainder of this problem, we assume that equilibrium prevails in the labor market so that $w = w^* = h'(\ell^*)$, where $w^*$ solves

$$\ell^s(w^*) = \ell^d(w^*). \tag{1.C.19}$$

The two differential equations in $\lambda_1$ and $\lambda_2$, the condition $\partial H^*/\partial u = 0$, and the definition

---

[8]Again, see Intriligator (1971, Ch. 14). The necessary mathematical techniques for solving this problem are presented in more detail in Chapter 8.

$u = \dot{m}$ may be manipulated to obtain the following differential equation in $m$:

$$\ddot{m} - r\dot{m} - \frac{1}{\eta}\left(r + \frac{\partial\gamma}{\partial m}\right) = 0. \tag{1.C.20}$$

Let us now assume that $\gamma(m, y)$ is approximately quadratic in $m$, so that

$$\frac{\partial\gamma}{\partial m} = \frac{\partial\gamma(m^*, y)}{\partial m} + \frac{\partial^2\gamma}{\partial m^2}(m - m^*), \tag{1.C.21}$$

where $m^*$ solves $r = -\partial\gamma/\partial m$.

The above differential equation in $m$ is now a second-order, linear differential equation with constant coefficients. The roots of this differential equation are given by

$$s_i = \frac{1}{2}\left[r \pm \left(r^2 + \frac{4}{\eta}\frac{\partial^2\gamma}{\partial m^2}\right)^{1/2}\right]. \tag{1.C.22}$$

However, only one of these two roots is negative. Therefore, the only stable solution is of the form

$$m(t) = m^* + [m(0) - m^*]e^{s_1 t}, \tag{1.C.23}$$

where

$$s_1 = \frac{1}{2}\left[r - \left(r^2 + \frac{4}{\eta}\frac{\partial^2\gamma}{\partial m^2}\right)^{1/2}\right] < 0. \tag{1.C.24}$$

We have now derived an optimal money accumulation function, which, evaluated at time zero, is given by

$$\dot{m}^d = \xi_m[m^* - m(0)] = \xi_m\left[\left(\frac{M}{P}\right)^d(y, r) - \frac{M}{P}\right], \tag{1.C.25}$$

where

$$\xi_m \equiv -s_1 > 0 \tag{1.C.26}$$

and

$$\left(\frac{M}{P}\right)^d(y, r) \quad \text{solves} \quad r = -\frac{\partial\gamma(m, y)}{\partial m}. \tag{1.C.27}$$

This form of the optimal money accumulation function is identical in form to the one postulated in Section 1.2.

We next turn our attention to the consumption function. The asset accumulation function can be solved to yield

$$f(t) = f(0)e^{rt} + \int_0^t\left[w^*\ell^* - c - \tau - \gamma(m, y) - u - \frac{\eta u^2}{2}\right]e^{r(t-s)}\,ds. \tag{1.C.28}$$

Optimal consumption behavior always results in an exhaustion of assets at the end of the planning horizon. That is, we always have

$$f(N) + m(N) = 0 \tag{1.C.29}$$

for any optimal plan. Multiplying through the above expression by $e^{-rt}$ and evaluating at $t = N$, we obtain

$$\int_0^N c(s)e^{-rs}\,ds = f(0) + m(N)e^{-rN}$$
$$+ \int_0^N\left[w^*\ell^* - \tau - \gamma(m, y) - u - \frac{\eta u^2}{2}\right]e^{-rs}\,ds. \tag{1.C.30}$$

One particularly easy case to analyze is that of the logarithmic utility function $U(\cdot) = \ln(\cdot)$. In this case, optimal consumption spending is given by

$$c(t) = h(\ell^*) + \frac{e^{(r-\beta)t}}{\lambda_2(0)}. \tag{1.C.31}$$

With the determination of the optimal paths of $\ell(t)$ and $m(t)$ already solved for, equations (1.C.30) and (1.C.31) are two simultaneous equations in $c$ and $\lambda_2$. However, solution for $c(t)$ is greatly complicated by the evolution of $m(t)$ over time. This difficulty can be avoided by assuming that $m(0) \simeq m^* \simeq m(N)$. In this case, $u = 0$ for all $t$ and the optimal consumption path is given by

$$c(t) = h(\ell^*) + \frac{\beta}{r} e^{(r-\beta)t}$$
$$\times \left\{ \frac{B}{P} + \Pi + rm^* e^{-rN} + [w^*\ell^* - h(\ell^*) - \tau - \gamma(m^*, y)](1 - e^{-rN}) \right\} \tag{1.C.32}$$

The case that is most closely comparable to the assumed form of the consumption function adopted in Section 1.2 is the case in which $r > \beta$ and $N \to +\infty$. As long as $N$ is finite, $r > \beta$ requires a rising, although strictly finite, consumption path. But as $N \to +\infty$, consumption rises indefinitely as $t \to +\infty$. For $N$ large but finite, there is no problem. However, the case of the infinite-horizon problem with $r > \beta$ has no proper, steady-state solution although, as pointed out in Section 8.3, the appropriate transversality conditions are unambiguously satisfied with $r > \beta$.

With this caveat in mind, let us take the limit as $N \to +\infty$ and evaluate at $t = 0$ to obtain

$$c^d = \frac{r-\beta}{r} h(\ell^*) + \frac{\beta}{r} \left[ \frac{B}{P} + \Pi + w^*\ell^* - \tau - \gamma(m^*, y) \right]. \tag{1.C.33}$$

Finally, recalling that $y = w\ell + \Pi$, due to the homogeneity of the production function, we obtain

$$c^d = \frac{r-\beta}{r} h(\ell^*) + \frac{\beta}{r} \left[ y + \frac{B}{P} - \tau - \gamma(m^*, y) \right]. \tag{1.C.34}$$

As long as aggregate transaction costs $\gamma$ are small relative to the other components of disposable income, this form of the consumption function is equivalent to that of Section 1.2.

# REFERENCES

Abel, Andrew B., "Empirical Investment Equations: An Integrative Framework," in Karl Brunner and Allan H. Meltzer, eds., *On the State of Macro-Economics,* Carnegie-Rochester Series on Public Policy, Amsterdam, North Holland, Spring 1980.

Archibald, G. C., and R. G. Lipsey, "Monetary and Value Theory: A Critique of Lange and Patinkin," *Review of Economic Studies,* October, 1958, 1–22.

Barro, Robert J., and Herschel I. Grossman, *Money, Employment and Inflation,* Cambridge, England, Cambridge University Press, 1976.

Baumol, William J., "The Transactions Demand for Cash: An Inventory Theoretic Approach," *Quarterly Journal of Economics,* November, 1952, 545–556.

Carr, Jack, and Michael R. Darby, "The Role of Money Supply Shocks in the Short-Run Demand for Money," *Journal of Monetary Economics,* September, 1981, 183–199.

Friedman, Milton, *A Theory of the Consumption Function,* Princeton, NJ, Princeton University Press, 1957.

Gould, John P., "Adjustment Costs in the Theory of Investment of the Firm," *Review of Economic Studies,* January, 1968, 47–55.

Hayashi, Fumio, "Tobin's Marginal *q* and Average *q*: A Neoclassical Interpretation," *Econometrica,* January, 1982, 213–224.

Intriligator, Michael D., *Mathematical Optimization and Economic Theory,* Englewood Cliffs, NJ, Prentice-Hall, 1971.

Jorgenson, Dale W., "Capital Theory and Investment Behavior," *American Economic Review,* May, 1963, 47–59.

Jorgenson, Dale W., "Econometric Studies of Investment Behavior: A Survey," *Journal of Economic Literature,* December, 1971, 1111–1147.

Judd, John P., and John L. Scadding, "The Search for a Stable Money Demand Function: A Survey of the Post-1973 Literature," *Journal of Economic Literature,* September, 1982, 993–1023.

Laidler, David, *Monetarist Perspectives,* Cambridge, MA, Harvard University Press, 1982.

Laidler, David, "The Buffer Stock Notion in Monetary Economics," *Economic Journal,* Supplement, 1984, 17–34.

Lucas, Robert E., Jr., "Adjustment Costs and the Theory of Supply," *Journal of Political Economy,* August, 1967, 321–334.

Santomero, Anthony M., and John J. Seater, "Partial Adjustment in the Demand for Money: Theory and Empirics," *American Economic Review,* September, 1981, 566–578.

Sargent, Thomas J., *Macroeconomic Theory,* 2nd ed., Orlando, FL, Academic, 1987.

Tobin, James, "The Interest-Elasticity of the Transaction Demand for Cash," *Review of Economics and Statistics,* August, 1956, 241–247.

Tobin, James, "Liquidity Preference as Behavior Toward Risk," *Review of Economic Studies,* February, 1958, 65–86.

Tobin, James, "A General Equilibrium Approach to Monetary Theory," *Journal of Money, Credit and Banking,* February, 1969, 15–29.

# Chapter 2

## Equilibrium Macroeconomic Models

This chapter analyzes the market-level and economywide implications of the assumptions about household, firm, and government behavior developed in Chapter 1. Throughout this chapter, we assume that wages and goods and asset prices continuously adjust to clear markets. The implications of potential wage and price inflexibilities are postponed for further discussion in later chapters.

Section 2.1 carefully discusses the market-clearing conditions in the markets for goods, earning assets, and money and characterizes general equilibrium for the economy as a whole. Section 2.2 utilizes the method of comparative statics to analyze the effects of changes in government policy parameters and other exogenous disturbances on the equilibrium interest rate and the equilibrium aggregate price level in the absence of government-issued bonds. Section 2.3 introduces government-issued bonds into the model and analyzes the effects of government fiscal and open-market policies.

Sections 2.4 and 2.5 extend the basic model in several directions to investigate whether the results derived in earlier sections generalize to models with alternative but equally plausible sets of assumptions about household behavior. Section 2.4 introduces the possibility of wealth as an argument in the consumption and money demand functions. Section 2.5 introduces the possibility that households may not view equities and government-issued bonds as perfect substitutes in their portfolios. In general, Sections 2.4 and 2.5 demonstrate that the neutrality of equiproportional increases in money and government bonds is robust to these alternative sets of assumptions but also demonstrates that the question of whether the composition of the government's liabilities matters for the allocation of resources is far less settled.

# 2.1 MARKET-CLEARING CONDITIONS AND ECONOMYWIDE EQUILIBRIUM

In this section, we analyze the interaction of supply and demand in the markets for goods, earning assets, and money, each first considered in isolation. These partial-equilibrium exercises then permit us to develop a graphical apparatus that proves most useful in answering questions about the effects of exogenous disturbances on the values of the endogenous variables consistent with general equilibrium. In the process of this analysis, we also show how Walras's law provides important and useful restrictions on the nature of economywide equilibrium.

In order to get a good grasp on the intuition behind market interactions in the model, we begin with the analysis of a particularly simple case. We temporarily abstract from complications introduced by the existence of government-issued bonds and so set $B = \dot{b}^s = 0$. We also temporarily abstract from wealth effects on consumption and on desired holdings of real money balances.

## Goods Market Equilibrium (GME)

Let us first consider market clearing in the market for current output of goods and services, the goods market. Equilibrium in the goods market requires the equality of goods supply and goods demand. The set of assumptions adopted in Chapter 1 guarantees that the level of output supply is exogenously determined by forces in a separate market for labor services. Denote aggregate goods supply by $y^*$.

Aggregate output demand consists of the sum of the demand of households $c^d$, the demand of firms $i^d$, and the demand of the government $g$. We also assume that the level of output produced is always equal to the level of aggregate supply. These assumptions generate the following market-clearing condition:

$$y^* = \underset{(+)}{c^d(z)} + \underset{(-)}{i^d(r)} + g, \tag{2.1.1}$$

where pluses and minuses indicate the sign of the derivative of a function with respect to the appropriate argument. Recalling that $z = y^* - \tau$, equation (2.1.1) may be rewritten as

$$y^* = c^d(y^* - \tau) + i^d(r) + g. \tag{2.1.2}$$

It is useful to graph the levels of aggregate goods supply $y^s$ and aggregate goods demand $y^d$ against the rate of interest $r$. As noted above, aggregate goods supply is equal to the exogenous constant level $y^*$. In particular, $y^*$ is independent of the rate of interest, and hence aggregate supply is drawn as a vertical line in Figure 2.1.

Next consider aggregate goods demand. Since we assume that actual output is always equal to aggregate supply, disposable income, in the absence of government bonds, is equal to $z = y^* - \tau$. The level of consumption demand is therefore independent of the rate of interest. We also continue to assume that government spending is exogenous and therefore $g$ is independent of the rate of interest as well. Aggregate goods demand is therefore inversely related to the rate of interest solely because the level of investment is

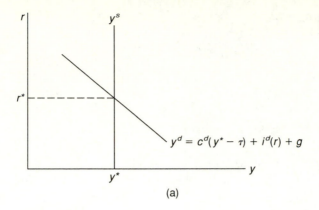

(a)

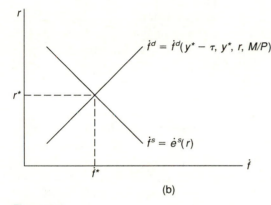

(b)

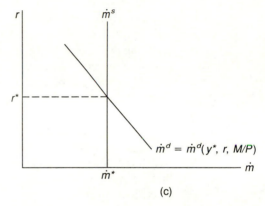

(c)

**Figure 2.1**

inversely related to the rate of interest. The downward-sloping aggregate demand sched-ule depicted in Figure 2.1 incorporates this effect of changes in the rate of interest on the level of investment spending.

For given values of $y^*$, $\tau$, and $g$, $r^*$ denotes the unique interest rate consistent with market clearing in the goods market. At interest rates below $r^*$, aggregate demand ex-ceeds aggregate supply. An increase in the rate of interest is needed to reduce investment demand and bring $y^d$ back down to the fixed level of aggregate supply, $y^*$. Above $r^*$, aggregate supply exceeds aggregate demand. A reduction in the interest rate is therefore needed to stimulate investment demand and bring $y^d$ back up to the fixed level of aggre-gate supply, $y^*$.

## Financial Market Equilibrium (FME)

Earning asset market equilibrium requires that the real demand for additional earning assets by households equal the total real supply of additional earning assets. Since we are assuming that the government is not selling any bonds, additional earning asset supply $\dot{f}^s$ is equal to the supply of additional equities by firms, $\dot{e}^s$. Market clearing in the financial market therefore requires that

$$\dot{f}^d\left(\underset{(+)}{z}, \underset{(-)}{y^*}, \underset{(+)}{r}, \underset{(+)}{\frac{M}{P}}\right) = \underset{(-)}{\dot{f}^s(r)} \equiv \underset{(-)}{\dot{e}^s(r)}. \tag{2.1.3}$$

With $y = y^*$ and $B = 0$, $z = y^* - \tau$. We therefore obtain

$$\dot{f}^d\left(y^* - \tau, y^*, r, \frac{M}{P}\right) = \dot{f}^s(r). \tag{2.1.4}$$

As with the goods market, it is useful to plot the supply of and demand for additional earning assets against the rate of interest $r$. The supply of additional earning assets is equal to the supply of additional equities, which is inversely related to the rate of interest. The earning asset supply curve is therefore drawn in Figure 2.1 as downward sloping.

The demand for additional earning assets depends on the level of disposable income, $y^* - \tau$, and the level of output as a proxy for the volume of transactions, $y^*$. At this stage of the analysis, both of these quantities are viewed as exogenous. Earning asset demand also depends on the level of real money balances $M/P$ and the rate of interest $r$. However, we temporarily postpone an analysis of the determination of the equilibrium level of real money balances. The earning asset demand curve is therefore plotted as upward sloping against the rate of interest in Figure 2.1.

For given values of $y^*$, $\tau$, and $M/P$, the rate of interest $r^*$ in Figure 2.1 is the unique value of the interest rate consistent with market clearing in the earning asset market. Recall that the price of a government bond is $1/r$ and the price of an equity is $P\Pi/rE$, so that the vertical axis in Figure 2.1 is proportional to the inverse of the price of an earning asset. If the demand for earning assets exceeds the supply of earning assets, the price of earning assets will tend to rise and hence the interest rate will tend to fall. If the supply of earning assets exceeds the demand for earning assets, the price of earning assets will tend to fall and hence the interest rate will tend to rise. Appropriate movements in the interest rate are therefore capable of restoring equilibrium in the earning asset market.

## Money Market Equilibrium (MME)

For money market equilibrium, we require that the real demand for additional money balances by household equals the real supply of additional money balances by the government. That is,

$$\dot{m}^s = \dot{m}^d\left(\underset{(+)}{y^*}, \underset{(-)}{r}, \underset{(-)}{\frac{M}{P}}\right). \tag{2.1.5}$$

At this stage of the analysis, we continue to postpone a discussion of the determination of the equilibrium stock of real money balances $M/P$. The real supply of additional money balances is exogenously set by government policy. In particular, the real supply of additional money balances is assumed to be independent of the rate of interest. The real supply of additional money balances is therefore depicted in Figure 2.1 as a vertical line. Holding the level of output $y^*$ and the stock of real money balances $M/P$ constant, the real demand for additional money balances is related only to the rate of interest $r$. Since the real demand for additional money balances is inversely related to the rate of interest, the real additional money balance demand schedule is depicted in Figure 2.1 as downward sloping.

For given values of $y^*$, $\dot{m}^s$, and $M/P$, the rate of interest $r^*$ in Figure 2.1 represents the unique level of the interest rate consistent with market clearing in the market for real additional money balances. Above $r^*$, the real supply of additional money balances exceeds the demand. A reduction in the interest rate is needed to stimulate $\dot{m}^d$ back up to the constant level of $\dot{m}^s$. Below $r^*$, the real demand for additional money balances exceeds the supply. An increase in the interest rate is needed to reduce $\dot{m}^d$ back down to the constant level of $\dot{m}^s$.

## Economywide Equilibrium

Simultaneous equilibrium in the markets for goods, earning assets, and money may be summarized by the following statement of our complete formal model of the economy:

### Market-clearing Conditions

Goods:

$$c^d(\underset{(+)}{z}) + i^d(\underset{(-)}{r}) + g - y^* = 0. \tag{2.1.6}$$

Earning assets:

$$\dot{f}^d\left(\underset{(+)}{z}, \underset{(-)}{y^*}, \underset{(+)}{r}, \underset{(+)}{\frac{M}{P}}\right) - \dot{f}^s(\underset{(-)}{r}) = 0. \tag{2.1.7}$$

Money:

$$\dot{m}^d\left(\underset{(+)}{y^*}, \underset{(-)}{r}, \underset{(-)}{\frac{M}{P}}\right) - \dot{m}^s = 0. \tag{2.1.8}$$

### Definitions and Identities

Government budget constraint: $g - \tau = \dot{m}^s$.
Disposable income: $z = y^* - \tau$.

### Exogenous Variables

Real: $y^*$, potential shift parameters, two among $g$, $\tau$, and $\dot{m}^s$.
Nominal: M.

### Endogenous Variables

Real: $r$ and one among $g$, $\tau$, and $\dot{m}^s$.
Nominal: $P$.

In our discussion of the representative household's demand for additional earning assets, we made use of the representative household's budget constraint $z = c^d + \dot{f}^d + \dot{m}^d$. The function $\dot{f}^s$ similarly incorporates the representative firm's budget constraint $i^d = \dot{e}^s = \dot{f}^s$. In an analogous manner, once the government sets two of its policy variables, the third policy variable is determined endogenously by the government budget constraint. Therefore, in the statement of the model above, only two of $g$, $\tau$, and $\dot{m}^s$ are listed as exogenous. The third policy variable must be listed as endogenous.

Once the third government policy variable has been fixed by the government's selection of values for the other two government policy variables, the model above has the two remaining endogenous variables $r$ and $P$ to be solved for. There are, however, three market-clearing conditions available to solve for these two endogenous variables. There appears to be one extra equation. However, as shown below, one of the above equations is always redundant by Walras's law.

## Walras's Law

Consider the aggregate plans of all economic agents. Even if they are not consistent with each other due to disequilibrium values of the endogenous variables, these aggregate plans must be internally consistent. On net, households can only buy more than current disposable income by attempting to sell earning assets or by running down money balances. Government can only run deficits by printing more money. Business can only invest by selling equities to finance the investment. Aggregating these sectoral budget constraints implies that the sum of aggregate excess demands is identically equal to zero. To see this, recall that we earlier showed that the household, firm, and government budget constraints were given by:

Households: $y* - \tau = c^d + \dot{f}^d + \dot{m}^d$. $\qquad(2.1.9)$

Firms: $i^d = \dot{e}^s \equiv \dot{f}^s$. $\qquad(2.1.10)$

Government: $\dot{m}^s = g - \tau$. $\qquad(2.1.11)$

Substituting the third of the above equations into the first, we obtain

$$y* - g + \dot{m}^s = c^d + \dot{f}^d + \dot{m}^d, \qquad(2.1.12)$$

or

$$0 = c^d + g - y* + \dot{f}^d + \dot{m}^d - \dot{m}^s. \qquad(2.1.13)$$

Now adding zero in the form of $i^d - \dot{f}^s$ and rearranging, we obtain

$$0 = c^d + i^d + g - y* + \dot{f}^d - \dot{f}^s + \dot{m}^d - \dot{m}^s. \qquad(2.1.14)$$

The expression above is referred to as Walras's law. Walras's law has two main implications. One implication is that one of the three market-clearing conditions written above is redundant. If two markets are in equilibrium, the third market is automatically in equilibrium as well. The other implication of Walras's law is that when we differentiate the aggregate budget constraint with respect to any exogenous or endogenous variable, the resulting expression is also always equal to zero. Similarly, when we differentiate any of the individual sectoral budget constraints with respect to any exogenous or endogenous variable, we also obtain an expression that is an equality. These results hold because each budget constraint must hold as an identity. For example, differentiating the household's budget constraint with respect to $y^*$ and noting that with $d\tau = 0$, $dy^* = dz$, we obtain

$$\frac{\partial c^d}{\partial z} + \frac{\partial \dot{f}^d}{\partial z} + \frac{\partial \dot{f}^d}{\partial y^*} + \frac{\partial \dot{m}^d}{\partial y^*} = 1. \tag{2.1.15}$$

Alternatively, this same condition can be obtained by substituting the government budget constraint into the aggregate budget constraint and differentiating with respect to $y^*$. Sometimes identities like the above help resolve some apparent ambiguities.

## Market-clearing Loci

It is often useful in doing comparative statics exercises to utilize market-clearing loci. These loci represent combinations of the endogenous variables, in this case $P$ and $r$, that satisfy the market-clearing conditions in the three markets, each examined in isolation. The common intersection of these three loci then indicate the pair $P^*$, $r^*$ for which the whole economy is in equilibrium.[1]

First, consider the goods market equilibrium condition $y^d = y^*$, where $y^d \equiv c^d + i^d + g$. Differentiating the goods market equilibrium condition with respect to $r$ and $P$, we obtain

$$\frac{\partial i^d}{\partial r} \, dr + (0) \, dP = 0, \tag{2.1.16}$$

and so

$$\left. \frac{dr}{dP} \right|_{y^d = y^*} = 0. \tag{2.1.17}$$

This locus is horizontal because aggregate supply and aggregate demand are both independent of $P$. At first glance, this lack of dependence of aggregate supply and aggregate demand on the aggregate price level may appear paradoxical. However, changes in the aggregate price level imply equiproportional changes in all nominal prices. In particular, with the real wage $w$ fixed at $w^*$ to equilibrate the labor market, any change in $P$ must be accompanied by an equiproportional change in the nominal wage $W$. Therefore, although changes in $P$ generate changes in nominal income, such changes in $P$ do *not* generate changes in real income and therefore there is no reason for real consumption, real investment, or real aggregate supply to vary with such changes in $P$. The goods market equilibrium locus is depicted in Figure 2.2.

Below the $y^d = y^*$ locus, there is an excess demand for goods. This region below the goods-market-clearing locus corresponds to the points below $r^*$ in the goods market equilibrium diagram in Figure 2.1. At such points, an increase in the rate of interest is necessary to reduce aggregate demand back down to the fixed level of aggregate supply $y^*$. Above the $y^d = y^*$ locus, there is an excess supply of goods. This region corresponds

---

[1]Our construction of these market-clearing loci follows closely the analysis of Patinkin (1965).

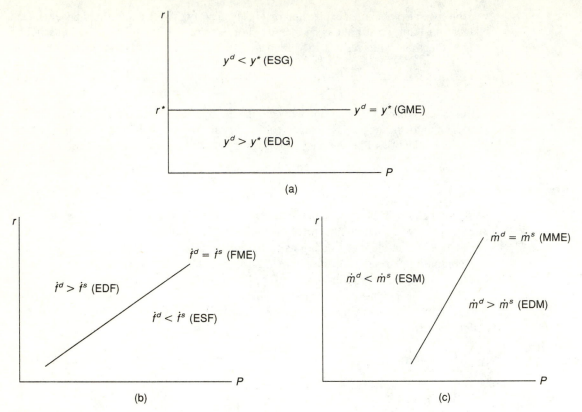

**Figure 2.2**

to those points above $r^*$ in the goods market equilibrium diagram in Figure 2.1. At such points a reduction in the rate of interest is necessary to stimulate investment spending and raise aggregate demand back up to the fixed level of aggregate supply $y^*$.

Next, consider the financial or earning asset market equilibrium condition, $\dot{f}^d = \dot{f}^s$. Differentiating this equilibrium condition with respect to $r$ and $P$, we obtain

$$\left[ \frac{\partial \dot{f}^d}{\partial r} - \frac{\partial \dot{f}^s}{\partial r} \right] dr - \frac{M}{P^2} \frac{\partial \dot{f}^d}{\partial (M/P)} dP = 0 \tag{2.1.18}$$

and so

$$\frac{dr}{dP} \bigg|_{\dot{f}^d = \dot{f}^s} = \frac{\dfrac{M}{P^2} \dfrac{\partial \dot{f}^d}{\partial (M/P)}}{[\partial \dot{f}^d / \partial r - \partial \dot{f}^s / \partial r]} > 0. \tag{2.1.19}$$

The financial market equilibrium locus is therefore upward sloping, as depicted in Figure 2.2. The intuition is as follows. An increase in $P$ lowers real money balances, therefore lowering the demand for additional earning assets and increasing the demand for additional money balances. In order to keep the financial market in equilibrium, we need a reduction in the price of equities and bonds and hence an increase in interest rates to raise the demand for and reduce the supply of additional earning assets.

Next consider points off the $\dot{f}^d = \dot{f}^s$ locus. Above and to the left of the financial market equilibrium locus, the interest rate is too high and hence the price of earning assets is too low. Points in this region correspond to points above $r^*$ in the earning asset market equilibrium diagram in Figure 2.1. At such points, there is an excess flow demand (EDF) for earning assets. Below and to the right of the financial market equilibrium locus, the interest rate is too low and the price of earning assets is too high. Points in this region correspond to points below $r^*$ in the earning asset market equilibrium diagram in Figure 2.1. At such points, there is an excess flow supply (ESF) of earning assets.

Finally, consider the money market equilibrium locus. The money market equilibrium condition is given by $\dot{m}^d = \dot{m}^s$. Differentiating this equilibrium condition with respect to $r$ and $P$, we obtain

$$\frac{\partial \dot{m}^d}{\partial r} dr - \frac{M}{P^2} \frac{\partial \dot{m}^d}{\partial (M/P)} dP = 0, \tag{2.1.20}$$

and therefore,

$$\frac{dr}{dP}\bigg|_{\dot{m}^d = \dot{m}^s} = \frac{M}{P^2} \frac{\partial \dot{m}^d / \partial (M/P)}{\partial \dot{m}^d / \partial r} > 0. \tag{2.1.21}$$

We therefore see that the money market equilibrium locus is upward sloping, as depicted in Figure 2.2. An increase in the price level reduces the stock of real money balances $M/P$. Households therefore wish to replenish their holdings of $M/P$ and so there is a tendency for $\dot{m}^d$ to rise. However, in order to keep $\dot{m}^d$ equal to the fixed value of $\dot{m}^s$, the interest rate must rise sufficiently to offset the incipient rise in $\dot{m}^d$.

Points above and to the left of the money market equilibrium locus are points of excess supply and therefore correspond to points above $r^*$ in the money market equilibrium diagram in Figure 2.1. A reduction in the interest rate is necessary to increase $\dot{m}^d$ and restore equality of $\dot{m}^d$ to the fixed value of $\dot{m}^s$. Alternatively, an increase in $P$ reduces $M/P$, and so a rightward movement in the diagram can also increase $\dot{m}^d$ and hence reequilibrate $\dot{m}^d$ and $\dot{m}^s$. Similarly, points below and to the right of the money market equilibrium locus are points of excess demand, corresponding to points below $r^*$ in the money market equilibrium diagram in Figure 2.1. In this situation an increase in $r$ or a reduction in $P$ is necessary to reduce $\dot{m}^d$ and restore equilibrium with the fixed value of $\dot{m}^s$.

From the household budget constraint we also know that

$$\frac{\partial \dot{m}^d}{\partial (M/P)} = -\frac{\partial \dot{f}^d}{\partial (M/P)} \quad \text{and} \quad \frac{\partial \dot{m}^d}{\partial r} = -\frac{\partial \dot{f}^d}{\partial r}. \tag{2.1.22}$$

Therefore,

$$\frac{dr}{dP}\bigg|_{\dot{m}^d = \dot{m}^s} = \frac{M}{P^2} \frac{\dfrac{\partial \dot{f}^d}{\partial (M/P)}}{\partial \dot{f}^d / \partial r} > \frac{M}{P^2} \frac{\dfrac{\partial \dot{f}^d}{\partial (M/P)}}{[\partial \dot{f}^d / \partial r - \partial \dot{f}^s / \partial r]} = \frac{dr}{dP}\bigg|_{\dot{f}^d = \dot{f}^s}. \tag{2.1.23}$$

Here we see not only that the money market equilibrium locus is upward sloping, but also that its slope is greater than that of the earning asset market equilibrium locus.

We may now draw all three market-clearing loci on the same diagram, as in Figure 2.3, and find the equilibrium values $r^*$ and $P^*$ at the common intersection of the three loci. We know that the three loci must have a common intersection as a consequence of

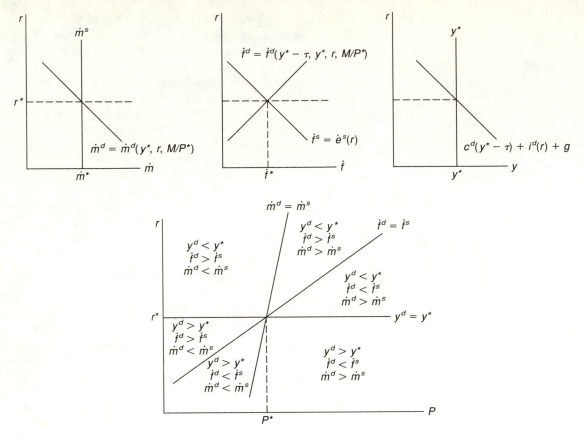

**Figure 2.3**

Walras's law. Consider the intersection of $y^d = y^*$ and $\dot{f}^d = \dot{f}^s$. At this point, the goods and earning asset markets must both be in equilibrium. However, if the goods and earning asset markets are both in equilibrium, Walras's law requires that the money market also be in equilibrium. Therefore, the point $r^*$, $P^*$ must lie on the money market equilibrium locus as well.

Figure 2.3 also depicts the supply and demand curves in each of the three individual markets and the resulting equilibrium values $\dot{m}^*$, $\dot{f}^*$, and $y^*$. Note that all three markets must equilibrate at a common interest rate $r^*$ if in fact $r^*$, $P^*$ is the correct solution to the original general equilibrium problem.

## Instantaneous Portfolio Adjustment

The assumption of gradual adjustment of actual to desired real money balances is conducive to clear thinking independent of whether this assumption is a particularly realistic one or not. While the question of realism of the gradual adjustment approach is still somewhat unresolved, the assumption of gradual adjustment forces us to specify earning asset and money demands as flow demands and therefore also forces us to realize that households' flow demands for goods, earning assets, and money must add up to disposable income regardless of the size of the speed of adjustment parameter $\xi_m$.

In the course of our analysis of comparative statics problems, we wish to be able to keep clear which results depend on the assumption of gradual portfolio adjustment and which do not. It is therefore most helpful to specify the model in such a way that it is straightforward to take the limit of our results as the speed of portfolio adjustment $\xi_m$ approaches infinity. Reassuringly, this exercise provides the same answer to questions that we would have obtained had we specified asset market equilibrium as stock equilibrium from the very beginning.

Utilizing the definition on $\dot{m}^d$ and the household budget constraint, the equilibrium conditions can be written in the following alternate forms:

Goods:

$$c^d(y^* - \tau) + i^d(r) + g - y^* = 0. \tag{2.1.24}$$

Earning assets:

$$y^* - \tau - c^d(y^* - \tau) - \xi_m\left[\left(\frac{M}{P}\right)^d - \frac{M}{P}\right] - \dot{f}^s(r) = 0. \tag{2.1.25}$$

Money:

$$\xi_m\left[\left(\frac{M}{P}\right)^d - \frac{M}{P}\right] - \dot{m}^s = 0. \tag{2.1.26}$$

Rearranging, we obtain:

Goods:

$$c^d(y^* - \tau) + i^d(r) + g - y^* = 0. \tag{2.1.27}$$

Earning assets:

$$\frac{1}{\xi_m}[y^* - \tau - c^d(y^* - \tau) - \dot{f}^s(r)] - \left(\frac{M}{P}\right)^d(y^*, r) + \frac{M}{P} = 0. \tag{2.1.28}$$

Money:

$$\left(\frac{M}{P}\right)^d(y^*, r) - \frac{M}{P} - \frac{1}{\xi_m}\dot{m}^s = 0. \tag{2.1.29}$$

Now taking the limit as $\xi_m \to +\infty$, the second and third of the above equations are both represented by

$$\left(\frac{M}{P}\right)^d - \frac{M}{P} = 0. \tag{2.1.30}$$

We therefore see that if portfolio adjustment is instantaneous, equilibrium for the model as a whole can be summarized by flow equilibrium in the goods market and stock equilibrium in the form of equality of actual and desired real money balances. These two equilibrium conditions should be familiar to those readers who are used to working with traditional IS-LM analysis. In terms of our graphical analysis of the preceding section, as the value of $\xi_m$ increases, the additional earning asset market equilibrium locus rotates toward the additional money balance market equilibrium locus until both become coincident as $\xi_m \to +\infty$.

The relationship of asset flow equilibrium with $\xi_m$ finite and asset stock equilibrium with $\xi_m$ infinite also brings up the question of the appropriate statement of Walras's law for stock excess demand functions. Temporarily ignoring the possible existence of government bonds (whose contribution to wealth we later question anyway), total real wealth is given by

$$\hat{\Omega} = \frac{P_e E}{P} + \frac{M}{P}. \tag{2.1.31}$$

The portfolio choice problem faced by the representative household consists of the decision, at current asset prices, of the distribution of wealth between money balances and equity. Therefore, denoting desired real equity holding as $(P_e E/P)^d$, desired money and equity holdings must satisfy

$$\hat{\Omega} = \left(\frac{P_e E}{P}\right)^d + \left(\frac{M}{P}\right)^d. \tag{2.1.32}$$

Combining the previous two equations, we see that Walras's law for asset stocks is therefore given by

$$\left[\left(\frac{P_e E}{P}\right)^d - \frac{P_e E}{P}\right] + \left[\left(\frac{M}{P}\right)^d - \frac{M}{P}\right] = 0. \tag{2.1.33}$$

In the limiting case in which $\xi_m \to +\infty$, desired and actual stocks of money balances are equated. Stock money market equilibrium therefore also has the property that actual and desired stocks of earning assets (in this case equities) are simultaneously equated.

In most of our subsequent analysis, both for ease in considering the limiting case of $\xi_m \to +\infty$ and because it generally provides more easily interpretable analytical results, we utilize Walras's law to eliminate the earning asset market equilibrium condition from our algebraic manipulations of the model. We therefore formally analyze the following specifications of goods and money market equilibrium:

Goods: $c^d(y^* - \tau) + i^d(r) + g - y^* = 0.$ \hfill (2.1.34)

Money: $(M/P)^d(y^*, r) - M/P - (1/\xi_m)\dot{m}^s = 0.$ \hfill (2.1.35)

Before proceeding with formal analysis of the model written above, it is useful to remind ourselves of a few of the limitations of this model. First of all, recall that consumption demand is assumed to be independent of the rate of interest $r$. While a case can be made for the lack of such an interest rate effect on the representative household's demand for perishable commodities like the composite good of this model, clearly the demand for durable consumption goods should, like the demand for investment goods by the representative firm, be inversely related to the rate of interest. Second, the demand for money, $(M/P)^d$, is the demand for money by the representative household. Throughout the analysis, we assume that the representative firm holds no money and therefore money demand is purely a household phenomenon. However, a more realistic approach recognizes the demand for money by firms and the potential repercussions such a firm demand for money might have on other components in the representative firm's budget constraint.

Fortunately, the demand for durable goods by households and the demand for money by firms are not likely to change many of the qualitative features of the basic model studied in this chapter. The demand for durable goods by households is likely to increase the sensitivity of aggregate demand to the rate of interest $r$. Similarly, the demand for money by firms is likely to increase the sensitivity of money demand to the rate of interest $r$ and the level of aggregate output $y$.

## 2.2 COMPARATIVE STATICS EXERCISES IN THE BASIC MODEL

In this section, we analyze the effects of changes in the exogenous variables on the equilibrium interest rate and price level in the basic model of the preceding section. We first analyze in some detail the response of the model to various changes in the government policy parameters. We then demonstrate an example analysis of the effect of a shift in one of the behavioral relationships, in particular, a shift in the firm's investment demand and additional equity supply schedules.

However, before proceeding, it is useful to reflect on why it is that we are interested in potential sources of such changes in prices and interest rates. Recall that the price level $P$ is the aggregate or average level of prices of all goods and services produced. Therefore, changes in $P$ do not signal changes in relative prices. In many of the models we analyze, the equilibrium value of this aggregate price level has no implications for household welfare or the allocation of resources. However, interest does attach to the process by which the aggregate price level is determined since prices do affect household welfare in some of the alternative models we analyze and because the study of price-level determination is a useful prelude to the analysis, presented in Chapter 6, of inflation.

A more fundamental economic question is the mechanism that determines the equilibrium interest rate. In the absence of secular inflation, as in the present model, 1 plus the interest rate represents the price of current consumption expressed in terms of future consumption. The interest rate is therefore a legitimate *relative* price in the terminology of microeconomics. In the present model, the only allocative impact of changes in the rate of interest are on the aggregate level of investment spending and on the composition of the fixed level of aggregate supply across consumption, investment, and government spending. However, in more general models, we can conceive of the interest rate playing a central role in the representative household's intertemporal optimization problem and the representative household's decision to allocate consumption and leisure across different time periods. Closer attention to these intertemporal substitution possibilities is temporarily postponed until our analysis of Chapter 5.

### Effects of Government Policy Changes

We begin our study of comparative statics by analyzing the effects of sudden, unanticipated step changes in the levels of the government's policy parameters $g$, $\tau$, and $\dot{m}^s$. Recall the government budget constraint

$$g - \tau = \dot{m}^s. \qquad (2.2.1)$$

Therefore, changes in government policies are constrained by

$$dg - d\tau = d\dot{m}^s. \tag{2.2.2}$$

In turn we analyze the effects of three government policy actions:

1. An increase in government spending financed by an increase in taxes.
2. A temporary increase in government spending financed by money creation.
3. A temporary tax cut financed by money creation.

Recall that an implication of Walras's law is that the effects of any exogenous disturbance may be analyzed by looking only at the equilibrium conditions of two of the three markets in our model. Differentiating the goods and money market equilibrium conditions (2.1.34) and (2.1.35) specified in the previous section with respect to $r$, $P$, and the government policy parameters $g$, $\tau$, and $\dot{m}^s$, we obtain

$$\begin{bmatrix} 0 & \dfrac{\partial i^d}{\partial r} \\[2ex] \dfrac{M}{P^2} & \dfrac{\partial (M/P)^d}{\partial r} \end{bmatrix} \begin{bmatrix} dP \\[2ex] dr \end{bmatrix} = \begin{bmatrix} \dfrac{\partial c^d}{\partial z} d\tau - dg \\[2ex] \dfrac{1}{\xi_m} d\dot{m}^s \end{bmatrix}, \tag{2.2.3}$$

subject to $dg - d\tau = d\dot{m}^s$. The determinant of the above matrix is given by

$$\Delta \equiv -\frac{M}{P^2} \frac{\partial i^d}{\partial r} > 0. \tag{2.2.4}$$

Applying Cramer's rule, we obtain

$$dr = \left( \frac{\partial i^d}{\partial r} \right)^{-1} \left[ \frac{\partial c^d}{\partial z} d\tau - dg \right], \tag{2.2.5}$$

$$dP = \frac{1}{\Delta} \left\{ \frac{\partial (M/P)^d}{\partial r} \left[ \frac{\partial c^d}{\partial z} d\tau - dg \right] - \frac{1}{\xi_m} \frac{\partial i^d}{\partial r} d\dot{m}^s \right\}. \tag{2.2.6}$$

**Case 1: $dg = d\tau$**   Let us first consider the case of a permanent increase in government expenditures financed by an increase in taxes. That is, assume that

$$dg = d\tau > 0, \quad \text{with } d\dot{m}^s = 0. \tag{2.2.7}$$

Plugging these values for the differentials in the above equations, we obtain the following comparative statics results:

$$\left. \frac{dr}{dg} \right|_{d\dot{m}^s=0} = -\left( 1 - \frac{\partial c^d}{\partial z} \right) \left( \frac{\partial i^d}{\partial r} \right)^{-1} > 0, \tag{2.2.8}$$

$$\left. \frac{dP}{dg} \right|_{d\dot{m}^s=0} = -\frac{1}{\Delta} \left( 1 - \frac{\partial c^d}{\partial z} \right) \frac{\partial (M/P)^d}{\partial r} > 0. \tag{2.2.9}$$

We therefore find that the tax-financed increase in government spending increases both the interest rate and the level of prices. We also note that these effects are independent of the rate of portfolio adjustment $\xi_m$.

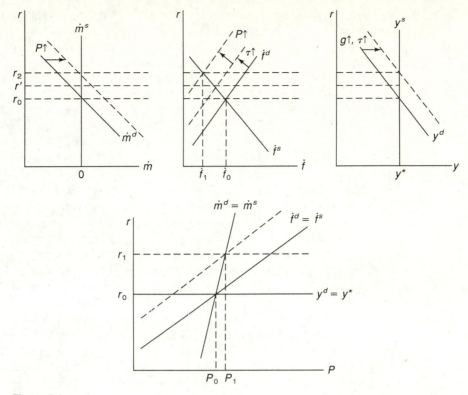

**Figure 2.4**

The effect of this policy change is also presented graphically in Figure 2.4. The increase in government spending increases aggregate demand one-for-one. The increase in taxes lowers aggregate demand, but as long as $\partial c^d / \partial z < 1$, the reduction in aggregate demand is less than one-for-one. Therefore, the $y^d = y^*$ locus shifts upward. The increase in taxes also reduces earning asset demand, and so the financial market equilibrium locus shifts upward as well. A new equilibrium is established at $r_1$, $P_1$.

Figure 2.4 also chronicles the developments in the three individual markets. The direct effect of the policy change itself is a rightward shift in the aggregate demand schedule and a leftward shift in the earning asset demand schedule. However, if the interest rate rose only to $r'$ to equilibrate the earning asset market at the original level of prices, we would still find an excess demand for goods and an excess supply of money. The excess demand for goods requires an increase in the aggregate price level. The resulting increase in prices generates a reduction in the stock of real money balances. This reduction in the stock of real money balances increases the flow demand for money and further reduces the flow demand for earning assets. Therefore, at the higher price level $P_1$, all three markets are able to equilibrate at the new equilibrium interest rate $r_1$.

The intuition behind these results is straightforward. As noted above, the impact effect of this policy move is a net increase in aggregate demand. However, since aggregate supply, government spending, and disposable income, the only explicit determinant of consumption spending, are all exogenous variables, the only remaining mechanism for equilibrating aggregate demand and aggregate supply is variations in the level of investment spending. Therefore the interest rate must rise by enough to make investment spending fall by the difference between the original increase in government spending and the reduction in consumption spending due to the increase in taxes.

Next consider the effect of the policy move on the price level. The real flow supply of money is fixed and the real flow demand for money is proportional to the difference between the desired and actual stocks of real money balances. The stock demand for real money balances falls due to the increase in the rate of interest. The stock supply of real money balances must therefore also fall to restore the proper balance between the actual and desired stocks of real money balances. The equilibrating rise in prices is just sufficient to reduce the actual stock of real money balances to the same extent as the original fall in the desired stock of real money balances due to the rise in interest rates.

In many fixed-price macroeconomic models like those of Chapter 3, an increase in government spending generates an increase in aggregate output $y$. However, in the present model, in which both wages and prices are fully flexible and satisfy market-clearing conditions in the goods and labor markets, there is no effect of an increase in government spending on aggregate output. The increase in prices from $P_0$ to $P_1$ would, with a fixed nominal wage, lead to a reduction in the real wage $W/P$ and hence an increase in labor demand and a reduction in labor supply. However, the resulting incipient excess demand for labor generates an increase in the nominal wage rate that is just sufficient to keep labor demand, labor supply, and employment all equal to their original levels. With no change in employment, there is also no change in aggregate output, which remains equal to $y^*$. Furthermore, the reader should be reminded that all such shifts in the aggregate demand schedule are neutral in their effects on aggregate output in this chapter's flexible-wage and flexible-price model.

While there is no effect of this policy change on the level of aggregate output, there is an effect of this policy change on the composition of output among its final purchasers: households, firms, and the government. Since the source of the disturbance is an increase in government spending, the share of government spending in total output obviously rises. Furthermore, since total output is fixed at $y^*$, the sum of consumption spending plus investment spending must fall by an equal amount. Consumption spending falls due to the increase in taxes. However, because consumption falls less than one-for-one with the increase in taxes ($\partial c^d/\partial z < 1$) and since the tax increase is equal in magnitude to the increase in government spending, it is apparent that investment spending must fall as well to accommodate the increase in government spending. Such a reduction in investment spending is accomplished through a rise in the rate of interest $r$. Therefore, the balanced-budget increase in government spending ''crowds out'' some consumption spending and some investment spending and thereby induces a shift in the command of resources away from the private sector and toward the public sector.

**Case 2: $dg = d\dot{m}^s$**    Let us next analyze the case of a temporary increase in government spending financed by money creation. Assume that we initially start with $\dot{m}^s = 0$ and with all three markets in equilibrium. (The relevant time paths of $g$ and $\dot{m}^s$ are depicted in Figure 2.7.) We begin our analysis by examining the impact effects of the policy change;

that is, the changes in the equilibrium values of $r$ and $P$ that occur immediately following the increases in $g$ and $\dot{m}^s$. With $dg = d\dot{m}^s > 0$ and $d\tau = 0$, we obtain

$$\left.\frac{dr}{d\dot{m}^s}\right|_{d\tau=0} = -\left(\frac{\partial i^d}{\partial r}\right)^{-1} > 0, \tag{2.2.10}$$

$$\left.\frac{dP}{d\dot{m}^s}\right|_{d\tau=0} = -\frac{1}{\Delta}\left(\frac{1}{\xi_m}\frac{\partial i^d}{\partial r} + \frac{\partial(M/P)^d}{\partial r}\right) > 0. \tag{2.2.11}$$

A money-financed increase in government spending initially raises both the interest rate and the level of prices. The qualitative nature of these results is also independent of the speed of portfolio adjustment $\xi_m$. However, note that the quantitative effect of the policy change on $P$ is reduced at higher values of $\xi_m$.

Graphically, the increase in government spending shifts the $y^d = y^*$ locus upward. The increase in the flow supply of money shifts the money market equilibrium locus downward and to the right. The financial market equilibrium locus is unaffected by the policy move. These impact effects are depicted in Figure 2.5.

Figure 2.5 also depicts the effects of the disturbance and the subsequent changes in $r$ and $P$ on the supply and demand curves in the three individual markets. As a direct result

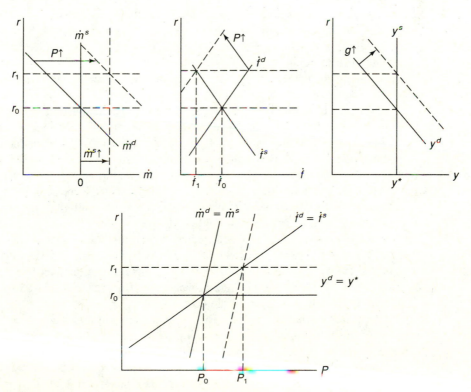

**Figure 2.5**

of the policy move, the aggregate demand curve shifts rightward due to the increase in $g$. The additional money demand curve also shifts to the right because new money is being issued to pay for the increase in government spending. The policy change therefore generates an excess demand for goods and an excess supply of money at the original values $r_0$ and $P_0$. The excess aggregate demand generates pressure for the aggregate price level to rise. This increase in prices lowers the stock of real money balances, and the additional earning asset demand curve therefore shifts leftward and the additional money demand curve shifts rightward. Equilibrium is restored in all three markets at $r_1$, $P_1$.

Some readers, particularly those whose earlier training included a heavy dose of sticky-price analysis, may find it surprising to see a policy action that could be considered a move toward a more ''expansionary'' monetary policy result in *higher* rather than lower interest rates. However, in the present, flexible-price model, the primary role for interest rate movements is to assure equality between aggregate demand and the fixed level of aggregate supply. The immediate goods market effect of the Case 2 policy experiment is the increase in goods demand due to the increase in government spending. The primary implication of the money financing of the increase in government spending is that, unlike the accompanying tax increase of Case 1, such money financing does not provide any direct offsetting effects on aggregate demand. Therefore, the interest rate must rise, in this circumstance, by enough to reduce investment spending by the full amount of the increase in government spending. That is, the increase in government spending ''crowds out'' an exactly equal amount of investment spending. We therefore find that the rise in the interest rate in Case 2 is quantitatively larger than the rise in the interest rate in Case 1, in which the crowding out of investment was less than one-for-one due to the induced decline in consumption spending.

Unlike Case 1, these impact effects are not the end of the story. In Case 2, there is another, permanent effect. With $\dot{m}^s > 0$, we also have $dM/dt > 0$. That is, the stock of money begins to grow over time. To properly analyze the dynamic effects of periods in which $dM/dt \neq 0$, we need to write down an explicitly dynamic model, an exercise we postpone until Chapter 6. We can, however, get a flavor of the dynamic effects of the implied evolution of $M$ over time by analyzing the effects of an unanticipated step change in the stock of money $M$. We may then pretend that at each instant of time at which $\dot{m}^s > 0$, there is a new, infinitesimally small, unanticipated increase in the money supply. This exercise then traces out a pseudodynamic adjustment pattern of the economy for the entire period of time in which $\dot{m}^s > 0$.

An increase in the stock of $M$, holding $P$ constant, results in an increase in $f^d$ and a reduction in $\dot{m}^d$. The earning asset equilibrium locus therefore shifts downward and to the right and the money market equilibrium locus therefore shifts even farther to the right. These shifts are depicted in Figure 2.6, where the effects of an increase in $M$ are depicted relative to the initial position of the economy at $r_0$, $P_0$.

We therefore find that as long as $\dot{m}^s > 0$, the level of prices continues to rise. When levels of government spending and money creation are restored to their original values, the impact effects of the government policy move disappear. However, the increased stock of money balances in the form of an increase in $M$ remains as a legacy of the policy. We can analyze the effects of a permanent increase in $M$ by differentiating the goods and money market equilibrium conditions with respect to $r$, $P$, and $M$. This procedure yields

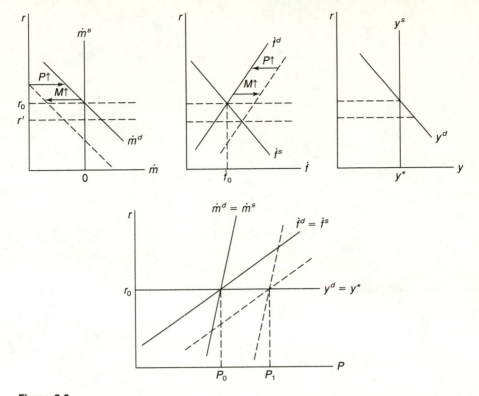

**Figure 2.6**

$$\begin{bmatrix} 0 & \dfrac{\partial i^d}{\partial r} \\[3mm] \dfrac{M}{P^2} & \dfrac{\partial (M/P)^d}{\partial r} \end{bmatrix} \begin{bmatrix} \dfrac{dP}{dM} \\[3mm] \dfrac{dr}{dM} \end{bmatrix} = \begin{bmatrix} 0 \\[3mm] \dfrac{1}{P} \end{bmatrix}.$$

$$(2.2.12)$$

Applying Cramer's rule, we obtain

$$\frac{dr}{dM} = \frac{1}{\Delta}(0) = 0,$$

$$(2.2.13)$$

$$\frac{dP}{dM} = -\frac{1}{\Delta}\left(\frac{1}{P}\,\frac{\partial i^d}{\partial r}\right) = \frac{P}{M}.$$

$$(2.2.14)$$

We therefore find that the permanent legacy of the money-financed, temporary increase in government expenditures is an increase in the level of prices proportional to the total increase in the money supply with no permanent change in the rate of interest. Note that these qualitative effects are independent of the speed of portfolio adjustment. The time patterns of the exogenous and endogenous variables for the entire scenario of Case 2 are depicted in Figure 2.7. The value of $P_3$ relative to the value of $P_1$ in Figure 2.7 depends on

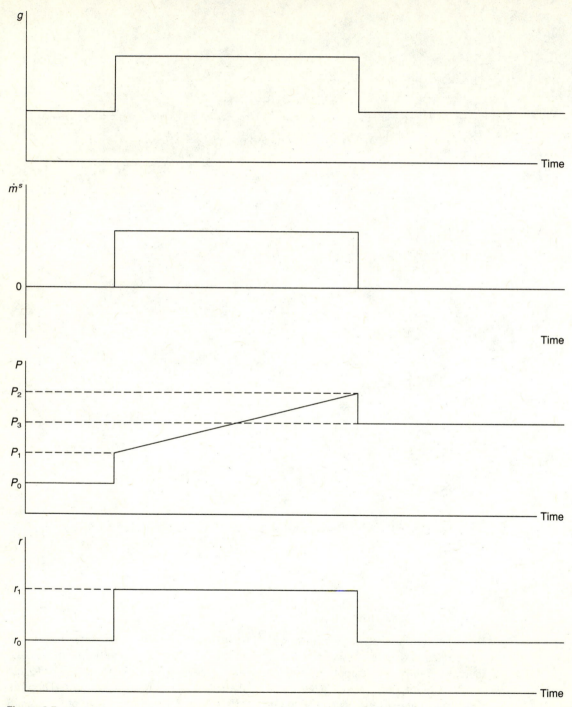

**Figure 2.7**

the slopes of the market-clearing loci, the size of the increase in government spending, and the amount of time the policy is pursued.

**Case 3: $d\dot{m}^s = -d\tau$**     We next analyze the case of a temporary tax cut financed by a temporary increase in the rate of expansion of the money supply. Again we begin the analysis with $\dot{m}^s = 0$ and assume that all three markets start out in equilibrium. Substituting $dg = 0$ and $d\dot{m}^s = -d\tau$ into the comparative statics solution from above, we obtain

$$\left.\frac{dr}{d\dot{m}^s}\right|_{dg=0} = -\frac{\partial c^d}{\partial z}\left(\frac{\partial i^d}{\partial r}\right)^{-1} > 0, \tag{2.2.15}$$

$$\left.\frac{dP}{d\dot{m}^s}\right|_{dg=0} = -\frac{1}{\Delta}\left[\frac{\partial (M/P)^d}{\partial r}\frac{\partial c^d}{\partial z} + \frac{1}{\xi_m}\frac{\partial i^d}{\partial r}\right] > 0. \tag{2.2.16}$$

These results are qualitatively the same as were obtained for the impact effects in Case 2. The interest rate and the level of prices both rise. However, it is straightforward to show that these effects are quantitatively smaller than those of Case 2 for an equal-sized increase in $\dot{m}^s$. Furthermore, we again find that these qualitative results are independent of the speed of portfolio adjustment $\xi_m$. However, faster portfolio adjustment does imply a smaller price response.

These impact effects are depicted graphically in Figure 2.8. The reduction in taxes generates an increase in aggregate goods demand and an increase in the demand for additional earning assets. The $y^d = y^*$ locus therefore shifts upward and the $\dot{f}^d = \dot{f}^s$ locus therefore shifts to the right. The increase in the flow supply of money finally shifts the $\dot{m}^d = \dot{m}^s$ locus to the right as well. Equilibrium in the three markets is restored at $r_1$, $P_1$.

Figure 2.8 also depicts the developments in each of the three individual markets as well. The tax cut shifts both the aggregate goods demand schedule and the demand for additional earning asset schedule to the right. The increase in $\dot{m}^s$ shifts the supply of additional money balances schedule to the right. If the interest rate immediately adjusted to $r'$ to clear the earning asset market at $P_0$, there would remain an excess demand for goods and an excess supply of money. The level of prices therefore rises to equate goods supply and goods demand. The higher price level also generates a reduction in the level of real money balances that results in an increase in the demand for additional money balances and a reduction in the demand for additional earning assets. Equilibrium in all three markets is finally attained at $r_1$, $P_1$.

As in Case 2, as long as $\dot{m}^s > 0$, the level of $M$ continues to increase over time. This increase in $M$ further shifts the $\dot{f}^d = \dot{f}^s$ and $\dot{m}^d = \dot{m}^s$ loci to the right, which generates continuing increases in the level of prices. Finally, when $\dot{m}^s$ returns to zero and $\tau$ returns to its original value, the impact effects disappear. However, just as in Case 2, the legacy of the increase in the money stock $M$ remains. Interestingly, the effect of the permanent increase in the money supply is exactly the same as it was in Case 2. We ultimately wind up with an equiproportional increase in $P$ with no change in $r$. That is, we still obtain

$$\frac{dr}{dM} = 0 \quad \text{and} \quad \frac{dP}{dM} = \frac{P}{M}. \tag{2.2.17}$$

Not surprisingly, the graphical representation of the effects of the resulting permanent increase in the money supply is exactly as it was in Figure 2.6.

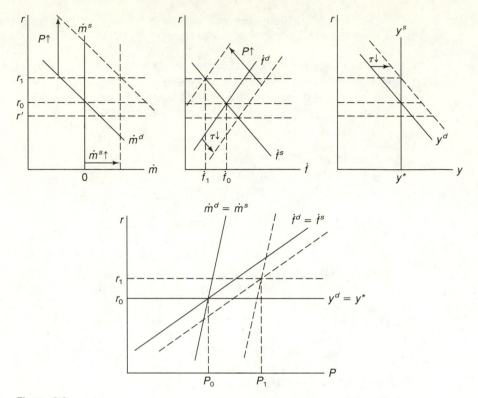

**Figure 2.8**

## The Neutrality of Money

An economic system is said to possess *neutrality* if an increase in all exogenous variables denominated in the unit of account (nominal exogenous variables) leads to an equiproportional increase in all endogenous variables denominated in the unit of account (nominal endogenous variables) with no change in the other endogenous variables (real endogenous variables).

Note that in the current model the only nominal exogenous variable is the nominal money supply $M$. We have seen above that an increase in $M$ leads to an equiproportional increase in $P$ with no change in the real endogenous variable $r$. Therefore the current model possesses neutrality. Neutrality of money has long been considered an important characteristic of equilibrium economic models. After all, since money possesses no special characteristics other than its acceptance as a medium of exchange, why should it matter for the conduct of real economic activity or for the determination of relative prices exactly how many dollars (or pesos, etc.) of it are in circulation.

## A Shift in Investment Demand and Earning Asset Supply

The method of comparative statics is useful, not only for analysis of the effects of changes in government policies, but also for analysis of the effects of exogenous shifts in the underlying behavioral relationships. As a representative example of this type of disturbance, let us consider the effects of a shift in the profitability of investment expenditures.

As noted in Chapter 1, business firms have an incentive to issue additional equities and purchase additional capital as long as the marginal product of newly installed capital exceeds the rate of return on financial assets (government bonds and equities). Let us now assume that the productivity of existing capital is unchanged so that the levels of employment and aggregate supply also remain unchanged. Let us further assume, however, that the invention of a new productive process raises the marginal product of newly installed capital. Such a disturbance raises the gap between $R$ and $r$ and therefore increases the representative firm's optimal rate of investment at the current rate of interest. Also, since the firm's budget constraint requires that $i^d \equiv \dot{e}^s$, we know that this disturbance implies an equal increase in the supply of additional earning assets.

It is often useful to introduce a shift parameter to capture the potential effects of such a disturbance. In the present case we denote the occurrence of the event of the introduction of the new production process by $\alpha$. The investment demand and earning asset supply functions are therefore given by

$$i^d = i^d(r, \alpha), \qquad \frac{\partial i^d}{\partial \alpha} > 0, \tag{2.2.18}$$

$$\dot{e}^s = \dot{e}^s(r, \alpha), \qquad \frac{\partial \dot{e}^s}{\partial \alpha} > 0. \tag{2.2.19}$$

Obviously, Walras's law requires that $\partial i^d/\partial \alpha = \partial \dot{e}^s/\partial \alpha$.

We now simply replace the original $i^d$ and $\dot{e}^s$ functions in the statement of the model with the modified behavioral relationships written above. With these substitutions in place, we are ready to formally analyze the effects of the change in investment opportunities (the change in $\alpha$) on the equilibrium interest rate and price level. As in all comparative statics exercises, we are free to choose to analyze this disturbance in any two of the three markets in our model. Again it is convenient to utilize the goods and money market equilibrium conditions for this purpose.

Differentiating the goods and money market equilibrium conditions with respect to $P$, $r$, and $\alpha$ and dividing through by $d\alpha$, we obtain

$$\begin{bmatrix} 0 & \dfrac{\partial i^d}{\partial r} \\[2ex] \dfrac{M}{P^2} & \dfrac{\partial (M/P)^d}{\partial r} \end{bmatrix} \begin{bmatrix} \dfrac{dP}{d\alpha} \\[2ex] \dfrac{dr}{d\alpha} \end{bmatrix} = \begin{bmatrix} -\dfrac{\partial i^d}{\partial \alpha} \\[2ex] 0 \end{bmatrix}. \tag{2.2.20}$$

Solution of the above equation by Cramer's rule yields

$$\frac{dr}{d\alpha} = \frac{1}{\Delta} \frac{M}{P^2} \frac{\partial i^d}{\partial \alpha} = -\frac{\partial i^d/\partial \alpha}{\partial i^d/\partial r} > 0, \tag{2.2.21}$$

$$\frac{dP}{d\alpha} = -\frac{1}{\Delta} \frac{\partial (M/P)^d}{\partial r} \frac{\partial i^d}{\partial \alpha} > 0. \tag{2.2.22}$$

We therefore find that the more favorable investment opportunities lead to an increase in the equilibrium interest rate and price level.

We can also analyze this disturbance graphically. The increase in investment demand shifts the $y^d = y^*$ locus upward and the increase in earning asset supply shifts the $\dot{f}^d = \dot{f}^s$ locus upward and to the left. Figure 2.9 depicts the resulting increase in the equilibrium values of $r$ and $P$. Figure 2.9 also depicts the effects of the change in $\alpha$ in the three individual markets. In the goods market, the increase in $i^d$ shifts the aggregate demand schedule to the right. In the earning asset market, the increase in equity supply shifts the earning asset supply curve to the right as well. If the interest rate adjusted immediately to equate earning asset supply and demand, the interest rate would move to $r'$. However, at $r'$ there is still an excess demand for goods and an excess supply of additional money balances.

The excess demand for goods generates an increase in the price level. This increase in the price level implies a reduction in the stock of real money balances. The reduction in the stock of real money balances induces households to try to restore their holdings of money by increasing $\dot{m}^d$ and reducing $\dot{f}^d$. Eventually, equilibrium is realized in all three markets at $r_1, P_1$.

It is also straightforward to demonstrate that in equilibrium the actual level of investment is unchanged from its previous value. Although this result may not be immediately obvious, it is easy to explain. In this experiment, the level of government spending remains constant. Similarly, since the levels of income and taxation are also constant, the

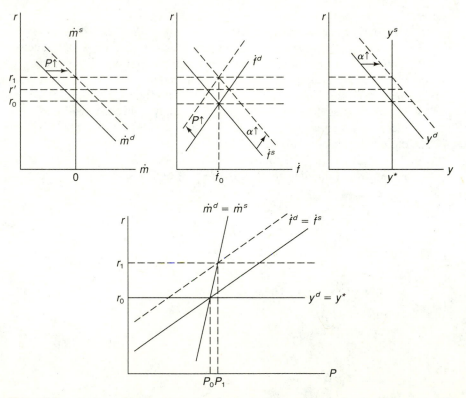

**Figure 2.9**

level of disposable income is unchanged. Therefore, if consumption demand depends only on the level of disposable income, there is no way in which the level of consumption can change in response to the change in $\alpha$. Therefore, the level of investment must be equal to $y^* - c^d - g$. With $c^d$ and $g$ fixed in this case, the increase in the equilibrium interest rate must just be enough to restore the level of investment demand to its original value.

Analysis of comparative statics exercises like that of a shift in the investment demand schedule is a main motivation for the construction of economic models in the first place. The reader is therefore encouraged to gain confidence in the ability to analyze such disturbances. In particular, the reader may wish to practice by analyzing the effects of disturbances such as

1. An increase in consumption demand financed by a reduction in earning asset demand.
2. An increase in the stock demand for money, $(M/P)^d$.

## 2.3 GOVERNMENT BONDS IN THE BASIC MODEL

We are now ready to reintroduce the possibility of government issuance of bonds. In this more general model, we may expect $B \neq 0$ and $\dot{b}^s \neq 0$. Earning asset supply $\dot{f}^s$ now consists of the sum of government bond supply $\dot{b}^s$ plus firm supply of additional equities $\dot{e}^s$. The assumption that bonds and equities are perfect substitutes allows these two assets to be aggregated in such a simple manner.

Since households now hold government bonds in their portfolios ($B > 0$), we need to change our specification of disposable income $z$. Because firm dividend payments to equity holders is always equal to $y - (W/P)\ell$, the sum of dividend plus labor income always exactly exhausts total production $y$. Therefore the composition of income between labor income and profits does not affect disposable income. However, the real value of interest payments on the government debt must be added to real disposable income and so, in general, we have

$$z = y + \frac{B}{P} - \tau. \tag{2.3.1}$$

A final complication generated by the inclusion of government bonds involves the government budget constraint. Recall that, in general,

$$g + \frac{B}{P} = \tau + \dot{m}^s + \dot{b}^s. \tag{2.3.2}$$

At any point in time, $B/P$ is a predetermined variable. This leaves government policymakers with four policy variables, any three of which may be set independently. The model is now given by:

### Market-clearing Conditions

Goods:

$$c^d(z) + i^d(r) + g - y^* = 0. \tag{2.3.3}$$
$$\underset{(+)}{\phantom{c^d(z)}} \quad \underset{(-)}{\phantom{i^d(r)}}$$

Earning assets:

$$\dot{f}^d\underset{(+)\ (-)\ (+)\ (+)}{\left( z\ ,\ y^*,\ r\ ,\ \frac{M}{P} \right)} - \underset{(-)}{\dot{e}^s(r)} - \dot{b}^s = 0. \tag{2.3.4}$$

Money

$$\dot{m}^d\underset{(+)\ (-)\ (-)}{\left( y^*,\ r\ ,\ \frac{M}{P} \right)} - \dot{m}^s = 0. \tag{2.3.5}$$

### Definitions and Identities

Government budget constraint: $g + B/P - \tau = \dot{m}^s + \dot{b}^s$.

Disposable income: $z = y^* + B/P - \tau$.

### Exogenous Variables

Real: $y^*$, potential shift parameters, three among $g$, $\tau$, $\dot{m}^s$, and $\dot{b}^s$.

Nominal: $M$, $B$.

### Endogenous Variables

Real: $r$ and one among $g$, $\tau$, $\dot{m}^s$, and $\dot{b}^s$.

Nominal: $P$.

Note that the model still possesses neutrality. Starting from equilibrium, an equi-proportional increase in $M$ and $B$ brings about an equiproportional increase in $P$ with no change in $r$. It is also straightforward to demonstrate that Walras's law still holds. The sectoral budget constraints are now given by:

Households: $y^* + B/P - \tau = c^d + \dot{f}^d + \dot{m}^d$. $\tag{2.3.6}$

Firms: $i^d = \dot{e}^s$. $\tag{2.3.7}$

Government: $\dot{m}^s + \dot{b}^s = g + B/P - \tau$. $\tag{2.3.8}$

Substituting equation (2.3.8) into equation (2.3.6), we obtain

$$y^* - g + \dot{m}^s + \dot{b}^s = c^d + \dot{f}^d + \dot{m}^d, \tag{2.3.9}$$

or

$$0 = c^d + g - y^* + \dot{f}^d - \dot{b}^s + \dot{m}^d - \dot{m}^s. \tag{2.3.10}$$

Now adding zero in the form of $i^d - \dot{e}^s$ and rearranging, we obtain

$$0 = c^d + i^d + g - y^* + \dot{f}^d - \dot{e}^s - \dot{b}^s + \dot{m}^d - \dot{m}^s. \tag{2.3.11}$$

The above equation is the modified version of Walras's law.

## Endogenous Government Policy Choice

In the previous analysis in which $B = \dot{b}^s = 0$, all of the variables in the government budget constraint, $g$, $\tau$, and $\dot{m}^s$, were real exogenous variables. While it may appear that $\dot{m}^s = (1/P)(dM/dt)$ contains the nominal endogenous variable $P$, this is in fact not the case. Recall that we specified the flow supply of money as a real exogenous variable because we implicitly assumed that the rate of change of the nominal money supply is governed by the relationship $dM/dt = P\dot{m}^s$. Therefore, increases in the price level automatically translate into changes in $dM/dt$, and so the government need not adjust either $g$ or $\tau$ in response to changes in the level of prices.[2]

With government bonds outstanding ($B > 0$), we need to be more careful about making explicit how the government responds to changes in $P$. Continue to assume that the flow supply of money $\dot{m}^s$ is specified in real terms and assume that the flow supply of government bonds is also specified in real terms, so that $dB/dt = P\dot{r}b^s$.[3] Analogous reasoning suggests that we specify interest payments on government bonds in real terms as well, that is, $B = P(B/P)$, with $B/P$ held fixed. However, this assumption only makes sense if government bond interest payments are indexed to the price level or if the government makes large separate tax or transfer payments in the form of bonds every time there is a change in the price level. While actual governments occasionally issue indexed bonds, such issuances are a rarity. Likewise, bond tax or transfer payments linked to the level of prices are a possible but not very realistic alternative. We therefore need to substitute some other assumption about how the government endogenously responds to changes in the price level.

One somewhat realistic possibility that also greatly simplifies the analysis of the effects of exogenous disturbances and other government policy changes is to allow the government to respond to changes in the real value of interest payments by changing the real level of taxation. That is, assume that real tax collections are given by

$$\tau = \tau_0 + \frac{B}{P}. \tag{2.3.12}$$

The basic level of taxation $\tau_0$ is now the government's exogenous policy choice variable. Once $\tau_0$ is chosen, total tax collections $\tau$ vary both with the level of prices $P$ and with changes over time in the level of government bonds outstanding. With this specification

---

[2] Differentiation of $m$ with respect to time yields

$$\dot{m} = \frac{d}{dt}\frac{M}{P} = \frac{1}{P}\frac{dM}{dt} - \frac{M}{P^2}\frac{dP}{dt}.$$

However, throughout the analysis of this chapter, we take the level of prices as constant and so $dP/dt = 0$. The assumption that $dP/dt = 0$ is consistent with the property of this model, that analysis is always conducted at a single point in time at which $P$ and $r$ are constant and equal to their market-clearing values. A change in $P$ in this context is to be interpreted as a comparison of equilibrium properties of the model across different circumstances with different values of the endogenous variables. Chapter 6 formally considers a truly dynamic analysis in which $dP/dt$ may be nonzero.

[3] This relationship requires the assumption that $dr/dt = 0$ as well as the assumption that $dP/dt = 0$.

for $\tau$, the model is given by:

### Market-clearing Conditions

Goods: $c^d(y^* - \tau_0) + i^d(r) + g - y^* = 0.$ (2.3.13)

Earning assets: $\dot{f}^d(y^* - \tau_0, y^*, r, M/P) - \dot{e}^s(r) - \dot{b}^s = 0.$ (2.3.14)

Money: $\dot{m}^d(y^*, r, M/P) - \dot{m}^s = 0.$ (2.3.15)

### Definitions and Identities

Government budget constraint: $g - \tau_0 = \dot{m}^s + \dot{b}^s.$

### Exogenous Variables

Real: $y^*$, potential shift parameters, three among $g$, $\tau_0$, $\dot{m}^s$, and $\dot{b}^s$.
Nominal: $M$, $B$.

### Endogenous Variables

Real: $r$ and one among $g$, $\tau_0$, $\dot{m}^s$, and $\dot{b}^s$.
Nominal: $P$.

Inspection of these market-clearing conditions will ensure the reader that this particular specification for $\tau$ also leaves the slopes of the market-clearing loci independent of $B$ and unchanged from the preceding section. We are therefore immediately able to proceed to an analysis of policy effects involving changes in the flow supply of bonds.

Using Walras's law to eliminate the earning asset market equilibrium condition and recalling the definition of $\dot{m}^d$, the equilibrium of the model may be written as

$$c^d(y^* - \tau_0) + i^d(r) + g - y^* = 0,$$ (2.3.16)

$$\left(\frac{M}{P}\right)^d (y^*, r) - \frac{M}{P} - \frac{1}{\xi_m}\dot{m}^s = 0.$$ (2.3.17)

Note that these expressions are unchanged from the model of the previous section in which $B = \dot{b}^s = 0$ except that $\tau_0$ replaces $\tau$ on the assumption that $\tau = \tau_0 + B/P$.

## Fiscal Policy

Pure fiscal policy actions involve changes in taxes financed by government sales or purchases of government bonds. Let us first consider the effects of an unanticipated, temporary tax cut financed by government bond sales. Assume that we are initially in equilibrium with $\dot{b}^s = \dot{m}^s = 0$. Now assume that $\tau_0$ falls and $\dot{b}^s$ rises by an equal amount.

Let us first analyze the effects of this policy move analytically. Differentiating the goods and money market equilibrium conditions with respect to $P$, $r$, $\tau_0$, and $\dot{b}^s$, we obtain

$$
\begin{bmatrix} 0 & \dfrac{\partial i^d}{\partial r} \\[2ex] \dfrac{M}{P^2} & \dfrac{\partial (M/P)^d}{\partial r} \end{bmatrix} \begin{bmatrix} \dfrac{dP}{d\tau_0} \\[2ex] \dfrac{dr}{d\tau_0} \end{bmatrix} = \begin{bmatrix} \dfrac{\partial c^d}{\partial z} \\[2ex] 0 \end{bmatrix}. \tag{2.3.18}
$$

Solving by Cramer's rule, we find that

$$
\left. \frac{dr}{d\tau_0} \right|_{d\dot{b}^s = -d\tau_0} = -\frac{1}{\Delta}\frac{M}{P^2}\frac{\partial c^d}{\partial z} < 0, \tag{2.3.19}
$$

$$
\left. \frac{dP}{d\tau_0} \right|_{d\dot{b}^s = -d\tau_0} = \frac{1}{\Delta}\frac{\partial (M/P)^d}{\partial r}\frac{\partial c^d}{\partial z} < 0. \tag{2.3.20}
$$

For the case of a tax cut, we have $d\tau_0 < 0$, and so the above expressions show that a bond-financed tax cut raises both interest rates and the level of prices. Note that these results are both independent of the size of $\xi_m$, the rate of portfolio adjustment.

We can also analyze the effect of this disturbance graphically. In the goods market the reduction in taxes increases consumption demand. Therefore the $y^d = y^*$ locus shifts upward. In the earning asset market, the flow supply of government bonds rises due to the policy action. The tax cut also increases earning asset demand, but by less than the rise in earning asset supply, since $\partial \dot{f}^d/\partial z = 1 - \partial c^d/\partial z < 1$. Therefore the earning asset market equilibrium locus shifts to the left. Finally, the flow demand for and flow supply of money are both unaffected, and so the position of the money market equilibrium locus remains unchanged. As shown in Figure 2.10, the interest rate and price level both unambiguously rise. The rise in prices also implies that $B/P$ falls. Our specification of the government budget constraint forces the government to spend this "inflation dividend" in the form of a further cut in taxes, so that $z = y^* + B/P - \tau$ remains constant.

Figure 2.10 also depicts the effects of the policy change in the three individual markets. The tax cut increases goods demand and therefore shifts the aggregate demand curve to the right. The tax cut also shifts the earning asset demand curve to the right. The increase in the flow supply of bonds shifts the earning asset supply curve to the right by a greater distance than the rightward shift in the earning asset demand curve. If the interest rate moved to clear the earning asset market with no change in the level of prices, the interest rate would move to $r'$. However, at $r'$, there is an excess demand for goods and an excess supply of additional money balances. Therefore the level of prices must rise. The rise in prices reduces $M/P$, which leads to an increase in $\dot{m}^d$ and a reduction in $\dot{f}^d$. Full equilibrium is reestablished at $r_1$, $P_1$.

Over time, with $\dot{b}^s > 0$, the outstanding stock of government bonds $B$ grows and so must nominal interest payments that need to be financed. However, our assumption that tax collections are automatically adjusted in response to changes in $B$ and $P$ guarantees that there are no further impacts on the market-clearing conditions. Eventually, the government resets $\dot{b}^s = 0$. At this point the levels of prices and interest rates revert to their initial values, $r_0$ and $P_0$. The only legacy of the experience is that taxes must be higher than they were originally in order to pay interest on the increase in government bonds outstanding.

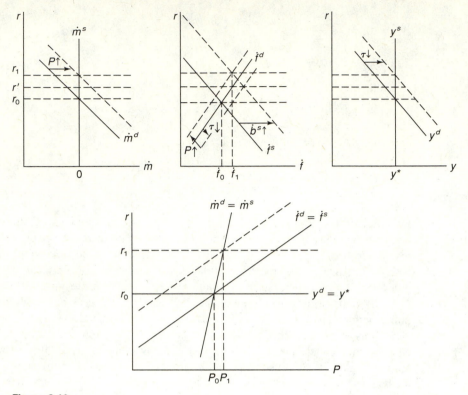

**Figure 2.10**

## Monetary Policy

Pure monetary policy involves open-market purchases and sales of government bonds by the government. These purchases and sales are generally conducted by the government's central bank. In the present model there are two ways that we can specify such open-market purchases and sales. One possibility is to allow the central bank to make a finite-size transaction in an instant of calendar time. That is, at any instant of time, we may consider the effect of a disturbance of the form

$$dM = -\frac{1}{r} \, dB. \tag{2.3.21}$$

With our current specification of the government budget constraint, in which we set $\tau = \tau_0 + B/P$, the effect of this type of policy move is identical to the effect of the corresponding change in the stock of money $M$ in the model of the preceding section without government bonds. So, for example, the effect of an open-market purchase of government bonds in the present model would be exactly the same as that depicted in Figure 2.6. The price level would rise in proportion to the increase in the money supply, and there would be no change in the rate of interest. The corresponding reduction in the level of government bonds outstanding would result in a reduction in government interest payments, but the resulting effects of the change in interest payments on disposable income would be neutralized by a simultaneous cut in taxes.

An alternate definition of open-market operations involves a disturbance of the form

$$d\dot{m}^s = -d\dot{b}^s. \tag{2.3.22}$$

This flow open-market operation involves offsetting changes in the flow supplies of money and government bonds holding $g$ and $\tau_0$ constant. Obviously, over time the effect of such a flow open-market purchase or sale is about the same as a stock open-market purchase or sale. However, if household's asset demand functions only gradually adjust to discrepancies between $(M/P)^d$ and $M/P$, such flow open-market operations will have an effect on the economy even before they translate into measurable changes in $M$ and $B$.

Let us therefore now consider a case in which the government temporarily increases the flow supply of money and reduces the flow supply of government bonds. Differentiating the goods and money market equilibrium conditions with respect to $P$, $r$, $\dot{m}^s$, and $\dot{b}^s$, we obtain

$$\begin{bmatrix} 0 & \dfrac{\partial i^d}{\partial r} \\[2ex] \dfrac{M}{P^2} & \dfrac{\partial (M/P)^d}{\partial r} \end{bmatrix} \begin{bmatrix} \dfrac{dP}{d\dot{m}^s} \\[2ex] \dfrac{dr}{d\dot{m}^s} \end{bmatrix} = \begin{bmatrix} 0 \\[2ex] \dfrac{1}{\xi_m} \end{bmatrix}. \tag{2.3.23}$$

Solving by Cramer's rule, we obtain

$$\left. \frac{dr}{d\dot{m}^s} \right|_{d\dot{m}^s = -d\dot{b}^s} = 0, \tag{2.3.24}$$

$$\left. \frac{dP}{d\dot{m}^s} \right|_{d\dot{m}^s = -d\dot{b}^s} = -\frac{1}{\xi_m \Delta} \frac{\partial i^d}{\partial r} > 0. \tag{2.3.25}$$

We therefore find that the flow open-market purchase, just like the stock open-market purchase, results in an increase in the level of prices with no change in the equilibrium interest rate. This result occurs in the present analysis even before the changes in $\dot{m}^s$ and $\dot{b}^s$ can translate into changes in the stocks of money and bonds. Note, however, that this impact effect on the price level only occurs in the case in which $\xi_m$, the rate of portfolio adjustment, is finite. Otherwise, changes in the flow supplies of money and government-issued bonds have no impact on financial markets.

If after a period of time $\dot{m}^s$ and $\dot{b}^s$ are reset to their initial values of zero, then these impact effects disappear. The ultimate effect of the temporary change in the growth rates of money and bonds is a change in the level of prices proportional to the ultimate effect of the policy move on the stock of money $M$. That is, we continue to find that $dr/dM = 0$ and $dP/dM = P/M$.

We can also analyze this disturbance graphically. The increase in $\dot{m}^s$ and the reduction in $\dot{b}^s$ generate no impact effects in the goods market and so the $y^d = y^*$ locus remains unchanged. In the earning asset market, the reduction in government bond supply shifts the earning asset market equilibrium locus downward and to the right. The increase in the flow supply of money shifts the money market equilibrium locus downward and to the

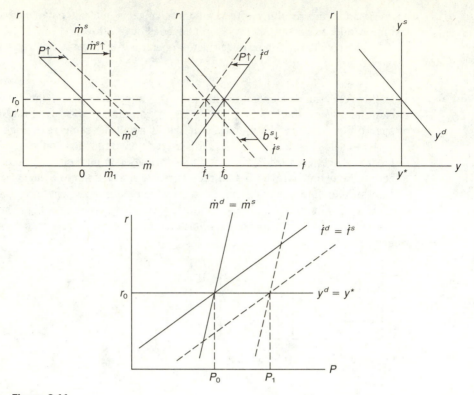

**Figure 2.11**

right as well. Therefore, we see that Figure 2.11 confirms the increase in $P$ and lack of a change in $r$ that we derived analytically above.

Figure 2.11 also depicts the effects of the flow open-market purchase on the three individual markets as well. The policy change shifts the supply of additional money balances schedule to the right and the supply of additional earning assets schedule to the left by an equal amount. If the interest rate reequated the earning asset market at $r'$, there would be an excess demand for goods and an excess supply of additional money balances. The excess demand for goods generates an increase in prices. The higher price level reduces the stock of real money balances, increasing the demand for additional money balances and reducing the demand for additional earning assets. All three markets finally equilibrate at $r_0$, $P_1$.

## An Alternative Formulation of Government Behavior

In the previous section, we pointed out that whenever there are government bonds outstanding, we need to specify how the government responds to changes in the real value of interest payments on those government bonds. We have analyzed the simple case in which tax collections are altered in such a way as to exactly offset any changes in the real value of interest payments. In this formulation $g$, $\dot{m}^s$, and $\dot{b}^s$ can all be properly viewed as strictly exogenous.

We now consider an alternative specification of how government might respond to changes in $B/P$. The motivation for this analysis is twofold. First of all, particularly over short periods of time, the current burden of debt service does not appear to be a compelling practical concern for most policymakers. Second, the extreme sort of neutrality results obtained with our original formulation do not square with most interpretations of the empirical record.

Now let us assume an alternative policy rule in which changes in $B/P$ are financed by changes in the flow supply of additional earning assets. In particular, let

$$\dot{b}^s = \dot{b}^s_0 + \frac{B}{P}, \qquad (2.3.26)$$

with $\dot{b}^s_0$ considered an exogenous policy parameter. In this formulation, government sets a basic rate of additional bond supply, $\dot{b}^s_0$, but then alters that basic supply of additional bonds one-for-one with changes in the real value of interest payments on the existing stock of bonds. This formulation isolates government's choice of $g$, $\tau$, and $\dot{m}^s$ so that these items do not have to be altered according to the current state of the economy. Since actual government policy is often set in terms of these policy parameters for significant periods of time, such a formulation may more closely mimic practical experience.

With this specification for government policy behavior, our model of the economy is reformulated as:

### Market-clearing Conditions

Goods: $c^d(y^* + B/P - \tau) + i^d(r) + g - y^* = 0.$       (2.3.27)

Earning assets: $\dot{f}^d(y^* + B/P - \tau, y^*, r, M/P) - \dot{e}^s(r) - \dot{b}^s_0 - B/P = 0.$     (2.3.28)

Money: $\dot{m}^d(y^*, r, M/P) - \dot{m}^s = 0.$       (2.3.29)

### Definitions and Identities

Government budget constraint: $g - \tau = \dot{m}^s + \dot{b}^s_0.$

### Exogenous Variables

Real: $y^*$, potential shift parameters, three among $g$, $\tau$, $\dot{m}^s$, and $\dot{b}^s_0$.
Nominal: $M$, $B$.

### Endogenous Variables

Real: $r$ and one among $g$, $\tau$, $\dot{m}^s$, and $\dot{b}^s_0$.
Nominal: $P$.

Differentiating these equilibrium conditions with respect to $r$ and $P$, we calculate the slopes of the resulting market-clearing loci as

$$\left.\frac{dr}{dP}\right|_{y^d=y^*} = \frac{B}{P^2}\frac{\partial c^d/\partial z}{\partial i^d/\partial r} < 0, \qquad (2.3.30)$$

$$\frac{dr}{dP}\bigg|_{\dot{f}^d=\dot{f}^s} = \frac{\dfrac{M}{P^2}\dfrac{\partial \dot{f}^d}{\partial(M/P)} - \dfrac{B}{P^2}\left(1 - \dfrac{\partial \dot{f}^d}{\partial z}\right)}{\partial \dot{f}^d/\partial r - \partial \dot{e}^s/\partial r} \gtreqless 0, \tag{2.3.31}$$

$$\frac{dr}{dP}\bigg|_{\dot{m}^d=\dot{m}^s} = \frac{M}{P^2}\frac{\partial \dot{m}^d/\partial(M/P)}{\partial \dot{m}^d/\partial r} > 0. \tag{2.3.32}$$

We therefore see that in the present formulation of the model, the goods market equilibrium locus is now downward sloping and the slope of the earning asset market equilibrium locus is now of ambiguous sign. However, Walras's law still guarantees that

$$\frac{dr}{dP}\bigg|_{y^d=y^*} < \frac{dr}{dP}\bigg|_{\dot{f}^d=\dot{f}^s} < \frac{dr}{dP}\bigg|_{\dot{m}^d=\dot{m}^s}. \tag{2.3.33}$$

It is again useful to utilize the goods and money market equilibrium conditions for our algebraic analysis of comparative statics exercises. Recalling the definition of $\dot{m}^d$, these equilibrium conditions can be written as

$$c^d\left(y^* + \frac{B}{P} - \tau\right) + i^d(r) + g - y^* = 0, \tag{2.3.34}$$

$$\left(\frac{M}{P}\right)^d(y^*, r) - \frac{M}{P} - \frac{1}{\xi_m}\dot{m}^s = 0. \tag{2.3.35}$$

Differentiating these equilibrium conditions with respect to $P$, $r$, and the government policy parameters, we obtain

$$\begin{bmatrix} -\dfrac{B}{P^2}\dfrac{\partial c^d}{\partial z} & \dfrac{\partial i^d}{\partial r} \\[2ex] \dfrac{M}{P^2} & \dfrac{\partial(M/P)^d}{\partial r} \end{bmatrix} \begin{bmatrix} dP \\[2ex] dr \end{bmatrix} = \begin{bmatrix} \dfrac{\partial c^d}{\partial z}\,d\tau - dg - \dfrac{1}{P}\dfrac{\partial c^d}{\partial z}\,dB \\[2ex] \dfrac{1}{P}\,dM + \dfrac{1}{\xi_m}\,d\dot{m}^s \end{bmatrix}. \tag{2.3.36}$$

Most of the effects of changes in those government policy parameters measured as flows (i.e., $g$, $\tau$, $\dot{m}^s$, and $\dot{b}^s_0$) are qualitatively unchanged from the analysis of the previous section. While there are some minor modifications attributable to the nonzero slope of the goods market equilibrium locus and the ambiguous sign of the earning asset market equilibrium locus, we leave the effects of such modifications to the interested reader.

Our principal current interest attaches to the effects of changes in $M$ and $B$ over time periods in which $\dot{m}^s \neq 0$ and/or $\dot{b}^s_0 \neq 0$. Evaluating the matrix expression above by use of Cramer's rule, we obtain

$$\frac{dr}{dM} = -\frac{1}{\Delta}\frac{B}{P^3}\frac{\partial c^d}{\partial z} < 0, \tag{2.3.37}$$

$$\frac{dP}{dM} = -\frac{1}{\Delta}\frac{1}{P}\frac{\partial i^d}{\partial r} = \frac{P}{M}\frac{\partial i^d/\partial r}{\dfrac{\partial i^d}{\partial r} + \dfrac{B}{M}\dfrac{\partial c^d}{\partial z}\dfrac{\partial(M/P)^d}{\partial r}} > 0, \tag{2.3.38}$$

$$\frac{dr}{dB} = \frac{1}{\Delta}\frac{M}{P^3}\frac{\partial c^d}{\partial z} > 0, \tag{2.3.39}$$

$$\frac{dP}{dB} = -\frac{1}{\Delta}\frac{1}{P}\frac{\partial c^d}{\partial z}\frac{\partial (M/P)^d}{\partial r} > 0, \tag{2.3.40}$$

where

$$\Delta = -\frac{1}{P}\left[\frac{B}{P}\frac{\partial c^d}{\partial z}\frac{\partial (M/P)^d}{\partial r} + \frac{M}{P}\frac{\partial i^d}{\partial r}\right] > 0. \tag{2.3.41}$$

We therefore find that increases in $M$ not matched by equiproportional increases in $B$ are no longer neutral. An increase in the money supply lowers the rate of interest and generates a less than proportional increase in prices since $dP/dM < P/M$.

These results are easily interpretable. The increase in the money supply increases the price level and lowers the real value of government bond interest payments. Consumption therefore falls. Interest rates must fall to increase investment and keep $y^d = y*$. The lower interest rate means that the demand for real money balances rises. Therefore the increase in prices must be less than in proportion to the original increase in the money supply so that the supply of real money balances can rise to meet the increase in demand.

The size of the stock of government bonds outstanding is no longer irrelevant for the determination of the equilibrium levels of $r$ and $P$. An increase in the stock of bonds now generates an increase in aggregate demand. Interest rates must rise to generate an offsetting reduction in investment demand. With higher interest rates, the demand for real money balances falls. Therefore prices rise to reduce the real value of the fixed nominal money supply.

A stock open-market purchase of government bonds involves changes in the supplies of both money and bonds such that $r\,dM = -dB > 0$. This disturbance has an effect similar to the effect of the increase in the money supply considered above. The interest rate now falls *both* due to the increase in $M$ and the coincident reduction in $B$. The effect on $P$ is formally ambiguous, however. Setting $r\,dM = -dB$ in the matrix expression above, we obtain, by application of Cramer's rule,

$$\left.\frac{dP}{dM}\right|_{dB=-r\,dM} = \frac{1}{P\Delta}\left[r\frac{\partial c^d}{\partial z}\frac{\partial (M/P)^d}{\partial r} - \frac{\partial i^d}{\partial r}\right] \gtreqless 0. \tag{2.3.42}$$

## An Alternative Parameterization of Government Liabilities

In our discussion of Section 2.2, we noted that money is neutral in the basic model without government bonds. An increase in the money supply in that model generates an equiproportional increase in the level of prices and has no effect on the rate of interest. In our earlier discussion in the present section, we noted that under one set of assumptions about government behavior money is neutral, and under another set of assumptions about government behavior money is not neutral. However, recall that in our original discussion of neutrality, we provided a general definition of neutrality that requires only that relative prices be independent of equiproportional changes in *all* nominal exogenous variables. As we demonstrate below, almost all flexible-price macroeconomic models are characterized by this form of neutrality.

In our current framework, the money supply $M$ and the supply of government bonds $B$ are the only two nominal exogenous variables. Therefore, one natural comparative statics experiment is an equiproportional increase in both money and government bonds.

If such a disturbance generates an equiproportional increase in $P$ with no change in $r$, then the economic system is neutral. To facilitate such an experiment, define the ratio of government bonds to money, $B/M \equiv \theta$. An increase in the money supply $M$ holding $\theta$ constant therefore constitutes an equiproportional change in both money and bonds.

In much of our later analysis, it turns out to be more convenient to parameterize the supply of government-issued liabilities by $\theta$ and $M$ rather than $B$ and $M$. Obviously, changes in $\theta$, $B$, and $M$ must satisfy

$$dB = \theta \, dM + M \, d\theta \tag{2.3.43}$$

or

$$d\theta = \frac{1}{M} \, dB - \frac{\theta}{M} \, dM. \tag{2.3.44}$$

Just as obvious is the fact that any exogenous disturbance originally parameterized in one set of policy variables is readily translated into the other set of policy variables. In particular,

$$dM \bigg|_{dB=0} \Rightarrow \begin{cases} d\theta = -\dfrac{\theta}{M} \, dM, \\ dM = dM, \end{cases} \tag{2.3.45}$$

$$dM \bigg|_{dB=-r\,dM} \Rightarrow \begin{cases} d\theta = -\dfrac{r+\theta}{M} \, dM, \\ dM = dM, \end{cases} \quad \text{(open-market operation)} \tag{2.3.46}$$

$$dB \bigg|_{dM=0} \Rightarrow \begin{cases} d\theta = \dfrac{1}{M} \, dB, \\ dM = 0. \end{cases} \tag{2.3.47}$$

Substituting $\theta$ into the equilibrium conditions of the current model, we obtain

$$c^d\left(y^* + \theta\frac{M}{P} - \tau\right) + i^d(r) + g - y^* = 0, \tag{2.3.48}$$

$$\left(\frac{M}{P}\right)^d (y^*, r) - \frac{M}{P} - \frac{1}{\xi_m}\dot{m}^s = 0. \tag{2.3.49}$$

Now differentiating the equilibrium conditions with respect to $P$, $r$, $M$, and $\theta$, we obtain

$$\begin{bmatrix} -\theta\dfrac{M}{P^2}\dfrac{\partial c^d}{\partial z} & \dfrac{\partial i^d}{\partial r} \\[3mm] \dfrac{M}{P^2} & \dfrac{\partial(M/P)^d}{\partial r} \end{bmatrix} \begin{bmatrix} dP \\[3mm] dr \end{bmatrix} = \begin{bmatrix} -\dfrac{M}{P}\dfrac{\partial c^d}{\partial z}\,d\theta - \dfrac{\theta}{P}\dfrac{\partial c^d}{\partial z}\,dM \\[3mm] \dfrac{1}{P}\,dM \end{bmatrix}. \tag{2.3.50}$$

Use of Cramer's rule facilitates the following results:

$$\frac{dr}{dM} = 0, \tag{2.3.51}$$

$$\frac{dP}{dM} = \frac{P}{M}, \tag{2.3.52}$$

$$\frac{dr}{d\theta} = \frac{1}{\Delta} \frac{M^2}{P^3} \frac{\partial c^d}{\partial z} > 0, \tag{2.3.53}$$

$$\frac{dP}{d\theta} = -\frac{1}{\Delta} \frac{M}{P} \frac{\partial c^d}{\partial z} \frac{\partial (M/P)^d}{\partial r} > 0, \tag{2.3.54}$$

where

$$\Delta \equiv -\left[ \theta \frac{M}{P} \frac{\partial c^d}{\partial z} \frac{\partial (M/P)^d}{\partial r} + \frac{M}{P^2} \frac{\partial i^d}{\partial r} \right] > 0. \tag{2.3.55}$$

Since $dr/dM = 0$ and $dP/dM = P/M$, the current economic model is characterized by neutrality. Furthermore, it is straightforward to reconstruct the results of the previous section by translating from these expressions in $M$ and $\theta$ to those expressions in $M$ and $B$ derived above.

The analysis above clearly indicates that the choice of assumption about how government responds to changes in $B/P$ can be crucial. In particular, if we assume that taxes adjust to keep $B/P - \tau$ constant, then holding constant the size of the money supply, the size of ratio of bonds to money, $\theta$, is irrelevant. Alternatively, if the government holds $B/P - \dot{b}^s$ constant, then changes in $\theta$ do affect the intertemporal terms of trade $r$ since we find that $dr/d\theta > 0$ in this case.

We shall reencounter this question of whether the composition of government liabilities between money and bonds or between non-interest-bearing and interest-bearing forms matters for the allocation of resources both in this chapter and in later chapters. Therefore, for purposes of comparison, it is important for us to realize exactly why any models that we study might provide such a channel of influence for changes in $\theta$.

In the present analysis, we need to realize that the assumptions we have chosen to work with are not, strictly speaking, logically compatible. We have been assuming that agents expect current levels of $P$, $r$, and $\tau$ to be constant into the indefinite future. However, starting with $\dot{b}^s = 0$ and with policy set to keep $B/P - \dot{b}^s$ constant, any disturbance that changes $B/P$ must force $\dot{b}^s \neq 0$. Therefore, over time, we get continuous changes in $B$ that force even further changes in $\dot{b}^s$. Eventually, if taxes are not adjusted, $P$ and/or $r$ must change, an occurrence that is inconsistent with agents' expectations. Unfortunately, more careful analysis of government policy and formation of consistent expectations must await the development of a formal dynamic specification of the model, a task we postpone until Chapter 6.

## 2.4 WEALTH EFFECTS

Formalization of the household's choice problem as a utility maximization problem over a finite horizon along the lines of Barro and Grossman (1976) suggests that the initial level of wealth should influence the household's demands for goods, earning assets, and money.[4] Wealth may also affect labor supply, but this complication is postponed until Chapter 5. First consider the consumption-saving decision. If a household has more real wealth, holding constant its lifetime income stream, it can consume more both now and in the future. Therefore, in response to an increase in real wealth, the representative household may plan to increase current and future consumption and reduce current saving.

## Components of Wealth

One component of wealth would be the real value of stocks of consumer durables and owner-occupied housing. Another component would be the real value of the stock of human capital owned by households. However, since the quantities of these items are predetermined at a point in time and change only slowly over time, they are assumed constant and are therefore suppressed throughout the analysis.

Next consider the liabilities of the government: money and government bonds. While it is clear that real money balances $M/P$ are wealth, it is not so clear whether government bonds should be counted as wealth. In this section we adopt our original parameterization of government policy in which taxes are expressed as $\tau = \tau_0 + B/P$. If we then further assume that taxes are adjusted to keep $\tau_0$ constant, it is likely that rational agents realize that higher government bond interest payments necessitate higher current and/or future taxes.

The rational expectation that such higher interest payments portend higher taxes therefore casts some doubt over whether households view government bonds as conferring net wealth. In particular, Barro (1974) catalogues a sizable collection of sets of alternative assumptions under which government bonds should not constitute net wealth. However, households see the present discounted value of tax payments as lasting over a finite time horizon, while the earning asset market values the government bond interest payments as lasting over an infinite time horizon. In particular, toward the end of the planning horizon, the representative household may plan to liquidate its holdings of government bonds and use the proceeds to purchase consumption goods while correctly perceiving that taxes need not be paid after death.[5]

There is also the possibility that the government may act as a financial intermediary if capital markets are not perfect. Moral hazard problems often prevent agents from borrowing against potential future earnings. Therefore, debt-financed current tax reductions for households with very little wealth, to be made up for with higher future tax levies on these same households, may result in an increase in current consumption normally frustrated by the assumed absence of perfect capital markets.

As this discussion of the wealth aspects of government bond holdings suggests, there are many ways to motivate wealth effects and many different specific functional forms could be justified as proxies for wealth. Furthermore, empirical evidence on the question

---

[4]Important early contributions to the general equilibrium analysis of such effects include Meltzer (1951) and Patinkin (1965).

[5]An explicit analysis of the representative household's consumption-saving choice was first presented in Appendix 1.C. In Appendix 2.A, we demonstrate how a finite planning horizon generates a consumption function with wealth as an argument.

of whether or not government bonds constitute net wealth is not yet conclusive.[6] Instead of presenting a lengthy discussion of these possibilities, we confine the analysis to a study of the theoretical implications of the specific functional form for consumption spending adopted by Patinkin (1965).

We therefore formally postulate that real consumption demand $c^d$ is given by

$$c^d = c^d(z^*, \Omega), \tag{2.4.1}$$
$$\underset{(+)}{\phantom{c^d = c^d(}} \underset{(+)}{\phantom{z^*,}} \phantom{\Omega)}$$

where $z^*$ represents expected disposable income and $\Omega$ represents wealth. The household wealth variable is assumed to be of the form

$$\Omega = \frac{M}{P} + \frac{\kappa B}{rP} + \frac{\Pi}{r}, \qquad 0 \le \kappa \le 1 \tag{2.4.2}$$

Barro (1974) would argue that $\kappa = 0$.

The variable $z^*$ includes those components of the representative household's endowment that are not included in $\Omega$. Such additional sources of revenue would include labor income (income from equity holdings is already included in $\Omega$) net of taxes. For the purposes of the present analysis, we adopt the assumption that $z^*$ and $\Omega$ are both exogenous. We further assume that exogenous shifts in $z^*$ and $\Omega$ are independent of one another.

In the analysis of Chapter 1, we motivated a stock demand for money based purely upon the representative household's optimal response to a particularly simple transaction technology. We further assumed that the representative household only slowly eliminated any divergence between actual and desired levels of real money balances. The analyses of Sections 2.1–2.3 are therefore based on a specification for real holdings of money balances in which the optimal stock of real money balances depends directly on the volume of transactions and the brokerage costs associated with sales of earning assets and inversely on the rate of interest. If we view the level of income $y$ as a proxy for the volume of transactions and suppress the presumably fixed real level of brokerage fees, we can summarize the inventory-theoretic approach of Baumol (1952) and Tobin (1956) by assuming that the representative household's desired holdings of real money balances are given by

$$\left(\frac{M}{P}\right)^d = \left(\frac{M}{P}\right)^d(y, r), \qquad \frac{\partial (M/P)^d}{\partial y} > 0, \qquad \frac{\partial (M/P)^d}{\partial r} < 0. \tag{2.4.3}$$

An alternative approach to the household portfolio allocation problem is provided by Tobin (1958). This alternative approach views money as a direct portfolio substitute for holdings of government bonds and equities. Government bonds and equities are subject to market price variability while money is not. Therefore, under conditions of uncertainty, agents may find it optimal to hold some money because the variance of money's pecuniary

---

[6]Feldstein (1982) presents evidence supporting the view that households value government debt as net wealth. Alternatively, Kormendi (1983) and Seater and Mariano (1985) find that the contribution of government bonds to net wealth is approximately offset by the present value of expected future tax liabilities.

rate of return is zero even though money offers a strictly lower average rate of return than earning assets.

While the portfolio approach views the money demand process in a very different light, the resulting implications for household behavior are very similar. The portfolio approach shares with the transactions approach the property that the optimal stock of real money balances is inversely related to the rate of return on earning assets (the rate of interest). The only principal difference between the two approaches is that the portfolio approach suggests using wealth as a scaling variable while the transactions approach suggests using income as a scaling variable. We therefore continue to utilize an income-related scale variable, actual aggregate income $y^*$, as an argument of $(M/P)^d(\cdot)$. However, for the remainder of Section 2.4, we analyze a model in which the demand for money depends both on the income variable $y^*$ as suggested by the transactions approach and the wealth variable $\Omega$ as suggested by the portfolio approach.

We therefore postulate a stock demand-for-money function of the form

$$\left(\frac{M}{P}\right)^d \underset{(+)\ (-)\ (+)}{(y^*,\ r\ ,\ \Omega)}, \qquad 0 < \frac{\partial(M/P)^d}{\partial\Omega} < 1. \tag{2.4.4}$$

If we retain the stock adjustment mechanism, the above stock demand-for-money function implies a flow demand for money of the form

$$\dot{m}^d = \xi_m \left[ \left(\frac{M}{P}\right)^d (y^*, r, \Omega) - \frac{M}{P} \right], \tag{2.4.5}$$

or

$$\dot{m}^d = \dot{m}^d \underset{(+)\ (-)\ (-)\ (+)}{\left(y^*,\ r\ ,\ \frac{M}{P},\ \Omega\right)}, \tag{2.4.6}$$

with

$$\frac{\partial\dot{m}^d}{\partial\Omega} < -\frac{\partial\dot{m}^d}{\partial(M/P)}. \tag{2.4.7}$$

The representative household's budget constraint therefore also implies

$$\dot{f}^d = z - c^d - \dot{m}^d = \dot{f}^d \underset{(+)\ (-)\ (-)\ (+)\ (+)\ (-)}{\left(z\ ,\ z^*,\ y^*,\ r\ ,\ \frac{M}{P},\ \Omega\right)}, \tag{2.4.8}$$

where

$$\frac{\partial\dot{f}^d}{\partial z} = 1.$$

$$\frac{\partial\dot{f}^d}{\partial\Omega} = -\frac{\partial c^d}{\partial\Omega} + \frac{\partial\dot{m}^d}{\partial\Omega} < 0. \tag{2.4.9}$$

This last partial derivative is unambiguously negative because we are increasing $\Omega$ holding $M/P$ constant. Note, however, that actual disposable income $z$ is not necessarily the same as the expected disposable income variable $z^*$.

## Market-clearing Conditions and Market-clearing Loci

As noted above, we now invoke our original assumption that taxes are given by $\tau = \tau_0 + B/P$. We also adopt the definition of nominal government-issued liabilities, $A \equiv M + \kappa B/r$. The model is therefore given by:

### Market-clearing Conditions

Goods:

$$c^d(\underset{(+)}{z^*},\ \underset{(+)}{\Omega}) + \underset{(-)}{i^d(r)} + g - y^* = 0. \tag{2.4.10}$$

Earning assets:

$$\dot{f}^d(\underset{(+)}{z},\ \underset{(-)}{z^*},\ \underset{(-)}{y^*},\ \underset{(+)}{r},\ \underset{(+)}{\frac{M}{P}},\ \underset{(-)}{\Omega}) - \underset{(-)}{\dot{e}^s(r)} - \dot{b}^s = 0. \tag{2.4.11}$$

Money:

$$\dot{m}^d(\underset{(+)}{y^*},\ \underset{(-)}{r},\ \underset{(-)}{\frac{M}{P}},\ \underset{(+)}{\Omega}) - \dot{m}^s = 0. \tag{2.4.12}$$

### Definitions and Identities

Government budget constraint: $g - \tau_0 = \dot{m}^s + \dot{b}^s$.

Actual disposable income: $z = y^* - \tau_0$.

Wealth: $\Omega = A/P + RK/r = M/P + \kappa B/rP + RK/r$.

### Exogenous Variables

Real: $y^*$, $z^*$, shift parameters, three among $g$, $\tau_0$, $\dot{m}^s$, and $\dot{b}^s$.

Nominal: $M$, $B$.

### Endogenous Variables

Real: $r$ and one among $g$, $\tau_0$, $\dot{m}^s$, and $\dot{b}^s$.

Nominal: $P$.

We now compute the slopes of the market-clearing loci. Differentiating the goods market equilibrium condition with respect to $P$ and $r$, we obtain

$$\left.\frac{dr}{dP}\right|_{y^d=y^*} = \frac{-\dfrac{A}{P^2}\dfrac{\partial c^d}{\partial \Omega}}{\dfrac{1}{r}\left(\dfrac{\kappa B}{rP} + \dfrac{RK}{r}\right)\dfrac{\partial c^d}{\partial \Omega} - \dfrac{\partial i^d}{\partial r}} < 0. \tag{2.4.13}$$

The slope of the goods market equilibrium locus is unambiguously negative. An increase in the price level reduces the real value of the money and bond components of wealth, lowering aggregate demand. In order to keep the goods market in equilibrium, we require a reduction in the rate of interest. The reduction in the interest rate directly stimulates investment spending. A reduction in the interest rate also increases the market values of government bonds and equities. The resulting increase in wealth reinforces the increase in investment demand with an increase in consumption demand.

Next, consider the money market. First let us rewrite the money market equilibrium condition in the form

$$\left(\frac{M}{P}\right)^d (y^*, r, \Omega) - \frac{M}{P} - \frac{1}{\xi_m} \dot{m}^s = 0. \tag{2.4.14}$$

Differentiating the money market equilibrium condition with respect to $P$ and $r$, we obtain

$$\left.\frac{dr}{dP}\right|_{\dot{m}^d = \dot{m}^s} = -\frac{\dfrac{1}{P}\left(\dfrac{M}{P} - \dfrac{A}{P}\dfrac{\partial (M/P)^d}{\partial \Omega}\right)}{\dfrac{\partial (M/P)^d}{\partial r} - \dfrac{1}{r}\left(\dfrac{\kappa B}{rP} + \dfrac{RK}{r}\right)\dfrac{\partial (M/P)^d}{\partial \Omega}}. \tag{2.4.15}$$

The denominator of this expression is unambiguously negative. An increase in the interest rate directly lowers money demand. An increase in the interest rate also reduces the market values of government bonds and equities. The resulting reduction in wealth reinforces the reduction in money demand. However, the sign of the numerator of the above expression is ambiguous.

An increase in the price level directly lowers the real value of the stock of money balances. However, the increase in prices also reduces the real value of nominally denominated assets (money and bonds) that are components of wealth. This wealth effect reduces the stock demand for money. Therefore the net effect on the flow demand for money is ambiguous. However, we normally assume that the direct effect on the real stock of money dominates, and so we now assume that

$$\left.\frac{dr}{dP}\right|_{\dot{m}^d = \dot{m}^s} > 0. \tag{2.4.16}$$

A necessary and sufficient condition for an upward-sloping money market equilibrium locus is that

$$\frac{\Omega}{M/P}\frac{\partial (M/P)^d}{\partial \Omega} < \frac{\Omega}{A/P} \quad \text{or} \quad \frac{A}{M}\frac{\partial (M/P)^d}{\partial \Omega} < 1. \tag{2.4.17}$$

This condition is almost surely satisfied. One sufficient condition is that the elasticity of the stock demand for money with respect to wealth be less than unity. That is, marginal increases in wealth must lower the desired ratio of money to wealth. The goods and money market equilibrium loci are depicted in Figure 2.12.

Finally, consider the earning asset market equilibrium condition. It is useful to write this equilibrium condition in the form

$$z - c^d(z^*, \Omega) - \xi_m\left[\left(\frac{M}{P}\right)^d (y^*, r, \Omega) - \frac{M}{P}\right] - i^d(r) - \dot{b}^s = 0. \tag{2.4.18}$$

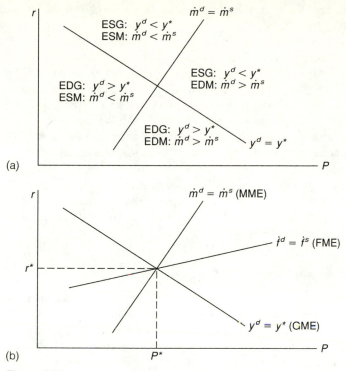

**Figure 2.12**

Differentiating with respect to $P$ and $r$, we obtain

$$\frac{dr}{dP}\bigg|_{\dot{f}^d=\dot{f}^s} = \frac{\dfrac{\xi_m}{P}\left(\dfrac{M}{P} - \dfrac{A}{P}\dfrac{\partial(M/P)^d}{\partial\Omega}\right) - \dfrac{1}{P}\dfrac{A}{P}\dfrac{\partial c^d}{\partial\Omega}}{\dfrac{1}{r}\left(\dfrac{\kappa B}{rP} + \dfrac{RK}{r}\right)\left[\dfrac{1}{\xi_m}\dfrac{\partial(M/P)^d}{\partial\Omega} + \dfrac{\partial c^d}{\partial\Omega}\right] - \xi_m\dfrac{\partial(M/P)^d}{\partial r} - \dfrac{\partial i^d}{\partial r}} . (2.4.19)$$

The denominator of this expression is unambiguously positive. An increase in interest rates lowers investment. As a consequence, equity supply falls and the excess demand for financial assets rises. An increase in the interest rate also induces a direct reduction in the demand for money. The demand for additional earning assets therefore rises as households adjust their portfolios. Finally, an increase in interest rates lowers the market values of bonds and equities. The resulting fall in wealth increases savings and lowers the demand for money. Both of these wealth effects tend to increase the excess demand for financial assets.

The sign of the numerator of this expression is ambiguous. An increase in the price level lowers the real value of nominally denominated assets. This effect leads to a reduction in consumption spending and an equal increase in the excess demand for additional earning assets. An increase in the price level also lowers both the level of real balances and the stock demand for real balances. However, we have already assumed that the net effect of an increase in the price level is an increase in the flow demand for money, which has as its counterpart a reduction in the flow demand for earning assets. Therefore, the net effect of an increase in the price level on the flow excess demand for additional earning assets is ambiguous.

While the slope of the earning asset market equilibrium locus is of ambiguous sign, Walras's law does provide some additional information about this locus. Walras's law states that the sum of the excess demands for goods, earning assets, and money must equal zero. Therefore, it is impossible to simultaneously have excess supplies of or excess demands for goods, earning assets, and money at the same time. Therefore, the diagram depicting the goods and money market equilibrium loci indicates that the slope of the earning asset market equilibrium locus must be greater than the slope of the goods market equilibrium locus but less than the slope of the money market equilibrium locus. All three market-clearing loci are depicted in the same diagram in Figure 2.12. The diagram is drawn with a positively sloped earning asset market equilibrium curve. The earning asset market equilibrium locus is upward sloping if the money market equilibrium locus is also upward sloping and if $\xi_m$, the rate at which actual real money balances are adjusted toward desired real money balances, is large.

## Comparative Statics Experiments

We are now ready to investigate whether the presence of wealth effects changes the comparative statics results derived earlier in this chapter in any important ways. For the most part, the results of those exogenous disturbances involving changes in flow magnitudes like $g$, $\tau$, $\dot{m}^s$, and $\dot{b}^s$ are unchanged. The only possibilities for change come about due to the downward slope of the goods market equilibrium locus and the ambiguous sign of the earning asset market equilibrium locus. The details of these comparative statics problems are left as exercises for the interested reader.

We therefore turn our attention to the effects of changes in the stocks of money and government-issued bonds. As noted in the previous section, we continue to find it easier to parameterize the model in terms of $\theta$ and $M$ instead of $B$ and $M$. Recalling that we have defined $\theta \equiv B/M$, the goods and money market equilibrium conditions can be written as

$$c^d\left( z^*, \frac{M}{P}\left( 1 + \frac{\kappa\theta}{r} \right) + \frac{RK}{r} \right) + i^d(r) + g - y^* = 0, \tag{2.4.20}$$

$$\left( \frac{M}{P} \right)^d\left( y^*, r, \frac{M}{P}\left( 1 + \frac{\kappa\theta}{r} \right) + \frac{RK}{r} \right) - \frac{M}{P} - \frac{1}{\xi_m}\dot{m}^s = 0. \tag{2.4.21}$$

Differentiating the above expressions with respect to $P$, $r$, $M$, and $\theta$ and noting that $(1 + \kappa\theta/r) = (A/P)/(M/P) = A/M$, we obtain

$$\begin{bmatrix} -\dfrac{A}{P^2}\dfrac{\partial c^d}{\partial \Omega} & \dfrac{\partial i^d}{\partial r} - \dfrac{1}{r}\left( \dfrac{\kappa B}{rP} + \dfrac{RK}{r} \right)\dfrac{\partial c^d}{\partial \Omega} \\[3mm] \dfrac{M}{P^2}\left[ 1 - \dfrac{A}{M}\dfrac{\partial (M/P)^d}{\partial \Omega} \right] & \dfrac{\partial (M/P)^d}{\partial r} - \dfrac{1}{r}\left( \dfrac{\kappa B}{rP} + \dfrac{RK}{r} \right)\dfrac{\partial (M/P)^d}{\partial \Omega} \end{bmatrix} \begin{bmatrix} dP \\[5mm] dr \end{bmatrix}$$
$$= \begin{bmatrix} -\dfrac{1}{P}\dfrac{A}{M}\dfrac{\partial c^d}{\partial \Omega} \, dM & -\dfrac{\kappa}{r}\dfrac{M}{P}\dfrac{\partial c^d}{\partial \Omega} \, d\theta \\[3mm] \dfrac{1}{P}\left[ 1 - \dfrac{A}{M}\dfrac{\partial (M/P)^d}{\partial \Omega} \right] dM & -\dfrac{\kappa}{r}\dfrac{M}{P}\dfrac{\partial (M/P)^d}{\partial \Omega} \, d\theta \end{bmatrix}. \tag{2.4.22}$$

Application of Cramer's rule facilitates the following results:

$$\frac{dr}{dM} = 0, \tag{2.4.23}$$

$$\frac{dP}{dM} = \frac{P}{M}, \tag{2.4.24}$$

$$\frac{dr}{d\theta} = \frac{1}{\Delta} \frac{\kappa}{r} \frac{M^2}{P^3} \frac{\partial c^d}{\partial \Omega} > 0, \tag{2.4.25}$$

$$\frac{dP}{d\theta} = \frac{1}{\Delta} \frac{\kappa}{r} \frac{M}{P} \left[ \frac{\partial i^d}{\partial r} \frac{\partial (M/P)^d}{\partial \Omega} - \frac{\partial c^d}{\partial \Omega} \frac{\partial (M/P)^d}{\partial r} \right], \tag{2.4.26}$$

where

$$\Delta = \frac{M}{P^2} \left[ -\frac{A}{M} \frac{\partial c^d}{\partial \Omega} \frac{\partial (M/P)^d}{\partial r} + \frac{1}{r} \left( \frac{\kappa B}{rP} + \frac{RK}{r} \right) \frac{\partial c^d}{\partial \Omega} \right.$$
$$\left. - \frac{\partial i^d}{\partial r} \left( 1 - \frac{A}{M} \frac{\partial (M/P)^d}{\partial \Omega} \right) \right]. \tag{2.4.27}$$

As long as

$$\frac{A}{M} \frac{\partial (M/P)^d}{\partial \Omega} = \left( 1 + \frac{\kappa \theta}{r} \right) \frac{\partial (M/P)^d}{\partial \Omega} < 1,$$

as we have been assuming, we are assured that $\Delta > 0$ unambiguously. Obviously, this is a sufficient but not necessary condition for $\Delta > 0$.

We therefore find that the presence of wealth effects does not alter the neutrality of the model. An increase in $M$, holding $\theta$ constant, is equivalent to an equiproportional increase in both $M$ and $B$. Such a balanced increase in government-issued liabilities generates an equiproportional increase in prices but has no impact on the allocation of resources through a change in the intertemporal terms of trade $r$.

A change in $\theta$, which, holding $M$ constant, amounts to an increase in the supply of government-issued bonds, unambiguously increases the interest rate but has an ambiguous effect on the level of prices. If the wealth effect on the demand for money is sufficiently weak, then an increase in bond supply, through its positive impact on consumption spending, unambiguously raises prices. Alternatively, if the effect of a change in wealth on consumption is sufficiently weak, then the main impact of the increase in government bond supply is an increase in the demand for money, which requires a reduction in the level of prices.

These disturbances may also be analyzed graphically. Holding $\theta$ constant, an increase in $M$ shifts all three market-clearing loci to the right by equal amounts. These shifts, depicted in Figure 2.13, are therefore consistent with the neutrality results derived algebraically above. Figure 2.13 also graphically depicts the effects of an increase in $\theta$. An increase in $\theta$ shifts all three loci upward. The interest rate therefore unambiguously rises. The effect of the increase in $\theta$ on $P$ depends on the relative slopes of the market-clearing loci and how far they shift in response to changes in $\theta$. The diagram in Figure 2.13 is drawn for the case in which $dP/d\theta > 0$.

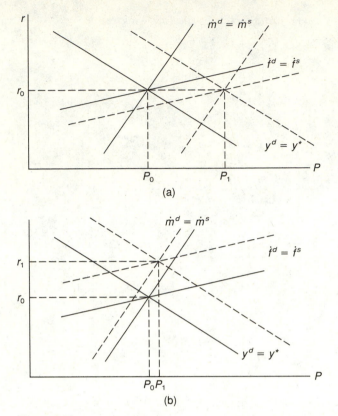

**Figure 2.13**

As noted in the previous section, it is important to fully understand and identify mechanisms by which any particular set of assumptions might generate a role for $\theta$ in influencing the intertemporal terms of trade. Note, however, that in this case, both the price and interest rate effects of a change in $\theta$ are only present if $\kappa > 0$. It is not the wealth effects per se but rather the inclusion of government bonds as a component of net wealth that provides a role for $\theta$ in affecting the allocation of resources.

Recall that we have already conceded that inclusion of $B$ in any way in the specification of net wealth is controversial. Why should it matter, for the allocation of resources, whether the government issues interest-bearing as opposed to non-interest-bearing debt to finance its liabilities as long as rational agents are aware that the government eventually needs to raise taxes to cover the interest payments on interest-bearing debt? To see how this policy decision might matter, we need to go back to the original arguments for the potential inclusion of some or all of $B$ as a component of $\Omega$.

As one possibility, we noted that with finite-lived agents the fact that taxes were only paid over a finite horizon while capital markets valued the stream of government bond interest payments over an infinite horizon might provide a wealth role for government bonds. Recall that when the government issues interest-bearing debt, it must eventually raise taxes to finance the necessary interest payments. In this particular case, the use of interest-bearing debt to finance current deficits is a way of shifting the burden of such taxation to future generations. Alternatively, issuing money to finance a deficit results in an immediate increase in prices, which exacts an instantaneous inflation tax only on currently living agents.

The alternative justification we offered for including government-issued bonds as wealth centered around government's potential role as a financial intermediary. In this case, government issue of interest-bearing debt mitigates the effects of a market failure—the capital market imperfection due to the inability of borrowers to guarantee repayment of loans for which human capital is the only form of collateral. However, it should not be surprising that when government has the capability of altering the effects of market imperfections, government actions in that direction may affect the allocation of resources.

We can also use the results derived above to calculate the effects of a change in the money supply holding $B$ constant. This type of disturbance accumulates after periods of purely money-financed deficits. Recalling the appropriate translations from the previous section, we obtain

$$\left.\frac{dr}{dM}\right|_{dB=0} = \frac{dr}{dM} - \frac{\theta}{M}\frac{dr}{d\theta} = -\frac{1}{\Delta}\frac{\kappa\theta}{rP}\frac{M}{P^2}\frac{\partial c^d}{\partial\Omega} < 0, \tag{2.4.28}$$

$$\left.\frac{dP}{dM}\right|_{dB=0} = \frac{dP}{dM} - \frac{\theta}{M}\frac{dP}{d\theta} = \frac{P}{M} - \frac{\theta}{M}\frac{dP}{d\theta}$$

$$= \frac{1}{P\Delta}\left[-\frac{\partial c^d}{\partial\Omega}\frac{\partial(M/P)^d}{\partial r} + \frac{1}{rP}\left(\frac{\kappa B}{rP} + \frac{RK}{r}\right)\frac{\partial c^d}{\partial\Omega}\right. \tag{2.4.29}$$

$$\left. - \frac{\partial i^d}{\partial r}\left(1 - \frac{\partial(M/P)^d}{\partial\Omega}\right)\right] > 0.$$

An increase in the money supply therefore unambiguously lowers the interest rate and raises prices. Whether prices rise more or less than in proportion to the increase in the money supply depends on whether government bonds raise prices or not. If an increase in the supply of government bonds raises prices, then an increase in the money supply results in a less than proportional increase in prices. If, instead, an increase in the supply of government bonds lowers prices, then an increase in the money supply results in a more than proportional increase in prices.

Finally, we can calculate the effects of an open-market purchase of government bonds by the monetary authority. Recall that this disturbance involves a change in $\theta$ such that $M\,d\theta = -(r + \theta)\,dM$. Some algebraic manipulations of the above expressions allows us to show that

$$\left.\frac{dr}{dM}\right|_{Md\theta=-(r+\theta)dM} = -\frac{1}{\Delta}\frac{r+\theta}{r}\frac{\kappa}{P}\frac{M}{P^2}\frac{\partial c^d}{\partial\Omega} < 0, \tag{2.4.30}$$

$$\left.\frac{dP}{dM}\right|_{Md\theta=-(r+\theta)dM} = \frac{1}{P\Delta}\left[-\frac{\partial i^d}{\partial r}\left(1 - (1-\kappa)\frac{\partial(M/P)^d}{\partial\Omega}\right)\right.$$

$$\left. - (1-\kappa)\frac{\partial c^d}{\partial\Omega}\frac{\partial(M/P)^d}{\partial r}\right. \tag{2.4.31}$$

$$\left. + \frac{1}{r}\left(\frac{\kappa B}{rP} + \frac{RK}{r}\right)\frac{\partial c^d}{\partial\Omega}\right] > 0.$$

Therefore, an open-market purchase of government bonds unambiguously raises the price level and reduces the rate of interest.

## An Alternative Specification of the Endogenous Variables

While we are certainly interested in the effects of changes in the exogenous variables on the level of prices, such interest in purely nominal effects is naturally secondary to an analysis of the real effects of such changes in the exogenous variables. The analysis of such real effects can be simplified somewhat if we specify the model in terms of the endogenous variables $r$ and $A/P \equiv M/P + \kappa B/rP$ instead of $r$ and $P$. Naturally, appropriate arithmetic calculations permit translation of changes in $r$ and $A/P$ into changes in $r$ and $P$, and vice versa. However, specification of the model in terms of $r$ and $A/P$ provides a neat alternative graphical presentation of the analysis and also provides a helpful introduction to the potentially cumbersome analysis of the next section, which introduces the possibility of imperfect substitutability between government bonds and equities.

Substituting the definition of $A/P$ into the goods and money market equilibrium conditions, we obtain the following:

$$c^d\left(z^*, \frac{A}{P} + \frac{RK}{r}\right) + i^d(r) + g - y^* = 0, \tag{2.4.32}$$

$$\left(1 + \frac{\kappa\theta}{r}\right)\left[\left(\frac{M}{P}\right)^d\left(y^*, r, \frac{A}{P} + \frac{RK}{r}\right) - \frac{1}{\xi_m}\dot{m}^s\right] - \frac{A}{P} = 0. \tag{2.4.33}$$

We can graph these equilibrium conditions in $r$, $A/P$ space. Differentiating the equilibrium conditions with respect to $r$ and $A/P$ and rearranging, we obtain

$$\left.\frac{dr}{d(A/P)}\right|_{y^d=y^*} = \left(\frac{\partial c^d}{\partial\Omega}\right)^{-1}\left(\frac{RK}{r^2}\frac{\partial c^d}{\partial\Omega} - \frac{\partial i^d}{\partial r}\right) > 0, \tag{2.4.34}$$

$$\left.\frac{dr}{d(A/P)}\right|_{(M/P)^d=M/P}$$

$$= \frac{1 - \left(1 + \dfrac{\kappa\theta}{r}\right)\dfrac{\partial(M/P)^d}{\partial\Omega}}{\left(1 + \dfrac{\kappa\theta}{r}\right)\left[\dfrac{\partial(M/P)^d}{\partial r} - \dfrac{RK}{r^2}\dfrac{\partial(M/P)^d}{\partial\Omega}\right] - \dfrac{\kappa\theta}{r^2}\dfrac{M}{P}} < 0. \tag{2.4.35}$$

We therefore see that the goods market equilibrium locus is upward sloping and we also see that the money market equilibrium locus is downward sloping as long as

$$\frac{A}{M}\frac{\partial(M/P)^d}{\partial\Omega} = \left(1 + \frac{\kappa\theta}{r}\right)\frac{\partial(M/P)^d}{\partial\Omega} < 1,$$

as we have been assuming. These market-clearing loci are depicted in Figure 2.14.

The present formulation can now be used to generate comparative statics results. Differentiating the equilibrium conditions with respect to $r$, $A/P$, $M$, and $\theta$ and recalling

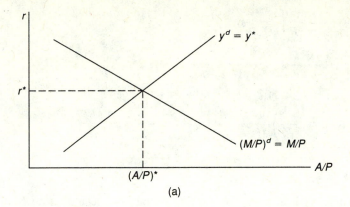

(a)

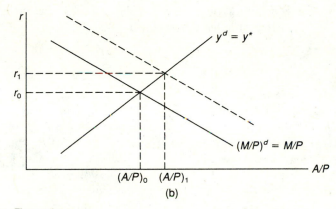

(b)

**Figure 2.14**

that $(1 + \kappa\theta/r) = A/M$, we obtain

$$
\left[
\begin{array}{cc}
-\dfrac{RK}{r^2}\dfrac{\partial c^d}{\partial \Omega} + \dfrac{\partial i^d}{\partial r} & \dfrac{\partial c^d}{\partial \Omega} \\[3mm]
-\dfrac{\kappa\theta}{r^2}\dfrac{M}{P} + \dfrac{A}{M}\left[\dfrac{\partial(M/P)^d}{\partial r} - \dfrac{RK}{r^2}\dfrac{\partial(M/P)^d}{\partial \Omega}\right] & -\left[1 - \dfrac{A}{M}\dfrac{\partial(M/P)^d}{\partial \Omega}\right]
\end{array}
\right]
$$
$$
\times \left[\begin{array}{c} dr \\[2mm] d\left(\dfrac{A}{P}\right) \end{array}\right] = \left[\begin{array}{c} 0 \\[2mm] -\dfrac{\kappa}{r}\dfrac{M}{P}\,d\theta \end{array}\right].
\tag{2.4.36}
$$

Use of Cramer's rule then permits us to derive the following results:

$$
\frac{dr}{dM} = 0,
\tag{2.4.37}
$$

$$
\frac{d(A/P)}{dM} = 0,
\tag{2.4.38}
$$

$$\frac{dr}{d\theta} = \frac{1}{\Delta} \frac{\kappa}{r} \frac{M}{P} \frac{\partial c^d}{\partial \Omega} > 0, \tag{2.4.39}$$

$$\frac{d(A/P)}{d\theta} = \frac{1}{\Delta} \frac{\kappa}{r} \frac{M}{P} \left( \frac{RK}{r^2} \frac{\partial c^d}{\partial \Omega} - \frac{\partial i^d}{\partial r} \right) > 0, \tag{2.4.40}$$

where

$$\Delta = \frac{M}{P} \left( \frac{RK}{r^2} + \frac{\kappa\theta}{r^2} \right) \frac{\partial c^d}{\partial \Omega} - \frac{\partial i^d}{\partial r} \left[ 1 - \left( 1 + \frac{\kappa\theta}{r} \right) \frac{\partial (M/P)^d}{\partial \Omega} \right]$$

$$- \left( 1 + \frac{\kappa\theta}{r} \right) \frac{\partial (M/P)^d}{\partial r} \frac{\partial c^d}{\partial \Omega} > 0. \tag{2.4.41}$$

As noted above, an increase in $M$, holding $\theta$ constant, results in an equiproportional increase in $P$ with no coincident change in $r$. The above results therefore reconfirm the result that $dr/dM = 0$. Also, since we have defined

$$\frac{A}{P} \equiv \frac{\kappa B}{rP} + \frac{M}{P}, \tag{2.4.42}$$

equiproportional increases in $M$, $B$, and $P$ holding $r$ fixed leave $A/P$ unchanged as well.

The above analysis also reconfirms that $dr/d\theta > 0$. However, since we earlier demonstrated that $dr/d\theta > 0$ and $dP/d\theta \gtreqless 0$, it would appear that the effect of changes in $\theta$ on the real value of the government-issued components of wealth, $A/P$, would be ambiguous. However, the present analysis proves that increases in $\theta$ unambiguously increase $A/P$. These results are depicted graphically in Figure 2.14. Following an increase in $\theta$, the goods market equilibrium locus is unaffected and the money market equilibrium locus shifts rightward. Therefore, $r$ and $A/P$ both unambiguously increase to $r_1$ and $(A/P)_1$ in Figure 2.14.

## 2.5 IMPERFECT ASSET SUBSTITUTABILITY

In Chapter 1, we defined the rate of return on government bonds and equities as the discount factor, which equates the price of the asset with the present value of the expected stream of income to which the asset entitles the bearer. We then adopted the assumption that agents expect that current dividend and interest streams will continue at current real rates with certainty into the indefinite future. If this assumption is valid, then potential asset holders should have no particular preference for one type of asset over the other and market forces should therefore ensure that equilibrium asset prices are such that the rates of return on the two assets are identical.

Clearly this assumption of perfect substitutability between equities and government bonds is not very realistic. While government's ability to raise taxes and issue fiat money allows the government to effectively guarantee the safety of the nominal value of the interest stream on government bonds, the government cannot guarantee the real value of that income stream nor can the government offer guarantees against changes in the market price of these securities. The prospects for equity holders are even more uncertain. Stock prices are notoriously volatile and dividend payments are not very predictable over extended periods of time.

These sources of uncertainty cry out for an explicit stochastic treatment of asset pricing and the capital asset-pricing model, as is summarized by Ross (1978), does provide such a framework. However, this framework is not very well suited for easy incorporation into macroeconomic models. We therefore seek to give a flavor of the complications arising from considerations of uncertainty while maintaining our certainty equivalent framework.

Recall from the preceding section the specification for total net wealth:

$$\Omega = \frac{M}{P} + \frac{\kappa B}{rP} + \frac{P_e E}{P}. \tag{2.5.1}$$

So far we have assumed that agents choose a desired decomposition of total wealth into desired holdings of money $M/P$ and desired holdings of earning assets, $\kappa B/rP + P_e E/P$. However, we have until now assumed that agents are completely indifferent as to the composition of their holdings of earning assets across government bonds and equities.

In this section, we assume that government bonds and equities may, in equilibrium, offer differing rates of return, and we further assume that agents have well-behaved preferences over these assets. Following Tobin (1969), assume that agents' stock demands for money, government bonds, and equities are given by

$$\left(\frac{M}{P}\right)^d \equiv m^d(y^*, \ r_b, \ r_e, \ \Omega), \tag{2.5.2}$$
$$\phantom{xxxxxxxxxxxxx}{\scriptstyle (+) \ \ (-) \ \ (-) \ \ (+)}$$

$$\left(\frac{\kappa B}{r_b P}\right)^d \equiv b^d(y^*, \ r_b, \ r_e, \ \Omega), \tag{2.5.3}$$
$$\phantom{xxxxxxxxxxxxx}{\scriptstyle (?) \ \ (+) \ \ (-) \ \ (+)}$$

$$\left(\frac{P_e E}{P}\right)^d \equiv e^d(y^*, \ r_b, \ r_e, \ \Omega), \tag{2.5.4}$$
$$\phantom{xxxxxxxxxxxxx}{\scriptstyle (?) \ \ (-) \ \ (+) \ \ (+)}$$

where $r_b$ and $r_e$ denote the rates of return on government bonds and equities, respectively, and where the signs under the arguments of the functions indicate the signs of the partial derivatives of that function with respect to the respective argument.

Each asset demand function depends directly on its own rate of return and inversely on the rates of return on competing assets. We retain the assumptions of zero expected inflation and no explicit interest on money holdings. Therefore, the constant (zero) pecuniary rate of return on money is suppressed from the functional forms above. Walras's law guarantees that

$$\frac{\partial m^d}{\partial \Omega} + \frac{\partial b^d}{\partial \Omega} + \frac{\partial e^d}{\partial \Omega} = 1, \tag{2.5.5}$$

$$\frac{\partial m^d}{\partial r_b} + \frac{\partial b^d}{\partial r_b} + \frac{\partial e^d}{\partial r_b} = 0, \tag{2.5.6}$$

$$\frac{\partial m^d}{\partial r_e} + \frac{\partial b^d}{\partial r_e} + \frac{\partial e^d}{\partial r_e} = 0, \tag{2.5.7}$$

$$\frac{\partial m^d}{\partial y^*} + \frac{\partial b^d}{\partial y^*} + \frac{\partial e^d}{\partial y^*} = 0. \tag{2.5.8}$$

Note that our earlier analysis was based on the (implicit) assumptions that

$$\frac{\partial b^d}{\partial r_b} = \frac{\partial e^d}{\partial r_e} \rightarrow +\infty, \tag{2.5.9}$$

$$\frac{\partial b^d}{\partial r_e} = \frac{\partial e^d}{\partial r_b} \rightarrow -\infty. \tag{2.5.10}$$

These assumptions on agent behavior would force $r_b = r_e = r$, in equilibrium.

We now wish to imbed this structure of asset preferences into our macroeconomic model. Principal current interest attaches to effects of changes in exogenous asset stocks. We therefore suppress the effects of changes in disposable income and measures of transaction activity from the behavioral relationships. We also assume that adjustment of actual to desired asset holdings is instantaneous. The resulting model of the economy is given by:

### Market-clearing conditions

Goods:

$$\underset{(+)}{c^d(\Omega)} + \underset{(-)}{i^d(r_e)} + g - y^* = 0. \tag{2.5.11}$$

Government bonds:

$$\underset{(+)\ \ (-)\ \ (+)}{b^d(r_b, r_e, \Omega)} - \frac{\kappa B}{r_b P} = 0. \tag{2.5.12}$$

Equities:

$$\underset{(-)\ \ (+)\ \ (+)}{e^d(r_b, r_e, \Omega)} - \frac{RK}{r_e} = 0. \tag{2.5.13}$$

Money:

$$\underset{(-)\ \ (-)\ \ (+)}{m^d(r_b, r_e, \Omega)} - \frac{M}{P} = 0. \tag{2.5.14}$$

### Definitions and Identities

Wealth:

$$\Omega = \frac{M}{P} + \frac{\kappa B}{r_b P} + \frac{P_e E}{P} = \frac{M}{P} + \frac{\kappa B}{r_b P} + \frac{RK}{r_e}.$$

### Exogenous Variables

Real: real potential shift parameters $RK$.

Nominal: $M, B$.

### Endogenous Variables

Real: $r_b$, $r_e$.

Nominal: $P$.

In order to simplify the analysis, first recall that Walras's law may be invoked to eliminate one of the market-clearing conditions as redundant. We choose to eliminate the bond market. Second, it is useful again to adopt the definition $\theta \equiv B/M$. Finally, it is also helpful to adopt the notation

$$\frac{A}{P} \equiv \frac{M}{P} + \frac{\kappa B}{r_b P}, \tag{2.5.15}$$

and hence

$$\frac{A}{P} = \frac{M}{P}\left(1 + \frac{\kappa\theta}{r_b}\right) \quad \text{and} \quad \Omega = \frac{A}{P} + \frac{RK}{r_e}. \tag{2.5.16}$$

The model can therefore be summarized by the following three equilibrium conditions:

$$c^d\left(\frac{A}{P} + \frac{RK}{r_e}\right) + i(r_e) + g - y^* = 0, \tag{2.5.17}$$

$$e^d\left(r_b, r_e, \frac{A}{P} + \frac{RK}{r_e}\right) - \frac{RK}{r_e} = 0, \tag{2.5.18}$$

$$\left(1 + \frac{\kappa\theta}{r_b}\right)m^d\left(r_b, r_e, \frac{A}{P} + \frac{RK}{r_e}\right) - \frac{A}{P} = 0. \tag{2.5.19}$$

We therefore have three equations in the three endogenous variables $r_b$, $r_e$, and $A/P$. The exogenous variables are $M$ and $\theta$. Note, however, that the exogenous variable $M$ does not explicitly appear in any of the equilibrium conditions.

Differentiating the equilibrium conditions with respect to $r_b$, $r_e$, and $A/P$ and noting that in equilibrium $A/P = (A/P)/(M/P) = (1 + \kappa\theta/r_b)$, we obtain

$$
\begin{bmatrix}
0 & \dfrac{\partial i^d}{\partial r_e} - \dfrac{RK}{r_e^2}\dfrac{\partial c^d}{\partial \Omega} & \dfrac{\partial c^d}{\partial \Omega} \\[3mm]
\dfrac{\partial e^d}{\partial r_b} & \dfrac{\partial e^d}{\partial r_e} + \dfrac{RK}{r_e^2}\left(1 - \dfrac{\partial e^d}{\partial \Omega}\right) & \dfrac{\partial e^d}{\partial \Omega} \\[3mm]
\dfrac{A}{M}\dfrac{\partial m^d}{\partial r_b} - \dfrac{\kappa\theta}{r_b^2}\dfrac{M}{P} & \dfrac{A}{M}\left(\dfrac{\partial m^d}{\partial r_e} - \dfrac{RK}{r_e^2}\dfrac{\partial m^d}{\partial \Omega}\right) & -\left(1 - \dfrac{A}{M}\dfrac{\partial m^d}{\partial \Omega}\right)
\end{bmatrix}
$$

$$
\times \begin{bmatrix} dr_b \\[2mm] dr_e \\[2mm] d\Omega \end{bmatrix} = \begin{bmatrix} 0 \\[2mm] 0 \\[2mm] -\dfrac{\kappa}{r_b}\dfrac{M}{P}d\theta \end{bmatrix}. \tag{2.5.20}
$$

The determinant of the partial derivative matrix is given by

$$
\Delta = \left( \frac{\partial i^d}{\partial r_e} - \frac{RK}{r_e^2} \frac{\partial c^d}{\partial \Omega} \right) \left[ \left( 1 - \frac{A}{M} \frac{\partial m^d}{\partial \Omega} \right) \frac{\partial e^d}{\partial r_b} \right.
$$

$$
\left. + \left( \frac{A}{M} \frac{\partial m^d}{\partial r_b} - \frac{\kappa \theta}{r_b^2} \frac{M}{P} \right) \frac{\partial e^d}{\partial \Omega} \right]
$$

$$
+ \frac{\partial c^d}{\partial \Omega} \left\{ \frac{A}{M} \left( \frac{\partial m^d}{\partial r_e} - \frac{RK}{r_e^2} \frac{\partial m^d}{\partial \Omega} \right) \frac{\partial e^d}{\partial r_b} \right.
$$

$$
\left. + \left[ \frac{\partial e^d}{\partial r_e} + \frac{RK}{r_e^2} \left( 1 - \frac{\partial e^d}{\partial \Omega} \right) \right] \left( \frac{\kappa \theta}{r_b^2} \frac{M}{P} - \frac{A}{M} \frac{\partial m^d}{\partial r_b} \right) \right\}.
$$

(2.5.21)

Note that as long as

$$
\frac{A}{M} \frac{\partial m^d}{\partial \Omega} = \left( 1 + \frac{\kappa \theta}{r_b} \right) \frac{\partial (M/P)^d}{\partial \Omega} < 1,
$$

(2.5.22)

we are assured that $\Delta > 0$. We continue to invoke this assumption throughout the present analysis.

Solving by Cramer's rule, we derive the following comparative statics results:

$$
\frac{dr_b}{dM} = \frac{dr_e}{dM} = \frac{d(A/P)}{dM} = 0,
$$

(2.5.23)

$$
\frac{dr_b}{d\theta} = -\frac{1}{\Delta} \frac{\kappa}{r_b} \frac{M}{P} \left\{ \frac{\partial e^d}{\partial \Omega} \left( \frac{\partial i^d}{\partial r_e} - \frac{RK}{r_e^2} \frac{\partial c^d}{\partial \Omega} \right) \right.
$$

$$
\left. - \frac{\partial c^d}{\partial \Omega} \left[ \frac{\partial e^d}{\partial r_e} + \frac{RK}{r_e^2} \left( 1 - \frac{\partial e^d}{\partial \Omega} \right) \right] \right\} > 0,
$$

(2.5.24)

$$
\frac{dr_e}{\partial \theta} = -\frac{1}{\Delta} \frac{\kappa}{r_b} \frac{M}{P} \frac{\partial c^d}{\partial \Omega} \left( \frac{A}{M} \frac{\partial m^d}{\partial r_b} - \frac{\kappa \theta}{r_b^2} \frac{M}{P} \right) > 0,
$$

(2.5.25)

$$
\frac{d(A/P)}{d\theta} = \frac{1}{\Delta} \frac{\kappa}{r_b} \frac{M}{P} \frac{\partial e^d}{\partial \Omega} \left( \frac{\partial i^d}{\partial r_e} - \frac{RK}{r_e^2} \frac{\partial c^d}{\partial \Omega} \right) > 0.
$$

(2.5.26)

We therefore find that the results of the previous section do generalize to this very simple case of imperfect asset substitutability. Money remains neutral. Equiproportional increases in $B$ and $M$ result in an equiproportional increase in $P$ with no change in the real endogenous variables $r_b$, $r_e$, and $A/P$. We also find that an increase in the supply of government bonds as captured by an increase in $\theta$ lowers the price of government bonds and increases the rate of return on government bonds $r_b$. The increase in the supply of government bonds also raises the rate of return on equities $r_e$ and increases government-issued net wealth $A/P$. Furthermore, since investment is inversely related to $r_e$, investment must fall and consumption must rise. Finally, since consumption is directly related only to the level of total real wealth and consumption rises, we therefore know that total real wealth must rise as well.

We can also compress this three-endogenous-variable system into a two-endogenous-variable system for the purposes of graphical analysis. Totally differentiating the money market equilibrium condition, we obtain

$$\left(\frac{A}{M}\frac{\partial m^d}{\partial r_b} - \frac{\kappa\theta}{r_b^2}\frac{M}{P}\right)dr_b + \frac{A}{M}\left(\frac{\partial m^d}{\partial r_e} - \frac{RK}{r_e^2}\frac{\partial m^d}{\partial\Omega}\right)dr_e$$

$$-\left(1 - \frac{A}{M}\frac{\partial m^d}{\partial\Omega}\right)d\left(\frac{A}{M}\right) + \frac{\kappa}{r_b}\frac{M}{P}\,d\theta = 0. \tag{2.5.27}$$

We therefore can construct the implicit function

$$r_b = r_b\left(r_e, \frac{A}{P}, \theta\right), \tag{2.5.28}$$

where

$$\frac{\partial r_b}{\partial r_e} = -\frac{\dfrac{A}{M}\left(\dfrac{\partial m^d}{\partial r_e} - \dfrac{RK}{r_e^2}\dfrac{\partial m^d}{\partial\Omega}\right)}{\dfrac{A}{M}\dfrac{\partial m^d}{\partial r_b} - \dfrac{\kappa\theta}{r_b^2}\dfrac{M}{P}} < 0, \tag{2.5.29}$$

$$\frac{\partial r_b}{\partial(AP)} = \frac{1 - \dfrac{A}{M}\dfrac{\partial m^d}{\partial\Omega}}{\dfrac{A}{M}\dfrac{\partial m^d}{\partial r_b} - \dfrac{\kappa\theta}{r_b^2}\dfrac{M}{P}} < 0, \tag{2.5.30}$$

$$\frac{\partial r_b}{\partial\theta} = -\frac{\dfrac{\kappa}{r_b}\dfrac{M}{P}}{\dfrac{A}{M}\dfrac{\partial m^d}{\partial r_b} - \dfrac{\kappa\theta}{r_b^2}\dfrac{M}{P}} > 0. \tag{2.5.31}$$

Substituting the implicit function $r_b(\cdot)$ for $r_b$ into the goods and equity market equilibrium conditions, we obtain the following two equations in $r_e$ and $A/P$:

$$c^d\left(\frac{A}{P} + \frac{RK}{r_e}\right) + i^d(r_e) + g - y^* = 0, \tag{2.5.32}$$

$$e^d\left(r_b\left(r_e, \frac{A}{P}, \theta\right), r_e, \frac{A}{P} + \frac{RK}{r_e}\right) - \frac{RK}{r_e} = 0. \tag{2.5.33}$$

We now construct two market-clearing loci in $r_e$, $A/P$ space. Differentiating the two above equilibrium conditions and rearranging, we obtain

$$\left.\frac{dr_e}{d(A/P)}\right|_{y^d=y^*} = -\frac{\partial c^d/\partial\Omega}{\dfrac{\partial i^d}{\partial r_e} - \dfrac{RK}{r_e^2}\dfrac{\partial c^d}{\partial\Omega}} > 0, \tag{2.5.34}$$

$$\left.\frac{dr_e}{d(A/P)}\right|_{e^d=RK/r_e} = -\frac{\dfrac{\partial e^d}{\partial r_b}\dfrac{\partial r_b}{\partial(A/P)} + \dfrac{\partial e^d}{\partial\Omega}}{\dfrac{\partial e^d}{\partial r_b}\dfrac{\partial r_b}{\partial r_e} + \dfrac{\partial e^d}{\partial r_e} + \left(1 - \dfrac{\partial e^d}{\partial\Omega}\right)\dfrac{RK}{r_e^2}} < 0. \tag{2.5.35}$$

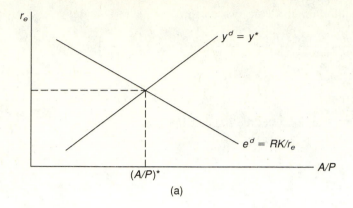

(a)

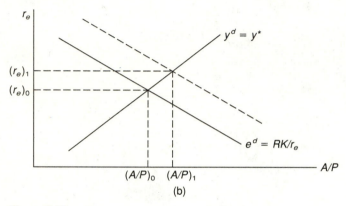

(b)

**Figure 2.15**

These market-clearing conditions are depicted in Figure 2.15. Figure 2.15 also graphically depicts the effects of an increase in $\theta$ on $r_e$ and $A/P$. The equity market equilibrium locus shifts upward and to the right. The goods market equilibrium locus is unaffected by the change in $\theta$. Therefore, consistent with our algebraic analysis, we find that the rate of return on equities rises to $(r_e)_1$ and the real value of government-issued wealth also rises to $(A/P)_1$.

# APPENDIX A: The Finite-Horizon Representative Household's Choice Problem

This appendix provides some motivation for the consumption function of Section 2.4, which includes a wealth variable of the form

$$\Omega = \frac{M}{P} + \frac{\kappa B}{rP} + \frac{\Pi}{r}.$$  (2.A.1)

To this end, let us consider a simplified version of the intertemporal maximization problem of

Appendix 1.C. In particular, let us assume that the portfolio adjustment cost parameter $\eta$ is equal to zero. Since $\eta = 0$, the level of real earning assets held by the representative household, $f(t)$, is no longer a state variable but rather a choice variable. The appropriate constraining variable for the household is now given by

$$\hat{\Omega}(0) = m(0) + f(0) = \hat{\Omega}_0 \tag{2.A.2}$$

since the representative household is free to instantaneously reallocate its wealth across its holdings of money and earning assets.

Let us now assume that the representative household's preferences are characterized by a no-wealth-effects instantaneous utility function and that the labor market is competitive. Furthermore, let us also assume that the representative household is constrained to retire at the exogenously determined date $N'$ and that the end of the representative household's planning horizon occurs with certainty at date $N > N'$. If we denote the representative household's labor income by $\hat{z}(t)$, these assumptions on labor market behavior imply a time path for $\hat{z}(t)$ given by

$$\hat{z}(t) = \begin{cases} \left(\dfrac{W}{P}\right)^* \ell^*, & 0 \le t \le N', \\ 0, & N' < t \le N, \end{cases} \tag{2.A.3}$$

where $(W/P)^*$ denotes the market-clearing real wage and $\ell^*$ denotes the equilibrium level of employment. The representative household expects no future shifts in the labor supply and labor demand schedules, and so labor income is expected to remain constant until $N'$, the exogenously determined date of retirement. Thereafter, the representative household expects no further wage income.

The representative household's choice problem is now given by

$$\max_{c(t),\, m(t)} V = \int_0^N U[c(t)]e^{-\beta t}\, dt \tag{2.A.4}$$

subject to

$$\frac{d\hat{\Omega}}{dt} = r(\hat{\Omega} - m) + \hat{z} - c - \tau - \gamma(m, y), \tag{2.A.5}$$

$$\hat{\Omega}(0) = \hat{\Omega}_0, \qquad \hat{\Omega}(N) = 0, \tag{2.A.6}$$

$$\hat{z}(t) = \begin{cases} \left(\dfrac{W}{P}\right)^* \ell^*, & 0 \le t \le N', \\ 0, & N' < t \le N. \end{cases} \tag{2.A.7}$$

In the absence of portfolio adjustment costs, optimal money holdings $m^*(t)$ solve

$$r = -\frac{\partial \gamma(m^*, y)}{\partial m} \Rightarrow m^*(t) = m^*(y, r), \quad \text{for all } t. \tag{2.A.8}$$

Since we are assuming that the representative household expects $y$ and $r$ to be constant into the indefinite future, we may rewrite the above maximization problem as

$$\max_{c(t)} V = \int_0^N U[c(t)]e^{-\beta t}\, dt \tag{2.A.9}$$

subject to

$$\frac{d\hat{\Omega}}{dt} = r(\hat{\Omega} - m^*) + \hat{z} - c - \tau - \gamma(m^*, y), \tag{2.A.10}$$

$$\hat{\Omega}(0) = \hat{\Omega}_0, \qquad \hat{\Omega}(N) = 0, \tag{2.A.11}$$

$$\hat{z}(t) = \begin{cases} \left(\dfrac{W}{P}\right)^* \ell^*, & 0 \le t \le N', \\ 0, & N' < t \le N. \end{cases} \tag{2.A.12}$$

First-order conditions for this maximization problem are given by[7]

$$\frac{\partial H^*}{\partial c} = U' - \lambda = 0, \tag{2.A.13}$$

$$\dot{\lambda} = -\frac{\partial H^*}{\partial \hat{\Omega}} + \beta\lambda = (\beta - r)\lambda \Rightarrow \lambda(t) = \lambda(0)e^{-(r-\beta)t}, \tag{2.A.14}$$

where

$$H^* \equiv U[c(t)] + \lambda[r(\hat{\Omega} - m^*) + \hat{z} - c - \tau - \gamma(m^*, y)]. \tag{2.A.15}$$

Solution of the intertemporal budget constraint yields

$$\int_0^N c(s)e^{-rs}\,ds = \hat{\Omega}(0) - m(0) + m^* e^{-rN} + \int_0^N \hat{z}(s) - \tau(s) - \gamma(m^*, y)]e^{-rs}\,ds. \tag{2.A.16}$$

We now follow the analysis of Appendix 1.C and assume an instantaneous utility function of the form $U(c) = \ln(c)$ and further assume that the representative household expects that the level of real taxes to be constant over time at a level $\tau$ given by

$$\tau = \tau_0 + \frac{B}{P}. \tag{2.A.17}$$

Denoting the equilibrium real wage by $w^*$, the intertemporal budget constraint may now be rewritten as

$$\int_0^N c(s)e^{-rs}\,ds = \hat{\Omega}(0) - \frac{B}{rP}(1 - e^{-rN})$$
$$+ \frac{w^*}{r}(1 - e^{-rN'}) - \frac{\tau_0 + \gamma(m^*, y) + rm^*}{r}(1 - e^{-rN}), \tag{2.A.18}$$

where we have made use of the fact that $m(0) = m^*$.

It is now useful to define the wealth variable:

$$\Omega \equiv \hat{\Omega} - \frac{B}{rP}(1 - e^{-rN}) = \frac{M}{P} + \frac{B}{rP}e^{-rN} + \frac{\Pi}{r}. \tag{2.A.19}$$

Solution of the representative household's choice problem now yields a time zero consumption function of the form

$$c^d = c(0) = \frac{\beta}{1 - e^{-\beta N}}\left[\Omega(0) + \frac{w^*}{r}(1 - e^{-rN'})\right.$$
$$\left. - \frac{\tau_0 + \gamma(m^*, y) + rm^*}{r}(1 - e^{-rN})\right]. \tag{2.A.20}$$

---

[7]See, for example, Intriligator (1971).

This form of the consumption function is similar to that adopted in Section 2.4, where

$$\Omega \equiv \frac{M}{P} + \frac{\kappa B}{rP} + \frac{\Pi}{r}, \qquad \kappa \equiv e^{-rN}, \tag{2.A.21}$$

$$z^* \equiv \frac{w^*}{r}(1 - e^{-rN'}) - \frac{\tau_0 + \gamma(m^*, y) + rm^*}{r}(1 - e^{-rN}). \tag{2.A.22}$$

Also note that if the representative firm's production function is given by the Cobb-Douglas form

$$\Phi(\ell, K) = \ell^{\alpha}K^{1-\alpha} \tag{2.A.23}$$

so that labor's share of total output is constant and equal to $\alpha$, then we obtain

$$z^* = \frac{\alpha}{r}(1 - e^{-rN'})y^* - \frac{\tau_0 + \gamma(m^*, y) + rm^*}{r}(1 - e^{-rN}). \tag{2.A.24}$$

However, one additional observation should be made about this particular solution. Note that the consumption function contains the two arguments:

$$\Omega(0) = m(0) + \frac{\kappa B}{rP} + \frac{\Pi}{r} \quad \text{and} \quad \gamma(m^*, y) + rm^*. \tag{2.A.25}$$

Since we are assuming that $m(t) = m^*$ throughout, it would appear that we could combine the $m(0)$ term with the $m^*$ terms above to permit further simplification of $c^d$. However, the component $m(0)$ in $\Omega(0)$ is part of what May (1970) and Foley (1975) would refer to as a "beginning-of-period" balance, while the component $m^*$ would be part of an "end-of-period" balance. If the representative household received an increased endowment of money at time $t = 0$, household wealth $\Omega(0)$ would rise one-for-one. While it is true that such an increased endowment would not change the representative household's desired money holdings $m^*$, such an increased endowment would nevertheless generate an increase in consumption. The representative household would, within the instant of time $t = 0$, both reallocate the increase in $m(0)$ across $B$ and $E$ to achieve $m(t + \varepsilon) = m^*$ and increase consumption due to the rise in $\Omega(0)$. While such subtleties do not often present problems in continuous-time models, they are potentially more troublesome in the analysis of discrete-time models.

# REFERENCES

Barro, Robert J., "Are Government Bonds Net Wealth?" *Journal of Political Economy*, November/December, 1974, 1095–1117.

Barro, Robert J., and Herschel I. Grossman, *Money, Employment and Inflation*, Cambridge, England, Cambridge University Press, 1976.

Baumol, William J., "The Transactions Demand for Cash: An Inventory Theoretic Approach," *Quarterly Journal of Economics*, November, 1952, 545–556.

Feldstein, Martin, "Government Deficits and Aggregate Demand," *Journal of Monetary Economics*, January, 1982, 1–20.

Foley, Duncan K., "On Two Specifications of Asset Equilibrium in Macroeconomic Models," *Journal of Political Economy*, April, 1975, 303–324.

Intriligator, Michael D., *Mathematical Optimization and Economic Theory*, Englewood Cliffs, NJ, Prentice-Hall, 1971.

Kormendi, Roger, C., "Government Debt, Government Spending, and Private Sector Behavior," *American Economic Review,* December, 1983, 994–1010.

May, Josef, "Period Analysis and Continuous Analysis in Patinkin's Macroeconomic Model," *Journal of Economic Theory,* March, 1970, 1–9.

Meltzer, Lloyd A., "Wealth, Saving and the Rate of Interest," *Journal of Political Economy,* April, 1951, 93–116.

Patinkin, Don, *Money, Interest, and Prices,* 2nd ed., New York, Harper & Row, 1965.

Ross, Steven, "The Current Status of the Capital Asset Pricing Model," *Journal of Finance,* June, 1978, 885–901.

Seater, John J., and Roberto S. Mariano, "New Tests of the Life Cycle and Tax Discounting Hypotheses," *Journal of Monetary Economics,* March, 1985, 195–215.

Tobin, James, "The Interest-Elasticity of the Transaction Demand for Cash," *Review of Economics and Statistics,* August, 1956, 241–247.

Tobin, James, "Liquidity Preference as Behavior Toward Risk," *Review of Economic Studies,* February, 1958, 65–86.

Tobin, James, "A General Equilibrium Approach to Monetary Theory," *Journal of Money, Credit and Banking,* February, 1969, 15–29.

# Chapter 3

## An Exogenous Price Model

While the model developed in Chapter 2 may reasonably approximate the medium-run workings of actual developed economies, some might question its usefulness for short-run analysis. That is, the model might not describe the behavior of economies on a quarter-to-quarter or even a year-to-year basis. Some would argue that on such a short-run basis the paradigm of perfectly competitive behavior and continuous market clearing is not a good description of reality. In particular, the short-run behavior of the economy may more closely mimic the outcomes of models in which goods prices fail to move to satisfy market-clearing conditions in a timely fashion.

This chapter examines in some detail the workings of a macroeconomic model that views the nominal price level as exogenously determined. Section 3.1 reconsiders those assumptions of the model of Chapter 2 that need to be modified in the context of fixed prices and sets up a formal fixed-price model. Section 3.2 performs comparative statics exercises in the model and discusses the relationship between the specific model under consideration and the traditional IS-LM model. Finally, Section 3.3 reintroduces wealth effects into the model and discusses the ways in which the presence of such wealth effects alters some of the basic results.

## 3.1 A BASIC FIXED-PRICE FRAMEWORK

The previous chapters assume profit maximizing behavior on the part of a large number of competitive, representative firms. Each firm has a predetermined endowment of capital, and the supply of labor depends only on the current real wage rate. Market clearing in the goods and labor market therefore guarantees the existence of equilibrium levels of employment and output that can be viewed as exogenous to the rest of the macroeconomic model. Chapter 2 analyzed adjustments to exogenous disturbances in the goods, earning assets, and money markets all under the assumption that the level of output remained fixed at this market-clearing level $y^*$. Since this equilibrium level of output $y^*$ is independent of the nominal price level, there was no further need to continually reconsider the representative firm's production decisions.

In this chapter, we simply assume that while the nominal wage rate may adjust to equate labor demand and labor supply, the nominal price level is exogenously fixed.[1] We also assume that firms are always able to expand their employment of labor services and that they always adjust this level of employment $\ell$ to keep the level of output $y$ equal to the level of aggregate demand $y^d$. Rather than attempting to justify a set of assumptions consistent with this fixed-price scenario, we simply note that many macroeconomists find the resulting model appealing for analysis of the short-run effects of exogenous disturbances and assert that an understanding of this model is a useful prelude to the study of more complex, yet more plausible aggregate demand–aggregate supply models.[2]

## Labor Market Equilibrium in the Fixed-Price Model

In this section, we more carefully examine the nature of representative firm behavior in the face of a clearing labor market and an excess supply of goods.[3] In particular, throughout this chapter, we adopt the maintained assumption that the prevailing wage–price–interest rate vector always has the property that

$$c^d\left(y + \frac{B}{P} - \tau\right) + i^d(r) + g < y^*, \tag{3.1.1}$$

where $y^*$ continues to denote the equilibrium level of output determined in the model of Chapter 2.

This possibility of the failure of the goods market to clear has important implications for the nature of representative firm decision making. In the analysis of Chapters 1 and 2, we assumed that the representative firm could purchase all the labor services it wanted at the prevailing wage rate $W$ and could sell all the output it wanted at the prevailing price level $P$. Based upon these assumptions of competitively functioning labor and goods markets, we derived the notional labor demand and goods supply schedules $\ell^d(w)$ and $y^s(w) \equiv \Phi(\ell^d(w), \overline{K})$, respectively.

However, in the present analysis, the representative firm's sales are constrained to a level $\overline{y}$ less than $y^s(w)$. In this case, the representative firm's marginal revenue product

---

[1]Formal models of stickyness in goods prices may be found in Barro (1972) and Rotemberg (1982). A macroeconomic model of household and firm behavior in the face of both wage and price stickyness is presented by Barro and Grossman (1971). Drazen (1980) provides an excellent survey of the microeconomic foundations of nominal stickyness as well as the macroeconomic implications of disequilibrium prices. More recent treatments of non-Walrasian models are summarized in Benassy (1986).

[2]Insightful essays by Grossman (1983) and McCallum (1986) offer broad perspective on many issues related to price stickyness. Gordon (1982) provides evidence in favor of sticky-price models as an accurate portrayal of short-run macroeconomic interactions.

[3]In Chapter 5, we consider the case in which the nominal price level is flexible while there is an excess supply of labor. Barro and Grossman (1971) consider the case in which both the price level and the wage rate are fixed and there is an excess supply of both goods and labor.

$P(\partial\Phi/\partial\ell)$ will generally exceed the nominal wage rate. If the goods market cleared, the representative firm would wish to increase its employment of labor services until the point at which its marginal revenue product equaled the nominal wage rate. However, with an excess supply of goods, the resulting increase in production would go unsold, and with perishable output, the representative firm's profits would unambiguously fall. Therefore, the disequilibrium in the goods market necessitates that the representative firm's notional demand for labor $\ell^d(w)$ be replaced with an effective demand for labor $\ell^{d'}$.

With sales constrained at $\bar{y} < y^s(w)$, the representative firm's current production decision is given by

$$\max_{\ell} \{P\Phi(\ell, \bar{K}) - W\ell\} \tag{3.1.2}$$

subject to

$$y \leq \bar{y}. \tag{3.1.3}$$

Solution of the above maximization problem leads to the effective labor demand schedule

$$\ell^{d'} = \ell^{d'}(\bar{y}, \bar{K}), \quad \text{where } \bar{y} = \Phi(\ell^{d'}, \bar{K}) \tag{3.1.4}$$

and

$$\frac{\partial \ell^{d'}}{\partial \bar{y}} = \left(\frac{\partial\Phi(\ell^{d'}, K)}{\partial\ell}\right)^{-1} > 0, \qquad \frac{\partial\ell^{d'}}{\partial\bar{K}} = -\frac{\partial\Phi/\partial K}{\partial\Phi/\partial\ell} < 0. \tag{3.1.5}$$

Clower (1965) denotes this substitution of an effective demand schedule for the analogous notional demand schedule as a consequence of what he terms the dual-decision hypothesis. Figure 3.1 depicts the notional and effective labor demand schedules.

As long as the wage rate moves to clear the labor market, labor market equilibrium will be characterized by the point of intersection of the notional labor supply schedule and the effective labor demand schedule. Such an intersection occurs in Figure 3.1 at the point $\hat{\ell}$, $\hat{w}$. Note that the equilibrium real wage rate $\hat{w}$ and the equilibrium employment level $\hat{\ell}$ in the fixed-price model are both unambiguously less than the equilibrium real wage rate $w^*$ and the equilibrium employment level $\ell^*$ that prevail when all markets clear, as in the analysis of Chapter 2.

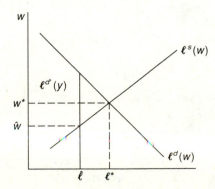

Figure 3.1

## Goods Market Equilibrium and the Multiplier Process

Before we proceed any farther with a formal analysis of fixed-priced macroeconomic models, it is now most helpful for the reader to develop a good early intuitive grasp of how the goods market equilibrates in such models. As a prelude to such an analysis, it is also important to reflect on whether changes in goods market behavior analogous to the substitution of an effective labor demand schedule for the notional labor demand schedule are necessary. At least for the time being, we take the level of government spending and taxation as fixed independent of the level of aggregate output. Furthermore, we also provisionally assume that investment demand is simply equal to the constant amount $\bar{i}^d$. This leaves us with a consideration of the determinants of consumption spending. However, since the labor market clears and since there is an excess supply of goods, the representative household faces no quantity constraints on its decision process. Therefore, representative household behavior, and in particular representative household consumption behavior, continues to be properly described by the notional consumption demand schedule $c^d(\cdot)$ derived in Chapter 1.

The fundamental feature of fixed-price models is that the goods market equilibrates through quantity adjustment, in particular adjustment in the level of aggregate output, rather than through price adjustment. As argued above, investment demand is exogenous, consumption demand continues to depend on disposable income denoted by $z = y + B/P_0 - \tau$, and the level of bond-financed government spending is the only policy variable. In this case, aggregate demand is given by

$$y^d = c^d\left(y + \frac{B}{P_0} - \tau\right) + \bar{i}^d + g. \tag{3.1.6}$$

The set of assumptions listed above guarantees that the only endogenous variable that aggregate demand is a function of is $y$, the level of aggregate output or income.

Goods market equilibrium in fixed-price models, as pointed out above, is characterized by equality between aggregate output $y$ and aggregate demand $y^d$. Recall that, by definition, output or income is identically given by

$$y \equiv c + i + g, \tag{3.1.7}$$

where $c$, $i$, and $g$ represent actual levels of real consumption, real investment, and real government spending, respectively. Goods market equilibrium is therefore given by

$$y = y^d = c^d\left(y + \frac{B}{P_0} - \tau\right) + \bar{i}^d + g. \tag{3.1.8}$$

If actual aggregate output $y = c + i + g$ differs from the level of aggregate output demand $y^d = c^d + i^d + g$ and if, as is generally assumed, desired and actual levels of government spending are always equal, it must be the case that either actual consumption and consumption demand are not equal or actual investment and investment demand are not equal, or both. Most fixed-price models assume that actual and desired levels of consumption are always equal (there is no ''forced saving''), and so $y$ and $y^d$ can only differ if desired and actual levels of investment are unequal. If we denote the level of undesired investment by $i^u$, then by definition

$$i \equiv i^d + i^u. \tag{3.1.9}$$

Actual investment includes all purchases by business firms, including firm purchases of new plant and equipment and changes in the level of inventories. Since most purchases of new plant and equipment occur only when firms actively make such purchases, $i^u$ is generally confined to undesired or unwanted changes in inventories, as might be expected if a new product does not sell as well as originally anticipated.

Recalling the definition of $i^u$, we may rewrite the goods market equilibrium condition $y = y^d$ as

$$y = c + i^d + i^u + g = c^d + i^d + g = y^d. \tag{3.1.10}$$

The assumption that actual and desired consumption are always equal means that the equilibrium condition $y = y^d$ has the alternate representation

$$i^u = 0. \tag{3.1.11}$$

We can therefore attach the following pseudodynamic interpretation to the goods market equilibrium condition. If actual output exceeds the level of aggregate demand, the representative firm finds that inventories are building up faster than desired, and so the level of production is cut back until $i^u$ is restored to zero. Alternatively, if the level of output is less than the level of aggregate demand, the representative firm finds that inventories are being depleted at a rate faster than desired, and so output is expanded in that case until $i^u$ is restored to zero.

It is helpful to visualize this process with the aid of a diagram. One common presentation is that depicted in Figure 3.2. In that figure, actual output $y$ is measured on the horizontal axis and aggregate demand $y^d$ is measured on the vertical axis. The equilibrium condition $y = y^d$ is represented by a straight line with slope of unity. Aggregate demand is a function of the level of total output because consumption depends on the level of disposable income, which is given by $z = y + B/P_0 - \tau$. The slope of the aggregate demand schedule is $dy^d/dy = \partial c^d/\partial z$. We generally assume that $\partial c^d/\partial z$ is positive but less than unity. Equilibrium in the goods market is therefore achieved at points like the one labeled $y_0$ in Figure 3.2.

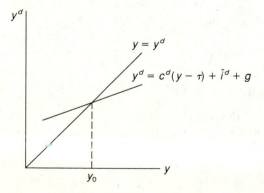

Figure 3.2

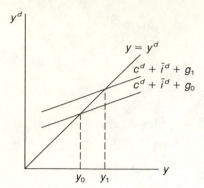

**Figure 3.3**

It is now useful to consider how a position of equilibrium like $y_0$ is disturbed if there is a change in one of the exogenous variables, like $g$. In this very simple case in which $y$ is the model's only endogenous variable, the comparative statics exercise of the effect of a change in $g$ is quite simple. Differentiating the goods market equilibrium condition with respect to $y$ and $g$, we obtain

$$\frac{dy}{dg} = \frac{1}{1 - \partial c^d / \partial z} > 0. \tag{3.1.12}$$

We therefore find that an increase in government spending raises the equilibrium level of output. The term $(1 - \partial c^d / \partial z)^{-1}$ is often referred to as the simple *Keynesian multiplier*. This expression is referred to as a multiplier since as long as $\partial c^d / \partial z < 1$, it always exceeds unity.

To help understand this simple comparative statics exercise, it is useful to refer to Figure 3.3. Suppose that there is a one-unit increase in government spending. If output remains equal to $y_0$ and if $c$ and $c^d$ remain equal as we have been assuming, then of necessity $i$ must drop below $\bar{i}^d$ by one unit and so we find that $i^u = -1$. Inventories are being depleted more rapidly than the representative firm wishes, and so the representative firm expands output.

However, if output is only expanded by one unit, the goods market cannot reequilibrate. This one-unit increase in output implies a one-unit increase in disposable income, and so desired consumption rises by $\partial c^d / \partial z$. Therefore, unless the level of output continues to rise, the level of undesired investment will again be negative. This process converges only when the full increase in output given by the multiplier expression above has been achieved. The new equilibrium level of output is denoted by $y_1$ in Figure 3.3.

## Investment Spending and the Equity Market

In the flexible-price model of the previous chapter, we assumed that all agents shared common expectations that the representative firm's profit stream $\Pi = y - (W/P)\ell$ would remain fixed indefinitely. With government bonds and equity viewed as perfect substitutes in earning asset portfolios, the value of equity shares is simply the present value of this constant expected profit stream discounted at $r$, the market rate of return on government bonds. We further assumed that agents expect $r$ to remain constant indefinitely, that firms pay workers the marginal product of their labor, and that production is governed by the constant-returns-to-scale production function $\Phi(\ell, K)$. These assumptions ensured that the total value of all equity claims equals $RK/r$, where $R$ denotes the marginal product of capital. Furthermore, these assumptions give rise to an investment demand function in which the level of investment spending is positively related to the difference between the marginal product of capital and the nominal rate of interest.

However, as noted above, the entire structure of the representative firm's decision-making process is changed by the existence of excess supply in the goods market. We have already taken note of the potential impact a sales constraint might have on the level of labor demand. We now consider potential effects on investment demand as well as potential interactions between investment demand and the demand for labor over time.

Suppose that the representative firm expects its sales to be constrained to $y = \bar{y}$ into the indefinite future.[4] The market price of the representative firm's equity shares is still equal to the discounted present value of its profit stream. With output fixed at $\bar{y}$, we therefore obtain

$$P_e = \frac{P}{E} \int_0^\infty \left( \bar{y} - \frac{W}{P} \ell \right) e^{-rt} \, dt. \tag{3.1.13}$$

In the absence of capital stock adjustment costs like those posited in Appendix 1.B, the representative firm should choose input paths $\ell(t)$ and $K(t)$ to maximize the current equity price $P_e$. However, just as in the analysis of Section 1.2, the lack of adjustment costs and the static nature of expectations lead to optimal paths for $\ell(t)$ and $K(t)$ that are constant over time. The representative firm's optimal behavior can therefore be captured by the solution to the static optimization problem:

$$\max_{\ell, K} P_e = \frac{P}{E} \int_0^\infty \left( \bar{y} - \frac{W}{P} \ell \right) e^{-rt} \, dt = \frac{P}{rE} \left( \bar{y} - \frac{W}{P} \ell \right) \tag{3.1.14}$$

subject to

$$\bar{y} - \Phi(\ell, K) = 0, \qquad P_e \, dE = P \, dK. \tag{3.1.15}$$

The representative firm therefore maximizes the Lagrangian expression

$$\mathcal{L} = \frac{P}{rE} \left( \bar{y} - \frac{W}{P} \ell \right) + \lambda[\bar{y} - \Phi(\ell, K)]. \tag{3.1.16}$$

First-order conditions for this maximization problem are given by

$$\frac{\partial \mathcal{L}}{\partial \ell} = -\frac{P}{rE} \frac{W}{P} - \lambda \frac{\partial \Phi}{\partial \ell} = 0, \tag{3.1.17}$$

$$\frac{\partial \mathcal{L}}{\partial K} = -\frac{P}{rE^2} \left( \bar{y} - \frac{W}{P} \ell \right) \frac{dE}{dK} - \lambda \frac{\partial \Phi}{\partial K} = -\frac{P}{E} - \lambda \frac{\partial \Phi}{\partial K} = 0, \tag{3.1.18}$$

---

[4]The representative firm's problem is slightly different in the case in which the period of excess-goods supply is expected to be temporary. However, while results in that case are quantitatively different, they are qualitatively unchanged.

$$\frac{\partial \mathcal{L}}{\partial \lambda} = \bar{y} - \Phi(\ell, K). \tag{3.1.19}$$

These first-order conditions are simply the solutions to the problem of the cost-minimizing method of production of $\bar{y}$ for factor prices $W/P$ and $r$. As long as the representative firm's expansion path for $(W/P)/r$ is increasing in both $\ell$ and $K$ (i.e., as long as both labor and capital are ''normal inputs''), then the representative firm's effective labor and capital demand schedules are given by

$$\ell^{d'} = \ell^{d'} \underset{(-) \;\; (+) \;\; (+)}{\left( \frac{W}{P}, \; r, \; \bar{y} \right)}, \qquad K^{*'} = K^{*'} \underset{(+) \;\; (-) \;\; (+)}{\left( \frac{W}{P}, \; r, \; \bar{y} \right)}. \tag{3.1.20}$$

As in the analysis of Section 1.2, we now invoke the possibility of capital stock adjustment costs as a way to intuitively motivate a finite-valued investment demand function. In particular, we assume that investment demand is given by

$$i^d = \xi_k \left[ K^{*'} \underset{(+) \;\; (-) \;\; (+)}{\left( \frac{W}{P}, \; r, \; \bar{y} \right)} - \bar{K} \right]. \tag{3.1.21}$$

However, with the capital stock temporarily fixed at $\bar{K}$, the equilibrium real wage rate is positively related to the exogenously determined level of output $\bar{y}$, as is apparent from Figure 3.1. We may therefore write the semi-reduced-form investment schedule as

$$i^d = i^d(r, y), \tag{3.1.22}$$

where $y$ denotes the level of current output that, from the point of view of the representative firm, is also the current constraint on the level of sales. While the current analysis therefore reconfirms the inverse relationship between the level of investment spending and the nominal rate of interest, the present analysis also points to the level of current income as an additional factor influencing investment spending. While the role of $y$ in determining $i^d$ is examined in more detail in Chapter 4 and is the subject of Grossman (1972), the formal analysis in the remainder of this chapter ignores this possibility and simply assumes that investment demand is given by $i^d = i^d(r)$.

As a final prelude to the analysis of Section 3.3, we now consider the contribution of equity shares to total wealth. The real market value of equity is given by

$$\frac{P_e E}{P} = \frac{1}{r} \left( \bar{y} - \frac{W}{P} \ell \right). \tag{3.1.23}$$

It is useful at this time to introduce the concept of the expected marginal product of capital $R^e$ as the natural counterpart to the actual marginal product of capital $R$ in Chapters 1 and 2. In particular, we formally define

$$R^e = \frac{\bar{y} - (W/P)\ell}{K}. \tag{3.1.24}$$

The equity component of wealth is therefore equal to

$$\frac{R^e K}{r} = \frac{1}{r} \left( \bar{y} - \frac{W}{P} \ell \right). \tag{3.1.25}$$

In general, we would expect $R^e$ to be an increasing function of $\bar{y}$, but we usually adopt the assumption that $R^e$ is exogenous and fixed in value.

## Rigid Prices and the Government Budget Constraint

As in Chapters 1 and 2, the government budget constraint is given by

$$g + \frac{B}{P} = \tau + \dot{m}^s + \dot{b}^s. \tag{3.1.26}$$

With flexible prices, changes in the price level imply changes in the real value of government bond interest payments. Therefore, at least one government policy parameter has to be explicitly linked to the price level so that the government budget constraint continues to be satisfied independent of the level of prices. We chose to specify the level of taxes as $\tau = \tau_0 + B/P$ with $\tau_0$ viewed as an exogenous policy parameter to purge the government budget constraint of all endogenous variables.

In the present case of fixed prices, the endogenous variables are the interest rate and the level of income. Since neither of these appears anywhere in the government budget constraint, we need not at this point employ such a convention. However, when we analyze the permanent effects of nonzero rates of $\dot{b}^s$ (i.e., the effects of changes in the stock of bonds $B$), we continue to assume that changes in the total interest payments on government bonds are financed through changes in taxes. We therefore continue to specify total tax collection as

$$\tau = \tau_0 + \frac{B}{P_0}, \tag{3.1.27}$$

with $P_0$ denoting the exogenously fixed price level.

A common alternate assumption in macroeconomic models is that the level of real taxes rises with the level of real income $y$. One formal possibility would be to specify $\tau = \tau_0 + \tau_1(y)$, $\tau_1' > 0$. In this case the government budget constraint would be given by

$$g + \frac{B}{P_0} = \tau_0 + \tau_1(y) + \dot{m}^s + \dot{b}^s. \tag{3.1.28}$$

However, we would again face the problem of the government being forced to change another of its policy variables in response to changes in an endogenous variable, this time the level of income $y$. One possible solution would be to simply let all changes in tax collections be offset with purchases and sales of government bonds. In this case, the real supply of additional government bonds per unit of time would be given by $\dot{b}^s = \dot{b}_0^s - \tau_1(y)$ with $\dot{b}_0^s$ viewed as the exogenous policy parameter.[5]

---

[5]Dynamic analyses along these lines are provided by Blinder and Solow (1973) and Christ (1979).

# 3.2 ECONOMYWIDE EQUILIBRIUM AND POLICY ANALYSIS

The equations describing the fixed-price model are formally very similar to those describing the flexible-price model. One obvious difference is that in the current model output $y$ is endogenous and prices $P_0$ are exogenous. In the flexible-price model the level of output is exogenously determined by the outcome of interactions in factor markets and is equal to $y^*$ while the level of prices $P$ is endogenous. The other major difference concerns our interpretation of the goods market equilibrium condition. In the flexible-price model, goods market equilibrium reflects equality between goods supply and goods demand. Alternatively, in this chapter, goods market equilibrium characterizes equality between the level of production and the level of aggregate demand.

## The Formal Model

In the absence of wealth effects in the savings and portfolio allocation decisions, our model is now given by:

### Market-clearing Conditions

Goods:

$$c^d(\underset{(+)}{z}) + i^d(\underset{(-)}{r}, \underset{(+)}{R^e}) + g - y = 0. \tag{3.2.1}$$

Earning assets:

$$\dot{f}^d\left(\underset{(+)}{z}, \underset{(-)}{y}, \underset{(+)}{r}, \underset{(+)}{\frac{M}{P_0}}\right) - \dot{e}^s(\underset{(-)}{r}, \underset{(+)}{R^e}) - \dot{b}^s = 0. \tag{3.2.2}$$

Money:

$$\dot{m}^d\left(\underset{(+)}{y}, \underset{(-)}{r}, \underset{(-)}{\frac{M}{P_0}}\right) - \dot{m}^s = 0. \tag{3.2.3}$$

### Definitions and Identities

Government budget constraint: $g - \tau_0 = \dot{m}^s + \dot{b}^s$.

Disposable income: $z = y - \tau_0$.

### Exogenous Variables

Real: $R^e$, three among $\tau_0$, $g$, $\dot{m}^s$, and $\dot{b}^s$, shift parameters.

Nominal: $M$, $B$, $P_0$, one among $\tau_0$, $g$, $\dot{m}^s$, and $\dot{b}^s$.

### Endogenous Variables

Real: $r$, $y$.

Nominal: None.

## Market Equilibrium Loci

Graphical analysis is changed slightly in the model since the endogenous variables are now $y$ and $r$ instead of $P$ and $r$. Therefore, the diagrammatical analysis is conducted in $y$, $r$ space instead of $P$, $r$ space. The slopes of the market equilibrium loci are now solved by differentiating the equilibrium conditions with respect to $y$ and $r$. The slope of the goods market equilibrium locus is given by

$$\frac{dr}{dy}\bigg|_{y=y^d} = \frac{1 - \partial c^d/\partial z}{\partial i^d/\partial r} < 0 \quad \text{(GME)}. \tag{3.2.4}$$

The goods market equilibrium curve is downward sloping under the usual assumption that the marginal propensity to consume, $\partial c^d/\partial z$, is less than unity.

The slope of the earning asset equilibrium locus is given by

$$\frac{dr}{dy}\bigg|_{\dot f^d=\dot f^s} = \frac{\partial \dot f^d/\partial z + \partial \dot f^d/\partial y}{\partial \dot e^s/\partial r - \partial \dot f^d/\partial r} \quad \text{(FME)}. \tag{3.2.5}$$

Substitution from the representative household's budget constraint allows this expression to be rewritten as

$$\frac{dr}{dy}\bigg|_{\dot f^d=\dot f^s} = \frac{\left(1 - \dfrac{\partial c^d}{\partial z}\right) - \xi_m \dfrac{\partial (M/P)^d}{\partial y}}{\partial \dot e^s/\partial r - \partial \dot f^d/\partial r} \quad \text{(FME)}. \tag{3.2.6}$$

The denominator of this expression is unambiguously negative while the numerator is of ambiguous sign. However, we generally assume that the rate of adjustment of actual to desired money balances, $\xi_m$, is large enough to guarantee that the numerator of this expression is negative. We therefore generally assume that the earning asset market equilibrium locus is upward sloping.

Finally, the slope of the money market equilibrium locus is given by

$$\frac{dr}{dy}\bigg|_{\dot m^d=\dot m^s} = -\frac{\partial \dot m^d/\partial y}{\partial \dot m^d/\partial r} = -\frac{\partial (M/P)^d/\partial y}{\partial (M/P)^d/\partial r} > 0 \quad \text{(MME)}. \tag{3.2.7}$$

This locus is unambiguously positively sloped. It is also straightforward to prove that the slope of the money market equilibrium locus is greater than the slope of the earning asset market equilibrium locus. All three loci are depicted graphically in Figure 3.4. The level of income $y_0$ represents the fixed-price equilibrium level of income and $r_0$ represents the fixed-price equilibrium interest rate.

## Effects of Exogenous Disturbances

As in our analysis of Chapter 2, one of the three market equilibrium conditions is always redundant by Walras's law. For the purposes of analysis, it is again convenient to work with the goods and money market equilibrium conditions. Recall that the real demand for additional money balances is given by

$$\dot m^d = \xi_m \left[\left(\frac{M}{P}\right)^d - \frac{M}{P}\right].$$

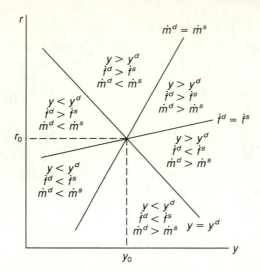

Figure 3.4

The goods and money market equilibrium conditions may therefore be written as

$$c^d(y - \tau_0) + i^d(r) + g - y = 0, \tag{3.2.8}$$

$$\left(\frac{M}{P}\right)^d(y, r) - \frac{M}{P_0} - \frac{1}{\xi_m}\dot{m}^s = 0. \tag{3.2.9}$$

Now differentiating with respect to $y$, $r$, $g$, $\tau_0$, $\dot{m}^s$, $\dot{b}^s$, $M$, and $B$, we obtain

$$\begin{bmatrix} -\left(1 - \dfrac{\partial c^d}{\partial z}\right) & \dfrac{\partial i^d}{\partial r} \\[2ex] \dfrac{\partial (M/P)^d}{\partial y} & \dfrac{\partial (M/P)^d}{\partial r} \end{bmatrix} \begin{bmatrix} dy \\[2ex] dr \end{bmatrix} = \begin{bmatrix} \dfrac{\partial c^d}{\partial z}\,d\tau_0 - dg \\[2ex] \dfrac{1}{P_0}\,dM + \dfrac{1}{\xi_m}\,d\dot{m}^s \end{bmatrix}. \tag{3.2.10}$$

The determinant of the matrix of partial derivatives above is given by

$$\Delta = -\left[\left(1 - \frac{\partial c^d}{\partial z}\right)\frac{\partial (M/P)^d}{\partial r} + \frac{\partial i^d}{\partial r}\frac{\partial (M/P)^d}{\partial y}\right] > 0. \tag{3.2.11}$$

Effects of combinations of exogenous disturbances on $y$ and $r$ may now be solved by application of Cramer's rule.

## Fiscal Policy

We first consider a temporary tax cut financed by the sale of bonds. This case corresponds to that in which $-d\tau_0 = db^s > 0$. Evaluating the total differential expression above, we obtain

$$\left.\frac{dy}{d\tau_0}\right|_{d\tau_0 = -db^s} = \frac{1}{\Delta}\frac{\partial c^d}{\partial z}\frac{\partial (M/P)^d}{\partial r} < 0, \tag{3.2.12}$$

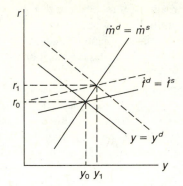

Figure 3.5

$$\frac{dr}{d\tau_0}\bigg|_{d\tau_0 = -d\dot{b}^s} = -\frac{1}{\Delta}\frac{\partial c^d}{\partial z}\frac{\partial(M/P)^d}{\partial y} < 0. \tag{3.2.13}$$

The impact effect of a bond-financed tax cut is to raise both the level of output and the interest rate.

Graphically, we see that the tax cut increases consumption demand shifting the $y = y^d$ locus to the right. The tax cut also raises earning asset demand but by less than the extent to which earning asset supply rises. Therefore, the $\dot{f}^d = \dot{f}^s$ locus shifts upward. The money market equilibrium locus is unaffected. The result is depicted in Figure 3.5. The level of income and the interest rate both rise unambiguously.

Over time, the increase in $\dot{b}^s$ from its assumed initial value of zero translates into an increase in the stock of government-issued bonds. However, inspection of the equilibrium conditions above should convince the reader that as long as there are no wealth effects and as long as the government raises the necessary taxes to pay the interest on the new debt, there will be no further effects of this policy on $y$ and $r$.

## Monetary Policy

Next consider purchases and sales of government-issued bonds by the monetary authority. As we pointed out in Chapter 2, such policy moves may be of two types. We refer to offsetting changes in the rates of growth of money and government bonds as flow open-market operations. Such flow open-market operations are characterized by $d\dot{m}^s = -d\dot{b}^s$. Alternatively, the monetary authority may make finite-sized purchases or sales of government securities at a single instant in time. We refer to such policy moves as stock open-market operations. They are characterized by $dM = -(1/r)\,dB$.

We first consider the effects on the economy of a flow open-market purchase, an increase in the rate of expansion of money balances combined with a reduction in the rate of expansion of government bonds. Application of Cramer's rule facilitates the analytical solutions:

$$\frac{dy}{d\dot{m}^s}\bigg|_{d\dot{m}^s = -d\dot{b}^s} = -\frac{1}{\xi_m\Delta}\frac{\partial i^d}{\partial r} > 0, \tag{3.2.14}$$

$$\frac{dr}{d\dot{m}^s}\bigg|_{d\dot{m}^s = -d\dot{b}^s} = -\frac{1}{\xi_m\Delta}\left(1 - \frac{\partial c^d}{\partial z}\right) < 0. \tag{3.2.15}$$

We therefore find that an increase in the flow supply of money combined with a reduction in the flow supply of bonds raises the equilibrium level of output and reduces the equilibrium interest rate. However, just as in our analysis of Chapter 2, such flow open-market operations become completely irrelevant in the case of instantaneous portfolio adjustment ($\xi_m \to +\infty$).

We can also analyze the effects of this policy move graphically. The increase in the flow supply of money shifts the money market equilibrium locus downward and to the right. The reduction in the flow supply of bonds shifts the earning asset market equilibrium locus downward and to the right. The results are depicted in Figure 3.6. We therefore reconfirm that the level of income rises unambiguously and the interest rate falls unambiguously. The reduction in interest rates induced by the increased rate of expansion of the money supply stimulates aggregate demand and the level of output rises.

Over time, the flow of open-market purchases of government bonds by the monetary authority translates into an increase in the stock of money in circulation and a reduction of the number of government bonds outstanding. Inspection of the market equilibrium conditions indicates that the reduction in the stock of bonds has no effect on the equilibrium levels of $y$ and $r$. The legacy of the temporary increase in $\dot{m}^s$ and the temporary reduction in $\dot{b}^s$ is therefore confined to the effects of the increase in the stock of money $M$. Solving the matrix equation above by Cramer's rule, we find that

$$\frac{dy}{dM} = -\frac{1}{P_0 \Delta} \frac{\partial i^d}{\partial r} > 0, \tag{3.2.16}$$

$$\frac{dr}{dM} = -\frac{1}{P_0 \Delta} \left( 1 - \frac{\partial c^d}{\partial z} \right) < 0. \tag{3.2.17}$$

We can also analyze the effects of an increase in the stock of money graphically. The increase in the stock of money lowers the flow demand for money and raises the flow demand for earning assets. Therefore, the $\dot{m}^d = \dot{m}^s$ and the $\dot{f}^d = \dot{f}^s$ loci both shift downward and to the right, as shown in Figure 3.7. The level of income rises and the rate of interest falls just as is predicted by the algebraic analysis presented above.

Next consider the effects of a stock open-market purchase in which the government

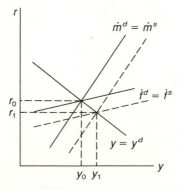

**Figure 3.6**

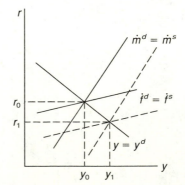

**Figure 3.7**

purchases a finite quantity of government bonds at a single instant in time. This policy is characterized by

$$r \, dM = -dB. \tag{3.2.18}$$

The effect of this policy is exactly the same as the cumulative effect of a flow open-market purchase. Again we find that the reduction in the stock of government bonds has no direct influence on any of the market equilibrium conditions. Furthermore, the effect of the increase in the stock of money is exactly the same as that described above. The interest rate falls to maintain money market equilibrium, and the level of income rises due to the resulting increase in investment spending.

One situation in which either a flow open-market operation or a stock open-market operation may become relatively impotent or completely ineffective is if the sensitivity of money demand to the rate of interest becomes very large or, in the limit, infinite. Inspection of the determinant of the partial derivative matrix above indicates that $dy/d\dot{m}^s$ does in fact approach zero as $\partial(M/P)^d/\partial r$ approaches minus infinity, the so-called liquidity trap.

However, as noted by Patinkin (1965, pp. 349–355), the plausibility of such an infinite responsiveness of money demand to the rate of interest is quite questionable. The traditional story is that at very low interest rates, agents expect that further declines in interest rates are quite unlikely and that a turnaround to rising interest rates and falling earning asset prices is more likely to occur. Therefore, agents anticipate capital losses on earning assets, and the demand for money may increase without bound.

The explicit microeconomic foundations of the representative household's choice problem presented in Chapter 1 are based on the assumption that agents hold expectations about the future with certainty. In particular, agents act as if there is no possibility that interest rates will ever change from their current levels. However, if uncertainty about the future is admitted as a possibility, a scenario in which agents consider the implications of unexpected changes in asset prices becomes more plausible. It is therefore useful at this point to rethink our earlier analysis of the representative household's decision to allocate its wealth across money and earning assets in light of such potential uncertainty about future interest rate movements.

Recall that the representative household's selection of a desired money stock is a by-product of its decision to allocate wealth across money and earning assets. Total net household wealth is given by

$$\Omega = \frac{M}{P} + \frac{\kappa B}{rP} + \frac{R^e K}{r}. \tag{3.2.19}$$

If we denote the representative household's desired stock of earning assets as $(F/P)^d$, then the representative household's wealth allocation problem is made subject to the constraint

$$\left(\frac{M}{P}\right)^d + \left(\frac{F}{P}\right)^d = \Omega. \tag{3.2.20}$$

An infinite negative responsiveness of money demand with respect to the rate of interest must therefore have as its counterpart an infinite positive responsiveness of the desired stock of earning assets with respect to the rate of interest. In principle, household holdings of earning assets need not be positive. The representative household may, subject to its wealth constraint, issue bonds (borrow) to augment its money holdings. An infinite responsiveness of money demand with respect to the rate of interest suggests that a further decline in interest rates will induce the representative household to issue bonds (borrow) without limit to finance additional money holding. But while the representative household expects earning asset prices to fall, there is at least some possibility that earning asset prices may rise instead. Having borrowed in unlimited quantities, the representative household will in this instance be unable to redeem the bonds it has issued and will instead be forced into bankruptcy. Risk aversion is likely to inhibit the representative household from exposing itself to so much risk, and therefore the existence of a liquidity trap is a quite remote possibility.

## An Alternative Formulation of Government Behavior

As we discussed in Chapter 2, changes in the stock of government bonds force the government to make an offsetting change in at least one other government policy parameter in order to satisfy the government budget constraint. In the preceding section, we assumed that the government raised taxes to finance increases in government bond interest payments.

In this section, we consider the alternative government policy strategy, first introduced in Chapter 2, in which the government responds to changes in $B$ by changing the rate of sales of new government bonds, $\dot{b}^s$. In particular, we now adopt the assumption that

$$\dot{b}^s = \dot{b}_0^s + \frac{B}{P_0}, \tag{3.2.21}$$

with $\dot{b}_0^s$ the fixed government policy parameter.

This modification does not involve changes in any agent's responses to the endogenous variables. Therefore, the slopes of the market equilibrium loci are unaffected by this change. However, there are changes in the goods and earning asset market equilibrium conditions. In the goods and earning asset markets, disposable income is now given by $z = y + B/P_0 - \tau$. Furthermore, in the earning asset market, the flow supply of government bonds is now given by $\dot{b}_0^s + B/P_0$. Finally, the money market equilibrium condition is unaltered by the change.

We continue to perform our algebraic analysis by utilizing the goods and money market equilibrium conditions. These equilibrium conditions are now given by

$$c^d\left(y + \frac{B}{P_0} - \tau\right) + i^d(r) + g - y = 0, \tag{3.2.22}$$

$$\left(\frac{M}{P}\right)^d(y, r) - \frac{M}{P_0} - \frac{1}{\xi_m}\dot{m}^s = 0. \tag{3.2.23}$$

Differentiating these equilibrium conditions with respect to the endogenous and exogenous variables, we obtain

$$\begin{bmatrix} -\left(1 - \dfrac{\partial c^d}{\partial z}\right) & \dfrac{\partial i^d}{\partial r} \\[3mm] \dfrac{\partial (M/P)^d}{\partial y} & \dfrac{\partial (M/P)^d}{\partial r} \end{bmatrix} \begin{bmatrix} dy \\[3mm] dr \end{bmatrix} = \begin{bmatrix} \dfrac{\partial c^d}{\partial z}\, d\tau - \dfrac{1}{P_0}\dfrac{\partial c^d}{\partial z}\, dB - dg \\[3mm] \dfrac{1}{P_0}\, dM + \dfrac{1}{\xi_m}\, d\dot m^s \end{bmatrix}. \tag{3.2.24}$$

The present change in government behavior leaves unchanged the response of the economy to changes in the government's flow policy parameters $g$, $\tau$, $\dot m^s$, and $\dot b^s$. However, there are important differences in the effects of policy moves that generate changes in the number of government bonds outstanding, $B$.

First consider the fiscal policy move of a temporary, bond-financed tax cut. In the preceding section, the legacy of this policy in the form of an increase in $B$ had no impact on the economy. In the present context, however, this is no longer the case. We now find that

$$\frac{dy}{dB} = -\frac{1}{P_0\Delta}\frac{\partial c^d}{\partial z}\frac{\partial (M/P)^d}{\partial r} > 0, \tag{3.2.25}$$

$$\frac{dr}{dB} = \frac{1}{P_0\Delta}\frac{\partial c^d}{\partial z}\frac{\partial (M/P)^d}{\partial y} > 0. \tag{3.2.26}$$

We therefore find that an increase in the stock of government bonds raises both the level of income and the rate of interest. The increase in $B$ raises disposable income directly through its effects on interest payments received by households. This increase in disposable income generates an increase in output through the usual channels. The resulting higher level of income generates an increase in the demand for money. This increase in the demand for money results in an increase in the rate of interest.

Graphically, the increase in the stock of government bonds shifts the $y = y^d$ locus to the right. The increase in $B$ also raises the supply of earning assets by more than it raises the demand for earning assets. The earning asset equilibrium locus therefore shifts upward and to the left. The effects of an increase in the stock of bonds is depicted in Figure 3.8.

Next consider the effects of this alternative policy formulation on the response of the

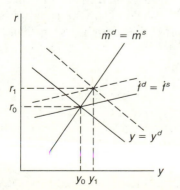

**Figure 3.8**

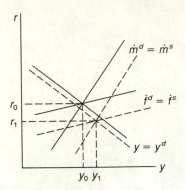

**Figure 3.9**

economy to open-market operations. As noted above, this change in government behavior does not alter the impact response of the economy to changes in flow policies, like those that result from a flow open-market operation. We therefore need only reconsider the effects of a stock open-market purchase, which are formally identical to the cumulative effects of a flow open-market purchase. Setting $r\,dM = -dB$ in the matrix expression above, we find that

$$\left.\frac{dy}{dM}\right|_{dB=-r\,dM} = \frac{1}{P_0\Delta}\left[r\frac{\partial c^d}{\partial z}\frac{\partial (M/P)^d}{\partial r} - \frac{\partial i^d}{\partial r}\right], \tag{3.2.27}$$

$$\left.\frac{dr}{dM}\right|_{dB=-r\,dM} = -\frac{1}{P_0\Delta}\left[r\frac{\partial c^d}{\partial z}\frac{\partial (M/P)^d}{\partial y} + \left(1 - \frac{\partial c^d}{\partial z}\right)\right] < 0. \tag{3.2.28}$$

We therefore see that a stock open-market purchase still unambiguously lowers the rate of interest. However, the lower interest rate and the coincident lower level of disposable income due to the reduction in $B$ now have offsetting effects on consumption spending and therefore the levels of aggregate demand and output.

We can also analyze this policy effect graphically, as is shown in Figure 3.9. The increase in $M$ shifts the money market and earning asset market equilibrium loci downward and to the right. The reduction in $B$ lowers earning asset supply by more than it lowers earning asset demand. Therefore, the coincident reduction in $B$ reinforces the shift in $\dot{f}^d = \dot{f}^s$ downward and to the right. The reduction in $B$ finally shifts the goods market equilibrium locus downward and to the left. While Figure 3.8 is drawn for the case in which $y$ rises, it should be apparent that a reduction in $y$ is also possible.

## Traditional IS-LM Analysis

The model we have studied throughout most of this chapter is very similar to the original presentation of the IS-LM model of Hicks (1937). In this section, we first discuss those minor differences between the models we have been studying and the traditional IS-LM model and then analyze the standard policy experiments in that model's framework.[6]

---

[6]Friedman (1970) provides an excellent discussion of policy issues in the language of the IS-LM model. Further discussion may be found in Brunner and Meltzer (1972), and Tobin (1972).

Throughout the analysis of this chapter, we have assumed that transaction costs make instantaneous adjustment of actual to desired money balances suboptimal. If such costs are trivial, then the representative household continuously adjusts its holdings of money and earning assets to keep $M/P = (M/P)^d$. We formally consider the effect of this possibility by taking limits as the speed of adjustment of actual to desired money balances, $\xi_m$, approaches infinity. In this case most of our results are only quantitatively, not qualitatively, affected.

However, we do find that flow open-market operations are completely ineffective if agents adjust their portfolios instantaneously. This failure of changes in $\dot{m}^s$ and $\dot{b}^s$ to affect the economy turns out to be a general phenomenon. As $\xi_m \to +\infty$, the earning asset and money market equilibrium conditions both converge to

$$\left(\frac{M}{P}\right)^d(y, r) = \frac{M}{P_0} \tag{3.2.29}$$

and the $\dot{f}^d = \dot{f}^s$ locus rotates until it converges with the $\dot{m}^d = \dot{m}^s$ locus.

Study of this limiting case in which $\xi_m \to \infty$ makes clear the principal difference between the models we have been studying and traditional IS-LM analysis. The only other difference concerns the implied specification of government budgetary policy. Traditional IS-LM analysis utilizes Walras's law to eliminate the earning asset market. As noted above, there is no particular problem in doing this except that care must still be taken to properly identify the full particulars of any policy change.

One common form of the IS-LM model is given by

$$c^d(y - \tau_0) + i^d(r, R^e) + g - y = 0, \tag{3.2.30}$$

$$\left(\frac{M}{P}\right)^d(y, r) - \frac{M}{P_0} = 0. \tag{3.2.31}$$

This model is formally identical to our original specification of the fixed-price model with $\tau = \tau_0 + B/P_0$. The only substantive difference is that in the IS-LM model, we let $\xi_m \to +\infty$. In this version of the IS-LM model, unmatched changes in government spending and taxation are implicitly assumed to be financed by purchases and sales of government bonds. All changes in $M$ are assumed to be accomplished through stock open-market operations. Any implied subsequent changes in $B$ are assumed to be offset by changes in taxes to keep net payments from households to the government, $\tau - B/P_0$, constant.

In the IS-LM formulation, the IS curve represents those combinations of $y$ and $r$ consistent with goods market equilibrium. The IS curve is therefore formally identical to the $y = y^d$ locus. The LM curve represents those combinations of $y$ and $r$ consistent with equilibrium in the money market. The LM curve is therefore formally identical to the common $\dot{f}^d = \dot{f}^s$ and $\dot{m}^d = \dot{m}^s$ loci that become coincident when $\xi_m \to +\infty$. The slopes of the IS and LM curves are given by

$$\left.\frac{dr}{dy}\right|_{IS} = \frac{1 - \partial c^d/\partial z}{\partial i^d/\partial r} < 0, \tag{3.2.32}$$

$$\left.\frac{dr}{dy}\right|_{LM} = -\frac{\partial(M/P)^d/\partial y}{\partial(M/P)^d/\partial r} > 0. \tag{3.2.33}$$

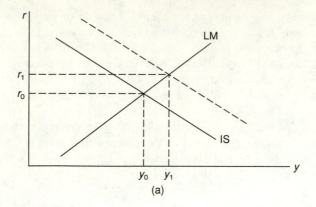

(a)

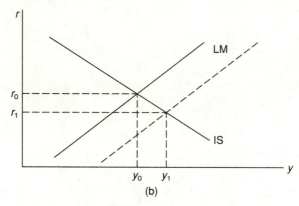

(b)

**Figure 3.10**

Fiscal and monetary policy effects in the IS-LM model can be summarized by the cases of a bond-financed tax cut and a stock open-market purchase. Recalling from above, the effects of these policy changes are given by

$$\frac{dy}{d\tau_0} = \frac{-\dfrac{\partial c^d}{\partial z}\dfrac{\partial (M/P)^d}{\partial r}}{\left(1 - \dfrac{\partial c^d}{\partial z}\right)\dfrac{\partial (M/P)^d}{\partial r} + \dfrac{\partial i^d}{\partial r}\dfrac{\partial (M/P)^d}{\partial y}} < 0, \tag{3.2.34}$$

$$\frac{dr}{d\tau_0} = \frac{\dfrac{\partial c^d}{\partial z}\dfrac{\partial (M/P)^d}{\partial y}}{\left(1 - \dfrac{\partial c^d}{\partial z}\right)\dfrac{\partial (M/P)^d}{\partial r} + \dfrac{\partial i^d}{\partial r}\dfrac{\partial (M/P)^d}{\partial y}} < 0, \tag{3.2.35}$$

$$\frac{dy}{dM} = \frac{\dfrac{1}{P_0}\dfrac{\partial i^d}{\partial r}}{\left(1 - \dfrac{\partial c^d}{\partial z}\right)\dfrac{\partial (M/P)^d}{\partial r} + \dfrac{\partial i^d}{\partial r}\dfrac{\partial (M/P)^d}{\partial y}} > 0, \tag{3.2.36}$$

$$\frac{dr}{dm} = \frac{\frac{1}{P_0}\left(1 - \frac{\partial c^d}{\partial z}\right)}{\left(1 - \frac{\partial c^d}{\partial z}\right)\frac{\partial (M/P)^d}{\partial r} + \frac{\partial i^d}{\partial r}\frac{\partial (M/P)^d}{\partial y}} < 0. \tag{3.2.37}$$

A tax cut shifts the IS curve upward and to the right. Output and the rate of interest both rise. An increase in the money stock shifts the LM curve downward and to the right. The interest rate falls and the level of output rises. These policy effects are depicted in Figure 3.10.

## Policy Effectiveness in the Basic IS-LM Model

It is also of interest to contemplate what behavioral characteristics lead to particularly large or particularly small quantitative effects of stimulative policy on output. Two characteristics are fairly straightforward. First, consider the marginal propensity to consume, $\partial c^d / \partial z$. As stimulative policy expands output, a high value for the marginal propensity to consume leads to bigger second-round increases in demand and hence a bigger cumulative increase in output. Next consider the sensitivity of money demand to income, $\partial (M/P)^d / \partial y$. As stimulative policy induces a higher level of income, the demand for money rises. However, if the demand for money rises elastically with increases in income, a bigger increase in the interest rate is necessary to keep money supply and money demand equal. The higher interest rate crowds out investment spending, leading to a smaller expansion in output.

The effects of changes in the interest sensitivity of investment and the interest sensitivity of the demand for money are less clear-cut. Both interest sensitivities enhance the effectiveness of one policy while reducing the effectiveness of the other. We begin by analyzing the effectiveness of stimulative fiscal policy in the form of reduced taxes. In any event, this policy results in a horizontal shift in the IS curve given by

$$-\frac{dy}{d\tau_0}\bigg|_{dr=0} = \frac{\partial c^d / \partial z}{1 - \partial c^d / \partial z} \equiv D > 0. \tag{3.2.38}$$

We first consider how changes in the sensitivity of investment to the rate of interest affect the effectiveness of this fiscal policy move as measured by the relative sizes of the resulting increases in output $y$. Consider two cases, one in which $\partial i^d / \partial r$ is large in absolute value and another in which $\partial i^d / \partial r$ is small in absolute value. These two cases are depicted graphically in Figure 3.11. As income rises, so too does the demand for money. To keep money demand equal to money supply, the interest rate must rise, which crowds out investment spending. If the sensitivity of investment to the rate of interest is large in absolute value, then a large amount of investment is crowded out and the increase in output is small.

We next consider how changes in the sensitivity of money demand to the rate of interest affect the effectiveness of fiscal policy measured again by the relative sizes of the resulting increases in output $y$. Again we consider two cases, one in which $\partial (M/P)^d / \partial r$ is small in absolute value and one in which $\partial (M/P)^d / \partial r$ is large in absolute value. These two cases are also depicted graphically in Figure 3.11.

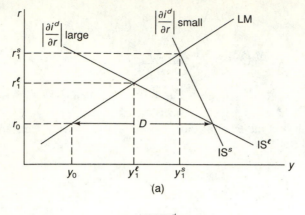

(a)

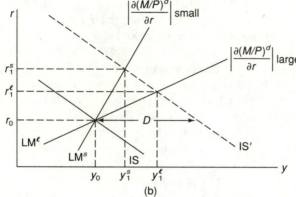

(b)

**Figure 3.11**

If the sensitivity of money demand to the interest rate is small, then as income rises and the demand for money tends to rise, it takes a large increase in the interest rate to keep money demand equal to the fixed supply. Therefore, a large amount of investment is crowded out, and less of an increase in income results. In the limiting case in which money demand is completely insensitive to the rate of interest, stimulative fiscal policy becomes completely impotent as the LM curve becomes vertical.

We next turn our attention to an analysis of the effectiveness of stimulative monetary policy. In any event, this policy shifts the LM curve horizontally by

$$\frac{dy}{dM}\bigg|_{dr=0} = \frac{1}{P_0}\left(\frac{\partial(M/P)^d}{\partial y}\right)^{-1} \equiv H > 0. \tag{3.2.39}$$

We first consider the impact on the effectiveness of monetary policy of the interest sensitivity of investment. If investment is very responsive to the rate of interest, then the reduction in the interest rate brought about by an increase in the money supply generates a large increase in investment and therefore a large increase in output. Alternatively, if the reduction in the interest rate brings forth little added investment spending, the increase in output will be small. Two representative cases are depicted in Figure 3.12.

Finally, consider the impact on the effectiveness of monetary policy of the interest sensitivity of money demand. If money demand is very interest sensitive, then when the

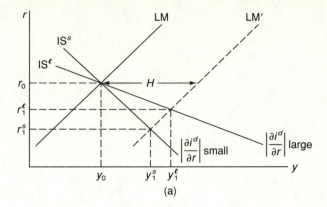

(a)

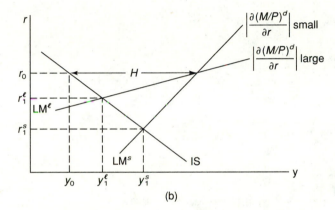

(b)

**Figure 3.12**

money supply is expanded, a very small reduction in the interest rate is enough to reequate money supply and money demand. With only a small reduction in the interest rate, less investment is stimulated, and therefore a smaller rise in output results. Again, two representative cases are depicted in Figure 3.12.

## 3.3 WEALTH EFFECTS IN THE FIXED-PRICE MODEL

Addition to the fixed-price model of the possibility of nonzero effects of wealth on consumption demand, the demand for additional earning assets, and the stock demand for money is now quite straightforward. In general, all of the basic qualitative results are unchanged, although the algebra is complicated somewhat. Retaining our basic policy assumption that $\tau = \tau_0 + B/P_0$, the model, appropriately amended, is given by

### Market-clearing Conditions

Goods:

$$c^d(\underset{(+)}{z}, \underset{(+)}{\Omega}) + i^d(\underset{(-)}{r}, \underset{(+)}{R^e}) + g - y = 0. \tag{3.3.1}$$

Earning assets:

$$\dot{f}^d\left(\underset{(+)}{z}, \underset{(-)}{y}, \underset{(+)}{r}, \underset{(-)}{\Omega}, \underset{(+)}{\frac{M}{P_0}}\right) - \underset{(-)\ (+)}{\dot{e}^s(r, R^e)} - \dot{b}^s = 0.$$    (3.3.2)

Money:

$$\dot{m}^d\left(\underset{(+)}{y}, \underset{(-)}{r}, \underset{(+)}{\Omega}, \underset{(-)}{\frac{M}{P_0}}\right) - \dot{m}^s = 0.$$    (3.3.3)

### Definitions and Identities

Government budget constraint: $g - \tau_0 = \dot{m}^s + \dot{b}^s$.

Disposable income: $z = y - \tau_0$.

Wealth: $\Omega = M/P_0 + \kappa B/rP_0 + R^e K/r$.

### Exogenous Variables

Real: $R^e$, three among $\tau_0$, $g$, $\dot{m}^s$, and $\dot{b}^s$, shift parameters.

Nominal: $M$, $B$, $P_0$, one among $\tau_0$, $g$, $\dot{m}^s$, and $\dot{b}^s$.

### Endogenous Variables

Real: $r$, $y$.

Nominal: None.

The slopes of the market equilibrium loci are given by

$$\left.\frac{dr}{dy}\right|_{y=y^d} = \frac{1 - \partial c^d/\partial z}{\dfrac{\partial i^d}{\partial r} - \dfrac{1}{r}\left(\dfrac{\kappa B}{rP_0} + \dfrac{R^e K}{r}\right)\dfrac{\partial c^d}{\partial \Omega}} < 0 \quad \text{(GME),}$$    (3.3.4)

$$\left.\frac{dr}{dy}\right|_{\dot{f}^d=\dot{f}^s} = \frac{\left(1 - \dfrac{\partial c^d}{\partial z}\right) - \xi_m \dfrac{\partial (M/P)^d}{\partial y}}{\dfrac{\partial \dot{e}^s}{\partial r} - \dfrac{\partial \dot{f}^d}{\partial r} + \dfrac{1}{r}\left(\dfrac{\kappa B}{rP_0} + \dfrac{R^e K}{r}\right)\dfrac{\partial \dot{f}^d}{\partial \Omega}} \quad \text{(FME),}$$    (3.3.5)

$$\left.\frac{dr}{dy}\right|_{\dot{m}^d=\dot{m}^s} = \frac{\partial \dot{m}^d/\partial y}{\dfrac{1}{r}\left(\dfrac{\kappa B}{rP_0} + \dfrac{R^e K}{r}\right)\dfrac{\partial \dot{m}^d}{\partial \Omega} - \dfrac{\partial \dot{m}^d}{\partial r}} > 0 \quad \text{(MME).}$$    (3.3.6)

The expressions for the slopes of the market equilibrium loci are only changed by the addition of terms reflecting the impact of changes in the rate of interest on the market values of equities and government bonds. This asset valuation effect in all cases reinforces the direct effects of changes in the rate of interest on the excess demand functions. Retaining the assumption that $\xi_m$ is large but finite, the slopes of the market equilibrium loci are qualitatively unchanged from our analysis of the preceding sections.

Differentiating the goods and money market equilibrium conditions with respect to the endogenous and exogenous variables, we obtain

$$
\begin{bmatrix}
-\left(1 - \dfrac{\partial c^d}{\partial z}\right) & \dfrac{\partial i^d}{\partial r} - \dfrac{1}{r}\left(\dfrac{\kappa B}{rP_0} + \dfrac{R^e K}{r}\right)\dfrac{\partial c^d}{\partial \Omega} \\[2ex]
\dfrac{\partial (M/P)^d}{\partial y} & \dfrac{\partial (M/P)^d}{\partial r} - \dfrac{1}{r}\left(\dfrac{\kappa B}{rP_0} + \dfrac{R^e K}{r}\right)\dfrac{\partial (M/P)^d}{\partial \Omega}
\end{bmatrix}
\begin{bmatrix} dy \\[2ex] dr \end{bmatrix}
$$

$$
= \begin{bmatrix}
\dfrac{\partial c^d}{\partial z}\, d\tau_0 - dg - \dfrac{1}{P_0}\dfrac{\partial c^d}{\partial \Omega}\left(dM + \dfrac{\kappa}{r}\, dB\right) \\[2ex]
\dfrac{1}{\xi_m}\, d\dot m^s + \dfrac{1}{P_0}\left(1 - \dfrac{\partial (M/P)^d}{\partial \Omega}\right) dM - \dfrac{\kappa}{rP_0}\dfrac{\partial (M/P)^d}{\partial \Omega}\, dB
\end{bmatrix},
\tag{3.3.7}
$$

where the determinant of the matrix in the above expression is given by

$$
\Delta = -\Bigg\{\left(1 - \dfrac{\partial c^d}{\partial z}\right)\dfrac{\partial (M/P)^d}{\partial r} + \dfrac{\partial i^d}{\partial r}\dfrac{\partial (M/P)^d}{\partial y}
$$
$$
- \dfrac{1}{r}\left(\dfrac{\kappa B}{rP_0} + \dfrac{R^e K}{r}\right)\left[\left(1 - \dfrac{\partial c^d}{\partial z}\right)\dfrac{\partial (M/P)^d}{\partial \Omega} + \dfrac{\partial (M/P)^d}{\partial y}\dfrac{\partial c^d}{\partial \Omega}\right]\Bigg\} > 0.
\tag{3.3.8}
$$

## Fiscal Policy

Let us first reanalyze the effects of a temporary, bond-financed tax cut. The impact effects of this policy may be computed by setting $-d\tau_0 = d\dot b^s > 0$ in the matrix expression above. Solving by means of Cramer's rule, we obtain the following results:

$$
\left.\dfrac{dy}{d\tau_0}\right|_{d\tau_0 = -d\dot b^s} = \dfrac{1}{\Delta}\dfrac{\partial c^d}{\partial z}\left[\dfrac{\partial (M/P)^d}{\partial r} - \dfrac{1}{r}\left(\dfrac{\kappa B}{rP_0} + \dfrac{R^e K}{r}\right)\dfrac{\partial (M/P)^d}{\partial \Omega}\right] < 0,
\tag{3.3.9}
$$

$$
\left.\dfrac{dr}{d\tau_0}\right|_{d\tau_0 = -d\dot b^s} = -\dfrac{1}{\Delta}\dfrac{\partial c^d}{\partial z}\dfrac{\partial (M/P)^d}{\partial y} < 0.
\tag{3.3.10}
$$

The impact effects derived above are qualitatively the same as those derived for the equivalent case in Section 3.2. Again we find that a bond-financed tax cut unambiguously raises both the rate of interest and the level of output.

One circumstance in which fiscal policy of this sort is often thought to be ineffective is that in which the stock demand for money in insensitive to the rate of interest—that is, the case in which $\partial (M/P)^d/\partial r = 0$. Evaluating $dy/d\tau$ for the model of Section 3.2, we find that

$$
\lim_{\partial (M/P)^d/\partial r \to 0}\left.\dfrac{dy}{d\tau_0}\right|_{d\tau_0 = -d\dot b^s} = 0.
\tag{3.3.11}
$$

However, as long as the stock demand for money depends positively on wealth, fiscal policy retains its effectiveness. If the demand for money is insensitive to both the rate of interest and the level of wealth, changes in the rate of interest cannot equilibrate the money market. In that circumstance, only changes in the level of income can keep money demand and money supply equal, and the interest rate must adjust to keep aggregate demand equal to this particular level of income. In response to reduced taxes, the interest rate must rise enough so that investment falls by the exact same amount that consumption rises. On net, there is no fiscal stimulus. Stimulative fiscal policy results in the complete crowding out of an identical amount of investment spending.

As long as money demand depends on wealth, however, some of the interest rate adjustment can still take place in the money market. A rise in the interest rate reduces the market value of government debt and firm equity. Therefore, if the demand for money is sensitive to changes in wealth, the demand for money can still fall when interest rates rise even if interest rates have no direct effect on the demand for money. The increase in money demand that accompanies rising income can now be accommodated by an equivalent fall in money demand as the market value of wealth falls.

Over time, the positive flow supply of bonds accompanying the tax cut leads to an increase in the stock of government bonds outstanding. Therefore, even after $\tau_0$ and $b^s$ are restored to their original levels, a legacy of the stimulative fiscal policy remains in the form of an increase in $B$. In the absence of wealth effects, this resulting increase in $B$ has no effect on the model's equilibrium conditions. With wealth effects, changes in the stock of bonds are no longer irrelevant. Evaluating the matrix expression above by Cramer's rule, we find that

$$\frac{dy}{dB} = \frac{\kappa}{rP_0\Delta}\left[\frac{\partial i^d}{\partial r}\frac{\partial (M/P)^d}{\partial \Omega} - \frac{\partial c^d}{\partial \Omega}\frac{\partial (M/P)^d}{\partial r}\right], \tag{3.3.12}$$

$$\frac{dr}{dB} = \frac{\kappa}{rP_0\Delta}\left[\frac{\partial (M/P)^d}{\partial y}\frac{\partial c^d}{\partial \Omega} + \left(1 - \frac{\partial c^d}{dz}\right)\frac{\partial (M/P)^d}{\partial \Omega}\right] > 0. \tag{3.3.13}$$

We therefore see that an increase in the stock of bonds unambiguously raises the rate of interest but has an ambiguous effect on the level of output. However, the expression for $dy/dB$ above should look familiar. The conditions under which the sign of $dy/dB$ is positive (negative) are precisely the same as the conditions under which the sign of $dP/dB$ is positive (negative) in the equivalent flexible-price model of Chapter 2. The increase in the stock of bonds raises wealth, therefore generating increases in consumption demand and the demand for money. The increase in the stock of government bonds tends to stimulate an increase in output if the sensitivity of money demand to the rate of interest and the wealth effect on consumption are large in absolute value. On the other hand, a strong effect of wealth on money demand combined with an interest-sensitive investment demand schedule tend to make increased government debt restrictive.

We can also analyze this policy effect graphically. The increase in the stock of bonds shifts all three market equilibrium loci upward, as is depicted in Figure 3.13. The interest rises unambiguously, as predicted by the algebraic analysis above. However, while Figure 3.13 is drawn for the case in which $dy/dB$ is positive, the reader should be able to verify that the sign of $dy/dB$ is ambiguous.

If an increase in the stock of bonds lowers the equilibrium level of income, then a temporary, bond-financed tax cut will always eventually turn out to be restrictive in nature. Typical time paths of $\tau_0$, $B$, and $y$ for the case in which $dy/dB < 0$ are depicted in

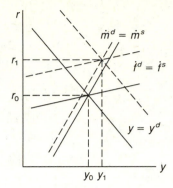

**Figure 3.13**

Figure 3.14. From time $\hat{t}$ onward, in that example, the net effect of the policy move is to reduce the level of income relative to its initial value $y_0$.

## Monetary Policy

We finally wish to reanalyze the effects of monetary policy. In particular, we now reconsider the impact effects of a flow open-market purchase and the accumulated effects of such a flow open-market purchase over time or, equivalently, the effects of a stock open-market purchase. A flow open-market purchase may be characterized by $d\dot{m}^s = -d\dot{b}^s > 0$. Evaluating the matrix equation above by means of Cramer's rule, we find that the impact effects of such a flow open-market purchase are given by

$$\left.\frac{dy}{d\dot{m}^s}\right|_{d\dot{m}^s=-d\dot{b}^s} = -\frac{1}{\xi_m \Delta}\left[\frac{\partial i^d}{\partial r} - \frac{1}{r}\left(\frac{\kappa B}{rP_0} + \frac{R^e K}{r}\right)\frac{\partial c^d}{\partial \Omega}\right] > 0, \qquad (3.3.14)$$

$$\left.\frac{dr}{d\dot{m}^s}\right|_{d\dot{m}^s=-d\dot{b}^s} = -\frac{1}{\xi_m \Delta}\left(1 - \frac{\partial c^d}{\partial z}\right) < 0. \qquad (3.3.15)$$

We therefore continue to find that the impact effects of a flow open-market purchase are an increase in the level of output and a reduction in the rate of interest. We also continue to find that flow open-market operations are only effective as long as the speed of portfolio adjustment $\xi_m$ is strictly finite. In the limiting case in which $\xi_m \to +\infty$, we find that $dy/d\dot{m}^s = dr/d\dot{m}^s = 0$, as we found in Section 3.2.

We also noted in the preceding section that monetary policy tends to be relatively ineffective when the sensitivity of investment spending to the rate of interest is small in absolute value. In particular, in the absence of wealth effects, we find that

$$\lim_{\partial i^d/\partial r \to 0} \left.\frac{dy}{d\dot{m}^s}\right|_{d\dot{m}^s=-d\dot{b}^s} = 0. \qquad (3.3.16)$$

However, inspection of the solution for $dy/d\dot{m}^s$ above indicates that in the present case monetary policy may be effective even if $\partial i^d/\partial r = 0$. The reduction in interest rates generated by the more rapid rate of monetary expansion also results in increases in government bond and equity prices. Therefore, as long as consumption demand is positively related to the level of wealth, the equilibrium level of income still rises.

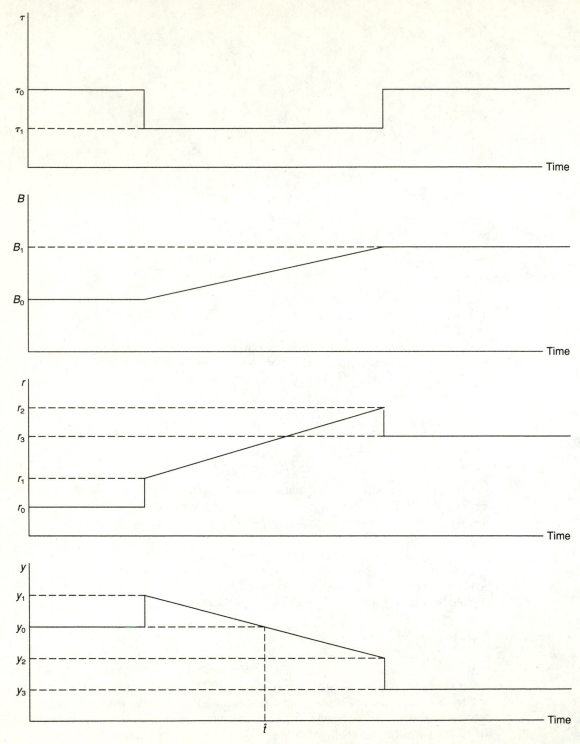

**Figure 3.14**

Over time, the flow of open-market purchases of government bonds by the monetary authority translates into an increase in the stock of money in circulation and a reduction of the number of government bonds outstanding. Assume that this substitution of money for bonds is approximately governed by $dM = -(1/r)\ dB$. [The exact relationships are $dM = P_0 \int_0^t \dot{m}^s(x)\ dx$ and $dB = P_0 \int_0^t r(x)\dot{b}^s(x)\ dx$.] We therefore see that the permanent effect of a temporary flow open-market purchase is precisely the same as the impact effect of a stock open-market purchase, just as was the case in the analysis of Section 3.2. Evaluating the matrix expression above by means of Cramer's rule, we therefore find that

$$\frac{dy}{dM}\bigg|_{dM=-dB/r} = \frac{1}{P_0\Delta}\left\{\left[\frac{1}{r}\left(\frac{\kappa B}{rP_0} + \frac{R^e K}{r}\right) - (1-\kappa)\frac{\partial(M/P)^d}{\partial r}\right]\frac{\partial c^d}{\partial\Omega}\right.$$
$$\left. - \left[1 - (1-\kappa)\frac{\partial(M/P)^d}{\partial\Omega}\right]\frac{\partial i^d}{\partial r}\right\} > 0,$$

$$(3.3.17)$$

$$\frac{dr}{dM}\bigg|_{dM=-dB/r} = \frac{1}{P_0\Delta}\left\{-\left(1 - \frac{\partial c^d}{\partial z}\right)\left[1 - (1-\kappa)\frac{\partial(M/P)^d}{\partial\Omega}\right]\right.$$
$$\left. + (1-\kappa)\frac{\partial c^d}{A/P}\frac{\partial(M/P)^d}{\partial y}\right\}\frac{\partial c^d}{\partial\Omega}\frac{\partial(M/P)^d}{\partial y} \gtreqless 0.$$

$$(3.3.18)$$

We therefore find that the stock effects of open-market purchases still include an unambiguous increase in the level of output. However, we are no longer able to unambiguously sign the stock effects of an open-market purchase on the rate of interest. One case in which a decline in the interest rate definitely occurs is when $\kappa = 1$. In this instance, increases in government debt increase wealth one-for-one. Therefore, the impact effect of an open-market operation on wealth is precisely zero. An open-market purchase increases the monetary component of wealth by exactly as much as it decreases the bond component of wealth. With only the liquidity effect of the increase in the stock of money operational, the interest rate falls unambiguously.

We can also analyze this comparative statics exercise graphically. The disturbance in question is composed of an increase in the money supply combined with a net increase in wealth as long as $\kappa < 1$. The increase in wealth shifts the goods market equilibrium locus upward and to the right. The increase in wealth also generates a reduction in the flow demand for earning assets. However, this wealth effect will likely be more than offset by a liquidity effect increasing the flow demand for earning assets. In this case, the earning asset market equilibrium locus shifts downward. Finally, the increase in the stock of money supplied is greater than the increase in money demand induced by the increase in wealth. Therefore, the money market equilibrium locus also likely shifts downward. The graphical representation of the open-market increase in the stock of money is presented in Figure 3.15.

We therefore reconfirm our algebraic result that the open-market increase in the stock of money unambiguously raises income. The effect on the interest rate, while drawn as negative, is, however, ambiguous. One case in which the interest rate declines unambiguously is that in which the earning asset market equilibrium locus is downward sloping. The earning asset market equilibrium locus slopes downward when increases in income raise saving by more than they increase the flow demand for money. Alternatively, wealth

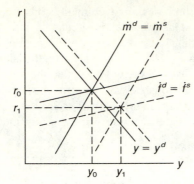

**Figure 3.15**

effects in the consumption function make a decline in the interest rate a less likely response to the stock open-market purchase. When there is no net wealth effect, there is no shift in the goods market equilibrium locus, and the interest rate must fall as we move downward along this locus.

Wealth effects in the consumption function also make the effectiveness of open-market purchases immune to the possibility of impotency in a liquidity trap. As the responsiveness of money demand to the rate of interest approaches minus infinity, increases in $M$ do not lead to changes in the interest rate. However, as long as $\kappa < 1$, the increase in the stock of money generates increased wealth, consumption demand rises, and therefore output rises as well. Finally, the presence of wealth effects also makes the effectiveness of open-market purchases immune to the possibility of a lack of interest rate responsiveness of investment demand. As long as wealth rises, either because $\kappa < 1$ or because a fall in the rate of interest raises the market value of earning assets, consumption demand rises and so output must increase.

# REFERENCES

Barro, Robert J., and Herschel I. Grossman, "A General Disequilibrium Model of Income and Employment," *American Economic Review,* March, 1971, 82–93.

Barro, Robert J., "A Theory of Monopolistic Price Adjustment," *Review of Economic Studies,* January, 1972, 17–26.

Benassy, Jean-Pascal, *Macroeconomics: An Introduction to the Non-Walrasian Approach,* Orlando, FL, Academic, 1986.

Blinder, Alan S., and Robert M. Solow, "Does Fiscal Policy Matter?" *Journal of Public Economics,* November, 1973, 319–337.

Brunner, Karl, and Allan H. Meltzer, "Friedman's Monetary Theory," *Journal of Political Economy,* September/October, 1972, 837–851.

Christ, Carl F., "On Fiscal and Monetary Policies and the Government Budget Restraint," *American Economic Review,* September, 1979, 526–538.

Clower, Robert W., "The Keynesian Counterrevolution: A Theoretical Appraisal," in F. Hahn and F. Brechling, eds., *The Theory of Interest Rates,* London, Macmillan, 1965.

Drazen, Allan, "Recent Developments in Macroeconomic Disequilibrium Theory," *Econometrica,* March, 1980, 283–306.

Friedman, Milton, "A Theoretical Framework for Monetary Analysis," *Journal of Political Economy,* March/April, 1970, 193–235.

Gordon, Robert J., "Price Inertia and Policy Ineffectiveness in the United States, 1890–1980," *Journal of Political Economy,* December, 1982, 1087–1117.

Grossman, Herschel I., "A Choice-Theoretic Model of an Income-Investment Accelerator," *American Economic Review,* September, 1972, 630–641.

Grossman, Herschel I., "The Natural-Rate Hypothesis, The Rational-Expectations Hypothesis, and the Remarkable Survival of Non-Market-Clearing Assumptions," in Karl Brunner and Allan Meltzer, eds., *Variability in Employment, Prices, and Money,* Carnegie-Rochester Conference Series on Public Policy, Amsterdam, North Holland, Autumn, 1983, 225–245.

Hicks, John R., "Mr. Keynes and the Classics: A Suggested Interpretation," *Econometrica,* April, 1937, 147–159.

McCallum, Bennett T., "On 'Real' and 'Sticky-Price' Theories of the Business Cycle," *Journal of Money, Credit and Banking,* November, 1986, 397–414.

Patinkin, Don, *Money, Interest, and Prices,* 2nd ed., New York, Harper & Row, 1965.

Rotemberg, Julio J., "Sticky Prices in the United States," *Journal of Political Economy,* December, 1982, 1187–1211.

Tobin, James, "Friedman's Theoretical Framework," *Journal of Political Economy,* September/October, 1972, 852–863.

# PART **TWO**

## DYNAMIC, DETERMINISTIC MACROECONOMIC MODELS

# Chapter **4**

## **Dynamic Models**

The macroeconomic models we have studied so far have all been formally static in nature. Any treatment of how economic variables move through time has been, of necessity, entirely intuitive in nature. The values of the endogenous variables are timeless, and there is therefore no need to date variables. Furthermore, equilibrium is reached without the passage of calendar time—there are no dynamic adjustments in the system.

Such a means of analysis is generally limited for two reasons. First, some variables naturally evolve over time as a result of economic activity. As one example, private saving evolves into privately held wealth. In a similar fashion, positive values for $\dot{m}^s$ and $\dot{b}^s$ translate into increases in $M$ and $B$ over time. Such considerations properly require formal treatment. Second, we are interested not only in equilibrium positions but also in how an economy evolves over time toward such an equilibrium. Furthermore, the more basic question of whether the economy moves toward or away from its static equilibrium (the stability of equilibrium) is a central issue in the study of dynamics.

This chapter first presents a brief, self-contained introduction to the sorts of differential equation models often employed in macroeconomic analysis. This introduction focuses primarily on the properties of linear, constant-coefficient differential equation systems. Since the solution to such systems takes a particularly simple functional form, we are able to develop a very natural definition of stability for such systems. We then demonstrate how more complex, nonlinear dynamic systems can be approximated by the more simple linear models and introduce an analogous concept of local stability for these nonlinear systems.

Mastery of the material in this chapter is an indispensible prerequisite to a clear understanding of the analyses of Chapters 5–9. Although we have already analyzed the effects of step changes in the supplies of money and government bonds and changes in the rates of expansion of money and government bonds in the models of Chapters 2 and 3, such analyses were, of necessity, technically quite crude. The material in this chapter therefore prepares the reader to properly calculate the resulting time paths of all of the endogenous variables following such policy experiments.

In Chapter 5, we analyze the dynamics of adjustment of wages and price expectations and how such adjustment processes affect the way in which a step change in the money supply affects the levels of employment and output over time. In Chapter 6, we study the effects of changes in the rate of expansion of the money supply and analyze how such disturbances affect the levels of interest rates and the rates of actual and expected inflation over time. Chapter 7 first models unemployment rate dynamics by examining the flows into and out of employment and then studies interactions between output dynamics and movements in the rate of inflation. In Chapter 8, we study how investment activities translate over time into changes in the level of capital per worker. Chapter 8 also introduces dynamic optimization techniques and applies these techniques to the problem of optimal capital accumulation over time. Finally, Chapter 9 studies the dynamics of exchange rate movements and the interactions between exchange rate movements and movements in the money supply and prices over time.

As a prelude to the analyses of these later chapters, we first consider two particularly simple dynamic models that contain the static models of Chapters 2 and 3 as special cases. Following Samuelson (1947), we also derive an important relationship between the stability conditions of these dynamic systems and expressions that are key to signing important comparative statics results.

Section 4.1 presents the basic properties of the linear, constant-coefficient system of differential equations. Section 4.2 demonstrates how nonlinear models can be approximated by linear models and derives local stability conditions for these nonlinear models. Sections 4.3 and 4.4 then apply dynamic analysis to the classical model with wealth effects of Section 2.5 and a variant of the IS–LM model of Section 3.2.

## 4.1 LINEAR SYSTEMS WITH CONSTANT COEFFICIENTS

Most of our analysis of dynamics involves systems of linear homogeneous differential equations with constant coefficients.[1] Such systems take the form

$$\dot{x} = Ax, \tag{4.1.1}$$

where $x$ is an $n \times 1$ vector of endogenous variables, $A$ is an $n \times n$ matrix of known constant coefficients, and a dot over a variable denotes the time derivative of that variable.

Let us pick a "trial" solution to the above equation of the form

$$x(t) = be^{\lambda t}, \tag{4.1.2}$$

where $b$ is an $n \times 1$ vector of yet to be determined constants and $\lambda$ is a (possibly complex) scalar. Taking the time derivative of the "guessed" solution and plugging into the dynamic equation above, we obtain

$$\lambda be^{\lambda t} = Abe^{\lambda t}. \tag{4.1.3}$$

---

[1]For an expanded treatment of this material see, e.g., Boyce and DiPrima (1986, Ch. 7). A good introduction to the use of differential equations in economic analysis is provided by Baumol (1970).

With $\lambda$ a scalar and $b$ a vector, this equation can be rewritten as

$$\lambda I b e^{\lambda t} = A b e^{\lambda t}, \tag{4.1.4}$$

where $I$ is the $n \times n$ identity matrix. Rearranging, we obtain

$$[\lambda I - A] b e^{\lambda t} = 0. \tag{4.1.5}$$

Since $e^{\lambda t}$ is a scalar, this equation may be rewritten as

$$[\lambda I - A] b = 0, \tag{4.1.6}$$

where $b$ is an undetermined $n \times 1$ vector and $\lambda$ is an undetermined scalar.

The above equation always has the solution $b \equiv 0$. However, the resulting solution of the differential equation system, that $x(t) \equiv 0$, $0 \le t < \infty$, is trivial. Nontrivial solutions for the vector $b$ ($b \ne 0$) exist for only a limited set of values of $\lambda$. The vector $b$ provides weights for the rows of the matrix $[\lambda I - A]$. In order to find weights (values of $b_i$) such that the weighted sum of the rows be zero, it is necessary that the rows of $\lambda I - A$ not all be linearly independent. Therefore $\lambda I - A$ must be of less than full rank, and so we must have $|\lambda I - A| = 0$. That is, we are only able to find nontrivial values of $b$ to solve what is called the *characteristic equation* for values of $\lambda$ such that $|\lambda I - A| = 0$. Such values of $\lambda$ are called the *characteristic roots* of $A$. For each such characteristic root $\lambda$, values of $b_i$ can be found such that

$$x(t) = b e^{\lambda t} \tag{4.1.7}$$

solves the set of differential equations $\dot{x} = Ax$.

In general, for an $n \times n$ matrix $A$, there will be $n$ values of $\lambda$ that satisfy the characteristic equation. Therefore, there will be $n$ solutions of the form $b_{(k)} e^{\lambda_k t}$, $k = 1, \ldots, n$, that satisfy the differential equation system $\dot{x} = Ax$. Linear systems with constant coefficients have the property that if $x(t) = y_1(t)$ and $x(t) = y_2(t)$ solve $\dot{x} = Ax$, then $x(t) = \alpha_1 y_1(t) + \alpha_2 y_2(t)$ also solves $\dot{x} = Ax$ for arbitrary constants $\alpha_1$, $\alpha_2$. Therefore, the most general solution to the system $\dot{x} = Ax$ is of the form

$$x = \alpha_1 b_{(1)} e^{\lambda_2 t} + \cdots + \alpha_n b_{(n)} e^{\lambda_n t}, \tag{4.1.8}$$

where $\alpha_i$ are arbitrary constants, $\lambda_k$ are the characteristic roots, and $b_k$ are the *characteristic vectors* corresponding to each characteristic root (the $b$'s that solve $[\lambda_k I - A] b_{(k)} = 0$).

It may well be the case that some of the characteristic roots are complex. Such complex roots always occur in pairs of the form

$$\lambda_k = \theta_1 + j\theta_2, \qquad \lambda_{k+1} = \theta_1 - j\theta_2, \tag{4.1.9}$$

where $\theta_1$ and $\theta_2$ are real numbers and $j \equiv \sqrt{-1}$. The solution of the differential equation system corresponding to these two roots takes the form

$$x(t) = \alpha_k b_{(k)} e^{\theta_1 t} \cos \theta_2 t + \alpha_{k+1} b_{(k+1)} e^{\theta_1 t} \sin \theta_2 t. \tag{4.1.10}$$

As long as $\theta_1 < 0$, this solution results in dampened oscillations.

It is also possible that some of the characteristic roots may occur more than once. Suppose, for example, that we had a characteristic equation of the form

$$(\lambda + 1)^2 = 0. \tag{4.1.11}$$

In this case, we would have $\lambda_1 = \lambda_2 = -1$. For the general case of a root repeated $m$ times, the solution corresponding to these roots $(l, l + 1, \ldots, l + m)$ takes the form

$$
\begin{aligned}
x(t) = {} & \alpha_l b_{(l)} e^{\lambda t} + \alpha_{l+1} b_{(l+1)} t e^{\lambda t} + \alpha_{l+2} b_{(l+2)} t^2 e^{\lambda t} + \cdots \\
& + \alpha_{l+m} b_{(l+m)} t^m e^{\lambda t}.
\end{aligned}
\tag{4.1.12}
$$

In such solutions, as $t \to +\infty$, the exponential terms always dominate the $t^{l+i}$ terms, and so for each value of $i$, $i = 1, \ldots, m$, and for $\lambda_l < 0$, we find that $\lim_{t \to \infty} t^{l+i} e^{\lambda t} = 0$.

## Solutions to the Characteristic Equation

The characteristic equation can be written as

$$
\beta_0 (-\lambda)^n + \beta_1 (-\lambda)^{n-1} + \cdots + \beta_{n-2} \lambda^2 - \beta_{n-1} \lambda + \beta_n = 0,
\tag{4.1.13}
$$

where the $\beta_i$ are the *order traces* of the matrix $A$.[2] In particular, the order traces are defined as follows:

$$
\begin{aligned}
& \beta_0 = 1, \\
& \beta_1 = a_{11} + a_{22} + \cdots + a_{nn} = \mathrm{tr}(A), \\
& \beta_2 = \sum_{k>j} \begin{vmatrix} a_{jj} & a_{jk} \\ a_{kj} & a_{kk} \end{vmatrix}, \\
& \beta_3 = \sum_{l>k>j} \begin{vmatrix} a_{jj} & a_{jk} & a_{jl} \\ a_{kj} & a_{kk} & a_{kl} \\ a_{lj} & a_{lk} & a_{ll} \end{vmatrix}, \\
& \quad \vdots \\
& \beta_n = \begin{vmatrix} a_{11} & \cdots & a_{1n} \\ \vdots & & \vdots \\ a_{n1} & \cdots & a_{nn} \end{vmatrix} = |A|.
\end{aligned}
\tag{4.1.14}
$$

The above equation can also be written in the equivalent form

$$
\lambda^n - \beta_1 \lambda^{n-1} + \beta_2 \lambda^{n-2} - \cdots + (-1)^{n-1} \beta_{n-1} \lambda + (-1)^n \beta_n = 0.
\tag{4.1.15}
$$

It can be shown that the characteristic roots of the matrix $A$ conform to the following restrictions:

$$
\begin{aligned}
& \beta_1 = \sum_{i=1}^{n} \lambda_i, \\
& \beta_2 = \sum_{j>i} \lambda_i \lambda_j, \\
& \beta_3 = \sum_{k>j>i} \lambda_i \lambda_j \lambda_k, \\
& \quad \vdots \\
& \beta_n = \lambda_1 \lambda_2 \cdots \lambda_n.
\end{aligned}
\tag{4.1.16}
$$

---

[2] For a representative proof, see Bloom (1979, pp. 354–359).

These equalities often generate useful insights into the properties of the characteristic roots.

## Stability of Equilibrium

A constant-coefficient linear system is said to be *stable* if and only if $x(t) \to 0$ as $t \to +\infty$. This stability property holds if and only if the real parts of all the roots ($\lambda$'s) of the characteristic equation are strictly negative. A sufficient condition for stability is that the matrix $A$ be negative definite.

Sometimes economic theory requires that the matrix $A$ be symmetric. In this symmetric case, necessary and sufficient conditions for $A$ to be negative definite and hence sufficient conditions for the system to be stable are

$$a_{11} < 0, \quad \begin{vmatrix} a_{11} & a_{12} \\ a_{21} & a_{22} \end{vmatrix} > 0, \ldots, (-1)^n \begin{vmatrix} a_{11} & \cdots & a_{1n} \\ \vdots & & \vdots \\ a_{n1} & \cdots & a_{nn} \end{vmatrix} > 0. \tag{4.1.17}$$

However, in many (if not most) cases, the matrix $A$ is not symmetric. In this more general case a necessary (although not sufficient) condition for stability is that

$$\beta_1 < 0, \ \beta_2 > 0, \ \beta_3 < 0, \ \ldots, (-1)^n \beta_{n-1} < 0, (-1)^n \beta_n > 0. \tag{4.1.18}$$

Note that the above condition has as a subset the condition that

$$(-1)^n \beta_n = (-1)^n |A| > 0. \tag{4.1.19}$$

The necessary condition on the signs of the $\beta_i$ terms above proves quite useful below. Furthermore, upon casual inspection, it would appear that this condition would be sufficient as well as necessary for stability. If all the coefficients of a polynomial in $\lambda$ are positive, how can a positive value of $\lambda$ make the polynomial equal to zero? The problem is that it is possible for the polynomial to have complex roots with positive real parts and the terms in the characteristic equation corresponding to such complex roots may, in fact, be negative. Such complex roots with positive real parts imply explosive oscillatory behavior that is inconsistent with stability. For example, consider the following polynomial:

$$\lambda^3 + \lambda^2 + 4\lambda + 30 = 0. \tag{4.1.20}$$

This polynomial equation may be factored in the following way:

$$(\lambda + 3)(\lambda - 1 + j3)(\lambda - 1 - j3) = 0, \tag{4.1.21}$$

where $j \equiv \sqrt{-1}$. The characteristic equation corresponding to this polynomial therefore has the following roots:

$$\lambda_1 = -3,$$

$$\lambda_2 = 1 - j3, \tag{4.1.22}$$

$$\lambda_3 = 1 + j3.$$

The portion of the solution to the original system of differential equations corresponding to the roots $\lambda_2$ and $\lambda_3$ is of the form

$$k_1 e^t \cos 3t + k_2 e^t \sin 3t. \tag{4.1.23}$$

Therefore, the differential equation system represented by the above characteristic equation is unstable.

In what follows, it is useful to define the quantities $c_i$ as

$$c_0 = 1,$$
$$c_1 = -\beta_1,$$
$$c_2 = \beta_2,$$
$$\vdots$$
$$c_{n-2} = (-1)^{n-2}\beta_{n-2},$$
$$c_{n-1} = (-1)^{n-1}\beta_{n-1},$$
$$c_n = (-1)^n\beta_n,$$
$$c_{n+1} = c_{n+2} = \cdots = 0.$$

(4.1.24)

We may now state the Routh-Hurvitz (RH) conditions for stability.[3] A linear constant-coefficient system of $n$ differential equations for which we have

$$(-1)^n\beta_n > 0 \tag{4.1.25}$$

is stable if and only if, for $k = 1, \ldots, n - 1$, the following determinants are all positive:

$$|c_1|,$$

$$\begin{vmatrix} c_1 & c_3 \\ c_0 & c_2 \end{vmatrix},$$

$$\begin{vmatrix} c_1 & c_3 & c_5 \\ c_0 & c_2 & c_4 \\ 0 & c_1 & c_3 \end{vmatrix},$$

$$\vdots$$

(4.1.26)

$$\begin{vmatrix} c_1 & c_3 & c_5 & \cdots & c_{2k-1} \\ c_0 & c_2 & c_4 & \cdots & c_{2k-2} \\ 0 & c_1 & c_3 & \cdots & c_{2k-3} \\ \vdots & \vdots & \vdots & & \vdots \\ 0 & 0 & 0 & \cdots & c_k \end{vmatrix}.$$

For $n$ reasonably small, these stability conditions are analytically tractable. For example, for $n = 1$, we require that $a_{11} < 0$. For $n = 2$, we require that

$$\beta_n = \beta_2 = |A| > 0, \tag{4.1.27}$$

$$|c_1| = -\beta_1 = -\text{tr}(A) > 0. \tag{4.1.28}$$

---

[3]See, e.g., Cronin (1980). A proof that the Routh-Hurvitz conditions guarantee that the real parts of the roots of the characteristic equation are negative is provided by Marden (1966).

For $n = 3$, the original necessary conditions on the signs of $\beta_i$ require that

$$\beta_3 = |A| < 0,$$

$$\beta_2 = \sum_{k>j} \begin{vmatrix} a_{jj} & a_{jk} \\ a_{kj} & a_{kk} \end{vmatrix} = \begin{vmatrix} a_{11} & a_{12} \\ a_{21} & a_{22} \end{vmatrix} + \begin{vmatrix} a_{11} & a_{13} \\ a_{31} & a_{33} \end{vmatrix} + \begin{vmatrix} a_{22} & a_{23} \\ a_{32} & a_{33} \end{vmatrix} > 0, \quad (4.1.29)$$

$$\beta_1 = \text{tr}(A) < 0.$$

The first of the RH determinant conditions in this case requires that $|c_1| = -\beta_1 = -\text{tr}(A) > 0$. This condition is a subset of the necessary conditions that the $\beta_i$ alternate in sign, listed above. The other RH determinant condition requires that

$$\begin{vmatrix} c_1 & c_3 \\ c_0 & c_2 \end{vmatrix} = \begin{vmatrix} -\text{tr}(A) & -|A| \\ 1 & \sum_{k>j} \begin{vmatrix} a_{jj} & a_{jk} \\ a_{kj} & a_{kk} \end{vmatrix} \end{vmatrix} > 0 \quad (4.1.30)$$

or

$$\sum_{k>j} \begin{vmatrix} a_{jj} & a_{jk} \\ a_{kj} & a_{kk} \end{vmatrix} [-\text{tr}(A)] + |A| > 0. \quad (4.1.31)$$

This condition is not redundant. The left-hand term above is unambiguously positive, while the second term above is unambiguously negative from the conditions on the signs of the $\beta_i$. One simple case in which the reader can be sure that the above condition does hold is that of $a_{ii} < 0$, $a_{ij} = 0$, $i \neq j$ ($A$ diagonal with all negative elements).

## 4.2 NONLINEAR SYSTEMS

We now consider the set of differential equations given by

$$\dot{s}_i = f_i(s_1, s_2, \ldots, s_n), \qquad i = 1, \ldots, n, \quad (4.2.1)$$

where the $f_i$ may in general be nonlinear functions of the $s_i$. A set of differential equations of this sort will not generally possess a closed-form solution as is the case with linear differential equations. However, if we define $x \equiv s - s^*$ (an $n \times 1$ vector), where $s^*$ solves $0 = f_i(s^*)$, $i = 1, \ldots, n$, the above set of differential equations can be approximated as a Taylor series expansion of the form

$$\dot{x} = \begin{bmatrix} \dfrac{\partial f_1}{\partial s_1}(s^*) & \cdots & \dfrac{\partial f_1}{\partial s_n}(s^*) \\ \vdots & & \vdots \\ \dfrac{\partial f_n}{\partial s_1}(s^*) & \cdots & \dfrac{\partial f_n}{\partial s_n}(s^*) \end{bmatrix} x + \cdots. \quad (4.2.2)$$

In general, stability conditions for nonlinear dynamic systems are difficult to find for any but a few special cases. However, stability of the linear approximation to the nonlinear system is a sufficient condition for local stability. A system of differential equations is said to be *locally stable* if, starting from a position arbitrarily close to the equilibrium point, we get the result that $\lim_{t \to \infty} x(t) = 0$. Local stability will in general be a necessary but not sufficient condition for global stability. A system of differential equations is *globally stable* if and only if, starting from arbitrary $x(0)$, we get $\lim_{t \to +\infty} x(t) = 0$. While there are techniques for proving systems to be globally stable like Liapunov's second method, such techniques are rarely easily applicable, if they are applicable at all.[4]

## Comparative Statics and the Correspondence Principle

We have already performed comparative statics experiments on static equilibrium conditions of the form

$$0 = f_i(s_1, \ldots, s_n), \qquad i = 1, \ldots, n. \tag{4.2.3}$$

If we denote an exogenous variable (suppressed in the notation above) as $\alpha$, use of Cramer's rule facilitates

$$\frac{ds_i}{d\alpha} = \frac{D_{i\alpha}}{\Delta}, \tag{4.2.4}$$

where

$$D_{i\alpha} \equiv \begin{vmatrix} \dfrac{\partial f_1}{\partial s_1} & \dfrac{\partial f_1}{\partial s_2} & \cdots & \dfrac{\partial f_1}{\partial s_{i-1}} & \dfrac{\partial f_1}{\partial \alpha} & \dfrac{\partial f_1}{\partial s_{i+1}} & \cdots & \dfrac{\partial f_1}{\partial s_n} \\ \vdots & \vdots & & \vdots & \vdots & \vdots & & \vdots \\ \dfrac{\partial f_n}{\partial s_1} & \dfrac{\partial f_n}{\partial s_2} & \cdots & \dfrac{\partial f_n}{\partial s_{i-1}} & \dfrac{\partial f_n}{\partial \alpha} & \dfrac{\partial f_n}{\partial s_{i+1}} & \cdots & \dfrac{\partial f_n}{\partial s_n} \end{vmatrix} \tag{4.2.5}$$

and

$$\Delta \equiv \begin{vmatrix} \dfrac{\partial f_1}{\partial s_n} & \cdots & \dfrac{\partial f_1}{\partial s_n} \\ \vdots & & \vdots \\ \dfrac{\partial f_n}{\partial s_1} & \cdots & \dfrac{\partial f_n}{\partial s_n} \end{vmatrix}. \tag{4.2.6}$$

Computing the sign of $ds_i/d\alpha$ therefore involves the evaluation of two determinants. However, the denominator $\Delta$ of the expression $ds_i/d\alpha$ is just the determinant of the matrix of partial derivatives in the linear approximation to the dynamic system $\dot{s}_i = f_i(s_1, \ldots, s_n)$. Therefore, if we view the static equilibrium conditions $f_i(s_1, \ldots, s_n) = 0$ to be the equilibrium conditions to the dynamic system $\dot{s} = 0$ and if we further have information leading us to believe that this dynamic system is stable, then we know by the

---

[4]See, e.g., La Salle and Lefschetz (1961).

necessary conditions for stability that the sign of the denominator above will be given by

$$(-1)^n \begin{vmatrix} \dfrac{\partial f_1}{\partial s_1} & \cdots & \dfrac{\partial f_1}{\partial s_n} \\ \vdots & & \vdots \\ \dfrac{\partial f_n}{\partial s_1} & \cdots & \dfrac{\partial f_n}{\partial s_n} \end{vmatrix} \tag{4.2.7}$$

Therefore, stability analysis provides half the information needed to determine the sign of $ds_i/d\alpha$.

In the theory of demand, we are often able to derive results that depend on the assumption that second-order conditions of a maximization problem are satisfied. So too, in dynamic analyses, we are sometimes able to generate results based on the assumption that stability conditions are satisfied. If we really believe that our model describes reality and if the economic system we describe appears stable, then the assumption of stability is not that heroic. The additional restrictions we get on our model from the assumption of stability are referred to by Samuelson (1947) as the "correspondence principle."

## Nonlinear Dynamic Models: The Two-Variable Case

Since most of the dynamic systems we work with are of no higher than second order, it is probably easiest to first present the complete analysis of the general, second-order, nonlinear system. Assume that we have an economic model whose static equilibrium conditions are given by

$$0 = f_1(s_1, s_2), \tag{4.2.8}$$

$$0 = f_2(s_1, s_2). \tag{4.2.9}$$

Further assume that this system of equations has the unique equilibrium values $s_1^*$, $s_2^*$.

Now let us also assume that these static equilibrium conditions are nested in the dynamic model:

$$\dot{s}_1 = \frac{ds_1}{dt} = f_1(s_1, s_2), \tag{4.2.10}$$

$$\dot{s}_2 = \frac{ds_2}{dt} = f_2(s_1, s_2). \tag{4.2.11}$$

Equilibrium for this dynamic system occurs at $\dot{s}_1 = \dot{s}_2 = 0$, and so the system's equilibrium conditions are $s_1 = s_1^*$ and $s_2 = s_2^*$.

Now take a Taylor series expansion of $f_1$ and $f_2$ around the equilibrium position $(s_1^*, s_2^*)$. Writing only the first-order terms, we obtain

$$f_1(s_1, s_2) \simeq \frac{\partial f_1}{\partial s_1}(s_1^*, s_2^*)(s_1 - s_1^*) + \frac{\partial f_1}{\partial s_2}(s_1^*, s_2^*)(s_2 - s_2^*), \tag{4.2.12}$$

$$f_2(s_1, s_2) \simeq \frac{\partial f_2}{\partial s_1}(s_1^*, s_2^*)(s_1 - s_1^*) + \frac{\partial f_2}{\partial s_2}(s_1^*, s_2^*)(s_2 - s_2^*). \tag{4.2.13}$$

Substituting these approximations into the above differential equations and writing them in matrix form, we obtain

$$
\begin{bmatrix} \dot{s}_1 \\ \dot{s}_2 \end{bmatrix} = \begin{bmatrix} \dfrac{\partial f_1}{\partial s_1}(s_1^*, s_2^*) & \dfrac{\partial f_1}{\partial s_2}(s_1^*, s_2^*) \\ \dfrac{\partial f_2}{\partial s_1}(s_1^*, s_2^*) & \dfrac{\partial f_2}{\partial s_2}(s_1^*, s_2^*) \end{bmatrix} \begin{bmatrix} s_1 - s_1^* \\ s_2 - s_2^* \end{bmatrix}.
\tag{4.2.14}
$$

It is next useful to adopt the following shorthand notation:

$$
x_1 \equiv s_1 - s_1^*, \qquad a_{11} \equiv \frac{\partial f_1}{\partial s_1}(s_1^*, s_2^*), \qquad a_{12} \equiv \frac{\partial f_1}{\partial s_2}(s_1^*, s_2^*),
\tag{4.2.15}
$$

$$
x_2 \equiv s_2 - s_2^*, \qquad a_{21} \equiv \frac{\partial f_2}{\partial s_1}(s_1^*, s_2^*), \qquad a_{22} \equiv \frac{\partial f_2}{\partial s_2}(s_1^*, s_2^*).
\tag{4.2.16}
$$

Since $s_1^*$ and $s_2^*$, the solution values to the original static equilibrium conditions, are simply constant numbers, we can differentiate $x_1$ and $x_2$ with respect to time to obtain

$$
\dot{x}_1 = \frac{d}{dt}(s_1 - s_1^*) = \dot{s}_1,
\tag{4.2.17}
$$

$$
\dot{x}_2 = \frac{d}{dt}(s_2 - s_2^*) = \dot{s}_2.
\tag{4.2.18}
$$

The linearization of the original equilibrium conditions therefore allows us to write an approximation to the dynamic model of the form

$$
\begin{bmatrix} \dot{x}_1 \\ \dot{x}_2 \end{bmatrix} = \begin{bmatrix} a_{11} & a_{12} \\ a_{11} & a_{22} \end{bmatrix} \begin{bmatrix} x_1 \\ x_2 \end{bmatrix} \equiv Ax.
\tag{4.2.19}
$$

## Stability Conditions and Comparative Statics

We are now ready to write down stability conditions for the first-order approximation to the set of nonlinear differential equations. Stability of this linear system ensures local stability of the nonlinear system. For the time being, we continue to suppress any exogenous variables.

For the linear, two-variable case, necessary and sufficient conditions for stability are given by

$$
\text{tr}(A) = a_{11} + a_{22} < 0,
\tag{4.2.20}
$$

$$
|A| = a_{11}a_{22} - a_{12}a_{21} > 0.
\tag{4.2.21}
$$

The characteristic roots for this system of equations are given by

$$
\lambda_i = \tfrac{1}{2}(\text{tr}(A) \pm \{[\text{tr}(A)]^2 - 4|A|\}^{1/2}).
\tag{4.2.22}
$$

These characteristic roots also satisfy

$$
\lambda_1 + \lambda_2 = \text{tr}(A) = a_{11} + a_{22},
\tag{4.2.23}
$$

$$
\lambda_1\lambda_2 = |A| = a_{11}a_{22} - a_{12}a_{21}.
\tag{4.2.24}
$$

It is often useful in the two-variable case to supplement our algebraic analysis with graphical techniques. One particularly useful technique is that of the phase diagram drawn in $x_1$, $x_2$ space. Here we plot combinations of $x_1$ and $x_2$ for which $\dot{x}_1 = 0$ and $\dot{x}_2 = 0$, respectively. We also find those parts of the $x_1$, $x_2$ space for which $\dot{x}_1 \gtreqless 0$ and $\dot{x}_2 \gtreqless 0$.

Differentiating the $\dot{x}_1 = 0$ and $\dot{x}_2 = 0$ conditions yields

$$\frac{dx_2}{dx_1}\bigg|_{\dot{x}_1 = 0} = -\frac{a_{11}}{a_{12}}, \tag{4.2.25}$$

$$\frac{dx_2}{dx_1}\bigg|_{\dot{x}_2 = 0} = -\frac{a_{21}}{a_{22}}. \tag{4.2.26}$$

Note that since the equilibrium of the dynamic system is given by $\dot{x}_1 = \dot{x}_2 = 0$, these phase diagram plots have the same mathematical interpretation as the equilibrium loci of our economic models.

For the original nonlinear set of static equilibrium conditions, slopes of the equilibrium loci can be computed as follows:

$$0 = \frac{\partial f_1}{\partial s_1}\,ds_1 + \frac{\partial f_1}{\partial f_2}\,ds_2, \tag{4.2.27}$$

$$0 = \frac{\partial f_2}{\partial s_1}\,ds_1 + \frac{\partial f_2}{\partial f_2}\,ds_2. \tag{4.2.28}$$

Rearranging we obtain

$$\frac{ds_2}{ds_1}\bigg|_{f_1 = 0} = -\frac{\partial f_1/\partial s_1}{\partial f_1/\partial s_s} = -\frac{a_{11}}{a_{12}} = \frac{dx_2}{dx_1}\bigg|_{\dot{x}_1 = 0}, \tag{4.2.29}$$

$$\frac{ds_2}{ds_1}\bigg|_{f_2 = 0} = -\frac{\partial f_2/\partial s_1}{\partial f_2/\partial s_2} = -\frac{a_{21}}{a_{22}} = \frac{dx_2}{dx_1}\bigg|_{\dot{x}_2 = 0}. \tag{4.2.30}$$

Let us now consider two cases:

Case I: $a_{22}a_{12} > 0$.

Case II: $a_{22}a_{12} < 0$.

Our determinant stability condition tells us that stability requires that

$$a_{11}a_{22} - a_{12}a_{21} > 0. \tag{4.2.31}$$

Therefore we get

Case I:

$$\frac{a_{11}}{a_{12}} > \frac{a_{21}}{a_{22}},$$

or

$$\frac{dx_2}{dx_1}\bigg|_{\dot{x}_1 = 0} < \frac{dx_2}{dx_1}\bigg|_{\dot{x}_2 = 0} \Rightarrow \frac{ds_2}{ds_1}\bigg|_{f_1 = 0} < \frac{ds_2}{ds_1}\bigg|_{f_2 = 0}.$$

Case II:

$$\frac{a_{11}}{a_{12}} < \frac{a_{21}}{a_{22}},$$

or

$$\left.\frac{dx_2}{dx_1}\right|_{\dot{x}_1=0} > \left.\frac{dx_2}{dx_1}\right|_{\dot{x}_2=0} \Rightarrow \left.\frac{ds_2}{ds_1}\right|_{f_1=0} > \left.\frac{ds_2}{ds_1}\right|_{f_2=0}.$$

Knowledge that the stability conditions are satisfied therefore gives us information about the relative slopes of the market-clearing loci.

The phase diagram can also give us some insight into likely dynamic paths of $x_1$ and $x_2$ over time. If we are off both the $\dot{x}_1 = 0$ and $\dot{x}_2 = 0$ loci, then both $x_1$ and $x_2$ must be moving. To see in what direction the system is moving, we merely compute the signs of $\dot{x}_1$ and $\dot{x}_2$ at any $x = (x_1, x_2)$. However, the locations of the $\dot{x}_1 = 0$ and $\dot{x}_2 = 0$ loci have already defined regions in which the signs of $\dot{x}_1$ and $\dot{x}_2$ are positive and negative. We need only look to the signs of $a_{11} = \partial\dot{x}_1/\partial x_1$ and $a_{22} = \partial\dot{x}_2/\partial x_2$ to see whether motion of $x_1$ and $x_2$ from points off the $\dot{x}_1 = 0$ and $\dot{x}_2 = 0$ loci, respectively, is toward or away from these market-clearing loci.

The requirement of local stability also gives us information about the comparative statics effects of changes in the exogenous variables on the original static system of equilibrium conditions. Since we have already developed restrictions on the slopes of the equilibrium loci and since manipulations of equilibrium loci have often been useful methods of analyzing comparative statics problems, this fact should not be surprising.

Let us now rewrite our original equilibrium conditions to explicitly consider the possible effects of changes in an exogenous variable, which we denote by $\alpha$:

$$0 = f_1(s_1, s_2, \alpha), \tag{4.2.32}$$

$$0 = f_2(s_1, s_2, \alpha). \tag{4.2.33}$$

Interest now focuses on the effects of changes in $\alpha$ on the equilibrium values $s_1^*$ and $s_2^*$. The method of comparative statics provides the solutions

$$\frac{ds_1}{d\alpha} = \frac{1}{\Delta}\begin{vmatrix} -\dfrac{\partial f_1}{\partial \alpha} & \dfrac{\partial f_1}{\partial s_2} \\[2ex] -\dfrac{\partial f_2}{\partial \alpha} & \dfrac{\partial f_2}{\partial s_2} \end{vmatrix}, \tag{4.2.34}$$

$$\frac{ds_2}{d\alpha} = \frac{1}{\Delta}\begin{vmatrix} \dfrac{\partial f_1}{\partial s_1} & -\dfrac{\partial f_1}{\partial \alpha} \\[2ex] \dfrac{\partial f_2}{\partial s_1} & -\dfrac{\partial f_2}{\partial \alpha} \end{vmatrix}, \tag{4.2.35}$$

where

$$\Delta \equiv \begin{vmatrix} \dfrac{\partial f_1}{\partial s_1} & \dfrac{\partial f_1}{\partial s_2} \\[2ex] \dfrac{\partial f_2}{\partial s_1} & \dfrac{\partial f_2}{\partial s_2} \end{vmatrix}. \tag{4.2.36}$$

In this problem we would normally be interested in the signs of $ds_1/d\alpha$ and $ds_2/d\alpha$. However, if we are willing to *assume* that the dynamic system whose equilibrium values are $s_1^*$ and $s_2^*$ is locally stable, then $\Delta$ must be positive. If $\Delta$ is not positive, the system is locally unstable and the model is not properly specified to begin with. Therefore, without further algebraic manipulation of the components of $\Delta$, we are often willing simply to assume that it is positive. If we choose to make this assumption, we are one-third of the way toward signing the effects of exogenous changes in $\alpha$ on the endogenous variables $s_1$ and $s_2$.

## 4.3 DYNAMICS IN THE CLASSICAL MODEL

Consider the classical model with wealth effects analyzed in Section 2.4. However, we relax the assumptions that the price level and the interest rate are always equal to their market-clearing values. Time enters the picture as $P$ and $r$ only gradually adjust toward equilibrium, although we continue to assume that such adjustment of $P$ and $r$ is rapid enough that we may retain our original assumption that $y = y^*$ throughout.

Excess demands for goods, earning assets, and money in that model are defined as

$$\text{EDG}(P, r) \equiv y^d - y^* = c^d\left( \underset{(+)}{z^*}, \underset{(+)}{\frac{M}{P} + \frac{\kappa B}{rP} + \frac{RK}{r}} \right) + \underset{(-)}{i^d(r)} + g - y^*, \qquad (4.3.1)$$

$$\text{EDF}(P, r) \equiv \dot{f}^d - \dot{f}^s = \dot{f}^d\left( \underset{(+)}{z}, \underset{(-)}{z^*}, \underset{(-)}{y^*}, \underset{(+)}{r}, \underset{(+)}{\frac{M}{P}}, \underset{(-)}{\frac{M}{P} + \frac{\kappa B}{rP} + \frac{RK}{r}} \right)$$

$$\underset{(-)}{- \dot{e}^s(r) - \dot{b}^s,} \qquad (4.3.2)$$

$$\text{EDM}(P, r) \equiv \dot{m}^d - \dot{m}^s = \dot{m}^d\left( \underset{(+)}{y^*}, \underset{(-)}{r}, \underset{(-)}{\frac{M}{P}}, \underset{(+)}{\frac{M}{P} + \frac{\kappa B}{rP} + \frac{RK}{r}} \right) - \dot{m}^s, \qquad (4.3.3)$$

where

$$g - \tau_0 = \dot{m}^s + \dot{b}^s. \qquad (4.3.4)$$

One plausible set of assumptions about the dynamic adjustments of $r$ and $P$ would be that

$$\frac{dP}{dt} = k_1[\text{EDG}(P, r)], \qquad (4.3.5)$$

$$\frac{dr}{dt} = -k_2[\text{EDF}(P, r)], \qquad (4.3.6)$$

where $k_1$ and $k_2$ are positive constants.

Equation (4.3.5) above indicates that prices rise when there is an excess demand for goods and prices fall when there is an excess supply of goods. Equation (4.3.6) above indicates that the interest rate falls when there is an excess demand for earning assets and rises when there is an excess supply of earning assets. Since the price of a government-issued bond is simply $1/r$ and since government-issued bonds and equities are viewed as perfect substitutes, this second assumption merely states that bond and equity prices rise (fall) when there is an excess demand (supply) for (of) bonds and equities (earning assets).

Linearization of the above system yields

$$\dot{P} \simeq k_1 \frac{\partial EDG(P, r)}{\partial P}(P - P^*) + k_1 \frac{\partial EDG(P, r)}{\partial r}(r - r^*), \tag{4.3.7}$$

$$\dot{r} \simeq -k_2 \frac{\partial EDF(P, r)}{\partial P}(P - P^*) - k_2 \frac{\partial EDF(P, r)}{\partial r}(r - r^*), \tag{4.3.8}$$

where $P^*$, $r^*$ solves EDG = EDF = 0. Now define $x_1 \equiv P - P^*$ and $x_2 \equiv r - r^*$ and note that since $dP^*/dt = dr^*/dt = 0$, we obtain

$$\dot{x}_1 = k_1 \frac{\partial EDG}{\partial P}x_1 + k_1 \frac{\partial EDG}{\partial r}x_2, \tag{4.3.9}$$

$$\dot{x}_2 = -k_2 \frac{\partial EDF}{\partial P}x_1 - k_2 \frac{\partial EDF}{\partial r}x_2. \tag{4.3.10}$$

The coefficient matrix for the linearized system is therefore given by

$$A \equiv \begin{bmatrix} k_1 \dfrac{\partial EDG}{\partial P} & k_1 \dfrac{\partial EDG}{\partial r} \\[2em] -k_2 \dfrac{\partial EDF}{\partial P} & -k_2 \dfrac{\partial EDF}{\partial r} \end{bmatrix}, \tag{4.3.11}$$

where

$$\frac{\partial EDG}{\partial P} = -\frac{1}{P}\left(\frac{M}{P} + \frac{\kappa B}{rP}\right)\frac{\partial c^d}{\partial \Omega} < 0, \tag{4.3.12}$$

$$\frac{\partial EDG}{\partial r} = -\frac{1}{r}\left(\frac{\kappa B}{rP} + \frac{RK}{r}\right)\frac{\partial c^d}{\partial \Omega} + \frac{\partial i^d}{\partial r} < 0, \tag{4.3.13}$$

$$\frac{\partial EDF}{\partial P} = -\frac{M}{P^2}\frac{\partial \dot{f}^d}{\partial(M/P)} - \frac{1}{P}\left(\frac{M}{P} + \frac{\kappa B}{rP}\right)\frac{\partial \dot{f}^d}{\partial \Omega} \gtrless 0, \tag{4.3.14}$$

$$\frac{\partial EDF}{\partial r} = \frac{\partial \dot{f}^d}{\partial r} - \frac{1}{r}\left(\frac{\kappa B}{rP} + \frac{RK}{r}\right)\frac{\partial \dot{f}^d}{\partial \Omega} - \frac{\partial \dot{e}^d}{\partial r} > 0. \tag{4.3.15}$$

The stability conditions for this dynamic system are therefore given by

$$tr(A) = k_1 \frac{\partial EDG}{\partial P} - k_2 \frac{\partial EDF}{\partial r} < 0 \tag{4.3.16}$$

and

$$|A| = -k_1 k_2 \left(\frac{\partial EDG}{\partial P}\frac{\partial EDF}{\partial r} - \frac{\partial EDF}{\partial P}\frac{\partial EDG}{\partial r}\right) > 0. \tag{4.3.17}$$

The first of these conditions is unambiguously satisfied. However, since we cannot unambiguously sign $\partial EDF/\partial P$, we cannot sign the determinant of $A$ and we therefore cannot rule out the possibility of instability.

The expressions for the partial derivatives of EDG and EDF above assure us that $(\partial EDF/\partial r)(\partial EDG/\partial r) < 0$. Dividing the stability condition $|A| > 0$ by this expression, we find that stability of the dynamic system requires that

$$0 > -\frac{\partial EDG/\partial P}{\partial EDG/\partial r} + \frac{\partial EDF/\partial P}{\partial EDF/\partial r}. \tag{4.3.18}$$

However, in Chapter 2, we identified these expressions with the slopes of the market-clearing loci. Stability of the dynamic process for $P$ and $r$ therefore requires that

$$\left.\frac{dr}{dP}\right|_{\dot{f}^d=\dot{f}^s} > \left.\frac{dr}{dP}\right|_{y^d=y^*}. \tag{4.3.19}$$

That is, if the earning asset market equilibrium locus is downward sloping, its slope must be smaller in absolute value than the slope of the goods market equilibrium locus. This inequality is often useful in graphical analysis of comparative statics problems.

Walras's law also tells us that

$$\frac{\partial EDF}{\partial P} = -\frac{\partial EDG}{\partial P} - \frac{\partial EDM}{\partial P} \quad \text{and} \quad \frac{\partial EDF}{\partial r} = -\frac{\partial EDG}{\partial r} - \frac{\partial EDM}{\partial r}. \tag{4.3.20}$$

Substituting these expressions for $\partial EDF/\partial P$ and $\partial EDF/\partial r$ into the $|A| > 0$ stability condition above, we find that this stability condition can also be written as

$$-\frac{\partial EDG}{\partial P}\frac{\partial EDF}{\partial r} + \frac{\partial EDF}{\partial P}\frac{\partial EDG}{\partial r} = \frac{\partial EDG}{\partial P}\frac{\partial EDG}{\partial r} + \frac{\partial EDG}{\partial P}\frac{\partial EDM}{\partial r}$$

$$-\frac{\partial EDG}{\partial r}\frac{\partial EDG}{\partial P} - \frac{\partial EDG}{\partial r}\frac{\partial EDM}{\partial P} = \frac{\partial EDG}{\partial P}\frac{\partial EDM}{\partial r} - \frac{\partial EDG}{\partial r}\frac{\partial EDM}{\partial P} > 0. \tag{4.3.21}$$

Furthermore, since we also know that $\partial EDG/\partial r < 0$ and $\partial EDM/\partial r < 0$, this condition requires that

$$\left.\frac{dr}{dP}\right|_{\dot{m}^d=\dot{m}^s} > \left.\frac{dr}{dP}\right|_{y^d=y^*} \tag{4.3.22}$$

Therefore, stability of the dynamic system ensures that the slopes of both the earning asset and money market equilibrium loci must be algebraically larger than the slope of the goods market equilibrium locus.

Finally, we can demonstrate that stability of the dynamic system also requires that the slope of the money market equilibrium locus must be algebraically greater than the slope of the earning asset market equilibrium locus. Adding $(\partial EDM/\partial r)(\partial EDM/\partial P)$ to both sides of inequality (4.3.21) above, we obtain

$$\frac{\partial EDM}{\partial r}\frac{\partial EDG}{\partial P} + \frac{\partial EDM}{\partial r}\frac{\partial EDM}{\partial P} > \frac{\partial EDG}{\partial r}\frac{\partial EDM}{\partial P} + \frac{\partial EDM}{\partial r}\frac{\partial EDM}{\partial P} > 0. \tag{4.3.23}$$

Factoring out $\partial EDM/\partial r$ and $\partial EDM/\partial P$ and substituting

$$\frac{\partial EDG}{\partial P} + \frac{\partial EDM}{\partial P} = -\frac{\partial EDF}{\partial P} \quad \text{and} \quad \frac{\partial EDG}{\partial r} + \frac{\partial EDM}{\partial r} = -\frac{\partial EDF}{\partial r}, \qquad (4.3.24)$$

by Walras's law, we obtain

$$-\frac{\partial EDM}{\partial r}\frac{\partial EDF}{\partial P} > -\frac{\partial EDM}{\partial P}\frac{\partial EDF}{\partial r}. \qquad (4.3.25)$$

Now, since $\partial EDM/\partial r = \partial \dot{m}^d/\partial r < 0$ and $\partial EDF/\partial r > 0$, from above, we may divide expression (4.3.25) through by $(\partial EDM/\partial r)(\partial EDF/\partial r) < 0$ to obtain

$$-\frac{\partial EDF/\partial P}{\partial EDF/\partial r} = \left.\frac{dr}{dP}\right|_{\dot{f}^d = \dot{f}^s} < \left.\frac{dr}{dP}\right|_{\dot{m}^d = \dot{m}^s} = -\frac{\partial EDM/\partial P}{\partial EDM/\partial r}. \qquad (4.3.26)$$

Therefore, if the dynamic system is stable, we require that

$$\left.\frac{dr}{dP}\right|_{\dot{m}^d = \dot{m}^s} > \left.\frac{dr}{dP}\right|_{\dot{f}^d = \dot{f}^s} > \left.\frac{dr}{dP}\right|_{y^d = y^*}. \qquad (4.3.27)$$

An alternative set of assumptions about movements of $P$ and $r$ out of equilibrium gives rise to the dynamic system

$$\frac{dP}{dt} = k_3(EDG), \qquad \frac{dr}{dt} = k_4(EDM). \qquad (4.3.28)$$

Here we assume that the interest rate adjusts to eliminate disequilibrium in the money market. Interestingly, stability of this dynamic system also requires that

$$\frac{\partial EDG}{\partial P}\frac{\partial EDM}{\partial r} - \frac{\partial EDG}{\partial r}\frac{\partial EDM}{\partial P} > 0. \qquad (4.3.29)$$

Therefore, stability of either of the dynamic systems above requires that the slope of the money market equilibrium locus be greater than the slope of the earning asset market equilibrium locus and that the slope of the earning asset market equilibrium locus be greater than the slope of the goods market equilibrium locus.

We next consider the dynamic adjustment of our original system under the more usual assumption that $\partial EDF/\partial P < 0$. In this case the dynamic system is unambiguously stable. Now recall that the loci of points at which $\dot{P} = \dot{x}_1 = 0$ and $\dot{r} = \dot{x}_2 = 0$ are equivalent to the market-clearing loci for the goods and earning asset markets, respectively. These loci are plotted in Figure 4.1 in $P$, $r$ space.

Adjustment of $P$ occurs any time $\dot{P} = \dot{x}_1 \neq 0$. To the right of the $\dot{P} = \dot{x}_1 = 0$ locus, we have $\dot{P} = \dot{x}_1 < 0$ since $\partial \dot{x}_1/\partial x_1 = k_1(\partial EDG/\partial P) < 0$. Therefore, $P$ must be falling. To the left of $\dot{P} = \dot{x}_1 = 0$, we have, by analogous reasoning, $\dot{P} = \dot{x}_1 > 0$. Motion of $P$ at points off the $\dot{P} = \dot{x}_1 = 0$ locus is therefore governed by the arrows in the top panel of Figure 4.2.

Adjustment of $r$ occurs any time $\dot{r} = \dot{x}_2 \neq 0$. At points above the $\dot{r} = \dot{x}_2 = 0$ locus, $r$ is falling since $\partial \dot{x}_2/\partial x_2 = -k_2(\partial EDF/\partial r) < 0$. By analogous reasoning, at points below the $\dot{r} = \dot{x}_2 = 0$ curve, $r$ is rising. Motion of $r$ at points off the $\dot{r} = \dot{x}_2 = 0$ locus is therefore governed by the arrows in the bottom panel of Figure 4.2.

The complete phase diagram is depicted in Figure 4.3. Starting from a point such as

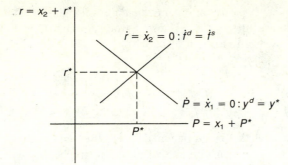

Figure 4.1

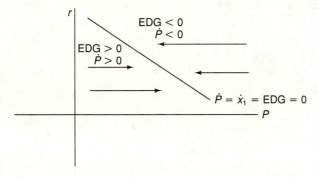

Figure 4.2

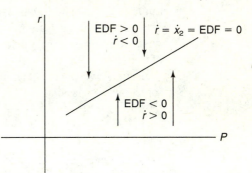

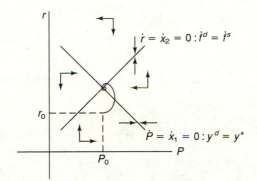

Figure 4.3

$P_0$, $r_0$, we might therefore expect motion like the counterclockwise arc in that diagram. In the case depicted in Figure 4.3, either real or complex roots appear possible. Therefore, dampened oscillations cannot be precluded in this case.

## 4.4 DYNAMICS IN THE IS-LM MODEL

We next consider the fixed-price equilibrium model. Although we could analyze dynamics in one of the more complex variants of this model, analysis of a simple IS-LM form of the model is particularly well suited to highlighting the usefulness of stability analysis as a tool of comparative statics. In particular, assume that portfolio adjustment is instantaneous ($\xi_m \rightarrow +\infty$) and that wealth effects are absent from the consumption and money demand functions. In this case it is useful to define

$$\text{EDG}(y, r) \equiv y^d - y = c^d(y - \tau) + i^d(r, R^e) + g - y, \tag{4.4.1}$$

$$\text{EDM}(y, r) \equiv \left(\frac{M}{P}\right)^d - \frac{M}{P} = \left(\frac{M}{P}\right)^d(y, r) - \frac{M}{P}. \tag{4.4.2}$$

When we first wrote down the fixed-price model, we observed that business expectations of the future path of the marginal product of capital $R^e$ might vary with the overall level of economic activity. In particular, if an increase in current output signals that future output will be higher relative to the size of the work force than was originally anticipated, expectations of the marginal product of capital might also be higher than they originally were. If this is the case, the level of desired investment must be directly related to the level of output as well. As it turns out, it is this potential effect of the level of output on the level of desired investment $i^d$ that makes the current example particularly interesting. We therefore now assume that

$$i^d = i^d(r, R^e(y)), \qquad \frac{\partial R^e}{\partial y} > 0, \tag{4.4.3}$$

or more concisely,

$$i^d = i^d(r, y), \qquad \frac{\partial i^d}{\partial y} > 0. \tag{4.4.4}$$

Now assume that dynamic adjustment is governed by

$$\frac{dy}{dt} = k_5[\text{EDG}(y, r)], \tag{4.4.5}$$

$$\frac{dr}{dt} = k_6[\text{EDM}(y, r)]. \tag{4.4.6}$$

The first equation above indicates that with prices fixed, output adjusts to eliminate any discrepancy between output and aggregate demand. If output and aggregate demand are not equal, inventories either are being built up or are being stripped away faster than firms want them to be. If actual sales are not equal to the level of desired sales, output will be adjusted to equal sales plus any desired change in inventories. Firms therefore attempt to avoid undesired inventory changes (those not included in $i^d$) by adjusting their level of production $y$ upward when demand (sales) exceeds the level of output and downward when demand (sales) falls short of the level of output.

The second equation above indicates that the interest rate adjusts to equalize money demand and money supply. With our assumption of instantaneous portfolio adjustment, recall that money market equilibrium and earning asset market equilibrium are synonymous. Therefore, this interest rate adjustment mechanism is equivalent to our earlier adjustment mechanism, which was based on the excess supply of earning assets:

$$\dot{y} \simeq k_5 \frac{\partial \text{EDG}(y_0, r_0)}{\partial y}(y - y_0) + k_5 \frac{\partial \text{EDG}(y_0, r_0)}{\partial r}(r - r_0), \tag{4.4.7}$$

$$\dot{r} \simeq k_6 \frac{\partial \text{EDM}(y_0, r_0)}{\partial y}(y - y_0) + k_6 \frac{\partial \text{EDM}(y_0, r_0)}{\partial r}(r - r_0), \tag{4.4.8}$$

where $y_0, r_0$ solves EDG = EDM = 0. Now define $x_1 \equiv y - y_0$ and $x_2 \equiv r - r_0$ and note that $dy_0/dt = dr_0/dt = 0$. We therefore obtain

$$\dot{x}_1 = k_5 \frac{\partial \text{EDG}}{\partial y} x_1 + k_5 \frac{\partial \text{EDG}}{\partial r} x_2, \tag{4.4.9}$$

$$\dot{x}_2 = k_6 \frac{\partial \text{EDM}}{\partial y} x_1 + k_6 \frac{\partial \text{EDM}}{\partial r} x_2. \tag{4.4.10}$$

The matrix of partial derivatives of $\dot{x}_1$ and $\dot{x}_2$ is given by

$$A \equiv \begin{bmatrix} k_5 \dfrac{\partial \text{EDG}}{\partial y} & k_5 \dfrac{\partial \text{EDG}}{\partial r} \\[2ex] k_6 \dfrac{\partial \text{EDM}}{\partial y} & k_6 \dfrac{\partial \text{EDM}}{\partial r} \end{bmatrix}, \tag{4.4.11}$$

where

$$\frac{\partial \text{EDG}}{\partial y} = -\left(1 - \frac{\partial c^d}{\partial z} - \frac{\partial i^d}{\partial y}\right), \tag{4.4.12}$$

$$\frac{\partial \text{EDG}}{\partial r} = \frac{\partial i^d}{\partial r} < 0, \tag{4.4.13}$$

$$\frac{\partial \text{EDM}}{\partial y} = \frac{\partial (M/P)^d}{\partial y} > 0, \tag{4.4.14}$$

$$\frac{\partial \text{EDM}}{\partial r} = \frac{\partial (M/P)^d}{\partial r} < 0. \tag{4.4.15}$$

Stability conditions for the dynamic system are given by

$$\text{tr}(A) = k_5 \frac{\partial \text{EDG}}{\partial y} + k_6 \frac{\partial \text{EDM}}{\partial r} = -k_5\left(1 - \frac{\partial c^d}{\partial z} - \frac{\partial i^d}{\partial y}\right) + k_6 \frac{\partial (M/P)^d}{\partial r} < 0, \tag{4.4.16}$$

$$|A| = k_5 k_6 \left(\frac{\partial \text{EDG}}{\partial y} \frac{\partial \text{EDM}}{\partial r} - \frac{\partial \text{EDM}}{\partial y} \frac{\partial \text{EDG}}{\partial r}\right) > 0. \tag{4.4.17}$$

Neither condition is unambiguously satisfied. A *sufficient* condition for stability is that $1 > \partial c^d/\partial z + \partial i^d/\partial y$. However, economic theory does not provide any justification for this assumption.

The slopes of the $\dot{y} = \dot{x}_1 = 0$ locus and the $\dot{r} = \dot{x}_2 = 0$ locus are given by

$$\left.\frac{dr}{dy}\right|_{\dot{y}=0} = \left.\frac{dx_2}{dx_1}\right|_{\dot{x}_1=0} = -\frac{\partial \text{EDG}/\partial y}{\partial \text{EDG}/\partial r} = \frac{1 - \partial c^d/\partial z - \partial i^d/\partial y}{\partial i^d/\partial r}, \tag{4.4.18}$$

$$\left.\frac{dr}{dy}\right|_{\dot{r}=0} = \left.\frac{dx_2}{dx_1}\right|_{\dot{x}_2=0} = -\frac{\partial \text{EDM}/\partial y}{\partial \text{EDM}/\partial r} = -\frac{\partial (M/P)^d/\partial y}{\partial (M/P)^d/\partial r} > 0. \tag{4.4.19}$$

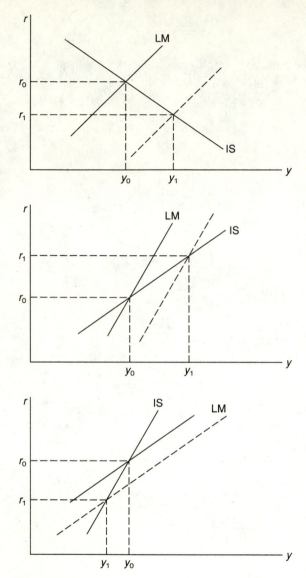

**Figure 4.4**

The second of these expressions is equal to the slope of the traditional LM curve, which is unambiguously positive. The first of these expressions gives the (negative) slope of the traditional IS curve when $\partial i^d / \partial y = 0$. However, in the more general case in which $\partial i^d / \partial y > 0$, we can have

$$\left. \frac{dx_2}{dx_1} \right|_{\dot{x}_1 = 0} > 0.$$

While the slope of the $\dot{y} = \dot{x}_1 = 0$ locus is theoretically ambiguous, stability analysis does give us some restrictions on this slope. In particular, if $\partial EDG/\partial y = -(1 - \partial c^d/\partial z - \partial i^d/\partial y) > 0$, then the determinant condition can be rewritten as

$$\frac{1 - \partial c^d/\partial z - \partial i^d/\partial y}{\partial i^d/\partial r} < -\frac{\partial (M/P)^d/\partial y}{\partial (M/P)^d/\partial r} \tag{4.4.20}$$

or

$$\left.\frac{dr}{dy}\right|_{IS} = \left.\frac{dx_2}{dx_1}\right|_{\dot{x}_1=0} < \left.\frac{dx_2}{dx_1}\right|_{\dot{x}_2=0} = \left.\frac{dr}{dy}\right|_{LM}. \tag{4.4.21}$$

For stability, if the IS curve is upward sloping, its slope must therefore be less than the slope of the LM curve. Note, however, that in cases in which the IS curve is upward sloping, we also require for stability that the trace of $A$ be negative. That the LM curve be more steeply positively sloped than the IS curve is neither necessary nor sufficient for $tr(A) < 0$. The stability condition on the sign of the trace of the partial derivative matrix has no obvious geometric representation.

Now consider the comparative statics effect of an expansion in the money supply. In the purely static case, all three cases depicted in Figure 4.4 would appear to be equally

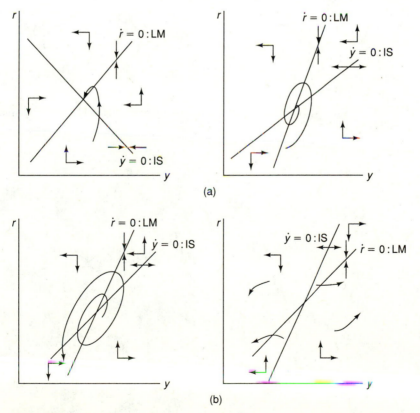

(a)

(b)

**Figure 4.5**

plausible. However, while the first two cases depicted are consistent with stable dynamics, the third one is not. Therefore, in a stable IS-LM model we know that expansionary monetary policy increases output. It is only the effect of an increase in the money supply on the interest rate that remains ambiguous.

The sign of $1 - \partial c^d/\partial z - \partial i^d/\partial y$ also has implications for whether the $y$ process is stable in isolation from the $r$ process since we know that $\partial \dot{y}/\partial y = k_5(\partial EDG/\partial y) = -k_5(1 - \partial c^d/\partial z - \partial i^d/\partial y)$. If $\partial \dot{y}/\partial y$ is positive, the $y$ process itself will be unstable, although as noted above, the differential equation *system* may still be stable if both the trace and determinant conditions are satisfied. Figure 4.5 shows four different dynamic possibilities; two are stable and two are unstable.

# REFERENCES

Baumol, William J., *Economic Dynamics: An Introduction,* 2nd ed., New York, Macmillan, 1970.

Bloom, David M., *Linear Algebra and Geometry,* Cambridge, England, Cambridge University Press, 1979.

Boyce, William E., and Richard C. DiPrima, *Elementary Differential Equations,* 4th ed., New York, Wiley, 1986.

Cronin, Jane, *Differential Equations: Introduction and Qualitative Theory,* New York, Dekker, 1980.

La Salle, Joseph, and Solomon Lefschetz, *Stability by Liapunov's Direct Method with Applications,* New York, Academic, 1961.

Marden, Morris, *Geometry of Polynomials,* 2nd ed., Providence, RI, American Mathematical Society, 1966.

Samuelson, Paul A., *Foundations of Economic Analysis,* Cambridge, MA, Harvard University Press, 1947.

# Chapter 5

## Macroeconomic Models of Employment and Output Determination

Chapters 2 and 3 present two highly stylized, yet very straightforward frameworks for analyzing the determination of equilibrium levels of employment and output. In Chapter 2, a simple labor supply–labor demand model generates an equilibrium employment level that is independent of any economic activity not impinging directly on the labor market. Alternatively, in Chapter 3, the labor market plays no meaningful role since the level of employment responds passively to increases in the demand for goods.

In this chapter, we consider models in which movements in the levels of employment and output occur as meaningful equilibrium outcomes. Section 5.1 presents a more careful analysis of labor market equilibrium emphasizing multiple sources of incentives for changes in the supply of labor. Section 5.2 presents a macroeconomic model of employment and output determination based upon the possibility of incomplete information on the part of labor suppliers. Section 5.3 presents a macroeconomic model of employment and output determination based upon the possibility of nominal wage rigidities. These analyses of Sections 5.2 and 5.3 highlight two of the more persuasive explanations of the possibility of monetary nonneutrality. Section 5.4 then presents a formal dynamic model of the adjustment of expectations and nominal wage rates that contains the models of Sections 5.2 and 5.3 as special cases.

Section 5.5 takes note of some important inconsistencies between the theoretical results of Sections 5.2–5.4 and empirical evidence on the cyclical pattern of real wage rates. Section 5.5 then presents an equilibrium model of employment and output determination and shows how the model economy's response to shocks to the marginal product of labor may replicate many of the ''stylized facts'' of typical business cycles. The equilibrium model of Section 5.5 is then used to analyze how fiscal policy may generate permanent changes in the levels of employment and output. Finally, Section 5.6 introduces the aggregate supply–aggregate demand framework and demonstrates how this framework may be used to depict the major results of Sections 5.2–5.5.

# 5.1 THE MICROECONOMICS OF LABOR SUPPLY AND LABOR DEMAND

This section presents Lucas and Rapping's (1969) two-period model of labor supply and consumption demand. A main agenda of this model is to identify the possibility of intertemporal substitution of leisure as a potentially important source of variations in labor supply. While the model is first presented in a certainty equivalent framework, this section also considers possible problems of incomplete information agents may encounter in making their labor supply decisions. This section concludes with a review of labor demand and a discussion of labor market equilibrium.

## The Household's Intertemporal Time Allocation Problem

Assume that the representative household faces a two-period planning problem. At the beginning of the first period (indexed by $t$), the household decides on current consumption of the composite good $c_t$ and current labor supply $\ell_t$. At the same time, the household also makes a contingency plan for second-period (indexed by $t + 1$), consumption $c_{t+1}$ and second-period labor supply $\ell_{t+1}$.

We begin our analysis by assuming that the representative household correctly believes that it can sell all the labor services it wants at the known nominal wage rates $W_t$ and $W_{t+1}$ and can buy all of the consumption good it wants at the known prices $P_t$ and $P_{t+1}$. The representative household begins with a predetermined level of wealth $\Omega$ measured in units of the current consumption good and may carry over to period $t + 1$ any funds left at the end of period $t$ earning interest at the known rate $r$. The consumption good itself, however, is strictly perishable.

As long as the representative household is not satiated in period $t + 1$ consumption, the nominal value of second-period consumption is equal to the proceeds from second-period work plus the principal and interest earned on first-period savings. First-period savings equals the nominal value of initial wealth plus the nominal value of first-period labor income minus the nominal value of first-period consumption. The representative household's intertemporal budget constraint is therefore given by

$$P_{t+1}c_{t+1} = W_{t+1}\ell_{t+1} + (1 + r)(P_t\Omega + W_t\ell_t - P_tc_t), \qquad (5.1.1)$$

or, upon rearranging,

$$c_t - \frac{W_t}{P_t}\ell_t + \frac{P_{t+1}}{P_t(1 + r)}c_{t+1} - \frac{W_{t+1}}{P_t(1 + r)}\ell_{t+1} - \Omega = 0. \qquad (5.1.2)$$

Let us further assume that $c_t$, $c_{t+1}$, $\ell_t$, and $\ell_{t+1}$ are chosen to maximize a time-separable utility function of the form

$$V = U(c_t, \ell_t) + \frac{1}{1 + \beta}U(c_{t+1}, \ell_{t+1}), \qquad (5.1.3)$$

where $U$ is a concave, single-period utility function and $\beta > 0$ is the representative household's rate of time preference.

The representative household therefore maximizes the Lagrangian

$$\mathcal{L} = U(c_t, \ell_t) + \frac{1}{1 + \beta} U(c_{t+1}, \ell_{t+1})$$

$$+ \lambda \left( \Omega - c_t + \frac{W_t}{P_t} \ell_t - \frac{P_{t+1}}{P_t(1 + r)} c_{t+1} + \frac{W_{t+1}}{P_t(1 + r)} \ell_{t+1} \right).$$

(5.1.4)

First-order conditions for this maximization problem are given by

$$\frac{\partial \mathcal{L}}{\partial c_t} = U_{1,t} - \lambda = 0, \qquad \frac{\partial \mathcal{L}}{\partial \ell_t} = U_{2,t} + \lambda \frac{W_t}{P_t} = 0,$$

(5.1.5)

$$\frac{\partial \mathcal{L}}{\partial c_{t+1}} = \frac{1}{1 + \beta} U_{1,t+1} - \lambda \frac{P_{t+1}}{P_t(1 + r)} = 0,$$

(5.1.6)

$$\frac{\partial \mathcal{L}}{\partial \ell_{t+1}} = \frac{1}{1 + \beta} U_{2,t+1} + \lambda \frac{W_{t+1}}{P_t(1 + r)} = 0,$$

(5.1.7)

$$\frac{\partial \mathcal{L}}{\partial \lambda} = \Omega - c_t + \frac{W_t}{P_t} \ell_t - \frac{P_{t+1}}{P_t(1 + r)} c_{t+1} + \frac{W_{t+1}}{P_t(1 + r)} \ell_{t+1} = 0,$$

(5.1.8)

where

$$U_{i,j} = \begin{cases} \partial U(c_j, \ell_j)/\partial c_j & \text{if } i = 1, \\ \partial U(c_j, \ell_j)/\partial l_j & \text{if } i = 2. \end{cases}$$

(5.1.9)

These first-order conditions may also be rearranged in the more intuitive forms

$$-\frac{U_{2,t}}{U_{1,t}} = \frac{W_t}{P_t},$$

$$-\frac{U_{2,t+1}}{U_{1,t+1}} = \frac{W_{t+1}}{P_{t+1}},$$

$$\frac{1}{1 + \beta} \frac{U_{1,t+1}}{U_{1,t}} = \frac{P_{t+1}}{P_t(1 + r)}.$$

(5.1.10)

The first two first-order conditions require that the marginal rate of substitution between goods and leisure equal the real wage in each of the two periods. The third first-order condition requires that the marginal rate of substitution between first- and second-period consumption equals the intertemporal terms of trade.

One particularly simple, special case is that of the logarithmic single-period utility function

$$U = (1 - \sigma)\ln c_t + \sigma \ln(1 - \ell_t),$$

(5.1.11)

where $\sigma$ denotes the weight of leisure relative to consumption in the utility function and units have been chosen such that $\ell_t$ represents the fraction of the total time available that is allocated to market work.

For this special case, the first-order conditions may be evaluated to obtain

$$c_t = (1 - \sigma)\frac{1 + \beta}{2 + \beta}\left[\Omega + \frac{W_t}{P_t} + \frac{W_{t+1}}{P_t(1 + r)}\right], \tag{5.1.12}$$

$$c_{t+1} = \frac{1 - \sigma}{2 + \beta}\left[\Omega + \frac{W_t}{P_t} + \frac{W_{t+1}}{P_t(1 + r)}\right], \tag{5.1.13}$$

$$\ell_t = 1 - \sigma\frac{1 + \beta}{2 + \beta}\left[1 + \frac{P_t}{W_t}\left(\Omega + \frac{W_{t+1}}{P_t(1 + r)}\right)\right], \tag{5.1.14}$$

$$\ell_{t+1} = 1 - \frac{\sigma}{2 + \beta}\left[1 + \frac{P_t(1 + r)}{W_{t+1}}\left(\Omega + \frac{W_t}{P_t}\right)\right]. \tag{5.1.15}$$

For this simple example, we find that an increase in wealth, $\Omega$, unambiguously raises both current and future consumption and unambiguously reduces both current and future labor supply. An increase in the current real wage, $W_t/P_t$, as well as an increase in the present value of the future real wage, $W_{t+1}/P_t(1 + r)$, both increase both current and future consumption. However, a higher current real wage raises current labor supply and lowers future labor supply, while an increase in the present value of the future real wage raises future labor supply and lowers current labor supply.

While the representative household's optimization problem implies choices for all of the decision variables, our principal present interest lies in the determinates of current labor supply $\ell_t$. In a more general setting, most of the effects of changes in the exogenous variables on current labor supply $\ell_t$ are ambiguous, as they involve offsetting income and substitution effects. If substitution effects dominate and if leisure is a normal good, aggregation of a large number of identical representative households results in an aggregate current labor supply function of the form

$$
\ell^s = f\left(\underset{(+)}{\frac{W_t}{P_t}}, \underset{(-)}{\frac{W_{t+1}}{P_t(1 + r)}}, \underset{(-)}{\frac{P_{t+1}}{P_t(1 + r)}}, \underset{(-)}{\Omega}\right)
$$

$$
\tag{5.1.16}
$$

$$
= f\left(\underset{(+)}{\frac{W_t}{P_t}}, \underset{(-)}{\frac{W_{t+1}}{P_{t+1}}} \frac{P_{t+1}}{P_t(1 + r)}, \underset{(-)}{\frac{P_{t+1}}{P_t(1 + r)}}, \underset{(-)}{\Omega}\right).
$$

This expression can therefore be reexpressed as

$$
\ell^s = g\left(\underset{(+)}{\frac{W_t}{P_t}}, \underset{(-)}{\frac{W_{t+1}}{P_{t+1}}}, \underset{(-)}{\frac{P_{t+1}}{P_t(1 + r)}}, \underset{(-)}{\Omega}\right). \tag{5.1.17}
$$

Current labor supply therefore depends directly on the current real wage $W_t/P_t$ and inversely on the future real wage $W_{t+1}/P_{t+1}$, the relative price of future consumption in terms of present consumption, $P_{t+1}/P_t(1 + r)$, and initial wealth $\Omega$.[1]

---

[1] Empirical evidence of intertemporal substitution effects on labor supply is provided by MaCurdy (1981) and Altonji (1986). Indirect evidence of intertemporal substitution effects based on the relationship between movements in output and the real interest rate is provided by Merrick (1984).

Although the two-period maximization problem analyzed above is somewhat more complicated than its single-period counterpart, the richer insights available from the above labor supply function make the added complications worthwhile. In a two-period context, the assumed positive sign for the effect of the real wage on current labor supply is intuitively more satisfying. If we were analyzing a long single period (like a full working life), we would surely have to conclude that a truly astronomically higher real wage (like $1,000 or $1,000,000 per hour) would certainly result in a reduction in labor supply. However, if we took the alternative extreme case in which the current period were today and the future period is the rest of one's working life, then today's supply of labor is quite likely to increase in response to such an astronomical, although temporary, increase in the real wage. A temporary real wage increase induces the representative household to substitute future leisure for current leisure.

Increases in the future real wage promote symmetric increases in future work effort and corresponding reductions in current work effort. Effects of changes in intertemporal relative prices more closely mimic the effects of changes in wealth. Clearly, increases in actual wealth $\Omega$ permit simultaneous increases in present and future consumption $c_t$ and $c_{t+1}$ and reductions in current and future work effort $\ell_t$ and $\ell_{t+1}$. Similarly, if future consumption becomes more expensive in terms of current consumption, the representative household works less, consumes less, and enjoys more leisure. The representative household is also likely in this case to shift toward more current consumption and less future consumption and, for given $W_{t+1}/P_{t+1}$, to work relatively more in the future as opposed to working in the present as the more efficient way of obtaining future consumption.

Before proceeding with our analysis of the labor market, it is useful to make one further modification to the functional form of the labor supply function. We have already assumed that the supply of labor is monotonically related to $P_{t+1}/P_t(1 + r)$. Therefore, since the natural logarithm is a monotonic function, labor supply must also be monotonically related to $\ln[P_{t+1}/P_t(1 + r)] = \ln(P_{t+1}/P_t) - \ln(1 + r)$. Now approximating,

$$\ln(1 + r) \simeq r, \tag{5.1.18}$$

and noting that $r - \ln(P_{t+1}/P_t) = -\{\ln[P_{t+1}/P_t] - r\}$, we can rewrite the labor supply function as

$$\ell^s = h\left(\underset{(+)}{\frac{W_t}{P_t}}, \underset{(-)}{\frac{W_{t+1}}{P_{t+1}}}, \underset{(+)}{r - \ln(P_{t+1}/P_t)}, \underset{(-)}{\Omega}\right). \tag{5.1.19}$$

This particular formulation proves most useful in Chapter 7, but it is also somewhat helpful in the present analysis.

## Speculative and Incomplete Information Models of Labor Supply

An important objective of this chapter is to identify ways in which aggregate demand shocks generate increases in output. If the labor market continuously clears, such increases in output can only occur if there is a corresponding increase in labor supply. One possible chain of causality is for increases in the nominal price level to lead to increases in labor supply.

Upon inspection of the function $h(\cdot)$, it would appear that purely nominal disturbances should not generate changes in labor supply. A permanent increase in the money supply, for example, is likely to raise $P_t$, $P_{t+1}$, $W_t$, and $W_{t+1}$ equiproportionately while generating no change in $r$ or $\Omega$. Such an increase in the money supply would be neutral in its effects on labor supply. How could such a purely nominal disturbance lead to changes in labor supply? There are at least two possible channels of influence, and both involve the possibility that labor suppliers may be imperfectly informed about the true incentives they face.

As one possibility, suppose, as is quite likely, that agents do not have perfect information about future wages and prices $W_{t+1}$ and $P_{t+1}$. Assume for now that expectations of $W_{t+1}$ and $P_{t+1}$ are purely static, that is, independent of changes in current economic events. Denote $w^e \equiv W_{t+1}^e / P_{t+1}^e$ and $P^e \equiv P_{t+1}^e$, where the superscript $e$ indicates the expectation of a variable. Now suppressing the current time index $t$, labor supply is given by

$$\ell^s = h(w, w^e, r - \ln(P^e/P), \Omega), \qquad (5.1.20)$$

where $w \equiv W_t/P_t$.

With $P^e$, $w$, and $w^e$ fixed, we find that labor supply now does respond to purely nominal disturbances. In particular,

$$\frac{\partial \ell^s}{\partial P} = \frac{\partial h}{\partial[r - \ln(P_{t+1}/P_t)]} \frac{P}{P^e} \frac{P^e}{P^2} = \frac{h_3}{P} > 0, \qquad (5.1.21)$$

where $h_3 \equiv \partial h/\partial[r - \ln(P_{t+1}/P_t)]$. With $P^e$ determined exogenously, increases in the nominal price level are viewed as purely transitory. Therefore, increases in prices generate expectations of a future decline in prices. Holding constant the nominal rate of interest and current and (expected) future real wages, this means that agents perceive an incentive to work more in the current period to save up for the future period of lower expected prices. Labor supply therefore rises with increases in $P$.[2]

An alternative way of motivating the nominal price level as a determinate of labor supply stresses uncertainty about the current level of prices $P_t$. Although our formal analysis is of an economy with a homogeneous consumption good as well as homogeneous labor inputs, let us at least for now think of this formulation merely as a convenient approximation of a multigood economy. In such an economy, agents know the nominal wage they are paid and they therefore immediately perceive any change in $W_t$. However, with $P_t$ interpreted in such a context as a price index, although it still makes sense for labor supply to depend on the perceived real wage $W_t/P_t$, it is less clear whether it is reasonable to presume that agents know the current value of $P_t$ when they make their labor supply decision.

It might be reasonable in such a multigood economy to presume that households continuously monitor some prices, while other prices may go unobserved for substantial amounts of time. Therefore, if there is a general rise in the level of prices, such a price change may be perceived as a rise in the relative price of the more frequently purchased commodities under the misperception that the general price level has risen little, if at all.

---

[2]This scenario is emphasized by Lucas and Rapping (1969).

Let us now consider the extreme case of this possibility in which individuals do not observe any current (or future) prices. Therefore, in the expression for labor supply all wages and prices except for $W_t$ and $r$ must be replaced by their expectations. In particular, let us assume that $w^e \equiv W_{t+1}^e/P_{t+1}^e$ is fixed. Let us further assume that $P_t^e = P_{t+1}^e$ is also fixed and therefore $\ln(P_{t+1}^e/P_t^e) = 0$. In this case the labor supply function is given by

$$\ell^s = h\left(\frac{W}{P^e}, w^e, r, \Omega\right) = h\left(\frac{W}{P}\frac{P}{P^e}, w^e, r, \Omega\right) = h\left(w\frac{P}{P^e}, w^e, r, \Omega\right). \quad (5.1.22)$$

We therefore observe that

$$\frac{\partial \ell^s}{\partial P} = \frac{\partial h}{\partial(W/P^e)}\frac{w}{P^e} = \frac{wh_1}{P^e} > 0, \quad (5.1.23)$$

where $h_1 \equiv \partial h/\partial(W/P^e)$. With the current price level perceived as fixed, any increase in the nominal wage is perceived as an equiproportional increase in the real wage independent of whether the nominal price level also moves in an equiproportional manner. Alternatively, holding the actual real wage fixed, an increase in the price level induces the perception of a rise in the expected real wage, which induces an increase in labor supply.[3]

Interestingly, both the possibility of potentially incorrect expectations of the future combined with intertemporal substitution effects or the possibility of misperceptions about the present combined with contemporaneous real wage effects lead to identical functional forms for the aggregate labor supply function. In both cases, we obtain

$$\ell^s = \ell^s\left(w, \frac{P}{P^e}, r\right),$$
$$\quad\; {\scriptstyle(+)\;\;(+)\;\;\;(+)} \qquad\qquad\qquad (5.1.24)$$

where, for ease of exposition, $w^e$ and $\Omega$ have temporarily been suppressed as arguments of the labor supply function. The only difference in the interpretation of the above equation comes in whether $P^e$ is interpreted as $P_{t+1}^e$ or $P_t^e$.

## Labor Demand and Labor Market Equilibrium

Our current analysis of the demand for labor is identical to that of Chapter 2. The representative firm may hire all the labor services it wishes at the prevailing nominal wage rate $W$ and sell all the output it wishes at the prevailing nominal price level $P$. With a predetermined stock of capital $\overline{K}$, the firm's problem is to choose $\ell$ and hence $y$ to maximize

$$\Pi = P\Phi(\ell, \overline{K}) - W\ell, \quad (5.1.25)$$

where $\Phi$ denotes the representative firm's production function.

Maximizing the above expression with respect to $\ell$ and aggregating over firms, we derive an aggregate labor demand schedule of the form

$$\ell^d = \ell^d(w), \qquad \frac{\partial \ell^d}{\partial w} = \left(\frac{\partial^2 \Phi}{\partial \ell^2}\right)^{-1} < 0. \quad (5.1.26)$$

---

[3]This scenario is emphasized by Lucas (1973).

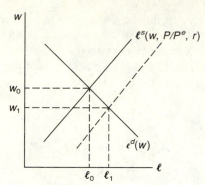

**Figure 5.1**

As long as $\Phi$ is concave, the relationship between labor demand and the real wage is unambiguously monotonic and inverse. Furthermore, even if we are considering a multi-good economy, because firms know both their input and output prices, there is no possibility of informational failures as we aggregate across industries. Finally, as long as capital is always fully employed and output is nonstorable, firms have no motivation to try to profit from intertemporal speculation. Therefore, there can be no effects of changes in $P^e$ on the demand for labor.

Throughout the present analysis, we assume that the labor market can properly be described by conditions of perfect competition. The real wage rate therefore adjusts to equate labor demand and labor supply. Labor market equilibrium is graphed in Figure 5.1. Figure 5.1 also depicts the partial-equilibrium effects of an increase in either $P$ or $r$ on the supply and demand for labor. Such an increase in $P$ or $r$ shifts the labor supply curve to the right, resulting in an increase in equilibrium employment and a reduction in the equilibrium real wage. As we shall later point out, the fact that incomplete information explanations of movements in output and employment predict an unambiguously inverse relationship between employment and the real wage is a frequently cited criticism of this approach.[4]

## 5.2 AN INCOMPLETE INFORMATION MODEL OF OUTPUT AND EMPLOYMENT

This section incorporates the labor market model of the preceding section into a simple macroeconomic model. The model is then used to show how changes in the money supply may affect employment and output even if prices and wages are completely flexible.

### The Formal Model

In this chapter, the main focus of interest is on the workings of the labor market and on interactions between the labor market and the goods and money markets. Therefore, in

---

[4]See, e.g., Grossman (1973).

order to highlight the implications of alternate labor market assumptions, we abstract from several interesting complications more carefully considered in earlier chapters.

We begin the discussion with a specification of goods market equilibrium. For the present, we abstract from complications associated with government bonds and therefore set $B = 0$. In this case, disposable income is simply $z = y - \tau$. Although the analysis of the preceding section also suggests that disposable income is more properly a choice variable chosen by the representative household jointly with its selection of current labor supply and that consumption more properly depends on expected relative prices, we continue to assume, as in Chapters 2 and 3, that

$$c^d = c^d(y - \tau) \tag{5.2.1}$$

on the assumption that $\partial c^d / \partial \Omega = 0$. This kind of specification may be defended by noting that as long as the production function exhibits constant returns to scale, average total disposable income, including dividend income, is equal to $y$ independent of the level of labor supply. Although a case could be made for the inclusion of variables like $r$ and $P^e_{t+1}/P_t$ in the consumption function, such complications increase the analytical complexity without offering much in the way of added insights.

The level of output supply is equal to total production evaluated at the level of labor demand on the assumption that in equilibrium firms can hire as much labor as they wish at the prevailing real wage. We therefore assume that

$$y^s = \Phi[\ell^d(w), \overline{K}] \equiv y^s(w), \qquad \frac{\partial y^s}{\partial w} = \frac{\partial \Phi}{\partial \ell} \frac{\partial \ell^d}{\partial w} < 0. \tag{5.2.2}$$

$$\underset{(-)}{}$$

Retaining our assumptions on the form of the investment demand function and the exogenous nature of government expenditures, goods market equilibrium is given by

$$c^d[y^s(w) - \tau] + i^d(r) + g - y^s(w) = 0. \tag{5.2.3}$$

Next consider the money market. As in the formulation of the goods market above, we temporarily abstract from the possibility of wealth effects, and so we assume that $\partial (M/P)^d / \partial \Omega = 0$. We further assume that adjustment of desired to actual real money balances is instantaneous, and so we let $\xi_m \to +\infty$. These assumptions result in a money market equilibrium condition of the form

$$\left(\frac{M}{P}\right)^d [y^s(w), r] - \frac{M}{P} = 0. \tag{5.2.4}$$

Finally, consider the labor market. We continue to utilize the basic functional forms for labor supply and labor demand from the preceding section. We also assume that agents' expectations of the future real wage are completely static and that wealth effects in the labor supply function are negligible. Furthermore, we assume that the real wage adjusts instantaneously to equate the supply and demand for labor. Now combing the equilibrium conditions of the goods, money, and labor markets, our formal model is given by

### Market-Clearing Conditions

Goods: $c^d[y^s(w) - \tau] + i^d(r) + g - y^s(w) = 0.$ $\qquad$ (5.2.5)

Money: $(M/P)^d[y^s(w), r] - M/P = 0.$ $\qquad$ (5.2.6)

Labor: $\ell^d(w) - \ell^s(w, P/P^e, r) = 0.$ $\qquad$ (5.2.7)

### Exogenous Variables

Real: $g$, $\tau$, potential shift parameters.

Nominal: $M$, $P^e$.

### Endogenous Variables    $r$, $P$, $w$.

## Money and Employment

We are now ready to reexamine the effects of a permanent, unanticipated monetary shock on the levels of output and employment. In the classical model of Chapter 2, when $B = 0$, such a disturbance generates an equiproportional increase in the price level with no change in $r$ or $y$. In the fixed-price model of Chapter 3, such an increase in the money supply has by definition no effect on $P$ but generates an increase in $y$ and a reduction in $r$.

Let us first analyze this disturbance by differentiating the goods, money, and labor market equilibrium conditions with respect to $r$, $P$, $w$, and $M$ to obtain

$$
\begin{bmatrix}
\dfrac{\partial i^d}{\partial r} & 0 & -\left(1 - \dfrac{\partial c^d}{\partial z}\right)\dfrac{\partial y^s}{\partial w} \\[3mm]
\dfrac{\partial (M/P)^d}{\partial r} & \dfrac{M}{P^2} & \dfrac{\partial (M/P)^d}{\partial y}\dfrac{\partial y^s}{\partial w} \\[3mm]
-\dfrac{\partial \ell^s}{\partial r} & -\dfrac{1}{P^e}\dfrac{\partial \ell^s}{\partial (P/P^e)} & \dfrac{\partial \ell^d}{\partial w} - \dfrac{\partial \ell^s}{\partial w}
\end{bmatrix}
\begin{bmatrix}
\dfrac{dr}{dM} \\[3mm]
\dfrac{dP}{dM} \\[3mm]
\dfrac{dw}{dM}
\end{bmatrix}
=
\begin{bmatrix}
0 \\[3mm]
\dfrac{1}{P} \\[3mm]
0
\end{bmatrix}.
\qquad (5.2.8)
$$

Cramer's rule now facilitates the following results:

$$
\frac{dr}{dM} = \frac{1}{P\Delta}\left[\frac{1}{P^e}\frac{\partial \ell^s}{\partial (P/P^e)}\left(1 - \frac{\partial c^d}{\partial z}\right)\frac{\partial y^s}{\partial w}\right] < 0,
\qquad (5.2.9)
$$

$$
\frac{dP}{dM} = \frac{1}{P\Delta}\left[\frac{\partial i^d}{\partial r}\left(\frac{\partial \ell^d}{\partial w} - \frac{\partial \ell^s}{\partial w}\right) - \frac{\partial \ell^s}{\partial r}\left(1 - \frac{\partial c^d}{\partial z}\right)\frac{\partial y^s}{\partial w}\right] > 0,
\qquad (5.2.10)
$$

$$
\frac{dw}{dM} = \frac{1}{P\Delta}\left(\frac{1}{P^e}\frac{\partial \ell^s}{\partial (P/P^e)}\frac{\partial i^d}{\partial r}\right) < 0,
\qquad (5.2.11)
$$

where

$$\Delta \equiv \frac{\partial i^d}{\partial r}\left[\frac{M}{P^2}\left(\frac{\partial \ell^d}{\partial w} - \frac{\partial \ell^s}{\partial w}\right) + \frac{1}{P^e}\frac{\partial \ell^s}{\partial(P/P^e)}\frac{\partial(M/P)^d}{\partial y}\frac{\partial y^s}{\partial w}\right]$$

$$+ \left(1 - \frac{\partial c^d}{\partial z}\right)\frac{\partial y^s}{\partial w}\left[\frac{1}{P^e}\frac{\partial \ell^s}{\partial(P/P^e)}\frac{\partial(M/P)^d}{\partial r} - \frac{M}{P^2}\frac{\partial \ell^s}{\partial r}\right] > 0. \qquad (5.2.12)$$

We therefore find that an increase in the money supply results in a reduction in the rate of interest, an increase in the level of prices, and a reduction in the real wage. Furthermore, since labor demand is inversely related to the real wage, an increase in the money supply therefore also results in an increase in the levels of employment and output. Finally, it is straightforward to show from the algebra above that $dP/dM < P/M$, and so real balances rise as a result of the increase in nominal money balances.

As a check on these results, let us reconsider the case in which there are no speculative and/or incomplete information effects. In that case, we find that $\partial \ell^s/\partial(P/P^e) = 0$. As we might anticipate, money is neutral in this instance. The above expressions reduce to $dr/dM = 0$, $dP/dM = P/M$, and $dw/dM = 0$. These results are identical to those derived in Chapter 2 when there are no government bonds and/or wealth effects.

Let us now examine what happens in each of the three markets. In the goods market, the reduction in $w$ guarantees that aggregate supply increases. The fall in the rate of interest combined with the increase in income generates an equal increase in aggregate demand. Next consider the money market. The increase in the money supply brings about a less than equiproportionate increase in the price level as long as $\partial \ell^s/\partial(P/P^e) > 0$. Therefore, the real money supply rises. The increase in income and the reduction in the rate of interest ensure an equal increase in money demand. In the labor market, the increase in prices generates an increase in labor supply. This increase in labor supply is partially offset by reductions in the real wage and the rate of interest. However, the lower real wage ensures that labor demand unambiguously rises, and therefore since the labor market is assumed to remain in equilibrium, we know that, on net, labor supply must increase.

Although for simplicity we have assumed that the supply of labor does not respond to changes in wealth, it is fairly straightforward to examine how the results would be affected by a wealth effect in the labor supply function. Abstracting from government-issued bonds, the level of wealth is equal to the level of real money balances. As noted above, the increase in the nominal money supply causes real money balances to rise in the present example, and so the presence of a wealth effect would tend to offset the increase in employment and output generated by the associated unperceived increase in the price level.

## A Graphical Representation

The form of the model studied above is not well suited for a graphical presentation. Since there are three endogenous variables, a three-dimensional representation would be needed. However, we can solve the money market equilibrium condition for $P$ as an implicit function of $r$, $w$, and $M$ and then substitute for $P$ in the labor market equilibrium condition to yield a two-equation model in $r$ and $w$.

Differentiating the money market equilibrium condition with respect to $r$, $P$, $w$, and $M$, we obtain

$$\frac{\partial (M/P)^d}{\partial r}\, dr + \frac{M}{P^2}\, dP + \frac{\partial (M/P)^d}{\partial y}\, \frac{\partial y^s}{\partial w}\, dw - \frac{1}{P}\, dM = 0. \tag{5.2.13}$$

We therefore derive the function $P$, where

$$P = P(r, w, M), \tag{5.2.14}$$

and

$$\frac{\partial P}{\partial r} = -P\frac{\partial (M/P)^d/\partial r}{M/P} > 0, \tag{5.2.15}$$

$$\frac{\partial P}{\partial w} = -P\frac{\partial (M/P)^d}{\partial y}\, \frac{\partial y^s}{\partial w} > 0, \tag{5.2.16}$$

$$\frac{\partial P}{\partial M} = \frac{P}{M} > 0. \tag{5.2.17}$$

The model can now be written as:

### Market-clearing Conditions

Goods: $c^d[y^s(w) - \tau] + i^d(r) + g - y^s(w) = 0.$ \hfill (5.2.18)

Labor: $\ell^d(w) - \ell^s\!\left(w, \frac{1}{P^e}P(r, w, M), r\right) = 0.$

$$\tag{5.2.19}$$

### Exogenous Variables

Real: $g$, $\tau$, potential shift parameters.
Nominal: $M$, $P^e$.

### Endogenous Variables   $r$, $w$.

Differentiating the goods and labor market equilibrium conditions with respect to $r$ and $w$, we obtain

$$\left.\frac{dr}{dw}\right|_{y^d = y^s} = \frac{\left(1 - \dfrac{\partial c^d}{\partial z}\right)\dfrac{\partial y^s}{\partial w}}{\partial i^d/\partial r} > 0, \tag{5.2.20}$$

$$\left.\frac{dr}{dw}\right|_{\ell^d = \ell^s} = \frac{\dfrac{\partial \ell^d}{\partial w} - \dfrac{\partial \ell^s}{\partial w} - \dfrac{\partial \ell^s}{\partial (P/P^e)}\dfrac{1}{P^e}\dfrac{\partial P}{\partial w}}{\dfrac{\partial P/\partial r}{P^e}\dfrac{\partial \ell^s}{\partial (P/P^e)} + \dfrac{\partial \ell^s}{\partial r}} < 0. \tag{5.2.21}$$

These market-clearing loci are depicted in Figure 5.2.

Let us first consider the goods market equilibrium locus. A reduction in $w$ increases aggregate supply more than it increases aggregate demand since $\partial c^d/\partial z < 1$. A coincident

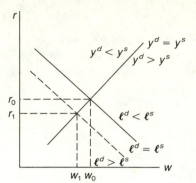

**Figure 5.2**

reduction in the rate of interest is therefore necessary to reequate aggregate supply and aggregate demand. Furthermore, since aggregate demand is inversely related to the rate of interest, we know that $y^d < y^s$ above and to the left of the $y^d = y^s$ locus. Finally, since aggregate supply is inversely related to the real wage, we know that as we move upward and to the right along the $y^d = y^s$ locus, successive points on the curve correspond to decreased output levels.

The labor market equilibrium locus is slightly more involved. An increase in the real wage reduces labor demand and increases labor supply, resulting in $\ell^d < \ell^s$. A reduction in the rate of interest directly reduces labor supply, providing a partial offset to the potential labor market disequilibrium. The lower interest rate also increases the demand for money. To maintain money market equilibrium, the price level must fall. The lower price level provides a second source of reduced labor supply, which keeps labor supply and labor demand equal along $\ell^d = \ell^s$. As noted above, an increase in $w$ reduces labor demand and increases labor supply. Therefore, to the right of and above $\ell^d = \ell^s$, there is an excess supply of labor. To the left of and below $\ell^d = \ell^s$, there is an excess demand for labor.

We are now ready to present a graphical analysis of the effects of an increase in the money supply. An increase in $M$ generates an increase in $P$ since $P_3 > 0$. The increase in $P$ generates an increase in labor supply. A reduction in $r$ and/or a reduction in $w$ is required to maintain labor market equilibrium. The $\ell^d = \ell^s$ locus therefore shifts downward and to the left. The equilibrium interest rate and real wage fall to $r_1$ and $w_1$. This graphical analysis therefore generates the same results as the algebraic analysis above.

# 5.3 A FIXED NOMINAL WAGE MODEL OF EMPLOYMENT AND OUTPUT

This section considers a model in which the nominal wage rate is rigid but in which the nominal price level is completely flexible. This case stands in contrast to the models of Chapter 3 in which the nominal wage rate is flexible and the nominal price level is rigid. In the present model, we show that the effects of a permanent increase in the money supply are very similar to those obtained in the model of the preceding section.

### Rigid Wages and Flexible Prices

An alternative rationale for nonneutral effects of changes in the money supply can be based on nominal wage rigidities. Suppose that goods prices adjust to satisfy market-clearing conditions but that nominal wages are predetermined. If we further assume that employment is demand determined, we obtain

$$\ell = \ell^d\!\left(\frac{\overline{W}}{P}\right), \tag{5.3.1}$$

where $\overline{W}$ is the predetermined nominal wage rate. Output supply is therefore given by

$$y^s = \Phi\!\left[\ell^d\!\left(\frac{\overline{W}}{P}\right), \overline{K}\right] = y^s(w). \tag{5.3.2}$$

Sticky-wage models are built on the presumption that a pool of unemployed workers exists who are willing to work at the prevailing wage rate. Some form of market failure must therefore prevent market forces from guaranteeing employment to all who wish to work. Unfortunately, the microeconomic foundations of such models are generally weak or nonexistent. However, if such models do offer an accurate picture of reality, the welfare implications of increased employment are fairly clear-cut. Increases in output and employment in such models are almost always welfare improving.

The sticky-wage model is analytically simpler to work with than equilibrium models because with $W$ fixed at $\overline{W}$, the variables $w \equiv W/P$ and $P$ can no longer both be endogenous. While we can use the fact that $W = Pw$ to substitute for either $w$ or $P$, for the time being we substitute $P = \overline{W}/w$ and analyze the model with $r$ and $w$ as the two remaining endogenous variables. The resulting model is given by:

#### Market Equilibrium Conditions

Goods: $c^d[y^s(w) - \tau] + i^d(r) + g - y^s(w) = 0.$ (5.3.3)

Money: $(M/P)^d[y^s(w), r] - w(M/\overline{W}) = 0.$ (5.3.4)

#### Exogenous Variables

Real: $g$, $\tau$, potential shift parameters.
Nominal: $M$, $\overline{W}$.

#### Endogenous Variables   $r$, $w$.

The equilibrium levels of output and employment can then be solved sequentially as

$$\ell = \ell^d(w) \quad \text{and} \quad y = \Phi[\ell^d(w), \overline{K}]. \tag{5.3.5}$$

With only two basic endogenous variables, the model of this section much more naturally permits a graphical analysis. Differentiating the goods and money market equilibrium conditions with respect to $r$ and $w$, we obtain, after some rearrangement,

$$\left.\frac{dr}{dw}\right|_{y^d=y^s} = \frac{\left(1 - \dfrac{\partial c^d}{\partial z}\right)\dfrac{\partial y^s}{\partial w}}{\partial i^d/\partial r} > 0, \tag{5.3.6}$$

$$\frac{dr}{dw}\bigg|_{(M/P)^d=M/P} = \frac{\dfrac{M}{\overline{W}} - \dfrac{\partial(M/P)^d}{\partial y}\dfrac{\partial y^s}{\partial w}}{\dfrac{\partial(M/P)^d}{\partial r}} < 0. \tag{5.3.7}$$

The goods market equilibrium locus for this model is identical to the goods market equilibrium locus for the model of the preceding section. However, the second market-clearing locus, although similar in appearance to the $\ell^d = \ell^s$ locus of the preceding section, has a substantially different interpretation. With the nominal wage fixed, an increase in the real wage rate implies a reduction in the price level. A lower price level implies an increased supply of real money balances. Furthermore, the increase in the real wage depresses output and therefore reduces the demand for real money balances. Both by increasing the real supply and reducing the real demand, we see that the increase in $w$ generates an excess supply of real money balances. We therefore need a coincident reduction in the rate of interest to keep the money market in equilibrium.

## Money and Employment

We are now ready to repeat our experiment of the preceding section in which we analyzed the effects of an unanticipated increase in the nominal money supply. Differentiating the equilibrium conditions, we find that

$$\begin{bmatrix} \dfrac{\partial i^d}{\partial r} & -\left(1 - \dfrac{\partial c^d}{\partial z}\right)\dfrac{\partial y^s}{\partial w} \\[4mm] \dfrac{\partial(M/P)^d}{\partial r} & \dfrac{\partial(M/P)^d}{\partial y}\dfrac{\partial y^s}{\partial w} - \dfrac{M}{\overline{W}} \end{bmatrix} \begin{bmatrix} \dfrac{dr}{dM} \\[4mm] \dfrac{dw}{dM} \end{bmatrix} = \begin{bmatrix} 0 \\[4mm] \dfrac{w}{\overline{W}} \end{bmatrix}. \tag{5.3.8}$$

Solving by Cramer's rule, we find that

$$\frac{dr}{dM} = \frac{w/\overline{W}}{\Delta}\left(1 - \frac{\partial c^d}{\partial z}\right)\frac{\partial y^s}{\partial w} < 0, \tag{5.3.9}$$

$$\frac{dw}{dM} = \frac{w/\overline{W}}{\Delta}\frac{\partial i^d}{\partial r} < 0, \tag{5.3.10}$$

where

$$\Delta = \frac{\partial i^d}{\partial r}\left(\frac{\partial(M/P)^d}{\partial y}\frac{\partial y^s}{\partial w} - \frac{M}{\overline{W}}\right) + \left(1 - \frac{\partial c^d}{\partial z}\right)\frac{\partial(M/P)^d}{\partial r}\frac{\partial y^s}{\partial w} > 0. \tag{5.3.11}$$

The interest rate and the real wage both fall following the increase in the money supply. The lower real wage also generates an increase in employment and output as the demand for labor expands. These results are depicted in Figure 5.3. In addition to our interest in the effects of changes in $M$ on $r$, $w$, $y$, and $\ell$, we are also interested in the effects of changes in $M$ on $P$. Not surprisingly, the increase in $M$ results in an increase in $P$. However, is this effect more or less than proportional? We can answer this question by

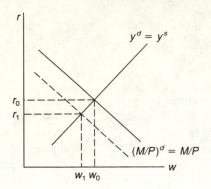

**Figure 5.3**

noting that since $P = \overline{W}/w$, we obtain

$$\frac{dP}{dM} = -\frac{\overline{W}}{w^2}\frac{dw}{dM}.$$

(5.3.12)

Evaluating from above, we find that

$$0 < \frac{dP}{dM} = \frac{1}{\dfrac{M}{P} - w\dfrac{\partial y^s}{\partial w}\left[\dfrac{\partial (M/P)^d}{\partial y} + \dfrac{\partial (M/P)^d/\partial r}{\partial i^d/\partial r}\left(1 - \dfrac{\partial c^d}{\partial z}\right)\right]} < \frac{P}{M}$$

(5.3.13)

Therefore, the supply of real money balances rises. This is not surprising since the increase in $y$ and the fall in $r$ both work to raise the demand for real money balances. While we continue to abstract from a wealth effect in the labor supply function, it is straightforward to see how the results of this analysis would be affected by such a wealth effect. Since the increase in the money supply causes a less than proportional increase in prices, in the absence of government-issued bonds, wealth unambiguously rises. Therefore, there would be an offsetting reduction in labor supply, and the ultimate effect on employment and output of the increase in the money supply would be reduced.

## 5.4 A DYNAMIC MODEL OF EMPLOYMENT AND OUTPUT

In this section, we specify a dynamic model of employment and output determination in the tradition of the models of the preceding two sections. This model possesses an equilibrium that avoids the puzzling features of completely rigid wages or completely exogenous price expectations. The model also has the property of money neutrality in the steady state while retaining the kinds of short-run nonneutralities of the sticky-wage and incomplete information models of the preceding sections.

## Wage and Expectation Adjustment

Surely, no one would suggest that wages are so rigid that the labor market never equilibrates. One intuitively pleasing model of wage adjustment is the so-called law of supply and demand. In this formulation, the percentage rate of wage change is proportional to the excess demand for labor. Recalling our formulations for labor supply and labor demand from above, this type of wage adjustment mechanism can be characterized by

$$\frac{\dot{W}}{W} = \lambda\left[\ell^d(w) - \ell^s\left(w, \frac{P}{P^e}, r\right)\right], \qquad \lambda > 0, \quad \text{a constant.} \tag{5.4.1}$$

With very low values for $\lambda$, wage adjustment is very slow, so that the sticky-wage model may be a very good approximation. On the other hand, for sufficiently large values of $\lambda$, completely flexible wages may be a more appropriate approximation. In any event, as long as $\lambda$ is strictly positive, the above model always predicts eventual labor market equilibration.

The wage adjustment mechanism above relates changes in the *nominal* wage to the level of excess labor demand. Another possibility would make the rate of change in the *real* wage proportional to the level of excess labor demand. This second possibility would more accurately describe a situation in which the wage rate were automatically indexed on a one-to-one basis with the rate of price change (the rate of inflation). If, on the other hand, the wage-setting agent ignores current price changes except to the extent that they are already reflected in $\ell^d - \ell^s$, then the formulation chosen above would be the more correct alternative. Fortunately, the particular one of these two forms chosen makes little difference in almost all of the results generated below. In the very few instances in which this choice of assumption does make a difference, the resulting differences are duly noted.

We also adopt the assumption that the expected price level adjusts over time in such a way that expected and actual prices are equal in the steady state. If $P^e$ denotes the expected value of the current price, then the process we wish to describe is one in which, for a given constant price level, agents eventually learn the correct price level, and so $P^e = P$.

If $P^e$ is instead interpreted as the expected future price level, then the sort of adjustment we have in mind is somewhat different. A sudden jump in the price level is perceived instantaneously in this case. Immediately following such an increase in the price level, since agents expect the price increase to be temporary, they therefore expect a future reduction in $P$. However, if agents are confronted with what turns out to be a permanent price increase, expectations of the future price level slowly rise until agents no longer expect a future price reduction, and again we find that $P^e = P$.

Let us formalize this process by assuming that

$$\dot{P}^e = \psi(P - P^e), \qquad \psi > 0, \quad \text{a constant.} \tag{5.4.2}$$

Large values of $\psi$ imply that the expected price level adjusts very rapidly while small values of $\psi$ correspond to very slow adjustment in $P^e$. However, as long as $\psi$ is strictly positive and the equilibrium price level is constant, the equilibrium expected and actual price levels are equal. We defer analysis of price expectation formation in an inflationary economy to Chapters 6 and 7. In that analysis, we see that while the economic landscape looks superficially different, most of the results of the present section carry over with only slightly altered interpretation.

## The Formal Dynamic Model

Our formal model consists of three algebraic equations in addition to the two differential equations postulated above. The resulting model is given by

$$0 = c^d[y^s(w) - \tau] + i^d(r) + g - y^s(w), \tag{5.4.3}$$

$$0 = \left(\frac{M}{P}\right)^d [y^s(w), r] - \frac{M}{P}, \tag{5.4.4}$$

$$0 = W - Pw, \tag{5.4.5}$$

$$\frac{\dot{W}}{W} = \lambda \left[ \ell^d(w) - \ell^s\left(w, \frac{P}{P^e}, r\right) \right], \tag{5.4.6}$$

$$\dot{P}^e = \psi(P - P^e). \tag{5.4.7}$$

Differentiating the first three equations with respect to time and assuming that $dM/dt = 0$, we obtain

$$0 = -\left(1 - \frac{\partial c^d}{\partial z}\right) \frac{\partial y^s}{\partial w} \dot{w} + \frac{\partial i^d}{\partial r} \dot{r}, \tag{5.4.8}$$

$$0 = \frac{\partial(M/P)^d}{\partial y} \frac{\partial y^s}{\partial w} \dot{w} + \frac{\partial(M/P)^d}{\partial r} \dot{r} + \frac{M}{P} \frac{\dot{P}}{P}, \tag{5.4.9}$$

$$0 = \frac{\dot{W}}{W} - \frac{\dot{P}}{P} - \frac{\dot{w}}{w}. \tag{5.4.10}$$

Substituting for $\dot{r}$ and $\dot{P}/P$, we obtain

$$\frac{\partial y^s}{\partial w} \left[ \frac{\partial(M/P)^d}{\partial y} + \frac{\partial(M/P)^d/\partial r}{\partial i^d/\partial r} \left(1 - \frac{\partial c^d}{\partial z}\right) \right] \dot{w} + \frac{M}{P} \frac{\dot{W}}{W} - \frac{M}{P} \frac{\dot{w}}{w} = 0, \tag{5.4.11}$$

or

$$\left\{ \frac{M}{W} - \frac{\partial y^s}{\partial w} \left[ \frac{\partial(M/P)^d}{\partial y} + \frac{\partial(M/P)^d/\partial r}{\partial i^d/\partial r} \left(1 - \frac{\partial c^d}{\partial z}\right) \right] \right\} \dot{w} = \frac{M}{P} \frac{\dot{W}}{W}. \tag{5.4.12}$$

Now plugging in for $\dot{W}/W$ from the wage adjustment equation, we find that

$$\dot{w} = \frac{\lambda(M/P)}{\dfrac{M}{W} - \dfrac{\partial y^s}{\partial w} \left[ \dfrac{\partial(M/P)^d}{\partial y} + \dfrac{\partial(M/P)^d/\partial r}{\partial i^d/\partial r} \left(1 - \dfrac{\partial c^d}{\partial z}\right) \right]} (\ell^d - \ell^s), \tag{5.4.13}$$

or

$$\dot{w} = \lambda^* \left[ \ell^d(w) - \ell^s\left(w, \frac{P}{P^e}, r\right) \right], \tag{5.4.14}$$

with $\lambda^*$ defined as the above coefficient on $\ell^d - \ell^s$. In what follows, we linearize the dynamics and therefore assume that $\lambda^*$ is constant and positive.

The above dynamic equation in $\dot{w}$ and the equation $\dot{P}^e = \psi(P - P^e)$ potentially combine to form a differential equation system in the two state variables $w$ and $P^e$. However, the current forms of the two differential equations contain the additional endogenous variables $P$ and $r$. Therefore, in order to write the system solely in terms of $w$ and $P^e$, we need to express $P$ and $r$ as functions of $P^e$, $w$, and any exogenous variables that may be of interest.

Substitution of functional forms for the variables $P$ and $r$ may be accomplished by means of an appropriate analysis of the goods and money market equilibrium conditions above. Since $P^e$ does not appear in either of these equations, we know that solution of these equations for $P$ and $r$ result in functional forms for which $\partial P/\partial P^e$ and $\partial r/\partial P^e$ are both zero. Therefore, $P$ and $r$ must be functions of only $w$ and the principal exogenous variable of current interest, $M$. Furthermore, it is straightforward to show that the value of $r$ that satisfies the goods and money market equilibrium conditions is independent of $M$. Application of Cramer's rule to the equations

$$c^d[y^s(w) - \tau] + i^d(r) + g - y^s(w) = 0, \tag{5.4.15}$$

$$\left(\frac{M}{P}\right)^d [y^s(w), r] - \frac{M}{P} = 0 \tag{5.4.16}$$

permits derivation of:

$$P = P(w, M), \tag{5.4.17}$$

where

$$\frac{\partial P}{\partial w} = -\frac{P^2}{M}\frac{\partial y^s}{\partial w}\left[\left(1 - \frac{\partial c^d}{\partial z}\right)\frac{\partial(M/P)^d/\partial r}{\partial i^d/\partial r} + \frac{\partial(M/P)^d}{\partial y}\right] > 0, \tag{5.4.18}$$

$$\frac{\partial P}{\partial M} = \frac{P}{M} > 0, \tag{5.4.19}$$

and

$$r = r(w), \tag{5.4.20}$$

where

$$\frac{\partial r}{\partial w} = \frac{\partial y^s/\partial w}{\partial i^d/\partial r}\left(1 - \frac{\partial c^d}{\partial z}\right) > 0. \tag{5.4.21}$$

With the above substitutions, the model may be expressed as

$$\dot{w} = \lambda^*\left[l^d(w) - l^s\left(w, \frac{P(w, M)}{P^e}, r(w)\right)\right], \tag{5.4.22}$$

$$\dot{P}^e = \psi[P(w, M) - P^e]. \tag{5.4.23}$$

Equilibrium for this model is given by $\dot{w} = \dot{P}^e = 0$. Evaluating these equilibrium conditions, we find that

$$\ell^d(w) - \ell^s(w, \ell, r(w)) = 0 \rightarrow w^*, \tag{5.4.24}$$

$$P = P^e \rightarrow P^* = P(w^*, M), \tag{5.4.25}$$

where

$$\frac{\partial P^*}{\partial M} = \frac{\partial P}{\partial M} = \frac{P}{M}. \tag{5.4.26}$$

We therefore find that the labor market equilibrium condition is sufficient to solve for the equilibrium real wage $w^*$. The $P(\cdot)$ function can then be used to solve for $P^* = P^e$. Note that money is neutral in this model. Both $w^*$ and $r^*$ are independent of $M$ and $dP^*/dM = P/M$. The price level rises equiproportional to any increase in the money supply.

We are now ready to solve for the model's stability conditions and plot the system's phase diagram. Differentiating the dynamic adjustment equations, we find that

$$\frac{\partial \dot{w}}{\partial w} = \lambda^* \left[ \frac{\partial \ell^d}{\partial w} - \frac{\partial \ell^s}{\partial w} - \frac{1}{P^e} \frac{\partial \ell^s}{\partial (P/P^e)} \frac{\partial P}{\partial w} - \frac{\partial \ell^s}{\partial r} \frac{\partial r}{\partial w} \right] < 0, \tag{5.4.27}$$

$$\frac{\partial \dot{w}}{\partial P^e} = \lambda^* \left[ \frac{P}{(P^e)^2} \frac{\partial \ell^s}{\partial (P/P^e)} \right] > 0, \tag{5.4.28}$$

$$\frac{\partial \dot{P}^e}{\partial w} = \psi \frac{\partial P}{\partial w} > 0, \tag{5.4.29}$$

$$\frac{\partial \dot{P}^e}{\partial P^e} = -\psi < 0. \tag{5.4.30}$$

The slopes of the $\dot{w} = 0$ and $\dot{P}^e = 0$ loci are therefore given in the neighborhood of equilibrium by

$$\left. \frac{dw}{dP^e} \right|_{\dot{w}=0} = \frac{-\dfrac{1}{P^e} \dfrac{\partial \ell^s}{\partial (P/P^e)}}{\dfrac{\partial \ell^d}{\partial w} - \dfrac{\partial \ell^s}{\partial w} - \dfrac{1}{P^e} \dfrac{\partial \ell^s}{\partial (P/P^e)} \dfrac{\partial P}{\partial w} - \dfrac{\partial \ell^s}{\partial r} \dfrac{\partial r}{\partial w}} > 0, \tag{5.4.31}$$

$$\left. \frac{dw}{dP^e} \right|_{\dot{P}^e=0} = \frac{1}{\partial P/\partial w} > 0. \tag{5.4.32}$$

Furthermore, we also know that

$$\left. \frac{dw}{dP^e} \right|_{\dot{P}^e=0} - \left. \frac{dw}{dP^e} \right|_{\dot{w}=0}$$

$$= \frac{1}{\partial P/\partial w} \frac{\dfrac{\partial \ell^d}{\partial w} - \dfrac{\partial \ell^s}{\partial w} - \dfrac{\partial \ell^s}{\partial r} \dfrac{\partial r}{\partial w}}{\dfrac{\partial \ell^d}{\partial w} - \dfrac{\partial \ell^s}{\partial w} - \dfrac{1}{P^e} \dfrac{\partial \ell^s}{\partial (P/P^e)} \dfrac{\partial P}{\partial w} - \dfrac{\partial \ell^s}{\partial r} \dfrac{\partial r}{\partial w}} > 0. \tag{5.4.33}$$

The $\dot{P}^e = 0$ locus is therefore more steeply positively sloped than the $\dot{w} = 0$ locus. We also know that both the $w$ and $P^e$ processes are stable by themselves since $\partial \dot{w}/\partial w$ and $\partial \dot{P}^e/\partial P^e$ are both negative. The resulting phase diagram is depicted in Figure 5.4.

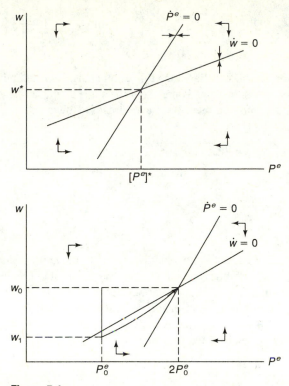

**Figure 5.4**

## Dynamic Response to an Increase in the Money Supply

In this section, we reanalyze the effects of a permanent, unanticipated step increase in the money supply on our model economy. We have already noted that the equilibrium effects of such a disturbance are equiproportional increases in $P$, $P^e$, and $W$ with no changes in $r$ or $w$. Therefore, in $w$, $P^e$ space, the $\dot{w} = 0$ locus and $\dot{P}^e = 0$ locus must both shift to the right by a distance proportional to the increase in $M$. Such a shift is depicted in Figure 5.4 for the case of a doubling in the money supply from $M_0$ to $2M_0$. The new equilibrium real wage is still $w_0$ while the new equilibrium expected price level is $P^e = 2P_0 = 2P_0^e$.

From the expected price adjustment equation, we see that at any instant in time, $P^e$ is predetermined. Therefore, immediately following the step increase in $M$, we continue to have $P^e = P_0^e$. The instantaneous behavior of the real wage is somewhat different and more complicated, however. Recall that we postulated an adjustment mechanism in which there is some stickyness in the *nominal* wage. Therefore, immediately following the increase in $M$, we observe $W = W_0$. Moreover, the price level immediately rises, and therefore $w$ falls to, say, $w_1$. We can compute the extent of this fall in $w$ by calculating the comparative statics effects of a change in $M$ on $w$ holding $W$ fixed by applying Cramer's rule to the three algebraic equations:

$$c^d[y^s(w)^s - \tau] + i^d(r) + g - y^s(w) = 0, \tag{5.4.34}$$

$$\left(\frac{M}{P}\right)^d [y^s(w), r] - \frac{M}{P} = 0, \tag{5.4.35}$$

$$W_0 - Pw = 0. \tag{5.4.36}$$

This calculation should look familiar since this exact analysis was conducted in Section 5.3. The present set of assumptions is precisely the same as those of the fixed-wage model analyzed in that section. We therefore have already shown that

$$\left.\frac{dw}{dM}\right|_{W=W_0} = \frac{1}{P\dfrac{\partial y^s}{\partial w}\left[\dfrac{\partial(M/P)^d}{\partial y} + \dfrac{\partial(M/P)^d/\partial r}{\partial i^d/\partial r}\left(1 - \dfrac{\partial c^d}{\partial z}\right) - \dfrac{M/W_0}{\partial y^s/\partial w}\right]}$$

$$= \frac{-1}{\dfrac{M}{P}\dfrac{\partial P}{\partial w} + \dfrac{PM}{W}} < 0. \tag{5.4.37}$$

What is not immediately apparent, however, is where to place the point $(P_0^e, w_1)$ on the $w, P^e$ phase diagram. In particular, does the point $(P_0^e, w_1)$ lie above or below the new $\dot{w} = 0$ locus? Does the point $(P_0^e, w_1)$ lie above or below the $\dot{P}^e = 0$ locus? We can answer these questions by determining the extent of the vertical shifts in the $\dot{w} = 0$ and $\dot{P}^e = 0$ loci following a change in $M$. First differentiating the $\dot{P}^e = 0$ equilibrium condition with respect to $w$ and $M$ and rearranging, we find that

$$\left.\frac{dw}{dM}\right|_{\substack{\dot{P}^e=0 \\ dP^e=0}} = \frac{-1}{\dfrac{M}{P}\dfrac{\partial P}{\partial w}} < 0. \tag{5.4.38}$$

We therefore note that

$$-\left.\frac{dw}{dM}\right|_{\substack{\dot{P}^e=0 \\ dP^e=0}} > -\left.\frac{dw}{dM}\right|_{W=W_0}, \tag{5.4.39}$$

and so the initial decline in $w$ is smaller than the downward vertical shift in the $\dot{P}^e = 0$ locus.

We next differentiate the $\dot{w} = 0$ equilibrium condition with respect to $w$ and $M$. Upon rearranging, we find that

$$\left.\frac{dw}{dM}\right|_{\substack{\dot{w}=0 \\ dP^e=0}} = \frac{-1}{\dfrac{M}{P}\dfrac{\partial P}{\partial w} + \dfrac{P^e M}{P}\left(\dfrac{\partial \ell^s}{\partial(P/P^e)}\right)^{-1}}\left(\dfrac{\partial \ell^s}{\partial w} - \dfrac{\partial \ell^d}{\partial w} + \dfrac{\partial \ell^s}{\partial r}\dfrac{\partial r}{\partial w}\right) < 0. \tag{5.4.40}$$

We therefore see that the absolute magnitude of the fall in $w$ is larger than the absolute magnitude of the downward shift in the $\dot{w} = 0$ locus as long as

$$\frac{\partial \ell^s}{\partial(P/P^e)} < -\frac{\partial \ell^d}{\partial w} + \frac{\partial \ell^s}{\partial w} + \frac{\partial \ell^s}{\partial r}\frac{\partial r}{\partial w}. \tag{5.4.41}$$

However, since this inequality is not unambiguously satisfied, we are unable to determine whether the point $(P_0^e, w_1)$ lies above or below the $\dot{w} = 0$ locus.

For those cases in which the inequality (5.4.41) is satisfied, the phase diagram is as depicted in Figure 5.4.[5] Given the assumed position and slopes of the equilibrium loci, most of the general characteristics of the dynamic adjustment paths of $w$ and $P^e$ are unambiguous. Following the initial downward jump in $w$, the real wage begins a monotonic rise back to its original value. Price expectations rise throughout. A typical adjustment path is depicted in Figure 5.4. Also, recall that with the nominal wage fixed, the instantaneous rise in $P$ is less than equiproportional. Therefore, after the impact effect of the change in $M$ on $P$, the price level must continue to rise over time until a full equiproportional increase in $P$ is accomplished.

We are now ready to demonstrate how the incomplete information and sticky-wage models of Sections 5.2 and 5.3 may be interpreted as special cases of the present analysis. First consider the flexible-wage and flexible-price model of Section 5.2. That case corresponds to the present model when $\lambda^* \to +\infty$ and $\psi = 0$. In that case, following an increase in $M$, the economy immediately jumps to point $A$ in Figure 5.5. The fall in the

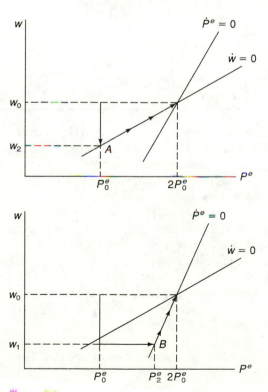

**Figure 5.5**

---

real wage is larger in absolute value than in the general case, and therefore the immediate increase in employment is also larger. If we now allow for $\psi > 0$, the economy moves along the $\dot{w} = 0$ locus until we gradually approach the equilibrium position $w_0, 2P_0$.

Alternatively, we can also consider the case in which $\lambda^* = 0$ and $\psi \rightarrow +\infty$. This case corresponds closely to but is not exactly the same as the sticky-wage case considered above. In that analysis, since we assumed that employment was demand determined and since the only effects of changes in $P^e$ are on labor supply, we left undetermined what process, if any, accounted for changes in $P^e$. If, in that analysis, we continually set $P^e = P$, then the current analysis would be an exact replica of that analysis.

The economy in this case instantaneously jumps to point $B$ in Figure 5.5 following the increase in $M$. We therefore see that as long as $w_2 < w_1$, as we have earlier assumed, the increase in employment in the sticky-wage model is unambiguously greater than the increase in employment in the incomplete information model. If we next relax the assumption that $\lambda^* = 0$, the economy proceeds directly along the $\dot{P}^e$ locus from point $B$ to the equilibrium point $w_0, 2P_0^e$. Finally, we noted that in the sticky-wage model, the price level rises less than equiproportionally to an increase in $M$. Therefore, as we move from point $B$ to the equilibrium position in which $dP/dM = P/M$, we know that the actual price level $P$ must also be rising.

# 5.5 AN EQUILIBRIUM MODEL OF EMPLOYMENT AND OUTPUT

An important objective of macroeconomic theory is to provide an internally consistent explanation of certain "stylized facts" of typical patterns of comovements in macroeconomic time series. One major such regularity is the positive correlation of movements in the money supply with movements in levels of employment and output. These correlations are certainly emphasized by Friedman and Schwartz (1963), who lean in the direction of identifying movements in the money supply as the principal cause of movements in employment and output. The models of Sections 5.2–5.4 continue in this tradition by presenting models in which the short-run impact of a monetary stock is a temporary increase in employment and output even though money is neutral in the long run.

Another implication of the models of Sections 5.2–5.4 is that money-induced increases in employment and output can only occur coincident with reductions in the real wage rate as firms always operate on their labor demand curves in these models. However, as pointed out by Grossman (1973), such a negative correlation between the real wage and the level of output is inconsistent with empirical evidence first presented by Kuh (1966) and Bodkin (1969) that found no such negative correlation. Even more damaging to these theories, Bils (1985), correcting for what he feels is a bias in the time series behavior of the average real wage rate, finds that real wages are strongly procyclical.

This section presents an analytical framework that proves useful in identifying alternative sources of output fluctuations. In particular, we temporarily abandon the possibilities of incomplete information and short-run wage stickyness and concentrate on so-called equilibrium models of business cycles. Formally, this analytical framework is identical to the steady state of the model of the preceding section.

## Shifts in the Aggregate Production Function

Work by Kydland and Prescott (1982) and Long and Plosser (1983) identify changes over time in labor's marginal product as potential sources of fluctuations in employment and output. While their analyses place more emphasis on the serial correlation properties of employment and output,[6] the possibility of shifts in the aggregate production function as a source of output movements is consistent with the observed procyclical pattern of real wage rates.

This section considers an equilibrium model of employment and output fluctuations based on shifts in the aggregate production function. This analysis is capable of generating a positive correlation between the real wage and the levels of employment and output. Assume that the aggregate production function is given by

$$y = \Phi(\ell, \nu), \tag{5.5.1}$$

where $\Phi$ is a concave production function and $\nu$ represents an exogenous "productivity shock." Throughout the analysis we assume that $\partial\Phi/\partial\nu > 0$. Physical capital, although still a factor of production, is employed in a constant amount, and therefore the level of capital is suppressed as an argument of the production function $\Phi$.

In order to highlight the effects of changes in $\nu$, we abstract from temporary wage rigidities and the possibility of imperfect information. We therefore set $P^e = P$ throughout. We also continue to assume that asset market adjustment is instantaneous, that prices continuously clear markets, and that wealth effects are unimportant. We further assume that all productivity shocks are unanticipated and viewed by agents as purely transitory. These assumptions ensure that shifts in the production function do not alter the incentives for firms to acquire new capital. The investment demand function is therefore properly written as independent of $\nu$. The model is therefore given by

$$c^d[\Phi(\ell^d(w, \nu), \nu) - \tau] + i^d(r) + g - \Phi(\ell^d(w, \nu), \nu) = 0, \tag{5.5.2}$$

$$\ell^d(w, \nu) - \ell^s(w, r) = 0. \tag{5.5.3}$$

With the level of $\nu$ exogenously determined, the demand for labor satisfies

$$w = \frac{\partial\Phi[\ell^d(w, \nu), \nu]}{\partial\ell}, \tag{5.5.4}$$

and so

$$\frac{\partial\ell^d}{\partial w} = \frac{1}{\partial^2\Phi/\partial\ell^2} < 0, \tag{5.5.5}$$

$$\frac{\partial\ell^d}{\partial \nu} = -\frac{\partial^2\Phi/\partial\ell\partial\nu}{\partial^2\Phi/\partial\ell^2}, \tag{5.5.6}$$

---

[6]Analysis of how shifts in the aggregate production function might affect the time series properties of employment and output is deferred to Chapter 15.

We further assume that $\ell$ and $\nu$ are both normal factors of production, and so, in particular,

$$\frac{\partial \Phi}{\partial \nu} + \frac{\partial \Phi}{\partial \ell} \frac{\partial \ell^d}{\partial \nu} > 0. \tag{5.5.7}$$

We are now ready to calculate the comparative statics effects of a change in $\nu$ on $w$, $r$, $\ell$, and $y$. Differentiating the equilibrium conditions with respect to $w$, $r$, and $\nu$, we obtain

$$\begin{bmatrix} -\left(1 - \dfrac{\partial c^d}{\partial z}\right) \dfrac{\partial \Phi}{\partial \ell} \dfrac{\partial \ell^d}{\partial w} & \dfrac{\partial i^d}{\partial r} \\[4mm] \dfrac{\partial \ell^d}{\partial w} - \dfrac{\partial \ell^s}{\partial w} & -\dfrac{\partial \ell^s}{\partial r} \end{bmatrix} \begin{bmatrix} \dfrac{dw}{d\nu} \\[4mm] \dfrac{dr}{d\nu} \end{bmatrix}$$
$$= \begin{bmatrix} \left(1 - \dfrac{\partial c^d}{\partial z}\right)\left(\dfrac{\partial \Phi}{\partial \nu} + \dfrac{\partial \Phi}{\partial \ell} \dfrac{\partial \ell^d}{\partial \nu}\right) \\[4mm] -\dfrac{\partial \ell^d}{\partial \nu} \end{bmatrix} \tag{5.5.8}$$

Use of Cramer's rule facilitates derivation of

$$\frac{dw}{d\nu} = \frac{1}{\Delta}\left[ -\left(1 - \frac{\partial c^d}{\partial z}\right)\frac{\partial \ell^s}{\partial r}\left(\frac{\partial \Phi}{\partial \nu} + \frac{\partial \Phi}{\partial \ell}\frac{\partial \ell^d}{\partial \nu}\right) + \frac{\partial i^d}{\partial r}\frac{\partial \ell^d}{\partial \nu}\right] > 0, \tag{5.5.9}$$

$$\frac{dr}{d\nu} = \frac{1}{\Delta}\left(1 - \frac{\partial c^d}{\partial z}\right)\left[\frac{\partial \ell^s}{\partial w}\left(\frac{\partial \Phi}{\partial \nu} + \frac{\partial \Phi}{\partial \ell}\frac{\partial \ell^d}{\partial \nu}\right) - \frac{\partial \ell^d}{\partial w}\frac{\partial \Phi}{\partial \nu}\right] < 0, \tag{5.5.10}$$

where

$$\Delta \equiv \left(1 - \frac{\partial c^d}{\partial z}\right)\left(\frac{\partial \Phi}{\partial \ell}\frac{\partial \ell^d}{\partial w}\frac{\partial \ell^s}{\partial r}\right) - \frac{\partial i^d}{\partial r}\left(\frac{\partial \ell^d}{\partial w} - \frac{\partial \ell^s}{\partial w}\right) < 0. \tag{5.5.11}$$

We therefore find that positive shocks to productivity lead to higher real wage rates and lower interest rates. We may further differentiate the production function and the labor demand function to obtain

$$\frac{d\ell}{d\nu} = \frac{\partial \ell^d}{\partial \nu} + \frac{\partial \ell^d}{\partial w}\frac{dw}{d\nu}, \tag{5.5.12}$$

$$\frac{dy}{d\nu} = \frac{\partial \Phi}{\partial \nu} + \frac{\partial \Phi}{\partial \ell}\left(\frac{\partial \ell^d}{\partial \nu} + \frac{\partial \ell^d}{\partial w}\frac{dw}{d\nu}\right). \tag{5.5.13}$$

Plugging in for $dw/d\nu$ and canceling some terms, we obtain

$$\frac{d\ell}{d\nu} = \frac{1}{\Delta}\left[\frac{\partial i^d}{\partial r}\frac{\partial \ell^s}{\partial w}\frac{\partial \ell^d}{\partial \nu} - \left(1 - \frac{\partial c^d}{\partial z}\right)\frac{\partial \ell^s}{\partial r}\frac{\partial \ell^d}{\partial w}\frac{\partial \Phi}{\partial \nu}\right], \tag{5.5.14}$$

$$\frac{dy}{d\nu} = \frac{\partial i^d/\partial r}{\Delta}\left[\frac{\partial \ell^s}{\partial w}\left(\frac{\partial \Phi}{\partial \nu} + \frac{\partial \Phi}{\partial \ell}\frac{\partial \ell^d}{\partial \nu}\right) - \frac{\partial \ell^d}{\partial w}\frac{\partial \Phi}{\partial \nu}\right] > 0. \tag{5.5.15}$$

We therefore find that a positive productivity shock unambiguously raises the level of output. This increase in output is not surprising. Since the interest rate unambiguously falls, investment must rise. Therefore, as long as the marginal propensity to consume is less than 1, the increase in investment demand can be matched by an increase in output supply above and beyond the induced increase in consumption demand only if the level of output rises.

The effect of the increase in $\nu$ on employment is, in general, ambiguous. However, as long as the increase in $\nu$ sufficiently increases the marginal product of labor, we find that an increase in employment is also possible. One case in which an increase in $\nu$ unambiguously increases employment is the case in which the supply of labor is independent of the rate of interest. Another case in which employment unambiguously rises is if the productivity shock changes only the marginal and not the average product of labor. In this case, while $\partial \ell^d / \partial \nu = -(\partial^2 \Phi / \partial \ell \partial \nu)/(\partial^2 \Phi / \partial \ell^2) > 0$, we now have $\partial \Phi / \partial \nu = 0$, and we therefore again find that $d\ell/d\nu > 0$.

Shocks to current labor productivity may therefore lead in the present model to coincident increases in employment, consumption, investment, output, employment, and the real wage. Furthermore, since in this example the level of income rises and the rate of interest falls, the demand for real money balances must rise. Therefore, either through this very simple mechanism or through more complicated mechanisms such as those proposed by King and Plosser (1984), we can also reconcile the observed positive correlation between real money balances and output as well. However, Barro and King (1982), among others, doubt the empirical relevance of the kinds of exogenous shifts to labor productivity necessary for this model to provide a reasonable description of actual economic events.

Throughout this example, we have abstracted from misinformation effects. However, at this point it is straightforward to see how the analysis would be affected by the possibility of incomplete information. In the absence of changes in the nominal money supply, since real money balances rise, the price level must fall. If this reduction in the price level were partially or completely unperceived, then the assumed increase in the level of employment would be mitigated. However, if the monetary authority were aware of the change in $\nu$, it could guarantee the full increase in employment by generating an increase in the nominal money supply of just the right magnitude to keep the actual (and expected) price level constant.

## Output Effects of Fiscal Policy

This section analyzes the effects of changes in government spending on the level of output. Sticky-price models like those of Chapter 3 always allow a strong channel of influence for changes in government spending to affect the levels of employment and output. However, many flexible-price models do not allow for such output effects of fiscal policy. In such models as the present analysis of Chapter 2, levels of employment and output are determined in an analytically separate labor market. As long as the real wage equilibrates labor supply and labor demand and as long as the labor supply function is independent of nominal disturbances, the equilibrium levels of employment and output are independent of the level of aggregate goods demand. Alternatively, the current model's recognition of the possibility of intertemporal substitution opportunities for labor suppliers opens the way for government spending to affect the levels of employment and output. As we demonstrate below, increases in government spending raise the interest rate and therefore generate incentives for increased current work effort.[7]

To formally analyze this effect, we retain the basic assumptions of the previous section. Since we again abstract from the possibility of shifts in the aggregate production function, we revert to our original notation of $y^s(w)$ for the level of production evaluated at the level of labor demand. The formal model is therefore given by

$$c^d[y^s(w) - \tau] + i^d(r) + g - y^s(w) = 0, \tag{5.5.16}$$

$$\ell^d(w) - \ell^s(w, r) = 0. \tag{5.5.17}$$

In order to avoid questions of whether the form of government finance of changes in government spending significantly affects the economy, we consider the least theoretically ambiguous case of a balanced-budget increase in government spending. Differentiating the above equilibrium conditions with respect to $w$, $r$, $g$, and $\tau$ and setting $dg = d\tau$, we obtain

$$\begin{bmatrix} -\left(1 - \dfrac{\partial c^d}{\partial z}\right)\dfrac{\partial y^s}{\partial w} & \dfrac{\partial i^d}{\partial r} \\[2ex] \dfrac{\partial \ell^d}{\partial w} - \dfrac{\partial \ell^s}{\partial w} & -\dfrac{\partial \ell^s}{\partial r} \end{bmatrix} \begin{bmatrix} \dfrac{dw}{dg} \\[2ex] \dfrac{dr}{dg} \end{bmatrix} = \begin{bmatrix} -\left(1 - \dfrac{\partial c^d}{\partial z}\right) \\[2ex] 0 \end{bmatrix} \tag{5.5.18}$$

Solving by Cramer's rule, we obtain

$$\frac{dw}{dg}\bigg|_{dg=d\tau} = \frac{1}{\Delta}\left(1 - \frac{\partial c^d}{\partial z}\right)\frac{\partial \ell^s}{\partial r} < 0, \tag{5.5.19}$$

$$\frac{dr}{dg}\bigg|_{dg=d\tau} = \frac{1}{\Delta}\left(1 - \frac{\partial c^d}{\partial z}\right)\left(\frac{\partial \ell^d}{\partial w} - \frac{\partial \ell^s}{\partial w}\right) > 0, \tag{5.5.20}$$

where

$$\Delta \equiv \left(1 - \frac{\partial c^d}{\partial z}\right)\frac{\partial \ell^s}{\partial r}\frac{\partial y^s}{\partial w} - \frac{\partial i^d}{\partial r}\left(\frac{\partial \ell^d}{\partial w} - \frac{\partial \ell^s}{\partial w}\right) < 0. \tag{5.5.21}$$

We therefore find that a balanced-budget increase in government spending unambiguously lowers the real wage and raises the interest rate. Since the real wage falls and the production function is unchanged, we also know that the levels of employment and output must both rise.

Since in this example we have assumed that the nominal money supply is kept constant, it is straightforward to analyze the effect of the increase in government spending on the level of prices. Differentiating the money market equilibrium condition, holding

---

[7]This analysis follows closely those of Hall (1980) and Barro (1981).

$dM = 0$, and rearranging, we obtain

$$\left.\frac{dP}{dg}\right|_{dg=d\tau} = -\frac{P^2}{M}\frac{1}{\Delta}\left(1 - \frac{\partial c^d}{\partial z}\right)$$

$$\times \left[\frac{\partial(M/P)^d}{\partial y}\frac{\partial y^s}{\partial w}\frac{\partial \ell^s}{\partial r} + \frac{\partial(M/P)^d}{\partial r}\left(\frac{\partial \ell^d}{\partial w} - \frac{\partial \ell^s}{\partial w}\right)\right]. \tag{5.5.22}$$

We therefore find that the effect of a balanced-budget increase in government spending on the level of prices is ambiguous. However, as long as the responsiveness of the supply of labor to the rate of interest is small, it is likely that an increase in government spending will raise prices. If prices do rise and if there is a wealth effect in the supply of labor, then the wealth effect enhances the employment- and output-increasing effects of the increase in government spending.

Although Barro's (1981) analysis demonstrates empirical support for positive output effects of both temporary and permanent increases in government spending, we must echo the same words of warning we voiced about the monetary effects of Sections 5.2–5.4. Government-spending-generated increases in output come about only through a reduction in the real wage and a subsequent increase in the demand for labor. However, as noted above, real wage rates are strongly procyclical. Furthermore, most studies of the consumption function confirm a strong positive correlation between the levels of consumption spending and output. Totally differentiating the consumption function with respect to the balanced-budget increase in government spending, we find

$$\left.\frac{dc^d}{dg}\right|_{dg=d\tau} = \frac{1}{\Delta}\frac{\partial c^d}{\partial z}\frac{\partial i^d}{\partial r}\left(\frac{\partial \ell^d}{\partial w} - \frac{\partial \ell^s}{\partial w}\right) < 0. \tag{5.5.23}$$

Therefore, we find that the present model predicts a negative effect of increases in the level of government spending on consumption. Furthermore, since increases in $g$ raise interest rates, we also know that such increases in $g$ must result in lower investment spending. However, the level of investment spending is also conceded to be positively correlated with the levels of employment and output. We therefore see that if fluctuations in government spending are the principal cause of business cycle movements in aggregate output, then the mechanisms by which such fluctuations in government spending influence aggregate output must be more complex than those captured by the admittedly very simple model presented here.

## 5.6 THE AGGREGATE SUPPLY–AGGREGATE DEMAND FRAMEWORK

Most of the analysis in this chapter has focused on the determination of the relative price variables $w$ and $r$. However, many macroeconomic analysts are more interested in the implications of exogenous disturbances and changes in government policies on the levels of output $y$ and prices $P$. The aggregate supply–aggregate demand framework is very useful for this purpose as it embodies $y$ and $P$ as its primary endogenous variables.

The basic modeling strategy of this framework is to construct two semireduced forms in $y$ and $P$ that then may be used to simultaneously determine the equilibrium levels of these two variables. One equation in $y$ and $P$ comes from the demand side of the model, in particular the goods and money market equilibrium conditions. In most of our preceding models these equilibrium conditions are given by

$$c^d(y - \tau) + i^d(r) + g - y = 0, \tag{5.6.1}$$

$$\left(\frac{M}{P}\right)^d (y, r) - \frac{M}{P} = 0. \tag{5.6.2}$$

Differentiating with respect to $y$, $P$, $r$, $M$, $g$, and $\tau$, we obtain

$$-\left(1 - \frac{\partial c^d}{\partial z}\right) dy + \frac{\partial i^d}{\partial r} dr - \frac{\partial c^d}{\partial z} d\tau + dg = 0, \tag{5.6.3}$$

$$\frac{\partial (M/P)^d}{\partial y} dy + \frac{\partial (M/P)^d}{\partial r} dr - \frac{1}{P} dM + \frac{M}{P^2} dP = 0. \tag{5.6.4}$$

Substituting for $dr$ yields

$$y^d = y^d(P, g, \tau, M), \tag{5.6.5}$$

where

$$\frac{\partial y^d}{\partial P} = \frac{1}{\Delta} \frac{M}{P^2} \frac{\partial i^d}{\partial r} < 0, \tag{5.6.6}$$

$$\frac{\partial y^d}{\partial g} = -\frac{1}{\Delta} \frac{\partial (M/P)^d}{\partial r} > 0, \tag{5.6.7}$$

$$\frac{\partial y^d}{\partial \tau} = \frac{1}{\Delta} \frac{\partial c^d}{\partial z} \frac{\partial (M/P)^d}{\partial r} < 0, \tag{5.6.8}$$

$$\frac{\partial y^d}{\partial M} = \frac{1}{\Delta} \frac{1}{P} \frac{\partial i^d}{\partial r} > 0, \tag{5.6.9}$$

where

$$\Delta \equiv -\left[\left(1 - \frac{\partial c^d}{\partial z}\right) \frac{\partial (M/P)^d}{\partial r} + \frac{\partial i^d}{\partial r} \frac{\partial (M/P)^d}{\partial y}\right] < 0. \tag{5.6.10}$$

The negative effect of a change in $P$ on $y^d$ comes from the following chain of causation. An increase in $P$ lowers the level of real money balances $M/P$. Money market equilibrium therefore requires a higher interest rate $r$. The higher interest rate causes a multiple contraction of output demand as investment demand and consumption demand both fall and output must also fall to keep output and aggregate demand equal. This chain of events closely follows the analysis of Chapter 3.

Let us now turn our attention to the aggregate supply side of the model. We again wish to construct a semireduced form equation in $y$ and $P$. However, such a relationship must be independent of any variables that have already been eliminated in the analysis of aggregate demand. In particular, the aggregate supply portion of the model must be independent of the interest rate $r$. This is so because the aggregate supply–aggregate demand framework is set up so that the equilibrium value of $r$ can only be identified after the analysis has been completed. Therefore, models that employ interest rate effects in labor supply cannot be analyzed with traditional aggregate supply–aggregate demand tools.

With this caveat in mind, we can now compute the aggregate supply curves for the models of Sections 5.2, 5.3, and 5.5 under the assumption of no interest rate effects on labor supply. The following analyses are all straightforward. In each case we simply solve out for the equilibrium real wage rate from the labor market equilibrium condition. We therefore obtain:

### The Incomplete Information Model

Solving

$$\ell^d(w) - \ell^s\left(w, \frac{P}{P^e}\right) = 0, \tag{5.6.11}$$

$$y - \Phi[\ell^d(w), \overline{K}] = 0, \tag{5.6.12}$$

we obtain

$$y^s = y^s(P, P^e), \tag{5.6.13}$$

$$\frac{\partial y^s}{\partial P} = \frac{\dfrac{\partial \Phi}{\partial \ell} \dfrac{\partial \ell^d}{\partial w} \dfrac{\partial \ell^s}{\partial (P/P^e)}}{P^e\left(\dfrac{\partial \ell^d}{\partial w} - \dfrac{\partial \ell^s}{\partial w}\right)} > 0, \tag{5.6.14}$$

$$\frac{\partial y^s}{\partial P^e} = \frac{-\dfrac{P}{P^e} \dfrac{\partial \Phi}{\partial \ell} \dfrac{\partial \ell^d}{\partial w} \dfrac{\partial \ell^s}{\partial (P/P^e)}}{P^e\left(\dfrac{\partial \ell^d}{\partial w} - \dfrac{\partial \ell^s}{\partial w}\right)} < 0. \tag{5.6.15}$$

### The Fixed Nominal Wage Model

Solving

$$y - \Phi\left[\ell^d\left(\frac{\overline{W}}{P}\right), \overline{K}\right] = 0, \tag{5.6.16}$$

we obtain

$$y^s = y^s(P, \overline{W}), \tag{5.6.17}$$

$$\frac{\partial y^s}{\partial P} = -\frac{\overline{W}}{P^2} \frac{\partial \Phi}{\partial \ell} \frac{\partial \ell^d}{\partial w} > 0, \tag{5.6.18}$$

$$\frac{\partial y^s}{\partial \overline{W}} = \frac{1}{P} \frac{\partial \Phi}{\partial \ell} \frac{\partial \ell^d}{\partial w} < 0. \tag{5.6.19}$$

### The Equilibrium Model

Solving

$$y - \Phi[\ell^d(w, \nu), \nu, \overline{K}] = 0, \tag{5.6.20}$$

$$\ell^d(w, \nu) - \ell^s(w) = 0, \tag{5.6.21}$$

we obtain

$$y^s = y^s(P, \nu), \tag{5.6.22}$$

$$\frac{\partial y^s}{\partial P} = 0, \tag{5.6.23}$$

$$\frac{\partial y^s}{\partial \nu} = \frac{\dfrac{\partial \Phi}{\partial \nu} \dfrac{\partial \ell^d}{\partial w} - \dfrac{\partial \ell^s}{\partial w}\left(\dfrac{\partial \Phi}{\partial \nu} + \dfrac{\partial \Phi}{\partial \ell} \dfrac{\partial \ell^d}{\partial \nu}\right)}{\dfrac{\partial \ell^d}{\partial w} - \dfrac{\partial \ell^s}{\partial w}} > 0. \tag{5.6.24}$$

We therefore see that the aggregate supply–aggregate demand framework consists in $P$, $y$ space of a downward-sloping aggregate demand curve and an upward-sloping (or vertical) aggregate supply curve. The aggregate supply–aggregate demand equilibrium is depicted in Figure 5.6.

The usefulness of the aggregate supply–aggregate demand framework may be demonstrated by reviewing our analysis of the effects of an unanticipated change in the money supply on the levels of output and prices in the three models. With labor supply independent of the rate of interest, the impact of changes in the money supply falls entirely on the demand side of the model. Holding $P$ fixed, we obtain from above

$$\left.\frac{dy^d}{dM}\right|_{dP=0} = -\frac{1}{\Delta}\frac{1}{P}\frac{\partial i^d}{\partial r} > 0. \tag{5.6.25}$$

This expression gives the extent of the horizontal shift in the aggregate demand schedule. The reader may remember that the above expression is exactly the same as the expression for the effect of an increase in the money supply on the level of output in the corresponding fixed-price model of Chapter 3. With the price level fixed at $P_0$ as in Figure 5.6, the level of output consistent with equality of output and aggregate demand is $y_1$. However, taking into account the interaction of aggregate supply and aggregate demand, the equilibrium effect of an increase in $M$ in the incomplete information and fixed-wage models is an increase in $y$ to only $y_2$ with a coincident rise in the price level to $P_2$.

We now proceed in turn to an interpretation of the equilibrium effects of the increase in $M$ in the three models. Let us first begin with the incomplete information model. Starting at $P_0$, $y_0$, the increase in the money supply generates an increase in aggregate demand, which, at $P_0$, implies a state of excess aggregate demand. However, at the initial real wage, firms are unwilling to hire more workers and expand output. Instead, the excess aggregate demand results in an increase in the price level. This increase in prices is not, however, immediately perceived by workers. While the higher price level causes workers to demand a higher *nominal* wage in exchange for working the same number of

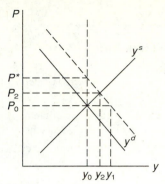

**Figure 5.6**

hours, these same workers turn out to be willing to work more hours at a lower *real* wage. Nominal wages and prices both rise, but wages rise less than in proportion to the increase in prices. Firms observe that actual real wages have declined. Workers believe that real wages have risen. Therefore, both labor demand and labor supply increase. Employment and output both expand.

If firms were willing to supply an unlimited amount of output at $P_0$, then output would expand all the way to $y_1$. However, firms are only willing to expand output if the price level rises and real wages fall. The resulting increase in price reduces demand relative to what it would have been and output only rises to $y_2$. The extent of the equilibrium increase in output depends on the slopes of the aggregate demand and aggregate supply curves.

In macroeconomics, there is a standard presumption that more employment and output is preferred to less. However, in the current example employment and output only expand because workers are fooled into working more hours at a lower real wage rate. Movements in output in this model in either direction from the level that corresponds to full information are likely to result in reduced welfare.

Next consider the case of an increase in the money supply in the fixed nominal wage model. Starting at $P_0$, $y_0$, the increase in the money supply causes a rightward shift in the aggregate demand curve, just as in the incomplete information model. At $P_0$ goods demand exceeds goods supply but firms are again unwilling to hire more workers and expand production. Prices then rise in response to the increase in demand. However, with rigid wages and higher prices, real wages are lower. Therefore, as long as employment is demand determined, firms hire more workers and output expands. With the increase in prices, demand falls somewhat from its peak level of $y_1$. Equilibrium is again attained at $P_2$, $y_2$.

Finally, consider the effects of an increase in the money supply in the equilibrium model. We again begin with a situation of excess aggregate demand. However, in this case the aggregate supply schedule is vertical at $y_0$. Therefore, wages and prices both continue to be bid upward until $W$ and $P$ both rise equiproportional to the original increase in $M$. The real wage and the levels of employment and output are all unchanged from their initial values. In Figure 5.6, equilibrium is reached at $y_0$, $P^*$. Money is neutral in this case.

# REFERENCES

Altonji, Joseph G., "Intertemporal Substitution in Labor Supply," *Journal of Political Economy*, June, 1986, Part 2, S176–215.

Barro, Robert J., "Output Effects of Government Purchases," *Journal of Political Economy*, December, 1981, 1086–1121.

Barro, Robert J., and Robert G. King, "Time-Separable Preferences and Intertemporal Substitution Models of Business Cycles," *Quarterly Journal of Economics*, November, 1982, 817–839.

Bils, Mark J., "Real Wages Over the Business Cycle: Evidence from Panel Data," *Journal of Political Economy*, August, 1985, 666–689.

Bodkin, Ronald G., "Real Wages and Cyclical Variations in Employment: A Reexamination of the Evidence," *Canadian Journal of Economics*, August, 1969, 353–374.

Friedman, Milton, and Anna Jacobson Schwartz, *A Monetary History of the United States 1867–1960*, Princeton, NJ, Princeton University Press, 1963.

Grossman, Herschel I., "Aggregate Demand, Job Search and Employment," *Journal of Political Economy*, November/December, 1973, 1353–1369.

Hall, Robert E., "Labor Supply and Aggregate Fluctuations," *Carnegie Rochester Series in Public Policy*, Amsterdam, North Holland, Spring, 1980, 7–33.

King, Robert G., and Charles I. Plosser, "The Behavior of Money, Credit and Prices in a Real Business Cycle," *American Economic Review*, June, 1984, 363–380.

Kuh, Edwin, "Unemployment, Production Functions, and Effective Demand," *Journal of Political Economy*, June, 1966, 238–249.

Kydland, Finn E., and Edward C. Prescott, "Time to Build and Aggregate Fluctuations," *Econometrica*, November, 1982, 1345–1370.

Long, John B., Jr., and Charles I. Plosser, "Real Business Cycles," *Journal of Political Economy*, February, 1983, 39–69.

Lucas, Robert E., Jr., and Leonard A. Rapping, "Real Wages, Employment, and Inflation," *Journal of Political Economy*, September/October, 1969, 721–754.

Lucas, Robert E., Jr., "Some International Evidence on Output-Inflation Tradeoffs," *American Economic Review*, June, 1973, 326–334.

McCurdy, Thomas E., "An Empirical Model of Labor Supply in a Life-Cycle Setting," *Journal of Political Economy*, December, 1981, 1059–1085.

Merrick, John J., Jr., "The Anticipated Real Interest Rate, Capital Utilization and the Cyclical Pattern of Real Wages," *Journal of Monetary Economics*, January, 1984, 17–30.

# Chapter **6**

## Inflation and Inflationary Expectations

Chapter 2 presents a model of the determination of the aggregate price level. In that model, changes in the exogenous variables generate once-and-for-all step changes in the price level. Although we acknowledged that sustained growth in the money supply or sustained growth in the number of government bonds outstanding would generate continual increases in the price level, there was at that time no formal analysis of inflation. We now define the *rate of inflation* as the percentage rate of change in prices over time. That is,

$$\pi \equiv \text{rate of inflation} \equiv \frac{1}{P} \frac{dP}{dt}. \qquad (6.0.1)$$

Much of this chapter centers around analyses of the determination of the rate of inflation.

In the course of our study of the actual rate of inflation, we also often have need to refer to the expected rate of inflation. Although a full description of any agent's expectations about the future course of inflation necessitates a listing of his or her expectations of the price level and its rate of change at every future instant of time, normally we neither need nor could handle, such a rich menu of possibilities. We therefore generally adopt the analytically more tractable assumption that agents expect the price level to rise at a constant percentage rate into the indefinite future. We denote the rate of such expected future inflation, or more simply the *expected rate of inflation,* as $\pi^e$. In much of what follows, we treat $\pi^e$ as exogenous, although we later present theories of the formation of inflationary expectations.

At a very superficial level, the environment in which agents engage in economic activity is clearly different at nonzero rates of inflation. In inflationary periods, prices quoted in the unit of account are routinely different at different points in time. However, a fundamental question of this chapter is the extent to which such differences are illusory or whether different rates of inflation generate different patterns of resource allocation.

One obvious way in which inflation might not be neutral in its effects is that changes in the rate of inflation might generate changes in the intertemporal terms of trade. Economist Irving Fisher argued that as long as borrowers and lenders could agree on the likely future course of inflation, they would simply agree to add an inflation premium to the interest rate paid by the borrower. This notion is formalized in the *Fisher hypothesis,* which states that nominal interest rates adjust one-for-one with perfectly anticipated, permanent changes in the rate of inflation.[1] Much of this chapter centers on sorting out those sets of assumptions under which the Fisher hypothesis does and does not hold.

The organization of this chapter is as follows. Section 6.1 introduces the concepts of inflation and inflationary expectations and presents the differential equation form of the quantity theory of money. Section 6.2 performs those alterations in the basic flexible price model that are required in an inflationary environment. Section 6.3 computes the dynamic adjustment paths of the endogenous variables when expectations of inflation are formed adaptively. Section 6.4 presents a formal dynamic analysis of the effects of policy changes that affect the underlying rate of inflation in a model without wealth effects, and Section 6.5 investigates the ways in which the presence of wealth effects changes some of the basic results. Finally, Appendix 6.A generalizes the choice-theoretic analyses of Appendices 1.B and 1.C to the case of a constant but nonzero expected rate of inflation.

# 6.1 INTRODUCTION TO INFLATION AND INFLATIONARY EXPECTATIONS

This section first recomputes equilibrium asset prices when asset market participants share common expectations of a nonzero rate of inflation. Based upon the implied movements of asset prices over time, we next generate a natural definition of the expected real rate of interest. Finally, as a prelude to more elaborate formal theories of the determination of the equilibrium rate of inflation, we study inflation rate determination in a simple version of the quantity theory of money.

## Interest Rates, Asset Yields, and Expected Inflation

Although several important modifications to the basic flexible-price model need to be made before we can properly analyze inflation, we can only understand these modifications after we have mastered the distinction between the nominal interest rate and the expected real interest rate. To get a handle on this distinction, we first return to the discussion of Chapter 1 of earning asset price determination.

In Chapter 1, we formally considered the case in which all agents unanimously hold expectations of a permanently constant price level and a permanently constant nominal interest rate. Obviously, consideration of the possibility of continual inflation requires a

---

[1] See Fisher (1930). Fama (1975) provides evidence strongly supportive of the Fisher hypothesis. Levi and Makin (1978) find support for an appropriately modified form of the Fisher hypothesis. Alternatively, evidence presented by Summers (1983) casts significant doubt on the overall usefulness of the Fisher hypothesis as a framework for predicting long-term movements in nominal interest rates. LeRoy (1984a,b) provides a good modern theoretical treatment of issues relating to the Fisher hypothesis.

change in this basic setup. While we continue to assume that all agents expect a constant (nominal) interest rate, we now assume that all agents expect a constant inflation rate instead of a constant price level.

With these assumptions about agents' expectations, the price of a government bond, a perpetuity paying the bearer a continuous stream of interest payments equal to \$1 per year forever, is still given by

$$P_b(t) = \int_t^\infty (\$1)e^{-r(s-t)} \, ds = \frac{\$1}{r}. \tag{6.1.1}$$

Define a bond's *current yield* as the ratio of its annual interest payment(s) to its market price. The current yield on government-issued perpetuities is therefore equal to the nominal interest rate. However, in an inflationary environment, the current yield is a particularly poor indicator of the absolute attractiveness of holding such a bond. We therefore seek to define a measure of bond performance that is inflation neutral. Such a measure is the expected real rate of return or the expected real rate of interest.

In order to adjust the current yield on a perpetuity to reflect the likely impact of future inflation, we need to take into account agents' expectations of future changes in purchasing power. The current market value of a perpetuity in terms of purchasing power is equal to $P_b/P = 1/rP$. Inspection of the formula for the price of a perpetuity, above, reveals that as long as the nominal interest rate $r$ is expected to remain constant over time, the nominal market price of the perpetuity is also expected to remain constant over time. Therefore, if inflation is expected to proceed at an annual rate $\pi^e$, then the percentage rate of change in the real market value of the perpetuity is expected to be given by

$$\frac{1}{P_b/P} \frac{d(P_b/P)}{dt} = \frac{P}{P_b}\left(\frac{1}{P}\frac{dP_b}{dt} - \frac{P_b}{P^2}\frac{dP}{dt}\right) = -\frac{1}{P}\frac{dP}{dt} = -\pi^e. \tag{6.1.2}$$

The expected real rate of return on a perpetuity must therefore include not only the current yield $r$ but also this additional term to reflect the expected rate of depreciation of the purchasing power inherent in the bond's market price. The expected real rate of return on the perpetuity will therefore be given by

Expected real rate of return on perpetuities = $r - \pi^e$. (6.1.3)

The expected real return on bonds is also referred to as the expected real rate of interest. The *expected real rate of interest* therefore equals the nominal rate of interest minus the expected rate of inflation. That is,

Expected real rate of interest $\equiv \rho \equiv r - \pi^e$. (6.1.4)

We continue to assume that asset market participants view government-issued perpetuities and equities as perfect substitutes. Agents are therefore indifferent to holding either bonds or equities as long as their nominal prices equal the present value of their nominal interest or dividend streams discounted at the nominal interest rate $r$. The price of an equity must therefore be given by

$$P_e(t) = \frac{1}{E} \int_t^\infty P(s)\Pi(s)e^{-r(s-t)} \, ds, \tag{6.1.5}$$

where $\Pi(s)$ denotes the expected future stream of real firm dividend payments and $P(s)$ denotes the expected future price of goods, both written as functions of the time index $s$.

While the formula for the market price of an equity is unchanged from our earlier analysis, we must now carefully consider how expectations of inflation may affect agents' expectations of how $P$ and $\Pi$ are likely to evolve over time. We have already assumed that agents expect inflation in the price of goods $P$ to proceed at the constant rate $\pi^e$ into the indefinite future. That is, agents expect future prices to be given by

$$P(s) = P(t)e^{\pi^e(s-t)} \quad \text{for all } s > t. \tag{6.1.6}$$

However, absent some fairly elaborate theory of inflationary distortions, it is likely that at first approximation agents expect real firm dividend payments (profits) to be independent of the rate of inflation. Therefore, ignoring future changes in the capital stock and assuming that agents expect no future changes in relative prices, agents expect $\Pi$ to remain constant over time. Recall that the analysis of Chapter 1 of equity prices in a noninflationary environment also assumes a constant value for agents' expectations of future real profits. Our expression above for the price of an equity can now be evaluated as

$$
\begin{aligned}
P_e(t) &= \frac{1}{E} \int_t^\infty P(t)e^{\pi^e(s-t)}\Pi e^{-r(s-t)} \, ds \\[2mm]
&= \frac{P(t)\Pi}{E} \int_t^\infty e^{-(r-\pi^e)(s-t)} \, ds = \frac{P(t)\Pi}{(r-\pi^e)E}.
\end{aligned}
\tag{6.1.7}
$$

As a check, we wish to verify that the properly defined expected real rate of return on equities equals the expected real rate of return on bonds, $r - \pi^e$. The current yield on equities equals the level of nominal dividends per share (profit per share) divided by the current nominal share price. That is,

$$\text{Current yield on equities} = \frac{P(t)\Pi/E}{P(t)\Pi/(r-\pi^e)E} = r - \pi^e. \tag{6.1.8}$$

As with government-issued perpetuities, the expected real rate of return on an equity share includes not only the current yield but also a term to reflect the expected rate of depreciation in the purchasing power implicit in the market price of the equity share. The real value (price) of an equity share is given by

$$\frac{P_e(t)}{P(t)} = \frac{\Pi}{(r-\pi^e)E}. \tag{6.1.9}$$

Since agents expect a constant nominal rate of interest, a constant rate of inflation, and a constant real dividend stream, agents must also expect a constant real equity price. Therefore, the adjustment to the current yield on equities to reflect expected future changes in purchasing power is zero, and the real rate of return on equities must be given by $r - \pi^e$, which is in fact equal to the expected real rate of return on government-issued perpetuities derived above.

We can also compute the expected nominal rate of return on equities. The expected nominal rate of return on equities equals the current yield plus the expected rate of change in the nominal share price $P_e$. The nominal price of an equity share is given by $P_e(t) =$

$P(t)[\Pi/(r - \pi^e)E]$. Therefore, consistent with our set of assumptions about agents' expectations, the expected rate of change of the nominal price of an equity share must equal the expected rate of inflation. Adding the expected rate of inflation to the current yield on equities, we find that the expected nominal rate of return on equities is equal to $r$, the nominal rate of return on government bonds.

In an inflationary environment, not only must the current nominal prices of equities and bonds be in proper relationship to one another for agents to willingly hold both in their portfolios but the expected future time paths $P_e(t)$ and $P_b(t)$ must also be in proper balance. Nominal equity prices are expected to rise over time while real equity prices are expected to remain constant. Nominal bond prices are expected to remain constant while real bond prices are expected to fall over time. The current market prices of each adjust so that their expected nominal and expected real rates of return are equalized. The necessary relationships are summarized in the table below and in Figure 6.1. Figure 6.1 is drawn under the assumption that the number of equity shares $E$ is equal to $rP(0)\Pi/(r - \pi^e)$. This value for the otherwise arbitrary number of equity shares is chosen to make $P_b(0) = P_e(0)$ simply for ease of comparison.

| | Nominal price | Real value | Current yield | Nominal return | Real return |
|---|---|---|---|---|---|
| Bond | $P_b = \dfrac{1}{r}$ | $\dfrac{1/r}{P(t)}$ | $r$ | $r$ | $r - \pi^e$ |
| Equity | $P_e = \dfrac{P(t)\Pi}{(r - \pi^e)E}$ | $\dfrac{\Pi}{(r - \pi^e)E}$ | $r - \pi^e$ | $r$ | $r - \pi^e$ |

We can gain some additional insight into the distinction between the nominal interest rate and the expected real rate of interest by considering the following simple example. If the loan is made for $\$V_0$ today, its repayment at time $T$ with continuous compounding at a nominal interest rate of $r$ must be

$$\$V_T = \$V_0 e^{rT}. \tag{6.1.10}$$

Suppose prices are expected to rise at a rate of $\pi^e$ per year over the course of the loan. The real value of the repayment is then expected to be given by

$$\text{Expected real repayment} = \frac{\$V_T}{P(T)} = \frac{\$V_T}{P(0)e^{\pi^e t}}. \tag{6.1.11}$$

Dividing the first equation above through by $P(0)e^{\pi^e T}$, we obtain

$$\frac{\$V_T}{P(0)e^{\pi^e t}} = \frac{\$V_0 e^{rT}}{P(0)e^{\pi^e t}} = \frac{\$V_0}{P(0)} e^{rT} e^{-\pi^e T} \tag{6.1.12}$$

or

$$\frac{\$V_T}{P(T)} = \frac{\$V_0}{P(0)} e^{(r - \pi^e)T} \equiv \frac{\$V_0}{P(0)} e^{\rho T}. \tag{6.1.13}$$

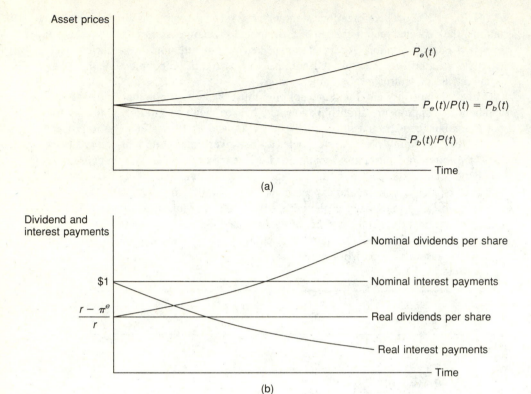

**Figure 6.1**

Since $\$V_0/P(0)$ is just the original real value of the amount of money first lent, it is sensible to define $\rho$ as the expected real rate of interest. The expected real rate of interest therefore denotes the anticipated real return in terms of command over goods from making the loan. Note that this definition of the expected real rate of interest is algebraically identical to the one given above.

The Fisher hypothesis, as stated above, requires that the nominal rate of interest adjust one-for-one with changes in the correctly anticipated rate of inflation. Our current discussion demonstrates that the Fisher hypothesis also implies that the expected real rate of interest be independent of the expected rate of inflation. The price of current consumption in terms of future consumption is 1 plus the expected real rate of interest. Therefore, if the Fisher hypothesis is correct, the intertemporal terms of trade are independent of the expected rate of inflation.

## The Simple Quantity Theory and Inflation

While we have said a great deal so far about the implications of nonzero expected rates of inflation, we have said much less about the causes of inflation. An inflationary situation cannot arise and perpetuate itself indefinitely without corresponding increases in the nominal quantity of money. The quantity theory of money provides a very simple and yet very accurate portrayal of the basic forces needed to generate persistent inflation. The quantity theory of money is based on the following assumptions:

1. The level of output is approximately equal to its equilibrium, or market-clearing, value.
2. The money demand function is stable.
3. Price adjustment is consistent with equality between money demand and money supply.

For now, let us assume that the nominal rate of interest is constant over time so that we may properly suppress $r$ as an argument of the money demand function. Let us also abstract from wealth effects and other subtleties of the specification of money demand. We therefore denote the stock demand for money as

$$\text{Real money demand} = \left(\frac{M}{P}\right)^d (y). \tag{6.1.14}$$

In equilibrium we would expect adjustment of desired to actual money balances to be complete, and so we now consider the limiting case of $\xi_m \to \infty$. We also continue to denote the equilibrium level of output by $y^*$. The quantity theory of money is therefore characterized by

$$\frac{M}{P} = \left(\frac{M}{P}\right)^d (y^*). \tag{6.1.15}$$

Differentiation of the above equation with respect to time yields

$$\frac{1}{P}\frac{dM}{dt} - \frac{M}{P^2}\frac{dP}{dt} = \frac{\partial (M/P)^d(y^*)}{\partial y^*}\frac{dy^*}{dt}. \tag{6.1.16}$$

We can rearrange the above equation as

$$\frac{1}{M}\frac{dM}{dt} = \frac{1}{P}\frac{dP}{dt} + \frac{1}{M/P}\frac{\partial (M/P)^d}{\partial y^*}\frac{dy^*}{dt}; \tag{6.1.17}$$

that is, growth in the money supply will be divided between increases in prices and increases in the demand for money due to growth in income over time. We can also write this equation as

$$\frac{1}{P}\frac{dP}{dt} = \frac{1}{M}\frac{dM}{dt} - \frac{1}{M/P}\frac{\partial (M/P)^d}{\partial y}\frac{dy^*}{dt}. \tag{6.1.18}$$

In long-run equilibrium, growth in the money supply in excess of the rate of growth of money demand will show up as inflation. While the above equation for the rate of inflation does not hold precisely on a day-to-day or even a year-to-year basis, over longer time periods the quantity theory of money provides a good accounting of the most important determinants of the rate of inflation.

# 6.2 INFLATIONARY EXPECTATIONS IN THE BASIC FLEXIBLE-PRICE MODEL

This section performs those alterations to the flexible-price model of Chapter 2 to take into account agents' expectations of nonzero rates of inflation. As we shall see, modifications are definitely needed in the investment demand and equity supply functions and the formulation for disposable income. We further consider whether changes are needed in the money demand function and whether adoption of an alternative specification of the government budget constraint may significantly economize on later algebraic manipulations.

## Expectations and Investment

A prime impact of changes in inflationary expectations on market behavior is likely to be felt on firm investment demand and therefore equity supply. It turns out that the representative firm's maximization problem in the case in which wages and prices are expected to rise at a constant percentage rate is formally almost identical to the representative firm's maximization problem in the case in which wages and prices are expected to remain constant. The only difference in an inflationary environment is that investment demand and equity supply are inversely related to the expected real rate of interest instead of the nominal rate of interest.

A formal derivation of the result that investment demand should depend upon the expected real rate of interest is presented in Appendix 6.A. However, we can get some insight into the intuition behind this result by considering the following thought experiment. Suppose that the expected rate of inflation rises and the nominal rate of interest remains constant. Obviously, this series of events implies a lower expected real rate of interest. With no change in the nominal interest rate, the number of dollars the representative firm would have to promise to pay to potential new equity holders would be unchanged. However, the number of dollars in profits generated by an investment expenditure would be expected to grow over time at the expected rate of inflation. Therefore, investment projects that originally may have been marginally unprofitable would now be marginally profitable and would therefore be undertaken. A fall in the expected real rate of interest stimulates investment spending even if the nominal rate of interest remains constant. We therefore summarize by assuming that

$$i^d = i^d(r - \pi^e) = i^d(\rho) = \dot{e}^s(\rho), \qquad \frac{\partial i^d}{\partial \rho} < 0. \tag{6.2.1}$$

## Expectations and Household Portfolio Behavior

In contrast to firms' incentives to acquire capital, households' incentives to hold earning assets instead of money are unaffected by changes in inflationary expectations. For a given level of the nominal rate of interest, an increase in inflationary expectations reduces the expected real rate of return to holding *both* money and earning assets. Because we continue to assume that all market participants share common expectations and view bonds and equities offering return packages of equal present value as perfect substitutes, both bonds and equities share common expected rates of return. The nominal rate of return on both equities and bonds is $r$, and the expected real rate of return on both equities and bonds is $\rho = r - \pi^e$. Money earns a nominal pecuniary rate of return of zero. The expected real pecuniary rate of return to holding money is minus the expected rate of inflation. Therefore, the difference between the common nominal (or real) expected rate of return on holding earning assets and the nominal (or real) expected rate of return on holding money is equal to the nominal interest rate. We therefore continue to assume that money demand and earning asset demand depend upon the nominal interest rate $r$[2].

## Anticipated Capital Losses to Inflation

Over time agents expect to suffer capital losses on money and government bonds due to inflation since the real values of both assets are expected to decline at a rate $\pi^e$. Alternatively, nominal equity prices are expected to rise over time and keep pace with inflation, and therefore agents expect neither capital gains nor losses in real terms on their holdings of equities. Market prices already reflect this difference in characteristics between equities and government-issued bonds, and holders of government bonds therefore need no further compensation for holding them even though they unanimously share expectations that suggest that their real value will decline over time.

However, in an inflationary environment, holders of money and government bonds realize that a part of disposable income must be earmarked for replenishing these holdings of money and government bonds just to keep their real value constant. Only such replenishment through current saving will enable households' holdings of money and government bonds to grow or at least remain constant in real terms over time. The net income expected to be available to households to allocate to consumption and augmenting their real wealth will therefore be given by their total income minus taxes minus the amount needed to keep their money and government bond holdings constant in real terms. Therefore, the proper measure of real disposable income in an inflationary economy is expected disposable income, which is given by[3]

$$z = y + \frac{B}{P} - \tau - \left( \frac{M}{P} + \frac{B}{rP} \right) \pi^e. \tag{6.2.2}$$

The fact that the current yield on government bonds exceeds the current yield on equities by the differential $\pi^e$ suggests a natural source of funds to replenish the inflationary losses on government bonds. However, because money earns no interest, inflationary losses on money holdings must be financed out of other income sources. That base money generally does not pay an inflation premium is the source of an important social cost of inflation.

---

[2] Appendix 6.A formally demonstrates that the demand for money is inversely related to the nominal rate of interest rather than the expected real rate of interest.

[3] Sargent (1987, Ch. 1) proposes a similar measure of disposable income. This measure of disposable income is also suggested by the generalization of Appendix 1.C to the case of a constant but nonzero expected rate of inflation presented in Appendix 6.A.

## The Formal Model: Static Equilibrium Conditions

Before we introduce any further inflationary complications, it is useful to write down the static equilibrium conditions of our formal model for cases in which $\pi^e \neq 0$. In order to keep things as simple as possible to start out, we abstract from wealth effects and assume that portfolio adjustment is instantaneous, that is, $\xi_m \to +\infty$. The model is now given by the following equations:

### Market-clearing Conditions

Goods:

$$c^d\left[y^* - \tau + \underset{(+)}{\frac{B}{P}} - \left(\frac{M}{P} + \frac{B}{rP}\right)\pi^e\right] + \underset{(-)}{i^d(r - \pi^e)} + g - y^* = 0. \qquad (6.2.3)$$

Money and earning assets:

$$\left(\frac{M}{P}\right)^d \underset{(+)\ (-)}{(y^*, r\ )} - \frac{M}{P} = 0. \qquad (6.2.4)$$

### Government Budget Constraint

$$g + \frac{B}{P} - \tau = \dot{m}^s + \dot{b}^s = \frac{1}{P}\frac{dM}{dt} + \frac{1}{rP}\frac{dB}{dt}. \qquad (6.2.5)$$

### Exogenous Variables

Real: $\pi^e$, shift parameters, three among $\tau$, $g$, $\dot{m}^s$, and $\dot{b}^s$.
Nominal: $M$, $B$.

### Endogenous Variables   $r$, $P$, $\rho = r - \pi^e$, one among $\tau$, $g$, $\dot{m}^s$, and $\dot{b}^s$.

## Inflation Policy Parameterization with Government Bonds

We began our discussion of the determination of the equilibrium rate of inflation by linking the rate of inflation to the rate of growth of the nominal money supply without any reference to whether the government is currently issuing bonds or has previously issued bonds in the past. The most natural extension of the concept of the rate of growth of the money supply in an economy in which there are government bonds outstanding is the rate of growth of total government liabilities holding the ratio of government bonds to money, $\theta \equiv B/M$, constant. We denote the growth rate of nominal government liabilities by $\mu$. In our present formulation, changes in the rate of expansion of the nominal money supply holding $\theta$ constant must involve changes in the growth rates of both money and government bonds. As we shall see, parameterization of government policy in terms of $\theta$ and $\mu$

is most useful in an inflationary environment. Our formal definition of $\mu$ is

$$\mu \equiv \frac{\dfrac{1}{r}\dfrac{dB}{dt} + \dfrac{dM}{dt}}{B/r + M}.$$ (6.2.6)

Before proceeding, it is useful to recall our earlier discussion of the government budget constraint. We have consistently asserted that any time one government policy parameter is changed, it is imperative to also specify which other item(s) in the government budget constraint change and which are held constant. In nominal terms, the government budget constraint can be written as

$$P(g - \tau) + B = P_b\frac{dB}{dt} + \frac{dM}{dt} = \frac{1}{r}\frac{dB}{dt} + \frac{dM}{dt}.$$ (6.2.7)

Unfortunately, this particular form of the government budget constraint is algebraically most difficult to work with. However, later analysis can be greatly simplified if we reexpress the government budget constraint in terms of the policy parameters $\mu$ and $\theta$. Clearly, any government policy action can be translated from one policy parameterization to another. The economy found in the use of $\mu$ and $\theta$ results from the fact, to be established below, that the equilibrium inflation rate is equal to $\mu$ independent of any other exogenous variable. Substitution of equation (6.2.6) into equation (6.2.7) yields

$$g - \tau + \frac{B}{P} = \mu\left(\frac{M}{P} + \frac{B}{rP}\right)$$ (6.2.8)

or

$$\frac{B}{P} - \tau = \mu\left(\frac{M}{P} + \frac{B}{rP}\right) - g = \frac{M}{P}\left(1 + \frac{\theta}{r}\right)\mu - g.$$ (6.2.9)

Just as in our analysis of Chapter 2, life here is also complicated by the presence of endogenous variables in the government budget constraint. This potential problem is dealt with most simply in the present analysis by substituting for $B/P - \tau$ from the government budget constraint directly into the expression for expected diposable income $z$. Expected disposable income is expressed above as

$$z = y^* + \frac{B}{P} - \tau - \left(\frac{M}{P} + \frac{B}{rP}\right)\pi^e.$$ (6.2.10)

Utilizing the definition of $\theta$ and the form of the government budget constraint above, we obtain

$$z = y^* - g - \frac{M}{P}\left(1 + \frac{\theta}{r}\right)(\pi^e - \mu).$$ (6.2.11)

This formulation avoids the need to make explicit assumptions directly linking the level of taxes to $B$ and/or $P$ as in Chapter 2. However, in much of what follows we again find it convenient to let the level of taxes act as the balancing item in the government budget.

# 6.3 A DYNAMIC MODEL OF INFLATION AND INFLATIONARY EXPECTATIONS

Before we consider an explicit dynamic model of the inflationary process, it is useful at this point to rewrite the static equilibrium conditions incorporating our reformulated policy parameters. Recalling the definition of the expected real rate of interest $\rho = r - \pi^e$, we can write the static equilibrium conditions as:

### Market-clearing Conditions

Goods:

$$c^d\left[y^* - g - \frac{M}{P}\underset{(+)}{\left(1 + \frac{\theta}{\rho + \pi^e}\right)}(\pi^e - \mu)\right] + \underset{(-)}{i^d(\rho)} + g - y^* = 0. \qquad (6.3.1)$$

Money and earning assets:

$$\left(\frac{M}{P}\right)^d\underset{(+)\quad(-)}{(y^*, \rho + \pi^e)} - \frac{M}{P} = 0. \qquad (6.3.2)$$

### Government Budget Constraint

$$g + \theta\frac{M}{P} - \tau = \frac{M}{P}\left(1 + \frac{\theta}{\rho + \pi^e}\right)\mu. \qquad (6.3.3)$$

### Exogenous Variables

Real: $\pi^e$, shift parameters, three among $\tau$, $g$, $\theta$, and $\mu$.

Nominal: none.

### Endogenous Variables    $\rho$, $M/P$, one among $\tau$, $g$, $\theta$, and $\mu$.

One significant change from the basic model of Chapter 2 is the listing of $M/P$ as an endogenous variable instead of listing $M$ as a separate exogenous variable and $P$ as a separate endogenous variable. This particular way of analyzing the model is much simpler because the levels of $M$ and $P$ are not constant in the dynamic steady state as long as $\mu \neq 0$. However, the ratio of $M$ to $P$, $M/P$, is constant in the steady state, and this is the principal advantage of this formulation.

## Adaptive Expectations

As a final prelude to our dynamic analysis of the effects of changes in the rate of growth of nominal government liabilities, we need to specify a mechanism for the formation of inflationary expectations. That is, we next need to specify how expectations of inflation are formed and how these expectations change over time. The subject of expectations formation has generated a lot of controversy over the years. Much of this controversy has centered upon whether expectations formation is "rational" or not and what difference the presence or absence of rationality makes for the behavior of economic models.[4] However, in the present application, the particular form of expectations formation is not a central concern. The only characteristics we require of an expectations formation mechanism at this point are that expectations be consistent with actual events in the steady state and that the dynamics of expectation formation themselves not inject instability into an otherwise stable dynamic process.

A natural candidate is that expectations of inflation adapt over time to the actual inflation rate. In particular, we assume that

$$\frac{d\pi^e}{dt} = \psi\left(\frac{1}{P}\frac{dP}{dt} - \pi^e\right), \qquad \psi > 0, \quad \text{a constant.} \tag{6.3.4}$$

This process has the property that when the actual rate of inflation exceeds expectations, expectations of inflation rise. When the actual rate of inflation is slower than expectations, expectations of inflation fall. Expectations of inflation only remain constant when these expectations are correct, that is, when the actual and expected rates of inflation are equal.

## The Dynamics of Inflationary Expectations

We are now ready to write down a formal model of the dynamics of inflation and inflationary expectations.[5] To start with the simplest example, consider the case in which the government policymaker keeps $\mu$, $\theta$, and $g$ constant and adjusts $\tau$ as may be necessary to satisfy the government budget constraint.

As a prelude, we now plug the money market-clearing condition into the goods market-clearing condition to obtain

$$c^d\left[y^* - g - \left(\frac{M}{P}\right)^d(y^*, \rho + \pi^e)\left(1 + \frac{\theta}{\rho + \pi^e}\right)(\pi^e - \mu)\right] \\ + i^d(\rho) + g - y^* = 0. \tag{6.3.5}$$

Note that this equation is of the form

$$H(\rho, \pi^e; g, \mu, \theta) = 0. \tag{6.3.6}$$

Differentiating equation (6.3.6) with respect to time and collecting terms, we obtain

$$\frac{d\rho}{dt} = -\frac{\partial H/\partial \pi^e}{\partial H/\partial \rho}\frac{d\pi^e}{dt} \quad \text{for} \quad \frac{dg}{dt} = \frac{d\mu}{dt} = \frac{d\theta}{dt} = 0. \tag{6.3.7}$$

The goods market-clearing condition therefore generates one relationship between $d\rho/dt$ and $d\pi^e/dt$.

---

[4] Rationally formed expectations are studied in some detail in Chapters 10 and 12. Furthermore, these chapters also explore the ways in which traditional macroeconomic results may be altered by the adoption of the assumption of rationally formed expectations.

[5] The formal model under consideration is similar to those of Pyle and Turnovsky (1976) and Turnovsky (1977, Ch. 7). Nguyen and Turnovsky (1979) present an interesting catalog of simulation results for models of this sort.

Differentiating the money market equilibrium condition, we obtain

$$\frac{\partial (M/P)^d}{\partial r}\left(\frac{d\rho}{dt} + \frac{d\pi^e}{dt}\right) = \frac{d(M/P)}{dt} = \frac{M}{P}(\mu - \pi). \tag{6.3.8}$$

This second equation in $d\rho/dt$ and $d\pi^e/dt$ can now be combined with the expectation adaptation equation (6.3.4) rewritten in the form

$$\pi = \pi^e + \frac{1}{\psi}\frac{d\pi^e}{dt} \tag{6.3.9}$$

to obtain

$$\frac{\partial(M/P)^d}{\partial r}\frac{d\rho}{dt} + \left[\frac{\partial(M/P)^d}{\partial r} + \frac{M/P}{\psi}\right]\frac{d\pi^e}{dt} = \frac{M}{P}(\mu - \pi^e). \tag{6.3.10}$$

We now have two differential equations in $d\rho/dt$ and $d\pi^e/dt$. Eliminating $d\rho/dt$, we obtain the following differential equation in $d\pi^e/dt$:

$$\frac{d\pi^e}{dt} = \frac{M}{P}\left[\frac{M/P}{\psi} + \frac{\partial(M/P)^d}{\partial r}\left(1 - \frac{\partial H/\partial \pi^e}{\partial H/\partial \rho}\right)\right]^{-1}(\mu - \pi^e). \tag{6.3.11}$$

The above relationship is a first-order, nonlinear differential equation in $\pi^e$. The equilibrium of this differential equation is simply $\pi^e = \mu = \pi$, just as in the case of the simple quantity theory.

## Stability of Equilibrium

The equilibrium conditions above are only of interest as long as the underlying dynamic process is stable. To investigate the likelihood of stability, consider the linearized form of the above differential equation. If the linearized system is stable, then the more general nonlinear case is at least locally stable.

For stability of the linearized system, we require that

$$\Lambda \equiv \frac{M}{P}\left[\frac{M/P}{\psi} + \frac{\partial(M/P)^d}{\partial r}\left(1 - \frac{\partial H/\partial \pi^e}{\partial H/\partial \rho}\right)\right]^{-1} > 0 \tag{6.3.12}$$

when evaluated at $\pi^e = \mu$.[6] We therefore need to evaluate $\partial H/\partial \rho$ and $\partial H/\partial \pi^e$ in the neighborhood of $\pi^e = \mu$. These expressions are given by

$$\left.\frac{\partial H}{\partial \rho}\right|_{\pi^e = \mu} = -\frac{\partial c^d}{\partial z}\left[\frac{\partial(M/P)^d}{\partial r}\left(1 + \frac{\theta}{\rho + \pi^e}\right) - \frac{\theta}{(\rho + \pi^e)^2}\frac{M}{P}\right](\pi^e - \mu)$$

$$+ \frac{\partial i^d}{\partial \rho} = \frac{\partial i^d}{\partial \rho} < 0. \tag{6.3.13}$$

---

[6]Cagan (1956) derives a similar stability condition.

$$\frac{\partial H}{d\pi^e}\bigg|_{\pi^e=\mu} = -\frac{\partial c^d}{\partial z}\left[\frac{\partial (M/P)^d}{\partial r}\left(1 + \frac{\theta}{\rho + \pi^e}\right) - \frac{\theta}{(\rho + \pi^e)^2}\frac{M}{P}\right](\pi^e - \mu)$$

$$-\frac{\partial c^d}{\partial z}\frac{M}{P}\left(1 + \frac{\theta}{\rho + \pi^e}\right) = -\frac{\partial c^d}{\partial z}\frac{M}{P}\left(1 + \frac{\theta}{\rho + \pi^e}\right) < 0. \tag{6.3.14}$$

Combining these equations, we obtain

$$\Lambda = \frac{M}{P}\left\{\frac{M/P}{\psi} + \frac{\partial (M/P)^d}{\partial r}\left[1 + \frac{M}{P}\left(1 + \frac{\theta}{\rho + \pi^e}\right)\frac{\partial c^d/\partial z}{\partial i^d/\partial \rho}\right]\right\}^{-1}. \tag{6.3.15}$$

Recall that $\Lambda > 0$ is required for stability. A sufficient condition for stability is therefore given by

$$-\frac{1}{M/P}\frac{\partial (M/P)^d}{\partial r} < \frac{1}{\psi}. \tag{6.3.16}$$

Weak sensitivity of money demand to the rate of interest and slow adjustment of inflationary expectations are likely to lead to stability. To get an intuitive feel for how fulfillment of this condition guarantees stability and to see how instability in the inflationary process might be possible, consider the case in which $\partial c^d/\partial z = 0$. In this case, as long as $\partial i^d/\partial \rho$ is finite, the stability condition above is both sufficient and necessary. With $\partial c^d/\partial z = 0$, consumption is constant at, say, $\bar{c}^d$. The goods market equilibrium condition becomes

$$\bar{c}^d + i^d(\rho) + g - y^* = 0. \tag{6.3.17}$$

Goods market clearing therefore determines a fixed equilibrium expected real interest rate.

Now suppose that we start out in equilibrium with $\pi = \pi^e = \mu_0$. Then suppose that $\pi^e$ is displaced above its equilibrium value. With the real interest rate pegged by the goods market-clearing condition, the nominal interest rate rises one-for-one with the increase in $\pi^e$. This increase in $r$ then reduces the demand for real money balances. To keep money demand and money supply equal, the inflation rate must rise above $\mu_0$ to reduce actual real money balances. This increase in $\pi$ may be even larger than the original displacement in $\pi^e$. If this is the case, the adaptive expectations mechanism requires a further increase in $\pi^e$, and the whole process may start over again. Therefore, we see that if money demand is sensitive to the nominal rate of interest and expectations adapt very quickly, a small displacement from equilibrium can generate an unstable buildup in inflation without any coincident increase in the growth rate of nominal government liabilities $\mu$.

Although the possibility of an explosive outburst of inflation is an inescapable consequence of our chosen set of assumptions, it is a most implausible scenario. The phenomenon described above is sometimes referred to as a *speculative hyperinflation*.[7] In such a hyperinflation, inflation accelerates only because agents expect ever faster inflation. However, even if such a process were to get started, agents' expectations are not likely in that instance to be well described by the simple mechanical adjustment mechanism we

---

[7] Obstfeld and Rogoff (1983) provide a useful discussion of this phenomenon.

have postulated. Agents are likely instead to realize that such an inflation is not sustainable, inflationary expectations are therefore likely to collapse, and the inflationary outburst will quickly end. Reflective of our confidence that such a phenomenon is not very realistic, we shall generally simply assume that this sufficient condition for stability is satisfied.

Formally, throughout the remainder of the analysis we assume that movement in $\pi^e$ can be approximated by the stable, first-order linear differential equation

$$\frac{d\pi^e}{dt} = \Lambda(\mu - \pi^e), \qquad \Lambda > 0, \tag{6.3.18}$$

and so

$$\pi^e(t) = \mu - [\mu - \pi^e(0)]e^{-\Lambda t}. \tag{6.3.19}$$

Having fully described the motion of $\pi^e$, we can now solve for the motions of $r$, $\rho$, and $M/P$ as functions of the gap between $\pi^e$ and $\mu$. To proceed along these lines, we recognize that $d\pi^e/dt$ is exogenous to the original $\rho$, $M/P$ system. Differentiating the equilibrium conditions of this static system with respect to time and evaluating at $\pi^e = \mu$, we obtain

$$\begin{bmatrix} \dfrac{\partial i^d}{\partial \rho} & 0 \\ \dfrac{\partial (M/P)^d}{\partial r} & -1 \end{bmatrix} \begin{bmatrix} \dfrac{d\rho}{dt} \\ \dfrac{d(M/P)}{dt} \end{bmatrix} = \begin{bmatrix} \dfrac{M}{P}\left(1 + \dfrac{\theta}{r}\right)\dfrac{\partial c^d}{\partial z} \\ -\dfrac{\partial (M/P)^d}{\partial r} \end{bmatrix} \dfrac{d\pi^e}{dt}. \tag{6.3.20}$$

Applying Cramer's rule and recalling that $d\pi^e/dt = \Lambda(\mu - \pi^e)$, we obtain

$$\frac{d\rho}{dt} = \Lambda\left[\frac{M}{P}\left(1 + \frac{\theta}{r}\right)\frac{\partial c^d/\partial z}{\partial i^d/\partial \rho}\right](\mu - \pi^e), \tag{6.3.21}$$

$$\frac{d(M/P)}{dt} = \Lambda\left[1 + \frac{M}{P}\left(1 + \frac{\theta}{r}\right)\frac{\partial c^d/\partial z}{\partial i^d/\partial \rho}\right]\frac{\partial (M/P)^d}{\partial r}(\mu - \pi^e). \tag{6.3.22}$$

Next, we utilize the relationships

$$r = \rho + \pi^e \quad \text{and} \quad \pi = \mu - \frac{\partial (M/P)^d/\partial r}{M/P}\frac{dr}{dt} \tag{6.3.23}$$

to obtain

$$\frac{dr}{dt} = \Lambda\left[1 + \frac{M}{P}\left(1 + \frac{\theta}{r}\right)\frac{\partial c^d/\partial z}{\partial i^d/\partial \rho}\right](\mu - \pi^e), \tag{6.3.24}$$

$$\pi = \mu - \Lambda\left[1 + \frac{M}{P}\left(1 + \frac{\theta}{r}\right)\frac{\partial c^d/\partial z}{\partial i^d/\partial \rho}\right]\frac{\partial (M/P)^d/\partial r}{M/P}(\mu - \pi^e). \tag{6.3.25}$$

These dynamic relationships prove most useful when we trace out the system response to exogenous disturbances in the next section.

# 6.4 DYNAMIC RESPONSE TO EXOGENOUS DISTURBANCES

The preceding sections provide almost all the necessary prerequisites for the analysis of the effects of changes in the exogenous variables. However, while all of the analysis can be done algebraically, it is also helpful to follow the movements in the exogenous and endogenous variables graphically. Differentiating the static equilibrium conditions and evaluating in the neighborhood of equilibrium, we obtain

$$
\begin{bmatrix} \dfrac{\partial i^d}{\partial \rho} & 0 \\[2ex] \dfrac{\partial (M/P)^d}{\partial r} & -1 \end{bmatrix} \begin{bmatrix} d\rho \\[2ex] d\!\left(\dfrac{M}{P}\right) \end{bmatrix}
$$

$$
= \begin{bmatrix} -\left(1 - \dfrac{\partial c^d}{\partial z}\right) dg + \left[\dfrac{M}{P}\left(1 + \dfrac{\theta}{r}\right)\dfrac{\partial c^d}{\partial z}\right] d\pi^e - \left[\dfrac{M}{P}\left(1 + \dfrac{\theta}{r}\right)\dfrac{\partial c^d}{\partial z}\right] d\mu \\[3ex] -\dfrac{\partial (M/P)^d}{\partial r}\, d\pi^e \end{bmatrix}
$$

(6.4.1)

or

$$
\left.\frac{d\rho}{d(M/P)}\right|_{y^d = y^*} = 0 \qquad \text{(GME)}, \tag{6.4.2}
$$

$$
\left.\frac{d\rho}{d(M/P)}\right|_{(M/P)^d = M/P} = \left[\frac{\partial (M/P)^d}{\partial r}\right]^{-1} < 0 \quad \text{(MME)}. \tag{6.4.3}
$$

The resulting goods and money market equilibrium loci are depicted in Figure 6.2, where $\rho^*$ and $(M/P)^*$, respectively, denote the equilibrium real interest rate and the equilibrium level of real money balances. Impact effects in this model are derived by setting $d\pi^e = 0$, while steady-state effects are solved by setting $d\pi^e = d\mu$.

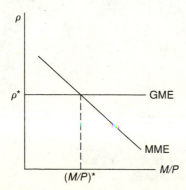

Figure 6.2

## An Inflationary Tax Cut

We now investigate the dynamic effects of a sudden, unanticipated increase in the rate of growth of government liabilities $\mu$ from $\mu_0$ to $\mu_1$, where $\mu_1 > \mu_0$. We start this experiment from a position of long-run equilibrium in which $\pi = \pi^e = \mu_0$. Following the step rise in $\mu$, we assume that there are no subsequent changes in $\mu$ and that $\theta$ and $g$ are held constant throughout at their initial values. With $\theta$ and $g$ held constant, taxes must fall simultaneous to the increase in $\mu$ to satisfy the government budget constraint. Thereafter, taxes must further be adjusted as may be required to continue to satisfy the government budget constraint as the endogenous variables evolve over time.

At any point in time, the expected rate of inflation is predetermined. Therefore, immediately following the increase in $\mu$, we find that

$$\mu - \pi^e = \mu_1 - \mu_0 > 0. \tag{6.4.4}$$

The impact effects of the increase in $\mu$ can be found by solving for $dr/d\mu$, $d\rho/d\mu$, and $d(M/P)/d\mu$ with $d\pi^e = dg = d\theta = 0$. Applying Cramer's rule, we find that

$$\left.\frac{dr}{d\mu}\right|_{\text{impact}} = \left.\frac{d\rho}{d\mu}\right|_{\text{impact}} = -\left[\frac{M}{P}\left(1 + \frac{\theta}{r}\right)\frac{\partial c^d/\partial z}{\partial i^d/\partial \rho}\right] > 0, \tag{6.4.5}$$

$$\left.\frac{d(M/P)}{d\mu}\right|_{\text{impact}} = -\left[\frac{M}{P}\left(1 + \frac{\theta}{r}\right)\frac{\partial c^d/\partial z}{\partial i^d/\partial \rho}\right]\frac{\partial (M/P)^d}{\partial r} < 0. \tag{6.4.6}$$

Throughout most of this analysis, we further assume that

$$1 + \frac{M}{P}\left(1 + \frac{\theta}{r}\right)\frac{\partial c^d/\partial z}{\partial i^d/\partial \rho} > 0 \quad \text{or} \quad \left.\frac{\partial(y^d - y^*)}{\partial \pi^e}\right|_{dr=0} > 0. \tag{6.4.7}$$

This assumption assures that while $r$ and $\rho$ unambiguously rise immediately after the jump in $\mu$, the increases in $r$ and $\rho$ are less than one-for-one. These impact effects are plotted in Figure 6.3. We find that $r$ rises to $r_1$, $\rho$ rises to $\rho_1$, and $M/P$ falls to $(M/P)_1$.

However, this is obviously not the end of the story. Since the increase in $\mu$ has opened up a gap between $\pi^e$ and $\mu$, all of the endogenous variables begin moving in response to the subsequent evolution of the expected rate of inflation through time. Recall the laws of motion derived above:

$$\pi = \mu - \Lambda\left[1 + \frac{M}{P}\left(1 + \frac{\theta}{r}\right)\frac{\partial c^d/\partial z}{\partial i^d/\partial \rho}\right]\frac{\partial (M/P)^d/\partial r}{M/P}(\mu - \pi^e), \tag{6.4.8}$$

$$\frac{dr}{dt} = \Lambda\left[1 + \frac{M}{P}\left(1 + \frac{\theta}{r}\right)\frac{\partial c^d/\partial z}{\partial i^d/\partial \rho}\right](\mu - \pi^e), \tag{6.4.9}$$

$$\frac{d\rho}{dt} = \Lambda\left[\frac{M}{P}\left(1 + \frac{\theta}{r}\right)\frac{\partial c^d/\partial z}{\partial i^d/\partial \rho}\right](\mu - \pi^e), \tag{6.4.10}$$

$$\frac{d(M/P)}{dt} = \Lambda\left[1 + \frac{M}{P}\left(1 + \frac{\theta}{r}\right)\frac{\partial c^d/\partial z}{\partial i^d/\partial \rho}\right]\frac{\partial (M/P)^d}{\partial r}(\mu - \pi^e). \tag{6.4.11}$$

Since we know that following the increase in $\mu$, $\mu > \pi^e$, and since we are assuming that $\partial(y^d - y^*)/\partial \pi^e|_{dr=0} > 0$, the four equations above establish the following results. Equation (6.4.8) reveals that the actual rate of inflation initially jumps to a value greater than

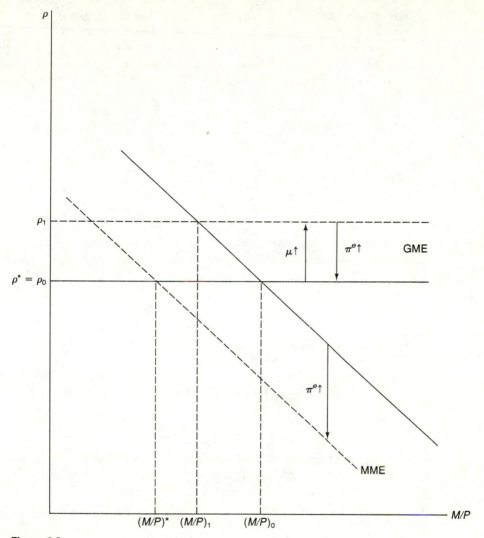

**Figure 6.3**

$\mu_1$ and then monotonically declines to its steady-state value of $\mu_1$. Equations (6.4.9) and (6.4.10) indicate that the nominal interest rate monotonically rises and the real interest rate monotonically falls throughout the adjustment process. Finally, equation (6.4.11) guarantees that $M/P$ monotonically falls throughout the adjustment process.

Now returning to the differential of the market-clearing conditions, we can solve for the steady-state effects of the increase in $\mu$ on $r$, $\rho$, and $M/P$. Since we know that in equilibrium $\pi^e = \mu$, we can evaluate equation (6.4.1) setting $d\pi^e = d\mu$. Use of Cramer's rule then allows us to show that

$$\left.\frac{dr}{d\mu}\right|_{SS} = 1, \qquad \left.\frac{d\rho}{d\mu}\right|_{SS} = 0, \qquad \left.\frac{d(M/P)}{d\mu}\right|_{SS} = \frac{\partial (M/P)^d}{\partial r} < 0. \qquad (6.4.12)$$

The resulting steady-state values $\rho*$ and $(M/P)*$ are also depicted in Figure 6.3. Furthermore, the time paths of $\mu$, $\pi$, $\pi^e$, $r$, $\rho$, and $M/P$ are all depicted in Figure 6.4.

We therefore see that our current set of assumptions guarantee that the Fisher hypothesis holds as a long-run equilibrium condition. However, unanticipated changes in $\mu$ can cause lasting changes in the expected real rate of interest as long as expectations of inflation do not immediately adjust to reflect the permanent change in the equilibrium rate of inflation. The analysis above predicts a temporary rise in the expected real rate of interest as the nominal rate of interest only gradually comes to reflect the full rise in the equilibrium rate of inflation.[8]

Finally, let us consider the effect of the increase in $\mu$ on the level of taxes $\tau$. The government budget constraint is given from above as

$$g + \theta \frac{M}{P} - \tau = \frac{M}{P}\left(1 + \frac{\theta}{r}\right)\mu. \tag{6.4.13}$$

Employing the equilibrium conditions $\pi = \pi^e = \mu$ and the definitions $\rho \equiv r - \pi^e$ and $\theta \equiv B/M$, we can write the equilibrium form of the government budget constraint as

$$g + \rho\left(\frac{B}{rP}\right) = \tau + \pi\left(\frac{M}{P}\right). \tag{6.4.14}$$

In this form, we see that government spending on goods and services $g$ plus the real interest payments on the government debt must be financed either through explicit taxation $\tau$ or through an inflation tax $\pi(M/P)$.

Totally differentiating the government budget constraint, we compute the following expression for the steady-state effect of an increase in $\mu$ on $\tau$:

$$\left.\frac{d\tau}{d\mu}\right|_{SS} = \frac{\rho}{r}\theta \frac{\partial(M/P)^d}{\partial r} - \frac{\rho}{r}\left(\frac{B}{rP}\right) - \left.\frac{d}{d\mu}\right|_{SS}\left(\pi\frac{M}{P}\right). \tag{6.4.15}$$

The first two terms are unambiguously negative. The last term reflects the effect of an increase in the inflation tax rate (the rate of inflation) on the total inflation tax revenue. This effect is given by

$$\frac{d}{dn}\left(\pi\frac{M}{P}\right) = \frac{M}{P} + \pi\frac{\partial(M/P)^d}{\partial r}. \tag{6.4.16}$$

This expression will be positive as long as we are on the upward-sloping portion of the inflationary "Laffer curve"; that is, as long as an increase in the rate of inflation increases the inflation tax revenue. This condition can be expressed as

$$-\frac{1}{M/P}\frac{\partial(M/P)^d}{\partial r} < \frac{1}{\pi}. \tag{6.4.17}$$

Recall, however, that we have already assumed that

$$-\frac{1}{M/P}\frac{\partial(M/P)^d}{\partial r} < \frac{1}{\psi} \tag{6.4.18}$$

---

[8] Sargent (1972) develops a dynamic model with similar properties. However, in his model expectations of inflation are exogenous and dynamics are introduced via lags in the consumption and investment functions.

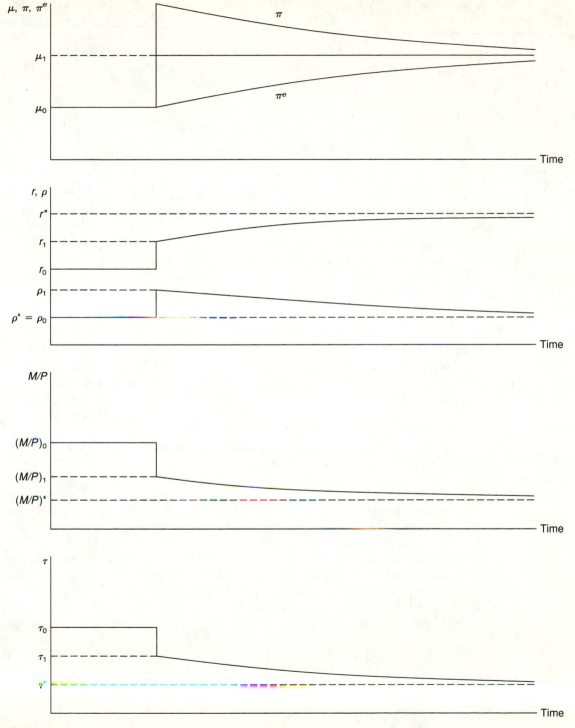

**Figure 6.4**

to guarantee stability. Therefore, as long as $1/\psi < 1/\pi$, or $\pi < \psi$, this earlier assumption is also sufficient to guarantee that inflation tax revenues rise with the equilibrium inflation rate. It is quite likely that the steady-state effect of an increase in $\mu$ on $\tau$ is negative.

Finally, however, it appears that we cannot generally rank the relative sizes of $d\tau/d\mu|_{\text{impact}}$ and $d\tau/d\mu|_{\text{SS}}$. Differentiating the government budget constraint with respect to $\tau$ and $\mu$ at impact and subtracting the steady-state effect, we obtain

$$\left( -\frac{d\tau}{d\mu}\Big|_{\text{SS}} \right) - \left( -\frac{d\tau}{d\mu}\Big|_{\text{impact}} \right) = \left( 1 - \frac{dr}{d\mu}\Big|_{\text{impact}} \right)$$

$$\times \left\{ \frac{\partial(M/P)^d/\partial r}{M/P} \left[ \pi\left(\frac{M}{P}\right) - \rho\left(\frac{B}{rP}\right) \right] - \frac{\pi}{r}\left(\frac{B}{rP}\right) \right\}.$$

(6.4.19)

While our earlier assumptions guarantee that $1 - dr/d\mu|_{\text{impact}} > 0$, the second term in the above expression may be either positive or negative. However, for sufficiently small rates of inflation the above expression is positive. In that case, following an inflationary tax cut, the steady-state reduction in taxes is greater than the impact reduction in taxes. Figure 6.4 is drawn under the assumption that the above expression is, in fact, positive.

## Perfect Foresight Expectations

Before proceeding to analysis of the effects of other exogenous disturbances, it is useful at this point to reflect on the extent to which the results of the previous section are dependent on the assumption of adaptive expectations. In many ways the types of models we have been studying up to this point are not well suited to very elaborate discussions of expectations formation. All policy changes and many related movements in endogenous variables are complete surprises. Such policy moves are not even viewed as possibilities. Furthermore, even in the face of such policy surprises, agents then revert to expectations that such future policy changes are impossible.

In order to more properly model the possibility of changes in exogenous variables and enlightened expectations about such changes in exogenous variables, it is necessary to formalize the stochastic structure under which movements in the exogenous variables might occur. In such richer models, it is then natural to assume that agents have some access to information about the stochastic structure of their environment. However, we presently leave this more ambitious project for later development.

A deterministic, continuous-time analogue to such "rational" expectations models is the assumption of perfect foresight expectations. More formally, perfect foresight requires that agents know the entire future time paths of all the exogenous and endogenous variables. One implication of such perfect foresight expectations is that the expected rate of inflation is always equal to the actual rate of inflation, that is, $\pi^e = \pi$. With this alternate expectational assumption and with the substitution $r = \rho - \pi^e$, the model is given by

$$c^d\left[ y^* - g - \frac{M}{P}\left(1 + \frac{\theta}{r}\right)(\pi - \mu) \right] + i^d(r - \pi) + g - y^* = 0,$$

(6.4.20)

$$\left(\frac{M}{P}\right)^d(y^*, r) - \frac{M}{P} = 0.$$

(6.4.21)

Differentiating the money market equilibrium condition, we obtain

$$\pi = \mu - \frac{\partial (M/P)^d/\partial r}{M/P} \frac{dr}{dt}. \tag{6.4.22}$$

Plugging into the goods market equilibrium condition yields

$$c^d\left[y^* - g + \left(\frac{M}{P}\right)^d (y^*, r)\left(1 + \frac{\theta}{r}\right)\left(\frac{\partial (M/P)^d/\partial r}{M/P}\right)\frac{dr}{dt}\right]$$
$$+ i^d\left[r - \mu + \frac{\partial (M/P)^d/\partial r}{M/P}\frac{dr}{dt}\right] + g - y^* = 0. \tag{6.4.23}$$

Therefore, the model can be expressed as a first-order, nonlinear differential equation in $r$. If we denote the static equilibrium level of $r$ as $r^*$, a first-order, linear approximation to the above equation may be obtained by differentiating the above expression with respect to $r$ and $dr/dt$. Upon rearranging, we find that

$$\frac{dr}{dt} = \frac{-\partial i^d/\partial \rho}{\dfrac{\partial (M/P)^d/\partial r}{M/P}\left[\dfrac{\partial i^d}{\partial \rho} - \left(1 + \dfrac{\theta}{r}\right)\dfrac{M}{P}\dfrac{\partial c^d}{\partial z}\right]}(r - r^*). \tag{6.4.24}$$

Perhaps not surprisingly, this equation can also be obtained by considering the limiting case of adaptive expectations in which $\psi \to +\infty$. Our earlier assumptions imply that the coefficient of $r - r^*$ in the above expression is positive and therefore this differential equation in $r$ is unstable. However, recall from Chapter 4 that the general form of the solution to such an equation is given by

$$r = r^* + be^{\lambda t}. \tag{6.4.25}$$

With $\lambda > 0$ as it is in this case, the only possible nonexplosive solution is $r = r^*$ with $b \equiv 0$. However, for such a solution to describe the actual time path of $r$, additional assumptions are needed to ensure that $b = 0$. Sometimes a condition such as $b = 0$ emerges from the transversality conditions of intertemporal maximization problems.[9] A less esoteric device is to simply assert that agents ignore those solutions corresponding to $b \neq 0$ and therefore assume that agents' expectational behavior guarantees stability.

If the perfect foresight equilibrium with $b = 0$ is the correct equilibrium for the model, then the solution involves instantaneous movement of all endogenous variables to those values described in the previous section as steady-state values. Therefore, the dynamic responses of the endogenous variables to a change in $\mu$ all mirror the movement in $\mu$ in Figure 6.4. Actual and expected inflation are identically equal to $\mu$ at every point in time. The expected real rate of interest is completely unchanged following changes in $\mu$ and the nominal rate of interest jumps up or down an amount exactly equal to the change in $\mu$. Perfect foresight expectations therefore imply in this case that the intertemporal terms of trade $\rho$ are completely immune to changes in inflation policy. This case is in contrast to the sticky-expectations case of adaptive expectations in which changes in $\mu$ can result in temporary, though not permanent, changes in $\rho$. Perfect foresight expectations therefore imply that the Fisher hypothesis holds at every point in time rather than only holding in equilibrium, as is the case with adaptive expectations.

---

[9] See, e.g., Brock (1974, 1975) and Benveniste and Scheinkman (1982).

## Effects of Other Exogenous Disturbances

Since we have already devoted considerable attention to the dynamics of adjustment, we now simply focus on the equilibrium effects of changes in the other exogenous disturbances. Retaining the convention of viewing the level of taxes as an endogenous variable, the only other explicit exogenous variables to consider are the level of government spending $g$ and the ratio of bonds to money $\theta$.

Rewriting the equilibrium conditions evaluated at $\pi = \pi^e = \mu$, we obtain:

### Market-clearing Conditions

Goods:

$$c^d(y^* - g) + i^d(\rho) + g - y^* = 0. \tag{6.4.26}$$
$$\underset{(+)}{\phantom{c^d(y^* - g)}} \quad \underset{(-)}{\phantom{i^d(\rho)}}$$

Money and earning assets:

$$\left(\frac{M}{P}\right)^d(y^*, \rho + \mu) - \frac{M}{P} = 0. \tag{6.4.27}$$
$$\underset{(+)}{\phantom{xx}} \quad \underset{(-)}{\phantom{xx}}$$

### Government Budget Constraint

$$g + \theta\frac{M}{P} - \tau = \frac{M}{P}\left(1 + \frac{\theta}{\rho + \mu}\right)\mu. \tag{6.4.28}$$

These steady-state equilibrium conditions are of a particularly simple form. The goods market equilibrium condition (6.4.26) suggests that the real interest rate $\rho$ depends only on the value of $y^* - g$. Therefore, it is the level of government spending that determines the real rate of interest independent of how that spending is financed. Furthermore, once $\rho$ has been determined, the nominal rate of interest is simply given by $r = \rho(y^* - g) + \mu$ and the level of real money balances is simply equal to the demand for money evaluated at $r = \rho(y^* - g) + \mu$.

Let us now explicitly consider the effects of an increase in government spending $g$. Differentiating the equilibrium conditions above, we obtain

$$\frac{d\rho}{dg} = \frac{dr}{dg} = -\frac{1 - \partial c^d/\partial z}{\partial i^d/\partial \rho} > 0, \tag{6.4.29}$$

$$\frac{d(M/P)}{dg} = -\left(\frac{1 - \partial c^d/\partial z}{\partial i^d/\partial \rho}\right)\frac{\partial(M/P)^d}{\partial r} < 0. \tag{6.4.30}$$

Real and nominal interest rates both rise and real money balances fall. The increase in the real interest rate is just sufficient to crowd out an equal amount of investment spending. The rise in the nominal interest rate reduces the demand for real money balances. The actual reduction in the level of real money balances is accomplished through a temporary rise in the inflation rate above its steady-state level $\mu$.

Differentiating the government budget constraint, we obtain

$$\frac{d\tau}{dg} = 1 - \left[\rho\left(\frac{B}{rP}\right) - \pi\left(\frac{M}{P}\right)\right]\frac{\partial(M/P)^d/\partial r}{M/P}\frac{\partial i^d\partial\rho}{1 - \partial c^d/\partial z}. \tag{6.4.31}$$

Although this expression is likely to be positive, we cannot in general say for sure whether taxes rise by more or by less than the increase in government spending.

The resulting decline in the equilibrium level of real money balances generates two offsetting effects. First, since the tax base for the inflation tax falls, inflationary revenue falls as well. This fall in revenue needs to be offset by an increase in explicit taxes. Second, with $\theta$ fixed, the decline in $M/P$ also translates into a decline in $B/rP$. Therefore, the real value of interest payments on the government debt falls. This effect implies a reduction in the need for explicit tax collections. However, for parameter values likely to correspond to recent U.S. experience, it is likely that $\rho(B/rP) > \pi(M/P)$, and so the increase in government spending requires a less than one-for-one increase in taxes.

We can now finally compute the effects of an increase in $\theta$, the ratio of government bonds to the monetary base. Changes in $\theta$ have no effect on the equilibrium values of $r$, $\rho$, or $M/P$. The only impact of changes in $\theta$ is in the form of a change in the level of explicit taxes. Differentiating the government budget constraint, we obtain

$$\frac{d\tau}{d\theta} = \frac{\rho}{\theta} \frac{B}{rP} > 0. \tag{6.4.32}$$

A larger volume of government bonds outstanding requires higher taxes to finance the increased level of real interest payments.

## 6.5 INFLATION AND WEALTH EFFECTS

In this section we reexamine some of the dynamic and comparative statics exercises of the preceding section to see if any of the principal results are changed in any important way if consumption and the demand for money depend on the level of wealth. To do this, we amend the basic inflation model in a manner analogous to the analysis of Section 2.6.

Wealth is composed of the level of real money balances, $M/P$, that portion of the real market value of government bonds above and beyond the discounted present value of any associated future tax payments ($\kappa B/rP$), and the real market value of equity shares. In Section 6.1, we calculated the real value of an equity share in an inflationary economy to be equal to $\Pi/\rho E$. Therefore, if the aggregate production function exhibits constant returns to scale and the capital stock is expected to remain constant over time, the aggregate level of real wealth can be represented by

$$\Omega \equiv \frac{M}{P} + \frac{\kappa B}{rP} + \frac{RK}{\rho}. \tag{6.5.1}$$

In much of what follows, it is useful to divide total wealth $\Omega$ into the government-issued portion

$$\frac{A}{P} \equiv \frac{M}{P} + \frac{\kappa B}{rP} \tag{6.5.2}$$

and net private wealth $RK/\rho$. Recalling the definition of $\theta$, we can rewrite the above expression as

$$\frac{A}{P} = \frac{M}{P}\left(1 + \frac{\kappa\theta}{r}\right). \tag{6.5.3}$$

Employing the above notation, the modified version of our Section 6.3 model is given by:

### Market-clearing Conditions

Goods:

$$c^d(\underset{(+)}{z}, \underset{(+)}{\Omega}) + \underset{(-)}{i^d(\rho)} + g - y^* = 0. \tag{6.5.4}$$

Money and earning assets:

$$\left(1 + \frac{\kappa\theta}{\rho + \pi^e}\right)\left(\frac{M}{P}\right)^d(\underset{(+)}{y^*}, \underset{(-)}{\rho + \pi^e}, \underset{(+)}{\Omega}) - \frac{A}{P} = 0. \tag{6.5.5}$$

### Government Budget Constraint

$$g + \theta\frac{M}{P} - \tau = \frac{M}{P}\left(1 + \frac{\theta}{\rho + \pi^e}\right)\mu. \tag{6.5.6}$$

### Definitions

Expected disposable income:

$$z = y^* - g - \frac{M}{P}\left(1 + \frac{\theta}{\rho + \pi^e}\right)(\pi^e - \mu).$$

Wealth:

$$\Omega = \frac{A}{P} + \frac{RK}{\rho}.$$

One natural way to proceed is to continue to assume that inflationary expectations are formed adaptively and conduct the analysis of the amended model in a manner closely comparable to the analysis of Section 6.3. However, the consideration of wealth effects does not dramatically alter the resulting dynamic response pattern of the model. Motion of all of the endogenous variables is still in proportion to the difference between $\pi^e$ and $\mu$, and the stability conditions are just as likely to hold.

In order to greatly simplify the analysis, we now adopt the alternate expectational assumption that expectations of inflation are asymptotically correct. The steady-state rate of inflation is still given by $\pi = \mu$. Therefore, it seems logical to assume that agents are able to correctly foresee this equilibrium outcome and therefore expect that the future inflation rate will be equal to $\mu$ under the assumption that any future changes in inflation policy are completely unanticipated. This expectational assumption therefore closely corresponds to the case of perfect foresight expectations considered in the previous section. Formally, the model can be rewritten in the somewhat simpler form:

### Market-clearing Conditions

Goods:

$$c^d\left(\underset{(+)}{z}, \underset{(+)}{\frac{A}{P} + \frac{RK}{\rho}}\right) + \underset{(-)}{i^d(\rho)} + g - y^* = 0. \tag{6.5.7}$$

Money and assets:

$$\left(1 + \frac{\kappa\theta}{\rho + \mu}\right)\left(\frac{M}{P}\right)^d\left(\underset{(+)}{y^*}, \underset{(-)}{\rho + \mu}, \underset{(+)}{\frac{A}{P} + \frac{RK}{\rho}}\right) - \frac{A}{P} = 0. \tag{6.5.8}$$

### Government Budget Constraint

$$g + \theta\frac{M}{P} - \tau = \frac{M}{P}\left(1 + \frac{\theta}{\rho + \mu}\right)\mu. \tag{6.5.9}$$

With this alternative expectational assumption, the actual inflation rate also turns out to equal $\mu$, except at discrete instants at which there is a change in one of the exogenous variables. At such instants, the price level generally jumps up or down while the appropriately defined time derivative of $P$ remains constant. However, while the assumption that $\pi^e = \mu$ changes the dynamic behavior of the model somewhat, the equilibrium properties are completely unaffected, and in this section we are most interested in how wealth effects change the model's equilibrium properties.

## A Graphical Representation

As a prelude to the derivation of comparative statics results, it is useful to adopt a graphical representation of the model. We again utilize the notation $\text{EDG} \equiv y^d - y^*$ and $\text{EDM} \equiv (1 + \kappa\theta/r)(M/P)^d - A/P$. However, instead of plotting the equilibrium loci against $r$ or $\rho$ and $M/P$, we now plot these loci against $\rho$ and $A/P$. Differentiating the equilibrium conditions with respect to $\rho$ and $A/P$, we obtain

$$\left.\frac{d\rho}{d(A/P)}\right|_{y^d=y^*} = -\frac{\partial \text{EDG}/\partial(A/P)}{\partial \text{EDG}/\partial\rho}, \tag{6.5.10}$$

$$\left.\frac{d\rho}{d(A/P)}\right|_{(M/P)^d=M/P} = -\frac{\partial \text{EDM}/\partial(A/P)}{\partial \text{EDM}/\partial\rho}, \tag{6.5.11}$$

where

$$\frac{\partial \text{EDG}}{\partial\rho} = \frac{\partial i^d}{\partial\rho} - \frac{RK}{\rho^2}\frac{\partial c^d}{\partial\Omega} < 0, \tag{6.5.12}$$

$$\frac{\partial \text{EDG}}{\partial(A/P)} = \frac{\partial c^d}{\partial\Omega} > 0, \tag{6.5.13}$$

$$\frac{\partial \text{EDM}}{\partial\rho} = -\frac{\kappa\theta}{r^2}\frac{M}{P} + \left(1 + \frac{\kappa\theta}{r}\right)\left[\frac{\partial(M/P)^d}{\partial r} - \frac{RK}{\rho^2}\frac{\partial(M/P)^d}{\partial\Omega}\right] < 0, \tag{6.5.14}$$

$$\frac{\partial \text{EDM}}{\partial(A/P)} = -\left[1 - \left(1 + \frac{\kappa\theta}{r}\right)\frac{\partial(M/P)^d}{\partial\Omega}\right]. \tag{6.5.15}$$

While the sign of $\partial \text{EDM}/\partial(A/P)$ is theoretically ambiguous, we assume that it is negative. This assumption is equivalent to the assumption that an increase in the level of prices generates an excess demand for money. Recall that we have already discussed and worked with this assumption in the analysis of Chapter 2. We therefore find that

$$\left.\frac{d\rho}{d(A/P)}\right|_{y^d=y^*} > 0, \qquad \left.\frac{d\rho}{d(A/P)}\right|_{(M/P)^d=M/P} < 0. \tag{6.5.16}$$

These diagrams are therefore closely comparable to the diagrams of the preceding section.

## An Inflationary Tax Cut Reconsidered

We are now ready to reconsider the effects of a tax cut financed by an increase in the growth rate of nominal government liabilities $\mu$. Differentiating equations (6.5.7) and (6.5.8), we obtain

$$\begin{bmatrix} \dfrac{\partial EDG}{\partial \rho} & \dfrac{\partial EDG}{\partial (A/P)} \\[2ex] \dfrac{\partial EDM}{\partial \rho} & \dfrac{\partial EDM}{\partial (A/P)} \end{bmatrix} \begin{bmatrix} \dfrac{d\rho}{d\mu} \\[2ex] \dfrac{d(A/P)}{d\mu} \end{bmatrix} = \begin{bmatrix} 0 \\[2ex] \dfrac{M}{P}\dfrac{\kappa\theta}{r^2} - \left(1+\dfrac{\kappa\theta}{r}\right)\dfrac{\partial (M/P)^d}{\partial r} \end{bmatrix}. \tag{6.5.17}$$

Cramer's rule facilitates the following results:

$$\frac{d\rho}{d\mu} = \frac{-\left[\dfrac{\kappa\theta}{r^2}\dfrac{M}{P} - \left(1+\dfrac{\kappa\theta}{r}\right)\dfrac{\partial (M/P)^d}{\partial r}\dfrac{\partial c^d}{\partial \Omega}\right]}{\dfrac{\kappa\theta}{r^2}\dfrac{M}{P} - \left(1+\dfrac{\kappa\theta}{r}\right)\dfrac{\partial (M/P)^d}{\partial r}\dfrac{\partial c^d}{\partial \Omega} - \dfrac{\partial i^d}{\partial \rho}\left[1-\left(1+\dfrac{\kappa\theta}{r}\right)\dfrac{\partial (M/P)^d}{\partial \Omega}\right]} < 0, \tag{6.5.18}$$

$$\frac{dr}{d\mu} = 1 + \frac{d\rho}{d\mu} \tag{6.5.19}$$

$$= \frac{-\dfrac{\partial i^d}{\partial \rho}\left[1-\left(1+\dfrac{\kappa\theta}{r}\right)\dfrac{\partial (M/P)^d}{\partial \Omega}\right]}{\dfrac{\kappa\theta}{r^2}\dfrac{M}{P} - \left(1+\dfrac{\kappa\theta}{r}\right)\dfrac{\partial (M/P)^d}{\partial r}\dfrac{\partial c^d}{\partial \Omega} - \dfrac{\partial i^d}{\partial \rho}\left[1-\left(1+\dfrac{\kappa\theta}{r}\right)\dfrac{\partial (M/P)^d}{\partial \Omega}\right]} > 0,$$

$$\frac{d(A/P)}{d\mu} = \frac{1}{\Delta}\left(\frac{\partial i^d}{\partial \rho} - \frac{RK}{\rho^2}\frac{\partial c^d}{\partial \Omega}\right)\left[\frac{\kappa\theta}{r^2}\frac{M}{P} - \left(1+\frac{\kappa\theta}{r}\right)\frac{\partial (M/P)^d}{\partial r}\right] < 0, \tag{6.5.20}$$

where

$$\Delta \equiv -\frac{\partial i^d}{\partial \rho}\left[1-\left(1+\frac{\kappa\theta}{r}\right)\frac{\partial (M/P)^d}{\partial \Omega}\right]$$
$$+ \frac{M}{P}\frac{\kappa\theta}{r^2} - \left(1+\frac{\kappa\theta}{r}\right)\frac{\partial (M/P)^d}{\partial r}\frac{\partial c^d}{\partial \Omega} > 0. \tag{6.5.21}$$

We therefore see that the increase in $\mu$ leads to a fall in the expected real rate of interest, a less than one-for-one rise in the nominal rate of interest, and a reduction in the real value of government-issued wealth. These results are depicted graphically in Figure 6.5. We therefore see that with wealth effects the Fisher hypothesis does not even hold in equilib-

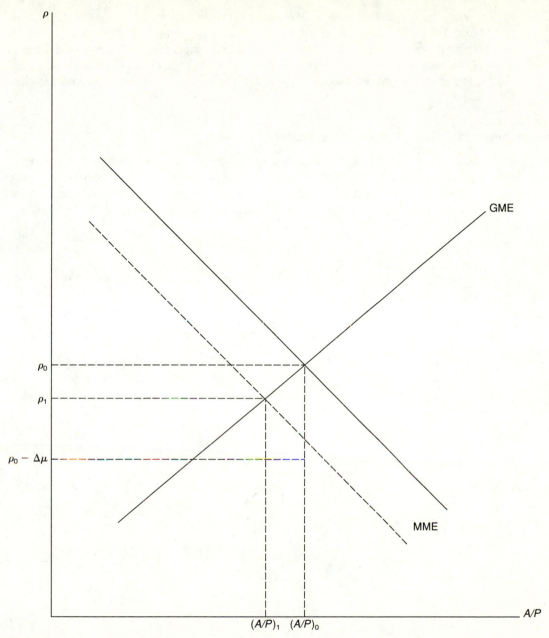

**Figure 6.5**

rium. Higher inflation rates correspond to lower expected real rates of interest. Following Mundell (1963) and Tobin (1965), this inverse relationship between the properly antici- pated rate of inflation and the real interest rate is known as the Mundell-Tobin effect.

The intuition behind the effect of changes in the rate of inflation on the expected real rate of interest is as follows. The increase in the rate of expansion of government liabilities raises the actual and expected rates of inflation and the nominal rate of interest subsequently also rises. The higher nominal rate of interest reduces the demand for real money balances. With a constant value for $\theta$, $B/rP$ also falls. The implied reduction in wealth reduces consumption demand. However, with total output fixed at $y^*$, total demand must be unchanged. Therefore, the expected real rate of interest must fall to stimulate investment spending and provide an offset to the decline in consumption demand described above.

## Government Liability Management Reconsidered

Also of interest are changes in the proportion of government debt monetized by the central bank. This type of policy is parameterized in the present analysis by $\theta \equiv B/M$. In Section 6.4, we demonstrated that in the absence of wealth effects changes in $\theta$ are neutral in that such changes have no impact on the expected real rate of interest.

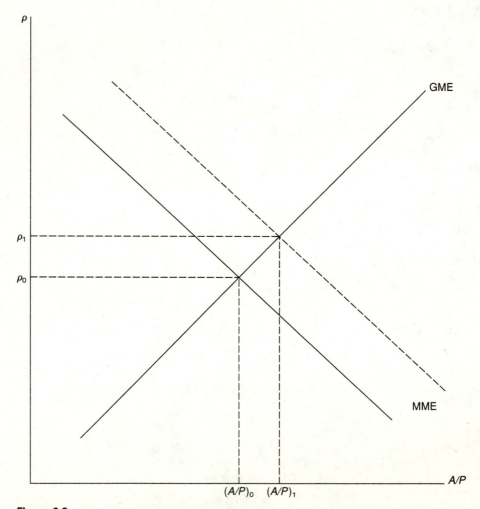

**Figure 6.6**

However, with nonzero wealth effects, this result no longer carries through. Differentiating the equilibrium conditions with respect to $\rho$, $A/P$, and $\theta$, we find that

$$
\begin{bmatrix}
\dfrac{\partial \text{EDG}}{\partial r} & \dfrac{\partial \text{EDG}}{\partial (A/P)} \\[2ex]
\dfrac{\partial \text{EDM}}{\partial r} & \dfrac{\partial \text{EDM}}{\partial (A/P)}
\end{bmatrix}
\begin{bmatrix}
\dfrac{d\rho}{d\theta} \\[2ex]
\dfrac{d(A/P)}{d\theta}
\end{bmatrix}
=
\begin{bmatrix}
0 \\[2ex]
-\left(\dfrac{\kappa}{\theta}\right)\left(\dfrac{B}{rP}\right)
\end{bmatrix}.
\tag{6.5.22}
$$

Solving by means of Cramer's rule, we obtain

$$
\frac{d\rho}{d\theta} = \frac{dr}{d\theta} = \frac{1}{\Delta}\,\frac{\kappa}{\theta}\,\frac{B}{rP}\,\frac{\partial c^d}{\partial \Omega} > 0,
\tag{6.5.23}
$$

$$
\frac{d(A/P)}{d\theta} = -\frac{1}{\Delta}\,\frac{\kappa}{\theta}\,\frac{B}{rP}\left(\frac{\partial i^d}{\partial \rho} - \frac{RK}{\rho^2}\,\frac{\partial c^d}{\partial z}\right) > 0.
\tag{6.5.24}
$$

Therefore, an increase in the ratio of bonds to money now increases nominal and expected real rates of interest and also leads to an increase in the real value of government-issued wealth. These effects are depicted in Figure 6.6.

Totally differentiating the government budget constraint with respect to $\theta$ and $\tau$, we obtain, upon rearranging terms,

$$
\frac{d\tau}{d\theta} = \frac{\rho}{\theta}\,\frac{B}{rP} + \left[\frac{\mu}{r}\,\frac{B}{rP} + \left(\rho\,\frac{B}{rP} - \pi\,\frac{M}{P}\right)\frac{\partial (M/P)^d/\partial r}{M/P}\right]\frac{dr}{d\theta}.
\tag{6.5.25}
$$

Although this expression is likely to be positive as long as wealth effects and hence $dr/d\theta$ are not large in absolute value, it is less clear whether the presence of wealth effects amplifies or moderates the increase in taxes necessitated by an increase in $\theta$.

# Appendix A: Inflation and the Representative Firm and Household Choice Problems

This appendix provides appropriate modifications to the analyses of Appendixes 1.B and 1.C for the case of constant but nonzero expected inflation. Throughout the analysis, we assume that all agents expect the future time paths of wages and prices to be given by

$$
W(t) = W(0)e^{\pi^f t},
\tag{6.A.1}
$$

$$
P(t) = P(0)e^{\pi^f t}.
\tag{6.A.2}
$$

Let us begin with the representative firm's investment decision. With $W$ and $P$ written as explicit functions of time, the problem of Appendix 1.B is given by

$$
\max_{\ell(t),u(t)} \frac{1}{E} \int_0^\infty \left\{ P(t)\Phi(\ell(t), K(t)) - W(t)\ell(t) - P(t)u(t) - P(t)\frac{\alpha}{2}[u(t)]^2 \right\} e^{-rt}\, dt
\tag{6.A.3}
$$

subject to

$$\dot{K}(t) = i = u. \tag{6.A.4}$$

Now plugging in for the expectational assumption above, and recalling that $w \equiv W/P$, the maximand may be rewritten as

$$\frac{P(0)}{E} \int_0^\infty \left\{ \Phi(\ell(t), K(t)) - w\ell(t) - u(t) - \frac{\alpha}{2}[u(t)]^2 \right\} e^{\pi^e t} e^{-rt} \, dt. \tag{6.A.5}$$

Finally, recalling the definition $\rho = r - \pi^e$, the problem may be recast as

$$\max_{\ell(t), u(t)} \frac{P(0)}{E} \int_0^\infty \left\{ \Phi(\ell(t), K(t)) - w\ell(t) - u(t) - \frac{\alpha}{2}[u(t)]^2 \right\} e^{-\rho t} \, dt \tag{6.A.6}$$

subject to

$$\dot{K}(t) = i = u. \tag{6.A.7}$$

We therefore find that this problem is identical to the problem of Appendix 1.B except that the expected real rate of interest $\rho$ replaces the nominal rate of interest $r$. Solution of this problem results in an investment demand function of the form

$$i^d = \xi_k(R - \rho). \tag{6.A.8}$$

We next consider the representative household's choice problem. Appropriate modifications here are just as straightforward but may not be quite so obvious. Let us begin with the representative household's instantaneous budget constraint. At any point in time, nominal savings equals nominal disposable income minus consumption and minus transaction and adjustment costs. Furthermore, nominal savings is divided between accumulation of additional money balances, accumulation of additional government bonds, and accumulation of additional equities. We therefore require that

$$\frac{dM}{dt} + \frac{1}{r}\frac{dB}{dt} + P_e\frac{dE}{dt} = W\ell + P\Pi + B - P\left[ c + \tau + \gamma + \frac{\eta}{2}(\dot{m})^2 \right]. \tag{6.A.9}$$

The budget constraint can also be expressed in real terms as

$$\frac{1}{P}\frac{dM}{dt} + \frac{1}{rP}\frac{dB}{dt} + \frac{P_e}{P}\frac{dE}{dt} = w\ell + \Pi + \frac{B}{P} - \left[ c + \tau + \gamma + \frac{\eta}{2}(\dot{m})^2 \right]. \tag{6.A.10}$$

Let us now define total real holdings of earning assets as

$$f \equiv \frac{B}{rP} + \frac{P_e E}{P} = \frac{B}{rP} + \frac{\Pi}{\rho}. \tag{6.A.11}$$

Taking the time derivative of the above expression and substituting the expectational assumptions

$$\frac{1}{P}\frac{dP}{dt} = \pi^e \quad \text{and} \quad \frac{dr}{dt} = \frac{d(P_e/P)}{dt} = 0, \tag{6.A.12}$$

we obtain

$$\frac{1}{rP}\frac{dB}{dt} + \frac{P_e}{P}\frac{dE}{dt} = \frac{df}{dt} + \frac{B}{rP}\pi^e. \tag{6.A.13}$$

We next take the time derivative of the definition $m \equiv M/P$ and again employ our expectational assumptions to obtain

$$\frac{1}{P}\frac{dM}{dt} = \frac{dm}{dt} + m\pi^e. \tag{6.A.14}$$

We can now plug identities (6.A.13) and (6.A.14) into the budget constraint (6.A.10) to obtain

$$\frac{df}{dt} = \rho f - \frac{dm}{dt} - m\pi^e + w\ell - \left[ c + \tau + \gamma + \frac{\eta}{2}(\dot{m})^2 \right]. \tag{6.A.15}$$

The representative household's choice problem, from Appendix 1.C, is now given by

$$\max_{\ell(t),c(t),u(t)} V = \int_0^N U(c(t), \ell(t))e^{-\beta t} \, dt \tag{6.A.16}$$

subject to

$$\dot{m} = u, \tag{6.A.17}$$

$$\dot{f} = \rho f(t) + w\ell(t) - c(t) - \tau - \gamma(m(t), y) - \frac{\eta}{2}[u(t)]^2 - u(t) - m(t)\pi^e. \tag{6.A.18}$$

Solution of the representative household's problem now follows closely the analysis of Appendix 1.C. The first-order conditions imply the following second-order differential equation in $m(t)$:

$$\ddot{m} - (r - \pi^e)\dot{m} - \frac{1}{\eta}\left( r + \frac{\partial\gamma}{\partial m} \right) = 0. \tag{6.A.19}$$

The steady-state equilibrium of this differential equation is given by

$$-\frac{\partial\gamma}{\partial m} = r. \tag{6.A.20}$$

This equilibrium condition therefore implies a money demand function in which the demand for money depends on the nominal rather than the expected real rate of interest. The expected real rate of interest may, however, affect the speed at which the representative household adjusts its actual to its desired level of real money balances. We now focus on the case in which $\eta \to 0$, in which actual real money balances instantaneously adjust to desired real money balances. The representative household's holdings of real money balances are therefore continuously given by

$$m(t) = \left( \frac{M}{P} \right)^d (y, r) \equiv m^*. \tag{6.A.21}$$

Next consider the differential equation governing the representative household's consumption-saving choice. Retaining the notation of Appendix 1.C, the solution of the representative household's consumption-saving problem is summarized by the first-order conditions

$$\frac{\partial U(c, \ell)}{\partial c} = \lambda_2(t), \tag{6.A.22}$$

$$\dot{\lambda}_2(t) = (\beta - \rho)\lambda_2(t) \to \lambda_2(t) = \lambda_2(0)e^{-(\rho - \beta)t}. \tag{6.A.23}$$

Note that in the differential equation for $\lambda_2(t)$, the expected real rate of interest $\rho$ replaces the nominal rate of interest $r$ that appears in the analogous equation of Appendix 1.C.

Solution of the representative household's intertemporal budget constraint results in the following specification for the representative household's real earning asset holdings over time:

$$f(t) = f(0)e^{\rho t} + \int_0^t [w^*\ell^* - c(s) - \tau - \gamma(m^*, y) - m^*\pi^e]e^{\rho(t-s)} \, ds. \tag{6.A.24}$$

If we now invoke the asset exhaustion condition $f(N) + m(N) = 0$, adopt the logarithmic instantaneous utility function $U(\cdot) = \ln(\cdot)$, and take the limit as $N \to +\infty$, the first-order conditions of the representative household's choice problem imply the following time path for consumption spending:

$$c(t) = h(l^*)\left(1 - \frac{\beta}{\rho}e^{(\rho-\beta)t}\right)$$

$$\times \frac{\beta}{\rho}\left[\frac{B}{P} + \Pi + w^*\ell^* - \tau - \gamma(m^*, y) - \left(\frac{M}{P} + \frac{B}{rP}\right)\pi^e\right]e^{(\rho-\beta)t}. \tag{6.A.25}$$

Evaluating at $t = 0$ and assuming that $\gamma \simeq 0$, we obtain the consumption function given in Section 6.2.

# REFERENCES

Benveniste, L. M., and José A. Scheinkman, ''Duality Theory for Dynamic Optimization Models of Economics: The Continuous Time Case,'' *Journal of Economic Theory,* June, 1982, 1–19.

Brock, William A., ''Money and Growth: The Case of Long Run Perfect Foresight,'' *International Economic Review,* October, 1974, 750–777.

Brock, William A., ''A Simple Perfect Foresight Monetary Model,'' *Journal of Monetary Economics,* April, 1975, 133–150.

Cagan, Phillip D., ''The Monetary Dynamics of Hyperinflation,'' in Milton Friedman, ed., *Studies in the Quantity Theory of Money,* Chicago, University of Chicago Press, 1956.

Fama, Eugene, F., ''Short-Term Interest Rates as Predictors of Inflation,'' *American Economic Review,* June, 1975, 269–282.

Fisher, Irving, *The Theory of Interest,* New York, Macmillan, 1930.

LeRoy, Stephen F., ''Nominal Prices and Interest Rates in General Equilibrium: Money Shocks,'' *Journal of Business,* April, 1984a, 177–195.

LeRoy, Stephen F., ''Nominal Prices and Interest Rates in General Equilibrium: Endowment Shocks,'' *Journal of Business,* April, 1984b, 197–213.

Levi, Maurice D., and John H. Makin, ''Anticipated Inflation and Interest Rates: Further Interpretation of Findings on the Fisher Equation,'' *American Economic Review,* December, 1978, 801–812.

Mundell, Robert, ''Inflation and Real Interest,'' *Journal of Political Economy,* June, 1963, 280–283.

Nguyen, Duc-Tho, and Stephen J. Turnovsky, ''Monetary and Fiscal Policies in an Inflationary Economy: A Simulation Approach,'' *Journal of Money, Credit and Banking,* August, 1979, 259–283.

Obstfeld, Maurice, and Kenneth Rogoff, ''Speculative Hyperinflations: Can We Rule Them Out?'' *Journal of Political Economy,* August, 1983, 675–687.

Pyle, David H., and Stephen J. Turnovsky, ''The Dynamics of Government Policy in an Inflationary Economy: An Intermediate-Run Analysis,'' *Journal of Money, Credit and Banking,* November, 1976, 411–437.

Sargent, Thomas J., ''Anticipated Inflation and the Nominal Interest Rate,'' *Quarterly Journal of Economics,* May, 1972, 212–225.

Sargent, Thomas J., Macroeconomic Theory, 2nd. ed., Orlando, FL, Academic, 1987.

Summers, Lawrence H., "The Nonadjustment of Nominal Interest Rates: A Study of the Fisher Effect," in James Tobin, ed., *Macroeconomics, Prices, and Quantities*, Washington, D.C., Brookings, 1983.

Tobin, James, "Money and Economic Growth," *Econometrica,* October, 1965, 671–684.

Turnovsky, Stephen J., *Macroeconomic Analysis and Stabilization Policy,* Cambridge, England, Cambridge University Press, 1977.

# Chapter **7**

## Unemployment and Inflation

This chapter discusses the phenomenon of unemployment and introduces dynamic models based on causal links that might exist between the rate of inflation and the level of unemployment. Section 7.1 discusses the phenomenon of unemployment and presents a very simple, static theory of unemployment. Section 7.2 considers the importance of worker-firm heterogeneity and shows how resulting frictions provide a richer, dynamic theory of unemployment. Section 7.3 introduces Phillips's study of inflation and unemployment and presents a theory capable of explaining both Phillips's original finding of a stable unemployment-inflation relationship and the much less stable association between inflation and unemployment apparent in more recent U.S. data. Section 7.4 embeds this theory in a complete macromodel and analyzes the dynamic adjustment of the economy to an acceleration in the rate of growth of the money supply. Section 7.5 considers an alternative dynamic model of the economy in which output responds to variations in the expected real rate of interest. Interestingly, the macroeconomic models of Sections 7.4 and 7.5 share a number of common characteristics in their responses to an acceleration in the rate of inflation.

## 7.1 A STATIC MODEL OF UNEMPLOYMENT

The discussion in Chapter 5 of aggregate supply analyzes the hours of current work decision of the representative household. Changes in the perceived current real wage, changes in expectations about the future, and changes in the rate of interest prompt changes in the number of hours of work, and such changes in work hours translate at the aggregate level into changes in total employment. In that discussion, attention centers on the hours-of-work decision because we postulate an aggregate production function that relates total output to total hours worked independent of the distribution of those hours worked across different individuals.

A basic foundation of our current discussion of unemployment is the realization that in order to define unemployment, one must treat working and being unemployed as two mutually exclusive labor market states. Therefore, if changes in the number of individuals who are employed are thought to be the primary source of changes in firms' employment of labor services, then by definition changes in hours worked per worker must be considered relatively unimportant.

Variability in hours worked is small if there are important economic factors inhibiting most workers from engaging in part-time work as a regular lifelong practice. Such part-time work may be relatively inefficient due to the existence of fixed employment costs like commuting expenses and the realization of productive externalities when many workers all work common hours. To the extent that part-time work is economically efficient, it is nevertheless likely that changes in total work hours among part-time employees are small relative to changes in total work hours due to changes in the number of full-time workers employed. This possibility is, in fact, supported by the data. Hansen (1985) attributes over half of the variations in aggregate fluctuations in recent U.S. employment to changes in the number of individuals working as opposed to changes in the numbers of hours worked per worker, which only account for about one-fifth of the total variation in employment.

To clarify our discussion of unemployment, it is therefore useful to recast the representative household's labor supply problem in an all-or-nothing framework. The representative household chooses to supply its single unit of labor if the expected net gain in utility from working and consuming the proceeds of the real wage is positive. Aggregate labor supply can then be computed simply by totaling the number of agents deciding to work. Furthermore, this setup makes unambiguous the effect of an increase in the perceived current real wage on aggregate labor supply since fixed working hours preclude the possibility of reductions in current hours worked by the individual as a response to an increase in the perceived current real wage. With only the substitution effect and not the income effect operational, increases in the perceived current real wage unambiguously increase current aggregate labor supply.

Treatment of labor supply as a binary decision variable at the individual level provides a clear-cut classification of individuals into suppliers and nonsuppliers of labor. The assumed unimportance of markets in part-time employment further provides a clear-cut classification of individuals into those employed and those not employed. However, we still require a further disaggregation of those not employed into those who are unemployed and those who are not in the labor force. Individuals with relatively long-lasting commitments to schooling, nonmarket domestic duties, and/or child-care duties and those whose poor health precludes labor market participation are those we normally classify as not in the labor force.

In order to proceed, it is useful simply to assume that demographic characteristics provide an unambiguous classification of those not working among those unemployed and those not in the labor force. Those not in the labor force are those households who choose not to work even under the most favorable circumstances one can realistically expect. Alternatively, the unemployed are those households who, for the time being, choose to consume their unit of labor as leisure and those households who would prefer to be employed but are currently unable to find suitable employment. For our purposes, the assumption of a fixed work force is not that bad an abstraction since most evidence supports the hypothesis that the size of the work force does not vary substantially over the course of the business cycle.

## Indivisible Labor and Employment

We formally assume that there are $N$ identical households each with one indivisible unit of labor who choose to participate in the labor force. We further assume that each household's level of utility is given by the concave, no-wealth-effects utility function

$$V = U[c - h(x)], \tag{7.1.1}$$

where

$$x = \begin{cases} 0 & \text{if unemployed,} \\ 1 & \text{if employed.} \end{cases} \tag{7.1.2}$$

Households prefer leisure to work and so we assume that $h(1) > h(0)$. Consumption of the composite good is given by $c$.

Denote the fraction of households who participate in the labor market but are unemployed by $u$. The fraction $1 - u$ of households who participate in the labor market are therefore employed. Total employment is denoted by

$$L = (1 - u)N. \tag{7.1.3}$$

We continue to assume that the representative firm produces output of the composite good according to the production function

$$y = \Phi(L, \overline{K}), \tag{7.1.4}$$

where $\overline{K}$ represents the fixed stock of capital and $L$ now represents the number of employed households.

Maximization of firm profits results in an employment demand function $L^d$, where $L^d$ represents the maximum integer for which

$$w \leq \Phi(L^d, \overline{K}) - \Phi(L^d - 1, \overline{K}). \tag{7.1.5}$$

However, we assume that the representative firm hires a large enough number of workers so that indivisibilities in employment are insignificant on the demand side, and so we simply assume a continuous employment demand function given by

$$L^d = L^d(w), \qquad \frac{\partial L^d}{\partial w} = \left( \frac{\partial^2 \Phi}{\partial L^2} \right)^{-1} < 0. \tag{7.1.6}$$

We next turn our attention to employment supply. At the level of the individual household, employment supply is either 1 or 0. At the aggregate level, employment supply measures the number of households who choose to work. An individual household wishes to be employed as long as

$$U[a + w - h(1)] \geq U[a - h(0)], \tag{7.1.7}$$

where $a$ represents real nonwage income.

The combined assumptions of indivisibilities in employment and identical households leads to an employment supply function of the form

$$L^s = \begin{cases} 0 & \text{if } w < h(1) - h(0), \\ N & \text{if } w \geq h(1) - h(0). \end{cases} \qquad (7.1.8)$$

We therefore find that the employment supply function is characterized by an important discontinuity. If the real wage is greater than or equal to $w^* \equiv h(1) - h(0)$, then all households wish to work. If the real wage is less than $w^*$, no households are willing to work and employment is zero. When $w = w^*$, all households are equally well off, whether they are employed or not, even though the unemployed households are willing to work at the prevailing real wage.

Figure 7.1 depicts equilibrium in the labor market. The equilibrium real wage is equal to $w^*$. Equilibrium employment $L^*$ is characterized by

$$w^* = \frac{\partial \Phi}{\partial L}(L^*, \overline{K}). \qquad (7.1.9)$$

Equilibrium unemployment is equal to

$$u^* = \frac{N - L^*}{N}. \qquad (7.1.10)$$

Indivisibilities in employment are therefore capable of supporting a very simple model in which unemployment exists as an equilibrium outcome. Furthermore, as noted

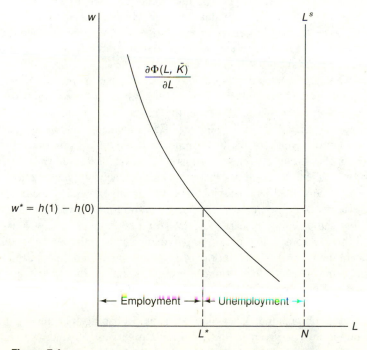

**Figure 7.1**

by Rogerson (1988), such models are consistent with empirical evidence on observed relative magnitudes of fluctuations in employment and real wages. However, an equilibrium in which the unemployed are willing to work is only consistent, in the present setup, with the assumption of identical households. If households differ in their taste for leisure (different $h$ functions) or in their levels of nonwage income (different $a$'s), then the model of this section would more closely mimic the labor supply analysis of Chapter 1, in which there were no indivisibilities in employment. We would again find an upward-sloping schedule of the supply of total labor services, and all households willing to work would always be employed. However, the model of this section might still have important implications for the division of labor across households and the movements of employment and real wages over time.

## 7.2 A DYNAMIC MODEL OF UNEMPLOYMENT

In this section, we retain the assumption of a clear-cut distinction between labor market participants and those households that choose to remain outside the labor force. However, we now consider job search as an alternative use of time as opposed to the presumption, in Section 7.1, that all nonworking households consume their unit of time as leisure.

### Unemployment and Job Turnover

This section abandons the timeless framework of Section 7.1 in favor of an explicitly dynamic formulation. In particular, we note that turnover in employment is an important characteristic of most labor markets and that, generally speaking, some amount of time is spent in unemployment when individuals change jobs or enter or reenter the labor market. To gain insight into how job turnover affects the levels of employment and unemployment, we now examine a simple dynamic model along the lines of Hall (1979), Darby, Haltiwanger, and Plant (1985), and Barro (1988).

To make things as simple as possible, we assume that the prevailing real wage generates equality between the number of jobs and the number of households seeking employment. We further assume, as noted above, that there are no changes over time either in the size of the labor force $N$ or in the number of jobs available. However, at any instant of time a constant fraction $s$ of the total number of individuals employed becomes unemployed. This characteristic of the labor market could be the result of a shifting pattern of demand for different commodities that would simultaneously generate job leavers in declining sectors combined with new job opportunities in expanding sectors. Alternatively, such separations could be the result of individual households reevaluating their terms of employment and deciding to search full time for a better opportunity. Finally, such turnover could result from a flow out of employment due to retirements or other exogenous factors combined with an equal inflow of new entrants or reentrants to the labor market with such entry or reentry occurring through an initial period of unemployment.

The second building block of the model is the process by which unemployed workers get matched with new jobs. The unemployed search over firms in an attempt to find a firm with a suitable job opening. We assume that the probability per unit of time of finding such an opportunity is given by the constant, exogenous job-finding rate $f$.

This simple job separation and job-finding technology implies a rate of flow into the unemployment pool equal to $s(1 - u)N$ and a rate of flow of workers into employment equal to $fuN$. We therefore obtain the following differential equation that summarizes the dynamics of unemployment:

$$\frac{d(uN)}{dt} = s(1 - u)N - fuN. \tag{7.2.1}$$

Since $N$ is assumed constant throughout, we may divide the above equation through by $N$ to obtain

$$\frac{du}{dt} = s - (s + f)u. \tag{7.2.2}$$

The above expression is a first-order, constant-coefficient differential equation in $u$, the unemployment rate. The solution of this equation is given by

$$u(t) = u^* + [u(0) - u^*]e^{-(s+f)t}, \tag{7.2.3}$$

where

$$u^* \equiv \frac{s}{s + f} = \frac{s/f}{1 + s/f}. \tag{7.2.4}$$

The term $u^*$ therefore represents the equilibrium unemployment rate. The convergence of $u$ to $u^*$ is stable as long as $s$ and $f$ are constant and their sum is positive. The equilibrium unemployment rate is a function of the ratio of $s$ to $f$. A higher separation rate implies a higher equilibrium unemployment rate, while a higher job-finding rate implies a lower equilibrium unemployment rate. Unemployment exists in equilibrium because workers need to be reallocated to different jobs and because job search for a new position takes time. Such unemployment exists even though, in the aggregate, the number of jobs and the number of workers are equal. Equality between the number of jobs and workers also suggests that there is no particular pressure for change in the prevailing real wage rate.

The formal model presented above adopts the assumption of worker and firm homogeneity. All workers have identical preferences and skills and all firms view workers as perfectly interchangeable in the production of a single, homogeneous composite good. However, the basic flavor of the model hopes to proxy for worker and firm heterogeneity. Workers may quit their jobs to seek a different job that is more closely suited to their particular package of skills and pays a higher wage in comparison to the general wage distribution. Similarly, different firms have job openings at different times and pay differing wage rates according to conditions of demand in the market for their particular type of output.

Formal consideration of heterogeneity in workers and firms makes results of the turnover model more compatible with existing empirical evidence on the behavior of unemployment. Average job separation and job-finding rates imply an equilibrium unemployment rate that is lower than those typically experienced, at least in post–World War II data for the United States. However, Clark and Summers (1979) point out that the bulk of unemployment may be experienced by a relatively small fraction of the population characterized by a higher than average separation rate and a lower than average job-finding rate.

Clark and Summers demonstrate that such heterogeneity in separation and finding rates imply a higher equilibrium unemployment rate than that calculated from the average separation and finding rates across all labor market participants.

Empirical evidence also points to greater persistence in the unemployment rate over time than that implied by the speed of adjustment in the simple differential equation in $u$ of the basic turnover model. However, Darby et al. (1985) point out that if there are two groups, one with higher than average values of both $s$ and $f$ and another group with lower than average values of both $s$ and $f$, movements in the aggregate unemployment rate may be much slower than that implied by the average values of $s$ and $f$.

## Productive Job Search and Unemployment

Another form of heterogeneity that has received considerable attention over time is the possibility that an unemployed job searcher may face considerable dispersion in the wage rates offered by different firms. Such variability in potential offers makes the possibility of turning down several job offers an economically worthwhile proposition. This phenomenon of job search for a particularly favorable wage rate was originally popularized by McCall (1970).

Following McCall, we assume that a job searcher receives exactly one job offer per period. Each job offer is viewed by the searcher as a random draw from the subjective probability density function $g(W)$. To simplify matters, we provisionally assume that the actual distribution of wage offers is identical to the searcher's subjective distribution of wage offers. In each period, the job searcher incurs a fixed cost $\xi$ in order to receive a wage offer. If the searcher accepts the wage offer, he expects to remain employed at the offering firm indefinitely, and he gives up subsequent search. If the searcher rejects the wage offer, he pays $\xi$ again and receives another offer. The cost of search $\xi$ may include out-of-pocket expenses incurred in the search process as well as the utility value of the time spent searching.

This very simple search technology possesses a constant acceptance wage strategy as the optimal stopping rule. In particular, the optimal search strategy is to accept any wage offer above the constant acceptance wage $W^*$ and to reject any wage offer below the acceptance wage $W^*$. Once a constant acceptance wage is chosen, the time spent searching is a random variable with a geometric probability distribution. The probability that any wage offer is accepted is given by

$$q \equiv \int_{W^*}^{\infty} (W - W^*)g(w)\, dW, \tag{7.2.5}$$

where $g(W)$ represents the wage offer density function. The expected duration of search is equal to $1/q$.

Total expected search costs are equal to the cost per search effort $\xi$ multiplied by the expected number of search attempts $1/q$. The expected value of the gross returns to search is equal to the expected value of $W$ given that $W$ exceeds $W^*$. Therefore,

$$\text{Net gains from search} = \frac{1}{q}\left[\int_{W^*}^{\infty} Wg(w)\, dW - \xi\right]. \tag{7.2.6}$$

Differentiating the above expression with respect to $W^*$ and rearranging, we find that the optimal acceptance wage satisfies

$$\xi = \int_{W^*}^{\infty} (W - W^*)g(w) \, dW. \tag{7.2.7}$$

The above first-order condition has a very simple economic interpretation. The left-hand side, $\xi$, is equal to the marginal cost of an additional wage offer. The right-hand side represents the expected gains from searching one more time given that the searcher has just been offered the wage offer $W^*$. The acceptance wage is that wage that exactly equates the marginal cost of continued search with the marginal benefits of continued search.

Comparative statics experiments on the above first-order condition generates several fairly intuitive results. An increase in the cost of search $\xi$ lowers the optimal acceptance wage and reduces the expected duration of search $1/q$. Alternatively, a favorable shift in the wage offer distribution increases the acceptance wage while having an ambiguous effect on the expected duration of search. This last result obtains because a more favorable wage distribution makes a wage higher than $W^*$ more likely at the same time that a higher value of $W^*$ makes an acceptable wage offer less likely. Lippman and McCall (1976) summarize these results as well as a number of important extensions of the basic search model.

## Job Search and Turnover Unemployment

Our earlier analysis of job turnover emphasized the job-finding rate $f$ as an important determinant of the level of unemployment. The analysis of job search above suggests that the job-finding rate should depend on optimal job search behavior in combination with the existing job search technology. In particular, the job-finding rate should be an increasing function of the probability of job acceptance $q$. Quite obviously, therefore, we should expect increased search costs to increase the rate of job finding and therefore lower the equilibrium unemployment rate. However, we should not necessarily view such a change as welfare improving. Presumably, a higher cost of job search implies poorer equilibrium matches between individual job and worker characteristics.

An important implication of the search and turnover model of unemployment concerns the effect of imperfect information about wage offer opportunities on the behavior of unemployment over time. Most search models assume fixed subjective and actual wage offer distributions. Some, like Jovanovic (1984), endogenize the distribution of opportunities faced by labor market participants. However, such more ambitious models, while important from the point of view of establishing the existence of equilibria with nondegenerate wage offer distributions, are not very amenable to easy macroeconomic applications.

A common way to proceed is to assume that a nondegenerate actual wage distribution exists and that this actual wage distribution may vary over time in a manner that differs from movements in the subjective distribution of wages. This approach is very similar to the treatment of movements in the actual as opposed to the expected price level presented in Chapter 5. In particular, suppose that movements in the actual wage distribution are parameterized by movements in the actual average wage across firms, which we denote by $W$. Alternatively, suppose that movements in the subjective wage distribution are parameterized by movements in the expected average wage across firms, denoted by $W^e$.

An increase in $W^e$ holding $W$ constant results in an increase in the acceptance wage $W^*$ and a reduction in the probability of finding an acceptable wage offer. An increase in $W$ holding $W^e$ constant results in no change in the acceptance wage $W^*$ along with an increase in the probability of finding an acceptable wage offer $q$. Recalling that the job-finding rate $f$ is an increasing function of the probability of finding an acceptable wage offer, it is reasonable to assume that the job-finding rate may be written as an increasing function of the ratio of the actual average wage $W$ to the expected average wage $W^e$.[1] We therefore postulate

$$f = f\left(\frac{W}{W^e}\right), \qquad \frac{\partial f}{\partial(W/W^e)} > 0. \tag{7.2.8}$$

We are now ready to construct a model of how imperfect information about the distribution of wage offers might affect the way the unemployment rate moves over time. First, let us rewrite the above job-finding rate function as

$$f = f\left(\frac{W}{P} \frac{P}{P^e} \frac{P^e}{W^e}\right). \tag{7.2.9}$$

If the supply and demand for employment are functions only of the real wage $W/P$, then the real wage is constant in equilibrium. Furthermore, with $W/P$ fixed in equilibrium, $W^e/P^e$ is also likely to remain constant over time. We have therefore generated a model in which the job-finding rate may be related in a simple way to the extent of misinformation about the aggregate price level as captured by the term $P/P^e$.

If we assume that the dynamic adjustment of the job turnover process is fairly rapid, then we can model the unemployment rate as the equilibrium unemployment rate of the job turnover process. We therefore obtain

$$u = \frac{s}{s + f(P/P^e)}. \tag{7.2.10}$$

Let us now define the normal, or frictional, unemployment rate $u^*$ as that unemployment rate that obtains when there is no imperfect information in the labor market, that is, when $P = P^e$. The level of $u^*$ is likely to be determined primarily by microeconomic considerations that affect the levels of $s$ and $f$. We therefore obtain

$$u^* \equiv \frac{s}{s + f(1)}. \tag{7.2.11}$$

Let us finally express the actual unemployment rate $u$ as the sum of the frictional

---

[1]In addition to the effect of $W/W^e$ on $f$, we should also expect changes in $W/W^e$ to affect the propensity of workers to quit their jobs to devote full-time attention to job search. This effect would lead to a dependence of the separation rate $s$ on the level of $W/W^e$, which works to enhance the effect of $W/W^e$ on $u$. For more discussion of job search and quit behavior, see Parsons (1973) and Barron and McCafferty (1977).

unemployment rate $u^*$ and a component that captures the effect of differences between $P$ and $P^e$. We may therefore write

$$u = u^* + \alpha\left(\frac{P}{P^e} - 1\right), \qquad \alpha(0) = 0, \qquad \alpha' < 0. \tag{7.2.12}$$

## 7.3 PHILLIPS'S WAGE RELATION

Probably the most striking piece of empirical evidence about unemployment and the business cycle is that presented by A. W. Phillips (1958) for the United Kingdom for the period 1861–1957 and subsequently confirmed for U.S. data by many other researchers. Phillips found a very stable relationship between unemployment and the rate of wage inflation. His observed relationship looks like that depicted in Figure 7.2. While his study and many of the others utilizing U.S. data plot the rate of wage inflation on the vertical axis, a corresponding relationship between the level of unemployment and the rate of price inflation has also been confirmed.[2]

Phillips's U.K. study spanned a period in which wage and price stability was very much the norm. Periods of inflation and deflation tended to be very short-lived and there was no considerable upward or downward secular drift in the aggregate price level. Alternatively, while Phillips's study found the relationship between unemployment and inflation to be very stable even over a period of almost 100 years, more recent studies have found this relationship to be much more unstable. Perhaps not inconsequentially, however, the time periods in which the inflation-unemployment relationship is most unstable are also those periods of very high and very variable rates of inflation. A major focus of macroeconomic research in the 1960s and 1970s centered on attempts to reconcile with economic theory the simultaneous existence of the original statistical regularity noted by Phillips and periods in which the relationship appeared to break down.

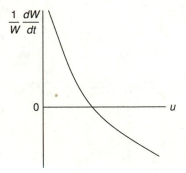

**Figure 7.2**

---

[2]Gordon (1976) provides an excellent overview of the Phillips curve literature.

## Imperfect Information Theories of the Phillips Curve

The analysis of search and turnover of Section 7.2 generated an unemployment relationship of the form

$$u = u^* + \alpha \left( \frac{P}{P^e} - 1 \right), \qquad \alpha(0) = 0, \qquad \alpha' < 0. \tag{7.3.1}$$

The above relationship is based on the possibility of shifts in the average level of wages relative to the expected level of wages that might result in changes over time in the rate at which unemployed job searchers accept employment.

Interestingly, the labor supply analysis of Chapter 5 also generates an identical relationship between $u$ and $P/P^e$. However, while the analysis of Section 7.2 focuses on imperfect information about the distribution of wages over space, the analysis of Chapter 5 is based on imperfect information about the real value of the current, uniform nominal wage rate.

In order to reinterpret the analysis of Chapter 5 in light of the indivisibility of labor introduced in Section 7.1, we need only replace the continuous variable in the analysis of Chapter 5 with the discrete variable $L^s = Nx$, $x = 0, 1$. With this substitution, the analysis of Chapter 5 goes through basically unchanged.[3] Such an analysis leads to an employment supply function of the form

$$L^s = \hat{L}^s \left( \frac{W_t}{P_t^e}, \frac{W_{t+1}^e}{P_{t+1}^e}, r - \ln \left( \frac{P_{t+1}^e}{P_t^e} \right), \Omega \right). \tag{7.3.2}$$

Let us provisionally assume that the effects of changes in the interest rate and wealth terms on employment supply are negligible and that the expected future real wage rate is constant. With identical households and indivisible labor, we again obtain an employment supply function with a discontinuity. Households now supply their unit of labor as long as the expected real wage rate $W_t/P_t^e$ exceeds some threshold real wage rate $\hat{w}$, where $\hat{w}$ is a function of the parameters of the representative household's utility function. We therefore obtain an equilibrium real wage rate $w^*$ given by

$$w^* = \frac{W_t}{P_t} = \frac{W_t}{P_t^e} \frac{P_t^e}{P_t} = \frac{\hat{w}}{P_t/P_t^e}. \tag{7.3.3}$$

The level of employment may now be computed as the level of employment demand evaluated at

$$w_t = \frac{\hat{w}}{P_t/P_t^e} \quad \text{or} \quad L = L^d \left( \frac{\hat{w}}{P_t/P_t^e} \right). \tag{7.3.4}$$

---

[3]Actually, the results of the analysis of Chapter 5 are strengthened by the substitution of $x$ for $\ell$. When employment is a binary choice, the usual income effects disappear at the margin, and so the presumption that substitution effects dominate is unambiguous.

The unemployment rate is therefore given by

$$u = \frac{N - L^d\left(\frac{\hat{w}}{P_t/P_t^e}\right)}{N} \qquad (7.3.5)$$

For given values of $N$ and $\hat{w}$, the above expression may be rewritten in the form

$$u = u^* + \alpha\left(\frac{P}{P^e} - 1\right), \qquad \alpha(0) = 0, \qquad \alpha' < 0, \qquad (7.3.6)$$

where

$$u^* \equiv \frac{N - L^d(\hat{w})}{N}. \qquad (7.3.7)$$

We therefore find that the analysis of imperfect current information about the price level presented in Chapter 5 generates an equivalent functional form for the unemployment rate as the search and turnover analysis of Section 7.2.

To obtain a theoretical relationship between the unemployment rate and the rate of inflation, we need only find a relationship between $P/P^e - 1$ and the rate of inflation. Assume that agents know the aggregate price level $P$ with a one-period lag. In order to form an expectation of the current aggregate price level, individuals update last period's observation of the price level by use of the currently expected rate of inflation, which we denote by $\pi_t^e$. In particular, the current value of the expected price index satisfies

$$P_t^e = P_{t-1}(1 + \pi_t^e), \qquad (7.3.8)$$

where $\pi_t^e$ denotes the currently expected rate of inflation.

The argument of the function $\alpha(\cdot)$ above can now be computed in the following way:

$$\frac{P_t}{P_t^e} - 1 = \frac{(P_t - P_{t-1})(1 + \pi_t^e) + P_t[1 - (1 + \pi_t^e)]}{P_{t-1}(1 + \pi_t^e)}. \qquad (7.3.9)$$

Defining $\pi_t \equiv (P_t - P_{t-1})/P_{t-1}$, the actual rate of inflation, the above relationship may be rewritten as

$$\frac{P_t}{P_t^e} - 1 = \pi_t - \frac{1 + \pi_t}{1 + \pi_t^e} \pi_t^e. \qquad (7.3.10)$$

If we linearize in the neighborhood of $\pi_t = \pi_t^e$, then we may postulate the approximate relationship

$$u = u^* + \alpha(\pi_t - \pi_t^e). \qquad (7.3.11)$$

Since $\alpha' < 0$, holding $\pi^e$ fixed generates a downward-sloping relationship between inflation and unemployment. Since the period of time for which Phillips did his study was one of relative price stability, it is likely that $\pi^e$ remained about constant and equal to zero. Therefore, he probably observed the above relationship between changes in $u$ and changes in $\pi_t$ holding $\pi_t^e$ constant. However, in more recent U.S. experience it is likely that changes in $\pi^e$ have been at least as common as changes in $\pi$. We therefore need to make the distinction between short-run and long-run Phillips curves. The short-run Phillips curve treats $\pi^e$ as fixed. However, in the long run we should anticipate the expected inflation rate and the actual inflation rate to be equal. In the present case, if $\pi^e = \pi$, we also find that $u = u^*$ and so the long-run Phillips curve must be vertical.[4]

## Inflation Policy and the Accelerationist Hypothesis

While the distinction between short- and long-run Phillips curves is now well documented, this distinction was not always well appreciated. It was originally thought that the Phillips curve represented an exploitable trade-off between inflation and unemployment. That is, it was thought that you could obtain a little less unemployment by tolerating a little more inflation. If any point along a short-run Phillips curve is viewed as permanently feasible, policymakers are tempted to try to maximize social welfare as defined by the policymaker's view of society's tastes for inflation and unemployment. Policy might then be utilized to lower the unemployment rate by generating inflation. However, while such a policy is temporarily feasible, it is not, at least as predicted by the models hypothesized above, permanently feasible.

According to the *accelerationist hypothesis,* attempts to keep $u$ below $u^*$ lead to accelerating inflation. To appreciate the economic rationale for the accelerationist hypothesis, consider the effects of a sudden increase in the rate of inflation. Because such inflation is probably initially unanticipated, the actual price level begins to rise faster than the expected price level, and so employment rises and unemployment falls. However, unless the rate of inflation accelerates further, individuals begin to anticipate a continuation of the increase in the rate of inflation, and so $\pi^e$ and hence $P^e$ adjust in such a way that the expected and actual price levels are likely to coincide again. Only the possibility of continually escalating inflation seems to have the potential for generating the permanent gap between expected and actual price levels necessary to maintain such a permanent reduction in unemployment below $u^*$.

Furthermore, even the temporary reduction in unemployment likely to be generated by such an acceleration in the rate of inflation is not likely to be a worthwhile goal of economic policy. Such reductions in the level of unemployment are only possible because individuals are fooled into accepting employment under terms under which they would actually prefer to remain unemployed. Therefore, such inflation-generated reductions in the level of unemployment imply reductions rather than increases in any sensibly defined measure of social welfare.

## Cycles in Inflation and Unemployment

The model of the Phillips curve sketched above is capable of reconciling economic theory with cycles in unemployment and inflation observed in post–World War II U.S. economic data. This experience is summarized in Figure 7.3, which plots yearly observations of the

---

[4]Phillips curve models of this type may be found in Phelps (1972). Friedman (1968) provides an excellent intuitive explanation of this phenomenon.

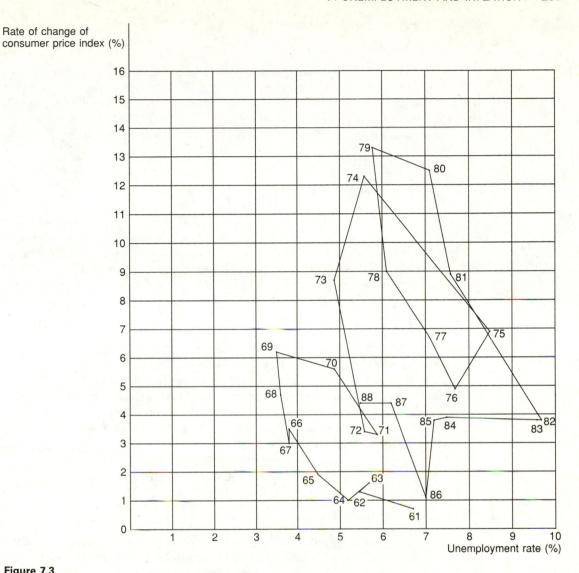

**Figure 7.3**

unemployment rate and the rate of price change. Typical unemployment-inflation cycles consist of periods of acceleration in the inflation rate in which unemployment is below average and periods of deceleration in the inflation rate in which unemployment is above average.

To mimic the experience of a typical cycle, assume that the actual inflation rate exhibits a cyclical pattern and that expectations of inflation are formed according to the adaptive expectations scheme introduced in Section 6.3. Suppose that we start with $u = u^*$ and $\pi = \pi^e = 0$. In this circumstance, movements in the level of unemployment will initially be governed by the relationship

$$u = u^* + \alpha(\pi). \qquad (7.3.12)$$

Now assume that the rate of inflation begins to accelerate. With the expected inflation rate initially equal to zero, the level of unemployment falls. However, the rise in the actual rate of inflation relative to the expected rate of inflation also sets in motion forces that push the level of unemployment back toward $u^*$. To set this, differentiate the unemployment equation and plug the resulting expression into the adaptive expectation equation to obtain

$$\frac{du}{dt} = \alpha' \frac{d\pi}{dt} - \alpha' \psi(\pi - \pi^e). \qquad (7.3.13)$$

The second term in this expression is positive as long as $\pi > \pi^e$. Once the run-up in the rate of inflation begins to subside, this second force dominates and the level of unemployment begins to rise toward $u^*$. If the inflation rate were then kept constant, the level of unemployment would eventually return to $u^*$. However, this high rate of inflation, which we denote by $\pi^{max}$, would then have to be maintained to keep the level of unemployment from rising above $u^*$. With the expected rate of inflation equal to $\pi^{max}$, we have

$$u = u^* + \alpha(\pi - \pi^{max}). \qquad (7.3.14)$$

If the cycle in inflation continues, the actual rate of inflation begins to fall at this point. Unemployment therefore begins to rise above $u^*$. However, just as forces dampened the original reduction in $u$, the downward adaptation of inflationary expectations now works to reverse this rise in unemployment. Ultimately, the deceleration of inflation ends, and if the inflation rate permanently stabilizes, the level of unemployment permanently returns to $u^*$. Alternatively, a continuation of the inflation cycle would perpetuate this cyclical pattern in unemployment as well. Such a cycle in the rate of inflation might result from a political process that vacillates between concern with reducing unemployment and concern with higher than desired rates of inflation.

## Disequilibrium and the Phillips Curve

In Section 5.3, we observed that sticky wages provides an alternative explanation of the aggregate supply process that is observationally very similar to an aggregate supply process based on misperceptions of the aggregate price level. Perhaps not surprisingly, a similar disequilibrium framework is capable of providing an explanation of inflation-unemployment behavior.[5] With sticky wages, we noted that increases in aggregate demand translate into increases in output and employment. Such increases in aggregate demand are also likely to result in reductions in unemployment. It is therefore reasonable to assume that sticky wages would be consistent with

$$u = u^* + \Gamma(y^d - y^s), \qquad \Gamma(0) = 0, \qquad \Gamma' < 0. \qquad (7.3.15)$$

In a generally noninflationary economy it is also reasonable to assume that move-

---

[5]Formal models along these lines may be found in Grossman (1974), Stein (1974), and Van Order (1976).

ments in the level of prices are governed by

$$\frac{dP}{dt} = k(y^d - y^s) \tag{7.3.16}$$

However, if inflation is the norm, it is likely that the price-setting agent continues to raise prices even if $y^d \leq y^s$. In particular, we might imagine the price-setting agent responding to two separate stimuli. In normal times, when $y^d = y^s$, the price-setting agent continues to adjust the price level based on expectations of the rate of change in the market-clearing price. Adjustments to this basic rate of inflation are then made according to whether aggregate demand is less than, equal to, or greater than aggregate supply. If the expected rate of change in the market-clearing price level is approximately equal to the expected rate of inflation, then this price-setting behavior can be summarized by

$$\pi = \pi^e + k(y^d - y^s). \tag{7.3.17}$$

Rearranging the above relationship, we find that

$$y^d - y^s = \frac{\pi - \pi^e}{k}. \tag{7.3.18}$$

Now combining this relationship with the unemployment relationship above, we obtain

$$u = u^* + \Gamma\left(\frac{\pi - \pi^e}{k}\right). \tag{7.3.19}$$

Note that this final relationship is formally identical to the relationship we derived earlier on the basis of incomplete information.

## 7.4 A SHORT-RUN DYNAMIC MACROECONOMIC MODEL

We are now ready to embed the expectations-augmented Phillips curve derived above into a short-run macromodel. Chapter 6 presented a dynamic analysis of inflation and inflationary expectations based on the classical assumption that output is always equal to its equilibrium level $y^*$. In the preceding section, we presented models in which the difference $u - u^*$ is inversely related to the difference $\pi - \pi^e$. In this section, we consider the possibility that output may differ from $y^*$ whenever the unemployment rate $u$ differs from the frictional unemployment rate $u^*$. If we further assume that the GNP gap $y - y^*$ is inversely related to the extent of abnormally high unemployment, $u - u^*$, then the accelerationist Phillips curve models of the preceding section may be translated into their inverse, or goods market, forms. In particular, we now assume that[6]

$$\pi = \pi^e + \zeta(y - y^*), \qquad \zeta(0) = 0, \qquad \zeta' > 0. \tag{7.4.1}$$

---

[6]Since $\alpha(0) = 0$, as noted above, the assumption that $\zeta(0) = 0$ implies that we are now interpreting the equilibrium level of real output $y^*$ as that level of real output consistent with $u = u^*$.

Next consider market clearing in the goods and money markets. A sensible way to proceed is to follow the convention of Chapter 5 and assume that when $y \neq y^*$, output is in any event equal to aggregate goods demand. We also assume that the nominal interest rate adjusts to keep money supply and money demand equal. Therefore, assume that at every point in time $y$, $P$, and $r$ satisfy

$$c^d \left[ y - g - \left(1 + \frac{\theta}{r}\right) \frac{M}{P} (\pi^e - \mu) \right] + i^d(r - \pi^e) + g - y = 0, \tag{7.4.2}$$

$$\left(\frac{M}{P}\right)^d (y, r) - \frac{M}{P} = 0. \tag{7.4.3}$$

We also continue to assume, as in Chapter 6, that the supplies of money and government bonds grow at the common rate $\mu$ on the assumption that the ratio of government bonds to money $\theta$ is constant. We further assume that $g$ is held constant and that any disturbance to other items in the government budget are offset by appropriate changes in the level of taxes.

We therefore begin our formal analysis by differentiating the goods and money market equilibrium conditions with respect to time to obtain

$$0 = -\left(1 - \frac{\partial c^d}{\partial z}\right) \frac{dy}{dt} + \left[ \frac{\partial i^d}{\partial \rho} + \frac{\theta}{r^2} \frac{M}{P} \frac{\partial c^d}{\partial z} (\pi^e - \mu) \right] \frac{dr}{dt}$$
$$- \left[ \frac{\partial i^d}{\partial \rho} + \left(1 + \frac{\theta}{r}\right) \frac{M}{P} \frac{\partial c^d}{\partial z} \right] \frac{d\pi^e}{dt} - \left(1 + \frac{\theta}{r}\right) \frac{M}{P} \frac{\partial c^d}{\partial z} (\pi^e - \mu)(\mu - \pi), \tag{7.4.4}$$

$$0 = \frac{\partial (M/P)^d}{\partial y} \frac{dy}{dt} + \frac{\partial (M/P)^d}{\partial r} \frac{dr}{dt} - \frac{M}{P} (\mu - \pi). \tag{7.4.5}$$

We next substitute the second of the above equations into the first to eliminate $dr/dt$ and evaluate in the neighborhood of the equilibrium condition $\pi^e = \mu$ to obtain, upon rearranging,

$$\frac{dy}{dt} = -\frac{M/P}{\Delta} \frac{\partial i^d}{\partial \rho} (\mu - \pi)$$
$$+ \frac{1}{\Delta} \left[ \frac{\partial i^d}{\partial \rho} + \left(1 + \frac{\theta}{r}\right) \frac{M}{P} \frac{\partial c^d}{\partial z} \right] \frac{\partial (M/P)^d}{\partial r} \frac{d\pi^e}{dt}, \tag{7.4.6}$$

where

$$\Delta \equiv -\left[ \left(1 - \frac{\partial c^d}{\partial z}\right) \frac{\partial (M/P)^d}{\partial r} + \frac{\partial i^d}{\partial \rho} \frac{\partial (M/P)^d}{\partial y} \right] > 0. \tag{7.4.7}$$

Next note that the assumption of adaptive expectations, $d\pi^e/dt = \psi(\pi - \pi^e)$, allows us to rearrange the Phillips curve assumption to obtain

$$\frac{d\pi^e}{dt} = \psi \zeta (y - y^*). \tag{7.4.8}$$

Now plugging in for $d\pi^e/dt$ and noting that $\mu - \pi = \mu - \pi^e - \zeta(y - y^*)$, the above differential equation in $y$ can be rearranged in the following form:

$$\frac{dy}{dt} = -\frac{M/P}{\Delta} \frac{\partial i^d}{\partial \rho}(\mu - \pi^e)$$

$$+ \frac{1}{\Delta}\left[\frac{M}{P}\frac{\partial i^d}{\partial \rho} + \psi\left(\frac{\partial i^d}{\partial \rho} + \left(1 + \frac{\theta}{r}\right)\frac{M}{P}\frac{\partial c^d}{\partial z}\right)\frac{\partial (M/P)^d}{\partial r}\right]\zeta(y - y^*). \tag{7.4.9}$$

We finally define

$$\Xi \equiv 1 + \frac{\psi}{M/P}\frac{\partial (M/P)^d}{\partial r} + \psi\left(1 + \frac{\theta}{r}\right)\frac{\partial c^d}{\partial z}\frac{\partial (M/P)^d/\partial r}{\partial i^d/\partial \rho}. \tag{7.4.10}$$

In the course of the analysis of Chapter 6, we have already assumed that $\Xi > 0$. Substituting the definition of $\Xi$ into the differential equation in $y$ and linearizing $\zeta(y - y^*)$ around $y - y^*$, we obtain

$$\frac{dy}{dt} = -\frac{M/P}{\Delta}\frac{\partial i^d}{\partial \rho}(\mu - \pi^e) + \frac{M/P}{\Delta}\frac{\partial i^d}{\partial \rho}\Xi\zeta'(y - y^*). \tag{7.4.11}$$

Now linearizing the differential equation $d\pi^e/dt = \psi\zeta(y - y^*)$ around $y - y^*$, we can write the following linear differential equation system:

$$\begin{bmatrix} \dot{y} \\ \dot{\pi}^e \end{bmatrix} = \begin{bmatrix} \dfrac{M/P}{\Delta}\Xi\zeta'\dfrac{\partial i^d}{\partial \rho} & \dfrac{M/P}{\Delta}\dfrac{\partial i^d}{\partial \rho} \\ \psi\zeta' & 0 \end{bmatrix}\begin{bmatrix} y - y^* \\ \pi^e - \mu \end{bmatrix}. \tag{7.4.12}$$

Stability conditions for this linearized dynamic model are that the trace of the above matrix be negative and the determinant of the above matrix be positive. The appropriate inequalities are given by

$$\frac{M}{P}\frac{\zeta'\Xi}{\Delta}\frac{\partial i^d}{\partial \rho} < 0, \qquad -\psi\frac{M}{P}\frac{\zeta'}{\Delta}\frac{\partial i^d}{\partial \rho} > 0. \tag{7.4.13}$$

These inequalities both hold unambiguously as long as $\Xi > 0$, which is a maintained assumption throughout.

## Dynamic Adjustment to an Acceleration of Inflation

In Chapter 6, we analyzed the effects of an increase in the rate of growth of government liabilities instituted to finance a cut in taxes. A working assumption in that analysis was that output remained fixed at the level of long-run aggregate supply $y^*$. In this section we repeat that analysis, now replacing the fixed output assumption with the assumption that output supply is dictated by the short-run Phillips curve derived in Section 7.3.

The equilibrium conditions for our dynamic system are given by

$$\pi^e = \mu \quad \text{and} \quad y = y^*. \tag{7.4.14}$$

The current policy experiment consists of a step increase in $\mu$ holding $g$ and $\theta$ constant and allowing taxes to change in whatever manner may be required to satisfy the government budget constraint. With these policy settings, the equilibrium effect of an increase in $\mu$ is an equiproportionate increase in $\pi = \pi^e$ with no change in $y$. This long-run result is unchanged from the analysis of Section 6.3, as we should well expect, since the Phillips curve has the equilibrium property that $y = y^*$ as long as the steady-state inflation rate is constant.

The major departure of the current analysis from that of Section 6.3 is the inclusion of formal dynamics for the time path of $y$. While the intrinsic dynamics of accumulation of money and government bonds and the inherent dynamics of the government budget constraint remain essentially unchanged from Section 6.3, we now study their interactions with the output adjustment dynamics governed by our Phillips curve assumptions. The current analysis is therefore a consolidation of the formal dynamic analysis of Section 6.3 with the more intuitive treatment of output dynamics presented in Section 7.4.

A natural starting point for this analysis is the phase diagram for the $y$, $\pi^e$ system. From above, we find that

$$\frac{\partial \dot{y}}{\partial y} = \frac{M/P}{\Delta} \Xi \zeta' \frac{\partial i^d}{\partial \rho} < 0, \tag{7.4.15}$$

$$\frac{\partial \dot{y}}{\partial \pi^e} = \frac{M/P}{\Delta} \frac{\partial i^d}{\partial \rho} < 0. \tag{7.4.16}$$

We therefore obtain

$$\left. \frac{d\pi^e}{dy} \right|_{\dot{y}=0} = -\Xi \zeta' < 0. \tag{7.4.17}$$

Therefore, the $\dot{y} = 0$ locus is downward sloping in $y$, $\pi^e$ space. Furthermore, the $\dot{y} = 0$ locus must pass through the equilibrium point $y^*$, $\mu$. Finally, since $\partial \dot{y}/\partial y < 0$, we know that $\dot{y} > 0$ to the left of the $\dot{y} = 0$ locus and $\dot{y} < 0$ to the right of the $\dot{y} = 0$ locus.

Inspection of the dynamic system above also reveals that the $\dot{\pi}^e = 0$ locus is vertical in $y$, $\pi^e$ space. However, since the coefficient of $\pi^e$ in the $\dot{\pi}^e = 0$ locus is zero, we cannot establish whether at points off the $\dot{\pi}^e = 0$ locus, motion is toward or away from the $\dot{\pi}^e = 0$ locus. Instead, we can establish that $\pi^e$ rises to the right of the $\dot{\pi}^e = 0$ locus and falls to the left of the $\dot{\pi}^e = 0$ locus. The phase diagram for the $y$, $\pi^e$ system is depicted in Figure 7.4.

Now suppose that the economy starts out in long-run equilibrium, with $y = y^*$ and

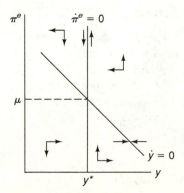

**Figure 7.4**

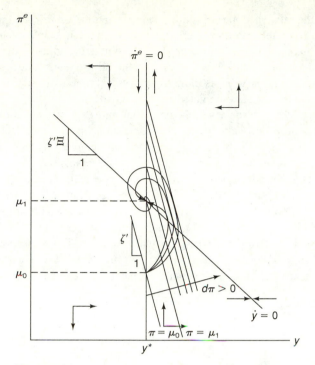

**Figure 7.5**

$\pi = \pi^e = \mu_0$, and that the growth rate of government liabilities rises to $\mu_1 > \mu_0$. The $\dot{y} = 0$ locus shifts up by $\mu_1 - \mu_0$ and $y$ and $\pi^e$ both begin to rise in response to the policy move. Convergence to $y^*$, $\mu_1$ may be characterized by dampened oscillations or may be characterized by one of the other more direct paths depicted in Figure 7.5.

While the dynamic system is most easily analyzed with $y$ and $\pi^e$ as the state variables, we are generally more interested in the path of the observable $\pi$ rather than the unobservable $\pi^e$. Fortunately, the path of $\pi$ may rather easily be inferred from the paths of $y$ and $\pi^e$. Recall the relationship $\pi = \pi^e + \zeta(y - y^*)$. In $y$, $\pi^e$ space this relationship defines loci of constant $\pi$ with slope $d\pi^e/dy|_{d\pi=0} = -\zeta' < 0$. The slope of these iso-$\pi$ loci will be greater in absolute value than the $\dot{y} = 0$ loci if $\zeta' > \Xi\zeta'$, or

$$\Xi - 1 = \frac{\psi}{M/P} \frac{\partial(M/P)^d}{\partial r} + \psi\left(1 + \frac{\theta}{r}\right) \frac{\partial c^d}{\partial z} \frac{\partial(M/P)^d/\partial r}{\partial i^d/\partial \rho} < 0. \tag{7.4.18}$$

The slope of the iso-$\pi$ loci will be less in absolute value than the $\dot{y} = 0$ locus otherwise. The above inequality is equivalent to the inequality

$$\frac{\partial(y^d - y^*)}{d\pi^e}\bigg|_{dr=0} = -\left[\frac{\partial i^d}{\partial \rho} + \frac{M}{P}\left(1 + \frac{\theta}{r}\right) \frac{\partial c^d}{\partial z}\right] > 0. \tag{7.4.19}$$

In Chapter 6, we assumed that this condition is satisfied, and Figure 7.5 is drawn accordingly.

Regardless of the relative slopes of the $\dot{y} = 0$ locus and the iso-$\pi$ loci, the actual rate of inflation rises immediately after the increase in $\mu$. With the loci as depicted in Figure 7.5, we also know that the inflation rate must at some point in the adjustment overshoot its long-run equilibrium value of $\mu_1$. This property of the adjustment process holds in this case even if convergence of $\pi^e$ to $\mu_1$ is monotonic. Typical time paths of $\mu$, $y$, $\pi^e$, and $\pi$ following a step increase in $\mu$ are depicted in Figure 7.6.

Figure 7.6 illustrates a case in which the actual and expected inflation rates both overshoot the new equilibrium value of $\mu_1$ but where adjustment is noncyclical. Output first rises above $y^*$ and then falls back to $y^*$ before finally converging to $y^*$ from below. As long as $y > y^*$, the relationship $\pi = \pi^e + \zeta(y - y^*)$ guarantees that $\pi > \pi^e$. Therefore, in the early stages of adjustment, both $\pi$ and $\pi^e$ rise with the actual inflation rate exceeding the expected inflation rate. As $y - y^*$ crosses zero, expected inflation reaches its peak value. At this point the actual inflation rate has already started to fall and now begins to drop below $\pi^e$ for the rest of the adjustment process. The level of $\pi$ must therefore peak sometime during the period in which $y > y^*$. From the point at which $y = y^*$ onward, $\pi^e$ adjusts monotonically to its equilibrium value of $\mu_1$. However, inspection of Figure 7.5 makes clear that $\pi$ may again overshoot $\mu_1$ before finally converging to $\mu_1$ from below.

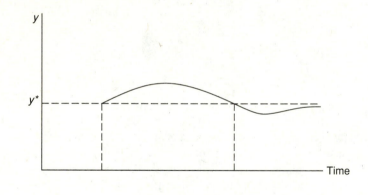

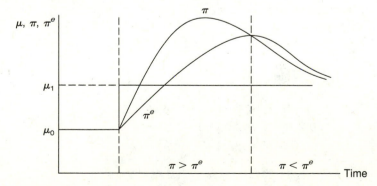

**Figure 7.6**

# 7.5 AN EXPECTED REAL INTEREST RATE MODEL OF THE PHILLIPS CURVE

In the previous section, we derived a macroeconomic model of the Phillips curve consistent with movements in output responding to variations in $P/P^e$. The formal model was based on the assumptions that expectations of inflation are formed adaptively along with

(i) $\begin{cases} \text{search unemployment is given by } u = \dfrac{s}{s + f(P/P^e)} \\[2ex] \qquad\qquad\qquad\text{or} \\[1ex] \text{employment supply is given by } L^s = L^s\!\left(w, \dfrac{P}{P^e}\right), \end{cases}$

(ii) there is a one-period lag in observing $P$, and

(iii) expected price is given by $P_t^e = P_{t-1}(1 + \pi^e)$.

In this section, we replace assumptions (i)–(iii) with the following:

(i′) Employment supply is given by $L^s(w, P/P^e, \rho)$ with $\partial L^s/\partial \rho > 0$.

(ii′) The price level is instantaneously observed so that $P^e = P$, and hence $P/P^e \equiv 1$.

The analysis of this section demonstrates that the combination of an aggregate supply function that depends upon the expected real rate of interest and the assumption of adaptively formed expectations of inflation also generate Phillips curves like comovements in inflation and output or unemployment.

To begin the analysis, recall the employment supply relationship postulated in Section 7.3:

$$L^s = \hat{L}^s\!\left( \frac{W_t}{P_t^e}, \frac{W_{t+1}^e}{P_{t+1}^e}, r - \ln\!\left( \frac{P_{t+1}^e}{P_t^e} \right), \Omega \right). \tag{7.5.1}$$

In this section, we are assuming that $P_t^e = P_t$. We also now adopt the assumptions that $W_{t+1}^e/P_{t+1}^e$ and $\Omega$ are approximately constant. The employment supply function is therefore given by

$$L^s = L^s\!\left( w, r - \ln\!\left( \frac{P_{t+1}^e}{P_t^e} \right) \right). \tag{7.5.2}$$

The discrete-time rate of inflation is now defined as

$$\pi_t = \frac{P_{t+1} - P_t}{P_t}. \tag{7.5.3}$$

We therefore find that

$$\frac{P_{t+1}}{P_t} = 1 + \pi_t. \tag{7.5.4}$$

Taking logarithms of both sides and approximating $\ln(1 + \pi_t) \simeq \pi_t$, we further find that

$$\ln\frac{P_{t+1}}{P_t} = \ln(1 + \pi_t) \simeq \pi_t. \tag{7.5.5}$$

Finally, replacing the unobservable and assumed constant rate of future inflation with its expected counterpart $\pi^e$, the employment supply function becomes

$$L^s = L^s(w, r - \pi^e) = L^s(w, \rho), \tag{7.5.6}$$

where $\rho$ denotes the expected real rate of interest, as in Chapter 6.

With indivisible labor and identical agents, we again find a kinked employment supply function with all households supplying their single unit of labor as long as the real wage rate exceeds some critical value $\hat{w}$ that depends on the representative household's tastes and endowment as well as on the expected real interest rate $\rho$. An increase in the expected real rate of interest increases the expected returns to current work. Therefore, the representative is willing to supply its single unit of labor at a lower real wage rate. However, a lower real wage rate implies an increase in employment demand and a simultaneous increase in aggregate supply. Summarizing this line of reasoning, we should expect the semireduced form

$$y^s = y^s(\rho), \qquad \frac{\partial y^s}{\partial \rho} > 0. \tag{7.5.7}$$

Now recall the real interest rate form of the model of Chapter 6, with $y^s(\rho)$ substituted for the constant level of output $y^*$. The goods and money market equilibrium conditions of this model are given by

$$c^d\left[ y^s(\rho) - g - \left(1 + \frac{\theta}{\rho + \pi^e}\right)\frac{M}{P}(\pi^e - \mu) \right] + i^d(\rho) + g - y^s(\rho) = 0, \tag{7.5.8}$$

$$\left(\frac{M}{P}\right)^d\left[ y^s(\rho), \rho + \pi^e \right] - \frac{M}{P} = 0. \tag{7.5.9}$$

The principal task of this section is to derive a differential equation in $\pi^e$ closely analogous to that of Section 6.3. In order to derive such a differential equation, we use the goods and money market equilibrium conditions in conjunction with the adaptive expectations mechanism to get two differential equations in $d\pi^e/dt$ and $d\rho/dt$ and subsequently solve for the desired relationship in $d\pi^e/dt$.

Differentiating the money market equilibrium condition and rearranging, we obtain

$$\pi = \mu - \frac{P}{M}\left[ \frac{\partial(M/P)^d}{\partial y}\frac{\partial y^s}{\partial \rho} + \frac{\partial(M/P)^d}{\partial r} \right]\frac{d\rho}{dt} - \frac{P}{M}\frac{\partial(M/P)^d}{\partial r}\frac{d\pi^e}{dt}. \tag{7.5.10}$$

We now use the above expression to substitute for $\pi$ in $d\pi^e/dt = \psi(\pi - \pi^e)$. Upon rearranging, we obtain

$$\psi(\mu - \pi^e) = \left[1 + \frac{\psi}{M/P} \frac{\partial (M/P)^d}{\partial r}\right] \frac{d\pi^e}{dt}$$

$$+ \frac{\psi}{M/P} \left[\frac{\partial (M/P)^d}{\partial y} \frac{\partial y^s}{\partial \rho} + \frac{\partial (M/P)^d}{\partial r}\right] \frac{d\rho}{dt}.$$

(7.5.11)

We next plug in $(M/P)^d[y^s(\rho), \rho + \pi^e]$ for $M/P$ in the goods market-clearing condition. Differentiating the resulting expression with respect to time, we obtain

$$0 = \left\{\frac{\partial i^d}{\partial \rho} - \left(1 - \frac{\partial c^d}{\partial z}\right) \frac{\partial y^s}{\partial \rho}\right.$$

$$+ \left[\frac{\theta}{r^2} \frac{M}{P} - \left(1 + \frac{\theta}{r}\right)\left(\frac{\partial (M/P)^d}{\partial y} \frac{\partial y^s}{\partial \rho} + \frac{\partial (M/P)^d}{\partial r}\right)\right] \frac{\partial c^d}{\partial z}(\pi^e - \mu)\right\} \frac{d\rho}{dt}$$

(7.5.12)

$$+ \left\{-\left(1 + \frac{\theta}{r}\right)\frac{M}{P} \frac{\partial c^d}{\partial z} + \left[\frac{\theta}{r^2} \frac{M}{P} - \left(1 + \frac{\theta}{r}\right) \frac{\partial (M/P)^d}{\partial r}\right] \frac{\partial c^d}{\partial z}(\pi^e - \mu)\right\} \frac{d\pi^e}{dt}.$$

Evaluating in the neighborhood of equilibrium ($\pi^e - \mu = 0$), we obtain

$$\frac{d\rho}{dt} = \frac{\left(1 + \dfrac{\theta}{r}\right)\dfrac{M}{P} \dfrac{\partial c^d}{\partial z}}{\dfrac{\partial i^d}{\partial \rho} - \left(1 - \dfrac{\partial c^d}{\partial z}\right) \dfrac{\partial y^s}{\partial \rho}} \frac{d\pi^e}{dt}.$$

(7.5.13)

Now plugging in the above equation for $d\rho/dt$ into the previous equation, we obtain

$$\left\{\left[1 + \frac{\psi}{M/P} \frac{\partial (M/P)^d}{\partial r}\right]\left[\frac{\partial i^d}{\partial \rho} - \left(1 - \frac{\partial c^d}{\partial z}\right) \frac{\partial y^s}{\partial \rho}\right]\right.$$

$$\left.+ \psi\left(1 + \frac{\theta}{r}\right) \frac{\partial c^d}{\partial z}\left[\frac{\partial (M/P)^d}{\partial y} \frac{\partial y^s}{\partial \rho} + \frac{\partial (M/P)^d}{\partial r}\right]\right\} \frac{d\pi^e}{dt}$$

(7.5.14)

$$= \psi\left[\frac{\partial i^d}{\partial \rho} - \left(1 - \frac{\partial c^d}{\partial z}\right) \frac{\partial y^s}{\partial \rho}\right](\mu - \pi^e).$$

Upon rearranging, we get the first-order differential equation

$$\frac{d\pi^e}{dt} = \lambda^*(\mu - \pi^e),$$

(7.5.15)

where

$$\lambda^* \equiv \psi\Delta\left[\frac{\partial i^d}{\partial \rho} - \left(1 - \frac{\partial c^d}{\partial z}\right) \frac{\partial y^s}{\partial \rho}\right],$$

(7.5.16)

$$\Delta \equiv \left[ 1 + \frac{\psi}{M/P} \frac{\partial (M/P)^d}{\partial r} \right] \left[ \frac{\partial i^d}{\partial \rho} - \left( 1 - \frac{\partial c^d}{\partial z} \right) \frac{\partial y^s}{\partial \rho} \right]$$
$$+ \psi \left( 1 + \frac{\theta}{r} \right) \left[ \frac{\partial (M/P)^d}{\partial y} \frac{\partial y^s}{\partial \rho} + \frac{\partial (M/P)^d}{\partial r} \right] \frac{\partial c^d}{\partial z}. \tag{7.5.17}$$

As a check, first note that the value of $\lambda^*$ is identical to that of Chapter 6 in the case in which $\partial y^s / \partial \rho = 0$, as we assume throughout Chapter 6. Next consider a likely set of sufficient conditions for stability. We continue to assume, as throughout most of Chapter 6, that

$$1 + \frac{\psi}{M/P} \frac{\partial (M/P)^d}{\partial r} > 0. \tag{7.5.18}$$

If we further assume that

$$\frac{\partial (M/P)^d}{\partial r} + \frac{\partial (M/P)^d}{\partial y} \frac{\partial y^s}{\partial \rho} < 0, \tag{7.5.19}$$

then the linearized process in $\pi^e$ is definitely stable. We assume that these two sufficient conditions for stability both hold in most of what follows.

## The Output Process and Inflation Response

Recall the following form of the goods market equilibrium condition:

$$c^d \left[ y^s(\rho) - g - \left( 1 + \frac{\theta}{\rho + \pi^e} \right) \left( \frac{M}{P} \right)^d (y^s(\rho), \rho + \pi^e)(\pi^e - \mu) \right]$$
$$+ i^d(\rho) + g - y^s(\rho) = 0. \tag{7.5.20}$$

This condition gives $\rho$ as an implicit function of (among other things) $\pi^e$ and $\mu$. Differentiating the above expression with respect to $\rho$, $\pi^e$, and $\mu$, we obtain

$$\frac{\partial \rho}{\partial \pi^e} = \frac{1}{Y} \left\{ \left( 1 + \frac{\theta}{r} \right) \frac{M}{P} \frac{\partial c^d}{\partial z} \right.$$
$$\left. + \left[ \frac{\theta}{r^2} \frac{M}{P} - \left( 1 + \frac{\theta}{r} \right) \frac{\partial (M/P)^d}{\partial r} \right] \frac{\partial c^d}{\partial z} (\pi^e - \mu) \right\}, \tag{7.5.21}$$

$$\frac{\partial \rho}{\partial \mu} = -\frac{1}{Y} \left( 1 + \frac{\theta}{r} \right) \frac{M}{P} \frac{\partial c^d}{\partial z}, \tag{7.5.22}$$

where

$$Y \equiv \left\{ \frac{\partial i^d}{\partial \rho} - \left( 1 - \frac{\partial c^d}{\partial z} \right) \frac{\partial y^s}{\partial \rho} \right.$$
$$\left. + \left[ \frac{\theta}{r^2} \frac{M}{P} - \left( 1 + \frac{\theta}{r} \right) \left( \frac{\partial (M/P)^d}{\partial y} \frac{\partial y^s}{\partial \rho} + \frac{\partial (M/P)^d}{\partial r} \right) \right] \frac{\partial c^d}{\partial z} (\pi^e - \mu) \right\}. \tag{7.5.23}$$

Evaluating these expressions in the neighborhood of the equilibrium condition $\pi^e = \mu$, we find that

$$\frac{\partial \rho}{\partial \pi^e} = -\frac{\partial \rho}{\partial \mu} = \frac{\left(1 + \dfrac{\theta}{r}\right)\dfrac{M}{P}\dfrac{\partial c^d}{\partial z}}{\dfrac{\partial i^d}{\partial \rho} - \left(1 - \dfrac{\partial c^d}{\partial z}\right)\dfrac{\partial y^s}{\partial \rho}} < 0. \tag{7.5.24}$$

We therefore approximate the implicit function (7.5.20) as

$$\rho = \rho(\mu - \pi^e), \tag{7.5.25}$$

where

$$\frac{\partial \rho}{\partial(\mu - \pi^e)} = -\frac{\left(1 + \dfrac{\theta}{r}\right)\dfrac{M}{P}\dfrac{\partial c^d}{\partial z}}{\dfrac{\partial i^d}{\partial \rho} - \left(1 - \dfrac{\partial c^d}{\partial z}\right)\dfrac{\partial y^s}{\partial \rho}} > 0.$$

These assumptions permit us to write a (semi) reduced form for output given by

$$y = y^s[\rho(\mu - \pi^e)], \qquad \frac{\partial y}{\partial(\mu - \pi^e)} > 0. \tag{7.5.26}$$

We are now ready to repeat our experiment of Section 7.3, an unanticipated step increase in the rate of growth of government liabilities. As long as $\partial y^s/\partial \rho$ is not too large, the behavior of most of the macroeconomic variables of interest is similar to that presented in Figure 6.4. At the instant after the increase in $\mu$, the level of $\pi^e$ remains fixed. Therefore, the expected real rate of interest unambiguously rises. Furthermore, the increase in $\rho$ shifts the labor supply curve to the right, resulting in a reduction in the real wage, an increase in employment and output, and therefore a reduction in unemployment. Over time, expectations of inflation begin to adapt to the resulting acceleration of inflation and hence $\mu - \pi^e$ and $\rho$ both begin to fall. Eventually, we get $\pi = \pi^e = \mu$, the expected real rate of interest falls back to its original value, and the levels of employment, output, and unemployment all return to their original values.

Response of the expected real interest rate model of this section to an acceleration of inflation closely mimics the response of the model of Section 7.4, which is explicitly based on incomplete contemporaneous information, to the same experiment. In both models, output temporarily rises before eventually returning to its original value, and in both cases $\pi$ and $\pi^e$ eventually adjust one-for-one to the increase in $\mu$. However, in the expected real interest rate model, the dynamics are first order, and therefore the possibility of dampened cyclical response is not present. Furthermore, in the incomplete information model, the level of actual inflation $\pi$ is directly tied to the state variables $\pi^e$ and $y$, and so the impact response of $\pi$ to changes in $\mu$ is always zero. Alternatively, in the expected real interest rate model of the current section, the actual inflation rate generally jumps coincident with the rise in $\mu$, as depicted in Figure 6.4. Therefore, the incomplete contemporaneous information model predicts less immediate responsiveness in the actual inflation rate than the expected real interest rate model.

# REFERENCES

Barro, Robert J., "The Persistence of Unemployment," *American Economic Review,* May, 1988, 32–37.

Barron, John, M., and Stephen McCafferty, "Job Search, Labor Supply, and the Quit Decision: Theory and Evidence," *American Economic Review,* September, 1977, 683–691.

Clark, Kim B., and Lawrence H. Summers, "Labor Market Dynamics and Unemployment: A Reconsideration," *Brookings Papers on Economic Activity,* vol. 1, 1979, 13–60.

Darby, Michael R., John Haltiwanger, and Mark Plant, "Unemployment Rate Dynamics and Persistent Unemployment Under Rational Expectations," *American Economic Review,* September, 1985, 614–637.

Friedman, Milton, "The Role of Monetary Policy," *American Economic Review,* March, 1968, 1–17.

Gordon, Robert J., "Recent Developments in the Theory of Inflation and Unemployment," *Journal of Monetary Economics,* April, 1976, 185–219.

Grossman, Herschel I., "The Cyclical Pattern of Unemployment and Wage Inflation," *Economica,* November, 1974, 403–413.

Hall, Robert E., "A Theory of the Natural Unemployment Rate and the Duration of Unemployment," *Journal of Monetary Economics,* April, 1979, 153–169.

Hansen, Gary D., "Indivisible Labor and the Business Cycle," *Journal of Monetary Economics,* November, 1985, 309–327.

Jovanovic, Boyan, "Matching, Turnover, and Unemployment," *Journal of Political Economy,* February, 1984, 108–122.

Lippman, Steven A., and John J. McCall, "The Economics of Job Search: A Survey," *Economic Inquiry,* June, 1976, 155–189.

McCall, John J., "Economics of Information and Job Search," *Quarterly Journal of Economics,* February, 1970, 113–126.

Parsons, Donald O., "Quit Rates Over Time: A Search and Information Approach," *American Economic Review,* March, 1973, 390–401.

Phelps, Edmund S., ed., *Microeconomic Foundations of Employment and Inflation Theory,* New York, Norton, 1972.

Phillips, A. W., "The Relationship between Unemployment and the Rate of Change of Money Wage Rates in the United Kingdom, 1861–1957," *Economica,* November, 1958.

Rogerson, Richard, "Indivisible Labor, Lotteries, and Equilibrium," *Journal of Monetary Economics,* January, 1988, 3–16.

Stein, Jerome L., "Unemployment, Inflation and Monetarism," *American Economic Review,* December, 1974, 867–887.

Van Order, Robert, "Unemployment, Inflation and Monetarism: A Further Analysis," *American Economic Review,* September, 1976, 741–746.

# Chapter **8**

## The Dynamics of Capital Accumulation

The dynamic analyses of Chapters 4–7 focus primarily on the dynamics of adjustment. In particular, we have studied how wages and prices might evolve toward market-clearing levels and how price-level and inflationary expectations might adjust or adapt to actual experience. Attention to more intrinsic dynamics of how commodity flows accumulate into changes in physical stocks has been of only secondary concern. While we have studied how different rates of change of money and government-issued bond supplies translate into different levels of government liabilities outstanding, such adjustment is generally only superficially dynamic in nature. While the nominal quantities of money and government bonds only gradually evolve over time, changes in the real values of money and government bonds outstanding are generally accomplished much more quickly through discrete jumps in the level of prices.

The focus of the present chapter is on the more fundamentally dynamic questions of the evolution over time of the supplies of capital and labor inputs and the resulting movement over time in the level of aggregate goods supply. Section 8.1 characterizes technology and market interactions in a highly stylized barter economy. Section 8.1 then studies the implications for growth over time of output and capital when savings behavior conforms to a very simple, yet admittedly ad hoc, mechanism. Section 8.2 poses and solves a general class of optimal control problems. Section 8.2 then considers the specific problem of the optimal intertemporal allocation of consumption and saving for a central planner responsible for maximizing welfare in an economy like that of Section 8.1.

Section 8.3 integrates the basic features of economic growth theory with the representative agent macroeconomic models we have studied in earlier chapters. We first analyze the representative household's consumption-savings problem and the representative firm's capital investment problem. Section 8.3 then demonstrates how market interactions of such optimizing households and firms may replicate the equilibrium of the optimal planner's problem of Section 8.2 and also proves that this model's equilibrium capital-labor ratio is independent of government monetary and fiscal policies. Section 8.4 introduces the Euler equation technique for solving dynamic optimization problems. Section 8.4 then reanalyzes the representative household, representative firm, and economic planner problems and generalizes the result of Section 8.4 on the optimality of equilibrium in the market economy. Finally, Section 8.5 presents a model in which government inflation and fiscal policies may influence the equilibrium quantity of capital per worker.

# 8.1 NEOCLASSICAL ECONOMIC GROWTH THEORY

We begin our analysis of capital accumulation with a study of the most simple possible structure capable of capturing the economic effects of growth over time in the factors of production, in particular, labor and capital. Therefore, in order to quickly generate some simple and unambiguous results, we delay the introduction of many complications that add realism until later sections.

## The Simple Analytics of Capital Accumulation

Assume that production is organized by firms and governed by the concave, linearly homogeneous production function

$$y = \Phi(L, K), \tag{8.1.1.}$$

where $L$ and $K$ denote the levels of employment of workers and capital, respectively. Firms hire the services of workers and rent the services of capital. Households are endowed with a single, nondivisible unit of labor services that they inelastically supply to the firms at the prevailing real wage rate $w$. Households also own all capital that they supply inelastically to the firms at the prevailing real rental rate $R$. Competition in the markets for labor and capital and homogeneity of the aggregate production function guarantee that factor payments exhaust all production. The equilibrium wage and rental rates are given by

$$w = \frac{\partial \Phi(L, K)}{\partial L} \quad \text{and} \quad R = \frac{\partial \Phi(L, K)}{\partial K}. \tag{8.1.2}$$

Output is chosen as the numeraire, and its price $P$ is set, for convenience, at unity.

Households receive all product produced by firms as income. There is, for now, no government sector, and so households pay no taxes. Households allocate output across consumption and saving. Output saved is available to augment the stock of capital owned by the household sector. Capital depreciates at the constant, exogenous rate $\delta$ independently of whether it is employed. Accumulation of capital is therefore governed by

$$\dot{K} \equiv \frac{dK}{dt} = y - \tilde{c}L - \delta K, \tag{8.1.3}$$

where $\tilde{c}$ denotes per capita consumption and $L$ denotes both the number of households and the level of employment on the assumptions that each household is endowed with one unit of labor services and that all labor services are continuously employed.

We start our analysis with the assumption that households save a fixed fraction $s$ of total income. Per capita consumption is therefore given by

$$\tilde{c} = (1 - s)\frac{y}{L}. \tag{8.1.4}$$

We further assume that $0 < s < 1$. The capital accumulation equation is therefore given by

$$\dot{K} = s\Phi(L, K) - \delta K. \tag{8.1.5}$$

Growth over time in the number of households and, equivalently, the supply of workers occurs at the constant, exogenous rate $n$. Employment is therefore governed by

$$\dot{L} = nL, \tag{8.1.6}$$

and so

$$L(t) = L(0)e^{nt}, \qquad n \geq 0.$$

We provisionally assume that the saving rate $s$ and the growth rate of the labor force $n$ are both independent of the level of output.

It is most convenient to express all variables in per capita terms. We therefore define

$$q \equiv \frac{y}{L} = \text{per capita output} \quad \text{and} \quad k \equiv \frac{K}{L} = \text{capital stock per worker.} \tag{8.1.7}$$

The homogeneity of the aggregate production function $\Phi(\cdot)$ now allows us to define the per capita production function $f(\cdot)$, where

$$q = \frac{\Phi(L, K)}{L} = \Phi(1, k) \equiv f(k). \tag{8.1.8}$$

It is straightforward to show that

$$f'(k) > 0 \quad \text{and} \quad f''(k) < 0 \tag{8.1.9}$$

as long as $\Phi(\cdot)$ is concave.

The capital accumulation equation can also be written in per capita terms. Differentiating $k = K/L$ with respect to time, we obtain

$$\dot{k} = \frac{\dot{K}}{L} - \frac{K}{L^2}\dot{L} = s\frac{\Phi(L, K)}{L} - \delta\frac{K}{L} - \frac{K}{L}\frac{\dot{L}}{L}, \tag{8.1.10}$$

or

$$\dot{k} = sf(k) - (\delta + n)k. \tag{8.1.11}$$

This simple differential equation describing the evolution over time in the capital-labor ratio $k$ is due to Solow (1956).

## Equilibrium, Stability, and Comparative Statics

The steady state of the differential equation of growth is given by

$$0 = sf(k^*) - (\delta + n)k^* \tag{8.1.12}$$

or

$$\frac{f(k^*)}{k^*} = \frac{(y/L)^*}{(K/L)^*} = \left(\frac{y}{K}\right)^* = \frac{\delta + n}{s}, \tag{8.1.13}$$

where the asterisks indicate the equilibrium levels of the respective variables. We therefore see that the equilibrium output-capital ratio is determined as a simple function of the savings rate, the rate of depreciation of the capital stock, and the growth rate of the labor force. Alternatively, we may view the above expression as determining the equilibrium levels of per capita output and capital per worker. Figure 8.1 plots the production function and the equilibrium values $q^*$ and $k^*$. Figure 8.1 also depicts the equilibrium levels of per capita consumption $\tilde{c}^*$ and per capita saving $\tilde{s}^* \equiv q^* - \tilde{c}^*$.

In equilibrium, the levels of output $y$ and employment $L$ as well as the levels of consumption and investment all grow at the same percentage rate $n$. That the growth rate of $L$ is equal to $n$ is straightforward. Growth in the labor force is exogenously determined. To see that the capital stock and output must also grow at the rate $n$, recall the capital accumulation equation

$$\frac{\dot{K}}{K} = s\frac{\Phi(L, K)}{K} - \delta = s\frac{y}{K} - \delta. \tag{8.1.14}$$

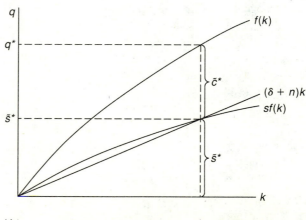

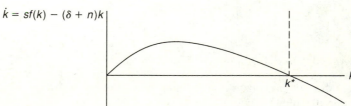

**Figure 8.1**

In equilibrium, we have $y/K = (y/K)^* = (\delta + n)/s$. Therefore, the above equation may be rewritten as

$$\frac{\dot{K}}{K} = s\frac{\delta + n}{s} - \delta = n. \tag{8.1.15}$$

Now differentiating the production function with respect to time and rearranging, we obtain

$$\frac{\dot{y}}{y} = \frac{1}{y}\left[\frac{\dot{L}}{L} + \frac{\partial\Phi}{\partial L}L + \frac{\dot{K}}{K}\frac{\partial\Phi}{\partial K}K\right] = n \tag{8.1.16}$$

since the production function is linearly homogeneous. Finally, since consumption is a fixed fraction $1 - s$ of $y$ and since savings and investment are both equal to $sy$, we know that, in equilibrium, consumption, savings, and investment must all grow at the same rate $n$.

We next examine whether the dynamic process determining $k^*$ is stable. For stability of the dynamic process, we require that

$$\frac{\partial\dot{k}}{\partial k} = sf'(k^*) - (\delta + n) < 0. \tag{8.1.17}$$

Plugging the equilibrium condition $sf(k^*)/k^* = \delta + n$ into the above inequality, stability also requires that

$$f'(k^*)k^* - f(k^*) < 0 \tag{8.1.18}$$

or

$$\frac{\partial(y/L)}{\partial(K/L)} = \frac{\partial\Phi(L, K)/\partial K}{L} < \frac{y}{K}. \tag{8.1.19}$$

That is, the per capita marginal product of capital must be less than the average product of capital. As long as the production function is sufficiently well behaved, this stability condition is unambiguously satisfied.[1]

The example depicted in Figure 8.1 is one in which a unique equilibrium exists and is globally stable. Rearranging the equation of growth above, we obtain

$$\dot{k} = k\left(\frac{\dot{K}}{K} - \frac{\dot{L}}{L}\right). \tag{8.1.20}$$

To the right of $k^*$ in Figure 8.1, we have $\dot{k} < 0$. Capital is growing more slowly than labor and so the capital-labor ratio tends to fall toward $k^*$. To the left of $k^*$, we have $\dot{k} > 0$. Capital is growing more quickly than labor, and so the capital-labor ratio tends to rise toward $k^*$. It is only at $k^*$ that capital and labor both grow at the common rate $n$ and the capital-labor ratio remains constant.

We may next investigate the comparative statics effects of changes in the savings rate

---

[1] For a representative proof, see Burmeister and Dobell (1970, Ch. 2).

$s$. Differentiating the equilibrium condition of the dynamic process and rearranging, we obtain

$$\frac{dk}{ds} = \frac{f(k)}{\delta + n - sf'(k)} = \frac{f(k)k/s}{f(k) - f'(k)k} > 0. \tag{8.1.21}$$

The equilibrium capital-labor ratio therefore unambiguously rises with an increase in the savings rate as long as the production function satisfies the stability condition.

While the sign of the effect of changes in the savings rate on the capital-labor ratio is unambiguously positive, the effect of changes in the savings rate on the level of per capita consumption is, in general, of ambiguous sign. Recalling that per capita consumption is given by $\tilde{c} = (1 - s)f(k)$, we may derive

$$\frac{d\tilde{c}}{ds} = (1 - s)f'\frac{dk}{ds} - f(k) = \frac{f(k)}{s}\frac{f'(k)k - sf(k)}{f(k) - f'(k)k}. \tag{8.1.22}$$

While the denominator of this expression must be positive for stability, the numerator may be of either sign.

Starting from equilibrium, an increase in the savings rate lowers consumption and raises savings and investment. Initially, the capital stock starts growing faster than the labor force, and hence the capital-labor ratio and per capita output both rise. However, the increased amount of capital per worker puts an added burden on the economy. As the labor force continues to grow, each new worker must be equipped with ever larger quantities of capital. Furthermore, the relatively larger capital stock implies more depreciation of capital per unit of time. These two drains on the economy therefore place a limit on the extent to which the increased savings can translate into a higher capital-labor ratio, and eventually the economy reequilibrates with output, labor, and capital all growing at the same rate again. It is also fairly straightforward why the equilibrium level of per capita consumption may either rise or fall. On the one hand, there is unambiguously more output per worker. However, maintaining the higher capital-labor ratio requires a higher level of per capita investment, and so per capita consumption may either rise or fall depending on how much added investment per worker is needed to maintain the higher level of capital per worker.

## 8.2 OPTIMAL CAPITAL ACCUMULATION IN THE COMMAND ECONOMY

This section provides an analysis of the optimal consumption path for an infinitely lived family of households endowed with a predetermined initial stock of capital and access to a fixed production technology but denied access to any trading opportunities with other economic agents. This problem may be posed as a straightforward application of the maximum principle, a very simple, yet powerful technique of optimal control theory that has many applications in intertemporal economic analysis. In the first part of this section, we state without proof the necessary conditions for solutions to this general class of problems. The remainder of this section presents the solution to the most basic optimal intertemporal consumption allocation problem.

## The Maximum Principle

In much of the analysis of this chapter, we make use of the maximum principle, a solution technique for constrained optimal control problems. While this technique is a very powerful tool that can handle a wide range of applications, the applications in this chapter and many others in economic theory are of a rather special functional form. In particular, we now consider maximization problems of the form

$$\max_{u(t)} J = \int_0^T I(x, u)e^{-\beta t}\, dt \tag{8.2.1}$$

subject to

$$\dot{x} = f(x, u), \tag{8.2.2}$$

$$x(0) = x_0, \qquad x(T) = x_T. \tag{8.2.3}$$

That is, we seek to maximize the present value of an integrand, $I(x(t), u(t))$, discounted at the given constant rate $\beta$ over a (possibly) finite time horizon stretching from the present ($t = 0$) to a specific terminal time ($t = T$). In attempting to maximize $J$, we seek to specify an optimal time function $u(t)$, which we denote the *control variable*, subject to its inclusion in some feasible set. The optimally chosen path of the control variable then implies a time path for the *state variable* subject to the given intrinsic dynamics $\dot{x} = f(x, u)$. As is apparent from the form of the integrand expression, $I(x, u)$, motion of the state variable may be a primary motivation for the choice of the time path $u(t)$. This maximization of $J$ is also made subject to the given initial and terminal values of the state variable, $x_0$ and $X_T$, respectively. However, in cases in which the time horizon takes the limiting value of $t \rightarrow +\infty$, the terminal constraint for the state variable may no longer be relevant.

To facilitate solution of this maximization problem, we define the current-value *Hamiltonian H\** as follows:

$$H^* \equiv I(x, u) + \lambda f(x, u), \tag{8.2.4}$$

where $\lambda$ represents the *costate variable*. The costate variable in a dynamic optimization problem, in general a function of time, is analogous to the Lagrange multiplier of static maximization problems. Necessary conditions for a maximum of the original optimization problem are given by[2]

$$\frac{\partial H^*}{\partial u} = 0, \qquad \dot{\lambda} = -\frac{\partial H^*}{\partial x} + \beta\lambda, \tag{8.2.5}$$

$$x(0) = x_0, \qquad x(T) = x_T. \tag{8.2.6}$$

In practice, it is often convenient to work with the so-called *canonical equations,* which

---

[2]See Intriligator (1971, Chs. 12, 14) for a derivation of these first-order conditions as well as conditions for solutions to more general optimal control problems.

are given by

$$\dot{\lambda} = -\frac{\partial H^*}{\partial x} + \beta\lambda, \tag{8.2.7}$$

$$\dot{x} = f(x, u). \tag{8.2.8}$$

These equations in combination with the first-order condition $\partial H^*/\partial u = 0$ summarize motion over time of the state variable, the control variable, and the costate variable along the optimal path.

As noted above, it is frequently the case in infinite-horizon problems that there is no explicit endpoint constraint that is analogous to $x(T) = x_T$. In such cases, the necessary conditions for a maximum also include a transversality condition.[3] If there is no restriction on the steady-state value of $x$, then the transversality condition is given by

$$\lim_{t \to +\infty} e^{-\beta t}\lambda(t) = 0. \tag{8.2.9}$$

Alternatively, if we also require that the steady state value of $x$ be strictly positive, then we require that

$$\lim_{t \to +\infty} e^{-\beta t}\lambda(t) \geq 0 \quad \text{and} \quad \lim_{t \to +\infty} e^{-\beta t}\lambda(t)x(t) = 0. \tag{8.2.10}$$

The similarity between Lagrange multipliers in the static optimization calculus and the costate variables in optimal control is more than just superficial. The usual interpretation of Lagrange multipliers is that they represent the marginal value of the constraining variable. For example, in traditional demand theory, the Lagrange multiplier has the interpretation of the marginal utility of additional income. In the optimal control problem, the initial value of the costate variable has the interpretation of the marginal value of a change in the initial value of the relevant state variable. As the units of the costate variables are often expressed as a price per unit of time, a costate variable is often construed as a shadow price of changes in the variable in question. Hopefully, the usefulness of these general observations can be clarified as we study specific applications of the maximum principle in the remainder of this section and in the next section.

## Optimal Consumption Over Time

In Section 8.1, we derived the capital accumulation equation

$$\frac{\dot{K}}{K} = \frac{y}{K} - \tilde{c}\frac{L}{K} - \delta, \tag{8.2.11}$$

where $\tilde{c}$ denotes per capita consumption. Recalling the definition $k \equiv K/L$, this equation may be rewritten as

$$\frac{\dot{K}}{K} = \frac{f(k) - \tilde{c}}{k} - \delta. \tag{8.2.12}$$

Now recalling that $\dot{k}/k = \dot{K}/K - \dot{L}/L = \dot{K}/K - n$, the per capita form of the above expres-

---

[3]Kamien and Schwartz (1981) provides considerable material on applications in which transversality conditions apply.

sion is given by

$$\dot{k} = f(k) - \tilde{c} - (\delta + n)k, \tag{8.2.13}$$

where $\tilde{c} = \tilde{c}(t)$ must satisfy $0 \le \tilde{c}(t) \le f(k)$; that is, per capita consumption must be non-negative and capital, once put in place, cannot be consumed.

Let us now consider the problem of a family composed of all the households in our economy of Section 8.1. Assume that this family's welfare can be represented by

$$V = \int_0^T U[\tilde{c}(t)]e^{-\beta t}\, dt, \tag{8.2.14}$$

where $U$ denotes a concave, instantaneous utility function defined over per capita consumption, $\beta$ is a constant rate of time preference, and $T$ is a possibly finite end of the planning horizon.

Suppose that this family has an initial endowment $k_0$ of capital per person and that the family is constrained to end up with $k_T$ capital per person at the end of the planning horizon. The family's choice problem is therefore amenable to solution by means of the maximum principle, as outlined above. One particularly simple and illustrative case of this problem is the infinite-horizon case in which $T \to +\infty$, and the terminal constraint on the level of capital per person is replaced with the appropriate transversality conditions. The family's problem is now given by

$$\max_{\tilde{c}(t)} \int_0^\infty U[\tilde{c}(t)]e^{-\beta t}\, dt \tag{8.2.15}$$

subject to

$$\dot{k} = f(k) - \tilde{c} - (\delta + n)k, \tag{8.2.16}$$

$$k(0) = k_0, \qquad k(\infty) \ge 0, \tag{8.2.17}$$

$$0 \le \tilde{c}(t) \le f(k). \tag{8.2.18}$$

The present-value Hamiltonian for this problem is given by

$$H^* = U[\tilde{c}(t)] + \lambda[f(k) - \tilde{c} - (\delta + n)k]. \tag{8.2.19}$$

An interior solution to this problem must therefore satisfy

$$\frac{\partial H^*}{\partial c} = U'[\tilde{c}(t)] - \lambda = 0, \tag{8.2.20}$$

$$\dot{\lambda} = -\frac{\partial H^*}{\partial k} + \beta\lambda = -\lambda[f'(k) - (\delta + n + \beta)], \tag{8.2.21}$$

$$k(0) = k_0, \qquad \lim_{t \to +\infty} e^{-\beta t}\lambda(t) \ge 0, \qquad \lim_{t \to +\infty} e^{-\beta t}\lambda(t)k(t) = 0. \tag{8.2.22}$$

The first of these first-order conditions requires that the marginal utility of per capita consumption equal the shadow value of an additional unit of capital per person. The second first-order condition may be rearranged as

$$f'(k) + \frac{\dot{\lambda}}{\lambda} = (\delta + n + \beta). \tag{8.2.23}$$

This expression may be interpreted as requiring that the marginal benefit of a permanent addition to the stock of capital per person be equal to the marginal cost of a permanent addition to the stock of capital per person. The marginal benefit of an additional unit of capital includes the addition to output per person, $f'(k)$, plus the capital gains accruing per unit of time due to changes in the shadow value of capital per person, $\dot{\lambda}/\lambda$. The costs of an increase in the stock of capital per person include the cost of losses due to depreciation of capital, $\delta$; the cost of equipping new workers with the additional amount of capital as the population grows, $n$; and the imputed interest cost of the foregone unit of consumption, $\beta$.

We may now differentiate equation (8.2.20) with respect to time to obtain

$$\dot{\lambda} = U''(\tilde{c})\dot{\tilde{c}}. \tag{8.2.24}$$

Now defining $\sigma(\tilde{c}) \equiv -\tilde{c}U''(\tilde{c})/U'(\tilde{c}),$[4] the above equation may be rewritten as

$$\frac{\dot{\lambda}}{\lambda} = \sigma(\tilde{c})\frac{\dot{\tilde{c}}}{\tilde{c}} \tag{8.2.25}$$

or

$$\frac{\dot{\tilde{c}}}{\tilde{c}} = \frac{1}{\sigma(\tilde{c})}[f'(k) - (\delta + n + \beta)]. \tag{8.2.26}$$

We may now combine this differential equation with the original differential equation in $k$,

$$\dot{k} = f(k) - \tilde{c} - (\delta + n)k, \tag{8.2.27}$$

to obtain a differential equation system in $\tilde{c}$ and $k$ that describes the motion of $\tilde{c}$ and $k$ over time when the optimal path for $\tilde{c}$ is implemented.

If the optimal path for $\tilde{c}$ is followed, eventually $\tilde{c}$ and $k$ take on values $\tilde{c}^*$ and $k^*$ that satisfy

$$f'(k^*) = \delta + n + \beta, \tag{8.2.28}$$

$$c^* = f(k^*) - (\delta + n)k^*. \tag{8.2.29}$$

We now consider the $\dot{\tilde{c}} = 0$ locus for the optimal control solution. This locus includes those points in $k$, $\tilde{c}$ space at which $f'(k) = \delta + n + \beta$. The $\dot{\tilde{c}} = 0$ locus is therefore vertical at $k = k^*$. The $\dot{\tilde{c}} = 0$ locus is depicted in Figure 8.2. Note that the direction of motion of $\tilde{c}$ at points off the $\dot{\tilde{c}} = 0$ locus is according to

$$\dot{\tilde{c}} \gtreqless 0 \quad \text{as } f'(k) \gtreqless \delta + n + \beta. \tag{8.2.30}$$

Since $f''(k) < 0$, we therefore see that $\dot{\tilde{c}} > 0$ if $k < k^*$ and $\dot{\tilde{c}} < 0$ if $k > k^*$.

Next consider the $\dot{k} = 0$ locus. The $\dot{k} = 0$ locus includes those points in $k$, $\tilde{c}$ space at which $\tilde{c} = f(k) - (\delta + n)k$. We therefore see that

$$\left.\frac{d\tilde{c}}{dk}\right|_{\dot{k}=0} = f'(k) - (\delta + n). \tag{8.2.31}$$

---

[4]The term $\sigma$ is often referred to as the Arrow-Pratt index of relative risk aversion.

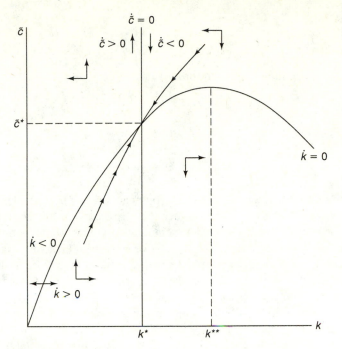

**Figure 8.2**

We normally assume that $f'(0) = +\infty$, and so $d\tilde{c}/dk|_{\dot{k}=0} > 0$ at $k = 0$. Since $d^2\tilde{c}/dk^2|_{\dot{k}=0}$ $= f''(k) < 0$, the $\dot{k} = 0$ locus is concave from below and reaches a maximum at $k^{**}$, where $f'(k^{**}) = \delta + n$. We therefore find that $d\tilde{c}/dk|_{\dot{k}=0} > 0$ to the left of $k^{**}$ and $d\tilde{c}/dk|_{\dot{k}=0} < 0$ to the right of $k^{**}$. Finally, motion of $k$ at points off the $\dot{k} = 0$ locus is according to

$$\dot{k} \gtreqless 0 \quad \text{as} \quad \tilde{c} \lesseqgtr f(k) - (\delta + n)k. \tag{8.2.32}$$

Therefore, we find that $\dot{k} < 0$ at points above the $\dot{k} = 0$ locus, and we find that $\dot{k} > 0$ at points below the $\dot{k} = 0$ locus. The $\dot{k} = 0$ locus is also depicted in Figure 8.2.

Motion of the optimal path of $\tilde{c}$ and $k$ is along the saddle path denoted by the locus of arrows in Figure 8.2. Such saddle path stability is a general property of the optimal path in optimal control problems. This saddle path property implies that the optimal path of $\tilde{c}$ and $k$ is the only stable solution to the canonical equations in $\tilde{c}$ and $k$. Starting at time $t = 0$, the level of consumption should discretely jump to the saddle path at the value of $k = k_0$. Thereafter, $\tilde{c}$ and $k$ should both monotonically converge to $\tilde{c}^*$, $k^*$ along the saddle path with $\tilde{c}$ and $k$ either gradually rising if $k_0 < k^*$ or with $\tilde{c}$ and $k$ gradually falling if $k_0 > k^*$.

To ensure that the solution to the maximization problem sketched above does, in fact, characterize a maximum, we also require that the transversality conditions are satisfied. Since

$$\lambda(t) = U'[\tilde{c}(t)], \tag{8.2.33}$$

we know that

$$\lim_{t \to +\infty} \lambda(t) = U'[f(k^*) - (\delta + n)k^*]. \tag{8.2.34}$$

The transversality conditions are therefore given by

$$\lim_{t \to +\infty} e^{-\beta t}\lambda(t) = \lim_{t \to +\infty} \{U'[f(k^*) - (\delta + n)k^*]\}e^{-\beta t} \geq 0, \tag{8.2.35}$$

$$\lim_{t \to +\infty} e^{-\beta t}\lambda(t)k(t) = \lim_{t \to +\infty} \{U'[f(k^*) - (\delta + n)k^*]\}e^{-\beta t}k^* = 0. \tag{8.2.36}$$

As long as $U' < +\infty$, for finite $\tilde{c}$, and $0 < k^* < +\infty$, these transversality conditions are unambiguously satisfied.

While the infinite-horizon version of the optimal consumption problem is easier to work with, it is also of interest to consider the characteristics of the solution to the finite-horizon version of the problem. In the finite-horizon form of the optimal consumption problem, the planner is constrained to achieve $k(T) = k_T$. Generally, the solution to this problem involves motion of $k$ toward $k^*$ until a point in time close to the end of the planning horizon at which point $k$ must begin motion toward $k_T$. Such finite-horizon optimal paths are sometimes referred to as growth *turnpikes*.[5]

Of final interest in this section is a comparison of the stationary state of the optimal control solution with the solution to the static optimal growth problem. The static optimal growth problem considers the question of the optimum quantity of capital per person that the planner would like to have subject to the constraint that the quantity of capital per person be indefinitely maintained. The static optimum growth solution maximizes per capita consumption along a feasible steady-state growth path. The static optimum value of capital per person is given by $k^{**}$ since it is at $k^{**}$ at which $\tilde{c}$ is maximized subject to $\dot{k} = 0$. The value $k^{**}$ and the growth path that maintains $k = k^{**}$ is referred to as the *golden rule of accumulation*. Note that it is only in the case in which $\beta = 0$ that the steady-state solution to the optimal control problem coincides with the golden rule path. When $\beta > 0$, preference for current consumption over future consumption precludes the optimality of the current sacrifice that may be required to raise the value of $k$ up to $k^{**}$.

# 8.3 CAPITAL ACCUMULATION IN THE MARKET ECONOMY

This section recasts the analysis of capital accumulation in the growing economy in the context of a representative agent, market model of the macroeconomy. A major motivation of this analysis is to demonstrate conditions under which a market economy can support the optimal accumulation path derived in the preceding section. To facilitate the analysis, we first consider the representative household's optimal consumption-saving problem when the household faces an exogenously determined interest rate path. We next analyze the representative firm's optimal investment-capital accumulation problem when the firm faces an exogenously determined interest rate path. Finally, we study the process

---

[5]See, e.g., Intriligator (1971, p. 413).

by which the equilibrium interest rate path is determined as well as the implied dynamic process describing evolution of the capital-labor ratio over time. A major result of this section is that, at least under a certain somewhat restrictive set of assumptions, the market economy does converge to the same steady-state capital-labor ratio as that of the central planner's problem of the preceding section. Furthermore, we find that this optimality of the market solution is unaffected by government's choice of its policy settings.

## Representative Household Behavior

We now turn our attention to the representative household's optimal consumption-saving problem in a growing economy. As a benchmark, we consider the case of an infinitely lived family whose preferences may be summarized by the instantaneous utility function $U(\cdot)$ defined over consumption of the composite good. As the careful reader may suspect, the present analysis follows closely those of Appendixes 1.C and 6.A.

The principal novelty of the current analysis is an explicit treatment of the possibility of growth over time in the number of workers in the economy. As one possibility, we could simply assume that the composition of each household remains the same over time and that growth in the population occurs through continual formation of new households. Alternatively, we could assume that the number of family members, and hence also the number of workers in each family, grows over time. This second possibility turns out to serve as a better point of comparison with the results of the preceding section since it forces the head of the representative household to explicitly deal with the implications of population growth, as must the central planner of Section 8.2 above.

We therefore assume that the head of the representative household chooses a time path for per capita consumption $\tilde{c}(t)$ for the family to maximize

$$V = \int_0^\infty U[\tilde{c}(t)]e^{-\beta t} \, dt, \tag{8.3.1}$$

where $\beta$ again represents an exogenously determined rate of time preference. The representative family sells all of its endowment $L$ of labor services in the labor market at the prevailing nominal wage rate $W(t)$ and may purchase as much of the composite good as it wishes for consumption purposes at the given, market-clearing price $P(t)$. Saving is accomplished through the purchase of government-issued bonds and firm-issued equities. The representative household views these securities as perfect substitutes that both earn the exogenously given nominal rate of interest $r(t)$.

It would be most preferable at this time to allow for the greatest degree of generality as possible for the processes $W(t)$, $P(t)$, and $r(t)$. We could then go on to derive the equilibrium paths for $W(t)$, $P(t)$, and $r(t)$ and adopt the assumption of perfect foresight on the part of the representative household about the properties of these paths. Unfortunately, such an ambitious task proves analytically most formidable. In order to keep the analysis tractable, we instead limit our attention to the case in which the representative household expects the evolution of the economy to generate the time paths $W(t) = W(0)e^{\pi^e t}$, $P(t) = P(0)e^{\pi^e t}$, and $r(t) = r(0)$. We later show that constant values of $W/P$ and $r$ are compatible with the steady-state solution of the market economy and that as long as the growth rate of government-issued liabilities is constant in the steady-state, equilibrium also implies a constant rate of inflation in $W$ and $P$ as well. Finally, we assume that population growth proceeds at the exogenously determined percentage rate $n$.

As a prelude to formal analysis of the representative household's maximization problem, let us first describe in a little more detail the dynamics of family wealth accumulation. Denote gross, nominal holdings of earning assets by the representative household as

$$F = \frac{B}{r} + \frac{P\Pi}{r - \pi^e}, \tag{8.3.2}$$

where $B$ denotes the number of government-issued bonds and $\Pi$ denotes real current and expected future firm profits. Although this particular formulation of the representative household's problem recognizes the possible existence of a government sector, we later demonstrate that the question of the potential existence of this government sector and the question of this government sector's choice of policy settings do not affect the optimality of the market equilibrium capital-labor ratio.

We next denote real, per capita holdings of earning assets by the representative household as

$$\phi \equiv \frac{F}{PL} = \frac{B}{rPL} + \frac{\Pi}{(r - \pi^e)L} = \frac{B}{rPL} + \frac{P_e E}{PL}. \tag{8.3.3}$$

Invoking the assumptions that $P(t) = P(0)e^{\pi^e t}$, $r(t) = r(0)$, $(d/dt)[P_e(t)/P(t)] = 0$, and $(1/L)(dL/dt) = n$, we may differentiate the above expression with respect to time to obtain

$$\frac{d\phi}{dt} = \frac{1}{L}\left(\frac{1}{rP}\frac{dB}{dt} + \frac{P_e}{P}\frac{dE}{dt}\right) - n\phi - \frac{B}{rPL}\pi^e. \tag{8.3.4}$$

The representative household's nominal savings equals nominal disposable income $WL + P\Pi + B - P\tau$ minus nominal consumption $Pc$. Nominal savings is divided among accumulation of additional money balances $dM/dt$, accumulation of additional government bonds $(1/r)(dB/dt)$, and accumulation of additional equities $P_e(dE/dt)$. Therefore, dividing the representative household's budget constraint through by $P$, we obtain

$$\frac{1}{P}\frac{dM}{dt} + \frac{1}{rP}\frac{dB}{dt} + \frac{P_e}{P}\frac{dE}{dt} = wL + \Pi + \frac{B}{P} - c - \tau. \tag{8.3.5}$$

For our current purposes, it is helpful to abstract from the microeconomic details of the representative household's allocation of wealth between money and earning assets. Consistent with the spirit of earlier discussions of this topic in Chapters 1 and 6, we simply assume that real, per capita holdings of money, $\tilde{m} \equiv M/PL$, are given by

$$\tilde{m} = \tilde{m}^d(q, r), \qquad \frac{\partial \tilde{m}^d}{\partial q} > 0, \qquad \frac{\partial \tilde{m}^d}{\partial r} < 0. \tag{8.3.6}$$

Differentiating the definition of $\tilde{m}$ with respect to time, we find that

$$\frac{1}{P}\frac{dM}{dt} = L\frac{d\tilde{m}}{dt} + L\tilde{m}(\pi^e + n). \tag{8.3.7}$$

Now combining the differential equations (8.3.4) and (8.3.7) with the representative household's budget constraint, equation (8.3.5), we obtain, after collecting terms,

$$\frac{d\phi}{dt} = (\rho - n)\phi + w - \tilde{c} - \tilde{\tau} - \frac{d\tilde{m}}{dt} - \tilde{m}(\pi^e + n), \tag{8.3.8}$$

where $\tilde{c}$ represents per capita consumption $C/L$ and $\tilde{\tau}$ represents per capita taxes $\tau/L$. Throughout the analysis, we assume that the representative household expects the real rate of interest $\rho = r - \pi^e$ as well as $w$, $n$, and $\tilde{\tau}$ to remain constant over time. Furthermore, the assumptions that the representative household expects $r$ and $q$ to remain constant over time assures us that $d\tilde{m}/dt = 0$ as well.

The representative household's maximization problem may now be specified as

$$\max_{\tilde{c}(t)} V = \int_0^\infty U[\tilde{c}(t)]e^{-\beta t}\, dt \tag{8.3.9}$$

subject to

$$\frac{d\phi}{dt} = (\rho - n)\phi + w - \tilde{c}(t) - \tilde{\tau} - \tilde{m}(\pi^e + n), \tag{8.3.10}$$

$$\phi(0) = \phi_0, \qquad \phi(\infty) \geq 0, \qquad \tilde{m} = \tilde{m}(q(0), r(0)). \tag{8.3.11}$$

The present-value Hamiltonian for this problem is given by

$$H^* = U[\tilde{c}(t)] + \lambda[(\rho - n)\phi + w - \tilde{c}(t) - \tilde{\tau} - \tilde{m}(\pi^e + n)]. \tag{8.3.12}$$

First-order conditions for this problem are given by

$$\frac{\partial H^*}{\partial c} = U'[\tilde{c}(t)] - \lambda(t) = 0, \tag{8.3.13}$$

$$\dot{\lambda} = -\frac{\partial H^*}{\partial \phi} + \beta\lambda = -(\rho - n - \beta)\lambda \Rightarrow \lambda(t) = \lambda(0)e^{-(\rho - n - \beta)t}. \tag{8.3.14}$$

The transversality conditions for this problem are given by

$$\lim_{t \to +\infty} e^{-\beta t}\lambda(t) \geq 0 \quad \text{and} \quad \lim_{t \to +\infty} e^{-\beta t}\lambda(t)\phi(t) = 0. \tag{8.3.15}$$

It is useful to begin our analysis with further inspection of the transversality conditions. With $\lambda(t)$ given directly from the differential equation in $\lambda$, we obtain

$$\lim_{t \to +\infty} e^{-\beta t}\lambda(t) \geq 0 = \lim_{t \to +\infty} \lambda(0)e^{-(\rho - n)t} \geq 0. \tag{8.3.16}$$

Sufficient conditions for this inequality to hold are that $\lambda(0)$ be finite and that $\rho \geq n$. The second transversality condition is given by

$$\lim_{t \to +\infty} e^{-\beta t}\lambda(t)\phi(t) = 0 = \lim_{t \to +\infty} \lambda(0)\phi(t)e^{-(\rho - n)t} = 0. \tag{8.3.17}$$

In order to check this second transversality condition, we need to solve explicitly for $\phi(t)$. The solution to the differential equation in $\phi(t)$ is given by inspection of the representative household's budget constraint (8.3.8) as

$$\phi(t) = \phi(0)e^{(\rho - n)t} + e^{(\rho - n)t}\int_0^t [w - \tilde{m}(\pi^e - n) - \tilde{\tau} - \tilde{c}(s)]e^{-(\rho - n)s}\, ds. \tag{8.3.18}$$

Since the representative household expects $w$, $\tilde{m}$, $\pi^e$, $n$, and $\tilde{\tau}$ to remain constant over time, the above equation may be rewritten as

$$\phi(t) = \phi(0)e^{(\rho - n)t} + e^{(\rho - n)t}\frac{w - \tilde{m}(\pi^e + n) - \tilde{\tau}}{\rho - n}(1 - e^{-(\rho - n)t})$$

$$-e^{(\rho - n)t}\int_0^t \tilde{c}(s)e^{-(\rho - n)s}\,ds. \tag{8.3.19}$$

The second transversality condition may therefore be expressed as

$$\lim_{t \to +\infty} e^{-\beta t}\lambda(t)\phi(t) = \lim_{t \to +\infty} \lambda(0)$$

$$\times \left[\phi(0) + \frac{w - \tilde{m}(\pi^e + n) - \tilde{\tau}}{\rho - n}(1 - e^{-(\rho - n)t}) - \int_0^t \tilde{c}(s)e^{-(\rho - n)s}\,ds\right] = 0. \tag{8.3.20}$$

The above expression may be rearranged as

$$\int_0^t \tilde{c}(s)e^{-(\rho - n)s}\,ds = \frac{B}{rPL} + \frac{\Pi}{\rho L} + \frac{w - \tilde{m}(\pi^e + n) - \tilde{\tau}}{\rho - n}. \tag{8.3.21}$$

Solution of the maximization problem is therefore given by

$$U'[\tilde{c}(t)] = \lambda(0)e^{-(\rho - n - \beta)t}, \tag{8.3.22}$$

$$\int_0^t \tilde{c}(s)e^{-(\rho - n)s}\,ds = \frac{B}{rPL} + \frac{\Pi}{\rho L} + \frac{w - \tilde{m}(\pi^e + n) - \tilde{\tau}}{\rho - n}. \tag{8.3.23}$$

These last two expressions represent two simultaneous equations in $\tilde{c}(t)$ and $\lambda(0)$, which may be used to solve for $\tilde{c}(t)$. One particularly simple case is that in which $U(\tilde{c}) = \ln \tilde{c}$. In this case, the first-order condition for $\tilde{c}(t)$ becomes

$$\tilde{c}(t) = \frac{e^{(\rho - n - \beta)t}}{\lambda(0)}. \tag{8.3.24}$$

Upon eliminating $\lambda(0)$, we therefore obtain

$$\tilde{c}(t) = \frac{\beta}{\rho - n}\left[w + \frac{\Pi}{L} + \frac{B}{PL} - \tilde{\tau} - \left(\frac{B}{rPL} + \tilde{m}\right)\pi^e\right.$$

$$\left. - \left(\frac{B}{rPL} + \frac{\Pi}{\rho L} + \tilde{m}\right)n\right]e^{(\rho - n - \beta)t}. \tag{8.3.25}$$

Appeal to the government budget constraint allows further simplification of the representative household's optimal consumption plan. In per capita terms, the government budget constraint is given by

$$\tilde{g} - \tilde{\tau} + \frac{B}{PL} = \mu\left(1 + \frac{\theta}{r}\right)\tilde{m}, \tag{8.3.26}$$

where $\mu$ represents the rate of growth of the nominal money supply, $\tilde{g}$ represents real, per capita government spending, and $\theta$ represents the ratio of government bonds to money.

Combining the government budget constraint with the consumption function and evaluating at $t = 0$, we obtain

$$\tilde{c} = \frac{\beta}{\rho - n}\left[ w + \frac{\Pi}{L} + - \tilde{g} + \left(1 + \frac{\theta}{r}\right)\tilde{m}^d(q, r)(\mu - \pi^e - n) - \frac{\Pi}{\rho L}n \right]. \quad (8.3.27)$$

## Representative Firm Behavior

Representative firm investment behavior was first analyzed in Chapter 1. The analysis of Section 1.2 viewed the representative firm's investment decision as the selection of the size of the capital stock that maximizes the market value of existing shareholders' equity. Section 1.2 then presented a heuristic argument that conjectured that optimal firm investment behavior only slowly closes the gap between the existing stock of capital and the optimal stock of capital.

In Appendixes 1.B and 6.A, we demonstrated how the presence of capital stock adjustment costs permits formal derivation of such an investment demand function. This section reviews the analysis of investment behavior in the presence of adjustment costs for those readers whose only familiarity with optimal control techniques has been achieved by working through Section 8.2. Furthermore, this section also extends the analysis of Appendix 6.A to the case of an economy with a growing labor force and a stock of capital that depreciates over time.

Assume that the price of a share of equity in the representative firm is given by[6]

$$P_e = \frac{1}{E}\int_0^\infty P(s)[\phi(L(s), K(s)) - w(s)L(s) - \delta K(s) - \dot{K}(s) - C(\dot{K})]e^{-rs}\, ds. \quad (8.3.28)$$

That is, the market price of an existing share of equity is equal to the present value of the firm's future cash flow discounted at the market rate of interest $r$. As long as earning asset market participants consider government-issued bonds and equities to be perfect substitutes and as long as all economic agents expect the nominal rate of return $r$ on earning assets to remain constant into the indefinite future, the above expression will be correct independent of whether the representative firm accounts for periods of nonzero cash flow by purchases and sales of equity claims or bonds. In the above expression, $C(\dot{K})$ denotes the real resource costs of installing new capital, $w$ denotes the (assumed constant) real wage, $\delta K$ denotes the physical cost of depreciation, and $\dot{K}(t)$ denotes the cost of the new output that is being installed as capital by the representative firm.

Although the most general form of the representative firm's choice problem involves selection of the optimal paths $L(t)$ and $K(t)$, homogeneity of the production function leads to problems resulting from the indeterminacy of firm size in a competitive equilibrium with constant returns to scale. One particularly simple way to sidestep such problems is to assume that the representative firm correctly perceives that, in equilibrium, full employment of the growing labor force, $L(t) = L(0)e^{nt}$, should prevail at a constant real wage $w$. We therefore simply take the employment level of the representative firm as exogenously given and restrict the analysis to the representative firm's selection of an optimal path of

---

[6]The analysis of this section closely parallels that provided by Sargent (1987, Ch. 6).

$K(t)$ over time. If the firm also expects the future course of the price level to be given by $P(t) = P(0)e^{\pi^e t}$, then the above expression for $P_e$ may be expressed as

$$P_e = \frac{P(0)L(t)}{E} \int_0^\infty \left\{ \Phi\left(1, \frac{K(t)}{L(t)}\right) - w - \frac{\dot{K}(t)}{L(t)} \right.$$
$$\left. - \delta\frac{K(t)}{L(t)} - \frac{C[\dot{K}(t)]}{L(t)} \right\} e^{-(r - \pi^e)t}\, dt. \tag{8.3.29}$$

With $L(t)$ exogenously determined, we may view the representative firm's choice problem equivalently as one of selecting an optimal path for $K(t)$ or as selecting an optimal path for $k(t) \equiv K(t)/L(t)$. Utilizing the definition of $k$ and noting that $\rho = r - \pi^e$ and $\dot{K}/L = \dot{k} + nk$, the above expression may be rewritten as

$$P_e = \frac{P(0)L(t)}{E} \int_0^\infty \left\{ f(k) - w - (\delta + n)k - \dot{k} - \frac{C[\dot{K}(t)]}{L(t)} \right\} e^{-\rho s}\, ds. \tag{8.3.30}$$

We now turn our attention in some detail to the likely form of the capital-stock adjustment term in a growing economy. The basic idea behind the existence of this term is that attempts to very rapidly install a large quantity of new capital may be prohibitively expensive. However, what constitutes sensible assumptions about the relative size of such costs as the aggregate economy and the absolute size of $\dot{K}$ grow over time? Furthermore, what constitutes a sensible assumption about the minimum cost rate of change of the capital stock?

In the growing economies of Sections 8.1 and 8.2 we found that, in equilibrium, the capital-labor ratio remains constant. However, such constancy in the capital-labor ratio requires continuous *gross* investment equal to $(\delta + n)K$. In the steady state, firms must therefore purchase and install new capital goods at this pace as a routine matter. Consequently, it might be reasonable to assume that it is deviations from this equilibrium rate of installation of new capital that might be particularly expensive. As noted above, it is quite obvious that particularly high rates of $\dot{K}$ may be expensive to implement. However, we might also expect rates of $\dot{K}$ that result in reductions in $k$ to be more expensive to implement than rates of $\dot{K}$ that simply maintain $k$ at its long-run equilibrium value. To deviate from the usual investment process by curtailing capital spending plans and retooling existing capital for production at a lower capital-labor ratio may involve incurring more than minimum capital adjustment costs. Second, we might expect that the absolute size of such costs of adjusting $k$ are likely to rise as the economy grows such that it is the per capita value of these costs that tends to remain constant in the steady state. One simple functional form that exhibits these properties is

$$C = \tfrac{1}{2}\alpha L(t)(\dot{k})^2. \tag{8.3.31}$$

Plugging this cost function into the above expression for $P_e$ and recalling that $L(t) = L(0)e^{nt}$, we obtain

$$P_e = \frac{P(0)L(0)}{E} \int_0^\infty \left[ f(k) - w - (\delta + n)k - \dot{k} - \frac{\alpha}{2}(\dot{k})^2 \right] e^{-(\rho - n)s}\, ds. \tag{8.3.32}$$

In posing the representative firm's choice problem, it is also useful to define the control variable $u(t) \equiv \dot{k}(t)$. The formal optimal control problem is therefore given by

$$\max_{u(t)} \int_0^\infty \left[ f(k) - w - (\delta + n)k - u - \frac{\alpha}{2}u^2 \right] e^{-(\rho - n)s} \, ds \tag{8.3.33}$$

subject to

$$\dot{k} = u, \tag{8.3.34}$$

$$k(0) = k_0, \qquad k(\infty) \geq 0. \tag{8.3.35}$$

The present-value Hamiltonian for this problem is therefore given by

$$H^* = f(k) - w - (\delta + n)k - u - \frac{\alpha}{2}u^2 + \lambda u. \tag{8.3.36}$$

Necessary conditions for a maximum are given by

$$\frac{\partial H^*}{\partial u} = -1 - \alpha u + \lambda = 0, \tag{8.3.37}$$

$$\dot{\lambda} = -\frac{\partial H^*}{\partial k} + (\rho - n)\lambda = -f'(k) + (\delta + n) + (\rho - n)\lambda. \tag{8.3.38}$$

The transversality conditions for this problem are given by

$$\lim_{t \to +\infty} \lambda(t)e^{-(\rho - n)t} \geq 0 \quad \text{and} \quad \lim_{t \to +\infty} \lambda(t)k(t)e^{-(\rho - n)t} = 0. \tag{8.3.39}$$

We may differentiate the first of the first-order conditions to obtain

$$\dot{\lambda} = \alpha \dot{u} = \alpha \ddot{k}. \tag{8.3.40}$$

Now plugging this expression for $\ddot{k}$ as well as the expression $\lambda = 1 + \alpha \dot{k}$ into the above differential equation for $\lambda$, we obtain

$$\alpha \ddot{k} = -f'(k) + (\delta + n) + (\rho - n) + \alpha(\rho - n)\dot{k}. \tag{8.3.41}$$

Upon rearranging, we obtain the following second-order, nonlinear, nonhomogeneous differential equation in $k$:

$$\ddot{k} - (\rho - n)\dot{k} + \frac{f'(k) - (\delta + \rho)}{\alpha} = 0. \tag{8.3.42}$$

The homogeneous part of the solution for the optimal path of $k$ is therefore governed by

$$\ddot{k} - (\rho - n)\dot{k} + \frac{f'(k)}{\alpha} = 0. \tag{8.3.43}$$

One particularly simple case in which a closed-form solution $k(t)$ to this differential equation may be obtained is that in which the production function is quadratic. In this case, we obtain $f'(k) = f'(k^*) + f''(k - k^*)$ for an arbitrarily selected $k^*$. In this case, the optimal path of $k$ is governed by a linear, second-order differential equation in $k$ with characteristic roots that satisfy

$$s_i = \frac{1}{2}\left\{(\rho - n) \pm \left[(\rho - n)^2 - \left(\frac{4f''}{\alpha}\right)\right]^{1/2}\right\}. \tag{8.3.44}$$

As we later discover, the equilibrium value of $\rho$ is such that $\rho - n > 0$. Therefore, one value of $s_i$ is negative and one value of $s_i$ is positive. The only nonexplosive time function $k(t)$ that satisfies the necessary conditions for an optimum is therefore given by

$$k(t) = k^* + (k_0 - k^*)e^{s_1 t}, \tag{8.3.45}$$

where $s_1$ denotes the negative root and $s_2$ denotes the positive root of the above characteristic equation. Furthermore, it is only the stable root of this characteristic equation that satisfies the transversality conditions. Finally, the steady-state value $k^*$ of $k$ must satisfy

$$\ddot{k} = \dot{k} = 0 \Rightarrow f'(k^*) = \rho + \delta. \tag{8.3.46}$$

The optimal path $k(t)$ of $k$ therefore also satisfies

$$\dot{k}(t) = s_1(k_0 - k^*)e^{s_1 t}. \tag{8.3.47}$$

However, we also know that

$$\begin{aligned} f'(k) - (\rho + \delta) &= f'(k^*) + f''(k - k^*) - (\rho + \delta) \\ &= f''(k - k^*) \end{aligned} \tag{8.3.48}$$

in general for any $k$ and for $k = k_0$ in particular. We therefore obtain

$$k_0 - k^* = \frac{f'(k_0) - (\rho + \delta)}{f''}. \tag{8.3.49}$$

Finally, evaluating $\dot{k}(t)$ at $t = 0$, we obtain

$$\dot{k}(0) = s_1(k_0 - k^*), \tag{8.3.50}$$

or

$$\dot{k}(0) = \frac{s_1}{f''}[f'(k_0) - (\rho + \delta)]. \tag{8.3.51}$$

Therefore, denoting per capita net investment $\dot{K}/L = i/L = \dot{k} + nk \equiv \tilde{i}$, we obtain

$$\tilde{i} = \xi_k[f'(k) - (\delta + \rho)] + nk, \qquad \xi_k = \frac{s_1}{f''} > 0. \tag{8.3.52}$$

## Growth Equilibrium in the Market Economy

As a prelude to a dynamic analysis of capital accumulation in the market economy, we first turn our attention to properties of the steady state in which the capital-labor ratio is constant. An important motivation of this part of the analysis is to provide a proof that the representative agent behavior derived in the two previous sections is in fact consistent with a dynamic equilibrium in which the capital-labor ratio is equal to the socially optimal capital-labor ratio $k^*$ of Section 8.2.

In this section, we retain the behavioral relationships $\tilde{c}(\cdot)$ and $\tilde{i}(\cdot)$ derived above for desired per capita consumption and net investment, respectively. We also assume that per capita government spending $\tilde{g}$ is constant. However, before proceeding, we need to more carefully specify some of the components of the argument of the consumption function $\tilde{c}^d(\cdot)$. For consistency with our assumption that the representative household expects that $(d/dt)(P_e/P) = 0$, at least in the steady state, it must be the case that the representative firm only distribute profits net of depreciation and capital stock adjustment costs. We therefore have

$$\frac{\Pi}{L} = q - w - \delta k - \frac{\alpha}{2}(\dot{k})^2. \tag{8.3.53}$$

The assumption that factor markets are competitive requires that the real wage equal the marginal product of labor, or

$$w = \frac{\partial \Phi(L, K)}{\partial L} = \frac{\partial}{\partial L}\left[ Lf\left(\frac{K}{L}\right)\right] = q - kf'(k). \tag{8.3.54}$$

We therefore get the alternate expression for $\Pi/L$:

$$\frac{\Pi}{L} = [f'(k)k - \delta] - \frac{\alpha}{2}(\dot{k})^2. \tag{8.3.55}$$

Plugging these two expressions for $\Pi/L$ into the consumption function, we obtain

$$\tilde{c}^d = \frac{\beta}{\rho - n}\left[ q - \left(\delta + \frac{f'(k) - \delta}{\rho}n\right)k - \frac{\alpha}{2}\frac{\rho - n}{\rho}(\dot{k})^2 \right.$$
$$\left. - \tilde{g} + \left(1 + \frac{\theta}{r}\right)\tilde{m}^d(q, \rho + \pi^e)(\mu - \pi^e - n)\right]. \tag{8.3.56}$$

The economywide budget constraint is given by

$$q = \tilde{c} + \frac{\dot{K}}{L} + \delta K + \frac{\alpha}{2}(\dot{k})^2 + \tilde{g}. \tag{8.3.57}$$

Goods market equilibrium obtains when per capita aggregate demand—per capita consumption demand $\tilde{c}^d$ plus gross per capita investment demand $\dot{K}/L + \delta K + \frac{1}{2}(\dot{k})^2 = \tilde{i}^d + (n + \delta)k + \frac{1}{2}(\dot{k})^2$ plus per capita government spending $\tilde{g}$—equals per capita aggregate supply, or

$$\tilde{c}^d(\cdot) + \tilde{i}^d(\cdot) + (n + \delta)k + \frac{\alpha}{2}(\dot{k})^2 - q = 0 \tag{8.3.58}$$

or

$$\frac{\beta}{\rho - n}\left[ q - \left(\delta + \frac{f'(k) - \delta}{\rho}n\right)k - \frac{\alpha}{2}\frac{\rho - n}{\rho}(\dot{k})^2 - \tilde{g} \right.$$
$$\left. + \left(1 + \frac{\theta}{r}\right)\tilde{m}^d(q, \rho + \pi^e)(\mu - \pi^e - n)\right] \tag{8.3.59}$$
$$+ \xi_k[f'(k) - (\rho + \delta)] + (n + \delta)k + \frac{\alpha}{2}(\dot{k})^2 + \tilde{g} - q = 0.$$

Let us now consider dynamic adjustment in the model. Differentiating the definition of $\tilde{m}$ with respect to time, we find that

$$\frac{\dot{\tilde{m}}}{\tilde{m}} = \mu - \pi - n. \tag{8.3.60}$$

Representative firm investment behavior implies the additional dynamic relationship

$$\dot{k} = \xi_k[f'(k) - (\delta + \rho)]. \tag{8.3.61}$$

We now consider dynamic equilibrium. For a stationary state, we require that

$$\dot{k} = \frac{\dot{\tilde{m}}}{\tilde{m}} = 0. \tag{8.3.62}$$

We should also expect that, in equilibrium, $\pi = \pi^e$. These three equilibrium conditions together require that

$$\pi = \pi^e = \mu - n \tag{8.3.63}$$

and

$$f'(k) - \delta = \rho = r - \pi^e \quad \text{or} \quad r = f'(k) - \delta + \pi^e. \tag{8.3.64}$$

Plugging these two relationships into the goods market equilibrium condition and recalling that, in equilibrium, $\dot{k} = 0$, we obtain

$$\frac{\beta}{\rho - n}[f(k) - (\delta + n)k - \tilde{g}] + (\delta + n)k + \tilde{g} - f(k) = 0. \tag{8.3.65}$$

As long as $\tilde{c} \neq 0$, goods market equilibrium therefore requires that

$$\beta = \rho - n \quad \text{or} \quad r = \beta + \pi^e + n. \tag{8.3.66}$$

We have therefore established that dynamic equilibrium of the representative agent, market model of the macroeconomy requires that

$$f'(k) = \delta + n + \beta. \tag{8.3.67}$$

Per capita consumption and net investment in the steady state are therefore given by

$$\tilde{c}^* \equiv f(k^*) - (\delta + n)k^* - \tilde{g}, \tag{8.3.68}$$

$$\tilde{i}^* \equiv nk^*. \tag{8.3.69}$$

Interestingly, the condition on $f'(k)$ in equation (8.3.67) above is precisely the same condition that defined $k^*$, the long-run equilibrium capital-labor ratio of the optimal planner problem of Section 8.2. We have therefore established that if the market economy equilibrium exists and is stable, the resulting asymptotic capital-labor ratio is precisely the same as that obtained in the optimal control solution to the central planner's problem. It is also of interest to note that the achievement of the Pareto-optimal capital-labor ratio is independent of the rate of expansion of government liabilities and the rate of inflation.[7]

---

[7]This independence of the optimum capital intensity from the rate of inflation in an infinite-horizon, utility-maximizing framework is demonstrated by Sidrauski (1967).

We have therefore proven that the market economy can, at least in the steady state, optimally coordinate the privately optimal plans of the atomistic representative households and firms.[8] However, this result obtains precisely because we have carefully set up the household and firm choice problems in such a way that there are no externalities and have therefore presented the steady state as a particularly straightforward example in which a competitive equilibrium is capable of supporting a Pareto-optimal allocation.

Notice that our assumption that population growth occurs through increases in the sizes of existing families rather than through the formation of new families is crucial. If the representative household ignored household population growth from its maximization calculus, equilibrium would instead be characterized by

$$\frac{\beta}{\rho - n}\left[f(k) - \delta k - \tilde{g} + n\left(1 + \frac{\theta}{r}\right)\tilde{m}\right] + \tilde{g} + (\delta + n)k - f(k) = 0. \qquad (8.3.70)$$

In this case, it is fairly straightforward to show that

$$f'(k) = \delta + n + \beta + \frac{\beta n[k + (1 + \theta/r)\tilde{m}]}{f(k) - (\delta + n)k - \tilde{g}}$$

$$= \delta + n + \beta + \frac{\beta n}{\tilde{c}}\left[k + \left(1 + \frac{\theta}{r}\right)\tilde{m}\right]. \qquad (8.3.71)$$

We therefore find that $f'(k) > f'(k^*)$, and so the equilibrium capital-labor ratio is less than the Pareto-optimal level. Individual households do not recognize the externalities imposed by population growth and therefore save less than the optimal amount.

It is also clear that other types of externalities would lead to similar divergences from the Pareto optimum. What is important, however, is that at least some plausible set of assumptions does reconcile the market equilibrium outcome with the socially optimum solution.

## Dynamics in the Market Economy

We are now ready to formally analyze the dynamic process of capital accumulation in the market economy. Recall the instantaneous goods and money market equilibrium conditions

$$\frac{\beta}{\rho - n}\left\{f(k) - \left(\delta + \frac{f'(k) - \delta}{\rho}n\right)k - \frac{\alpha}{2}\frac{\rho - n}{\rho}\xi_k^2[f'(k) - \rho - \delta)]^2 - \tilde{g}\right.$$

$$\left. + \left(1 + \frac{\theta}{r}\right)\tilde{m}^d(q, \rho + \pi^e)(\mu - \pi^e - n)\right\} + \xi_k[f'(k) - \rho - \delta)] \qquad (8.3.72)$$

$$+ (n + \delta)k + \frac{\alpha}{2}\xi_k^2[f'(k) - \rho - \delta)]^2 + \tilde{g} - q = 0,$$

$$\tilde{m}^d[f(k), \rho + \pi^e] - \tilde{m} = 0. \qquad (8.3.73)$$

---

[8]Stein (1971, Ch. 7) contains an expanded discussion of those conditions under which a market economy can and cannot support an optimal growth plan.

These two equilibrium conditions provide two equations in the variables $\rho$, $\pi^e$, $k$, and $\tilde{m}$ that must hold at each point in time. As we demonstrate below, the formal dynamic model of the capital accumulation process is one in two state variables. The choice of which two of these four variables to designate as the state variables of the dynamic system is quite arbitrary. The system consisting of the state variables $k$ and $\tilde{m}$ proves particularly illuminating, and so our formal analysis employs these two quantities as the system's state variables.

As a useful prelude, we now wish to construct the implicit functions

$$\rho = \rho(k, \tilde{m}), \qquad \pi^e = \pi^e(k, \tilde{m}) \tag{8.3.74}$$

from the goods and money market equilibrium conditions. Differentiating these two static equilibrium conditions in the neighborhood of the dynamic equilibrium conditions $\rho = f' - \delta = \beta + n$ and $\pi^e = \mu - n$ with respect to $\rho$, $\pi^e$, $k$, and $\tilde{m}$ and rearranging, we find that

$$\begin{bmatrix} -\left[ \dfrac{\tilde{c}^*}{\beta} + \left( \xi_k - \dfrac{nk}{\beta+n} \right) \right] & -\left( 1 + \dfrac{\theta}{r} \right)\tilde{m} \\[2em] \dfrac{\partial \tilde{m}^d}{\partial r} & \dfrac{\partial \tilde{m}^d}{\partial r} \end{bmatrix} \begin{bmatrix} d\rho \\[2em] d\pi^e \end{bmatrix}$$

$$= \begin{bmatrix} -f''\left( \xi_k - \dfrac{nk}{\beta+n} \right) dk \\[2em] -\dfrac{\partial \tilde{m}^d}{\partial y} f' \, dk + d\tilde{m} \end{bmatrix}. \tag{8.3.75}$$

The determinant of this matrix is given by

$$\Delta = \frac{\partial \tilde{m}^d}{\partial r} \left[ -\frac{\tilde{c}^*}{\beta} - \left( \xi_k - \frac{nk}{\beta+n} \right) + \left( 1 + \frac{\theta}{r} \right)\tilde{m} \right]. \tag{8.3.76}$$

Throughout the analysis, we assume that $\Delta > 0$. This assumption is equivalent to the assumption that an increase in $\pi^e$ holding $r$ constant raises excess aggregate demand. Recall that we adopted an analogous assumption earlier in Chapter 6.

Application of Cramer's rule facilitates the following preliminary results:

$$\frac{\partial \rho}{\partial k} = -\frac{1}{\Delta} \left[ f'' \frac{\partial \tilde{m}^d}{\partial r} \left( \xi_k - \frac{nk}{\beta+n} \right) + f' \frac{\partial \tilde{m}^d}{\partial y} \left( 1 + \frac{\theta}{r} \right)\tilde{m} \right] < 0, \tag{8.3.77}$$

$$\frac{\partial \rho}{\partial \tilde{m}} = \frac{1}{\Delta} \left( 1 + \frac{\theta}{r} \right)\tilde{m} > 0, \tag{8.3.78}$$

$$\frac{\partial \pi^e}{\partial k} = \frac{1}{\Delta} \left[ \frac{\partial \tilde{m}^d}{\partial y} f' \frac{\tilde{c}^*}{\beta} + \left( \frac{\partial \tilde{m}^d}{\partial y} f' + \frac{\partial \tilde{m}^d}{\partial r} f'' \right)\left( \xi_k - \frac{nk}{\beta+n} \right) \right] > 0, \tag{8.3.79}$$

$$\frac{\partial \pi^e}{\partial \tilde{m}} = -\frac{1}{\Delta} \left[ \frac{\tilde{c}^*}{\beta} + \left( \xi_k - \frac{nk}{\beta+n} \right) \right] < 0. \tag{8.3.80}$$

The signs of these partial derivatives are all straightforward as long as $\Delta > 0$, as we are assuming throughout, and as long as $\xi_k > nk/(\beta + n)$. We are assured that $\xi_k -$

$nk(\beta + n) > 0$ as long as an increase in the real interest rate reduces investment demand by more than it reduces $n$ times the market value of equity. Obviously, this assumption is always valid for sufficiently small $n$.

We first consider the dynamic adjustment of $k$, the capital-labor ratio. As noted above, adjustment of $k$ is described by[9]

$$\dot{k} = \xi_k[f'(k) - \delta - \rho] = \xi_k[f'(k) - \delta - \rho(k, \tilde{m})]. \tag{8.3.81}$$

Differentiating this expression with respect to $k$, we obtain

$$\frac{\partial \dot{k}}{\partial k} = \frac{\xi_k}{\Delta}\left[-f'' \frac{\partial \tilde{m}^d}{\partial r} \frac{\tilde{c}^*}{\beta} + \left(f' \frac{\partial \tilde{m}^d}{\partial y} + f'' \frac{\partial \tilde{m}^d}{\partial r}\right)\left(1 + \frac{\theta}{r}\right)\tilde{m}\right]. \tag{8.3.82}$$

Although this expression is formally of ambiguous sign, we assume throughout that $\partial \dot{k}/\partial k < 0$. We next differentiate $\dot{k}$ with respect to $\tilde{m}$ to obtain

$$\frac{\partial \dot{k}}{\partial \tilde{m}} = \frac{-\xi_k}{\Delta}\left(1 + \frac{\theta}{r}\right)\tilde{m} < 0. \tag{8.3.83}$$

We therefore find that

$$\left.\frac{d\tilde{m}}{dk}\right|_{\dot{k}=0} = \frac{-f'' \dfrac{\partial \tilde{m}^d}{\partial r} \dfrac{\tilde{c}^*}{\beta} + \left(f' \dfrac{\partial \tilde{m}^d}{\partial y} + f'' \dfrac{\partial \tilde{m}^d}{\partial r}\right)\left(1 + \dfrac{\theta}{r}\right)\tilde{m}}{(1 + \theta/r)\tilde{m}} < 0 \tag{8.3.84}$$

as long as $\partial \dot{k}/\partial k < 0$, as we have already assumed.

We next consider the dynamics of motion of $\tilde{m}$. Differentiating the definition of $\tilde{m}$ with respect to time, we again obtain

$$\frac{\dot{\tilde{m}}}{\tilde{m}} = \mu - \pi - n. \tag{8.3.85}$$

As in Chapter 6, we employ the assumption of adaptive expectation. We may then consider perfect foresight expectations as the limit in which such adaptation is instantaneous. In particular, we assume that

$$\dot{\pi}^e = \psi(\pi - \pi^e) \Rightarrow \pi = \pi^e + \frac{1}{\psi}\dot{\pi}^e. \tag{8.3.86}$$

Combining these last two equations, we obtain

$$\frac{\dot{\tilde{m}}}{\tilde{m}} = [\mu - n - \pi^e(k, \tilde{m})] - \frac{1}{\psi}\dot{\pi}^e. \tag{8.3.87}$$

However, since we have already defined the implicit function $\pi^e = \pi^e(k, \tilde{m})$, we may rewrite this last expression as

$$\frac{\dot{\tilde{m}}}{\tilde{m}} = [\mu - n - \pi^e(k, \tilde{m})] - \frac{1}{\psi} \frac{\partial \pi^e}{\partial k}\dot{k} - \frac{\tilde{m}}{\psi} \frac{\partial \pi^e}{\partial \tilde{m}} \frac{\dot{\tilde{m}}}{\tilde{m}}. \tag{8.3.88}$$

---

[9]This explicit link between the capital formation process and the representative firm's investment behavior, as opposed to the representative household's savings behavior, is an important characteristic of Stein's (1970b) Keynes-Wicksell model.

Rearranging, we find that

$$\frac{\dot{\tilde{m}}}{\tilde{m}} = A\left[ (\mu - n - \pi^e(k, \tilde{m})) - \frac{1}{\psi} \frac{\partial \pi^e}{\partial k} \dot{k} \right], \tag{8.3.89}$$

where

$$A \equiv \frac{1}{1 + \dfrac{\tilde{m}}{\psi} \dfrac{\partial \pi^e}{\partial \tilde{m}}}. \tag{8.3.90}$$

Since $\partial \pi^e / \partial \tilde{m} < 0$, we see that $A < 0$ for sufficiently small values of $\psi$ and that $A > 0$ for sufficiently large values of $\psi$.

We are now ready to derive the properties of the $\dot{\tilde{m}}/\tilde{m} = 0$ locus. Differentiating the expression for $\dot{\tilde{m}}/\tilde{m}$ above, first with respect to $\tilde{m}$, we obtain

$$\frac{\partial (\dot{\tilde{m}}/\tilde{m})}{\partial \tilde{m}} = -A\left( \frac{\partial \pi^e}{\partial \tilde{m}} + \frac{1}{\psi} \frac{\partial \pi^e}{\partial k} \frac{\partial \dot{k}}{\partial \tilde{m}} \right). \tag{8.3.91}$$

Since we have already demonstrated that $\partial \pi^e / \partial \tilde{m} < 0$, $\partial \pi^e / \partial k > 0$, and since from equation (8.3.83) we are assured that $\partial \dot{k} / \partial \tilde{m} < 0$, we see that

$$\text{sgn}\left( \frac{\partial (\dot{\tilde{m}}/\tilde{m})}{\partial \tilde{m}} \right) = \text{sgn}(A). \tag{8.3.92}$$

We next differentiate the expression for $\dot{\tilde{m}}/\tilde{m}$ with respect to $k$ to obtain

$$\frac{\partial (\dot{\tilde{m}}/\tilde{m})}{\partial k} = -A \frac{\partial \pi^e}{\partial k}\left( 1 + \frac{1}{\psi} \frac{\partial \dot{k}}{\partial k} \right). \tag{8.3.93}$$

This expression is of ambiguous sign, both because $A$ is of ambiguous sign and because $\partial \dot{k} / \partial k$ is assumed to be negative. We may finally combine these last two expressions to obtain

$$\frac{d\tilde{m}}{dk}\bigg|_{\dot{\tilde{m}}/\tilde{m} = 0} = -\frac{\partial (\dot{\tilde{m}}/\tilde{m})/\partial k}{\partial (\dot{\tilde{m}}/\tilde{m})/\partial \tilde{m}} = \frac{-\dfrac{\partial \pi^e}{\partial k}\left( 1 + \dfrac{1}{\psi} \dfrac{\partial \dot{k}}{\partial k} \right)}{\dfrac{\partial \pi^e}{\partial \tilde{m}} + \dfrac{1}{\psi} \dfrac{\partial \pi^e}{\partial k} \dfrac{\partial \dot{k}}{\partial \tilde{m}}}. \tag{8.3.94}$$

This expression is also of ambiguous sign. However, we do know that the denominator of this last expression is negative, that $\partial \pi^e / \partial k$ is positive, and that $\partial \dot{k} / \partial k$ is negative. We are therefore assured that

$$\text{sgn}\left( \frac{d\tilde{m}}{dk}\bigg|_{\dot{\tilde{m}}/\tilde{m} = 0} \right) = \text{sgn}\left( 1 + \frac{1}{\psi} \frac{\partial \dot{k}}{\partial k} \right). \tag{8.3.95}$$

## Dynamics with Slowly Adapting Expectations

Let us begin a formal dynamic analysis with the case of slowly adapting inflationary expectations. In particular, we assume that $\psi$ is small and that the traditional dynamic stability conditions are satisfied. With $\psi \simeq 0$, we find that

$$A < 0 \quad \text{and} \quad 1 + \frac{1}{\psi}\frac{\partial \dot{k}}{\partial k} < 0. \tag{8.3.96}$$

We therefore are assured that

$$\frac{\partial(\dot{\tilde{m}}/\tilde{m})}{\partial \tilde{m}} < 0 \quad \text{and} \quad \frac{d\tilde{m}}{dk}\bigg|_{\dot{\tilde{m}}/\tilde{m}=0} < 0. \tag{8.3.97}$$

These last two inequalities combine with our earlier results that

$$\frac{\partial \dot{k}}{\partial k} < 0 \quad \text{and} \quad \frac{d\tilde{m}}{dk}\bigg|_{\dot{k}=0} < 0, \tag{8.3.98}$$

which are independent of the size of $\psi$.

The only additional piece of information needed to draw the phase diagram of the $k, \tilde{m}$ system is the magnitude of the slope of the $\dot{k} = 0$ locus relative to the slope of the $\dot{\tilde{m}}/\tilde{m} = 0$ locus. However, as long as the determinant of the matrix of partial derivatives is positive, as it must be to satisfy the stability conditions, we know that

$$\frac{\partial \dot{k}}{\partial k}\frac{\partial(\dot{\tilde{m}}/\tilde{m})}{\partial \tilde{m}} - \frac{\partial \dot{k}}{\partial \tilde{m}}\frac{\partial(\dot{\tilde{m}}/\tilde{m})}{\partial k} > 0. \tag{8.3.99}$$

Since we also know in this case that $\partial(\dot{\tilde{m}}/\tilde{m})/\partial\tilde{m} < 0$ and $\partial\dot{k}/\partial\tilde{m} < 0$, this last inequality guarantees that

$$-\frac{d\tilde{m}}{dk}\bigg|_{\dot{k}=0} = \frac{\partial\dot{k}/\partial k}{\partial\dot{k}/\partial\tilde{m}} > \frac{\partial(\dot{\tilde{m}}/\tilde{m})/\partial k}{\partial(\dot{\tilde{m}}/\tilde{m})\partial\tilde{m}} = -\frac{d\tilde{m}}{dk}\bigg|_{\dot{\tilde{m}}/\tilde{m}=0}. \tag{8.3.100}$$

We therefore know that the $\dot{k} = 0$ locus must be more steeply negatively sloped than the $\dot{\tilde{m}}/\tilde{m} = 0$ locus. The phase diagram for the dynamic system is therefore as depicted in Figure 8.3.

We are now ready to analyze the dynamics of adjustment of the economy to exogenous disturbances. One particularly interesting case is that of an unanticipated increase in the rate of expansion of government liabilities $\mu$. It is straightforward from our analysis of the steady state that an increase in $\mu$ has no lasting effect on $k$. An increase in $\mu$ does,

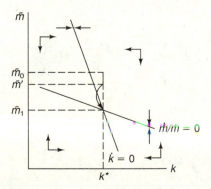

**Figure 8.3**

however, result in one-for-one increases in $\pi$ and $r$ and a consequent reduction in $\tilde{m}$.

Following a unit increase in $\mu$, the $\dot{k} = 0$ and $\dot{\tilde{m}}/\tilde{m} = 0$ loci both shift downward by $\partial\tilde{m}^d/\partial r$. We also experience instantaneous changes in $\rho$, $r$, and $\tilde{m}$. Since $\pi^e$ and $k$ are fixed in the very short run, we may use the goods market equilibrium condition to demonstrate that

$$\left.\frac{d\rho}{d\mu}\right|_{\text{impact}} = \frac{(1 + \theta/r)\tilde{m}}{\dfrac{\tilde{c}^*}{\beta} + \left(\xi_k - \dfrac{nk}{\beta + n}\right)}. \tag{8.3.101}$$

Our earlier assumption that $\Delta > 0$ guarantees that $0 < d\rho/d\mu|_{\text{impact}} < 1$. Therefore, $\tilde{m}$ immediately falls, but $\tilde{m}$ falls by less than the amount of the steady-state decline in $\tilde{m}$. In Figure 8.3, we depict the instantaneous drop in $\tilde{m}$ from $\tilde{m}_0$ to $\tilde{m}'$.

Over time, the expected rate of inflation and the capital-labor ratio both begin to evolve according to the system dynamics. As shown in Figure 8.3, this dynamic adjustment path includes a gradual decline in $\tilde{m}$ from $\tilde{m}'$, to $\tilde{m}_1$. We also find that $k$ and therefore $q = f(k)$ both initially fall, with $k$ first declining to levels below $k^*$ before gradually rising back to $k^*$ in the steady state. This last result demonstrates that an acceleration in the money growth rate brings about a temporary *reduction* in per capita output. Although this last result may be somewhat counterintuitive, it should not, upon some reflection, be that surprising.

Recall that the model we analyzed in Chapter 6 is very similar to the present model. The principal difference is that the current model explicitly allows for the dynamics of capital accumulation. In the model of Chapter 6, an acceleration in $\mu$ induced a temporary increase in the expected real rate of interest. However, a higher expected real rate of interest results in less investment and more consumption. As investment falls, the capital-labor ratio also begins to fall, and with less capital per worker, output per worker must fall as well. It is only after the expected real rate of interest reverts to its original level and the investment process can restore the original capital-labor ratio that the level of per capita output can rise back up to its original level.

## Dynamics with Perfect Foresight Expectations

We can gain some additional insight into the dynamics of capital accumulation by considering the perfect foresight version of the model. Perfect foresight ($\pi^e = \pi$) obtains in the limit as $\psi \to +\infty$. In this case, we know that

$$A > 0 \quad \text{and so} \quad \frac{\partial(\dot{\tilde{m}}/\tilde{m})}{\partial\tilde{m}} > 0. \tag{8.3.102}$$

Furthermore, we also know that

$$\left.\frac{d\tilde{m}}{dk}\right|_{\dot{\tilde{m}}/\tilde{m} = 0} = -\frac{\partial\pi^e/\partial k}{\partial\pi^e/\partial\tilde{m}} > 0. \tag{8.3.103}$$

The phase diagram is therefore as is depicted in Figure 8.4.

In the analysis of Chapter 6, we noted that perfect foresight expectations rendered the formal dynamic process unstable. We therefore had to rely upon an auxiliary assumption

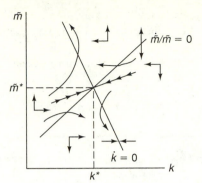

**Figure 8.4**

that the coefficient on the unstable part of the solution to the differential equation in $r$ was identically equal to zero. The rationale behind this argument was the idea that rational economic agents are likely to ignore such explosive roots in the formation of their expectations. With this potential instability purged from agents' expectations, there is no need for an explosive price and/or interest rate process to maintain equality of market-clearing conditions. The price and interest rate processes are, instead, determined by so-called market fundamentals like the rate of growth of government liabilities. In the present analysis, the dynamic process is second order and therefore the linear approximation to the solution includes two characteristic roots. In general, we find in this perfect foresight version of the model that one root is negative and the other root is positive. Therefore, the only stable solution to this system of differential equations is a saddle path like that indicated by the arrows in Figure 8.4. We assume that representative household and firm behavior guarantees instantaneous motion toward and then along this unique, stable path.

Therefore, starting out at $k \neq k^*$, motion of $k$ and $\tilde{m}$ is monotonic toward the dynamic equilibrium. So, for example, starting out at $k_0 < k^*$, the capital-labor ratio and per capita real money balances both begin to rise after an initial upward or downward jump in $\tilde{m}$ to the saddle path. The subsequent gradual rise in $\tilde{m}$ also guarantees that since

$$\frac{\dot{\tilde{m}}}{\tilde{m}} = \mu - \pi - n, \tag{8.3.104}$$

we have $\pi = \pi^e < \mu - n$ as we approach $k = k^*$. We therefore experience a period of less than steady-state inflation as the capital-labor ratio grows toward $k^*$. Furthermore, we also know that the period of rising $k$ requires a transition period in which $\tilde{c} < \tilde{c}^*$ and $\tilde{i} > \tilde{i}^*$.

It is also of interest to repeat our experiment of an unanticipated increase in the rate of growth of government liabilities $\mu$. However, with perfect foresight expectations, the response to such a disturbance is particularly simple. An instantaneous upward jump in $P$ accomplishes the necessary instantaneous decline in $\tilde{m}$ to its new long-run equilibrium position. Since the adjustment in $\tilde{m}$ occurs without the passage of calendar time, there is no reason for $k$ to diverge, even temporarily, from its initial and long-run equilibrium value of $k^*$. There is therefore no transition period of temporarily low per capita output in this case. Furthermore, $\pi$, $\pi^e$, and the nominal interest rate $r$ all rise instantaneously one-for-one with the increase in $\mu$ as well. The expected real rate of interest $\rho$ remains constant. In this case, money is superneutral in both the short and long runs. Not only is the level of the nominal money supply irrelevant to the real level of economic activity and to the pattern of resource allocation, so too is the rate of growth of the money supply irrelevant to the level of economic activity and to the pattern of resource allocation.[10]

# 8.4 THE EULER EQUATION APPROACH TO OPTIMAL GROWTH

The analysis of Section 8.3 makes heavy use of the maximum principle of optimal control theory. The maximum principle is a natural extension of static constrained optimization theory with the costate variables performing a role quite similar to the role of Lagrange multipliers in static analysis. Alternatively, the Euler equation approach is formally more similar to static techniques of unconstrained optimization. Side constraints, if any, must be substituted into the objective function before the maximization problem may be solved.

Optimal control techniques are helpful because they often facilitate calculation of closed-form solutions for the trajectory of the optimal path of the control variable. In addition, optimal control techniques are directly amenable to phase diagram analysis even when closed-form solutions are not possible. Finally, optimal control is also helpful because the costate variables often have readily intuitive interpretations.

However, the ease with which optimal control techniques can be used to compute the entire future time paths of the state and control variables comes at some cost. Generally, we need to specify the entire future time paths of any exogenous variables. In the analysis of Section 8.3, such exogenous variables include a wide range of government policy variables as well as agents' expectations about the future time paths of endogenous variables like the rate of interest and the size of the capital stock.

This section first summarizes necessary conditions for a maximum to problems like those posed in Section 8.2. Next, we analyze the representative household and firm maximization problems of Section 8.3 with the help of Euler equation techniques. Finally, we compare the equilibrium of a market economy with the optimal solution to an analogous central planner problem. Interestingly, market equilibrium in the market economy replicates the solution of the central planner problem at every point in time, not merely in the steady state.

## Euler Equation Techniques

In Section 8.2, we analyzed problems of the form

$$\max_{u(t)} J = \int_0^T I(x, u)e^{-\beta t}\, dt \tag{8.4.1}$$

subject to

$$\dot{x} = f(x, u), \tag{8.4.2}$$

---

[10]Sargent (1987, pp. 125–130) derives similar results for the perfect foresight case in an analogous model.

$$x(0) = x_0, \qquad x(T) = x_T. \tag{8.4.3}$$

Often, problems of this form can be expressed in the alternate form

$$\max_{u(t)} J = \int_0^T G(x, \dot{x}) e^{-\beta t} \, dt \tag{8.4.4}$$

subject to

$$x(0) = x_0, \qquad x(T) = x_T. \tag{8.4.5}$$

In particular, the equation $\dot{x} = f(x, u)$ can generally be inverted to obtain an expression with the control variable $u$ written as a function of $x$ and $\dot{x}$. We then need only plug this latter function into the integral expression $J$ to obtain the second form of the problem written above.

Necessary conditions for a solution of the above problem are given by[11]

$$\frac{\partial G}{\partial x} = \frac{\partial^2 G}{\partial \dot{x} \, \partial t} - \beta \frac{\partial G}{\partial \dot{x}}, \tag{8.4.6}$$

$$x(0) = x_0, \qquad x(T) = x_T. \tag{8.4.7}$$

As noted in Section 8.2, we noted that we are often interested in solutions to the infinite-horizon version of the basic optimization problem. Just as in the case of the maximum principle, we now abandon the terminal condition on $x(t)$ and replace it with a transversality condition. In particular, we now have

$$\lim_{t \to +\infty} e^{-\beta t} \frac{\partial G}{\partial \dot{x}} = 0 \tag{8.4.8}$$

when $x(\infty)$ is unconstrained and

$$\lim_{t \to +\infty} e^{-\beta t} \frac{\partial G}{\partial \dot{x}} \geq 0, \qquad \lim_{t \to +\infty} e^{-\beta t} \frac{\partial G}{\partial \dot{x}} x(t) = 0 \tag{8.4.9}$$

when $x(\infty)$ is constrained to be nonnegative.

## Euler Equation Solutions to Representative Agent and Central Planner Problems

Let us now pose and solve the representative household and representative firm optimization problems of Section 8.3 with the use of Euler equation methods. We first consider the representative household's consumption-savings problem. Using the budget constraint to solve for $\tilde{c}(t)$ in the household's utility function, we obtain the following form of the problem:

$$\max_{\phi(t)} V = \int_0^\infty U\left( -\frac{d\phi}{dt} + (\rho - n)\phi + w - \tilde{\tau} - \tilde{m}(\pi^e + n) - \frac{d\tilde{m}}{dt} \right) e^{-\beta t} \, dt \tag{8.4.10}$$

---

[11]See, e.g., Kamien and Schwartz (1981).

subject to

$$\phi(0) = \phi_0, \qquad \phi(\infty) \geq 0. \tag{8.4.11}$$

Differentiating $U$ with respect to $\phi$ and $d\phi/dt$, we obtain the first-order condition

$$\frac{d\tilde{c}}{dt} = -\frac{U'(\tilde{c})}{U''(\tilde{c})}(\rho - n - \beta), \tag{8.4.12}$$

where we have made use of the relationship

$$\frac{d}{dt}U'(\cdot) = U''(\cdot)\frac{d\tilde{c}}{dt}. \tag{8.4.13}$$

The above first-order condition in $\tilde{c}(t)$ may then be combined with the economywide budget constraint

$$\tilde{c}(t) = f(k) - (n + \delta)k - \frac{\alpha}{2}(\dot{k})^2 - \tilde{g} \tag{8.4.14}$$

to solve for $\tilde{c}(t)$ and $k(t)$ along the optimal path.

We next reconsider the representative firm's investment problem also considered in Section 8.3. Using the differential equation in $k$, $\dot{k} = u$, we obtain

$$\max_{k(t)} \int_0^\infty \left[ f(k) - w - (\delta + n)k - \dot{k} - \frac{\alpha}{2}(\dot{k})^2 \right] e^{-(\rho - n)s}\, ds \tag{8.4.15}$$

subject to

$$k(0) = k_0, \qquad k(\infty) \geq 0. \tag{8.4.16}$$

The Euler equation for this problem is given by

$$\alpha\ddot{k} - (\rho - n)(1 + \alpha\dot{k}) + f'(k) - (\delta + n) = 0. \tag{8.4.17}$$

The above expression is a second-order differential equation in $k$ that may be used to solve for the optimal time path $k(t)$.

Note that the Euler equation technique does not directly generate explicit behavioral relationships $\tilde{c}(\cdot)$ and $\tilde{i}(\cdot)$. In the analyses of Section 8.3, such explicit relationships were solved, and then these behavioral relationships were plugged into the goods market equilibrium condition to solve for the economy's instantaneous equilibrium position.

How to proceed with equilibrium analysis in this section is less transparent. However, let us assume that households and firms share common expectations about the future course of the economic variables they face. In particular, assume that households and firms share common inflationary expectations $\pi^e$. If households and firms also participate in the same earning asset market, they must also face a common nominal interest rate, $r$ and a common expected real interest rate $\rho = r - \pi^e$. Eliminating $\rho$ from the Euler equations above, we obtain

$$\frac{d\tilde{c}}{dt} = -\frac{U'}{U''}\left[ \frac{\alpha\ddot{k} - \beta(1 + \alpha\dot{k}) + f'(k) - (\delta + n)}{1 + \alpha\dot{k}} \right]. \tag{8.4.18}$$

This expression in $\tilde{c}(t)$ and $k(t)$ can then be combined with the economywide budget constraint to solve for $\tilde{c}(t)$ and $k(t)$.

Let us finally consider the solution to an economic planner's problem in which the planner seeks to maximize the present value of the representative household's level of utility given the size of government spending and given the technology of capital stock installation. The planner's problem is given by

$$\max_{\tilde{c}(t)} \int_0^\infty U[\tilde{c}(s)]e^{-\beta s}\,ds \tag{8.4.19}$$

subject to

$$\dot{k} = f(k) - (\delta + n)k - \frac{\alpha}{2}(\dot{k})^2 - \tilde{c}(t), \tag{8.4.20}$$

$$k(0) = k_0, \qquad k(\infty) \geq 0. \tag{8.4.21}$$

This problem may be rewritten as

$$\max_{k(t)} \int_0^\infty U\left(-\dot{k} + f(k) - (\delta + n)k - \frac{\alpha}{2}(\dot{k})^2\right)e^{-\beta s}\,ds \tag{8.4.22}$$

subject to

$$k(0) = k_0, \qquad k(\infty) \geq 0. \tag{8.4.23}$$

The Euler equation for the above problem may be solved as

$$\frac{d\tilde{c}}{dt} = -\frac{U'}{U''}\left[\frac{\alpha\ddot{k} - \beta(1 + \alpha\dot{k}) + f'(k) - (\delta + n)}{1 + \alpha\dot{k}}\right]. \tag{8.4.24}$$

By inspection, we note that the necessary condition for maximization of the planner's problem is exactly the same as the market equilibrium condition of the market economy given above. Therefore, as long as all agents have common expectations about the future time paths of the economic variables they face, the market solution is identical to the planner's solution at every point in time, not merely in equilibrium, as was the case in the analysis of Section 8.3.

## 8.5 MONEY AND ECONOMIC GROWTH

The model of Section 8.3 has the property that, at least in long-run equilibrium, government policy actions have no potential for influencing the real interest rate, the capital-labor ratio, or the level of per capita output. Chapter 6 provides a prelude to these results in the context of a model with a fixed capital stock. However, the analysis of Chapter 6 also demonstrates that such policy irrelevance results depend crucially on the particular functional form for aggregate consumption predicted by the solution to an infinitely lived, representative household's intertemporal utility maximization problem. The analysis of Chapter 6 also contrasts these policy irrelevance results with results derived in a specification in which wealth affects consumption spending and shows that such a consumption function provides a channel for government inflation and debt management policies to affect the equilibrium expected real interest rate.

In this section, we generalize the analysis of Section 6.5 to the case in which the capital-labor ratio evolves endogenously over time. This analysis demonstrates that in the presence of wealth effects in the consumption function, monetary and fiscal policies may be able to influence the equilibrium real interest rate, capital-labor ratio, and level of per capita output. This analysis also demonstrates how such government policy parameters might optimally be selected in the context of an economy whose behavior closely parallels that of this section's model economy.

## Wealth, Consumption, and Capital Accumulation

Chapter 2 presents a formal, finite-horizon, representative household intertemporal utility maximization problem that motivates an aggregate consumption function in which consumption depends both on a current-income term and a wealth term. In this section, our primary purpose is to provide a brief overview of the kinds of policy options wealth effects confer on government policymakers. Therefore, instead of analyzing the most general or the most rigorous possible functional form for the consumption function, we instead choose to study what may be the most simple possible functional form that generates a typical set of results. The interested reader is invited to investigate how the principal results of this section might be altered by the selection of more elaborate and/or more realistic specifications.

Assume that aggregate per capita consumption is positively related to aggregate per capita real net wealth. In particular, assume that

$$\tilde{c}^d = \tilde{c}^d(\omega), \qquad \partial \tilde{c}^d / \partial \omega > 0, \tag{8.5.1}$$

where $\omega$ denotes per capita real net wealth. We further assume that per capita real net wealth is given by

$$\omega = \frac{y - \delta K}{L\rho} + \frac{M}{PL} + \frac{\kappa B}{rPL}, \qquad 0 < \kappa < 1. \tag{8.5.2}$$

Here we assume that the wealth component due to the present value of wage and dividend income is given by the capitalized value of the flow of real net national product discounted at the real interest rate $\rho$. This specification ignores subtleties like the possibility of different time horizons for the receipt of wage and dividend income and differences between the current and expected future marginal productivities of capital. Alternatively, the terms reflecting the contributions to wealth of households' holdings of government liabilities are unchanged from the specifications of Chapters 2 and 6. We further assume in the current analysis, however, that government policy acts to keep the ratio of the market value of government bonds outstanding, $B/r$, to the size of the nominal money supply $M$ constant and equal to the fixed value $\theta'$. Summarizing, per capita consumption is given by

$$\tilde{c}^d = \tilde{c}^d\left(\frac{f(k) - \delta k}{\rho} + (1 + \kappa\theta')\tilde{m}\right). \tag{8.5.3}$$

If we further define $\hat{\theta} \equiv 1 + \kappa\theta'$, then we may express this relationship in the slightly more compact form

$$\tilde{c}^d = \tilde{c}^d\left(\frac{f(k) - \delta k}{\rho} + \hat{\theta}\tilde{m}\right). \tag{8.5.4}$$

Although we could follow up on the more general formulation for money demand set down in Section 2.4, we instead choose to work with the same money demand schedule we adopted in Section 8.3. In particular, we continue to assume that

$$\tilde{m}^d = \tilde{m}^d(q, r) = \tilde{m}^d(f(k), \rho + \pi^e). \tag{8.5.5}$$

Furthermore, we continue to assume that per capita net investment is equal to $\tilde{i} = \xi_k[f'(k) - \delta - \rho]$, that aggregate goods demand and aggregate goods supply are equal at every instant of time, and that money demand and money supply are also always equal at every instant of time. We further simplify the analysis by ignoring the presence of the adjustment cost term $\frac{1}{2}(\dot{k})^2$ in the goods market equilibrium condition. Goods and money market equilibrium therefore generate the algebraic relationships

$$\tilde{c}^d\left(\frac{f(k) - \delta k}{\rho} + \hat{\theta}\tilde{m}\right) + \xi_k[f'(k) - \delta - \rho] + \tilde{g} - (\delta + n)k - f(k) = 0, \tag{8.5.6}$$

$$\tilde{m}^d(f(k), \rho + \pi^e) - \tilde{m} = 0. \tag{8.5.7}$$

Evolution of the state variables $k$ and $\tilde{m}$ conform to

$$\dot{k} = \xi_k[f'(k) - \delta - \rho], \tag{8.5.8}$$

$$\frac{\dot{\tilde{m}}}{\tilde{m}} = \mu - \pi - n. \tag{8.5.9}$$

Long-run equilibrium is therefore characterized by

$$f'(k) - \delta = \rho, \qquad \pi = \mu - n = \pi^e. \tag{8.5.10}$$

The algebraic equilibrium conditions (8.5.6) and (8.5.7) above may be used to express $\rho$ and $\pi^e$ as implicit functions of $k$, $\tilde{m}$, and any exogenous variables of interest. Differentiating these algebraic equilibrium conditions with respect to $\rho$, $\pi^e$, $k$, $\tilde{m}$, $\mu$, $\hat{\theta}$, and $\tilde{g}$ and evaluating in the neighborhood of the dynamic equilibrium characterized above, we obtain

$$\begin{bmatrix} -\left(\xi_k + \dfrac{q - \delta k}{\rho^2}\dfrac{\partial \tilde{c}^d}{\partial \omega}\right) & 0 \\[3ex] \dfrac{\partial \tilde{m}^d}{\partial r} & \dfrac{\partial \tilde{m}^d}{\partial r} \end{bmatrix}\begin{bmatrix} d\rho \\[3ex] d\pi^e \end{bmatrix}$$

$$= \begin{bmatrix} \left[f' - \dfrac{\partial \tilde{c}^d}{\partial \omega} - \xi_k f'' - (\delta + n)\right]dk - \hat{\theta}\dfrac{\partial \tilde{c}^d}{\partial \omega}d\tilde{m} - \tilde{m}\dfrac{\partial \tilde{c}^d}{\partial \omega}d\hat{\theta} - d\tilde{g} \\[3ex] -\dfrac{\partial \tilde{m}^d}{\partial q}dk + d\tilde{m} \end{bmatrix}. \tag{8.5.11}$$

Application of Cramer's rule facilitates the following results:

$$\frac{\partial \rho}{\partial k} = \frac{1}{\Delta} \frac{\partial \tilde{m}^d}{\partial r} \left[ f' - \frac{\partial \tilde{c}^d}{\partial \omega} - \xi_k f'' - (\delta + n) \right] < 0, \tag{8.5.12}$$

$$\frac{\partial \rho}{\partial \tilde{m}} = -\frac{1}{\Delta} \hat{\theta} \frac{\partial \tilde{m}^d}{\partial r} \frac{\partial \tilde{c}^d}{\partial \omega} > 0, \tag{8.5.13}$$

$$\frac{\partial \pi^e}{\partial k} = \frac{1}{\Delta} \left[ \frac{\partial \tilde{m}^d}{\partial q} \left( \xi_k + \frac{q - \delta k}{\rho^2} \frac{\partial \tilde{c}^d}{\partial \omega} \right) \right.$$
$$\left. - \frac{\partial \tilde{m}^d}{\partial r} \left( f' - \frac{\partial \tilde{c}^d}{\partial \omega} - \xi_k f'' - (\delta + n) \right) \right] > 0, \tag{8.5.14}$$

$$\frac{\partial \pi^e}{\partial \tilde{m}} = -\frac{1}{\Delta} \left[ \left( \xi_k + \frac{q - \delta k}{\rho^2} \frac{\partial \tilde{c}^d}{\partial \omega} \right) - \hat{\theta} \frac{\partial \tilde{m}^d}{\partial r} \frac{\partial \tilde{c}^d}{\partial \omega} \right] < 0, \tag{8.5.15}$$

$$\frac{\partial \rho}{\partial \mu} = \frac{\partial \pi^e}{\partial \mu} = 0, \tag{8.5.16}$$

$$\frac{\partial \rho}{\partial \hat{\theta}} = -\frac{\partial \pi^e}{\partial \hat{\theta}} = -\frac{1}{\Delta} \tilde{m} \frac{\partial \tilde{m}^d}{\partial r} \frac{\partial \tilde{c}^d}{\partial \omega} > 0, \tag{8.5.17}$$

$$\frac{\partial \rho}{\partial \tilde{g}} = -\frac{\partial \pi^e}{\partial \tilde{g}} = -\frac{1}{\Delta} \frac{\partial \tilde{m}^d}{\partial r} > 0, \tag{8.5.18}$$

where

$$\Delta \equiv -\frac{\partial \tilde{m}^d}{\partial r} \left( \xi_k + \frac{q - \delta k}{\rho^2} \frac{\partial \tilde{c}^d}{\partial \omega} \right) > 0. \tag{8.5.19}$$

The signs of these expressions are all straightforward as long as we assume that

$$f' - \frac{\partial \tilde{c}^d}{\partial \omega} - \xi_k f'' - (\delta + n) > 0. \tag{8.5.20}$$

Just as in the analysis of Section 8.3, dynamic analysis of this system may now proceed along the following lines. First, we substitute for $\pi$ from the adaptive expectation equation into the differential equation for $\tilde{m}$. Next, we substitute the implicit functions for $\rho$ and $\pi^e$ derived above into the differential equations for $k$ and $\tilde{m}$ to obtain

$$\dot{k} = \xi_k [f'(k) - \delta - \rho(k, \tilde{m}, \ldots)], \tag{8.5.21}$$

$$\frac{\dot{\tilde{m}}}{\tilde{m}} = A \left[ (\mu - n - \pi^e(k, \tilde{m}, \ldots)) - \frac{1}{\psi} \frac{\partial \pi^e}{\partial k} \dot{k}(k, \tilde{m}, \ldots) \right]. \tag{8.5.22}$$

Since the signs of the partial derivatives of $\rho$ and $\pi^e$ with respect to $k$ and $\tilde{m}$ are precisely the same as those of the analysis of Section 8.3, the phase diagram of this system in $k$, $\tilde{m}$ space has the same qualitative characteristics as those of the analysis of Section 8.3. We therefore choose to leave the formal details of the analogous dynamic analysis of the present system to the interested reader. We again find that with $\psi$ sufficiently small the

$k, \tilde{m}$ system is unambiguously stable and that with $\psi$ sufficiently large the $k, \tilde{m}$ system possesses a saddle path solution. However, one important quantitative aspect of the dynamic analysis is an important prelude to our equilibrium analysis of this system presented below. Differentiating the expression for $\dot{k}$ with respect to $k$, we find that

$$\frac{\partial \dot{k}}{\partial k} = \xi_k\left(f'' - \frac{\partial \rho}{\partial k}\right). \tag{8.5.23}$$

Plugging in the expressions for $\partial \rho / \partial k$ and $\Delta$ derived above allows derivation of

$$\frac{\partial \dot{k}}{\partial k} = -\frac{\xi_k}{\Delta}\frac{\partial \tilde{m}^d}{\partial r}\left[f' - (\delta + n) - \frac{\partial \tilde{c}^d}{\partial \omega}\left(1 - f''\frac{q - \delta k}{\rho^2}\right)\right]. \tag{8.5.24}$$

Throughout the analysis we assume that

$$f' - (\delta + n) - \frac{\partial \tilde{c}^d}{\partial \omega}\left(1 - f''\frac{q - \delta k}{\rho^2}\right) < 0, \tag{8.5.25}$$

and so we again have the result that $\partial \dot{k}/\partial k < 0$, which is necessary for stability in at least the perfect foresight version of the model.

## Equilibrium Policy Effects

We are now ready to compute the effects of changes in the government policy parameters $\mu$, $\hat{\theta}$, and $\tilde{g}$ on the steady-state values of $k$ and $\tilde{m}$. Recall that in the steady state equilibrium requires that

$$f'(k) - \delta - \rho = 0 \Rightarrow \rho = f'(k) - \delta, \tag{8.5.26}$$

$$\pi = \pi^e = \mu - n. \tag{8.5.27}$$

Plugging these two relationships into the goods and money market equilibrium conditions, we obtain the following two simultaneous equations in the steady-state values of $k$ and $\tilde{m}$:

$$\tilde{c}^d\left[\frac{f(k) - \delta k}{f'(k) - \delta} + \hat{\theta}\tilde{m}\right] + \xi_k(0) + (n + \delta)k + \tilde{g} - f(k) = 0, \tag{8.5.28}$$

$$\tilde{m}^d[f(k), f'(k) - \delta + \mu - n] - \tilde{m} = 0. \tag{8.5.29}$$

As an aid to our analysis of policy effects and as an aid to the analysis of the steady-state effects of changes in other exogenous variables, it is useful to graph these two equilibrium relationships, which we denote by LGME and LMME, respectively, in $k, \tilde{m}$ space. Differentiating these long-run equilibrium conditions with respect to $k$ and $\tilde{m}$, we find that

$$\frac{d\tilde{m}}{dk}\bigg|_{\text{LGME}} = \frac{f' - (n + \delta) - (\partial \tilde{c}^d/\partial \omega)\{1 - f''[(q - \delta k)/\rho^2]\}}{\hat{\theta}(\partial \tilde{c}^d/\partial \omega)} < 0, \tag{8.5.30}$$

$$\frac{d\tilde{m}}{dk}\bigg|_{\text{LMME}} = f'\frac{\partial \tilde{m}^d}{\partial q} + f''\frac{\partial \tilde{m}^d}{\partial r} > 0. \tag{8.5.31}$$

Note that the LGME locus is upward sloping as long as the capital accumulation process is stable when viewed in isolation, that is, as long as $\partial k/\partial k < 0$. The interested reader should also be able to demonstrate that the analogous equilibrium locus for the model of Section 8.3 is vertical at the equilibrium capital intensity.

Now differentiating LGME and LMME with respect to $k$, $\tilde{m}$, $\mu$, $\hat{\theta}$, and $\tilde{g}$, we find that

$$
\begin{bmatrix} -\left[ f' - (\delta + n) - \dfrac{\partial \tilde{c}^d}{\partial \omega}\left( 1 - f'' \dfrac{q - \delta k}{\rho^2} \right) \right] & \hat{\theta} \dfrac{\partial \tilde{c}^d}{\partial \omega} \\[2ex] f' \dfrac{\partial \tilde{m}^d}{\partial q} + f'' \dfrac{\partial \tilde{m}^d}{\partial r} & -1 \end{bmatrix} \begin{bmatrix} dk \\[2ex] d\tilde{m} \end{bmatrix}
$$

$$
= \begin{bmatrix} -\tilde{m} \dfrac{\partial \tilde{c}^d}{\partial \omega} d\hat{\theta} - d\tilde{g} \\[2ex] -\dfrac{\partial \tilde{m}^d}{\partial r} d\mu \end{bmatrix} . \tag{8.5.32}
$$

Application of Cramer's rule now facilitates the following results:

$$
\frac{dk}{d\mu} = \frac{1}{\Delta} \hat{\theta} \frac{\partial \tilde{c}^d}{\partial \omega} \frac{\partial \tilde{m}^d}{\partial r} > 0, \tag{8.5.33}
$$

$$
\frac{d\tilde{m}}{d\mu} = \frac{1}{\Delta} \frac{\partial \tilde{m}^d}{\partial r} \left[ f' - (\delta + n) - \frac{\partial \tilde{c}^d}{\partial \omega}\left( 1 - f'' \frac{q - \delta k}{\rho^2} \right) \right] < 0, \tag{8.5.34}
$$

$$
\frac{dk}{d\hat{\theta}} = \frac{\tilde{m}}{\Delta} \frac{\partial \tilde{c}^d}{\partial \omega} < 0, \tag{8.5.35}
$$

$$
\frac{d\tilde{m}}{d\hat{\theta}} = \frac{\tilde{m}}{\Delta} \frac{\partial \tilde{c}^d}{\partial \omega} \left( f' \frac{\partial \tilde{m}^d}{\partial q} + f'' \frac{\partial \tilde{m}^d}{\partial r} \right) < 0, \tag{8.5.36}
$$

$$
\frac{dk}{d\tilde{g}} = \frac{1}{\Delta} < 0, \tag{8.5.37}
$$

$$
\frac{d\tilde{m}}{d\tilde{g}} = \frac{1}{\Delta} \left( f' \frac{\partial \tilde{m}^d}{\partial q} + f'' \frac{\partial \tilde{m}^d}{\partial r} \right) < 0, \tag{8.5.38}
$$

where

$$
\Delta \equiv \left[ f' - (n + \delta) - \frac{\partial \tilde{c}^d}{\partial \omega}\left( 1 - f'' \frac{q - \delta k}{\rho^2} \right) \right]
$$

$$
- \hat{\theta}\left( f' \frac{\partial \tilde{m}^d}{\partial q} + f'' \frac{\partial \tilde{m}^d}{\partial r} \right) \frac{\partial \tilde{c}^d}{\partial \omega} < 0. \tag{8.5.39}
$$

These algebraic results are also confirmed by graphical analysis. An increase in the rate of growth of government liabilities $\mu$ shifts the LMME locus downward and to the right, resulting in an increase in the equilibrium quantity of capital per worker and a

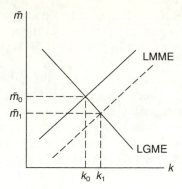

**Figure 8.5**

decrease in the per capita level of real money balances.[12] These effects are depicted in Figure 8.5. The increase in $\mu$ clearly results in an increase in the equilibrium rate of inflation, $\pi = \mu - n$. This increase in the rate of inflation implies a higher nominal rate of interest, which reduces the demand for per capita real money balances. Furthermore, this reduction in $\tilde{m}$ implies a lower amount of per capita real net wealth, and less wealth results in less consumption and more saving. However, this increase in per capita saving can only be consistent with a constant quantity of capital per worker at a higher capital intensity $k$. Finally, a higher value of $k$ implies a lower equilibrium real interest rate since, in equilibrium, we require that $\rho = f'(k) - \delta$ and since $f'' < 0$.

Next, consider the effects of an increase in the ratio of government bonds to money, parameterized by $\hat{\theta}$. An increase in $\hat{\theta}$ shifts the LGME locus downward and to the left, resulting in reductions in both $k$ and $\tilde{m}$.[13] The increase in $\hat{\theta}$ has the impact effect of raising wealth and therefore lowering saving and raising consumption. The growth process then results in a reduction in $k$, which can only come about at a higher real interest rate, since we again require that $f'(k) = \rho + \delta$. Finally, the higher real (and nominal) interest rate combines with a reduction in $q = f(k)$ to result in a reduction in per capita real money balances.

Finally, consider the effects of an increase in $\tilde{g}$, real per capita government spending. An increase in $\tilde{g}$ also shifts the LGME locus downward and to the left, again resulting in reductions in both $k$ and $\tilde{m}$ and simultaneously increasing both $\rho$ and $r$. More government spending crowds out investment spending, which eventually brings about a reduction in $k$. This reduction in $k$ requires a higher real interest rate $\rho$, and the lower $k$ and higher $\rho$ combine with a constant expected rate of inflation $\pi^e = \pi = \mu - n$ to induce a lower value for $\tilde{m}$.[14]

---

[12]This result was first demonstrated by Tobin (1965). For a more extensive discussion of the assumptions needed to generate this result, see Stein (1970b).

[13]This result is demonstrated by Stein (1966).

[14]These results depend crucially on the functional form chosen for the consumption function and the parameterization chosen for the government policy variables. For some alternative possibilities, see Turnovsky (1977, Ch. 8).

Having fully outlined the likely effects of government policy on long-run equilibrium in the present model, it is natural to consider what might constitute optimal government policy choice. We consider the three government policy parameters $\tilde{g}$, $\mu$, and $\hat{\theta}$, each in turn.

Macroeconomic theory has the least to say about the choice of the optimal level of per capita government spending. Public finance theory suggests that the optimal size of government spending involves equating the marginal utility of the composite good in consumption with the marginal utility of the composite good in distribution as a public good. The only bearing the present analysis has on this decision process is the explicit recognition of the possibilities of changing the intertemporal distribution of public goods provisions.

Next consider the optimum rate of monetary expansion and the related questions of the optimal inflation rate and the optimal quantity of money holdings. Although the analysis of Section 8.3 ignores the representative household's decision to allocate wealth between interest-bearing and non-interest-bearing forms, this question could be formalized by including real money balances as an argument of the utility function. Within such a framework, Friedman (1969) provides a natural policy proscription for the optimal rate of monetary growth.

The opportunity cost of holding money is simply the difference between the rate of return on money and the rate of return on earning assets, which equals the nominal rate of interest $r$. However, in long-run equilibrium, the nominal rate of interest is given by

$$r = \rho + \pi = f'(k) - \delta + \mu - n. \tag{8.5.40}$$

This expression makes clear that the appropriate choice of $\mu$ can, for any arbitrarily selected value of $k$, achieve any desired nominal interest rate. In particular, the government need only set $\mu = \delta + n - f'(k)$ to achieve a nominal interest rate of zero. Such a zero nominal interest rate implies a zero opportunity cost of holding money, and the representative household may therefore satiate itself with real money balance holdings. Furthermore, there is no social cost to the achievement of this satiation since the rate of inflation need not, as we demonstrate below, affect the achievement of the optimum quantities of per capita output and capital per worker. This optimal monetary policy simply requires an inflation rate equal to minus the real rate of interest, $\rho = f'(k) - \delta$.[15]

Having proscribed policy rules for $\tilde{g}$ and $\mu$, we are left with the optimal choice of $\hat{\theta}$; that is, government's optimal liability management policy. Obviously, if government bonds are not viewed as net wealth ($\kappa = 0$), then the choice of $\hat{\theta}$ is irrelevant. However, in such a case, the private economy is likely to independently equilibrate at the socially optimal value of $k$, and so there is no particular policy problem in this case. Alternatively, in cases in which $\kappa \neq 0$, the private economy's steady-state capital-labor ratio only coincidently equals the social optimum. Now appropriate choice of $\hat{\theta}$ can always ensure that the social optimum value of $k$ is attained. This ability of government policy to rectify the effects of any externalities in the growth process obtains because as long as $\kappa \neq 0$, the

---

[15]Stein (1970a) points out some practical implementation problems with this policy. Brock (1975) develops necessary conditions for an optimum anticipated rate of deflation in a utility-maximizing model without capital.

government has the three independent policy tools $\tilde{g}$, $\mu$, and $\hat{\theta}$ with which to control the three policy objectives $\tilde{g}$, $\tilde{m}$, and $k$.

# REFERENCES

Brock, William A., "A Simple Perfect Foresight Monetary Model," *Journal of Monetary Economics,* April, 1975, 133–150.

Burmeister, Edwin, and A. Rodney Dobell, *Mathematical Theories of Economic Growth,* New York, Macmillan, 1970.

Friedman, Milton, *The Optimum Quantity of Money,* Chicago, Aldine, 1969.

Intriligator, Michael D., *Mathematical Optimization and Economic Theory,* Englewood Cliffs, NJ, Prentice-Hall, 1971.

Kamien, Morton I., and Nancy L. Schwartz, *The Calculus of Variations and Optimal Control in Economics and Management,* New York, Elsevier North Holland, 1981.

Sargent, Thomas J., *Macroeconomic Theory,* 2nd. ed., Orlando, FL, Academic, 1987.

Sidrauski, Miguel, "Rational Choice and Patterns of Growth in a Monetary Economy," *American Economic Review,* May, 1967, 534–544.

Solow, Robert M., "A Contribution to the Theory of Economic Growth," *Quarterly Journal of Economics,* February, 1956, 65–94.

Stein, Jerome L., "Money and Capacity Growth," *Journal of Political Economy,* October, 1966, 451–465.

Stein, Jerome L., "Monetary Growth Theory in Perspective," *American Economic Review,* March, 1970a, 85–106.

Stein, Jerome L., "The Optimum Quantity of Money," *Journal of Money, Credit and Banking,* November, 1970b, 397–419.

Stein, Jerome L., *Money and Capacity Growth,* New York, Columbia University Press, 1971.

Tobin, James, "Money and Economic Growth," *Econometrica,* October, 1965, 671–684.

Turnovsky, Stephen J., *Macroeconomic Analysis and Stabilization Policy,* Cambridge, England, Cambridge University Press, 1977.

# Chapter 9

## Open-Economy Macroeconomic Models

While the analyses of Chapters 5–8 extend the basic equilibrium macroeconomic model of Chapters 1 and 2 in many important and fruitful ways, all of these extensions are in the context of a closed economy. However, recent growth in the volume of international trade and recent concern with the variability of exchange rates since most industrialized nations adopted a system of floating exchange rates in 1973 has made the traditional fiction of the closed-economy assumption a most glaring oversight for even the largest and most economically self-sufficient nations.

In this chapter, we extend the basic model of Chapters 1 and 2 to allow for the possibilities of specialization in production and mobility of financial capital across national boundaries. Section 9.1 introduces the concepts of trade in goods and earning assets and demonstrates how a system of flexible exchange rates is capable of balancing such trade in goods and earning assets. Section 9.2 then develops the mechanics of adjustment in a fixed exchange rate system and demonstrates the irrelevance of the exchange rate regime for the equilibrium allocation of resources. Section 9.3 demonstrates how sluggish adjustment of domestic goods prices may exacerbate the degree of volatility of the exchange rate in a flexible exchange rate system. Finally, Appendix 9.A solves a typical intertemporal optimization problem for the representative domestic household.

## 9.1 FLEXIBLE EXCHANGE RATE SYSTEMS

The history of the international monetary system includes considerable experience with many types of international payments arrangements ranging from purely fixed to purely flexible exchange rate regimes. Since from at least a notational point of view, the possibility of floating exchange rates requires a slightly more general framework, it is useful to begin our discussion of open-economy macroeconomic issues in the context of such a purely flexible exchange rate system. Therefore, in the remainder of this section, we first modify our closed-economy model to allow for international transactions and the possibility of changes in the rate of exchange between national currencies and then go on to examine issues of comparative statics and the dynamics of adjustment in the context of this flexible exchange rate model.

## The Goods Market in the Open Economy

The sheer volume of analysis in the theory of international trade suggests the goods market as the most obvious part of the macroeconomic model that needs to be altered to account for the possibility of international transactions. However, while most microeconomic analyses of international trade allow for production of (at least) two goods in (at least) two countries, we adopt the alternative, simpler assumption of perfect specialization in production.

Production of the single domestically produced good is denoted by $y$, and the domestic price of this good is denoted by $P$. A foreign-produced good is available in unlimited supply to purchasers in the small domestic economy at a price of $P^f$ denominated in units of the foreign currency. To translate the price of the foreign good into units of domestic currency, it is necessary to multiply the foreign price $P^f$ by the spot exchange rate $s$. The spot exchange rate denotes the domestic currency price of the foreign currency (i.e., the number of U.S. dollars per British pound for the case of the United States as the home country and the United Kingdom as the foreign country). Therefore, the domestic currency price of the foreign good is equal to $sP^f$. Furthermore, the relative price of the domestic good is denoted by $p \equiv P/sP^f$ in units of foreign goods per unit of domestic goods.

As in Chapter 1 and throughout most of the subsequent chapters, we continue to assume that production of the domestically produced good is governed by the aggregate production function $y = \Phi(\ell, K)$, where $K$ denotes the fixed current supply of capital goods in the domestic economy and $\ell$ denotes domestic employment. Profit maximization by the representative domestic firm results in a labor demand function of the form

$$\ell^d = \ell^d\left(\frac{W}{P}\right), \qquad \frac{\partial \ell^d}{\partial(W/P)} = \frac{1}{\partial^2\Phi/\partial\ell^2} < 0. \tag{9.1.1}$$

Complete specialization of production in the domestic economy leads in the open-economy case to an identical functional form for the labor demand schedule as in the case of the closed economy. However, the explicit consideration of the possibility of two separate consumption goods leads to nontrivial changes in the representative household's maximization problem. The representative household now chooses consumption levels for both types of goods as well as deciding on a supply of labor and holdings of real money balances. We continue to assume that the representative household's instantaneous utility function is of the no-wealth-effects variety. In particular, we adopt the form

$$U = U[c_d^\alpha(c_d^f)^{1-\alpha} - h(\ell)], \tag{9.1.2}$$

where $c_d$ denotes domestic consumption of the domestic good, $c_d^f$ denotes domestic consumption of the foreign good, and $\alpha$ is a constant between zero and 1.

The representative household's solution of its intertemporal utility maximization problem results in a labor supply function of the form[1]

$$\ell^s = \ell^s\left(\frac{W}{P}, \frac{P}{sP^f}\right), \qquad \frac{\partial \ell^s}{\partial(W/P)} > 0, \qquad \frac{\partial \ell^s}{\partial(P/sP^f)} > 0. \tag{9.1.3}$$

Labor market equilibrium is now given by

$$\ell^d\left(\frac{W}{P}\right) = \ell^s\left(\frac{W}{P}, \frac{P}{sP^f}\right). \tag{9.1.4}$$

This labor market equilibrium condition may be solved for the equilibrium domestic real wage $W/P$ and the domestic level of employment $\ell$ as functions of the relative price of the domestic good $p = P/sP^f$. Now plugging the equilibrium employment level back into the aggregate domestic production function, we derive the aggregate domestic supply schedule

$$y^s = y^s(p), \qquad \frac{\partial y^s}{\partial p} > 0. \tag{9.1.5}$$

We next turn our attention to the demand for domestically produced goods. Assume that all domestic government purchases $g$ and all domestic firm purchases $i$ are purchases of the *domestic* good. Furthermore, assume that domestic investment demand is inversely related to the nominal interest rate $r$ and that domestic government spending is exogenous. Finally, assume that all foreign investment and government spending represents purchases of the foreign good. Aggregate demand for the domestic good is therefore given by

$$y^d = c^d + i^d(r) + g, \tag{9.1.6}$$

where $c^d$ now represents total consumption spending on the domestic good both by domestic *and* foreign households.

As in earlier chapters, we continue to assume that domestic consumption of both the domestic and the imported good depends directly on domestic disposable income $z$. Domestic disposable income, measured in units of the domestically produced good, includes all domestic production $y$ plus net interest income minus taxes $\tau$. Net interest income includes interest payments on domestic government bonds $B/P$ plus interest received from net holdings of an internationally traded bond. We denote the net holdings of such internationally traded bonds by $B^f$ measured in units of foreign currency. These internationally traded bonds are one-period bonds paying interest at an exogenously given nominal rate $r^f$. Net interest on holdings of internationally traded bonds for domestic residents is therefore equal to $r^f B^f$ measured in units of foreign currency. To translate these interest payments into units of the domestically produced good, we need to multiply $r^f B^f$ by $s/P$. We again assume, as in Chapter 2, that domestic taxes $\tau$ are adjusted to offset changes in the real value of interest payments on the domestic government's debt, and so we have

---

[1] Appendix 9.A presents a typical specification of and solution to the representative domestic household's intertemporal optimization problem.

$\tau = \tau_0 + B/P$. Domestic disposable income is therefore given by

$$z = y + r^f\left(\frac{sB^f}{P}\right) - \tau_0. \tag{9.1.7}$$

Foreign consumption of both the domestic and the foreign goods depends on foreign disposable income. However, throughout the analysis we assume that foreign disposable income $z^f$ is constant and exogenous. We finally assume that the proportions of both domestic and foreign consumption that consist of the domestic good depend inversely on the relative price of the domestically produced good $p$. Market clearing in the domestic goods market is therefore given by[2]

$$0 = \underset{(+)\,(-)}{c^d(z, p)} + \underset{(-)}{i^d(r)} + g - \underset{(+)}{y^s(p)}, \tag{9.1.8}$$

$$p \equiv \frac{P}{sP^f}, \tag{9.1.9}$$

$$z = y + r^f\left(\frac{sB^f}{P}\right) - \tau_0. \tag{9.1.10}$$

## The Foreign Exchange and Domestic Money Markets

Proper modeling of the open macroeconomy also requires formal recognition of the existence of multiple currencies. For our simple case of a single small domestic economy trading with a larger rest of the world, there are two currencies, a domestic currency and a foreign currency. As noted above, the domestic currency price of the foreign currency is equal to the spot exchange rate $s$, which represents the terms of trade for international currency transactions.

International trade both in goods and in earning assets necessitates such transactions between currencies. Domestic purchases of foreign goods and internationally traded earning assets and other payments by domestic residents to foreigners imply a demand for the corresponding amount of the foreign currency. In the case of flexible exchange rates, the spot exchange rate varies in such a way as to equate the supply of and demand for foreign exchange.

The supply of foreign currency (measured in units of foreign currency) resulting from the export of domestic goods equals the physical volume of exports in units of domestic goods times the price of domestic goods $P$ divided by the exchange rate $s$. The demand for foreign currency resulting from the import of foreign goods (measured in units of foreign currency) equals the physical volume of imports times the price of the foreign good $P^f$.

---

[2] Appendix 9.A suggests equation (9.1.10) as the particular form for the disposable income term $z$ in the domestic good demand function $c^d$. The analysis of Appendix 9.A also demonstrates that for the case of the Cobb-Douglas utility function, *domestic* consumption of the domestic good $\hat{c}_d$ is independent of the relative price term $p$. However, as long as foreign demand for the domestic good is sensitive to relative price movements, we still find that $\partial c^d/\partial p < 0$.

The net supply of foreign currency from international purchases and sales of goods is referred to as the trade balance:

$$\text{Balance of trade (£)} = \frac{P}{s} \times \text{exports} - P^f \times \text{imports}, \qquad (9.1.11)$$

here measured in units of foreign currency.

We assume that the physical volume of export demand depends inversely on the relative price $p$ of the domestic good and that the physical volume of import demand depends directly on the relative price $p$ of the domestic good. We further assume that import demand depends on the level of domestic disposable income $z$. While analogous reasoning requires that export demand depend on the level of foreign disposable income $z^f$, we continue to assume that $z^f$ is exogenous and constant. The balance of trade is therefore given by

$$\text{Balance of trade (£)} = P^f[\underset{(-)}{p \times \text{exports}(p)} - \underset{(+)(+)}{\text{imports}(z, p)}], \qquad (9.1.12)$$

measured in units of the foreign currency.

Denoting the trade balance measured in units of the domestic good by $T$, we have

$$T = \text{exports}(p) - \frac{1}{p} \times \text{imports}(z, p). \qquad (9.1.13)$$

Throughout the analysis, we make the assumption, standard in international economics, that $\partial T/\partial p < 0$. That $\partial T/\partial z < 0$ follows directly from the assumed direct relationship between import demand and the level of domestic disposable income. It is also standard to assume that $-\partial T/\partial z < 1$, that is, that the marginal propensity to import out of disposable income is less than unity.

In order to translate the trade balance back into units of the foreign currency, as a necessary step in deriving the foreign exchange market-clearing condition, we need to multiply $T$ by $pP^f$. We therefore have

$$\text{Demand for foreign exchange resulting from trade balance} = pP^fT(z, p). \quad (9.1.14)$$

Surpluses and deficits in the balance of trade must be offset by capital flows in order for the foreign exchange market to clear. Such capital flows result from purchases and sales of internationally traded earning assets by domestic residents. We follow a common convention in adopting the assumption that foreigners neither hold nor issue earning assets denominated in the domestic currency. However, we do allow for the possibility of domestic residents borrowing from abroad by issuing foreign bonds. As noted above, we denote holdings by domestic residents of assets denominated in foreign currency by $B^f$ measured in units of foreign currency. We assume that all such assets may be aggregated in the form of a single short-term bond paying the exogenously determined nominal rate of interest $r^f$. The resulting net receipt per unit of time of interest payments by domestic residents from holdings of foreign assets is therefore equal to $r^fB^f$.

As in the analysis of Section 2.5, we assume that while all domestic assets are perfect substitutes for one another, domestic and foreign assets are imperfect substitutes in domestic residents' portfolios.[3] The net demand for foreign assets by domestic residents is therefore assumed to depend directly on the rate of return on foreign earning assets relative to the rate of return on domestic earning assets. The rate of return on foreign assets includes both the foreign interest rate $r^f$ plus any expected appreciation or depreciation due to anticipated changes in the exchange rate $s$. The rate of return on domestic earning assets is simply equal to the domestic rate of interest. Driskill and McCafferty (1987), among others, motivate a net domestic demand function for foreign earning assets of the form

$$\left(\frac{sB^f}{P}\right)^d = \left(\frac{sB^f}{P}\right)^d(x), \qquad \frac{\partial(sB^f/P)^d}{\partial x} > 0, \tag{9.1.15}$$

where

$$x \equiv r^f + \dot{s}^e - r \tag{9.1.16}$$

and where $\dot{s}^e$ denotes the expected rate of change of the spot exchange rate $s$. The analysis of Driskill and McCafferty (1987) argues that the proper units of measure for the function $(sB^f/P)^d$ are units of the domestic good. Therefore, the net nominal demand for foreign earning assets, denominated in units of foreign currency, is given by

$$\frac{P}{s}\left(\frac{sB^f}{P}\right)^d = P^f p\left(\frac{sB^f}{P}\right)^d. \tag{9.1.17}$$

The demand for foreign exchange originating out of transactions in foreign earning assets includes the desired change in holdings of foreign earning assets minus interest earnings on previously accumulated foreign earning assets. The capital account portion of the demand for foreign exchange is therefore given by

$$\frac{d}{dt}\left[P^f p\left(\frac{sB^f}{P}\right)^d(r^f + \dot{s}^e - r)\right] - r^f P^f p\left(\frac{sB^f}{P}\right)^d(r^f + \dot{s}^e - r) \tag{9.1.18}$$

measured in units of foreign currency. With the foreign price level $P^f$ constant and exogenously given, the market-clearing condition in the foreign exchange market is given by

$$P^f p T(z, p) - P^f \frac{d}{dt}\left[p\left(\frac{sB^f}{P}\right)^d(r^f + \dot{s}^e - r)\right]$$
$$+ r^f P^f p\left(\frac{sB^f}{P}\right)^d(r^f + \dot{s}^e - r) = 0 \tag{9.1.19}$$

or

$$T\left[y^s(p) + r^f\left(\frac{sB^f}{P}\right)^d(x) - \tau_0, p\right] - \frac{1}{p}\frac{d}{dt}\left[p\left(\frac{sB^f}{P}\right)^d(x)\right] + r^f\left(\frac{sB^f}{P}\right)^d(x) = 0. \tag{9.1.20}$$

---

[3] The choice-theoretic analysis of Appendix 9.A is built upon a framework in which foreign and domestic bonds are *perfect* substitutes. Motivation of a foreign asset demand function consistent with imperfect capital substitutability generally requires the explicit introduction of uncertainty. Unfortunately, such a generalization of the analysis of Appendix 1.C to an uncertain environment requires considerably more technical methodology.

This last expression requires that the excess demand for foreign currency measured in units of domestic goods be equal to zero.

We continue to assume that all domestic transactions are conducted by means of the domestic currency and that domestic residents hold only domestic money. We also continue to assume that the demand for domestic money is of the form

$$\left(\frac{M}{P}\right)^d = \left(\frac{M}{P}\right)^d (y, r). \tag{9.1.21}$$

If we further continue to assume that actual and desired money balances are always equal, money market equilibrium is characterized by

$$\left(\frac{M}{P}\right)^d (y^s(p), r) - \frac{M}{P} = 0. \tag{9.1.22}$$

However, recalling the definition of the relative price $p$, the money market equilibrium condition may also be written in the alternate form

$$sp\left(\frac{M}{P}\right)^d \left[y^s(p), r\right] - \frac{M}{P^f} = 0. \tag{9.1.23}$$

## Equilibrium in the Goods, Money, and Foreign Exchange Markets

The market-clearing conditions in the goods, money, and foreign exchange markets are therefore summarized as follows:

$$c^d(z, p) + i^d(r) + g - y^s(p) = 0, \tag{9.1.24}$$

$$sp\left(\frac{M}{P}\right)^d \left[y^s(p), r\right] - \frac{M}{P^f} = 0, \tag{9.1.25}$$

$$T(z, p) + r^f\left(\frac{sB^f}{P}\right)^d (x) - \frac{1}{p}\frac{d}{dt}\left[p\left(\frac{sB^f}{P}\right)^d (x)\right] = 0, \tag{9.1.26}$$

where

$$p \equiv \frac{P}{sP^f}, \tag{9.1.27}$$

$$z \equiv y - \tau_0 + r^f\left(\frac{sB^f}{P}\right)^d, \tag{9.1.28}$$

$$x \equiv \dot{s}^e + r^f - r. \tag{9.1.29}$$

The form of the foreign exchange market equilibrium condition makes this model inherently dynamic in nature. We therefore cannot simply perform comparative statics exercises on the above system without first formally considering these dynamics.

The first task we face in evaluating the term $(d/dt)[p(sB^f/P)^d(x)]$ is to provide a functional form for $\dot{s}^e$, the expected rate of depreciation of the spot exchange rate. A reasonable analogue to the assumption of adaptive expectations employed in earlier chapters is to assume that agents expect the exchange rate to gradually adjust back to its long-run equilibrium value whenever the exchange rate differs from its long-run equilibrium value. Therefore, it is reasonable to assume that

$$\dot{s}^e = \psi(\bar{s} - s), \qquad \psi > 0, \tag{9.1.30}$$

where $\bar{s}$ denotes the long-run equilibrium exchange rate, which is momentarily assumed to be constant. For the time being we also assume that $\psi$ is an exogenous constant. However, we later show that for an appropriately chosen value of $\psi$, the above expectational assumption corresponds to perfect foresight expectations as defined in earlier chapters.

The equilibrium conditions may now be rewritten as

$$c^d\left( y^s(p) - \tau_0 + r^f\left(\frac{sB^f}{P}\right)^d [\psi(\bar{s} - s) + r^f - r], \, p \right) + i^d(r) + g - y^s(p) = 0, \tag{9.1.31}$$

$$sp\left(\frac{M}{P}\right)^d [y^s(p), \, r] - \frac{M}{P^f} = 0, \tag{9.1.32}$$

$$T(y^s(p) - \tau_0 + r^f\left(\frac{sB^f}{P}\right)^d [\psi(\bar{s} - s) + r^f - r], \, p)$$

$$+ r^f\left(\frac{sB^f}{P}\right)^d (\psi(\bar{s} - s) + r^f - r) \tag{9.1.33}$$

$$- \frac{1}{p} \frac{d}{dt}\left[ p\left(\frac{sB^f}{P}\right)^d [\psi(\bar{s} - s) + r^f - r] \right] = 0.$$

Formal analysis of the above system is greatly complicated by the presence of terms of the form $r^f(sB^f/P)^d$, which measures the domestic interest income on net holdings of foreign-denominated assets. This term is often referred to as the service balance and is generally negligible in magnitude. Therefore, since the analysis of the above system is greatly complicated by formal consideration of these presumably negligible terms, most analyses simply ignore such terms. One formal way to handle this problem is to assume that the foreign interest rate $r^f$ is constant and approximately equal to zero. The above system simplifies, in the neighborhood of $r^f = 0$, to

$$c^d(y^s(p) - \tau_0, \, p) + i^d(r) + g - y^s(p) = 0, \tag{9.1.34}$$

$$sp\left(\frac{M}{P}\right)^d [y^s(p), \, r] - \frac{M}{P^f} = 0, \tag{9.1.35}$$

$$T(y^s(p) - \tau_0, \, p) - \frac{1}{p} \frac{d}{dt}\left[ p\left(\frac{sB^f}{P}\right)^d [\psi(\bar{s} - s) + r^f - r] \right] = 0. \tag{9.1.36}$$

## Dynamics of Adjustment Under Flexible Exchange Rates

The above model therefore consists of two algebraic equations and one differential equation in the endogenous variables $p$, $r$, and $s$. As a prelude to the solution of the model, we first consider the subsystem composed of the algebraic equilibrium conditions in the markets for goods and money. It is useful to view this subsystem as defining $p$ and $r$ as implicit functions of $s$. We momentarily postpone the analysis of how the state variable $s$

evolves over time. Differentiating the goods and money market equilibrium conditions with respect to $p$, $r$, and $s$, we obtain

$$
\begin{bmatrix}
-\left(1 - \dfrac{\partial c^d}{\partial z}\right)\dfrac{\partial y^s}{\partial p} + \dfrac{\partial c^d}{\partial p} & \dfrac{\partial i^d}{\partial r} \\[2ex]
s\dfrac{M}{P} + sp\dfrac{\partial (M/P)^d}{\partial y}\dfrac{\partial y^s}{\partial p} & sp\dfrac{\partial (M/P)^d}{\partial r}
\end{bmatrix}
\begin{bmatrix}
dp \\[2ex]
dr
\end{bmatrix}
=
\begin{bmatrix}
0 \\[2ex]
-p\dfrac{M}{P}ds
\end{bmatrix}
\tag{9.1.37}
$$

The above expression defines the implicit functions $p(s)$ and $r(s)$ such that

$$
\frac{\partial p}{\partial s} = \frac{\dfrac{1}{s}\dfrac{\partial i^d}{\partial r}}{\left[\dfrac{\partial c^d}{\partial p} - \left(1 - \dfrac{\partial c^d}{\partial z}\right)\dfrac{\partial y^s}{\partial p}\right]\dfrac{\partial (M/P)^d/\partial r}{M/P} - \left[\dfrac{1}{p} + \dfrac{\partial (M/P)^d/\partial y}{M/P}\dfrac{\partial y^s}{\partial p}\right]\dfrac{\partial i^d}{\partial r}}, \tag{9.1.38}
$$

$$
\frac{\partial r}{\partial s} = \frac{-\dfrac{1}{s}\left[\dfrac{\partial c^d}{\partial p} - \left(1 - \dfrac{\partial c^d}{\partial z}\right)\dfrac{\partial y^s}{\partial p}\right]}{\left[\dfrac{\partial c^d}{\partial p} - \left(1 - \dfrac{\partial c^d}{\partial z}\right)\dfrac{\partial y^s}{\partial p}\right]\dfrac{\partial (M/P)^d/\partial r}{M/P} - \left[\dfrac{1}{p} + \dfrac{\partial (M/P)^d/\partial y}{M/P}\dfrac{\partial y^s}{\partial p}\right]\dfrac{\partial i^d}{\partial r}}. \tag{9.1.39}
$$

We therefore find that $\partial p/\partial s < 0$ and $\partial r/\partial s > 0$ unambiguously.

The dynamics of adjustment in the model may now be summarized by

$$
T[y^s(p(s)) - \tau_0, p(s)] - \frac{1}{p(s)}\frac{d}{dt}\left[p(s)\left(\frac{sB^f}{P}\right)[\psi(\bar{s} - s) - r(s)]\right] = 0. \tag{9.1.40}
$$

We may now approximate the above first-order differential equation by expanding in a Taylor series around the point $s = \bar{s}$. Ignoring second- and higher-order terms, we therefore obtain

$$
\frac{ds}{dt} = \frac{\dfrac{\partial T}{\partial z}\dfrac{\partial y^s}{\partial p} + \dfrac{\partial T}{\partial p}}{\left[\dfrac{1}{p}\dfrac{\partial p}{\partial s}\left(\dfrac{sB^f}{P}\right)^d - \left(\psi + \dfrac{\partial r}{\partial s}\right)\dfrac{\partial (sB^f/P)^d}{\partial x}\right]}(s - \bar{s}). \tag{9.1.41}
$$

Stability requires that

$$
\frac{1}{p}\frac{\partial p}{\partial s}\frac{sB^f}{P} - \left(\psi + \frac{\partial r}{\partial s}\right)\frac{\partial (sB/P)^d}{\partial x} < 0. \tag{9.1.42}
$$

Sufficient conditions for stability are that $\psi \geq 0$ and that $B^f \geq 0$. We assume that this process is stable throughout.

The first-order differential equation in $s$ above is compatible with the expectational assumption that

$$
\dot{s}^e = \psi(\bar{s} - s). \tag{9.1.43}
$$

In particular, a unique value of $\psi$ always exists such that this expectational assumption is

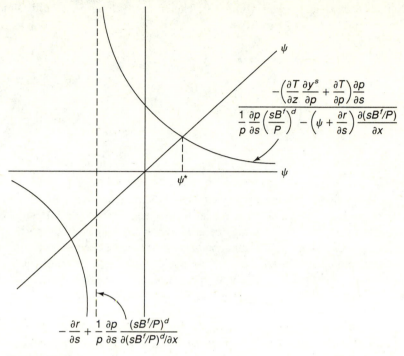

**Figure 9.1**

equivalent to perfect foresight expectations. The appropriate value of $\psi$ solves

$$\psi = \frac{-\left[\dfrac{\partial T}{\partial z}\dfrac{\partial y^s}{\partial p} + \dfrac{\partial T}{\partial p}\right]\dfrac{\partial p}{\partial s}}{\left[\dfrac{1}{p}\dfrac{\partial p}{\partial s}\left(\dfrac{sB^f}{P}\right)^d - \left(\psi + \dfrac{\partial r}{\partial s}\right)\dfrac{\partial (sB^f/P)^d}{\partial x}\right]}. \tag{9.1.44}$$

A solution $\psi^*$ to this equation is depicted in Figure 9.1.

## Steady-State Equilibrium and Comparative Statics Experiments

The dynamic path of $s$ is determined by the solution to the above first-order differential equation in $s$. Once the solution path of $s$ has been solved for, the algebraic relationships $p(s)$ and $r(s)$ may then be used to complete the analysis of motion of the three endogenous variables $p$, $r$, and $s$.

Recall the foreign exchange market equilibrium condition

$$T[y^s(p) - \tau_0, p] - \left[\frac{1}{p}\frac{\partial p}{\partial s}\left(\frac{sB^f}{P}\right) - \left(\psi + \frac{\partial r}{\partial s}\right)\frac{\partial (sB^f/P)^d}{\partial x}\right]\frac{ds}{dt} = 0. \tag{9.1.45}$$

In the steady state, we have $ds/dt = 0$. Therefore, the long-run equilibrium values $\bar{p}$ of $p$, $\bar{r}$ of $r$, and $\bar{s}$ of $s$ must satisfy

$$c^d[y^s(\bar{p}) - \tau_0, \bar{p}] + i^d(\bar{r}) + g - y^s(\bar{p}) = 0, \tag{9.1.46}$$

$$\bar{s}\bar{p}\left(\frac{M}{P}\right)^d[y^s(\bar{p}), \bar{r}] - \frac{M}{P^f} = 0, \tag{9.1.47}$$

$$T[y^s(\bar{p}) - \tau_0, \bar{p}] = 0. \tag{9.1.48}$$

Although the model is in the form of three simultaneous equations in the three endogenous variables $\bar{p}$, $\bar{r}$, and $\bar{s}$, the model solves recursively. The foreign exchange market equilibrium condition $T = 0$ may be used to solve for the equilibrium relative price ratio $p$. The goods market equilibrium condition may then be used to solve for the equilibrium domestic nominal interest rate $r$. Note that the equilibrium values of both $p$ and $r$ are independent of $M$ and $P^f$. Finally, the money market equilibrium condition may be used to solve for the equilibrium exchange rate $s$ in terms of $M$, $P^f$, and the equilibrium values of $p$ and $r$.

The recursive nature of the model helps to easily demonstrate the comparative statics effects of changes in $M$ and $P^f$. Differentiating the money market equilibrium condition and observing that $d\bar{p}/dM = d\bar{r}/dM = d\bar{p}/dP^f = d\bar{r}/dP^f = 0$, we obtain

$$\frac{d\bar{s}}{\bar{s}} = \frac{dM}{M} \quad \text{and} \quad \frac{d\bar{s}}{\bar{s}} = -\frac{dP^f}{P^f}. \tag{9.1.49}$$

Therefore, an increase in the nominal money supply results in an equiproportional increase in the exchange rate, while an increase in the nominal foreign currency price of the foreign good results in an equiproportional reduction in the exchange rate. Furthermore, recalling that $\bar{P} = \bar{s}\bar{p}P^f$, it is also straightforward to show that

$$\frac{d\bar{P}}{\bar{P}} = \frac{dM}{M} \quad \text{and} \quad \frac{d\bar{P}}{dP^f} = 0. \tag{9.1.50}$$

Therefore, at least in the steady state, nominal endogenous variables like the exchange rate and the domestic price level are in strict proportion to nominal exogenous variables like the domestic money supply and the foreign price level.

Although unanticipated, permanent changes in the money supply have no impact on the equilibrium values of the interest rate and the relative price level, fiscal policy changes generally do have permanent effects. For example, consider a permanent increase in government spending financed by an increase in taxes. Setting $d\tau_0 = dg$ and differentiating the goods, money, and foreign exchange market equilibrium conditions with respect to $\bar{p}$, $\bar{r}$, $\bar{s}$, and $g$, we obtain

$$
\begin{bmatrix}
\dfrac{\partial c^d}{\partial p} - \left(1 - \dfrac{\partial c^d}{\partial z}\right)\dfrac{\partial y^s}{\partial p} & \dfrac{\partial i^d}{\partial r} & 0 \\[2ex]
\left[\dfrac{1}{p} + \dfrac{\partial (M/P)^d/\partial y}{M/P}\dfrac{\partial y^s}{\partial p}\right]\dfrac{M}{P^f} & \dfrac{\partial (M/P)^d/\partial r}{M/P}\dfrac{M}{P^f} & \dfrac{1}{s}\dfrac{M}{P^f} \\[2ex]
\dfrac{\partial T}{\partial p} + \dfrac{\partial T}{\partial z}\dfrac{\partial y^s}{\partial p} & 0 & 0
\end{bmatrix}
\begin{bmatrix}
\dfrac{dp}{dg} \\[2ex]
\dfrac{a\bar r}{dg} \\[2ex]
\dfrac{ds}{dg}
\end{bmatrix}
=
\begin{bmatrix}
-\left(1 - \dfrac{\partial c^d}{\partial z}\right) \\[2ex]
0 \\[2ex]
\dfrac{\partial T}{\partial z}
\end{bmatrix}.
$$

$$(9.1.51)$$

Cramer's rule facilitates derivation of the following comparative statics results:

$$
\frac{d\bar p}{dg} = \frac{\partial T/\partial z}{\dfrac{\partial T}{\partial p} + \dfrac{\partial T}{\partial z}\dfrac{\partial y^s}{\partial p}} > 0,
\tag{9.1.52}
$$

$$
\frac{d\bar r}{dg} = -\frac{\dfrac{\partial c^d}{\partial p}\dfrac{\partial T}{\partial z} + \left(1 - \dfrac{\partial c^d}{\partial z}\right)\dfrac{\partial T}{\partial p}}{\left(\dfrac{\partial T}{\partial p} + \dfrac{\partial T}{\partial z}\dfrac{\partial y^s}{\partial p}\right)\dfrac{\partial i^d}{\partial r}} \gtreqless 0,
\tag{9.1.53}
$$

$$
\frac{d\bar s}{dg} = \frac{\bar s D}{\left(\dfrac{\partial T}{\partial p} + \dfrac{\partial T}{\partial z}\dfrac{\partial y^s}{\partial p}\right)\dfrac{\partial i^d}{\partial r}} \gtreqless 0,
\tag{9.1.54}
$$

where

$$
D \equiv \left[\left(1 - \frac{\partial c^d}{\partial z}\right)\frac{\partial T}{\partial p} + \frac{\partial T}{\partial z}\frac{\partial c^d}{\partial p}\right]\frac{\partial (M/P)^d/\partial r}{M/P}
$$
$$
- \left[\frac{1}{p} + \frac{\partial (M/P)^d/\partial y}{M/P}\frac{\partial y^s}{\partial p}\right]\frac{\partial i^d}{\partial r}\frac{\partial T}{\partial z}.
\tag{9.1.55}
$$

We therefore see that a balanced-budget increase in government spending on domestic goods unambiguously raises the relative price of the domestic good but has ambiguous effects on the interest rate and the exchange rate.

To understand these ambiguous effects, let us first consider the foreign exchange market equilibrium condition $T = 0$. Since we are assuming that $\partial T/\partial z < 0$ and $\partial T/\partial p < 0$, the fact that the increase in government spending raises relative prices also implies that the increase in government spending must lower disposable income. Now let us reconsider the goods market equilibrium condition. By definition, government spending rises. However, both due to a decline in disposable income and an increase in the relative price of the domestic good, foreign and domestic demand for the domestic good fall. Therefore, even in the absence of a rise in aggregate supply, it would be unclear whether investment demand would have to rise or fall to keep aggregate domestic demand and supply equal. Therefore, the interest rate may either fall or rise.

One case in which the interest rate unambiguously rises as it does in this same policy experiment in the analyses of Chapters 2, 3, and 5 is if consumption of the domestic good is insensitive to changes in relative prices, $\partial c^d / \partial p = 0$. In this case, in the absence of a rise in the interest rate, aggregate domestic demand rises by more than aggregate domestic supply, and an increase in the interest rate is needed to reduce investment spending and keep aggregate demand and supply equal.

Next consider the effect of the increase in government spending on the exchange rate. By inspection of the money market equilibrium condition, we see that if the increase in government spending raises domestic output (as it unambiguously does) and *lowers* the rate of interest, then the exchange rate must fall to keep money supply and money demand equal. That is, the domestic currency must appreciate. Therefore, if the interest rate rises, then the effect of the increase in government spending on the exchange rate is ambiguous. However, if the interest sensitivity of money demand is sufficiently small, then the exchange rate must appreciate even if the interest rate does rise.

Finally, consider the effect of a balanced-budget increase in government spending on the domestic price level $P$. Since, by definition, $P \equiv spP^f$, we must have

$$\frac{d\overline{P}}{dg} = P^f \left( \overline{s} \frac{d\overline{p}}{dg} + \overline{p} \frac{d\overline{s}}{dg} \right). \tag{9.1.56}$$

Combining the above expressions for $d\overline{p}/dg$ and $d\overline{s}/dg$, we obtain

$$\frac{d\overline{P}}{dg} = \frac{\overline{P}D'}{\left( \dfrac{\partial T}{\partial p} + \dfrac{\partial T}{\partial z} \dfrac{\partial y^s}{\partial p} \right) \dfrac{\partial i^d}{\partial r}} \gtreqless 0, \tag{9.1.57}$$

where

$$D' \equiv \left[ \left( 1 - \frac{\partial c^d}{\partial z} \right) \frac{\partial T}{\partial p} + \frac{\partial T}{\partial z} \frac{\partial c^d}{\partial p} \right] \frac{\partial (M/P)^d / \partial r}{M/P} - \frac{\partial y^s}{\partial p} \frac{\partial i^d}{\partial r} \frac{\partial T}{\partial z} \frac{\partial (M/P)^d / \partial y}{M/P}. \tag{9.1.58}$$

We therefore find that the effect of an increase in government spending on the domestic price level is also ambiguous. However, if aggregate supply is insensitive to changes in relative prices, that is, $\partial y^s / \partial p = 0$, and if the increase in government spending raises the interest rate, that is,

$$\left( 1 - \frac{\partial c^d}{\partial z} \right) \frac{\partial T}{\partial p} + \frac{\partial T}{\partial z} \frac{\partial c^d}{\partial p} < 0,$$

then the domestic price level unambiguously rises, as it does in response to the same policy experiment in the analyses of Chapters 2, 3, and 5.

## Impact Effects

In addition to our interest in the steady-state effects of changes in the exogenous variables on the endogenous variables in our model, we are also interested in the impact effects of such exogenous disturbances. Although relative prices, the interest rate, and the exchange rate may all change instantaneously to clear markets at any point in time, domestic nominal net holdings of foreign-denominated assets are predetermined. Therefore, although instantaneous changes in the endogenous variables may result in an instantaneous change in $(sB^f/P)^d$, the value of this expression denominated in units of foreign currency, $(P/s)(sB^f/P)^d = pP^f(sB^f/P)^d \equiv B_0^f$, may not change instantaneously. Therefore, the immediate, postimpact values of $p$, $r$, and $s$ must satisfy

$$c^d[y^s(p) - \tau_0, p] + i^d(r) + g - y^s(p) = 0, \tag{9.1.59}$$

$$sp\left(\frac{M}{P}\right)^d[y^s(p), r] - \frac{M}{P^f} = 0, \tag{9.1.60}$$

$$pP^f\left(\frac{sB^f}{P}\right)^d[\psi(\bar{s} - s) + r^f - r] - B_0^f = 0. \tag{9.1.61}$$

In the previous section, we demonstrated that the long-run effects of a change in the money supply were felt only on the nominal endogenous variables $s$ and $P$ but not on the real endogenous variables $p$ and $r$. Analysis of the above system guarantees that changes in the money supply also have no effect on the values of $p$ and $r$ even in the very short run. Furthermore, these neutrality results are independent of the quantitative size of $\psi$ and whether or not the value of $\psi$ is compatible with perfect foresight expectations. By inspection of the above equilibrium conditions, if in response to an increase in $M$ we find that the values of $p$ and $r$ are unaffected, then the domestic goods market is also undisturbed. Furthermore, with $p$ and $r$ unchanged, equiproportional changes in $M$ and $s$ leave the money market in equilibrium as well. Finally, inspection of the condition that nominal holdings of foreign earning assets be unchanged in the very short run assures us that this condition is also maintained as long as $p$ and $r$ are unchanged and as long as the change in $\bar{s}$ is the same as the change in $s$. Therefore, all three equilibrium conditions are in fact maintained when both $s$ and $\bar{s}$ respond equiproportionally to changes in $M$, and so money must be neutral in both the short and the long runs.

Let us now turn our attention to the impact effects of a balanced-budget increase in government spending. In our earlier analysis, we argued that it appeared sensible to assume that the net interest earnings on foreign asset holdings are negligible, and so we evaluated the model in the neighborhood of $r^f = 0$. In the present analysis it also makes sense to assume that $B_0^f$ is close to zero as well. Differentiating the above equilibrium conditions with respect to $p$, $r$, $s$, $g$, and $\tau_0$ and setting $dg = d\tau_0$ and $B_0^f = 0$, we obtain

$$\begin{bmatrix} \dfrac{\partial c^d}{\partial p} - \left(1 - \dfrac{\partial c^d}{\partial z}\right)\dfrac{\partial y^s}{\partial p} & \dfrac{\partial i^d}{\partial r} & 0 \\[3ex] \left[\dfrac{1}{p} + \dfrac{\partial(M/P)^d/\partial y}{M/P}\dfrac{\partial y^s}{\partial p}\right]\dfrac{M}{P^f} & \dfrac{\partial(M/P)^d/\partial r}{M/P}\dfrac{M}{P^f} & \dfrac{1}{s}\dfrac{M}{P^f} \\[3ex] 0 & -1 & -\psi \end{bmatrix}\begin{bmatrix} \dfrac{dp}{dg} \\[2ex] \dfrac{dr}{dg} \\[2ex] \dfrac{ds}{dg} \end{bmatrix} = \begin{bmatrix} -\left(1 - \dfrac{\partial c^d}{\partial z}\right) \\[2ex] 0 \\[2ex] -\psi\dfrac{d\bar{s}}{dg} \end{bmatrix}.$$

$$\tag{9.1.62}$$

In the transition from impact to the steady state, earlier analysis showed that $p$ and $r$ were monotonically related to $s$ during such transition. Therefore, it suffices to show how $s$ moves toward $\bar{s}$ after impact and the corresponding movements in $p$ and $r$ may readily be

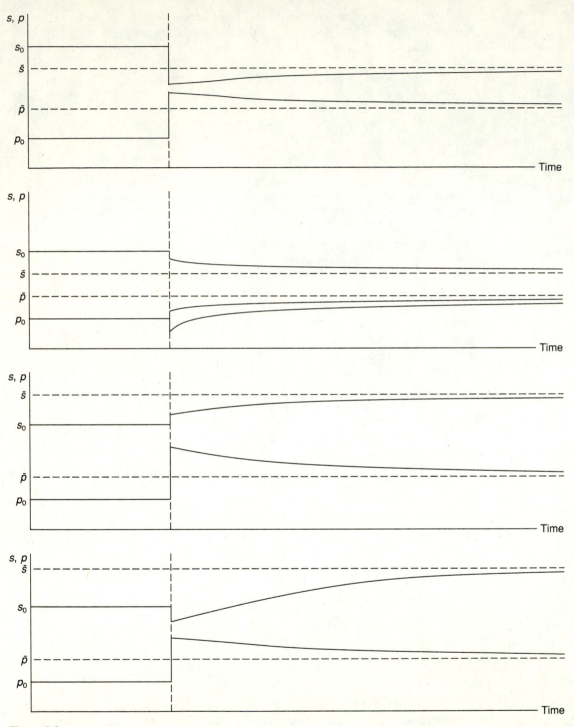

**Figure 9.2**

inferred. Use of Cramer's rule permits derivation of

$$
\frac{ds}{dg} = \frac{1 - \partial c^d/\partial z}{\Delta}\left[\frac{1}{p} + \frac{\partial(M/P)^d/\partial y}{M/P}\right]\frac{\partial y^s}{\partial p}\frac{M}{P^f}
$$

$$
- \frac{\psi}{\Delta}\left[\frac{\partial c^d}{\partial p}\frac{\partial(M/P)^d/\partial r}{M/P} - \frac{\partial i^d}{\partial r}\left(\frac{1}{p} + \frac{\partial(M/P)^d/\partial y}{M/P}\right)\right]\frac{M}{P^f}\frac{d\bar{s}}{dg},
$$

(9.1.63)

where

$$
\Delta \equiv \frac{1}{s}\left[\frac{\partial c^d}{\partial p} - \left(1 - \frac{\partial c^d}{\partial z}\right)\frac{\partial y^s}{\partial p}\right]\frac{M}{P^f} - \psi
$$

$$
\times \left\{\left[\frac{\partial c^d}{\partial p} - \left(1 - \frac{\partial c^d}{\partial z}\right)\frac{\partial y^s}{\partial p}\right]\frac{\partial(M/P)^d/\partial r}{M/P} - \frac{\partial i^d}{\partial r}\left(\frac{1}{p} + \frac{\partial(M/P)^d/\partial y}{M/P}\right)\right\}\frac{M}{P^f} < 0.
$$

(9.1.64)

Inspection of the above expressions reveals that $ds/dg$ consists of two terms. The first term is a negative constant independent of the size and sign of $d\bar{s}/dg$. The second term consists of a negative fraction multiplied by $d\bar{s}/dg$. Therefore, if $d\bar{s}/dg < 0$, a case considered above, then the impact effect of an increase in $g$ on $s$ is unambiguously negative. However, the absolute value of the impact effect on $s$ may be greater or less than the long-run effect and so $s$ may either rise or fall as equilibrium is approached. Alternatively, if $d\bar{s}/dg$ is positive, then we cannot be sure whether $s$ instantaneously rises or falls. However, we do know in this case that the exchange rate rises in the transition from the impact effect to the steady-state equilibrium. Several possible transition paths are depicted in Figure 9.2.

## 9.2 FIXED EXCHANGE RATE SYSTEMS

Throughout the analysis of Section 9.1, the exchange rate adjusts continuously to equate the supply of and demand for foreign exchange. Domestic monetary policy is characterized by a fixed value for the domestic nominal money supply. These assumptions are standard for the case of purely floating exchange rates.

In this section, we consider the alternative, polar case of a system of purely fixed exchange rates. With fixed exchange rates, a predetermined, often constant time path is chosen in advance for the nominal exchange rate. If at the predetermined exchange rate there is a private excess supply or excess demand for foreign exchange, the domestic monetary authority stands ready to buy or sell foreign exchange from its holdings of international reserves in unlimited quantities to maintain the prearranged level of the exchange rate. Furthermore, in the pure version of a fixed exchange rate system, the domestic monetary authority expands or contracts the domestic money supply one-for-one with changes in its holdings of international reserves.

### The Foreign Exchange Market Under Fixed Exchange Rates

The principal alterations to the basic open-economy macroeconomic model necessary to consider the case of fixed exchange rates involve the market-clearing condition in the foreign exchange market. The remaining modifications of the model of Section 9.1 are all purely cosmetic in nature.

First consider the demand for foreign-denominated assets, $(sB^f/P)^d$. In the most basic fixed exchange rate case, the spot exchange rate is expected to remain constant into the indefinite future due to agents' beliefs that the monetary authority will in fact carry through with its stated policy. Therefore, the relative-rate-of-return variable $x$ is now given by

$$x = \dot{s}^e + r^f - r = r^f - r, \tag{9.2.1}$$

since $\dot{s}^e \equiv 0$ in this case.

However, the difference between the trade balance and the rate of accumulation of privately held, foreign-denominated assets is no longer identically equal to zero, except by coincidence. Now any discrepancy between the private supplies and demands for foreign exchange shows up as a change in the domestic money supply. More precisely, let $R$ denote the level of domestic holdings of international reserves denominated in units of foreign currency. The domestic country's monetary policy may now be characterized by

$$M = \hat{s}R, \tag{9.2.2}$$

where $\hat{s}$ denotes the fixed value of the exchange rate. Therefore, the domestic money supply is equal to the volume of international reserves valued in units of domestic currency.

The evolution of the domestic country's reserve holdings is given by

$$\frac{dR}{dt} = P^f pT - P^f \frac{d}{dt}\left[ p\left(\frac{sB^f}{P}\right)^d (r^f - r) \right], \tag{9.2.3}$$

where we again adopt the assumption that interest income on net domestic holdings of foreign-denominated assets is negligible. The above expression is identical to the analogous expression of Section 9.1 except that we have converted each term to units of foreign currency and have replaced the exchange rate with the domestic holdings of reserves as the adjusting variable.

It is now useful to define the monetary variable

$$m' = \frac{M}{\hat{s}P^f}. \tag{9.2.4}$$

The variable $m'$ is equal to the domestic money supply measured in units of the foreign good.

Differentiating the monetary policy rule and the definition of $m'$, we obtain

$$\frac{dM}{dt} = \hat{s}\frac{dR}{dt} + R\frac{d\hat{s}}{dt}, \tag{9.2.5}$$

$$\frac{dm'}{dt} = \frac{1}{\hat{s}P^f}\frac{dM}{dt} - \frac{M}{\hat{s}P^f}\frac{1}{\hat{s}}\frac{d\hat{s}}{dt} - \frac{M}{\hat{s}P^f}\frac{1}{P^f}\frac{dP^f}{dt}. \tag{9.2.6}$$

Combining these two expressions to eliminate $M$, we obtain

$$\frac{dm'}{dt} = \frac{1}{P^f}\frac{dR}{dt} - \frac{m'}{P^f}\frac{dP^f}{dt}. \tag{9.2.7}$$

Now setting $dP^f/dt = 0$ and combining this last expression with the above differential equation in domestic reserve holdings $R$, we obtain

$$\frac{dm'}{dt} = pT(z, p) - \frac{d}{dt}\left[p\left(\frac{sB^f}{P}\right)^d (r^f - r)\right].$$

(9.2.8)

Finally, the full fixed exchange rate open-economy macromodel consists of the above differential equation in $m'$ plus the algebraic goods and money market equilibrium conditions

$$c^d[y^s(p) - \tau_0, p] + i^d(r) + g - y^s(p) = 0,$$

(9.2.9)

$$p\left(\frac{M}{P}\right)^d [y^s(p), r] - m' = 0.$$

(9.2.10)

## Dynamics of Adjustment Under Fixed Exchange Rates

In order to write down the solution to the above dynamic system, it is first useful to solve the goods and money market equilibrium conditions for the implicit functions $p(m')$ and $r(m')$. Differentiating the goods and money market equilibrium conditions with respect to $p$, $r$, and $m'$, we obtain

$$\begin{bmatrix} \dfrac{\partial c^d}{\partial p} - \left(1 - \dfrac{\partial c^d}{\partial z}\right)\dfrac{\partial y^s}{\partial p} & \dfrac{\partial i^d}{\partial r} \\[3mm] \left[1 + p\dfrac{\partial (M/P)^d/\partial y}{M/P}\dfrac{\partial y^s}{\partial p}\right]\dfrac{M}{P} & p\dfrac{\partial (M/P)^d}{\partial r} \end{bmatrix}\begin{bmatrix} dp \\[3mm] dr \end{bmatrix} = \begin{bmatrix} 0 \\[3mm] dm' \end{bmatrix}.$$

(9.2.11)

Solving by Cramer's rule, we obtain

$$\frac{\partial p}{\partial m'} = -\frac{1}{\Delta}\frac{\partial i^d}{\partial r} > 0,$$

(9.2.12)

$$\frac{\partial r}{\partial m'} = \frac{1}{\Delta}\left[\frac{\partial c^d}{\partial p} - \left(1 - \frac{\partial c^d}{\partial z}\right)\frac{\partial y^s}{\partial p}\right] < 0,$$

(9.2.13)

where

$$\Delta = p\left[\frac{\partial c^d}{\partial p} - \left(1 - \frac{\partial c^d}{\partial z}\right)\frac{\partial y^s}{\partial p}\right]\frac{\partial (M/P)^d}{\partial r}$$

$$- \left[1 + p\frac{\partial (M/P)^d/\partial y}{M/P}\frac{\partial y^s}{\partial p}\right]\frac{\partial i^d}{\partial r}\frac{M}{P} > 0.$$

(9.2.14)

We may now linearize the differential equation in $m'$ around its equilibrium value, which we denote by $\overline{m}'$. Collecting terms, we obtain

$$\frac{dm'}{dt}\left[1 + \left(\frac{sB^f}{P}\right)\frac{\partial p}{\partial m'} - p\frac{\partial (sB^f/P)^d}{\partial x}\frac{\partial r}{\partial m'}\right]$$

$$= \left[T\frac{\partial p}{\partial m'} + p\left(\frac{\partial T}{\partial z}\frac{\partial y^s}{\partial p} + \frac{\partial T}{\partial p}\right)\frac{\partial p}{\partial m'}\right](m' - \overline{m}').$$

(9.2.15)

The system dynamics are therefore captured by the first-order differential equation

$$\frac{dm'}{dt} = \frac{T\dfrac{\partial p}{\partial m'} + p\left(\dfrac{\partial T}{\partial z}\dfrac{\partial y^s}{\partial p} + \dfrac{\partial T}{\partial p}\right)\dfrac{\partial p}{\partial m'}}{1 + \left(\dfrac{sB^f}{P}\right)\dfrac{\partial p}{\partial m'} - p\dfrac{\partial(sB^f/P)^d}{\partial x}\dfrac{\partial r}{\partial m'}}(m' - \overline{m}'). \tag{9.2.16}$$

The dynamics of adjustment of $m'$ are stable as long as the above coefficient on $m' - \overline{m}'$ is negative.

Equilibrium, if it exists and if the system is stable, is characterized by $dm'/dt = 0$. Full equilibrium is therefore governed by the following:

$$c^d[y^s(\overline{p}) - \tau_0, \overline{p}] + i^d(\overline{r}) + g - y^s(\overline{p}) = 0, \tag{9.2.17}$$

$$\overline{p}\left(\frac{M}{P}\right)^d[y^s(\overline{p}), \overline{r}] - \overline{m}' = 0, \tag{9.2.18}$$

$$T[y^s(\overline{p}) - \tau_0, \overline{p}] = 0. \tag{9.2.19}$$

We therefore find that, in equilibrium, $T \equiv 0$. If we also assume that $sB^f/P \simeq 0$, then the above stability condition, evaluated in the neighborhood of equilibrium, is given by

$$\frac{\overline{p}\left(\dfrac{\partial T}{\partial z}\dfrac{\partial y^s}{\partial p} + \dfrac{\partial T}{\partial p}\right)\dfrac{\partial p}{\partial m'}}{1 - \overline{p}\dfrac{\partial(sB^f/P)^d}{\partial x}\dfrac{\partial r}{\partial m'}} < 0. \tag{9.2.20}$$

This condition is unambiguously satisfied, and so the dynamics of adjustment of $m'$ are always stable.

## Steady-State Equilibrium and Comparative Statics Experiments

Once the path of motion of $m'$ has been solved for, the algebraic functions $p(m')$ and $r(m')$ may be used to solve for the paths of $p$ and $r$. Furthermore, since $\hat{s}$ and $P^f$ are both assumed constant, the motion of $M$ is simply proportional to the motion of $m'$. Finally, the path of $\hat{s}$ is trivial since, by definition, the exchange rate is fixed.

One important property of the current model, which is typical of most equilibrium open-economy macromodels, is that the equilibrium allocation of resources is independent of the exchange rate regime. In both the flexible and fixed exchange rate systems, the equilibrium values $\overline{p}$ and $\overline{r}$ may be solved for by means of the goods market equilibrium condition and the property that, in either system, the trade balance $T$ is equal to zero in equilibrium. The money market equilibrium condition may then be used recursively to solve either for the equilibrium exchange rate in the flexible exchange case or for the equilibrium nominal money supply in the fixed exchange rate case.

Since the conditions determining the equilibrium values $\overline{p}$ and $\overline{r}$ are identical under the fixed and floating rate regimes, the steady-state comparative statics effects of changes in the exogenous variables on $p$ and $r$ must also be identical. Therefore, the analyses of the steady-state effects of changes in $g$ and $P^f$ are unchanged from the analysis of Section 9.1. However, since in the fixed exchange rate case, the nominal money supply is an endogenous rather than an exogenous variable, the comparative statics effects of changes in $M$ in the fixed exchange rate system are meaningless.

However, in a fixed exchange rate system, there is a policy change whose impact closely resembles that of a change in the money supply in a flexible exchange rate system. This policy change is that of an unanticipated, permanent change in the nominal exchange rate, a policy change referred to as a devaluation.

A devaluation is an exogenous increase in the value of $\hat{s}$. Such an increase in $\hat{s}$ involves an increase in the domestic currency price of foreign exchange and a corresponding increase in the domestic currency value of holdings of international reserves. Devaluation also implies a reduction in the international value of a unit of domestic currency.

As long as the domestic monetary authority continues to adhere to its monetary rule that

$$M = \hat{s}R, \tag{9.2.21}$$

the devaluation also involves a simultaneous, equiproportional increase in the nominal domestic money supply. However, the value of the domestic money supply measured in units of foreign goods is equal to

$$m' = \frac{M}{\hat{s}P^f} = \frac{R}{P^f}. \tag{9.2.22}$$

Therefore, the real value of the domestic money supply is unchanged by the devaluation, and so too are the levels of $p$ and $r$ unchanged since both $p$ and $r$ are directly linked to $m'$. The effects of the devaluation are therefore confined to equiproportional increases in the nominal domestic money supply and the domestic price level:

$$P = \hat{s}\frac{p}{P^f}. \tag{9.2.23}$$

One case in which a devaluation does have temporary real effects is the case in which the domestic monetary authority insulates the domestic money supply from the change in the exchange rate. Consider the alternative policy rule

$$M = k\hat{s}R \tag{9.2.24}$$

and suppose that $k$ is simultaneously adjusted to keep the money supply unchanged immediately following the increase in $\hat{s}$. In this case, the value of $m'$ immediately falls following the devaluation. Therefore, in the present flexible-price model, relative prices $p$ temporarily fall and the interest rate $r$ temporarily rises. The devaluation is therefore followed by a period of lower domestic output until the value of $m'$ is restored, through a period of surplus in the trade balance, to its original level.

## 9.3 SLUGGISH PRICE ADJUSTMENT IN THE OPEN ECONOMY

The models of Sections 9.1 and 9.2 are both characterized by a general tendency toward less than instantaneous adjustment to disturbances. The basic rationale for this dynamic response pattern is that time is required for any adjustment that involves a change in holdings of internationally traded earning assets or international reserves.

However, even acknowledging this important source of friction, we still note that some nominal disturbances trigger instantaneous adjustments even when capital is imperfectly mobile as it is in the models of the previous sections. In particular, Section 9.1 demonstrates that with flexible exchange rates, an increase in the domestic money supply results in immediate, equiproportional increases in the exchange rate and the domestic price level without even a temporary change in the pattern of resource allocation due to temporary changes in the interest rate or relative prices.

In this section, we introduce a model characterized by less than instantaneous adjustment to nominal disturbances. The basic building block of this model is the assumption of less than instantaneous adjustment in the domestic nominal price level. This model is therefore somewhat similar to that of Section 4.3, which introduced sluggish price dynamics into the classical model of Chapter 2. The present model is also somewhat similar to that of Section 5.4, which considered the case of sluggish nominal wage adjustment.

## Perfect Capital Mobility

In this section, we hope to prominently feature those properties of open-economy macroeconomic models that are primarily indigenous to less than instantaneous goods price adjustment. It is therefore helpful to try to set up the basic model of this section with those auxiliary assumptions that are least likely to inject any further complications to the process of dynamic adjustment.

In Sections 9.1 and 9.2, nontrivial dynamics were due to the fact that time is required in those models for domestic agents to build up or deplete their holdings of foreign-denominated assets. This process is similar in form to the case of less than instantaneous adjustment of actual to desired holdings of money balances that we considered in Chapters 1 and 2.

We now consider a case in which such adjustments occur without the passage of calendar time. In particular, suppose that the demand for internationally traded earning assets is infinitely elastic at the point $x = 0$. In this case, huge incipient portfolio adjustments prevent any changes in the expected relative rates of return on domestic and foreign assets. We may therefore replace the foreign exchange market equilibrium condition with the asset market arbitrage condition

$$\dot{s}^e + r^f - r \equiv 0. \tag{9.3.1}$$

Although it is possible to generate the case of perfect capital mobility smoothly as a limiting case of models like those of Sections 9.1 and 9.2, we have not chosen to present that exercise here. With imperfect capital mobility, the trade balance $T$ must equal zero but only in the steady state. Alternatively, the relative-rate-of-return variable $x$ is unconstrained both in and out of the steady state in that case. Finally, holdings of foreign-denominated assets $sB^f/P$ take on an equilibrium value determined by the equilibrium value of $x$.

With perfect capital mobility, the relative-rate-of-return variable $x$ is identically equal to zero at all times whether the economy is or is not in steady-state equilibrium. Alternatively, the trade balance $T$ is not constrained to zero even in the steady state. The trade balance simply falls out as a residual variable driven by any changes in foreign asset holdings that may be required to maintain the equality in expected yields between domestic and internationally traded earning assets.

## Price Adjustment

The basic building block of this section is a price adjustment mechanism that links the percentage rate of change of the domestic price level to the level of excess demand for the domestic good. In particular, assume that adjustment in $P$ is given by

$$\frac{\dot{P}}{P} = \lambda\{c^d[y^s(p) - \tau_0, p] + i^d(r) + g - y^s(p)\}. \tag{9.3.2}$$

The above equation implies that it is the nominal domestic price $P$ rather than the real relative price term $p$ that adjusts in the face of disequilibrium in the domestic goods market. This potential distinction between a real price adjustment mechanism and a nominal price adjustment mechanism is similar to the choice necessitated in Section 5.4 between labor market adjustment of the real wage as opposed to the nominal wage. Choice of a nominal price adjustment mechanism is chosen here both for consistency with plausible stories of how firms might actually set prices and by a desire to keep the present analysis as closely comparable as possible to most of the relevant existing literature.

Consider the relative price term $p \equiv P/sP^f$. For domestic firms to adjust $p$ in a manner consistent with a price adjustment mechanism in $\dot{p}$ like that presented above in $\dot{P}$, firms would have to make sure that motion in $p$ over time was smooth. In particular, instantaneous adjustments in $P$ would be required to match any sudden movements in $s$ or $P^f$. However, it is not likely that most sellers of domestic goods would be able, nor would they find it desirable, to constantly adjust the nominal price $P$ one-for-one with every momentary change in the foreign exchange rate $s$, for example.

To see the implied mechanical relationship between $\dot{P}$ and $\dot{p}$, we may differentiate the definition $p \equiv P/sP^f$ with respect to time. Upon rearranging terms, we obtain

$$\frac{1}{p}\frac{dp}{dt} = \frac{1}{P}\frac{dP}{dt} - \frac{1}{s}\frac{ds}{dt} - \frac{1}{P^f}\frac{dP^f}{dt}. \tag{9.3.3}$$

We may therefore specify the underlying dynamics of adjustment either in terms of $p$ or $P$. The above identity may then be employed to solve for the coincident rate of change in the other price variable. Throughout most of the analysis, we take the foreign price level $P^f$ as fixed. Therefore, the difference in the percentage rates of change in $p$ and $P$ is simply equal to the percentage rate of change in the exchange rate $s$.

## Price and Exchange Rate Dynamics

We are now ready to investigate the implications of the price adjustment mechanism we have postulated on the dynamic path of the exchange rate. The formal analysis presented below is very similar to that of Dornbusch (1976). A primary result of his analysis is that sluggish price adjustment may lead to exaggerated adjustments in the exchange rate under a system of flexible exchange rates.

However, before proceeding with our analysis of disequilibrium dynamics, it is necessary to observe that the model is not fully determined outside of the steady state. In equilibrium, domestic output is equal both to domestic aggregate demand and domestic aggregate supply. However, when there is disequilibrium in the domestic goods market, it is also necessary to specify a mechanism for determining the actual level of domestic production. Our analysis of Chapter 3 and the original Dornbusch model both adopt the assumption that output is demand determined out of equilibrium. However, in the present analysis, in which domestic output demand and domestic output supply both depend on the relative price term $p$, it is much simpler to assume that output is supply determined out of equilibrium.[4] Fortunately, the close parallels between the results of this section and those of Dornbusch (1976) suggest that this assumption is not crucial to most of the results.

Adopting the assumptions of perfect capital mobility and slowly adjusting domestic prices, our flexible exchange rate model is now summarized by

$$\frac{\dot{P}}{P} = \lambda\{c^d[y^s(p) - \tau_0, p] + i^d(r) + g - y^s(p)\}, \tag{9.3.4}$$

$$0 = sp\left(\frac{M}{P}\right)^d [y^s(p), r] - \frac{M}{P^f}, \tag{9.3.5}$$

$$0 = r - r^f - \psi(\bar{s} - s), \tag{9.3.6}$$

$$0 = spP^f - P. \tag{9.3.7}$$

Note that we have retained our earlier assumption that the expected path of the exchange rate is given by

$$\dot{s}^e = \psi(\bar{s} - s), \tag{9.3.8}$$

where $\bar{s}$ denotes the long-run equilibrium exchange rate and $\psi$ is a positive constant. As in Section 9.1, we later demonstrate that a value of $\psi$ exists that makes this expectational assumption compatible with perfect foresight expectations.

Before we proceed with an analysis of the dynamic properties of the model, it is useful to briefly note a few similarities and differences in the steady-state properties of this model and that of Section 9.1. In the present model, steady-state equilibrium always requires a unified world capital market in which $r = r^f$. Therefore, the equilibrium domestic interest rate is exogenous. With $r$ determined by external forces, the goods and money market equilibrium conditions may then be used to solve for the equilibrium levels of $p$ and $s$.

One obvious common feature of the present model and the model of Section 9.1 concerns the steady-state effects of an increase in the nominal domestic money supply $M$. An increase in $M$ again brings about equiproportional increases in $P$ and $s$ with no change in either $p$ or $r$. However, while in Section 9.1 adjustment to such a disturbance is instantaneous, a prominent part of the present analysis centers on the richer menu of possible adjustment dynamics to this disturbance when goods prices are somewhat sticky.

The plan of analysis is as follows. First, we use the money market equilibrium condition and the perfect capital mobility assumption to express $r$ and $s$ as implicit functions of $p$, the relative price of the domestic good. We may then use the relationship between $\dot{P}$ and $\dot{p}$ developed above to derive a dynamic equation solely in terms of $p$. Once we solve for the motion of $p$ over time, motion of the other endogenous variables may be solved for algebraically.

---

[4] This complication is less important in the Dornbusch (1976) analysis, which assumes that domestic aggregate supply is fixed.

Differentiating the money market equilibrium condition (9.3.5) and the perfect capital mobility assumption (9.3.6) with respect to $r$, $s$, and $p$, we may obtain, by application of Cramer's rule,

$$\frac{\partial r}{\partial p} = \frac{\psi\left[\dfrac{1}{p} + \dfrac{\partial(M/P)^d/\partial y}{M/P} \dfrac{\partial y^s}{\partial p}\right]}{\dfrac{1}{s}\left[1 - s\psi\dfrac{\partial(M/P)^d/\partial r}{M/P}\right]} > 0, \tag{9.3.9}$$

$$\frac{\partial s}{\partial p} = \frac{-\left[\dfrac{1}{p} + \dfrac{\partial(M/P)^d/\partial y}{M/P} \dfrac{\partial y^s}{\partial p}\right]}{\dfrac{1}{s}\left[1 - s\psi\dfrac{\partial(M/P)^d/\partial r}{M/P}\right]} < 0. \tag{9.3.10}$$

The dynamics of price adjustment may now be written as

$$\frac{\dot{P}}{P} = \lambda\{c^d[y^s(p) - \tau_0, p] + i^d[r(p)] + g - y^s(p)\}. \tag{9.3.11}$$

Next consider the relationship between the rates of change of $P$ and $p$. With $s$ given as an implicit function of $p$, we may write

$$\frac{ds}{dt} = \frac{\partial s}{\partial p} \frac{dp}{dt}. \tag{9.3.12}$$

Combining this relationship with the equation

$$\frac{1}{p}\frac{dp}{dt} = \frac{1}{P}\frac{dP}{dt} - \frac{1}{s}\frac{ds}{dt}, \tag{9.3.13}$$

we obtain

$$\frac{1}{p}\frac{dp}{dt} = \frac{\dfrac{1}{P}\dfrac{dP}{dt}}{1 + \dfrac{p}{s}\dfrac{\partial s}{\partial p}}. \tag{9.3.14}$$

Now plugging in for $\partial s/\partial p$, we may, upon rearranging, obtain

$$\frac{1}{p}\frac{dp}{dt} = -\frac{1 - s\psi\dfrac{\partial(M/P)^d/\partial r}{M/P}}{s\psi\dfrac{\partial(M/P)^d/\partial r}{M/P} + p\dfrac{\partial(M/P)^d/\partial y}{M/P}\dfrac{\partial y^s}{\partial p}}\frac{1}{P}\frac{dP}{dt}. \tag{9.3.15}$$

However, we have already derived an expression for $\dot{P}/P$ solely as a function of $p$. We now expand that expression in a Taylor series around the equilibrium value $p = \bar{p}$. Ignoring terms higher than second order, we obtain

$$\frac{\dot{P}}{P} = \lambda\left[\frac{\partial c^d}{\partial p} - \left(1 - \frac{\partial c^d}{\partial z}\right)\frac{\partial y^s}{\partial p} + \frac{\partial i^d}{\partial r}\frac{\partial r}{\partial p}\right](p - \bar{p}). \tag{9.3.16}$$

Now plugging in for $\partial r/\partial p$ and combining with the above expression for $\dot{p}/p$, we obtain:

$$\frac{\dot{p}}{p} = \frac{-\lambda D(p - \bar{p})}{s\psi \dfrac{\partial(M/P)^d/\partial r}{M/P} + p\dfrac{\partial(M/P)^d/\partial y}{M/P}\dfrac{\partial y^s}{\partial p}}, \tag{9.3.17}$$

where

$$D \equiv \left[\frac{\partial c^d}{\partial p} - \left(1 - \frac{\partial c^d}{\partial z}\right)\frac{\partial y^s}{\partial p}\right]\left[1 - s\psi\frac{\partial(M/P)^d/\partial r}{M/P}\right]$$

$$+ s\psi\frac{\partial i^d}{\partial r}\left[\frac{1}{p} + \frac{\partial(M/P)^d\partial y}{M/P}\frac{\partial y^s}{\partial p}\right] < 0. \tag{9.3.18}$$

We have therefore summarized the dynamics of adjustment in the model in a single first-order differential equation in the state variable $p$. Once the solution trajectory for $p$ has been derived, the paths of $s$ and $r$ may be inferred by means of the implicit functions $s(p)$ and $r(p)$. Finally, motion of $P$ may be derived by means of the definition $p \equiv P/sP^f$.

The dynamic process in $p$ is stable as long as

$$s\psi\frac{\partial(M/P)^d/\partial r}{M/P} + p\frac{\partial(M/P)^d/\partial y}{M/P}\frac{\partial y^s}{\partial p} < 0. \tag{9.3.19}$$

Obviously, this inequality holds unambiguously as long as $\psi \geq 0$ and $\partial y^s/\partial p = 0$. This is the case originally analyzed by Dornbusch (1976). Although in the more general case in which $\partial y^s/\partial p > 0$, we cannot be assured that the $p$ process is stable, as long as $\partial y^s/\partial p$ is relatively small in absolute value and/or $\psi$ is relatively large in absolute value, the above stability condition is likely to be satisfied.

As in Section 9.1, one case of particular interest is that of perfect foresight expectations. Just as in the earlier analysis of Section 9.1, we are again able to find a value of $\psi$ that makes our original expectational assumption consistent with perfect foresight. To see that this is the case, we first must transform the above differential equation in $p$ into a differential equation in $s$.

Differentiating the implicit function $s(p)$ with respect to time, we obtain

$$\frac{ds}{dt} = p\frac{\partial s}{\partial p}\left[\frac{1}{p}\frac{dp}{dt}\right]. \tag{9.3.20}$$

We next employ the Taylor series approximation:

$$(s - \bar{s}) = \frac{\partial p}{\partial s}(p - \bar{p}). \tag{9.3.21}$$

These last two expressions may be combined with the above differential equation in $p$ to obtain

$$\frac{ds}{dt} = \frac{-\lambda p D(s - \bar{s})}{s\psi\dfrac{\partial(M/P)^d/\partial r}{M/P} + p\dfrac{\partial(M/P)^d/\partial y}{M/P}\dfrac{\partial y^s}{\partial p}}. \tag{9.3.22}$$

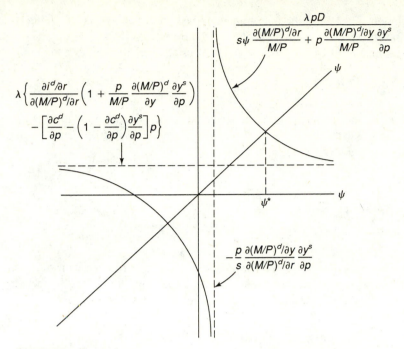

**Figure 9.3**

Finally, recalling that expectations about movements in the exchange rate are given by

$$\dot{s}^e = \psi(\bar{s} - s),$$  (9.3.23)

we find that perfect foresight requires a value of $\psi$ that satisfies

$$\psi = \frac{\lambda pD}{s\psi\dfrac{\partial(M/P)^d/\partial r}{M/P} + p\dfrac{\partial(M/P)^d/\partial y}{M/P}\dfrac{\partial y^s}{\partial p}}.$$  (9.3.24)

The left- and right-hand sides of the above equation are depicted in Figure 9.3. Note that a unique positive value of $\psi$ may always be found that is consistent with the above equality. We also note that this perfect foresight value $\psi^*$ of $\psi$ also guarantees stability of the original dynamic process in $p$.

## Dynamic Response to an Increase in the Money Supply

We have already demonstrated that the steady-state effects of an unanticipated increase in the money supply are equiproportional increases in the exchange rate and the domestic price level with no changes in the relative price of the domestic good or the domestic nominal interest rate. We also know that any impact effects of such an increase in the money supply slowly dissipate over time as the economy converges to this steady-state solution. Therefore, the only remaining task in our analysis of the effects of such a step jump in the money supply center on these impact effects.

Since the trajectory of the nominal price level $P$ is subject to

$$\frac{\dot{P}}{P} = \lambda[c^d + i^d + g - y^s], \tag{9.3.25}$$

we know that, at any point in time, the domestic nominal price level is predetermined. If we denote the initial level of $P$ by $P_0$, then the values of $p$, $r$, and $s$ must, immediately following any disturbance, be governed by

$$spP^f - P_0 = 0, \tag{9.3.26}$$

$$sp\left(\frac{M}{P}\right)^d [y^s(p), r] - \frac{M}{P^f} = 0, \tag{9.3.27}$$

$$r - r^f - \psi(\bar{s} - s) = 0. \tag{9.3.28}$$

We may now compute the impact effects of an increase in the money supply by differentiating these three equations with respect to $p$, $r$, $s$, and $M$. Recalling the dependence of $s$ on $M$, this procedure results in the following:

$$\left[\begin{array}{ccc} sP^f & 0 & pP^f \\ s\left[1 + p\dfrac{\partial(M/P)^d/\partial y}{M/P}\dfrac{\partial y^s}{\partial p}\right]\dfrac{M}{P} & sp\dfrac{\partial(M/P)^d}{\partial r} & p\dfrac{M}{P}\psi \\ 0 & 1 & \psi \end{array}\right] \left[\begin{array}{c} dp \\ dr \\ ds \end{array}\right] = \left[\begin{array}{c} 0 \\ \dfrac{sp}{P}\,dM \\ \psi\dfrac{d\bar{s}}{dM}\,dM \end{array}\right]. \tag{9.3.29}$$

Application of Cramer's rule, the earlier result that $d\bar{s}/dM = \bar{s}/M$, and some algebraic manipulation allows derivation of

$$\frac{ds}{dM} = \frac{s}{M} \frac{s\psi\dfrac{\partial(M/P)^d/\partial r}{M/P} - 1}{s\psi\dfrac{\partial(M/P)^d/\partial r}{M/P} + p\dfrac{\partial(M/P)^d/\partial y}{M/P}\dfrac{\partial y^s}{\partial p}}. \tag{9.3.30}$$

The numerator of this expression is unambiguously negative. The denominator of this expression is also negative if and only if the stability condition for the dynamic process in $p$ is satisfied, which we have already shown to be the case for the case of perfect foresight expectations. Therefore, as long as the dynamic process is stable, the impact effect of an increase in the money supply on the exchange rate is unambiguously positive. Furthermore, we have already shown that the steady-state effect of the increase in the money supply is given by

$$\frac{d\bar{s}}{dM} = \frac{\bar{s}}{M}. \tag{9.3.31}$$

On the right-hand side of the above expression for the impact effect of an increase in $M$ on $s$, we also know that the term that multiplies $s/M$ is unambiguously greater than unity. This is clearly the case because the numerator is always greater than $-s\psi(\partial(M/P)^d/\partial r)P/M$

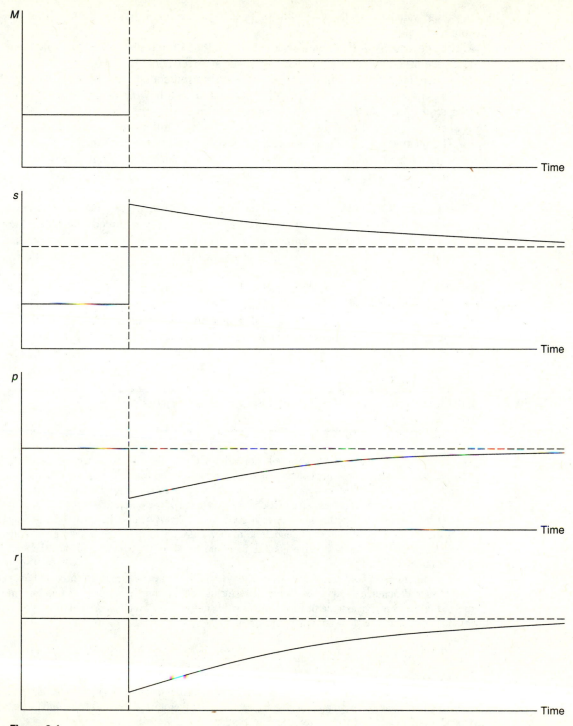

**Figure 9.4**

in absolute value while the denominator is always less than $-s\psi(\partial(M/P)^d/\partial r)P/M$ in absolute value.

The above analysis therefore confirms the result of Dornbusch (1976) that following an increase in the money supply, the exchange rate overshoots its long-run equilibrium value. Therefore, gradual adjustment to the new long-run equilibrium exchange rate involves a period of exchange rate appreciation (a fall in $s$) following the initial jump in $s$. Furthermore, since we have already demonstrated that $p$ and $r$ are algebraically related to $s$, it is easy to plot out the dynamic responses of $p$ and $r$ following an increase in $M$ as well. The relative price of the domestic good instantaneously falls and then slowly rises back to its original value. The domestic interest rate also instantaneously falls before rising back to its original value. Typical time paths $s$, $p$, $r$, and $M$ are depicted in Figure 9.4.

Finally, since dynamic adjustment to the increase in $M$ involves a period of time in which $p$ is below its long-run level and since aggregate supply is directly related to the level of $p$, we see that the dynamic response of this model economy to an increase in the nominal money supply involves a period of temporarily depressed output. This result is in contrast to most closed-economy models in which money is temporarily nonneutral. However, this result of a negative short-run output response to an increase in the nominal money supply is crucially dependent on the assumptions that output is always supply determined and aggregate output supply depends directly on the relative price of the domestic good. It is a simple enough exercise to construct sticky-price open-economy models in which increases in the money supply generate temporary increases in output.

# APPENDIX A: The Domestic Representative Household's Maximization Problem

In this appendix, we recast the analysis of Appendix 1.C for the case in which the domestic representative household consumes both a domestically produced good and a foreign-produced good and holds bonds denominated in both the domestic currency and the foreign currency.

Denote the domestic representative household's purchases of the domestically produced good by $c_d$ and its purchases of the foreign-produced good by $c_d^f$. Let $P$ denote the domestic currency price of the domestic good and let $P^f$ denote the foreign currency price of the foreign good. The domestic currency price of the foreign good is therefore equal to $sP^f$, where $s$ denotes the spot exchange rate.

Domestic residents hold domestic money $M$, domestic equities $E$, domestic government bonds $B$, and foreign-denominated bonds $B^f$. Domestic residents hold no foreign currency and no foreign equities. Furthermore, we assume that the representative household's holdings of domestic money, measured in units of the domestic good, are given by

$$m(t) = \left(\frac{M}{P}\right)^d (y, r) \quad \text{for all } t, \tag{9.A.1}$$

where $y$ denotes real gross domestic product and $r$ denotes the domestic nominal interest rate. We further assume that the representative household expects that $y$ and $r$ will be constant into the indefinite future, and so the representative household must therefore also expect that $m(t) = m^*$ independent of time.

To get a flavor for the most basic complications that arise from international transactions, we abstract from domestic and foreign inflation as well as from anticipated changes in the market value of earning assets. We therefore formally assume that the representative household expects

$$\frac{dr}{dt} = \frac{dr^f}{dt} = \frac{d}{dt}\left(\frac{P^e}{P}\right) = \frac{d}{dt}\left(\frac{sP^f}{P}\right) = \frac{dP}{dt} = \frac{dP^f}{dt} = \frac{ds}{dt} = 0. \tag{9.A.2}$$

We are now ready to write down the representative household's budget constraint. The representative household receives nominal income from wage earnings $W\ell$ plus nominal domestic dividends $P\Pi$ plus nominal domestic interest $B$. The representative household also receives interest income from its holdings of foreign bonds. In domestic currency units, foreign interest income is equal to $sr^fB^f$, where $r^f$ denotes the foreign nominal interest rate.[5] The representative household uses its income to purchase domestic goods $Pc_d$ and foreign goods $sP^fc_d^f$. Any remaining income is used to acquire earning assets (recall that domestic money holdings are constant).

Just as in Appendix 1.C, it is useful to let $f$ denote the real value of the representative household's holdings of earning assets. With the inclusion of foreign-denominated earning assets, we obtain

$$f \equiv \frac{B}{rP} + \frac{\Pi}{r} + \frac{sB^f}{P}. \tag{9.A.3}$$

The representative household's budget constraint may therefore be written as

$$\dot{f} = \frac{1}{rP}\frac{dB}{dt} + \frac{P^e}{P}\frac{dE}{dt} + \frac{s}{P}\frac{dB^f}{dt}$$

$$= w\ell + r\left(\frac{B}{rP} + \frac{\Pi}{r} + \frac{sr^f}{Pr}B^f\right) - c_d - \frac{sP^f}{P}c_d^f - \tau. \tag{9.A.4}$$

If we assume that capital is perfectly mobile, then the real and nominal (recall that $dP/dt = dP^f/dt = ds/dt = 0$) rates of return on foreign and domestic bonds must be equal, so that $r = r^f$. Therefore, the representative household's budget constraint may be rewritten as

$$\dot{f} = rf + w\ell - c_d - \frac{sP^f}{P}c_d^f - \tau. \tag{9.A.5}$$

We are now ready to write down and solve the representative household's intertemporal optimization problem. As noted in Section 9.1, we adopt a single-period utility function of the form

$$U = c_d^\alpha(c_d^f)^{1-\alpha} - h(\ell), \qquad 0 \le \alpha \le 1, \qquad h' > 0, \qquad h'' < 0. \tag{9.A.6}$$

The representative household's problem may now be written as

$$\max_{c_d,c_d^f,\ell} \int_0^\infty [c_d^\alpha(c_d^f)^{1-\alpha} - h(\ell)]e^{-\beta t}\, dt \tag{9.A.7}$$

subject to

$$\dot{f} = rf + w\ell - c_d - \frac{sP^f}{P}c_d^f - \tau, \tag{9.A.8}$$

$$f(0) = \hat{\Omega}_0 - m^*, \tag{9.A.9}$$

$$\hat{\Omega}_0 \equiv \frac{M(0)}{P} + \frac{B(0)}{rP} + \frac{P^eE(0)}{P} + \frac{sB^f(0)}{P}. \tag{9.A.10}$$

---

[5] Recall that $B^f$ denotes the foreign currency *value* of foreign bond holdings, whereas $B$ denotes the *number* of domestic government bonds each paying \$1 per unit of time in interest.

First-order conditions for this maximization problem are given by

$$\frac{\partial H^*}{\partial c_d} = \alpha \left( \frac{c_d^f}{c_d} \right)^{1-\alpha} - \lambda = 0, \tag{9.A.11}$$

$$\frac{\partial H^*}{c_d^f} = (1 - \alpha) \left( \frac{c_d^f}{c_d} \right)^{-\alpha} - \frac{sP^f}{P} \lambda = 0, \tag{9.A.12}$$

$$\frac{\partial H^*}{\partial \ell} = -h' + w\lambda = 0, \tag{9.A.13}$$

$$\dot{\lambda} = -\frac{\partial H^*}{\partial f} + \beta \lambda = -(r - \beta)\lambda \Rightarrow \lambda(t) = \lambda(0)e^{-(r-\beta)t}, \tag{9.A.14}$$

where

$$H^* \equiv [c_d^\alpha (c_d^f)^{1-\alpha} - h(\ell)] + \lambda \left( rf + w\ell - c_d - \frac{sP^f}{P} c_d^f - \tau \right). \tag{9.A.15}$$

Combining equations (9.A.11), (9.A.12), and (9.A.13), we find that

$$\frac{c_d^f}{c_d} = \frac{1 - \alpha}{\alpha} \frac{P}{sP^f}, \tag{9.A.16}$$

$$h'(\ell) = \alpha w \left( \frac{1-\alpha}{\alpha} \right)^{1-\alpha} \left( \frac{P}{sP^f} \right)^{1-\alpha}. \tag{9.A.17}$$

Equation (9.A.17) therefore implicitly defines $\ell^s$ as

$$\ell^s = \ell^s \left( \underset{(+)}{w}, \underset{(+)}{\frac{P}{sP^f}} \right), \tag{9.A.18}$$

just as asserted in Section 9.1. Finally, the differential equation in $\lambda$ can be combined with the transversality condition to obtain

$$c_d(0) = \alpha \left[ \frac{r - \beta}{r} h(\ell^*) + \frac{\beta}{r} z \right], \tag{9.A.19}$$

$$c_d^f(0) = (1 - \alpha) \left[ \frac{r - \beta}{r} h(\ell^*) + \frac{\beta}{r} z \right], \tag{9.A.20}$$

where

$$z \equiv y + \frac{B}{P} + \frac{r^f s B^f}{P} - \tau \tag{9.A.21}$$

and $\ell^*$ solves

$$\ell = \ell^d(w) = \ell^s \left( w, \frac{P}{sP^f} \right). \tag{9.A.22}$$

# REFERENCES

Dornbusch, Rudiger, ''Expectations and Exchange Rate Dynamics,'' *Journal of Political Economy,* December, 1976, 1161–1176.

Driskill, Robert, and Stephen McCafferty, ''Exchange Rate Determination: An Equilibrium Approach With Imperfect Capital Mobility,'' *Journal of International Economics,* November, 1987, 241–261.

# PART THREE

## STOCHASTIC MACROECONOMIC MODELS AND RECENT TOPICS IN MACROECONOMIC THEORY

# Chapter **10**

## An Introduction to Stochastic Macroeconomic Models

The topics of study in Chapters 1–9 are all presented in the context of deterministic models. Alternatively, the analyses of the remaining chapters are almost exclusively presented in the context of stochastic models. One important reason for the study of stochastic models is that such models represent a natural link between macroeconomics and econometrics. Empirical models are traditionally presented in the form of sets of linear equations with stochastic error terms. Such models are routinely used by policy advisors and economic forecasters.

Two topics considered in detail in subsequent chapters can best be analyzed only in stochastic settings. The first topic concerns the effects uncertainty might have on the practical conduct of macroeconomic policymaking. Analyses of policymaking that utilize deterministic models implicitly assume that policymakers have complete knowledge of the workings of the economy (they have an exact and correct model) and that they know precisely the nature of exogenous disturbances and the effects policy actions have on macroeconomic variables. A natural question, therefore, is whether the explicit introduction of uncertainty in such models affects the optimal conduct of policy. In particular, should policymakers simply make their best guess of the effects of disturbances and the effects of policies they utilize to combat these disturbances or should policymaking be tempered in light of such an uncertain environment? We identify situations in which this "certainty equivalence" result does and does not hold. We then go on to analyze policy-makers' likely information sets and how specific informational limitations can affect the proper conduct of policy. Chapter 11 considers this question in the context of a fixed-price macroeconomic model and Chapter 12 expands the analysis to the case of flexible-price models.

The second topic that requires study in a stochastic setting is the analysis of macroeconomic models in which private economic agents have only limited information about their environment. A natural consequence of such a stochastic setting is that it pays for agents to efficiently utilize all relevant information. Maximizing behavior therefore requires that individuals form their expectations "rationally." With rationally formed expectations policymakers must realize that changes in their conduct of policy affect the way private agents form expectations and therefore the way they behave. One key result here is that under certain circumstances optimizing behavior by private agents renders macroeconomic stabilization policy totally impotent.

Policymaking in a macroeconomic model with rational expectations is an important topic in Chapter 12. Informational problems also dominate the analysis of labor contracts in Chapter 13 and the equilibrium macroeconomic modeling strategy presented in Chapter 14. In Chapter 15, the study of real business models is based on an analysis of production planning and consumption-saving choice under uncertainty.

This chapter's focus is primarily on providing an introduction to some of the important concepts and techniques used in later chapters. Section 10.1 discusses discrete-time modeling and the signal extraction problem. Section 10.2 provides a general introduction to the concept of rational expectation. Sections 10.3 and 10.4 then provide some practice in applying the concepts and techniques presented in Sections 10.1 and 10.2.

Section 10.3 replicates the analysis of Muth (1960), which is one of the most heavily cited of the early works on rational expectations and provides good practice in understanding how the techniques of rational expectations should be applied in economic model building. Section 10.3 also demonstrates the use of difference equation methodology for solving for the rational expectations equilibrium. Section 10.4 introduces a very basic stochastic macroeconomic model and demonstrates use of the method of undetermined coefficients as a means for solving for the rational expectations equilibrium. Furthermore, Section 10.4 also introduces the Lucas critique of econometric policy evaluation and the policy ineffectiveness proposition. However, since most of the analysis of Sections 10.3 and 10.4 are provided as practice in using some important tools of modern macroeconomic analysis, they may be skipped without losing much in the way of purely economic insight.

# 10.1 MATHEMATICAL PRELIMINARIES

Before turning our attention to the analysis of stochastic macroeconomic models, it is useful first to develop two mathematical tools that have widespread applicability in work with such models. The first is the difference equation, in particular the first-order linear difference equation, and the second is the least-squares projection with particular reference to the signal extraction problem.

## Lag Operators and Difference Equations

In work with discrete-time stochastic models we routinely utilize dated variables. In such analyses, it is useful to define the backward shift or lag operator as

$$Lx_t = x_{t-1}, \tag{10.1.1}$$

or more generally,

$$L^n x_t = x_{t-n}. \tag{10.1.2}$$

Positive powers of $L$ instruct us to shift the variable multiplied by the operator backward in time by $n$ periods. Similarly, negative powers of $L$ instruct us to shift the variable forward in time by $n$ periods. The operator $L$ works as a standard linear operator and can be manipulated algebraically just like any other constant or variable.

To exemplify the usefulness of the lag operator, consider the first-order difference equation

$$y_t = \lambda y_{t-1} + bx_t + a. \qquad (10.1.3)$$

Use of the lag operator allows this equation to be rewritten as

$$y_t = \lambda L y_t + bx_t + a \qquad (10.1.4)$$

or

$$(1 - \lambda L)y_t = bx_t + a. \qquad (10.1.5)$$

Dividing both sides by $1 - \lambda L$, we obtain

$$y_t = \frac{b}{1 - \lambda L}x_t + \frac{a}{1 - \lambda L}. \qquad (10.1.6)$$

Since $L$ can be treated as an ordinary variable, terms like those that appear above can be solved by the use of the following formula from the analysis of infinite series:

$$\frac{1}{1 - c} = 1 + c + c^2 + c^3 + \cdots \qquad (10.1.7)$$

for $-1 < c < 1$. Applying this formula to our difference equation above, we obtain

$$y_t = b(1 + \lambda L + \lambda^2 L^2 + \cdots)x_t + a(1 + \lambda L + \lambda^2 L^2 + \cdots) \times 1. \qquad (10.1.8)$$

In summation notation, we have

$$y_t = b \sum_{i=0}^{\infty} \lambda^i x_{t-i} + \frac{a}{1 - \lambda} \qquad (10.1.9)$$

as long as $-1 < \lambda < 1$ for a process that started in the indefinite past ($t = -\infty$) or

$$y_t = b \sum_{i=0}^{t+T} \lambda^i x_{t-1} + a\frac{1 - \lambda^{t+T}}{1 - \lambda} \qquad (10.1.10)$$

for a process that began T periods ago. Including a term to reflect an arbitrary ''constant of integration'' to take into account initial conditions, the general solution to the first-order difference equation is given by

$$y_t = \frac{a}{1 - \lambda} + b \sum_{i=0}^{\infty} \lambda^i x_{t-i} + c\lambda^t, \qquad (10.1.11)$$

where $c$ is a constant whose values can be determined by an initial-value or final-value condition.

The above solution technique is only valid if $|\lambda| < 1$ or if the process has been in motion for a finite period of time. However, solutions to the first-order difference equation posed above often have meaning for cases in which $|\lambda| > 1$. In such cases, we simply multiply the numerator and denominator of the above equation by the term $-\lambda^{-1}L^{-1}$ to obtain

$$
\begin{aligned}
y_t &= \frac{-\lambda^{-1}L^{-1}}{1 - \lambda^{-1}L^{-1}}bx_t + \frac{a}{1 - \lambda} \\
&= -\frac{1}{\lambda}L^{-1}\left(1 + \frac{1}{\lambda}L^{-1} + \left(\frac{1}{\lambda}\right)^2 L^{-2} + \left(\frac{1}{\lambda}\right)^3 L^{-3} + \cdots\right)bx_t + \frac{a}{1 - \lambda} \\
&= -\frac{b}{\lambda}L^{-1}\left(x_t + \frac{1}{\lambda}x_{t+1} + \frac{1}{\lambda^2}x_{t+2} + \cdots\right) + \frac{a}{1 - \lambda} \\
&= -b\left(\frac{1}{\lambda}x_{t+1} + \left(\frac{1}{\lambda}\right)^2 x_{t+2} + \left(\frac{1}{\lambda}\right)^3 x_{t+3} \cdots\right) + \frac{a}{1 - \lambda} \\
&= -b\sum_{i=0}^{\infty}\left(\frac{1}{\lambda}\right)^i x_{t+i+1} + \frac{a}{1 - \lambda}.
\end{aligned}
\tag{10.1.12}
$$

Incorporating the constant-of-integration term, we get as a general solution

$$
y_t = \frac{a}{1 - \lambda} - b\sum_{i=0}^{\infty}\left(\frac{1}{\lambda}\right)^i x_{t+i+1} + d\lambda^t.
\tag{10.1.13}
$$

While we have formally considered only solutions to the first-order difference equation, this solution methodology readily generalizes to the case of $n$th order difference equations.[1]

## Least-Squares Projections

In later chapters, we repeatedly encounter problems that require the construction of estimates of the outcome of one random variable based upon observations of the outcomes of related random variables. For example, in Section 11.2, an economic policymaker may wish to infer whether an unanticipated interest rate movement is due to a stochastic shock to the goods market or a stochastic shock to the money market. In Section 13.2, agents wish to disentangle whether an unanticipated price movement is due to a real disturbance or a nominal disturbance. In Section 14.2 agents wish to construct an estimate of appropriate relative price and wealth variables based upon observations of "local" and "global" signals.

These problems are all examples of the signal extraction problem. However, the signal extraction problem is itself an example of a more general class of problems that can be solved by the method of least-squares projections. This general class of problems is similar to regression analysis, but there are a number of important differences. First, we

---

[1]Sargent (1987, Ch. 9) provides an excellent introduction to the analysis of difference equations.

are not interested in estimating parameters, instead we assume full knowledge of the structure of the model. Second, we are interested in optimal estimates of unobservable outcomes rather than in the results of statistical tests.

Consider, for example, estimation of the outcome or a random variable $y$ based upon observations of the random variables $x_1, \ldots, x_n$, which are statistically related to $y$. Assume that we know the first and second moments of $y, x_1, \ldots, x_n$ and that all these moments exist.[2] In particular, assume that we know

$$
\begin{bmatrix}
Eyx_1 & Ex_1^2 & Ex_1x_2 & \cdots & Ex_1x_n \\
Eyx_2 & Ex_2x_1 & Ex_2^2 & \cdots & Ex_2x_n \\
\vdots & \vdots & \vdots & & \vdots \\
Eyx_n & Ex_nx_1 & Ex_nx_2 & \cdots & Ex_n^2
\end{bmatrix}.
\tag{10.1.14}
$$

To make things even simpler, suppose that we confine ourselves to linear estimates of $y$ based on the $x_i$:

$$
\hat{y} = a_0 + a_1x_1 + \cdots + a_nx_n.
\tag{10.1.15}
$$

In particular, consider the minimum-variance estimator $\hat{y}$, the estimator that minimizes $E(y - \hat{y})^2$. Necessary and sufficient conditions for this minimization are given by

$$
E\{[y - (a_0 + a_1x_1 + \cdots + a_nx_n)]x_i\} = 0, \qquad i = 1, \ldots, n
\tag{10.1.16}
$$

or

$$
E[(y - \hat{y})x_i] = 0.
\tag{10.1.17}
$$

The error of estimate $y - y$ must therefore be independent of or *orthogonal* to all the $x_i$. To prove this assertion, we differentiate the expression

$$
J \equiv E\left(y - \sum_{i=0}^{n} a_ix_i\right)^2
\tag{10.1.18}
$$

with respect to $a_k$ to obtain

$$
\frac{\partial J}{\partial a_k} = -2E\left(y - \sum_{i=0}^{n} a_ix_i\right)x_k = 0, \qquad k = 1, \ldots, n
\tag{10.1.19}
$$

which are just the orthogonality conditions given above. These orthogonality conditions may also be rewritten as

$$
Eyx_k - \sum_{i=0}^{n} a_iEx_ix_k = 0,
\tag{10.1.20}
$$

or in matrix notation,

$$
Eyx = (Ex'x)a.
\tag{10.1.21}
$$

---

[2] A more exhaustive treatment of this subject is provided by Sargent (1987, Ch. 10).

We can also rearrange the orthogonality conditions into the familiar least-squares normal equations:

$$
\begin{bmatrix} Ey \\ Eyx_1 \\ Eyx_2 \\ \vdots \\ Eyx_n \end{bmatrix} = \begin{bmatrix} 1 & Ex_1 & Ex_2 & \cdots & Ex_n \\ Ex_1 & Ex_1^2 & Ex_1x_2 & & Ex_1x_n \\ Ex_2 & Ex_1x_2 & Ex_2^2 & & Ex_2x_n \\ \vdots & \vdots & \vdots & & \vdots \\ Ex_n & Ex_1x_n & Ex_2x_n & \cdots & Ex_n^2 \end{bmatrix} \begin{bmatrix} a_0 \\ a_1 \\ a_2 \\ \vdots \\ a_n \end{bmatrix},
\tag{10.1.22}
$$

or

$$
\begin{bmatrix} a_0 \\ a_1 \\ \vdots \\ a_n \end{bmatrix} = [Ex_ix_j]^{-1}[Eyx_k].
\tag{10.1.23}
$$

For the two-variable case we obtain

$$
\begin{bmatrix} Ey \\ Eyx \end{bmatrix} = \begin{bmatrix} 1 & Ex \\ Ex & Ex^2 \end{bmatrix} \begin{bmatrix} a_0 \\ a_1 \end{bmatrix}.
\tag{10.1.24}
$$

Use of Cramer's rule generates the following:

$$
a_0 = \frac{EyEx^2 - EyxEx}{Ex^2 - (Ex)^2} = \frac{Ey[Ex^2 - (Ex)^2] - Ex(Eyx - ExEy)}{Ex^2 - (Ex)^2},
\tag{10.1.25}
$$

$$
a_1 = \frac{Eyx - EyEx}{Ex^2 - (Ex)^2}.
\tag{10.1.26}
$$

Rearranging, we find that

$$
a_0 = Ey - a_1Ex,
\tag{10.1.27}
$$

$$
a_1 = \frac{E[(y - Ey)(x - Ex)]}{E(x - Ex)^2},
\tag{10.1.28}
$$

and so

$$
\hat{y} = Ey + a_1(x - Ex).
\tag{10.1.29}
$$

The constructed estimate $\hat{y}$ is referred to as the projection of $y$ on $x$ and is denoted $P(y|1, x)$. If $y$ and $x$ are jointly normally distributed, the projection of $y$ on $x$ gives the conditional expected value of $y$.

## The Signal Extraction Problem

The theory of projections can now be used to construct an estimate of a signal contaminated with noise. As noted above, the signal extraction problem has many applications in macroeconomics, and we shall encounter several of these applications in later chapters. One example of an application of the technique would be the estimation of relative price signals contaminated by inflationary ''noise.''[3] For example, suppose we wish to estimate $s$ but observe

$$x = s + n, \tag{10.1.30}$$

where $E(s) = E(n) = E(sn) = 0$, $E(s^2) = \sigma_s^2$, $E(n^2) = \sigma_n^2$. In the above notation $y$ corresponds to $s$ and $x$ is exactly as above. Therefore, we have

$$Ex^2 = \sigma_s^2 + \sigma_n^2 \quad \text{and} \quad Eyx = E[s(s + n)] = \sigma_s^2. \tag{10.1.31}$$

The *projection* of $s$ on $x$ is denoted as

$$P[s \,|\, 1, x] = a_0 + a_1 x, \tag{10.1.32}$$

where $a_0$ and $a_1$ are given by the least-squares normal equations above. Plugging in the assumed statistical properties of $s$ and $n$, we obtain

$$a_0 = 0, \qquad a_1 = \frac{\sigma_s^2}{\sigma_s^2 + \sigma_n^2}. \tag{10.1.33}$$

The projection of $s$ on a constant and $x$ is therefore given by

$$\hat{s} = \frac{\sigma_s^2}{\sigma_s^2 + \sigma_n^2}(s + n) = \frac{\sigma_s^2}{\sigma_s^2 + \sigma_n^2}x. \tag{10.1.34}$$

If the noise component $n$ of the observation $s + n$ has very little variance, the best estimate of $s$ is equal to the observation. If on the other hand the variance of the noise is very large compared to the variance of the signal, our best estimate of $s$ is closer to its unconditional mean of zero ($Es = 0$).

## 10.2 RATIONAL EXPECTATIONS AND ECONOMIC THEORY

The concept of rational expectations in economic modeling has been the instigator of considerable controversy. Much of this controversy has centered on specific implications of rational expectations *in combination with* certain other controversial assumptions. However, the logical foundation of the hypothesis of rationally formed expectations is well within the tradition of other typical assumptions about maximizing behavior. The basic idea is that when information is important to economic agents, such agents are likely to come to learn the probability distributions of the random variables that are important to their decision making.

More formally, the assumption of rational expectations requires that economic agents act as if they know the conditional probability distributions of the relevant random variables given all information available to them. Any other expectational assumption implies that agents are systematically wrong. Implications of economic theory based on such systematic misinformation should therefore be viewed with some skepticism. Viewed in

---

[3] An important early treatment of this problem is provided by Muth (1960).

this light, rational expectations may be viewed as a neutral assumption to be abandoned only when a given alternative is clearly preferable for the specific situation.

However, there are also some valid reasons for questioning the underlying validity of rational expectations as an approximation of economic agents' behavior. While it may well be reasonable to assume that agents have enough information about their endowments and relative prices to solve deterministic maximization problems, it is less clear whether agents are likely to have full information about probability density functions. In particular, precise information about the probability density function of a random variable requires an infinite number of observations of realizations from that random variable's distribution. The assumption that agents possess such information may therefore be a realistic assumption only when looking at a stochastic steady state whose structure never changes.

Such a situation is not likely to be observed in practice. Changes in the behavior of policymakers and other economic agents and changes in the stochastic structure of nature make agents' information about their environment obsolete. Although such considerations are very hard to model, the spirit of such objections to the rational expectations approach should inspire some caution in the application of the rational expectations assumption to the modeling of economic phenomenon.[4]

One important application of rational expectations is in the determination of financial asset prices. One example would be the determination of equity share prices. If all asset traders have the same information, their trading behavior would force the prices of each equity share to the point where all shares have the same risk-adjusted expected yield.[5] Therefore, any new information about the profitability of a specific firm would be fully and immediately reflected in the price of its shares. Such information therefore does *not* lead traders to buy shares in this particular firm over others because this information has already been incorporated in the price of the firm's shares. Equity prices therefore incorporate all information about a given firm's expected future earnings.

## Examples of Rationally Formed Expectations

Consider a series of stochastic processes for the (logarithm of the) price level. We may then compute the rationally expected price levels and rates of inflation. As a prelude, first look at the relationship between price levels and the rate of inflation. The rate of inflation is defined as

$$\pi_t = \frac{P_t - P_{t-1}}{P_{t-1}}. \tag{10.2.1}$$

Therefore, we can also write

$$\frac{P_t}{P_{t-1}} = 1 + \pi_t. \tag{10.2.2}$$

---

[4]Friedman (1979) summarizes many of these objections to the use of rational expectations. Taylor (1975) models the convergence to a steady state in which agents possess rational expectations.

[5]See, e.g., Samuelson (1965).

Taking logarithms, we obtain

$$p_t - p_{t-1} = \ln(1 + \pi_t) \simeq \pi_t \quad \text{for small } \pi. \tag{10.2.3}$$

In what follows we take the approximation of $\pi_t = p_t - p_{t-1}$ as sufficiently close to being exact.

Once the logarithm-of-price process has been specified, computation of the expected price level and the expected rate of inflation is straightforward. In particular, consider the following price processes:

1. $p_t = \bar{p} + \varepsilon_t, \bar{p}$ a constant.
2. $p_t = p_{t-1} + \varepsilon_t$.
3. $p_t = p_{t-1} + \mu + \varepsilon_t, \mu$ a constant.
4. $p_t = (1 + \rho)p_{t-1} - \rho p_{t-2} + \mu + \varepsilon_t, 0 < \rho < 1, \mu$, constants.

In each case we assume that $\varepsilon_t$ is a zero-mean, serially uncorrelated random variable.

If agents are aware of the above stochastic processes, they may use this information in calculating expectations. Let us assume that agents are interested in computing expected (logarithm) price levels and inflation rates for period $t$ based upon all information available through period $t - 1$. The expected (logarithm) price level is simply given by $E_{t-1}p_t$, where $E_{t-1}$ represents the expectations operator conditional upon the information set $\{p_{t-1}, p_{t-2}, \ldots, E(\varepsilon_t), \text{Var}(\varepsilon_t)\}$. The expected inflation rate is simply $E_{t-1}(p_t - p_{t-1}) = E_{t-1}p_t - p_{t-1}$. The table below gives expected prices, inflation rates, and expectational errors for the four processes.

| Process | Expected price, $E_{t-1}p_t$ | Expectational error, $p_t - E_{t-1}p_t$ | Expected inflation $E_{t-1}\pi_t = E_{t-1}p_t - p_{t-1}$ |
|---|---|---|---|
| 1 | $\bar{p}$ | $\varepsilon_t$ | 0 |
| 2 | $p_{t-1}$ | $\varepsilon_t$ | 0 |
| 3 | $p_{t-1} + \mu$ | $\varepsilon_t$ | $\mu$ |
| 4 | $(1 + \rho)p_{t-1} - \rho p_{t-2} + \mu$ | $\varepsilon_t$ | $\rho(p_{t-1} - p_{t-2}) + \mu = \rho\pi_{t-1} + \mu$ |

One of the key features of rational expectations concerns properties of expectational errors. Such expectational errors are always uncorrelated with any variable known by the economic agent constructing the estimate. That is, expectational errors are always white noise. If this is not the case, some useful bit of information is being ignored in the formation of the expectation.

To gain some early insight into the way in which the assumption of rational expectations dramatically altered macroeconomic thinking, let us briefly consider how the assumption of rational expectations affects the behavior of the employment and output model of Section 5.2. In that model, movements in employment and output are due to shifts in the labor supply function. Such shifts in the labor supply function are due to movements in the expected price level relative to the actual price level. In particular, suppose that output supply is positively related to $p_t - E_{t-1}p_t$ as a proxy for $P/P^e$.[6] From the table above, we see that for any of the stochastic price processes under consideration, equilibrium movements in employment and output will be described by a white-noise stochastic process independent of the nature of the stochastic process generating the rate of inflation. Any observation of a "Phillips curve" would therefore, of necessity, be a statistical artifact if expectations are rational and movements in $P/P^e$ are the sole source of employment and output fluctuations.

# 10.3 RATIONAL EXPECTATIONS: A MICROECONOMIC EXAMPLE

In order to get some practice using the tools of Section 10.1 and the concept of rational expectations presented in Section 10.2, it is useful first to consider an important microeconomic application of the concept. This exercise is useful because the underlying properties of microeconomic models are often more familiar than the properties of macroeconomic models and because the results of such exercises are generally less controversial. Furthermore, the specific model we examine is one of the most heavily cited early examples of an application of rational expectations.

## Muth's Model of Inventory Speculation

An important early contribution to the literature on rational expectations is a paper by Muth (1961) that applies the technique to a model of the market for an agricultural commodity. In this analysis, current demand for the commodity is assumed to be a linear function of the current price $p_t$:

$$D_t = -\beta p_t. \tag{10.3.1}$$

The supply of the commodity depends directly on the amount planted plus a random disturbance that represents the influences of weather and other exogenous factors. In the absence of a futures market,[7] the amount planted depends on the one-period-ahead forecast of the market price, $p_t^e$. We therefore write

$$S_t = \gamma p_t^e + u_t, \tag{10.3.2}$$

where $u_t$ is serially uncorrelated with $E(u_t) = 0$, $E(u_t^2) = \sigma_u^2$.

In addition to primary demanders and suppliers, Muth posits the existence of speculators who attempt to profit from expected changes in the market price of the commodity. These speculators buy the commodity in period $t$ at price $p_t$ and hope to sell the commodity for a profit in period $t + 1$ at price $p_{t+1}$.

Suppose that these speculators maximize the expected value of a one-period utility function $U$ defined over the level of speculative profits. The utility value of speculators is

---

[6]The motivation for such an aggregate supply function in a stochastic setting is provided in Section 10.4.

[7]A futures market is easily incorporated into the model without changing its basic characteristics. See, e.g., Driskill, McCafferty, and Sheffrin (1988).

therefore given by

$$U = U[I_t(p_{t+1}^e - p_t)],$$ (10.3.3)

where $I_t$ represents the speculative inventory of the commodity at the end of period $t$ to be carried over and sold in period $t + 1$.

Expanding the above expression in a Taylor series and neglecting terms higher than second order, we obtain

$$U \simeq U(0) + U'(0)I_t(p_{t+1}^e - p_t) + \tfrac{1}{2}U''(0)I_t^2(p_{t+1}^e - p_t)^2.$$ (10.3.4)

Expected utility of speculators is therefore given by

$$E(U) \simeq U(0) + U'(0)I_t(p_{t+1}^e - p_t) + \tfrac{1}{2}U''(0)I_t^2[\sigma_{t,1}^2 + (p_{t+1}^e - p_t)^2],$$ (10.3.5)

where $\sigma_{t,1}^2$ represents the one-period-ahead forecast variance of $p_t$. Maximization of the above expression with respect to $I_t$ yields the first-order condition

$$I_t = \frac{-U'(0)}{U''(0)[\sigma_{t,1}^2 + (p_{t+1}^e - p_t)^2]}(p_{t+1}^e - p_t).$$ (10.3.6)

If we further assume that the square of the expected price change is small in comparison to the price variance, then we may approximate the above expression as

$$I_t \simeq -\frac{U'(0)}{U''(0)\sigma_{t,1}^2}(p_{t+1}^e - p_t) \equiv \frac{K}{\sigma_{t,1}^2}(p_{t+1}^e - p_t) \equiv \alpha(p_{t+1}^e - p_t),$$ (10.3.7)

where $K$ is an inverse measure of speculator risk aversion.

Now combining the purchases and sales of speculators to the supplies and demands of primary market participants, we derive the period $t$ market-clearing condition

$$I_t + D_t = I_{t-1} + S_t.$$ (10.3.8)

At this point we also follow Muth in substituting for market participants' price expectations $p_t^e$ the mathematically expected one-period-ahead price forecast conditional on all information available at the time the forecast is made. That is, we assume that

$$p_t^e = E_{t-1}p_t,$$ (10.3.9)

where $E_{t-1}$ denotes the expectation operator contingent upon the information set $\Omega_{t-1} \equiv \{p_{t-1}, p_{t-2}, \ldots\}$.

Now plugging the supply function, the primary demand function, and the speculative demand function into the market-clearing condition, we obtain

$$E_t p_{t+1} - p_t - E_{t-1}p_t + p_{t-1} = \frac{\gamma}{\alpha}E_{t-1}p_t + \frac{1}{\alpha}u_t + \frac{\beta}{\alpha}p_t.$$ (10.3.10)

This equilibrium condition is valid for any arbitrarily selected period of time. Looking $j$ periods into the future, we therefore obtain

$$E_{t+j}p_{t+j+1} - \left(1 + \frac{\beta}{\alpha}\right)p_{t+j} - \left(1 + \frac{\gamma}{\alpha}\right)E_{t+j-1}p_{t+j} + p_{t+j-1} = \frac{1}{\alpha}u_t.$$ (10.3.11)

Taking the expected value of the above expression with respect to $\Omega_{t-1}$ and recalling that $E_{t-1}E_{t+k}x_t = E_{t-1}x_t$ and $E_{t-1}u_{t+k} = 0$ for all $k \geq 0$, we obtain

$$E_{t-1}p_{t+j+1} - \left(2 + \frac{\beta + \gamma}{\alpha}\right)E_{t-1}p_{t+j} + E_{t-1}p_{t+j-1} = 0. \tag{10.3.12}$$

This expression is a difference equation in the expectational terms. A necessary condition for the price expectational process to be rational is that this process be governed by the solution to this difference equation. Use of the lag operator allows the substitutions

$$E_{t-1}p_{t+j+1} = L^{-1}E_{t-1}p_{t+j}, \tag{10.3.13}$$

$$E_{t-1}p_{t+j-1} = LE_{t-1}p_{t+j}. \tag{10.3.14}$$

We therefore obtain

$$\left[L^2 - \left(2 + \frac{\beta + \gamma}{\alpha}\right)L + 1\right]E_{t-1}p_{t+j} = 0. \tag{10.3.15}$$

Therefore, either we require that $E_{t-1}p_{t+j} \equiv 0$ for all $j$ or we require that the quadratic expression in $L$ be identically equal to zero. Therefore, a nontrivial solution requires that

$$L^2 - \left(2 + \frac{\beta + \gamma}{\alpha}\right)L + 1 = 0. \tag{10.3.16}$$

Denote the roots of this quadratic equation by $\lambda_i$, $i = 1, 2$. A result presented in Chapter 4 on such equations requires that

$$\lambda_1\lambda_2 = 1 \quad \text{and} \quad \lambda_1 + \lambda_2 = 2 + \frac{\beta + \gamma}{\alpha}. \tag{10.3.17}$$

Furthermore, the general solution to a homogeneous difference equation of this type is given by[8]

$$E_{t-1}p_{t+j} = c\lambda_1^j + d\lambda_2^j, \tag{10.3.18}$$

with $c$ and $d$ determined by an initial-value condition. In particular, we know that

$$E_{t-1}p_{t-1} = p_{t-1}, \tag{10.3.19}$$

and so for $j = -1$, we obtain

$$p_{t-1} = c\lambda_1^{-1} + d\lambda_2^{-1}. \tag{10.3.20}$$

Finally, since $\lambda_1\lambda_2 = 1$ and since $\lambda_1 + \lambda_2 > 2$, it must be true that one root, $\lambda_i$, is greater than 1 and the other root, $\lambda_i$, is less than 1. The above equation in $E_{t-1}p_{t+j}$ can therefore be nonexplosive only if the constant ($c$ or $d$) corresponding to the greater root is identically equal to zero.

Now define $\lambda \equiv \lambda_1 < \lambda_2$, where $\lambda_1$ is arbitrarily selected as the smaller of the two roots. In this case we require that $d \equiv 0$, and therefore, for $j = 1$, the above equation becomes

---

[8]See, e.g., Sargent (1987, Ch. 9).

$$E_{t-1}p_{t-1} = p_{t-1} = c\lambda^{-1},$$
(10.3.21)

and so

$$c = \lambda p_{t-1}.$$
(10.3.22)

Therefore, the rational price expectation process is given by

$$E_{t-1}p_{t+j} = \lambda^{j+1}p_{t-1},$$
(10.3.23)

where the root $\lambda$ solves

$$\lambda = 1 + \frac{\beta + \gamma}{2\alpha} - \frac{\eta + \gamma}{2\alpha}\left(1 + \frac{4\alpha}{\beta + \gamma}\right)^{1/2}.$$
(10.3.24)

The rational expectation solution also allows us to substitute

$$E_{t-1}p_t = \lambda p_{t-1} \quad \text{and} \quad E_t p_{t+1} = \lambda p_t$$
(10.3.25)

into the market-clearing condition to obtain

$$-(1 - \lambda)p_t + (1 - \lambda)p_{t-1} = \frac{\gamma\lambda}{\alpha}p_{t-1} + \frac{b}{\alpha}p_t + \frac{u_t}{\alpha}.$$
(10.3.26)

Collecting terms, we therefore find that

$$p_t = \frac{\alpha(1 - \lambda) - \gamma\lambda}{\beta + \alpha(1 - \lambda)}p_{t-1} - \frac{u_t}{\beta + \alpha(1 - \lambda)}.$$
(10.3.27)

Rationality therefore also requires that

$$\lambda = \frac{\alpha(1 - \lambda) - \gamma\lambda}{\beta + \alpha(1 - \lambda)}$$
(10.3.28)

since

$$E_{t-1}p_t = \frac{\alpha(1 - \lambda) - \gamma\lambda}{\beta + \alpha(1 - \lambda)}p_{t-1}$$

from above. Rearrangement of the above equation allows it to be expressed as

$$\lambda - \left(2 + \frac{\beta + \gamma}{\alpha}\right)\lambda + 1 = 0,$$
(10.3.29)

which is just the quadratic equation that the equilibrium value of $\lambda$ has already been shown to satisfy. In any event, the important point to recognize is that for $\lambda$ satisfying the rational expectations condition, we find that

$$p_t^e = \lambda p_{t-1} = E_{t-1}p_t.$$
(10.3.30)

## Comparative Statics in Rational Expectations Models

In this section, we preview important results presented in Lucas (1976). Lucas argues that in performing comparative statics exercises in models involving expectational variables, it is not, in general, correct to hold fixed the rules by which agents form their expectations.

In particular, in the model of Muth (1961), it is not correct to view $\lambda$ as a fixed parameter of agents' (unchanging) rule for forming the expectations $p_t^e$ and $p_{t+1}^e$.

As a prelude to the kinds of considerations involved in this issue, let us first recall that the parameter $\alpha$ must be consistent with

$$\alpha = \frac{K}{\sigma_{t,1}^2}. \tag{10.3.31}$$

However, from the reduced-form expression for $p_t$ derived in the previous section, we know that the one-period-ahead forecast variance for $p_t$ is given by

$$\sigma_{t,1}^2 = \frac{\sigma_u^2}{[\beta + \alpha(1 - \lambda)]^2}, \tag{10.3.32}$$

and so the value of $\alpha$ must be consistent with

$$\alpha = \frac{K[\beta + \alpha(1 - \lambda)]^2}{\sigma_u^2}. \tag{10.3.33}$$

But we have already shown that $\lambda$ (and hence $\alpha$) must also satisfy

$$\lambda = \frac{\alpha(1 - \lambda) - \gamma\lambda}{\beta + \alpha(1 - \lambda)}. \tag{10.3.34}$$

We therefore have two simultaneous equations (10.3.33) and (10.3.34) that must be solved in order to express the equilibrium values of $\alpha$ and $\lambda$ as functions of the underlying parameters $\beta$, $\gamma$, $K$, and $\sigma_u^2$.

As a useful intermediate step, note that the original quadratic equation in $\lambda$ and $\alpha$ may also be written in either of the following two alternate forms:

$$\alpha = \frac{(\beta + \gamma)\lambda}{(1 - \lambda)^2} \quad \text{and} \quad \beta + \alpha(1 - \lambda) = \frac{\beta + \gamma\lambda}{1 - \lambda}. \tag{10.3.35}$$

We now rewrite the first half of equation (10.3.35) and plug the second half of equation (10.3.35) into the relationship between $\alpha$ and $\sigma_u^2$ (equation (10.3.33)) to obtain the following two independent relationships between $\alpha$ and $\lambda$:

$$\alpha(1 - \lambda)^2 = (\beta + \gamma)\lambda \quad \text{(RE)}, \tag{10.3.36}$$

$$\alpha(1 - \lambda)^2 = \frac{K}{\sigma_u^2}(\beta + \gamma\lambda)^2 \quad \text{(SB)}. \tag{10.3.37}$$

The first of these expressions is denoted RE as a reminder that it is a necessary condition for the expectational process to be rational. The second expression is denoted SB as a reminder that it is a transformation of the first-order condition for optimal speculative behavior.

The equations RE and SB are graphed in Figure 10.1 as functions of $\lambda$. While McCafferty and Driskill (1980) demonstrate that this model may possess no equilibrium, a single equilibrium, or two equilibria, Figure 10.1 is drawn on the assumption that a single equilibrium exists. For this to be the case, it must be true that the RE curve intersect the SB curve from below on the interval [0, 1]. For this to be the case, we require that

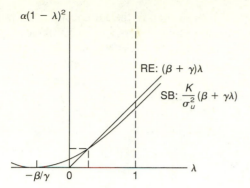

**Figure 10.1**

$RE(1) > SB(1)$. For the remainder of the analysis we adopt the assumption that a single equilibrium exists.

We may therefore be assured that

$$1 > \frac{2K\gamma}{\sigma_u^2}. \tag{10.3.38}$$

As a corollary, we are also guaranteed that

$$\beta + \gamma > \frac{2K\gamma}{\sigma_u^2}(\beta + \gamma\lambda) \quad \text{for all } 0 \le \lambda \le 1, \tag{10.3.39}$$

which is sufficient for the slope of the RE curve to exceed the slope of the SB curve at the equilibrium value of $\lambda$.

We are now ready to perform comparative statics experiments in this model. One important question in models such as this one is whether speculation is stabilizing or destabilizing. This general question is usually interpreted as inquiring as to whether an increase in speculative activity raises or lowers the conditional variance of $p_t$. Recall that the one-period-ahead forecast variance of $p_t$ is given by

$$\sigma_{t,1}^2 = \frac{\sigma_u^2}{[\beta + \alpha(1 - \lambda)]^2}. \tag{10.3.40}$$

A casual approach to measuring the volume of speculative activity might identify the parameter $\alpha$ as an index of the extent of such activity. This approach is followed by Muth (1960). A more careful approach recognizes that $\alpha$ is an endogenous variable and therefore may not properly be treated as an exogenous variable in comparative statics exercises. A more appropriate procedure identifies exogenous changes in the volume of speculation with changes in $K$, a measure of speculators' taste for risk bearing. Shift parameters in utility or production functions like $K$ are often referred to as ''deep parameters'' of taste and technology.[9]

---

[9]See Lucas and Sargent (1978) and Sargent (1981) for detailed discussions about the distinction between exogenous and endogenous variables in economic models.

Referring back to the original specification of the SB equation, it would appear that since $\alpha = K/\sigma_{t,1}^2$, an increase in the taste for risk parameter $K$ would lead to an automatic increase in $\alpha$. It would further appear that since $\sigma_{t,1}^2 = \sigma_u^2/[\beta + \alpha(1 - \lambda)]^2$, an increase in $\alpha$ unambiguously lowers $\sigma_{t,1}^2$. However, at least in principle, this may not be the case. As we demonstrate below, an increase in $K$ also results in an increase in $\lambda$. Since the equilibrium value of $\lambda$ always satisfies the inequality $0 \le \lambda \le 1$, the induced increase in $\lambda$ tends to *increase* $\sigma_{t,1}^2$.

More formally, differentiating the above expression for $\sigma_{t,1}^2$, we find that

$$\frac{d\sigma_{t,1}^2}{dK} = \frac{-2\sigma_u^2}{[\beta + \alpha(1 - \lambda)]^3}\left[(1 - \lambda)\frac{d\alpha}{dK} - \alpha\frac{d\lambda}{dK}\right]. \tag{10.3.41}$$

In order to evaluate this expression, we must first perform comparative statics on the system of equations RE and SB. Differentiating these expressions with respect to $\alpha$, $\lambda$, and $K$, we obtain

$$\begin{bmatrix} (1 - \lambda)^2 & -2\alpha(1 - \lambda) - (\beta + \gamma) \\ (1 - \lambda)^2\sigma_u^2 & -2[\alpha(1 - \lambda)^2\sigma_u^2 + \gamma(\beta + \gamma\lambda)K] \end{bmatrix}\begin{bmatrix} d\alpha \\ d\lambda \end{bmatrix}$$
$$= \begin{bmatrix} 0 \\ (\beta + \gamma\lambda)^2\,dK \end{bmatrix}. \tag{10.3.42}$$

Application of Cramer's rule allows derivation of

$$\frac{d\alpha}{dK} = \frac{1}{\Delta}(\beta + \gamma\lambda)^2[2\alpha(1 - \lambda) + (\beta + \gamma)] > 0, \tag{10.3.43}$$

$$\frac{d\lambda}{dK} = \frac{1}{\Delta}(1 - \lambda)^2(\beta + \gamma\lambda)^2 > 0, \tag{10.3.44}$$

where

$$\Delta \equiv (1 - \lambda)^2[(\beta + \gamma)\sigma_u^2 - 2\gamma K(\beta + \gamma\lambda)] > 0. \tag{10.3.45}$$

We are assured that $\Delta > 0$ as long as the equilibrium of the model is unique and the RE and SB curves are configured as they are depicted in Figure 10.1.

Now combining the above expressions for $d\alpha/dK$ and $d\lambda/dK$ with the earlier expression for $d\sigma_{t,1}^2/dK$, we find that

$$\frac{d\sigma_{t,1}^2}{dK} = \frac{-2\sigma_u^2}{[\beta + \alpha(1 - \lambda)]^3\Delta}(\beta + \gamma\lambda)^2(1 - \lambda)[\alpha(1 - \lambda) + (\beta + \gamma)] < 0. \tag{10.3.46}$$

We have therefore demonstrated that an increase in speculators' taste for risk unambiguously reduces the one-period-ahead price forecast variance. Since this result would also obtain with both $\alpha$ and $\lambda$ viewed as exogenous variables, this exercise may give the misleading impression that careful specification of the endogeneity of expectations in economic models is not important. Such precision may even be viewed as theoretical nitpicking. However, the attention or inattention to such theoretical niceties turns out to make a dramatic difference in many of the more important characteristics of macroeconomic models. Such important questions as whether even short-run trade-offs between unemployment and inflation exist and whether routine stabilization policies have any effect on the behavior of production and employment often turn on whether the underlying model is carefully specified or not with regard to the way agents form expectations and the way in which equilibrium is characterized.

# 10.4 RATIONAL EXPECTATIONS: A MACROECONOMIC EXAMPLE

We next turn our attention to some examples of the application of rational expectations techniques in macroeconomic models. Such macroeconomic models often include expectational variables like the expected real wage and the expected rate of inflation. This section outlines procedures for endogenizing these expectations and previews some important differences between the rational expectations and previews some important differences between the rational expectations models of subsequent chapters and the adaptive expectations models of Chapters 5–8. Furthermore, the analysis of this section provides a helpful introduction to the method of undetermined coefficients, which is often useful in solving rational expectations macromodels.

## Expectations and Employment Fluctuations

In Section 5.2, we studied equilibrium in an individual labor market characterized by incomplete information as[10]

$$\ell^d(w) = \ell^s\left(w, \frac{P}{P^e}\right) \Rightarrow w = w\left(\frac{P}{P^e}\right), \qquad \frac{dw}{d(P/P^e)} < 0, \tag{10.4.1}$$

where   $\ell^d$ = labor demand
$\ell^s$ = labor supply
$w$ = real wage
$P$ = price level
$P^e$ = expected price level

Combining the above equilibrium condition with an output expression derived from the production function

$$y = \Phi(\ell, \overline{K}), \tag{10.4.2}$$

we obtain

$$y = \Phi\left[\ell^d\left(\frac{P}{P^e}\right), \overline{K}\right]. \tag{10.4.3}$$

We now adopt the following functional form for this relationship:

$$e^y = e^{y*}\left(\frac{P}{P^e}\right)^\beta, \quad \text{where } y* \equiv \Phi[\ell^d(w(1), \overline{K}]. \tag{10.4.4}$$

---

[10]We temporarily suppress the effect of the interest rate on the level of labor supply.

The term $y*$ has the interpretation of the normal, or "natural," level of output. Taking logarithms, we obtain

$$y = y* + \beta(p - p^e), \tag{10.4.5}$$

where $p$ and $p^e$ denote the logarithms of the price level and expected price level.

## A Stochastic Macroeconomic Supply Function

The supply schedule above motivates a log-linear relationship between output and price expectation errors. However, until an information structure is specified, the analysis is incomplete. One common way to close the output-employment sector of the model is the so-called island paradigm popularized by Phelps (1970, Introduction), among others.

Following Lucas (1973), we posit a large number of informationally distinct local markets. There is no contemporaneous trade across markets (no interisland trade), and therefore the price of the single good in each market $p_{it}$ is, in general, different. What producers (labor suppliers) are interested in is purchasing power across goods in general (they expect to travel to other islands in the future), and so they deflate nominal quantities by the expected aggregate (logarithm) price $p_t$. With the local wage based on the local output price $p_{it}$, the local supply will be based on $(p_{it} - p_{it}^e)$, where $p_{it}^e$ is the local expectation of the current price level $p_t$. Therefore, at the local level we obtain

$$y_{it} = y_{it}^* + \beta(p_{it} - p_{it}^e). \tag{10.4.6}$$

Each agent in the macroeconomy has information on all one-period lagged aggregate macroeconomic variables as well as all current local (island-specific) information. The current aggregate price level is given by a common one-period-ahead expected price $E_{t-1}p_t$ plus an economywide current disturbance $\varepsilon$. Therefore the aggregate price level is given by

$$p_t = E_{t-1}p_t + \varepsilon_t, \tag{10.4.7}$$

where $\varepsilon_t$ is white noise. We assume that $\varepsilon_t$ is normally distributed with zero mean and variance $\sigma_\varepsilon^2$.

At the local level, prices are equal to the current aggregate price $p_t$ plus a purely local random disturbance $z_{it}$, where $z_{it}$ is normally distributed with zero mean and variance $\sigma_z^2$. All local disturbances are uncorrelated with each other and with the current aggregate disturbance. Taking the limit as $N$, the number of markets, approaches infinity, we find that

$$\lim_{N \to +\infty} \frac{1}{N} \sum_{i=1}^{N} z_{it} = 0. \tag{10.4.8}$$

The local price in each market is given by

$$p_{it} = p_t + z_{it}. \tag{10.4.9}$$

The assumption of a continuum of markets guarantees that

$$p_t \equiv \lim_{N \to +\infty} \frac{1}{N} \sum_{i=1}^{N} p_{it} = \lim_{N \to +\infty} \frac{1}{N} \sum_{i=1}^{N} (p_t + z_{it}) = p_t, \tag{10.4.10}$$

and so the specification of the local and aggregate price levels is consistent.

With the unconditional expectation of the aggregate price level denoted by $E_{t-1}p_t$, each agent observes a local price given by

$$p_{it} = E_{t-1}p_t + \varepsilon_t + z_{it}. \tag{10.4.11}$$

From this observation the agent wishes to make the best (rational) estimate of the current aggregate price $p_t$. Since $p_{it} - E_{t-1}p_t = \varepsilon_t + z_{it}$ is observable and since the agent needs to estimate $\varepsilon_t$ to estimate $p_t = E_{t-1} + \varepsilon_t$, he or she must calculate

$$E[\varepsilon_t \mid \varepsilon_t + z_{it}]. \tag{10.4.12}$$

As noted in Section 10.1, with normally distributed random variables, this expectation is given by

$$E[\varepsilon_t \mid \varepsilon_t + z_t] = \frac{\sigma_\varepsilon^2}{\sigma_\varepsilon^2 + \sigma_z^2}(\varepsilon_t + z_t) = \frac{\sigma_\varepsilon^2}{\sigma_\varepsilon^2 + \sigma_z^2}(p_{it} - E_{t-1}p_t). \tag{10.4.13}$$

Now define $\theta = [\sigma_\varepsilon^2/(\sigma_\varepsilon^2 + \sigma_z^2)]$. The best estimate of the aggregate price level for an agent in market $i$ is given by

$$p_{it}^e = E_{t-1}p_t + \theta[p_{it} - E_{t-1}p_t], \tag{10.4.14}$$

or

$$p_{it}^e = \theta p_{it} + (1 - \theta)E_{t-1}p_t. \tag{10.4.15}$$

Local aggregate supply is therefore given by

$$y_{it} = y_{it}^* + \beta(1 - \theta)(p_{it} - E_{t-1}p_t). \tag{10.4.16}$$

Now aggregating across markets we get an average output level given by

$$y_t = \frac{1}{N} \sum_{i=1}^{N} y_{it}^* + \beta(1 - \theta) \lim_{N \to +\infty} \left[ \frac{1}{N} \sum_{i=1}^{N} (p_{it} - E_{t-1}p_t) \right] \tag{10.4.17}$$

or with $y_t^* \equiv \lim_{N \to +\infty} [(1/N) \sum_{i=1}^{N} y_{it}^*]$, we obtain

$$y_t = y_t^* + \beta(1 - \theta)(p_t - E_{t-1}p_t). \tag{10.4.18}$$

This aggregate supply schedule is often referred to as the *Lucas supply function*.

## Theoretical and Empirical Phillips Curves

Defining $\beta^* \equiv \beta(1 - \theta)$, the aggregate Lucas supply function is given by

$$y_t = y_t^* + \beta^*(p_t - E_{t-1}p_t), \tag{10.4.19}$$

where $y_t^*$ represents the possibly time-varying, "normal" level of output and $p_t - E_{t-1}p_t$ is an aggregate price surprise. In Section 10.1, we analyzed a number of price processes.

Some were consistent with no sustained inflation (1 and 2), one with steady inflation (3), and one with steady inflation combined with serially correlated movements away from the average inflation rate. However, as is *always* the case with rational expectations, the expectational error for these processes, $p_t - E_{t-1}p_t$, is uncorrelated with the underlying or expected inflation rate. That is, we always have $E_{t-1}[(p_t - E_{t-1}p_t)E_{t-1}(p_t - p_{t-1})] = 0$. In the present model, inflation can only affect output and employment through this price surprise channel if the inflation is unexpected. More fundamentally, we find that

$$y_t = y_t^* + \beta^* \varepsilon_t. \tag{10.4.20}$$

Therefore, a stable Phillips curve only exists if inflation affects the "normal" level of output. That is, $E(y_t^* \varepsilon_t) \neq 0$ is required for an inflation-output trade-off.

While the theoretical underpinnings of a stable Phillips curve based upon incomplete information microeconomic foundations are, at best, quite weak, very casual data manipulation in some cases might lead one to the belief that a Phillips curve phenomena does exist even if such a Phillips curve is purely a statistical artifact. For each of the original cases of Section 10.1, let us write the unexpected price change in terms of the actual price and the predetermined expectation:

| Case | $P_t - E_{t-1}p_t$ |
|---|---|
| 1 | $p_t - \bar{p} = (p_t - p_{t-1}) + (p_{t-1} - \bar{p})$ |
| 2 | $p_t - p_{t-1}$ |
| 3 | $p_t - p_{t-1} - \mu$ |
| 4 | $p_t - p_{t-1} - \rho(p_{t-1} - p_{t-2}) - \mu$ |

In all of these cases we know that the proper reduced form of the correct model is given by $y = y_t^* + \beta^* \varepsilon_t$. However, a regression of the current output level $y_t$ on the current rate of inflation $\pi_t = p_t - p_{t-1}$, as noted from the above table, is likely to pick up considerable spurious correlation between $y_t$ and $p_t - p_{t-1}$. Therefore, a careless researcher might "discover" a Phillips curve, *especially* if he or she is looking for one.

Let us now look a little more carefully at cases 3 and 4. One way to write the reduced-form output equations would be

**3.** $y_t = y_t^* + \beta^*(p_t - p_{t-1}) - \beta^*\mu.$
**4.** $y_t = y_t^* + \beta^*(p_t - p_{t-1}) - \rho\beta^*(p_{t-1} - p_{t-2}) - \beta^*\mu.$ $\qquad(10.4.21)$

As one possible example let us assume that $y_t^* = \bar{y} + u_t$, where $u_t$ has zero mean and is serially uncorrelated. We therefore obtain

**3.** $y_t = (\bar{y} - \beta^*\mu) + \beta^*(p_t - p_{t-1}) + u_t.$
**4.** $y_t = (\bar{y} - \beta^*\mu) + \beta^*(p_t - p_{t-1}) - \rho\beta^*(p_{t-1} - p_{t-2}) + u_t.$ $\qquad(10.4.22)$

Now consider regression equations of the form

**3′.** $y_t = \alpha_0 + \alpha_1 \pi_t + v_t.$
**4′.** $y_t = \alpha_0 + \alpha_1 \pi_t + \alpha_2 \pi_{t-1} + v_t.$ $\qquad(10.4.23)$

One would very likely get positive and statistically significant $\hat{\alpha}_1$. Is this an interesting and useful finding? Of course not. It is purely a statistical artifact of a misspecified model.

## The Lucas Critique of Econometric Policy Evaluation

Suppose that the average inflation rate were constant, but inflation fluctuated some from year to year. Such a world would have price processes given by 3 and 4 above. Presumably agents would eventually become aware that these processes governed prices and inflation and base their expectations accordingly. However, regression analysis in such a world would generate positive estimates of $\alpha_1$. It might therefore appear plausible that a permanently higher rate of inflation might result in permanently higher levels of output.

While this argument looks plausible, it is not supported by the theoretical structure presented earlier in this section. A *permanent* increase in the rate of inflation involves an increase in the parameter $\mu$ in the price-generating process. While agents may temporarily be fooled into thinking that they are observing aberrantly high prices (positive values for $\varepsilon_t$) and on the basis of these surprises output may rise, such an effect cannot be lasting. Eventually agents will learn that $\mu$ has risen, expectation formation will be appropriately revised, and again we find that

$$y_t = y_t^* + \beta^* \varepsilon_t \tag{10.4.24}$$

independent of $\mu$. Therefore, while a Phillips curve phenomenon might exist out of the stochastic steady state, such a phenomenon would eventually disappear.

This example is an application of the "Lucas critique" of econometric policy evaluation.[11] Policy prescriptions based upon regressions like those discussed above often generate misleading results. It is not correct to presume that variations in some variable (like the inflation rate) *within* one policy regime that are correlated with movements in proposed target variables (like the level of output) within the *same* policy regime offer proof that a change in policy regimes to a different average level of this same variable will result in the same type of movement in the average level of the target variable. In the current situation inflation is correlated with output only when it is unanticipated. It is impossible to generate permanently unexpected inflation in a stable world of rational agents.

## The Policy Ineffectiveness Proposition

Under certain circumstances, the combined assumptions of rational expectations, the Lucas supply function, and symmetrically informed policymakers and private agents imply that stabilization policies have absolutely no effect on the levels of employment and output in the stochastic steady state. This policy ineffectiveness proposition goes beyond the accelerationist hypothesis discussed in Chapter 7, which argues that policy cannot affect the average levels of employment and output. The policy ineffectiveness proposition rather asserts that policy cannot even induce short-run deviations in the time paths of employment and output relative to their average levels.[12] That is, the policy ineffectiveness proposition asserts that policy cannot mitigate random fluctuations in output and employment relative to their normal levels over time.

In order to facilitate the analysis, we need to define and explain what we mean by a

---

[11]See Lucas (1976).

[12]This characteristic of macroeconomic models is developed in Lucas (1972), Sargent (1973), and Sargent and Wallace (1975). McCallum (1980) provides an excellent survey of this literature.

policy rule. In any given circumstance, if there is an optimal policy, we must be able to define it over measurable macroeconomic variables. Once properly specified over observable variables, such a policy will be time invariant. Consider monetary policy and assume that the policy is implemented with the same information set that private agents have. If we assume that individuals receive aggregate information with a one-period lag, one possibility would be a monetary policy in which the logarithm of the nominal money supply $m_t$ follows

$$m_t = ap_{t-1},$$
(10.4.25)

where $a$ is a constant.

This policy rule is now combined with the following very simple specifications of aggregate supply and demand:

$$y_t^s = \beta^*(p_t - E_{t-1}p_t),$$
(10.4.26)

$$y_t^d = \gamma(m_t - p_t) + u_t,$$
(10.4.27)

where $u_t$ is a zero-mean serially uncorrelated random variable. Plugging in our policy rule and solving for the market-clearing price yields

$$p_t = \frac{\beta^*}{\beta^* + \gamma}E_{t-1}p_t + \frac{\alpha\gamma}{\beta^* + \gamma}p_{t-1} + \frac{u_t}{\beta^* + \gamma}.$$
(10.4.28)

At this point our market-clearing condition contains the unobservable $E_{t-1}p_t$. We also note that the stochastic process for $p_t$ is now endogenous. Therefore, computation of $E_{t-1}p_t$ along rational expectation lines is not trivial. As an alternative to the solution strategy adopted in the previous section, we now employ the solution strategy of Lucas (1973) and Muth (1961). As a first step, we posit a "trial" solution for $p_t$ of the form

$$p_t = \Pi_1 p_{t-1} + \Pi_2 u_t.$$
(10.4.29)

It is straightforward to demonstrate that any other variables used in such a trial solution would necessarily have coefficients of zero. If our guessed solution of $p_t$ is correct, we obtain

$$E_{t-1}p_t = \Pi_1 p_{t-1},$$
(10.4.30)

since $E_{t-1}u_t = 0$ Now plugging in for $E_{t-1}p_t$ above, we obtain

$$p_t = \frac{a\gamma + \beta^*\Pi_1}{\beta^* + \gamma}p_{t-1} + \frac{u_t}{\beta^* + \gamma}.$$
(10.4.31)

For consistency with our postulated trial solution for $p_t$, we require

$$\Pi_1 = \frac{a\gamma + \beta^*\Pi_1}{\beta^* + \gamma} \quad \text{and} \quad \Pi_2 = \frac{1}{\beta^* + \gamma}.$$
(10.4.32)

Solving for $\Pi_1$, we obtain $\Pi_1 = a$. We therefore have

$$p_t = ap_{t-1} + \frac{u_t}{\beta^* + \gamma}.$$
(10.4.33)

The output equation is given by

$$y_t = y^* + \frac{\beta^*}{\beta^* + \gamma} u_t.$$

(10.4.34)

The important thing to notice is that the policy parameter $a$ does not appear in the reduced-form output equation. Other possible policy feedback rules also have no effect on output. This is not surprising. Policy rules that are known by agents and are functions only of variables known by agents cannot produce price surprises. Therefore, with flexible prices and the Lucas supply function, such policy rules cannot affect the time paths of output and employment. In Chapters 12 and 14, we extend this result to a much broader class of macroeconomic models.

# REFERENCES

Driskill, Robert, Stephen McCafferty, and Steven M. Sheffrin, "Speculative Intensity and Spot and Futures Price Variability," mimeo, Ohio State University, July 1988.

Friedman, Benjamin M., "Optimal Expectations and the Extreme Informational Assumptions of 'Rational Expectations' Macromodels," *Journal of Monetary Economics*, January, 1979, 23–41.

Lucas, Robert E., Jr., "Expectations and the Neutrality of Money," *Journal of Economic Theory*, April, 1972, 103–124.

Lucas, Robert E., Jr., "Some International Evidence on Output—Inflation Tradeoffs," *American Economic Review*, June, 1973, 326–334.

Lucas, Robert E., Jr., "Econometric Policy Evaluation: A Critique," in *The Phillips' Curve and Labor Markets,* Carnegie-Rochester Conference Series on Public Policy, Amsterdam, North Holland, 1976.

Lucas, Robert E., Jr., and Thomas J. Sargent, "After Keynesian Macroeconomics," in *After the Phillips' Curve: Persistence of High Inflation and High Unemployment,* Federal Reserve Bank of Boston Conference, vol. 19, Boston, Federal Reserve Bank of Boston, 1978, 49–72.

McCafferty, Stephen, and Robert Driskill, "Problems of Existence and Uniqueness in Nonlinear Rational Expectations Models," *Econometrica*, July, 1980, 1313–1317.

McCallum, Bennett T., "Rational Expectations and Macroeconomic Stabilization Policy," *Journal of Money, Credit, and Banking*, November, 1980, Part 2, 716–746.

Muth, John F., "Optimal Properties of Exponentially Weighted Forecasts," *Journal of the American Statistical Association*, June, 1960, 299–306.

Muth, John F., "Rational Expectations and the Theory of Price Movements," *Econometrica*, July, 1961, 315–335.

Phelps, Edmund S., *Microeconomic Foundations of Employment and Inflation Theory*, New York, Norton, 1970.

Samuelson, Paul A., "Proof That Properly Anticipated Prices Fluctuate Randomly," *Industrial Management Review*, Spring, 1965, 41–49.

Sargent, Thomas J., "Rational Expectations, the Real Rate of Interest, and the Natural Rate of Unemployment," *Brookings Papers on Economic Activity*, vol. 2, 1973, 429–472.

Sargent, Thomas J., ''Interpreting Economic Time Series,'' *Journal of Political Economy,* April, 1981, 213–248.

Sargent, Thomas J., *Macroeconomic Theory,* 2nd ed., Orlando, FL, Academic, 1987.

Sargent, Thomas J., and Neil Wallace, ''Rational Expectations, the Optimal Monetary Instrument, and the Optimal Money Supply Rule,'' *Journal of Political Economy,* April, 1975, 241–254.

Taylor, John B., ''Monetary Policy During a Transition to Rational Expectations,'' *Journal of Political Economy,* October, 1975, 1009–1021.

# Chapter **11**

## Policymaking Under Uncertainty

Chapter 10 previews the policy ineffectiveness proposition by demonstrating circumstances in which the choice of the macroeconomic policy setting is irrelevant to the stochastic process governing movements in employment and output. Alternatively, the analysis of Chapter 3 indicates that at least in the context of traditional fixed-price macroeconomic models, the choice of the policy setting may have very important employment and output ramifications. The analysis of the present chapter sidesteps this important issue of policy ineffectiveness by working exclusively with models in which the choice of the policy setting is an important consideration.

The focus of this chapter is on the implications of the existence of uncertainty on policy choice vis-à-vis policy choice in a deterministic setting. We therefore analyze economic policymaking in a stochastic environment and pose the question of whether the existence of uncertainty represents simply a minor unavoidable inconvenience for the policymaker or such uncertainty profoundly alters the nature of the policymaker's environment.

Section 11.1 develops some of the important basic concepts of the stochastic policy problem and demonstrates a fundamental "certainty equivalent" result. Section 11.2 then develops in some detail a specific application of the theory to a stochastic IS-LM macromodel and demonstrates how the choice-of-policy-instruments problem can be recast as a signal extraction problem.

The questions considered in this chapter, while of substantial interest in their own right, also provide very illustrative points of comparison for the results generated in subsequent chapters. The stochastic IS-LM model developed in Section 11.2 represents a situation perhaps most conducive to the application of beneficial macroeconomic policy. Considerations introduced in later chapters almost always weaken the case for an activist policy stance because such considerations render policies ineffective or even counterproductive.

## 11.1 BASIC CONCEPTS AND RESULTS

In a determinist setting, an optimal macroeconomic policy can usually be determined as a (possibly linear) function of the exogenous variables and the parameters of the economic model. In order to consider the possible effects of uncertainty, we now need to expand our set of potential exogenous variables to include the outcomes of random processes. We then wish to study whether in the presence of such exogenous random variables the optimal policies are the same as the optimal deterministic policies for the case in which with the random exogenous variables are replaced by their expected values, the so-called certainty equivalence policy.

### A Simple Stochastic Model with Additive Uncertainty

Consider first the case of additive uncertainty. Assume the following simple linear stochastic model:

$$y = \hat{y} + b + aM + u, \tag{11.1.1}$$

$$E(u) = 0, \ \text{Var}(u) = \sigma_u^2. \tag{11.1.2}$$

In this formulation $y$ might represent real output and $M$ might represent a policy parameter capable of generating increases in $y$. The constant term $\hat{y}$ would then correspond to desired output and the constant term $b$ would represent the expected deviation of $y$ from $\hat{y}$, when the policy variable, $M$, is set equal to zero. The unique feature of the present analysis vis-à-vis models like those of Chapter 3 is the addition of $u$, a random disturbance representing uncertainty either about policy effects or disturbance effects. Notice that $u$ is additive in nature rather than multiplicative. The term $b$ represents our best guess as to the (undesired) output response to some predicted "disturbance."

Assume that the policymaker wants to keep $y$ equal to some full-employment level $\hat{y}$. This output level may minimize inflation while keeping employment at a sufficiently high level. Further assume that the policymaker's loss function is quadratic in the difference between actual output and full-employment output. Such a loss function implies that positive and negative discrepancies of $y$ from $\hat{y}$ are equally costly. The policymaker therefore seeks to minimize

$$
\begin{aligned}
\mathscr{L} &= E\{(y - \hat{y})^2\} \\
&= E\{(aM + b + u)^2\} \\
&= E\{(aM + b)^2 + 2(aM + b)u + u^2\} \\
&= (aM + b)^2 + \sigma_u^2.
\end{aligned} \tag{11.1.3}
$$

Since $E(u) = 0$ and $E(u^2) = \sigma_u^2$, differentiation of the above expression with respect to $M$ yields a first-order condition for expected loss minimization given by

$$\frac{\partial \mathscr{L}}{\partial M} = 2a(aM + b) = 0 \tag{11.1.4}$$

or

$$aM + b = 0 \Rightarrow M = -\frac{b}{a}. \tag{11.1.5}$$

This expression implies that

$$y = aM + b + \hat{y} + u$$

$$= a\left(-\frac{b}{a}\right) + b + \hat{y} + u \qquad (11.1.6)$$

$$= \hat{y} + u,$$

and so

$$E(y) = \hat{y} + E(u) = \hat{y}. \qquad (11.1.7)$$

We have therefore demonstrated the optimality of what Theil (1964) refers to as the *"certainty equivalent"* policy for the case of strictly additive uncertainty. The policy-maker should act as if randomness does not exist. This certainty equivalence result is due entirely to the additive nature of the uncertainty. Such uncertainty cannot be avoided, and therefore the policymaker may just as well ignore it. Optimal policy should aim directly at the target such that $E(y) = \hat{y}$ no matter what the value of $b$ is.

We can gain some additional insight into this result by noting that the variance of output is equal to $\sigma_y^2 = \sigma_u^2$ independent of the level of $M$. Therefore, since the choice of $M$ cannot affect the variance of output, the appropriate policy should try to make the expected value of $y$ equal to $\hat{y}$.

## Multiplicative Uncertainty

The case analyzed above considered only additive uncertainty. We next consider multiplicative uncertainty, as in Brainard (1967). With multiplicative uncertainty, the policy-maker does not know the exact potency of the policy variable. Output is now given by

$$y = \hat{y} + (a + w)M + b + u, \qquad (11.1.8)$$

where

$$E(w) = E(u) = 0, \qquad E(wu) = 0, \qquad (11.1.9)$$

$$\text{Var}(w) = \sigma_w^2, \qquad \text{Var}(u) = \sigma_u^2. \qquad (11.1.10)$$

Therefore, the random variable $w$ represents uncertainty in the impact of the level of the policy variable $M$ on the level of output $y$. Furthermore, we now note that the variance of $y$ will depend upon the level of $M$. Since the present setup implicitly defines $M$ as the minimum-variance policy level, it might be wise to interpret values of $M$ as deviations of the policy variable from its normal or average value.

We continue to posit the quadratic loss function

$$\mathcal{L} = E\{(y - \hat{y})^2\} = E\{[aM + wM + b + u]^2\}. \qquad (11.1.11)$$

Expanding the above expression and taking the expectation, we find that

$$\mathcal{L} = (aM + b)^2 + \sigma_w^2 M^2 + \sigma_u^2. \qquad (11.1.12)$$

Differentiating the loss function with respect to $M$ and setting the resulting expression equal to zero, we derive the first-order condition

$$\frac{\partial \mathcal{L}}{\partial M} = 2(aM + b)a + 2\sigma_w^2 M = 0 \tag{11.1.13}$$

or

$$(2a^2 + w\sigma_w^2)M + 2ab = 0. \tag{11.1.14}$$

We therefore find that the optimal policy setting solves

$$M = \frac{-2ab}{2(a^2 + \sigma_w^2)} = \frac{-ab}{a^2 + \sigma_w^2} = -\frac{b}{a}\frac{a^2}{a^2 + \sigma_w^2}. \tag{11.1.15}$$

Plugging this expression for the optimal policy setting back into our original output equation, we obtain:

$$y = \hat{y} + (a + w)M + b + u = \hat{y} + (a + w)\frac{-ab}{a^2 + \sigma_w^2} + b + u, \tag{11.1.16}$$

*(handwritten: E(w) = 0,   E(u) = 0)*

and therefore

*(handwritten: $E(y) = \hat{y} + \frac{-a^2 b}{a^2 - \sigma_w^2} + b$)*

$$E(y) = \hat{y} + b\left(1 - \frac{a^2}{a^2 + \sigma_w^2}\right) = \hat{y} + \frac{\sigma_w^2}{a^2 + \sigma_w^2}b. \tag{11.1.17}$$

*(handwritten left margin: common denom.  $b\left(\frac{a^2 + \sigma_w^2 - a^2}{a^2 + \sigma_w^2}\right)$)*

Note that in this case the policymaker does not compensate for the full expected effect of $b$. Use of policy is costly here because deviations of the policy variable from its minimum-variance level add output variance the policymaker wants to avoid.

## The Policy Instruments Problem

In many circumstances policymakers may have two or more distinct although interrelated policy instruments to choose from in an attempt to control a single target variable. In a world of certainty it is generally the case that it does not matter exactly with which instrument policy is conducted.[1] After all, each policy variable's effect on the economy is precisely known, as is the unwanted effects of the exogenous disturbances.

Consider, for example, the fixed-price IS-LM model of Chapter 3 without wealth effects. Monetary policy may be implemented to affect the level of output and keep it equal to any desired level, such as $\hat{y}$. In our formal analysis we express such policies in terms of the level of the money supply $\overline{M}$. Through open-market operations, the policymaker can shift the LM curve in such a way as to intersect the relevant IS curve at $y = \hat{y}$.

We can, however, just as easily express monetary policy in terms of an interest rate rule. Money stock policies may be carried out via open-market operations quantified in terms of a specific number of government bonds to be bought or sold on the open market at whatever price the market will bear (through sealed bid auctions). Alternatively, the policymaker can instead simply stand ready to buy or sell as many government bonds as

---

[1]Tinberger (1952) shows that in the linear, deterministic case, a policymaker needs only as many policy instruments as target variables in order to exactly hit all the targets.

private agents wish to sell or buy, respectively, at a preannounced price. Given the one-to-one correspondence between interest rates and bond prices ($P_b = 1/r$), this policy amounts to pegging the nominal interest rate $r$. Such a policy therefore results in a horizontal LM curve. The policymaker may therefore also position this LM curve by selection of the appropriate nominal interest rate to intersect the relevant IS curve such that $y = \hat{y}$. In the absence of uncertainty, money stock policies and interest rate policies are equally capable of keeping income at its desired level. However, the optimal choice between a money stock policy and an interest rate policy in a more general, stochastic framework is a central concern of the following section.

# 11.2 POLICYMAKING IN A SIMPLE STOCHASTIC IS-LM MODEL

In this section, we formally amend the IS-LM model of Section 3.2 to allow for the possibility of uncertainty. We then consider optimal policymaking in this model and solve the optimal policy variable problem first posed by Poole (1970).

Assume the following linear, stochastic goods market equilibrium condition:

$$y = a_0 - a_1 r + u, \tag{11.2.1}$$

where $a_1 > 0$ and $a_0$ are constants and $u$ is a random variable with $E(u) = 0$, $E(u^2) = \sigma_u^2$. Further assume the following linear, stochastic money market equilibrium condition:

$$m = b_0 + b_1 y - b_2 r + v, \tag{11.2.2}$$

where $m \equiv M/P$ and where $b_1$, $b_2 > 0$ and $b_0$ are constants and $v$ is a random variable such that $E(v) = E(uv) = 0$, $E(v^2) = \sigma_v^2$. Since this model is a fixed-price model, the policymaker can always control $m$ by the appropriate choice of $M$. In what follows we assume that the policymaker instantaneously observes the interest rate $r$ that clears the financial asset market. However, while the level of output instantaneously adjusts to its equilibrium value, the contemporaneous output level is not readily observable by anyone including the policymaker. Only in later periods are statistics on current $y$ processed and announced. We now turn our attention to the question of whether the pegging of interest rates at an appropriate level is a better policy than controlling the supply of money at an appropriate level when undertaking policymaking in an uncertain environment.

## The Optimal Money Stock Policy

First consider the selection of an optimal value for the money supply, $m = \bar{m}$, which attempts to keep the level of output close to $\hat{y}$. We assume that the money stock is selected before values of $u$ and $v$ are realized. We further assume that no subsequent changes in $m$ are permissible. With the money stock as a control variable our system is given by

$$\begin{bmatrix} 1 & a_1 \\ -b_1 & b_2 \end{bmatrix} \begin{bmatrix} y \\ r \end{bmatrix} = \begin{bmatrix} a_0 + u \\ b_0 - \bar{m} + v \end{bmatrix}. \tag{11.2.3}$$

The solution to this system is easily found by Cramer's rule as

$$y = \frac{a_0 b_2 + a_1(\overline{m} - b_0)}{b_2 + a_1 b_1} + \frac{b_2 u - a_1 v}{b_2 + a_1 b_1}, \qquad \text{[handwritten: } E u \doteq E v = 0 \text{]}$$

(11.2.4)

$$r = \frac{a_0 b_1 + b_0 - \overline{m}}{b_2 + a_1 b_1} + \frac{b_1 u + v}{b_2 + a_1 b_1}.$$

(11.2.5)

*[handwritten left margin: minus the Estimated white noise]*

The fixed-price IS-LM model above is equivalent to the simple stochastic model with additive uncertainty analyzed above. In such a case, minimization of $E[(y - \hat{y})^2]$ is accomplished by choosing the policy variable, in this case $m$, to satisfy $E(y) = \hat{y}$. We therefore choose a value of $\overline{m}$ that satisfies

$$\hat{y} = \frac{a_0 b_2 + a_1(\overline{m} - b_0)}{b_2 + a_1 b_1}$$

(11.2.6)

or

$$\overline{m} = \left( b_0 - \frac{b_2 a_0}{a_1} \right) + \left( b_1 + \frac{b_2}{a_1} \right) \hat{y}.$$

(11.2.7)

Plugging the optimal value of $m$, $\overline{m}$ into the reduced forms for $y$ and $r$ yields

$$y = \hat{y} + \frac{b_2 u - a_1 v}{b_2 + a_1 b_1},$$

(11.2.8)

$$r = \frac{a_0 - \hat{y}}{a_1} + \frac{b_1 u + v}{b_2 + a_1 b_1}.$$

(11.2.9)

The loss function evaluated with the optimal money stock policy is given by

$$\mathcal{L}_m = E[(y - \hat{y})^2] = \frac{b_2^2 \sigma_u^2 + a_1^2 \sigma_v^2}{(b_2 + a_1 b_1)^2} = \frac{\sigma_u^2 + (a_1/b_2)^2 \sigma_v^2}{(1 + a_1 b_1/b_2)^2}.$$

(11.2.10)

## The Optimal Interest Rate Policy

By standing willing to buy and sell government bonds in unlimited quantities at a fixed price, the policymaker is able to peg the nominal interest rate. With the policymaker pegging the interest rate at $\overline{r}$, we obtain the following reduced forms for $y$ and $r$:

*[handwritten left margin: Read again]*

$$y = a_0 - a_1 \overline{r} + u,$$

$$r = \overline{r}.$$

(11.2.11)

To set $E(y) = \hat{y}$, the policymaker needs to set the nominal interest rate at

$$\overline{r} = \frac{a_0 - \hat{y}}{a_1},$$

(11.2.12)

so that $y = \hat{y} + u$. Note that this interest rate is also equal to the unconditional expectation of the interest rate under the optimal money stock policy. Obviously in the nonstochastic case of $u \equiv v \equiv 0$, both policies are identical.

Before proceeding with our analysis, we should note that the careful reader of Chapters 3 and 6 may detect a potential problem with attempts to control the nominal rate of interest in models with short-run price rigidities. Suppose that we start with zero expected and actual inflation. Further suppose that the policymaker implements a policy of pegging the nominal rate of interest at a level that is less than the initial nominal (and expected real) rate of interest. With sticky prices, a lower nominal rate of interest requires an increase in the rate of expansion of the money supply. However, over time, such an increase in the rate of expansion of the money generates positive actual and expected inflation. Now the nominal rate of interest begins to exceed the expected real rate of interest. Therefore, to achieve the objective of a constant nominal interest rate, the expected real rate of interest must be driven down even farther by an even faster rate of expansion of the money supply. The potential therefore exists for an attempt to peg the nominal rate of interest too low to lead to accelerating inflation.[2]

However, as long as the interest-rate-pegging policy is feasible, loss under the optimal interest rate policy is given by

$$\mathcal{L}_r = \sigma_u^2. \tag{11.2.13}$$

Clearly, the interest rate policy dominates if and only if

$$\sigma_u^2 < \frac{\sigma_u^2 + (a_1/b_2)^2 \sigma_v^2}{(1 + a_1 b_1/b_2)^2} \quad \text{or} \quad b_1^2 \left(1 + \frac{2b_2}{a_1 b_1}\right)\sigma_u^2 < \sigma_v^2. \tag{11.2.14}$$

We therefore find that a policy of pegging the nominal interest rate tends to be superior when shocks are primarily monetary in nature ($\sigma_v^2 \gg \sigma_u^2$) and when investment spending is very sensitive to changes in interest rates ($a_1 \gg 0$). Alternatively, strong responsiveness of money demand to income and interest rates ($b_1, b_2 \gg 0$) as well as highly variable aggregate demand ($\sigma_u^2 \gg \sigma_v^2$) favors a money stock policy.

Before proceeding, it is useful to reflect for a moment on interactions between the choice-of-instruments problem and the question of whether certainty equivalence is the appropriate policy. The certainty equivalence result was shown, in the previous section, to only obtain when uncertainty is strictly additive in nature. With only additive uncertainty, the optimal money stock policy and the optimal interest rate policy are both of the certainty equivalent variety. The choice of instrument then comes down to the selection of the certainty equivalent policy that offers the lowest output variance. Suppose, however, that we also have multiplicative uncertainty for both the money stock and interest rate policies. In this case, we would still compare the optimal money stock and interest rate policies as appropriately modified by the Brainard (1967) analysis. Again we would choose the policy with the smallest optimal value of the loss function.

However, it is not clear, in this case, what implications the Brainard analysis would have for the optimal variance of the money stock or interest rates. Presumably, the variance of whichever policy instrument is optimal will be smaller to the extent that there is multiplicative uncertainty about its effect on the level of output. However, if the optimal policy instrument is the money stock, multiplicative uncertainty may lead to a nearly constant money supply and a very variable interest rate. Alternatively, if the optimal

---

[2]For a detailed discussion of these and related issues, see McCallum (1986).

policy instrument is the interest rate, multiplicative uncertainty may lead to a nearly constant interest rate and a highly variable money stock. It is therefore not generally possible to tell whether multiplicative uncertainty argues for a more stable level of the money supply or more stable interest rates or whether multiplicative uncertainty affects the choice of policy instrument.

## The Optimal Combination Policy

Both the optimal money stock policy and the optimal interest rate policy are dominated by an optimal combination policy. Note that both such policies involve precommitment of either $m$ or $r$ before the values of $u$ and $v$ are realized. Recall that the reduced form for output is given by

$$y = \frac{a_0 b_2 + a_1(\overline{m} - b_0) + b_1 u + v}{b_2 + a_1 b_1}. \tag{11.2.15}$$

If the policymaker could infer the values of $u$ and $v$ prior to setting the value of $m$, a value $\overline{m}$ could always be chosen so as to equate $y = \hat{y}$ with no error. However, in our setup, the policymaker does not know $u$ and $v$ before he or she sets policy. Fortuitously, policy interactions with the bond market of a specific sort turn out to be equivalent to having some information about the realizations of $u$ and $v$. In particular, the optimal combination policy consists of setting an excess demand *schedule* for government bonds. Such a policy makes the money supply interest elastic. Later, we show exactly what sort of information such a combination policy imparts to the policymaker.

Following Poole (1970), a combination policy takes the specific form

$$m = c_0 + c_1 r, \tag{11.2.16}$$

where $c_0$ and $c_1$ are as-yet-to-be-determined constants. Plugging this money supply function into our simple IS-LM setup yields

$$\begin{bmatrix} 1 & a_1 \\ -b_1 & b_2 + c_1 \end{bmatrix} \begin{bmatrix} y \\ r \end{bmatrix} = \begin{bmatrix} a_0 + u \\ (b_0 - c_0) + v \end{bmatrix}. \tag{11.2.17}$$

Use of Cramer's rule facilitates the following solutions for $y$ and $r$:

$$y = \frac{a_0(b_2 + c_1) + a_1(c_0 - b_0)}{b_2 + c_1 + a_1 b_1} + \frac{(b_2 + c_1)u - a_1 v}{b_2 + c_1 + a_1 b_1}, \tag{11.2.18}$$

$$r = \frac{b_0 - c_0 + a_0 b_1}{b_2 + c_1 + a_1 b_1} + \frac{b_1 u + v}{b_2 + c_1 + a_1 b_1}. \tag{11.2.19}$$

These reduced-form equations contain the two policy parameters $c_0$ and $c_1$. Inspection of the output equation above reveals that it is possible to set $c_0$ so that $E(y) = \hat{y}$. This model is also a linear model with additive uncertainty. Therefore, the optimal policy is again of the certainty equivalence variety. The policymaker should set $c_0$ to make the first term of the first expression above equal to $\hat{y}$. The policymaker then has free reign to optimize with respect to $c_1$ to try to reduce the impact of nonzero values of $u$ and $v$ on $y$. The appropriate choice of $c_0$ therefore satisfies

$$c_0 = \frac{1}{a}\{[a_1b_1 + (b_2 + c_2)]\hat{y} + [a_1b_0 - a_0(b_2 + c_1)]\}. \tag{11.2.20}$$

Now plugging in for $c_0$ in the above equations and rearranging, we obtain

$$y = \hat{y} + \frac{(b_2 + c_1)u - a_1v}{(b_2 + c_1) + a_1b_1}, \tag{11.2.21}$$

$$r = \frac{a_0 - \hat{y}}{a_1} + \frac{b_1u + v}{(b_2 + c_1) + a_1b_1}. \tag{11.2.22}$$

We may now solve for $c_1$, the optimal responsiveness of the money supply to the rate of interest. The loss function $E[(y - \hat{y})^2] = \sigma_y^2$ is now given by

$$\sigma_y^2 = \frac{(b_2 + c_1)^2\sigma_u^2 + a_1^2\sigma_v^2}{(b_2 + c_1 + a_1b_1)^2}. \tag{11.2.23}$$

Differentiating with respect to $c_1$ and setting this derivative equal to zero, we obtain

$$0 = a_1b_1(b_2 + c_1)\sigma_u^2 - a_1^2\sigma_v^2. \tag{11.2.24}$$

Upon rearranging, we find that

$$b_2 + c_1 = \frac{a_1\sigma_v^2}{b_1\sigma_u^2} \quad \text{or} \quad c_1 = \frac{a_1\sigma_v^2 - b_1b_2\sigma_u^2}{b_1\sigma_u^2}. \tag{11.2.25}$$

Plugging in for $c_0$ and $c_1$ in the original money supply relationship and rearranging, we find that with the optimal policy,

$$m = (b_0 + b_1\hat{y} - b_2\bar{r}) + \frac{a_1\sigma_v^2 - b_1b_2\sigma_u^2}{b_1\sigma_u^2}(r - \bar{r}). \tag{11.2.26}$$

This money supply function then implies the following reduced forms for the level of output and the interest rate:

$$y = \hat{y} + \frac{\sigma_v^2 u - b_1\sigma_u^2 v}{\sigma_v^2 + b_1^2\sigma_u^2}, \tag{11.2.27}$$

$$r = \bar{r} + \frac{1}{a_1}\frac{b_1^2\sigma_u^2}{\sigma_v^2 + b_1^2\sigma_u^2}\left(u + \frac{v}{b_1}\right). \tag{11.2.28}$$

Several things are worth noting about the behavior of the model with the optimal combination policy. First, if either disturbance is identically zero ($\sigma_u^2 = 0$ or $\sigma_v^2 = 0$), then the policymaker is always able to achieve $y = \hat{y}$. The optimal combination policy is able to completely insulate the economy from disturbances. Second, the sign of the coefficient of $r$ in the optimal money supply function is the same as the sign of

$$a_1\sigma_v^2 - b_1b_2\sigma_u^2. \tag{11.2.29}$$

Therefore, whether the policy rule amplifies or dampens interest rate fluctuations depends on the respective disturbance term variances as well as on structural parameters. Finally, the loss under the combination policy is given by

$$\mathscr{L}_c = \frac{\sigma_u^2 \sigma_v^2}{\sigma_v^2 + b_1^2 \sigma_u^2}.$$

(11.2.30)

Some relatively tedious algebraic manipulations prove that this expression for the loss incurred under the combination policy is unambiguously less than the expressions for the losses that obtain in the money stock and interest rate policy cases. Alternatively, note that the money stock and interest rate policies are simply special cases of the combination policy with $c_1 = 0$ and $c_1 = +\infty$, respectively. Therefore, the optimal selection of $c_1$ with $c_1$ unconstrained must lead to a loss that is less than or equal to the loss that obtains with $c_1$ constrained to either $c_1 = 0$ or $c_1 = +\infty$.

The money market equilibrium condition is given by

$$c_0 + c_1 r = b_0 + b_1 y - b_2 r + v,$$

(11.2.31)

or

$$r = \frac{b_0 - c_0}{c_1 + b_2} + \frac{b_1}{c_1 + b_2} y + \frac{v}{c_1 + b_2}.$$

(11.2.32)

The slope of the LM curve under the optimal combination policy is therefore

$$\left. \frac{dr}{dy} \right|_{\mathrm{LM}_c} = \frac{b_1}{c_1 + b_2} = \frac{b_1^2 \sigma_u^2}{a_1 \sigma_v^2}$$

(11.2.33)

We therefore see that if there are only money demand shocks, the LM curve is horizontal, as in the case of the interest rate policy. Alternatively, with only goods market disturbances, the optimal LM curve will be vertical at $y = \hat{y}$. With both types of shocks the LM curve takes on intermediate slopes.

## Optimal Policy and the Informational Content of Interest Rates

In the previous section, we noted that the interaction with the bond market implicit in the implementation of the optimal combination policy generated information as to the likely source(s) of the disturbance(s). Such information permits the policymaker to improve over the performances of the pure money stock and pure interest rate policies. In this section, we more explicitly identify the nature of the information available in the money market and provide an alternative institutional setup that replicates the performance of the optimal combination policy. The primary motivations for the analysis of this section are first to demonstrate how information may optimally be inferred from observations of contemporaneous interest rate movements and second to recognize how the optimal combination policy implicitly exploits this information.

Some might argue that a fundamental difficulty with the combination policy is that it is not operational. The mechanics of implementation of a money supply function go something like this. First, an auctioneer is needed to call out interest rates, observe both the private and public excess bond demands, and continue doing so until the market clears. Only then can trade take place. For the policymaker to behave as described, he or she cannot make any trades until the equilibrium interest rate is known, and yet by definition, in order for policy to make a difference, the policymaker's trades need to be big enough to affect the market-clearing interest rate. Therefore, without recontracting, the policymaker is making trades before knowing what net bond market position he or she ultimately wants to take.

Whether such practical problems are significant or not is not the central point here. The main purpose is to motivate consideration of the following alternative institutional setting. Suppose we allow the policymaker to observe the equilibrium interest rate (but not the equilibrium output level) based upon some arbitrary initial setting for $m$. Now allow *one* and only one change in $m$ and then let the economy reequilibrate. Although implementation is different, we demonstrate below that the economy winds up in the same equilibrium position as it does in the case of the optimal combination policy.

How does optimal policy work in this setting? With an arbitrarily selected initial level of the real money supply denoted by $m_0$, the equilibrium interest rate is given by

$$r = \frac{a_0 b_1 + b_0 - m_0}{b_2 + a_1 b_1} + \frac{b_1 u + v}{b_2 + a_1 b_1} = r_0 + \frac{b_1 u + v}{b_2 + a_1 b_1}, \tag{11.2.34}$$

where $r_0$ is defined as the expected value of $r$ when $m = m_0$. The policymaker is assumed to be able to observe the market-clearing value of $r$. By assumption, he or she also knows the correct model of the economy and therefore knows the magnitude of the first right-hand-side term above, which is equal to $r_0$. The policymaker therefore also knows the magnitude of $r - r_0$, the second right-hand-side term above. The policymaker is now free to change $m$ (but only once). Once the change is made, output will be given by

$$y = \frac{a_0 b_2 + a_1(m - b_0)}{b_2 + a_1 b_1} + \frac{b_2 u - a_1 v}{b_2 + a_1 b_1} = y_0 + \frac{a_1(m - m_0)}{b_2 + a_1 b_1} + \frac{b_2 u - a_1 v}{b_2 + a_1 b_1}, \tag{11.2.35}$$

where $y_0$ is the expected value of $y$ when $m = m_0$. If the magnitude of $b_2 u - a_1 v$ is known, the policymaker could exactly offset it and set $y = \hat{y}$. However, knowledge of $b_1 u + v$ can help provide an *estimate* of $b_2 u - a_1 v$—an estimate that, on average, will be more accurate than this term's unconditional expected value of zero.

Recall that we observe

$$r - r_0 = \frac{b_1 u + v}{b_2 + a_1 b_1}. \tag{11.2.36}$$

Therefore, we can infer that

$$b_1 u + v = (a_1 b_1 + b_2)(r - r_0). \tag{11.2.37}$$

If we now further assume that $u$ and $v$ are normally distributed, then solution to the signal extraction problem developed in Section 10.1 tells us that

$$E(b_1 u | r) = \frac{b_1^2 \sigma_u^2}{b_1^2 \sigma_u^2 + \sigma_v^2} (a_1 b_1 + b_2)(r - r_0), \tag{11.2.38}$$

$$E(v | r) = \frac{\sigma_v^2}{b_1^2 \sigma_u^2 + \sigma_v^2} (a_1 b_1 + b_2)(r - r_0). \tag{11.2.39}$$

Our best estimate of the output disturbance term is therefore

$$
E\left[\frac{b_2 u - a_1 v}{a_1 b_1 + b_2}\bigg| r\right] = \frac{b_1 b_2 \sigma_u^2 (r - r_0)}{b_1^2 \sigma_u^2 + \sigma_v^2} - \frac{a_1 \sigma_v^2 (r - r_0)}{b_1^2 \sigma_u^2 + \sigma_v^2}
$$

$$
= \frac{b_1 b_2 \sigma_u^2 - a_1 \sigma_v^2}{b_1^2 \sigma_u^2 + \sigma_v^2}(r - r_0). \tag{11.2.40}
$$

Taking the expected value of the output equation above, we therefore obtain

$$
E(y) = y_0 + \frac{a_1(m - m_0)}{b_2 + a_1 b_1} + \frac{b_1 b_2 \sigma_u^2 - a_1 \sigma_v^2}{b_1^2 \sigma_u^2 + \sigma_v^2}(r - r_0). \tag{11.2.41}
$$

The optimal monetary policy now involves setting this expression equal to $\hat{y}$. We therefore obtain

$$
m^* = m_0 + \frac{a_1 b_1 + b_2}{a_1}\left[(\hat{y} - y_0) - \frac{b_1 b_2 \sigma_u^2 - a_1 \sigma_v^2}{b_1^2 \sigma_u^2 + \sigma_v^2}(r - r_0)\right]. \tag{11.2.42}
$$

As we noted in Chapter 3, an increase in the money supply, ceteris paribus, reduces the equilibrium interest rate in this model. Therefore, in the present example, the optimal monetary policy dampens interest rate movements if and only if the coefficient on $r - r_0$ in the $m^*$ equation above is positive. Therefore, whether optimal monetary policy amplifies or dampens interest rate movements again depends on the sign of $a_1 \sigma_v^2 - b_1 b_2 \sigma_u^2$, just as it did in the case of the optimal combination policy.

Plugging the value of $m^*$ into the original output equation, we obtain

$$
y = \hat{y} + \frac{b_2 u - a_1 v}{b_2 + a_1 b_1} - E\left[\frac{b_2 u - a_1 v}{b_2 + a_1 b_1}\bigg| r\right]. \tag{11.2.43}
$$

That is, policy tries to offset the expected effect of the disturbance given the information available. Now since

$$
E\left[\frac{b_2 u - a_1 v}{b_2 + a_1 b_1}\bigg| r\right] = \frac{b_1 b_2 \sigma_u^2 - a_1 \sigma_v^2}{b_1^2 \sigma_u^2 + \sigma_v^2}\frac{b_1 u + v}{b_2 + a_1 b_1}, \tag{11.2.44}
$$

we obtain, upon collecting and rearranging terms,

$$
y = \hat{y} + \frac{\sigma_v^2 u - b_1 \sigma_u^2 v}{\sigma_v^2 + b_1^2 \sigma_u^2}. \tag{11.2.45}
$$

As was previewed earlier, this output expression is identical to that which obtains under the optimal combination policy. Therefore, the informational content of observing the initial equilibrium interest rate is the same from the point of view of the conduct of policy as the informational content of observing the market response to a money supply schedule.

## Alternative Information Structures: An Example

To give a little more intuition to the similarities of the two approaches, consider the following specific example. First of all, assume that $b_1 b_2 \sigma_u^2 > a_1 \sigma_v^2$; that is, aggregate demand shocks are the primary source of output disturbances.

In the case of a pure money stock policy or in the case of the two-step procedure of the previous section, the slope of the LM curve is given by

$$\left.\frac{dr}{dy}\right|_{LM_m} = \frac{b_1}{b_2}. \tag{11.2.46}$$

In the case of the optimal combination policy, the slope of the LM curve is given by

$$\left.\frac{dr}{dy}\right|_{LM_c} = \frac{b_1^2 \sigma_u^2}{a_1 \sigma_v^2}. \tag{11.2.47}$$

But since $b_1 b_2 \sigma_u^2 > a_1 \sigma_v^2$, we get

$$\frac{b_1^2 \sigma_u^2}{a_1 \sigma_v^2} > \frac{b_1}{b_2}, \tag{11.2.48}$$

and so

$$\left.\frac{dr}{dy}\right|_{LM_c} > \left.\frac{dr}{dy}\right|_{LM_m}. \tag{11.2.49}$$

Let us further assume that the level of $m$ in the first state of the two-stage information-based policy is chosen such that $y_0 = \hat{y}$. We then get the configuration depicted in Figure 11.1. In Figure 11.1, the IS and LM curves are drawn for the case of $u = v = 0$.

Now suppose that we observe a state in which $v = 0$ and $u > 0$, an expansionary goods market disturbance and no money market disturbance. The IS curve shifts rightward. However, with the optimal combination policy, the more steeply sloped LM curve in Figure 11.2 dampens the effect of $u$ on $y$.

In the two-step procedure the goods market disturbance raises the interest rate to $r_0'$. Since $b_1 b_2 \sigma_u^2 > a_1 \sigma_v^2$, this shock is (correctly) perceived to be an expansionary goods market disturbance, and the money supply is therefore reduced according to

$$m^* - m_0 = \frac{a_1 b_1 + b_2}{a_1} \frac{a_1 \sigma_v^2 - b_1 b_2 \sigma_u^2}{\sigma_v^2 + b_1^2 \sigma_u^2}(r_0' - r_0). \tag{11.2.50}$$

Optimal policy therefore shifts the LM curve to the left by $(1/b_1)(m^* - m_0)$. In Figure 11.2, the LM curve shifts back to $LM(m = m^*)$, and we again find that $y = y_1$.

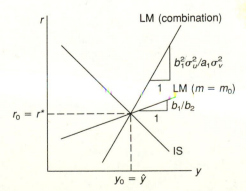

**Figure 11.1**

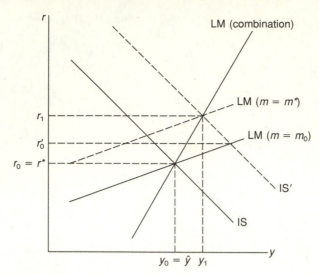

**Figure 11.2**

## Some General Lessons About Uncertainty and Economic Policy

The analysis of this chapter provides some basic insights into the extent to which uncertainty should affect the optimal conduct of macroeconomic policymaking. In Section 10.1, we noted that as long as uncertainty is strictly additive, such additive uncertainty should in no way affect optimal policymaking. Alternatively, when the selection of policy levels that depart from normal policy levels adds variance to the level of the target variable, then the variability of the policy variable should be reduced.

Uncertainty can also be an important consideration when there are several potential policy instruments available to the policymaker. In a deterministic setting, this choice-of-instruments question is irrelevant. The policymaker needs only be sure to have at least as many linearly independent policy instruments as policy targets. Alternatively, in the face of uncertainty, some policy instruments may prove to be superior to others. Furthermore, some appropriate combination of policy instruments may be superior to any single policy instrument. Such a combination policy may prove to be equivalent to an increase in the amount of information available to the policymaker or, alternatively, a reduction in the effective extent of the uncertainty that the policymaker seeks to avoid.

As a final note, it must be remembered that the analysis of this chapter applies only to situations in which the policymaker has complete knowledge of the stochastic structure of the economy. That is, the policymaker is always presumed to have the correct model of the economy when formulating policy plans. This assumption is quite likely to be rather questionable in actual practice. In particular, a much more likely source of uncertainty facing the practical conduct of policy centers around uncertainty about which macroeconomic model is the correct one. Economic analysis has a long way to go until we can specify models with as little residual uncertainty as the ones posited in this chapter, and unfortunately economic analysis has little to say about the appropriate conduct of policy when there is uncertainty as to the correct model of the economy. Therefore, the actual practical usefulness of the analyses of this chapter may be quite limited.

# REFERENCES

Brainard, William, ''Uncertainty and the Effectiveness of Policy,'' *American Economic Review,* May, 1967, 411–425.

McCallum, Bennett T., ''Some Issues Concerning Interest Rate Pegging, Price Level Determinacy, and the Real Bills Doctrine,'' *Journal of Monetary Economics,* January, 1986, 135–160.

Poole, William, ''Optimal Choice of Monetary Policy Instruments in a Simple Stochastic Macro Model,'' *Quarterly Journal of Economics,* May, 1970, 197–216.

Theil, Henri, *Optimal Decision Rules for Government and Industry,* Amsterdam, North-Holland, 1964.

Tinberger, Jan, *On the Theory of Economic Policy,* Amsterdam, North-Holland, 1952.

# Chapter 12

## Policymaking in Flexible-Price Macroeconomic Models

Throughout the analysis of Chapter 11, the macroeconomic policy problem is a legitimate "problem." That is, although the existence of uncertainty may not affect the optimal policy setting, it nevertheless does matter what policy setting the policymaker chooses. However, such results should not be surprising since the workings of the models of Chapter 11 closely mimic the workings of the fixed-price models of Chapter 3.

Alternatively, the models of this chapter are all based on the assumption of instantaneous price adjustment. In such models, as in the models of Chapters 2, 5, 6, and 7, money is often neutral, and therefore the optimal money supply problem is a trivial one. In the models of this chapter, the question of the potency of policy generally turns on whether expectations are formed "rationally" or not. This chapter therefore generalizes several such policy ineffectiveness results previewed in Chapter 10.

Section 12.1 first presents a linear, stochastic version of the flexible-price models of Chapters 5–7, quite similar to that of Sargent and Wallace (1975). We then pose and solve the optimal monetary policy problem for the case of exogenously formed expectations. As in the adaptive expectations models of Chapters 5–7, policy does have real effects on macroeconomic variables. Section 12.2 then repeats the analysis of Section 12.1 for the case of rational expectations. Here we show that in many circumstances policymaker actions can have no effect on real macroeconomic variables.

Finally, Section 12.3 considers the relative attractiveness of policy rules over policy discretion when the objectives of the policymaker and private agents appear inconsistent with one another. In particular, we point out policy problems inherent in the time inconsistency problem and show how games played between policymakers and private agents can lead to unambiguously worse economic performance. Although the analysis of this section is not, strictly speaking, stochastic in nature, it is built upon potential divergence between expected and actual economic outcomes.

The general theme of this chapter is that the optimism about macroeconomic policymaking that may have been implicit in the analysis of Chapter 11 may well be premature. In this chapter, we demonstrate that if price-level expectations are truly exogenous and fixed, then monetary policy is capable of achieving any desired target for the expected value of real output. Alternatively, when price-level expectations are formed rationally, monetary policy generally becomes ineffective. About the only hope for a positive role for policy comes about through the policymaker's optimal choice of the interest sensitivity of the money supply. However, such a choice cannot affect the expected value of real output, only its variance. Finally, we show that public perceptions about policymaking and game-playing aspects to policymaking may not only prevent policy from achieving its desired output goals but also impart an inflationary bias into an otherwise noninflationary environment.

## 12.1 AN EQUILIBRIUM MODEL WITH EXOGENOUS EXPECTATIONS

Throughout this chapter, we assume that goods prices are determined by a market-clearing condition and that aggregate output is determined by the equilibrium level of aggregate supply. In particular, we follow Lucas (1973) and assume that aggregate goods supply is positively related to aggregate price-level surprises. This aggregate supply function is first motivated in Chapter 5, and a stochastic version of it is introduced in Section 10.4.

Price-level flexibility naturally introduces the possibilities of both anticipated and unanticipated rates of price inflation. We must therefore carefully distinguish between the nominal and expected real rates of interest, as first discussed in Chapter 6. The expected real rate of interest is equal to the nominal rate of interest minus the expected rate of inflation. We continue to assume that aggregate goods demand is negatively related to the expected real rate of interest and that the demand for real money balances is negatively related to the nominal rate of interest.

Although such considerations turn out not to be crucial to the results that follow, we also assume that both aggregate demand and aggregate supply are positively related to past levels of actual aggregate output. Serial correlation in aggregate supply can be motivated by the existence of output adjustment costs, as in Sargent (1987, Ch. 18), and serial correlation in aggregate demand can be motivated by permanent income considerations, as in Hall (1978), or by capital stock adjustment costs, as in Lucas and Prescott (1971).

Without loss of generality, we specify the monetary policy variable as the sum of two component parts. One component, reminiscent of the combination monetary policy of Chapter 11, is linked to the contemporaneous value of the nominal interest rate. This component is given by $c_1 r_t$, where $c_1$ is the parameter set by the monetary authority. The other component of the monetary policy parameter may respond to lagged endogenous economic variables and may also contain a nonstochastic future path for the money supply. However, this component is not linked to contemporaneous or future values of the endogenous variables or any stochastic disturbance terms.

The appropriate modification of the model of Section 11.2 gives rise to the following macroeconomic model:

$$y_t^s = \beta(p_t - p_t^e) + \gamma y_{t-1} + u_{1t}, \tag{12.1.1}$$

$$y_t^d = a_0 y_{t-1} - a_1(r_t - \pi_t^e) + u_{2t}, \tag{12.1.2}$$

$$m_t^d = p_t + b_1 y_t - b_2 r_t + v_t, \tag{12.1.3}$$

$$m_t^s = c_1 r_t + \phi_t, \tag{12.1.4}$$

with the parameters $\beta$, $\gamma$, $a_0$, $a_1$, $b_1$, $b_2$ all positive constants and $\phi_t$, $-\infty \leq c_1 \leq +\infty$ monetary policy parameters. As in earlier chapters, $y_t$ represents the logarithm of output, $p_t$ represents the logarithm of the price level, $r_t$ represents the interest rate in natural units, and $m_t$ represents the logarithm of the money supply. The disturbance terms $u_{1t}$, $u_{2t}$ and $v_t$ are all mutually independent, serially uncorrelated, zero mean random variables with variances $\sigma_1^2$, $\sigma_2^2$, and $\sigma_v^2$, respectively. In this model, the expected rate of inflation $\pi_t^e$ is equal to the expected value of $p_{t+1} - p_t$. We assume that information on the current aggregate price level $p_t$ and the future aggregate price level $p_{t+1}$ is not available in period $t$. Therefore, the expected real rate of interest is given by $r_t - p_{t+1}^e + p_t^e$.

Solving the money market equilibrium condition for the nominal rate of interest, we obtain

$$r_t = \frac{p_t}{b_2 + c_1} - \frac{\phi_t}{b_2 + c_1} + \frac{b_1 y_t}{b_2 + c_1} + \frac{v_t}{b_2 + c_1}. \tag{12.1.5}$$

Now plugging in for $y_t = y_t^s$, we obtain

$$r_t = \frac{1 + \beta b_1}{b_2 + c_1} p_t - \frac{\beta b_1}{b_2 + c_1} p_t^e - \frac{\phi_t}{b_2 + c_1} + \frac{b_1 \gamma y_{t-1}}{b_2 + c_1} + \frac{v_t + b_1 u_{1t}}{b_2 + c_1}. \tag{12.1.6}$$

Goods market equilibrium is therefore given by

$$\beta(p_t - p_t^e) + \gamma y_{t-1} + u_{1t} = a_0 y_{t-1} - a_1 \left( \frac{1 + \beta b_1}{b_2 + c_1} p_t + \frac{b_2 + c_1 - \beta b_1}{b_2 + c_1} p_t^e \right.$$
$$\left. - \frac{\phi_t}{b_2 + c_1} + \frac{b_1 \gamma y_{t-1}}{b_2 + c_1} + \frac{v_t + b_1 u_{1t}}{b_2 + c_1} - p_{t+1}^e \right) + u_{2t}. \tag{12.1.7}$$

Rearranging yields

$$\frac{a_1 + \beta(b_2 + c_1 + a_1 b_1)}{b_2 + c_1} p_t$$

$$= \frac{(a_0 - \gamma)(b_2 + c_1) - a_1 b_1 \gamma}{b_2 + c_1} y_{t-1} + \frac{a_1}{b_2 + c_1} \phi_1$$

$$+ \frac{-a_1(b_2 + c_1) + \beta(b_2 + c_1 + a_1 b_1)}{b_2 + c_1} p_t^e + a_1 p_{t+1}^e \tag{12.1.8}$$

$$+ \frac{-[a_1 b_1 + (b_2 + c_1)]u_{1t} + (b_2 + c_1)u_{2t} - a_1 v_t}{b_2 + c_1}.$$

Solving for the price level, we obtain

$$p_t = \frac{(a_0 - \gamma)(b_2 + c_1) - a_1 b_1 \gamma}{a_1 + \beta(b_2 + c_1 + a_1 b_1)} y_{t-1} + \frac{a_1 \phi_t}{a_1 + \beta(b_2 + c_1 + a_1 b_1)}$$

$$+ \frac{-a_1(b_2 + c_1) + \beta(b_2 + c_1 + a_1 b_1)}{a_1 + \beta(b_2 + c_1 + a_1 b_1)} p_t^e$$

$$+ \frac{a_1(b_2 + c_1)}{a_1 + \beta(b_2 + c_1 + a_1 b_1)} p_{t+1}^e \qquad (12.1.9)$$

$$+ \frac{-[a_1 b_1 + (b_2 + c_1)]u_{1t} + (b_2 + c_1)u_{2t} - a_1 v_t}{a_1 + \beta(b_2 + c_1 + a_1 b_1)}.$$

The above expression for $p_t$ may now be combined with the aggregate supply relationship to obtain the following semireduced form for output:

$$y_t = \frac{a_0 \beta(b_2 + c_1) + a_1 \gamma}{a_1 + \beta(b_2 + c_1 + a_1 b_1)} y_{t-1} + \frac{a_1 \beta \phi_t}{a_1 + \beta(b_2 + c_1 + a_1 b_1)}$$

$$- \frac{a_1 \beta(1 + b_2 + c_1)}{a_1 + \beta(b_2 + c_1 + a_1 b_1)} p_t^e + \frac{a_1 \beta(b_2 + c_1)}{a_1 + \beta(b_2 + c_1 + a_1 b_1)} p_{t+1}^e \qquad (12.1.10)$$

$$+ \frac{a_1 u_{1t} + \beta(b_2 + c_1)u_{2t} - a_1 \beta v_t}{a_1 + \beta(b_2 + c_1 + a_1 b_1)}.$$

## Optimal Period-by-Period Policymaking

One particularly simple case of the optimal policy problem is that case in which price-level expectations are static. To analyze this case, let us assume that $p_t^e = p_{t+1}^e = \bar{p}$. The important characteristic of this particular case is that the expected price level is independent of the money supply rule. With price expectations fixed at $\bar{p}$, reduced forms for the levels of $p_t$ and $y_t$ are given by

$$p_t = \frac{a_1 \phi_t + \beta(b_2 + c_1 + a_1 b_1)\bar{p}}{a_1 + \beta(b_2 + c_1 + a_1 b_1)} + \frac{a_0(b_2 + c_1) - \gamma(b_2 + c_1 + a_1 b_1)}{a_1 + \beta(b_2 + c_1 + a_1 b_1)} y_{t-1}$$

$$+ \frac{-(b_2 + c_1 + a_1 b_1)u_{1t} + (b_2 + c_1)u_{2t} - a_1 v_t}{a_1 + \beta(b_2 + c_1 + a_1 b_1)}, \qquad (12.1.11)$$

$$y_t = \frac{a_1 \beta(\phi_t - \bar{p}) + [a_1 \gamma + a_0 \beta(b_2 + c_1)]y_{t-1}}{a_1 + \beta(b_2 + c_1 + a_1 b_1)}$$

$$+ \frac{a_1 u_{1t} + \beta(b_2 + c_1)u_{2t} - a_1 \beta v_t}{a_1 + \beta(b_2 + c_1 + a_1 b_1)}. \qquad (12.1.12)$$

This particular case is most conducive to the effective use of policy. Inspection of the above expression for $y_t$ makes clear that by appropriate selection of $\phi_t$, any desired time path for the expected value of output is always feasible even though prices are completely flexible in this model. However, successive substitution of more realistic expectational assumptions below demonstrates that such optimism about the potential effectiveness of policy may be quite premature.

In this example, we seek an optimal current period policy setting $\phi_t^*$ that solves the single-period minimization problem

$$\min_{\phi_t} E\{(y_t - \hat{y}_t)^2\}. \tag{12.1.13}$$

In this problem, expectations are predetermined and independent of the policy action. Also implicit in this specification is the assumption that the policymaker is not concerned with future output levels or future expectations held by agents.

The output equation above is linear with strictly additive uncertainty. We therefore have a case in which the certainty equivalence result applies. With the target level of output denoted by $\hat{y}$, for any arbitrarily selected value of $c_1$, the optimal value of $\phi_t$ satisfies

$$\hat{y} = \frac{a_1\beta(\phi_t - \bar{p}) + [a_1\gamma + a_0\beta(b_2 + c_1)]y_{t-1}}{a_1 + \beta(b_2 + c_1 + a_1b_1)}. \tag{12.1.14}$$

Solving the above expression for the optimal value of $\phi_t$, which we denote by $\phi_t^*$, we obtain

$$\phi_t^* = \bar{p} + \frac{[a_1 + \beta(b_2 + c_1 + a_1b_1)]\hat{y} - [a_1\gamma + a_0\beta(b_2 + c_1)]y_{t-1}}{a_1\beta}, \tag{12.1.15}$$

where $\phi_t^*$ is written as a function of the yet-to-be-specified value of $c_1$, the interest sensitivity of the money supply. Implementation of the optimal value of $\phi_t$ results in a reduced-form expression for output given by

$$y_t = \hat{y} + \frac{a_1u_{1t} + \beta(b_2 + c_1)u_{2t} - a_1\beta v_t}{a_1 + \beta(b_2 + c_1 + a_1b_1)}. \tag{12.1.16}$$

Since the expected value of $y_t$ is now given by $\hat{y}_t$, minimization of the policymaker's loss function with respect to the as-yet-to-be-specified value of $c_1$ is equivalent to the minimization of the variance of output. The variance of output, with $\phi_t = \phi_t^*$ as computed above, is given by

$$\sigma_y^2 = E\{(y_t - \hat{y}_t)^2\} = \frac{a_1^2\sigma_1^2 + \beta^2(b_2 + c_1)^2\sigma_2^2 + a_1^2\beta^2\sigma_v^2}{[a_1 + \beta(b_2 + c_1 + a_1b_1)]^2}. \tag{12.1.17}$$

Differentiating this expression with respect to $c_1$, we obtain

$$\frac{d\sigma_y^2}{dc_1} = \frac{2a_1\beta[-a_1\sigma_1^2 + \beta(b_2 + c_1)(1 + \beta b_1)\sigma_2^2 - a_1\beta^2\sigma_v^2]}{[a_1 + \beta(b_2 + c_1 + a_1b_1)]^3}. \tag{12.1.18}$$

Setting $d\sigma_y^2/dc_1 = 0$, we therefore derive the following expression for the optimal value $c_1^*$ of $c_1$:

$$c_1^* = -b_2 + \frac{a_1(\sigma_1^2 + \beta^2\sigma_v^2)}{\beta(1 + \beta b_1)\sigma_2^2}. \tag{12.1.19}$$

Some experimentation with the above expression demonstrates that the properties of $c_1^*$ in the current model are very similar to the properties of the optimal combination policy parameter in the simple stochastic IS-LM model analyzed in Section 11.2.

Plugging the optimal policy variable $\phi_t^*$ into the price equation derived above, we find that

$$p_t = \bar{p} + \frac{1}{\beta}\hat{y} - \frac{\gamma}{\beta}y_{t-1} + \frac{-(b_2 + c_1 + a_1b_1)u_{1t} + (b_2 + c_1)u_{2t} - a_1v_t}{a_1 + \beta(b_2 + c_1 + a_1b_1)}.$$

$$(12.1.20)$$

Note that unless $\hat{y}_t = \gamma y_{t-1}$, we find that the expected price level $\bar{p}$ is not equal to the conditional expected value of $p_t$. The current model with static expectations therefore has the somewhat troubling property that policy can generate any desired expected level of $y$ but such an outcome is only possible if $p_t \neq p_t^e$.

## Optimal Feedback Policies

In the preceding section, optimal policymaking is a purely period-by-period problem. That is, the current period's optimal policy parameter $\phi_t^*$ may continuously be recomputed on a period-by-period basis. In this section, we consider choices of the policy setting over current and future time. However, while the chosen value of the policy variable may change over time, the parameters of our model economy ($a_i$, $b_i$, $\beta$, $\gamma$) are time invariant. The condition of such time-invariant processes is completely summarized by the values of its state variables. In the current problem, the sole state variable for the economy is the value $y_{t-1}$.

If a particular policy setting is optimal in period $t$ for a particular state of a time-invariant process, such a policy setting is always optimal any time the process is in the same state. Therefore, if an optimal policy exists, such a policy may be written as a time-invariant function of the state of the economy. In the current example, a linear policy rule would be given by

$$\phi_t = \phi_0 + \phi_1 y_{t-1}, \qquad (12.1.21)$$

with $\phi_0$ and $\phi_1$ independent of time. Note that this functional form for $\phi_t$ is identical to the functional form for the single-period optimal policy derived in the preceding section.

The rule for $\phi_t$ above is an example of a feedback policy. Feedback policy rules relate the current value of the policy variable to current and/or lagged conditions of the economy. However, since the condition of a time-invariant system is completely summarized by the value of its state variable(s), an optimal policy, if such a policy exists, can always be written as a feedback policy.

We now assume that a feedback policy has been selected and observe the evolution of the economy assuming that this policy has been in place since $t = -\infty$. We then seek to solve for the optimal values of the policy parameters $\phi_0$ and $\phi_1$. Plugging the policy rule into the economy's equilibrium conditions, we may derive the following reduced forms for output and price:

$$y_t = \frac{a_1\beta(\phi_0 - \bar{p})}{a_1 + \beta(b_2 + c_1 + a_1b_1)} + \frac{a_1(\gamma + \beta\phi_1) + a_0\beta(b_2 + c_1)}{a_1 + \beta(b_2 + c_1 + a_1b_1)}y_{t-1}$$

$$+ \frac{a_1u_{1t} + \beta(b_2 + c_1)u_{2t} - a_1\beta v_t}{a_1 + \beta(b_2 + c_1 + a_1b_1)},$$

$$(12.1.22)$$

$$p_t = \frac{a_1\phi_0 + \beta(b_2 + c_1 + a_1b_1)\bar{p}}{a_1 + \beta(b_2 + c_1 + a_1b_1)}$$

$$+ \frac{a_0(b_2 + c_1) + a_1\phi_1 - \gamma(b_2 + c_1 + a_1b_1)}{a_1 + \beta(b_2 + c_1 + a_1b_1)} y_{t-1} \qquad (12.1.23)$$

$$+ \frac{-(b_2 + c_1 + a_1b_1)u_{1t} + (b_2 + c_1)u_{2t} - a_1v_t}{a_1 + \beta(b_2 + c_1 + a_1b_1)}.$$

Equation (12.1.22) above is a first-order, constant-coefficient difference equation in $y_t$. The solution for $y_t$ is therefore given by

$$y_t = \frac{a_1\beta(\phi_1 - \bar{p})}{a_1(1 - \gamma - \beta\phi_1) + \beta[a_1b_1 + (1 - a_0)(b_2 + c_1)]} + \sum_{i=0}^{\infty} k^i x_{t-1}, \qquad (12.1.24)$$

where

$$k \equiv \frac{a_1(\gamma + \beta\phi_1) + a_0\beta(b_2 + c_1)}{a_1 + \beta(b_2 + c_1 + a_1b_1)}, \qquad (12.1.25)$$

$$x_j \equiv \frac{a_1u_{1j} + \beta(b_2 + c_1)u_{2j} - a_1\beta v_j}{a_1 + \beta(b_2 + c_1 + a_1b_1)} \quad \text{for } -1 < k < 1. \qquad (12.1.26)$$

A sufficient condition for $|k| < 1$ is given by

$$\phi_1 < b_1 + \frac{(1 - \gamma)a_1 + (1 - a_0)\beta b_2}{a_1\beta}. \qquad (12.1.27)$$

As long as $\gamma < 1$ and $a_0 < 1$, as is usually thought to be the case, the above inequality is satisfied as long as money supply is less responsive to income than money demand.

Up until now, we have been assuming that expectations are purely static and therefore that $\bar{p}$ is exogenously determined. While the assumption of static expectations may or may not be reasonable, it should certainly be the case that with a given feedback policy in place for all time, the value of $\bar{p}$ is consistent with the unconditional expected value of $p$. Substituting the unconditional expected value of $y$ for $y_{t-1}$ in the $p_t$ equation and setting the resulting expected value equal to $\bar{p}$, we obtain:

$$\bar{p} - \phi_0 = \frac{\beta(\phi_0 - \bar{p})[a_0(b_2 + c_1) + a_1\phi_1 - \gamma(b_2 + c_1 + a_1b_1)]}{a_1(1 - \gamma - \beta\phi_1) + \beta[(1 - a_0)(b_2 + c_1) + a_1b_1]}. \qquad (12.1.28)$$

The only value of $\bar{p}$ for which the above equation is satisfied is $\bar{p} = \phi_0$. The output and price equations may now be rewritten as

$$y_t = \frac{a_1(\gamma + \beta\phi_1) + a_0\beta(b_2 + c_1)}{a_1 + \beta(b_2 + c_1 + a_1b_1)} y_{t-1} + \frac{a_1u_{1t} + \beta(b_2 + c_1)u_{2t} - a_1\beta v_t}{a_1 + \beta(b_2 + c_1 + a_1b_1)}, \qquad (12.1.29)$$

$$p_t = \bar{p} + \frac{a_0(b_2 + c_1) + a_1\phi_1 - \gamma(b_2 + c_1 + a_1b_1)}{a_1 + \beta(b_2 + c_1 + a_1b_1)} y_{t-1}$$

$$+ \frac{-(b_2 + c_1 + a_1b_1)u_{1t} + (b_2 + c_1)u_{2t} - a_1v_t}{a_1 + \beta(b_2 + c_1 + a_1b_1)}. \qquad (12.1.30)$$

Solution of the reduced form for output now simplifies to

$$y_t = \sum_{i=0}^{\infty} k^i x_{t-i}. \tag{12.1.31}$$

Here we see that the unconditional expected value of $y$ is zero independent of $\phi_0$ and $\phi_1$. In particular, note that the value of $\phi_0$ has no effect at all on the statistical properties of $y$. The value of $\phi_0$ only affects the value of $\bar{p}$.

Although the process for $y_t$ has an unconditional mean of zero, the evolution of output is governed by a process that exhibits first-order serial correlation. In particular, we find that

$$E(y_t y_{t-1}) = \frac{a_1(\gamma + \beta\phi_1) + a_0\beta(b_2 + c_1)}{a_1 + \beta(b_2 + c_1 + a_1b_1)}. \tag{12.1.32}$$

In the absence of vigorous countercyclical policy,[1] we generally expect that $\gamma + \beta\phi_1 > 0$ and $b_1 + c_1 > 0$, and so output exhibits positive serial correlation. This property of an output process is often referred to as a "business cycle." Output, when high, tends to remain high, and output, when low, tends to remain low. An important issue at hand is whether policy can or even should attempt to "smooth" such business cycle tendencies.

Recall the policy loss function

$$\mathscr{L} = E\{(y - \hat{y})^2\}. \tag{12.1.33}$$

Under the assumption that an appropriate feedback policy has been in place for all time, the only sensible interpretation of the above loss function would view the expectation in that expression as an unconditional expectation. If we denote the unconditional mean of $y_t$ by $\bar{y}$, then we may write

$$\begin{aligned}
\mathscr{L} &= E\{(y - \bar{y} + \bar{y} - \hat{y})^2\} \\
&= E\{(y - \bar{y})^2\} + 2E\{(y - \bar{y})(\bar{y} - \hat{y})\} + (\bar{y} - \hat{y})^2. \\
&= \sigma_y^2 + (\bar{y} - \hat{y})^2.
\end{aligned} \tag{12.1.34}$$

In the current example, we find that $\bar{y} = 0$ independent of the value of $\phi_1$. Minimization of $\mathscr{L}$ is therefore equivalent to minimization of $\sigma_y^2$, where $\sigma_y^2$ denotes the asymptotic variance of $y_t$, which is given by

$$\sigma_y^2 = \frac{1}{1 - \left[\dfrac{a_1(\gamma + \beta\phi_1) + a_0\beta(b_2 + c_1)}{a_1 + \beta(b_2 + c_1 + a_1b_1)}\right]^2} \times \frac{a_1^2\sigma_1^2 + \beta(b_2 + c_1)^2\sigma_2^2 + a_1^2\beta^2\sigma_v^2}{[a_1 + \beta(b_2 + c_1 + a_1b_1)]^2}. \tag{12.1.35}$$

In order to minimize $\sigma_y^2$, the policymaker can clearly do no better than to set $\phi_1$ such that

$$a_1(\gamma + \beta\phi_1) + a_0\beta(b_2 + c_1) = 0 \tag{12.1.36}$$

---

[1] A discussion of such policies follows.

or

$$\phi_1 = -\frac{\gamma}{\beta} - \frac{a_0}{a_1}(b_2 + c_1). \tag{12.1.37}$$

If the above value of $\phi_1$ has been in place for all time, the stochastic process governing $y_t$ is given by

$$y_t = \frac{a_1 u_{1t} + \beta(b_2 + c_1)u_{2t} - a_1\beta v_t}{a_1 + \beta(b_2 + c_1 + a_1 b_1)}. \tag{12.1.38}$$

Feedback policy that attempts to minimize $E[(y - \hat{y})^2]$ therefore purges output of serial correlation. That is, policy eliminates the business cycle.[2] Lagged output terms disappear from the output equation. As long as $b_2 + c_1 > 0$, such policies result in movements in the money supply in the opposite direction from lagged output movements. Such a property is normally the case with "countercyclical" monetary policies.

Further attempts to utilize an interest-rate-sensitive monetary policy to dampen output variance dictates a choice of $c_1$ that minimizes

$$\sigma_y^2 = \frac{a_1^2\sigma_1^2 + \beta(b_2 + c_1)^2\sigma_2^2 + a_1^2\beta^2\sigma_v^2}{[a_1 + \beta(b_2 + c_1 + a_1 b_1)]^2}. \tag{12.1.39}$$

Minimization of the above expression with respect to $c_1$ is precisely the same problem encountered earlier in the discussion of optimal period-by-period policymaking. The resulting optimal value for $c_1$ is given by

$$c_1^* = -b_2 + \frac{a_1(\sigma_1^2 + \beta^2\sigma_v^2)}{\beta(1 + \beta b_1)\sigma_2^2}. \tag{12.1.40}$$

In the present example, expectations, although static, are consistent in the sense that $p^e$ is equal to the unconditional expected value of $p$. This restriction on the expectational process generally frustrates policy attempts to achieve $E(y_t) = \hat{y}$, as is always feasible in the fixed-price IS-LM model of Section 11.2. However, we might at this time also question the desirability of minimizing the asymptotic variance of output and consequently eliminating the business cycle.

Recall the output supply schedule

$$y_t^s = \beta(p_t - p_t^e) + \gamma y_{t-1} + u_{1t}. \tag{12.1.41}$$

This output supply schedule presumably reflects optimal firm and/or household behavior. Might it not make sense, therefore, for policy to attempt to prevent output variations due to expectational errors? Following Barro (1976), let us define *full information output* as that level of output supply consistent with $p_t^e = p_t$. We therefore define

$$y_t^* \equiv \gamma y_{t-1} + u_{1t}. \tag{12.1.42}$$

Optimal policy may now be more appropriately geared toward minimizing the variance of output around its full information level. We therefore seek to minimize

$$\chi \equiv E\{(y_t - y_t^*)^2\}. \tag{12.1.43}$$

---

[2] See Sargent and Wallace (1976) for a discussion of this result.

In the current setup, minimization of $\chi$ corresponds to the minimization of

$$E\{(p_t - \bar{p})^2\} = E(p_t - E_{t-1}p_t)^2 + (E_{t-1}p_t - \bar{p})^2. \tag{12.1.44}$$

Expectational errors due to the static formation of expectations based upon the unconditional expectation of the price level as opposed to the conditional expectation of the price level are given by

$$E_{t-1}p_t - \bar{p} = \frac{a_0(b_2 + c_1) + a_1\phi_1 - \gamma(b_2 + c_1 + a_1b_1)}{a_1 + \beta(b_2 + c_1 + a_1b_1)}y_{t-1}. \tag{12.1.45}$$

Expectational errors due to the unforeseeable random disturbances are given by

$$p_t - E_{t-1}p_t = \frac{-(b_2 + c_1 + a_1b_1)u_{1t} + (b_2 + c_1)u_{2t} - a_1v_t}{a_1 + \beta(b_2 + c_1 + a_1b_1)}. \tag{12.1.46}$$

The first expression above, $E_{t-1}p_t - \bar{p}$, is zero independent of the level of $y_{t-1}$ as long as policy is set according to

$$\phi_1 = \frac{\gamma(b_2 + c_1 + a_1b_1) - a_0(b_2 + c_1)}{a_1}. \tag{12.1.47}$$

Output is now given by

$$y_t = \gamma y_{t-1} + \frac{a_1u_{1t} + \beta(b_2 + c_1)u_{2t} - a_1\beta v_t}{a_1 + \beta(b_2 + c_1 + a_1b_1)}. \tag{12.1.48}$$

The optimal value of $\phi_1$ ensures that the expected value of $p_t - \bar{p}$ equals zero for all $t$. The policymaker may now independently select a value of $c_1$ to further reduce the variance of the expectational error. The variance of the price expectational error is given by

$$\sigma^2_{(p-\bar{p})} = \frac{(b_2 + c_1 + a_1b_1)^2\sigma_1^2 + (b_2 + c_1)^2\sigma_2^2 + a_1^2\sigma_v^2}{[a_1 + \beta(b_2 + c_1 + a_1b_1)]^2}. \tag{12.1.49}$$

Differentiating the above expression with respect to $c_1$ and setting this derivative equal to zero, we obtain

$$b_2 + c_1^{**} = \frac{\beta a_1\sigma_v^2 - a_1b_1\sigma_1^2}{\sigma_1^2 + (1 + \beta b_1)\sigma_2^2}, \tag{12.1.50}$$

where $c_1^{**}$ denotes the appropriately redefined optimal value of $c_1$.

## 12.2 An Equilibrium Model with Endogenous Expectations

Many would argue that the policymaking exercises of the previous section make little sense because they all rely on the assumption of fixed expectational mechanisms. In particular, agents ignore the actions of the policymaker in forming $p_t^e$ and $p_{t+1}^e$. A more realistic assumption, especially in the case of feedback policies that are in place for long periods of time, is that the process by which agents form price expectations eventually comes to incorporate full knowledge of the structure of the economy as well as the policy feedback parameters. Such expectations mechanisms, as those introduced in Chapter 10, are, following Muth (1961), commonly referred to as "rational" expectations.

Let us now adopt the following notation. Define $\epsilon_t$ as the composite, contemporaneous error term in the price process as computed in the previous section. That is, define

$$\epsilon_t \equiv \frac{-(b_2 + c_1 + a_1 b_1)u_{1t} + (b_2 + c_1)u_{2t} - a_1 v_t}{a_1 + \beta(b_2 + c_1 + a_1 b_1)}. \tag{12.2.1}$$

Without loss of generality, we also now denote the interest inelastic component of the money supply process as

$$\phi_t \equiv \phi_1 y_{t-1} + \overline{m}_t, \tag{12.2.2}$$

where the sequence $\{\overline{m}_t\}$ for all $t$, $0 \leq t \leq +\infty$, is any deterministic sequence of real numbers. The reduced form for the price process may now be written as

$$\begin{aligned}
p_t = {} & \frac{a_1 \overline{m}_t}{a_1 + \beta(b_2 + c_1 + a_1 b_1)} - \frac{-a_1(b_2 + c_1) + \beta(b_2 + c_1 + a_1 b_1)}{a_1 + \beta(b_2 + c_1 + a_1 b_1)} p_t^e \\
& + \frac{a_1(b_2 + c_1)}{a_1 + \beta(b_2 + c_1 + a_1 b_1)} p_{t+1}^e \\
& + \frac{a_0(b_2 + c_1) + a_1\phi_1 - \gamma(b_2 + c_1 + a_1 b_1)}{a_1 + \beta(b_2 + c_1 + a_1 b_1)} y_{t-1} + \epsilon_t.
\end{aligned} \tag{12.2.3}$$

## Rational Expectations and Policy Ineffectiveness

In order to compute the rationally expected price levels $p_t^e$ and $p_{t+1}^e$, it is first necessary to carefully specify the information sets that agents have at their disposal when forming these expectations. We begin our analysis by assuming that agents know the values of all previous aggregate economic variables including $p_{t-1}, p_{t-2}, \ldots, y_{t-1}, y_{t-2}, \ldots, r_{t-1}, r_{t-2}, \ldots$. We further assume that agents know the policy feedback parameters $\phi_1$ and $c_2$. Finally, agents are aware of the workings of supply and demand in each aggregate market and therefore know the entire structure of the macroeconomy. We denote this information set by $\Omega_{t-1}$. Note, however, that $\Omega_{t-1}$ does not include information about any contemporaneous macroeconomic variable. In particular, at least for the present, agents do not know the current nominal interest rate $r_t$ when forming the expectations $p_t^e$ and $p_{t+1}^e$.

We therefore adopt the following notation:

$$p_t^e = E[p_t | \Omega_{t-1}] \equiv E_{t-1} p_t, \tag{12.2.4}$$

$$p_{t+1}^e = E[p_{t+1} | \Omega_{t-1}] \equiv E_{t-1} p_{t+1}. \tag{12.2.5}$$

In order to solve for the difference between the actual current price $p_t$ and the rationally expected current price $E_{t-1}p_t$, first note that

$$E[\epsilon_t | \Omega_{t-1}] \equiv E_{t-1}\epsilon_t = 0. \tag{12.2.6}$$

Now taking expectations of the above expression for $p_t$ conditional on $\Omega_{t-1}$, we obtain the following result:

$$p_t - p_t^e = p_t - E_{t-1}p_t = \epsilon_t. \tag{12.2.7}$$

Real output $y_t$, regardless of the value of $\phi_1$, is therefore governed by

$$y_t = y_t^s = \beta(p_t - E_{t-1}p_t) + \gamma y_{t-1} + u_{1t} \tag{12.2.8}$$

or

$$y_t = \gamma y_{t-1} + \beta\epsilon_t + u_{1t} = \gamma y_{t-1} + \frac{a_1 u_{1t} + \beta(b_2 + c_1)u_{2t} - \beta a_1 v_t}{a_1 + \beta(b_2 + c_1 + a_1 b_1)} \tag{12.2.9}$$

in the stochastic steady state of the model under consideration (recall that we assume that the feedback policy has been in effect since $t = -\infty$). This exercise therefore demonstrates the policy ineffectiveness proposition for the model under consideration. With expectations formed rationally, feedback parameters such as $\phi_1$ and alternative, additive, nonstochastic components of the money supply path, $\{\overline{m}_t\}$, are irrelevant to the determination of real output.

While in the present case the policymaker's choice of $\phi_1$ and $\{\overline{m}_t\}$ cannot affect their statistical properties of $y_t$, this case continues to imply a nontrivial choice problem in the selection of $c_1$. Recall the money supply rule

$$m_t^s = c_1 r_t + \phi_t. \tag{12.2.10}$$

This money supply process implies that the policymaker is able to respond to $r_t$ in setting $m_t^s$. Therefore, the present set of informational assumptions has the implication that the policymaker possesses superior information since private economic agents only have access to information on the lagged values of macroeconomic variables, including the nominal interest rate.

In this case, the optimal choice of $c_1$ still satisfies

$$b_2 + c_1^{**} = \frac{\beta a_1 \sigma_v^2 - a_1 b_1 \sigma_1^2}{\sigma_1^2 + (1 + \beta b_1)\sigma_2^2}. \tag{12.2.11}$$

In general, models like the one under current consideration allow for policy effectiveness only in cases like the present one in which the policymaker has access to superior information. If the policymaker also has access only to lagged values of the interest rate, then the policymaker would be constrained to a choice of $c_1 = 0$.

Feedback parameters like $\phi_1$ only affect the statistical properties of the output process if such feedback is able to respond to exogenous disturbances more quickly than private agents. In the current setup, the policymaker and private agents both have symmetric access to information about $y_{t-1}$, and so policymaker responses to economic disturbances through this particular channel have no effect on the output process.

## The Equilibrium Price Process

We next turn our attention to the derivation of a reduced form for the price process. Traditionally, it is assumed that policymakers are primarily concerned with the statistical properties of aggregate output. However, policymakers are often also concerned with the level of prices and/or the rate of inflation. In order to address this concern, it is therefore necessary to compute the implications of alternative monetary policies, in particular alternative sequences $\{\overline{m}_t\}$ for the path of prices over time. This exercise also proves useful practice in the methods of solution of stochastic difference equations.

Since we are now assuming that expectations are formed rationally and since we are dealing with the stochastic steady state of the model, the price expectations terms $p_t^e$ and $p_{t+1}^e$ are now given by the mathematical expectations of $p_t$ and $p_{t+1}$ conditional on the information set $\Omega_{t-1}$. The $j$-period-ahead future price level may therefore be written as

$$
\begin{aligned}
p_{t+j} = &\frac{a_1 \overline{m}_{t+j}}{a_1 + \beta(b_2 + c_1 + a_1 b_1)} \\
&+ \frac{-a_1(b_2 + c_1) + \beta(b_2 + c_1 + a_1 b_1)}{a_1 + \beta(b_2 + c_1 + a_1 b_1)} E_{t+j-1} p_{t+j} \\
&+ \frac{a_1(b_2 + c_1)}{a_1 + \beta(b_2 + c_1 + a_1 b_1)} E_{t+j-1} p_{t+j+1} \\
&+ \frac{a_0(b_2 + c_1) + a_1 \phi_1 - \gamma(b_2 + c_1 + a_1 b_1)}{a_1 + \beta(b_2 + c_1 + a_1 b_1)} y_{t+j-1} + \epsilon_{t+j}.
\end{aligned} \tag{12.2.12}
$$

In order to solve this general equation for $p_{t+j}$, we need first calculate the reduced form for expectational terms of the form $E_{t-1} p_{t+j}$. As a prelude, note that the expectation of a future expectation is simply the current expectation. That is,

$$
E_{t-1}(E_{t+j-1} P_{t+j}) = E_{t-1} p_{t+j}. \tag{12.2.13}
$$

Next, note that we have already solved for the output process. In particular, the future output level $y_{t+j}$ may be written as

$$
\begin{aligned}
y_{t+j} &= \gamma^{j+1} y_{t-1} + \sum_{i=0}^{j} \gamma^i [\beta \epsilon_{t+j-i} + u_{1t+j-i}] \\
&= \gamma^{j+1} y_{t-1} + \sum_{i=0}^{j} \gamma^i \frac{a_1 u_{1t+j-i} + \beta(b_2 + c_1) u_{2t+j-i} - \beta a_1 v_{t+j-i}}{a_1 + \beta(b_2 + c_1 + a_1 b_1)}.
\end{aligned} \tag{12.2.14}
$$

Taking the expectation of this expression conditional on $\Omega_{t-1}$, we therefore obtain

$$
E_{t-1} y_{t+j} = \gamma^{j+1} y_{t-1},
$$

and so

$$
E_{t-1} y_{t+j-1} = \gamma^j y_{t-1}. \tag{12.2.15}
$$

Finally, we have already noted that

$$
E_{t-1} \epsilon_{t+j} = 0 \quad \text{for all } j \geq 0. \tag{12.2.16}
$$

Therefore, taking the expectation of the above expression for $p_{t+j}$ conditional on

$\Omega_{t-1}$, we obtain

$$
E_{t-1}p_{t+j} = \frac{a_1\overline{m}_{t+j}}{a_1 + \beta(b_2 + c_1 + a_1b_1)}
$$

$$
+ \frac{-a_1(b_2 + c_1) + \beta(b_2 + c_1 + a_1b_1)}{a_1 + \beta(b_2 + c_1 + a_1b_1)} E_{t-1}p_{t+j}
$$

$$
+ \frac{a_1(b_2 + c_1)}{a_1 + \beta(b_2 + c_1 + a_1b_1)} E_{t-1}p_{t+j+1}
$$

$$
+ \frac{a_0(b_2 + c_1) + a_1\phi_1 - \gamma(b_2 + c_1 + a_1b_1)}{a_1 + \beta(b_2 + c_1 + a_1b_1)} \gamma^j y_{t-1}.
$$

(12.2.17)

This expression is simply a first-order difference equation in $E_{t-1}p_{t+j}$. Use of the lag operator allows us to write

$$
LE_{t-1}p_{t+j+1} = E_{t-1}p_{t+j} \quad \text{or} \quad E_{t-1}p_{t+j+1} = L^{-1}E_{t-1}p_{t+j}. \tag{12.2.18}
$$

This substitution allows the price expectations process to be rewritten as

$$
E_{t-1}p_{t+j} = \frac{a_1\overline{m}_{t+j}}{a_1 + \beta(b_2 + c_1 + a_1b_1)}
$$

$$
+ \frac{-a_1(b_2 + c_1) + \beta(b_2 + c_1 + a_1b_1)}{a_1 + \beta(b_2 + c_1 + a_1b_1)} E_{t-1}p_{t+j}
$$

$$
+ \frac{a_1(b_2 + c_1)}{a_1 + \beta(b_2 + c_1 + a_1b_1)} L^{-1}E_{t-1}p_{t+j}
$$

$$
+ \frac{a_0(b_2 + c_1) + a_1\phi_1 - \gamma(b_2 + c_1 + a_1b_1)}{a_1 + \beta(b_2 + c_1 + a_1b_1)} \gamma^j y_{t-1}.
$$

(12.2.19)

This expression may be rearranged in the form

$$
E_{t-1}p_{t+j} = \frac{1}{1 + b_2 + c_1} \frac{1}{1 - \dfrac{b_2 + c_1}{1 + b_2 + c_1}L^{-1}}
$$

$$
\times \left[ \overline{m}_{t+j} + \frac{a_0(b_2 + c_1) + a_1\phi_1 - \gamma(b_2 + c_1 + a_1b_1)}{a_1[a_1 + \beta(b_2 + c_1 + a_1b_1)]} \gamma^j y_{t-1} \right]
$$

(12.2.20)

Now noting that the lag operator in the above expression operates on the $j$ time subscript, we may solve this expression as

$$
E_{t-1}p_{t+j} = \frac{1}{1 + b_2 + c_1} \sum_{i=0}^{\infty} \left( \frac{b_2 + c_1}{1 + b_2 + c_1} \right)^i \overline{m}_{t+j+i}
$$

$$
+ \frac{a_0(b_2 + c_1) + a_1\phi_1 - \gamma(b_2 + c_1 + a_1b_1)}{a_1[1 + (1 - \gamma)(b_2 + c_1)]} \gamma^j y_{t-1}.
$$

(12.2.21)

Some tedious manipulations now allow us to solve for the following reduced form for the price process:

$$p_t = \frac{1}{1 + b_2 + c_1} \sum_{i=0}^{\infty} \left( \frac{b_2 + c_1}{1 + b_2 + c_1} \right)^i \overline{m}_{t+i} + \epsilon_t$$

$$+ \frac{a_0(b_2 + c_1) + a_1\phi_1 - \gamma(b_2 + c_1 + a_1b_1)}{a_1[1 + (1 - \gamma)(b_2 + c_1)]} y_{t-1},$$

(12.2.22)

or, plugging in for $y_{t-1}$ from a backwards iterated form of equation (12.2.8) above, we obtain the expression

$$p_t = \frac{1}{1 + b_2 + c_1} \sum_{i=0}^{\infty} \left( \frac{b_2 + c_1}{1 + b_2 + c_1} \right)^i \overline{m}_{t+i} + \epsilon_t$$

$$+ \frac{a_0(b_2 + c_1) + a_1\phi_1 - \gamma(b_2 + c_1 + a_1b_1)}{a_1[1 + (1 - \gamma)(b_2 + c_1)]}$$

(12.2.23)

$$\times \sum_{i=1}^{\infty} \gamma^i \frac{a_1 u_{1t-i} + \beta(b_2 + c_1)u_{2t-i} - \beta a_1 v_{t-i}}{a_1 + \beta(b_2 + c_1 + a_1b_1)}.$$

This reduced form for the price process expresses the price level as a sum of terms involving current and future money supply levels, the current composite disturbance $\epsilon_t$, and a sum of past disturbance terms operating through the effects of lagged output shocks impinging on current levels of output supply and demand.

Note, in the above expression, that the quantity theory of money does not hold on a period-by-period basis. That is, we do not observe that $E(p_t)$ is strictly proportional to $\overline{m}_t$. Instead, the sequence $\{p_t\}$ depends in a somewhat complicated fashion on the sequence $\{\overline{m}_t\}$. However, we still find that the long-run quantity theory of money holds in the sense that $E(p)$ is strictly proportional to $\overline{m}$ when the sequence $\{\overline{m}_t\}$ is simply equal to a constant $\overline{m}$ independent of $t$. We also find that the policymaker may achieve any price path he or she wishes, at least in the sense of being able to control $E_t(p_{t+i})$ precisely, even if this may entail complex movements in $\overline{m}_t$. Later, in Section 12.3, we find that even such control of the price level becomes a more complex issue.

## Contemporaneous Aggregate Information

The original version of the model of the preceding section is somewhat unrealistic. The policymaker has access to information on the level of the current nominal interest while private agents, in constructing their price expectations, do not. One possible way of reconciling this asymmetry is to make the alternate assumption that neither the policymaker nor private agents observe $r_t$ prior to the determination of the current output level $y_t$. This case was alluded to in the previous section when we considered the possibility of constraining $c_1$ to equal zero. However, even that case does not address the asymmetry presented by the simultaneous existence of an investment demand schedule that relates aggregate investment demand to the current nominal interest rate through its inclusion in the real interest rate term $r_t - E_{t-1}(p_{t+1} - p_t)$.

Analysis of a macroeconomic model with a consistently specified information structure awaits the analysis of Chapter 14. However, we should note that a more consistent version of the present model may be obtained if we adopt the alternate assumption that *all* agents possess information on the current nominal interest rate. In this case, the information set for private agents is given by

$$\Omega_{t-1}^+ = \{r_t, r_{t-1}, \ldots, p_{t-1}, \ldots, y_{t-1}, \ldots\}. \tag{12.2.24}$$

The level of output supply is now given by

$$y_t = \beta(p_t - E_{t-1}^+ p_t) + \gamma y_{t-1} + u_{1t}, \quad \text{where } E_{t-1}^+ p_t \equiv E[p_t | \Omega_{t-1}^+]. \tag{12.2.25}$$

The main difference in this formulation is that the observation of the contemporaneous interest rate assures us that

$$\text{Var}(p_t | \Omega_{t-1}^+) \leq \text{Var}(p_t | \Omega_{t-1}). \tag{12.2.26}$$

That is, the price-level forecast variance is, in general, lower in this form of the model because agents have more information from which to extract a more precise estimate of $p_t$.

Now plugging in for $p_t^e = E_{t-1}^+ p_t$ and $p_{t+1}^e = E_{t-1}^+ p_{t+1}$ into the semireduced form for $p_t$ allows us to rewrite that expression as

$$p_t = \frac{a_1 \overline{m}_t}{a_1 + \beta(b_2 + c_1 + a_1 b_1)} - \frac{-a_1(b_2 + c_1) + \beta(b_2 + c_1 + a_1 b_1)}{a_1 + \beta(b_2 + c_1 + a_1 b_1)} E_{t-1}^+ p_t$$

$$+ \frac{a_1(b_2 + c_1)}{a_1 + \beta(b_2 + c_1 + a_1 b_1)} E_{t-1}^+ p_{t+1} \tag{12.2.27}$$

$$+ \frac{a_0(b_2 + c_1) + a_1 \phi_1 - \gamma(b_2 + c_1 + a_1 b_1)}{a_1 + \beta(b_2 + c_1 + a_1 b_1)} y_{t-1} + \epsilon_t,$$

where

$$\epsilon_t \equiv \frac{-(b_2 + c_1 + a_1 b_1)u_{1t} + (b_2 + c_1)u_{2t} - a_1 v_t}{a_1 + \beta(b_2 + c_1 + a_1 b_1)}, \quad \text{as before.} \tag{12.2.28}$$

Now taking the expectation of the above expression with respect to $\Omega_{t-1}^+$ and subtracting from the original form of the equation yields

$$p_t - E_{t-1}^+ p_t = \epsilon_t - E_{t-1}^+ \epsilon_t, \tag{12.2.29}$$

and so

$$y_t = \beta(\epsilon_t - E_{t-1}^+ \epsilon_t) + \gamma y_{t-1} + u_{1t}. \tag{12.2.30}$$

The difference between this output specification and the one of the previous section is the addition of the term $E_{t-1}^+ \epsilon_t$. In that section's model, this term is identically equal to zero. In the present model, this is no longer the case. However, this case still retains the property that $y_t$ is independent of $\phi_1$ and $\overline{m}_t$. Feedback policy parameters that operate on $\Omega_{t-1}$ and deterministic components of the money supply both exert identical influences on $\epsilon_t$ and $E_{t-1}^+ \epsilon_t$.

Recall the present assumption that agents observe the current nominal interest rate $r_t$. Since agents also are assumed to know the full structure of the economy, they also must know $b_2$ and $c_1$, and so they therefore have information on $(b_2 + c_1)r_t$. From the money market equilibrium condition agents therefore must observe

$$s_t \equiv p_t + \beta b_1(p_t - E_{t-1}^+ p_t) + (\gamma b_1 - \phi_1)y_{t-1} - \overline{m}_t + (b_1 u_{1t} + v_t)$$
$$= (1 + \beta b_1)p_t + (b_1 u_{1t} + v_t) - \beta b_1 E_{t-1}^+ p_t + (\gamma b_1 - \phi_1)y_{t-1} - \overline{m}_t.$$

(12.2.31)

In the above expression, agents know $E_{t-1}^+ p_t$, $y_{t-1}$, $\overline{m}_t$, and all the parameters of the model. Therefore, from observation of $s_t$, it is in principle a straightforward signal extraction problem to determine $E_{t-1}^+ \epsilon_t$. Since the interest rate policy parameter $c_1$ is in general capable of affecting the covariance structure of $(p_t, u_{1t}, u_{2t}, v_t)$, selection of $c_1$ also affects the variance of $\epsilon_t - E_{t-1}^+ \epsilon_t$. That is, selection of $c_1$ may affect the information structure of the economy. However, any effect of policy on output arising from the selection of alternative values of $c_1$ does not come about from an ability of the policy-maker to systematically fool private agents but rather from an ability to change the informational content of the endogenous variable $r_t$. McCallum (1980) discusses this issue in some more detail.

As noted above, selection of values of $\phi_1$ and $\overline{m}_t$ cannot affect the statistical properties of $y_t$ and so, in that sense, the policy ineffectiveness proposition holds in this specification of the model as well as in earlier specifications. However, if we require that the selection of $c_1$ also be irrelevant for the policy ineffectiveness proposition to hold, then things become more complex. In the models of earlier sections, selection of $c_1$ has always at least affected the variances of $y_t$ and $p_t$. Whether selection of $c_1$ affects these variances in the present model is a more difficult question to answer. In general, selection of $c_1$ does matter. However, rather than more carefully pursuing this question at this time, we postpone this type of analysis to Chapter 14, whose model is more properly suited to answer questions that turn on policies that affect the informational structure of the economy.

## 12.3 INFLATION AND STRATEGIC MONETARY POLICY

This section discusses strategic models of macroeconomic policy. The literature we examine builds on the works of Kydland and Prescott (1977) and Barro and Gordon (1983a,b). Basic to this analysis are three considerations. First, the objectives of private agents and policymakers may be at odds with one another even if only for the policymaker's attempts to correct for the ill effects of externalities. Second, attempts by the policymaker to achieve the most preferred outcome may not only fail, but such attempts may achieve an outcome deemed inferior by both the policymaker and by private agents. Third, cooperative behavior by the policymaker may be optimal, but arrangements to ensure such cooperation may be difficult or impossible to achieve.

The basic setup of this section is similar to the period-by-period policy analysis of Section 12.1. The policymaker acts after private agents have already formed their expectations. Also, as in Section 12.2, private agents anticipate the policymaker's actions in forming their expectations. But unlike the analysis of Section 12.2, equilibrium in the economy does not come about contemporaneously with the actions of both the policymaker and the private agents. Instead, private agents first form their expectations, and then the policymaker takes his or her policy action.

As in Sections 12.1 and 12.2, the policymaker may wish to achieve a level of output different from (higher than) that rate of output consistent with $p = p^e$. However, just as in

Section 12.2, the policymaker fails to achieve this objective. The new insight is that the preference of the policymaker for a level of output higher than that consistent with $p = p^e$ now, of necessity, leads to a higher price level (inflation rate) than would otherwise occur. Despite the pessimistic nature of this result, we later note that there may exist alternative institutional arrangements that might alleviate this tendency.

## A Positive Theory of Inflation Policy

Recall our earlier analysis of policymaking in which expectations are formed rationally and in which the policymaker follows a fixed rule that is known by private agents. Since output responds only to price-level surprises, the determination of output is completely unaffected by the specific form of the policy rule. In such instances, if there are costs to high prices (high inflation), the optimal policy is to promote low prices (or, alternatively, to achieve zero inflation).

In this section, we consider policy interactions that occur over a single period of time. Clearly, in such a situation, a policy rule of the sort we studied in Section 12.2 is not a sensible construct. Therefore, we plan now to depart from the sort of stochastic steady-state models that have often been our primary focus of study. Within a single period of time, is it not conceivable that a policymaker might be able to induce a price-level surprise and raise output above the level consistent with $p = p^e$? Although intuition might suggest that this is possible, we demonstrate below that rational behavior on the part of private agents still precludes this possibility.

Our formal model is similar to those of previous sections. However, in order to concentrate on the specifics of the problem at hand, let us abstract from most of the macroeconomic detail. The abstractions we have in mind consist of ignoring aggregate demand and the specifics of the money market. We therefore simply assume that output is equal to aggregate supply. Let us further assume that a policymaker, perhaps a monetary policymaker, is able to precisely control the price level $p$. Finally, let us assume that there are no stochastic disturbances as such. The only possibility of "uncertainty" may be some doubt on the part of private agents as to how the policymaker will behave.

We continue to assume a specific functional form for the aggregate supply function given by

$$y = \beta(p - p^e), \tag{12.3.1}$$

where $y$ again represents the logarithm of output and $\beta$ represents the elasticity of output with respect to expectational errors. This supply relationship is meant to capture the actions of private agents. Implicit in this supply response is the notion that private agents would prefer to "know" the price level and produce at $y = 0$. Production levels that are higher or lower occur because private agents are "fooled" into producing more or less than they would prefer. The microeconomics of this aggregate supply function might therefore be implicit in the analysis of Chapter 5.[3]

---

[3]For this specific application, a motivation for the aggregate supply function based upon sticky wages or nominally denominated labor contracts is actually much more persuasive. It is after all difficult to explain local, aggregate price-level confusion when the monetary authority precisely controls the aggregate price level. However, all that is really necessary here is some relationship between the level of output and price-level or inflation rate surprises no matter how such a relationship is justified.

As noted above, the policymaker in this model sets $p$ after the private agents have formed their expectations $p^e$. In the absence of market imperfections or other distortions, there would seem to be no reason for the policymaker to do anything but set $p = p^e$ to achieve $y = 0$. This policy would presumably maximize private agent welfare.

However, the existence of proportional income taxes or the existence of unemployment compensation and minimum-wage laws among other potential distortions and market imperfections might cause the socially optimal output level $\hat{y}$ to deviate from the output level that would be generated by private sector behavior in the absence of price-level surprises, $y = 0$. We therefore simply assume that the private sector tends, on average, to produce too little output and hence that $\hat{y}$ is positive.

The policymaker in this model acts to minimize the value of a loss function that penalizes deviations of output away from the socially optimal level $\hat{y}$. The policymaker is also averse to price-level deviations. Such concern about the price level is an attempt to capture concern about the rate of inflation.[4] Such aversion to inflation could reflect concern with the need to economize on money holdings when nominal interest rates rise due to high actual and expected inflation. Concern over inflation could also be indicative of attempts to minimize the size of menu-type costs of price changes. In any event, we attempt to capture policymaker preferences with a loss function of the form

$$\mathcal{L} = \tfrac{1}{2}a(y - \hat{y})^2 + \tfrac{1}{2}bp^2. \tag{12.3.2}$$

The policymaker is able to generate any desired price level, and that price level is generated after private agents form their expectations. However, we assume that private agents are aware of the exact circumstances under which the policymaker sets the price level and there is no uncertainty in the system. Therefore, expectations turn out, ex post, to be correct.

This setup naturally leads to a Nash-type equilibrium game between the policymaker and the private agents. The policymaker acts as if agents' expectations are fixed in choosing an optimal price level. Private agents act as if the policymaker's method of choosing the price level is determined by maximizing behavior. Each of the two types of agents then maximizes given the presumably fixed behavior of the other. Equilibrium occurs when the choice rules of both parties are mutually consistent.

First, let us consider the choice problem of the policymaker. The policymaker selects the price level for a given value of the private agents' expected price level. The policymaker's formal problem is given by

$$\min_{p} [\tfrac{1}{2}a(y - \hat{y})^2 + \tfrac{1}{2}bp^2] \tag{12.3.3}$$

---

[4] The original Barro and Gordon papers specify a supply function given by

$$y = \beta(\pi - \pi^e).$$

However, if we assume that the previous period price level $p_{-1}$ is known, the two formulations are identical. In particular,

$$\pi - \pi^e = (p - p_{-1}) - (p^e - p_{-1}) = p - p^e.$$

Furthermore, with $p_{-1}$ given, concern about $\pi$ may properly be captured by concern about $p$. This type of relationship between $p_t - p_t^e$ and $\pi_t - \pi_t^e$ should be familiar from the analysis of Chapter 7.

subject to

$$y = \beta(p - p^e), \quad p^e \text{ exogenous.} \tag{12.3.4}$$

Differentiating expression (12.3.3) with respect to $p$ and collecting terms, we find that the optimal price level is given by

$$p = \frac{a\beta(\beta p^e + \hat{y})}{a\beta^2 + b}. \tag{12.3.5}$$

Implicit in the private agents' supply function is their desire to accurately predict the price level. Their preferences are therefore consistent with an attempt to minimize a loss function of the form $(p - p^e)^2$. Since they are assumed to know the policymaker's behavior in setting $p$, it is therefore reasonable to suppose that the private agents solve

$$\min_{p^e} (p - p^e)^2 \tag{12.3.6}$$

subject to

$$p = \frac{a\beta(\beta p^e + \hat{y})}{a\beta^2 + b}. \tag{12.3.7}$$

Trivially, the solution to this problem is given implicitly by

$$p^e = \frac{a\beta(\beta p^e + \hat{y})}{a\beta^2 + b}. \tag{12.3.8}$$

Now solving this implicit relationship in $p^e$, we find that

$$p^e = \frac{a\beta\hat{y}}{b}. \tag{12.3.9}$$

The Nash equilibrium for this problem must therefore be given by

$$p = p^e = \frac{a\beta\hat{y}}{b}. \tag{12.3.10}$$

Finally, we note that since $p = p^e$, it must be the case that $y = 0$.

## Equilibrium Inflation and the Time Inconsistency Problem

As we previewed earlier, the equilibrium level of (log) output in this model is just the natural level of zero. Second, we note that the equilibrium (log) price level is always strictly positive. These results obtain even though zero levels of both output and prices are clearly technically feasible, and such levels would be preferred by both the policymaker and the private agents to the equilibrium that actually occurs.

We also note that the greater the socially optimal level of output $\hat{y}$, the greater the level of prices and the worse off the economy is. This result suggests a channel through which a higher level of government activity, which might require a higher level of distorting taxes, might lead to higher inflation. However, we see in this example a chain of causation that is far from transparent.

Recall that the parameter $\beta$ represents the elasticity of output with respect to price-level surprises. This parameter often has a natural interpretation as the inverse slope of the output form of the short-run Phillips curve. We therefore find that a flatter Phillips curve leads to a higher equilibrium price level (i.e., more inflation). Note the similarity to the argument sometimes advanced by policymakers that a flat short-run Phillips curve makes it very costly to reduce inflation.

We finally note that the policymaker's tastes for output shortfalls and price-level changes have predictable equilibrium effects. When the policymaker finds losses in output relative to $\hat{y}$ to be very costly (a large value for the parameter $a$), the policymaker tolerates a very high price level (inflation rate) in his or her fruitless attempt to raise output. Alternatively, if the policymaker finds a high price level to be very costly (a high value for the parameter $b$), the equilibrium price level turns out to be lower than it otherwise would be.

At this stage in the analysis, it is natural to wonder about the feasibility of a policy of $p = 0$. Such a policy leads to the mimimum technically possible value of the policymaker's loss function. Furthermore, such a policy, if credible, allows private agents to perfectly predict the price level and therefore makes them as well off as is technically possible too. Unfortunately, in the context of the present model, as long as the policymaker is unable to rigidly precommit to a policy of $p = 0$, the private agents will not believe that this policy will be implemented. Finally, even if the private agents believe the policymaker, it would be in the policymaker's interests to renege on the choice of $p = 0$ after the fact.

The key to this dilemma is Kydland and Prescott's (1977) notion of the time inconsistency problem. A precommitment to $p = 0$ that is, in fact, honored is the optimal policy, but it is a time-inconsistent policy. The term *time inconsistency* refers to situations in which the public realizes that the policymaker has an incentive not to follow through with the optimal policy.

To gain some insight into the issue of time inconsistency, consider the following nonmacroeconomic examples, which are due to Kydland and Prescott (1977). First consider patent protection. Some form of patent protection is generally regarded as a socially useful policy. Presumably, more scientific discoveries will be made if the discoverers have the expectation of a period of monopoly rights on their inventions. However, once a discovery is made, society (in the form of the government) has an incentive to take the protection away in an attempt to extract the monopoly rents from the inventor.

Next consider flood control policy. What incentives govern the private decisions of whether to build houses and other structures in a flood plain? In the absence of costly public flood control projects, such areas routinely flood. The socially optimal outcome may therefore entail building neither structures nor costly flood control projects. However, potential builders realize that if enough construction is undertaken in the flood plain, the government is likely to step in and build the costly flood control project. Public announcements that the project will not be built under any circumstances are not credible.

Finally, consider taxation of the returns to capital. Public finance theory suggests that the taxation of factors that are supplied inelastically is the least distortionary of taxes when lump-sum taxes are not feasible. Therefore, once capital goods have been put in place, they are a very tempting source of tax revenue. Similar considerations would suggest taxing wealth instead of income. However, such policies, especially if they are preannounced, may not be optimal. Agents may not put as much capital in place, and they may choose to save less as to acquire less wealth if they expect that the returns to such activities will be heavily taxed. Optimal policy may well involve the promise not to heavily tax capital and wealth. However, such policies are time inconsistent because agents may fully expect that the policymaker will, ex post, impose severe capital and wealth taxes anyway.

In all of these cases, problems arise due to public expectations about future policy and the possible inability of policymakers to tie their hands on the conduct of future policy. That is, policymakers in each of these cases have an incentive to later deviate from the optimal policy. It is this kind of consideration that leads to the apparently unnecessary inflation in the present (Barro and Gordon, 1983b) model.

The issue of time inconsistency argues for policy rules over policy discretion. That is, time inconsistency argues for legal mandates for the policymaker to adhere to proscribed policies. However, at least in the macroeconomic policy area, discretion has long been viewed as a very valuable option for the policymaker. For example, Fischer (1980) points to a need for the monetary authority to be able to respond to bank panics and a desirability for the policymaker's ability to respond to changes in the nature of business cycles over time. Finally, the possibility that stochastic economic models may not be capable of even listing all possible states of nature that policy might wish to respond to argues against formally tying the hands of the macroeconomic policymaker.

## Policymaker Reputation as a Check on Inflation

Short of absolute and irrevocable policy rules, what sort of hope is there against the time inconsistency problem? One possibility first advanced by Barro and Gordon (1983a) is that policymakers value a reputation for not deviating from the optimal policy over long periods of time. The basic argument proceeds as follows. Suppose that the monetary policy game is to be played repeatedly. In such a repeated-game setup, private agents can compare their expectations about policymaker behavior with the actual evolution of policymaker behavior. In particular, if the policymaker consistently promises to observe a particular policy rule, then private agents can observe over time whether the policymaker carries through with his or her promises.

The Barro and Gordon (1983a) analysis assumes that, at least provisionally, private agents are willing to believe that the policymaker will adhere to a policy rule rather than resorting to discretionary inflation. Furthermore, as long as the policymaker continues to follow the rule, private agents continue to believe that the policymaker will persist in this course of action. However, should the policymaker deviate from the rule and adopt the discretionary policy instead, private agents will, for one period, refuse to believe that the policymaker will do anything other than resort to discretion.

The equilibrium to this modified version of the monetary policy game is intermediate between the optimal policy rule of $p = 0$ and the discretionary policy solution that we derived earlier. That is, a policy rule $p^*$ such that

$$0 < p^* < \frac{a\beta\hat{y}}{b} \tag{12.3.11}$$

turns out to be the equilibrium. Private agents believe that the policymaker will carry out this rule because they understand that the policymaker values his or her reputation for following the rule. The policymaker resists the temptation to cheat on the rule and adopt the discretionary policy because to do so would bring about an even worse state of affairs in the following period when private agents would refuse to believe any policy pronouncement other than that of $p = a\beta\hat{y}/b$.

A key question in this analysis concerns whether the equilibrium policy rule is closer to the optimal rule of $p = 0$ or closer to the discretionary equilibrium. This question turns primarily on the policymaker's rate of time preference. If the policymaker heavily discounts the future, then the equilibrium closely resembles the discretionary equilibrium. Alternatively, if the policymaker's discount rate is low, an equilibrium closer to the optimal policy of $p = 0$ becomes possible.

One problem with the Barro and Gordon (1983a) reputational analysis is the arbitrariness of the potential punishment faced by the policymaker for failing to adhere to the policy rule. That is, the private agent's response of failing to believe the policymaker for exactly one period following a lapse into discretion is not well grounded in maximizing behavior. Backus and Driffill (1985) attempt to remedy this problem by appealing to private agent uncertainty about the policymaker's preferences. In particular, they introduce the possibility of two types of policymaker (government): "wet" governments, who are very concerned with meeting their output goal but are relatively unconcerned about inflation, and "hard-nosed" governments, who are much more concerned about inflation relative to output shortfalls. Much of their policy game then centers around private agent attempts to discern whether the government is wet or hard-nosed.

The basic preference framework of Backus and Driffill (1985) has a natural extension to the economics of electoral politics. Alesina (1987) formalizes this notion by specifically allowing for the election of political parties with differing inflation-output preferences. Alesina (1987) demonstrates that such a model is capable of supporting a political business cycle in the sense of Nordhaus (1975). Alesina (1987) also demonstrates that such a two-party interaction can improve upon the purely discretionary equilibrium and also reduce the magnitude of economic fluctuations that would otherwise arise in his model.

Although Backus and Driffill (1985) introduce uncertainty about policymakers' preferences, their framework still assumes that the state of the economy is common knowledge both to the policymaker and to private agents. Alternatively, Canzoneri (1985) considers the possibility that the policymaker may have information that is not available to private agents. In particular, Canzoneri (1985) assumes that the policymaker knows the value of money demand shocks while private agents do not. This possibility makes it more difficult for private agents to verify whether or not the policymaker is adhering to his or her announced policy rule. The basic insight here is that even if institutional arrangements could, in principle, be implemented to solve the time inconsistency problem, monetary policy games of the sort envisioned by Barro and Gordon (1983b) might still prove problematic.

An insightful review of the monetary policy games literature is provided by Rogoff (1987). However, Fischer (1986) doubts that time inconsistency considerations constitute a real problem in the actual practice of monetary policy. He notes that the kind of inflationary bias implicit in this type of analysis does not seem to appear in many actual episodes of high inflation. He further notes the many instances in which countries have consciously pursued deflationary policies following wartime inflations and wonders how monetary policy games theory can account for greatly differing experiences with inflation across time and across countries.

## Some Concluding Remarks

The analysis of this chapter started with an examination of monetary policymaking in an equilibrium macroeconomic model with purely exogenous price-level expectations. In such a model, monetary policy is capable of achieving any desired level of economic activity. This scenario changed dramatically when we invoked the constraint that expectations be formed rationally. In that setting, some form of the policy ineffectiveness proposition was always shown to hold. The only hope for an effective monetary policy involved an appropriate setting for the interest sensitivity of money supply. However, even that type of policy was shown to be effective only to the extent that it alters the informational content of the interest rate.

Finally, we considered the possibility that monetary policy might be best modeled as a game played between the policymaker and private agents who have differing objectives. In this situation, we showed that while the general idea of policy ineffectiveness with respect to output levels continues to hold, an inflationary bias is injected into monetary policymaking that would not otherwise be present.

# REFERENCES

Alesina, Alberto, "Macroeconomic Policy in a Two-Party System as a Repeated Game," *Quarterly Journal of Economics,* August, 1987, 651–678.

Backus, David, and John Driffill, "Inflation and Reputation," *American Economic Review*, June, 1985, 530–538.

Barro, Robert J., "Rational Expectations and the Role of Monetary Policy," *Journal of Monetary Economics,* January, 1976, 1–32.

Barro, Robert J., and David B. Gordon, "Rules, Discretion and Reputation in a Model of Monetary Policy," *Journal of Monetary Economics,* July, 1983a, 101–121.

Barro, Robert J., and David B. Gordon, "A Positive Theory of Monetary Policy in a Natural Rate Model," *Journal of Political Economy,* August, 1983b, 589–610.

Canzoneri, Matthew B., "Monetary Policy Games and the Role of Private Information," *American Economic Review,* December, 1985, 1056–1070.

Fischer, Stanley, "On Activist Monetary Policy with Rational Expectations," in Stanley Fischer, ed., *Rational Expectations and Economic Policy,* Chicago, University of Chicago Press, 1980.

Fischer, Stanley, "Time Consistent Monetary and Fiscal Policies: A Survey," mimeo, Massachusetts Institute of Technology, 1986.

Hall, Robert E., "Stochastic Implications of the Life Cycle–Permanent Income Hypothesis: Theory and Evidence," *Journal of Political Economy,* December, 1978, 971–987.

Kydland, Finn E., and Edward C. Prescott, "Rules Rather Than Discretion: The Inconsistency of Optimal Plans," *Journal of Political Economy,* June, 1977, 473–491.

Lucas, Robert E., Jr., "Some International Evidence on Output-Inflation Tradeoffs," *American Economic Review,* June, 1973, 326–334.

Lucas, Robert E., Jr., and Edward C. Prescott, "Investment Under Uncertainty," *Econometrica,* September, 1971, 659–681.

McCallum, Bennett T., "Rational Expectations and Macroeconomic Stabilization Policy," *Journal of Money, Credit, and Banking,* November, 1980, Part 2, 716–746.

Muth, John F., "Rational Expectations and the Theory of Price Movements," *Econometrica,* July, 1961, 315–353.

Nordhaus, William, "The Political Business Cycle," *Review of Economic Studies,* April, 1975, 169–190.

Rogoff, Kenneth, "Reputational Constraints on Monetary Policy," *Carnegie-Rochester Conference Series on Public Policy,* Amsterdam, North-Holland, Spring, 1987, 141–182.

Sargent, Thomas J., *Macroeconomic Theory,* 2nd ed., Orlando, FL, Academic, 1987.

Sargent, Thomas J., and Neil Wallace, "Rational Expectations, the Optimal Monetary Instrument, and the Optimal Money Supply Rule," *Journal of Political Economy,* April, 1975, 241–254.

Sargent, Thomas J., and Neil Wallace, "Rational Expectations and the Theory of Economic Policy," *Journal of Monetary Economics,* April, 1976, 169–183.

# Chapter 13

## Employment Contracts and Wage Indexation

Although there is a long history of explicit employment contracts between workers and firms, such contracts cover a rather small and generally diminishing fraction of total employment. Pioneering papers by Azariadis (1975), Baily (1974), and Gordon (1974) have extended the idea of labor contracts to include "implicit" labor contracts. Such arrangements, although informal in nature, contain the same general types of provisions as explicit labor contracts. Though not legally binding, such arrangements may, as noted by Grossman (1977), be enforced through reputational considerations. Workers and firms that consistently renege on implicit contracts may lose the market ability to enter into such valuable agreements in the future.

An important rationale for explicit and implicit employment contracts is the possibility that there may be important investments that are specific to a particular worker-firm attachment. Once such investments are made, the physical productivity of the worker becomes highest in the firm in which he or she is employed, and the worker becomes the most productive available candidate for the position he or she fills in the firm.

With such specific investments in place, the labor market employment relationship becomes one of bilateral monopoly. In such circumstances, auction market allocation mechanisms may become infeasible. One possible alternative is ex post bargaining. However, if one of the parties (typically the firm) generally winds up in a significantly stronger bargaining position, the worker may find the original investment in the relationship unattractive even though it presents a generous expected return. A viable alternative solution to this potential "holdup problem" is for the worker and firm to enter into an agreement prior to the realization of the returns to the relationship. Such an agreement often takes the form of an explicit or implicit labor contract that may relate hours of employment and rate of pay to some readily observable outcomes of a set of random variables that determine the returns to the investment.

There are two main bodies of research that apply the analytical structure of labor

**387**

contracts to areas of interest to macroeconomists. The first area, although primarily microeconomic in nature, considers the addition of risk-shifting or risk-pooling arrangements to the basic labor contract. This enormous body of literature is well surveyed by Rosen (1985). These models generally have three important properties. First, such models generally imply the possibility of an outcome that appears as involuntary unemployment even if the Pareto-optimal amount of labor is employed. Second, these models almost always have the property that the observed real wage only inadvertently equals the marginal product of labor. Third, the possibility of equilibrium employment levels that are either greater than or less than the efficient employment level become possible depending upon the specific set of assumptions employed. Contracts of this type are analyzed in Section 13.1.

The second area of research analyzes how contracts may be written that try to correctly link wage and employment levels to real productivity shocks. Such a problem may be nontrivial if there is more than one type of shock and if the contracting technology precludes the possibility of writing fully contingent contracts. This body of literature is highlighted by papers by Fischer (1977a), Gray (1976), and Barro (1977), and it is reviewed in Section 13.2.

Contracts of this second type generally provide for nominally denominated contingencies and then allow employment to be demand determined at the contractually determined wage rate. Macroeconomic models that include such contracts behave in a manner quite similar to the sticky-wage model of Chapter 5. These models have somewhat stronger microeconomic foundations, however, and simultaneously provide a propagation mechanism for employment effects of several kinds of stochastic shocks. Finally, these models provide a role for a kind of policy activism that was missing in much of the analysis of Chapter 12.

## 13.1 RISK-SHIFTING CONTRACTS

In this section, we analyze ways in which employment contracts generate an appropriate level of employment in a series of spatially separate labor markets and simultaneously shift risk from risk-averse households to risk-neutral firms. We begin the analysis by considering a case in which households' labor endowment is divisible and derive optimal employment contracts that involve worksharing. We then go on to consider the nature of optimal contracts in cases in which households' endowments of time are indivisible. Such models generally yield equilibria in which the possibility of unemployment emerges, and such unemployment may appear to conform to common definitions of involuntary unemployment. However, such involuntary unemployment may be efficient even though some households may regret, ex post, agreeing, ex ante, to contract terms that were clearly in their best interests.

### Worksharing Contracts

When the level of employment at either the aggregate or firm level changes, there are at least two possible ways in which such a change may occur. As one possibility, the number of hours worked per worker could remain constant, and the change in employment could be facilitated through a change in the number of workers who work. Alternatively, the number of workers who work could remain constant, while the number of hours worked per worker could change. We refer to this second phenomenon as "worksharing."

Much of the microeconomic literature on employment contracts seeks to explain unemployment by positing circumstances in which worksharing is artificially precluded. Alternatively, we begin our analysis by examining worksharing contracts because such contracts are most clearly efficient and because the resulting equilibrium allocations most closely resemble the now familiar analysis of Chapter 5.

Consider a labor market inhabited by a large number of identical firms. Each firm produces a homogeneous, nonstorable product and has a fixed number of workers attached to it. These workers are assumed to be ex post immobile across firms in order to capture the spirit of past investments that have been made in the worker-firm relationship.

Each firm produces output according to

$$Y = e^{u+\epsilon}f(L), \qquad f' > 0, \qquad f'' < 0, \tag{13.1.1}$$

where $u$ represents an economywide productivity shock, $\epsilon$ represents a firm-specific productivity shock, and $L$ represents the total input of labor services at the firm. For most of the analysis, the realization of $u$ is taken to be common knowledge, known before the writing of any contracts or the production of any output. Alternatively, the random variable $\epsilon$ is realized after employment contracts have been agreed upon but before production takes place. In general, employment contracts are written contingent upon the mutually observable and verifiable realization of $\epsilon$.[1] The random variable $\epsilon$ is normally distributed with zero mean and variance $\sigma_\epsilon^2$. The number of firms is large enough that the sampling distribution of $\epsilon$ is also equal to the probability density function of $\epsilon$ with probability 1.

The utility level of each household under contract to the firm is given by

$$V = U[c - h(x)], \qquad U' > 0, \qquad U'' \le 0, \qquad h' > 0, \qquad h'' \ge 0, \tag{13.1.2}$$

where $c$ denotes household consumption of the single produced good and $x$ denotes the fraction of the household's total time endowment devoted to market work. Therefore, $0 \le x \le 1$. For simplicity, we suppress a subscript for each household as long as no confusion is likely to arise. One particularly convenient functional form for $h(\cdot)$ we formally adopt in Section 13.2 is given by[2]

$$h(x) = \beta x^{1+1/\eta}. \tag{13.1.3}$$

As long as $U'' < 0$ and $h'' > 0$, efficiency always requires that each household work the same amount as every other household in the same firm. Efficiency considerations also favor constant employment levels across firms, but this further efficiency move would, in general, only be possible if labor mobility across firms were an option. An

---

[1]Throughout this section, we only consider situations in which both the workers and the firm observe the realization of $\epsilon$. For a survey of cases of asymmetric information in which only the firm and not the workers observe $\epsilon$, see Rosen (1985). As Rosen demonstrates, considerations of asymmetric information greatly complicate the formal analysis.

[2]The usefulness of this particular functional form is that it implies a labor supply schedule with constant elasticity $\eta$.

important motivation for contracts in this economy, however, is that such labor mobility is not feasible.

Each firm contracts with $n$ households. With each of $n$ households supplying an amount of labor services given by $x$, total employment in the firm is given by

$$L = nx. \tag{13.1.4}$$

Employment contracts specify $x$ and $c$ in advance as functions of the yet-to-be-realized value of the random variable $\epsilon$. That is, a labor contract consists of functions $c(\epsilon)$ and $x(\epsilon)$.

The expected utility of each household in the firm is given by

$$E(V) = E_\epsilon\{U[c(\epsilon) - h(x(\epsilon))]\}. \tag{13.1.5}$$

The expected value of profits for the firm is given by

$$E(\Pi) = E_\epsilon\{e^{u+\epsilon}f[nx(\epsilon)] - nc(\epsilon)\}. \tag{13.1.6}$$

There are two ways to proceed to characterize an optimal employment contract. Many analyses maximize the expected value of profits subject to a constraint that the expected level of utility for the households be at least as great as some specified value $\overline{V}$. Alternatively, we specify the optimal contract as maximizing the expected value of utility for the representative household subject to a constraint that the firm's expected profit be at least as great as some specified value $\overline{\Pi}$. Clearly, either problem is the dual of the other, and solution of either problem is a contract that is Pareto optimal. However, absent a more elaborate theory about the supply of and demand for employment contracts, each contractual arrangement is the subject of a bilateral monopoly bargaining problem, and so we cannot more precisely determine which point on the contract curve the bargaining parties will settle upon.

We therefore seek to choose a contingent contract in the form of functions $c(\epsilon)$ and $x(\epsilon)$ that maximize the Lagrangian expression

$$E_\epsilon\{U[c(\epsilon) - h(x(\epsilon))] + \lambda[\overline{\Pi} - e^{u+\epsilon}f[nx(\epsilon)] + nc(\epsilon)]\}. \tag{13.1.7}$$

As discussed in Rosen (1985), the first-order conditions for this maximization problem may be expressed in the compact form

$$U'\{c(\epsilon) - h[x(\epsilon)]\} = -n\lambda, \tag{13.1.8}$$

$$U'\{c(\epsilon) - h[x(\epsilon)]\}h'[x(\epsilon)] + n\lambda e^{u+\epsilon}f'[nx(\epsilon)] = 0, \tag{13.1.9}$$

where these equations hold at each possible realization of $\epsilon$.

The first of these equations requires that the marginal utility of consumption be equal at every realization of $\epsilon$. As long as $U'' < 0$, this equation has the implication that the value of the term $c(\epsilon) - h[x(\epsilon)]$ must be independent of the value of $\epsilon$. Therefore, households are equally well off no matter what value of $\epsilon$ is realized.

Equivalently, workers in "less productive" firms enjoy the same level of utility as workers in "more productive" firms. Risk-neutral firms therefore absorb all of the risk of firm-specific productivity shocks. The firms are presumably capable of providing such insurance by engaging in trades among themselves in state-contingent claims. Such trading, although outside the realm of the formal model, is by assumption precluded to households due to moral hazard problems or prohibitively high transaction costs. We only require that, in the aggregate, output be at least as great as the total value of contractually specified consumption claims held by households.

Rearranging the first-order conditions, we find that

$$h'[x(\epsilon)] = e^{u+\epsilon}f'[nx(\epsilon)]. \tag{13.1.10}$$

This condition requires that at each value of $\epsilon$, the marginal product of labor equal the marginal utility of leisure, measured in units of the consumption good. Therefore, at each firm, in each state, the efficient level of employment always obtains. Since there are a large number of firms each experiencing a different value of $\epsilon$, the marginal product of labor differs across firms. However, ex post labor immobility precludes those further efficiency gains that would accrue if workers were reallocated from low-$\epsilon$ firms to high-$\epsilon$ firms.

The determination of the contractual level of employment per household, $x$, is demonstrated in Figure 13.1 for the specific $h(\cdot)$ function listed above and for a production function that is of very general form other than that it satisfies the so-called Inada conditions [in particular, $f'(0) \to +\infty$]. As the realization of $\epsilon$ increases, the level of employment per worker continues to increase until a value of $\epsilon$ is reached at which $x \equiv 1$. Further increases in $\epsilon$ then generate a situation in which the marginal product of labor exceeds the marginal utility of leisure but in which no more labor input can be forthcoming. More formally, at an interior solution for $x(\epsilon)$,

$$\frac{dx}{d\epsilon} = \frac{e^{u+\epsilon}f'}{h'' - ne^{u+\epsilon}f''} > 0. \tag{13.1.11}$$

Furthermore, since $U\{c(\epsilon) - h[x(\epsilon)]\} \equiv \overline{V}$, we know that

$$\frac{dc}{d\epsilon} = h'\frac{\partial x}{\partial \epsilon} > 0. \tag{13.1.12}$$

Therefore, workers at higher-productivity firms both work more and consume more than workers at lower-productivity firms. However, as noted above, such workers are neither better off nor worse off than workers in lower-productivity firms, who consume fewer goods but enjoy more leisure.

These results come about rather naturally from the insurance feature of the optimal

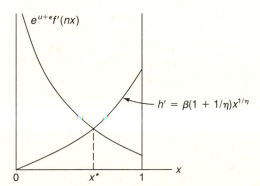

**Figure 13.1**

labor contracts. With the average value of $\epsilon$ across firms equal to zero by assumption and since firms are assumed able to trade among themselves in claims that are contingent on the values of $\epsilon$ actually realized, these risk-neutral firms are able to provide insurance to their workers against unfavorable own-firm draws of $\epsilon$. Therefore, if a low value of $\epsilon$ is realized, the additional amount of leisure enjoyed by the workers fully compensates them for the loss in wage income that they suffer. Alternatively, the additional amount of consumption available to workers fully compensates them for the loss in leisure that they suffer when a high value of $\epsilon$ is realized.

Such results would not obtain in an auction market version of the present model, at least not for the specific form of the $h(\cdot)$ function specified above. If employment and wages at each firm were given by the intersection of local labor supply and labor demand curves, it is straightforward to demonstrate that workers are unambiguously worse off when $\epsilon$ is low and unambiguously better off when $\epsilon$ is high. That is, the auction market outcome provides for an even larger reduction in consumption when equilibrium employment falls than does the optimal employment contract. Similarly, the auction market outcome provides for an even larger increase in consumption when equilibrium employment rises than does the optimal employment contract. It is therefore in the risk-averse workers' interests to accept contracts that call for a level of utility independent of the level of $\epsilon$.

Let us finally consider the possibility of aggregate productivity shocks, that is, changes in $u$. If such shocks occur before contracts are written, they may routinely be taken into account. Greater aggregate productivity simply results in increases in $x$ at all firms for which $x < 1$ with corresponding increases in $c$ at all firms (even those at which $x = 1$). Alternatively, suppose that $u$ is truly random and suppose that contracts are written contingent upon the realization of $u$. How would such a possibility change the analysis? As pointed out by Rosen (1985), the analysis, as formally stated above, would be unaffected.

The generality of this result is limited, though, because the above analysis is not really well suited for study of ex post changes in $u$. With $u$ fixed, ex ante, the choice of whether to maximize $V$, with $\Pi$ fixed, or to maximize $\Pi$, with $V$ fixed, is an inconsequential matter. However, note that when $u$ rises, the economy is unambiguously better off. What then determines the distribution of such gains between workers and firms when the value of $u$ is realized after contracts have already been written? One possibility is the familiar solution offered by the auction market outcome in which firms own all nonlabor inputs into the production process.

Alternatively, our simple contract form in which we maximize the expected value of $V$ subject to the expected value of $\Pi = \overline{\Pi}$ automatically allocates the effects of changes in $u$ to changes in worker utility levels.[3] Similarly, a setup in which the optimal contract maximizes the expected value of $\Pi$ subject to the expected value of $V = \overline{V}$ automatically allocates the effects of changes in $u$ to changes in profit levels.[4] Risk-averse workers

---

[3]Recall that the relevant expectations are taken over the range of $\epsilon$ with $u$ fixed. Therefore, $u$ acts as a simple, nonstochastic shift variable in the original maximization problems.

[4]Please realize, however, that the aggregate economy cannot transfer resources across states of nature. Therefore, no matter what the contract form, neither workers nor the owners of firms can be allocated more output than the aggregate level of output produced.

would presumably prefer the second alternative to the first, and therefore efficient risk shifting would call for contracts of this second form.[5] In any event, any optimal contract form still calls for a productive, efficient level of employment.

The above analysis, with its special set of assumptions, including the no-wealth-effects utility function, provides a very useful benchmark case. This case results in an exact replication of the employment level outcome of auction markets in labor services at each firm if each individual firm's local labor market could in fact operate in such a fashion. Employment contracts, per se, are neither a contribution nor a detriment to productive efficiency. However, employment contracts help promote overall efficiency by changing the nature of labor force compensation in such a way that risk is shifted away from risk-averse workers and toward risk-neutral firms. That is, employment contracts help complete markets by providing a mechanism for transactions in risk-bearing services. Contracts are also one simple means of solving the ex post bargaining problem in an efficient manner when labor is immobile across firms.

## Employment Contracts and Nondivisible Allocations of Time

The analysis of the preceding section predicted a worksharing solution in which all of the workers attached to a particular firm work exactly the same number of hours. In this section, we reintroduce a potential constraint first introduced in Chapter 7 that employment may be lumpy. In particular, diseconomies outside the formal model may preclude "part-time" work. To formally consider this possibility, we simply assume that each household's consumption of leisure is either zero or unity, with $0 < x < 1$ precluded by assumption.

In this instance, the solution for the optimal employment contract must be modified in a number of ways. First, as long as the realization of $\epsilon$ is such that it is optimal for $x < 1$, it is also optimal in the present analysis for there to be less than full employment. That is, some households are employed in the market ($x = 1$), while other households specialize in nonmarket activities ($x = 0$). Furthermore, since households are assumed to be identical, there is no particularly preferred way to choose which households work and which households consume leisure. We therefore assume that such assignments are made by random selection. However, the firm is in principle free to vary $c$ across households in any way it wishes subject to such arrangements having been specified in the contract. That is, it is entirely possible for firms to pay those workers who do not work. We therefore need to at least consider the possibility of private unemployment compensation as an equilibrium outcome.

The most general contract form specifies consumption levels to workers, $c_1$, consumption levels to those "unemployed," $c_0$, and the fraction $\psi$ of workers who work. Obviously, the realizations of $c_1$, $c_0$, and $\psi$ must be contingent upon the realization of $\epsilon$.[6] Since employment is determined in a purely random fashion once the value of $\epsilon$ has been

---

[5] The optimal allocation of the risks of aggregate shocks, $u$, goes beyond the scope of the present analysis. However, Azariadis (1978) considers in some more detail employment contracts that deal with such variations in aggregate productivity.

[6] We again retain the assumption that $u$ is predetermined.

realized, expected utility for the household is given by

$$E(V) = E_\epsilon\{\psi(\epsilon)U[c_1(\epsilon) - h(1)] + [1 - \psi(\epsilon)]U[c_0(\epsilon) - h(0)]\}. \tag{13.1.13}$$

Analogously, expected profit for the firm is given by

$$E(\Pi) = E_\epsilon\{e^{u+\epsilon}f[n\psi(\epsilon)] - n\psi(\epsilon)c_1(\epsilon) - n[1 - \psi(\epsilon)]c_0(\epsilon)\}. \tag{13.1.14}$$

An optimal employment contract therefore maximizes the Lagrangian expression

$$\mathcal{L} = E_\epsilon(\psi(\epsilon)U[c_1(\epsilon) - h(1)] + [1 - \psi(\epsilon)]U[c_0(\epsilon) - h(0)]$$
$$+ \lambda[\overline{\Pi} - e^{u+\epsilon}f[n\psi(\epsilon)] + n\psi(\epsilon)c_1(\epsilon) + n[1 - \psi(\epsilon)]c_0(\epsilon)]). \tag{13.1.15}$$

Again following the procedure of Rosen (1985), we obtain the following first-order conditions:

$$U'[c_1(\epsilon) - h(1)] = -n\lambda, \qquad U'[c_0(\epsilon) - h(0)] = -n\lambda, \tag{13.1.16}$$

$$U[c_1(\epsilon) - h(1)] - U[c_0(\epsilon) - h(0)] = n\lambda\{e^{u+\epsilon}f'[n\psi(\epsilon)] - c_1(\epsilon) - c_0(\epsilon)\}. \tag{13.1.17}$$

The first two of these expressions may be combined to yield

$$U'[c_1(\epsilon) - h(1)] = U'[c_0(\epsilon) - h(0)] \tag{13.1.18}$$

or

$$c_1(\epsilon) - h(1) = c_0(\epsilon) - h(0) \quad \text{for all } \epsilon. \tag{13.1.19}$$

We therefore find, as we did in the previous section, that the level of utility is independent of $\epsilon$; that is, there is a perfectly equal distribution of utility levels across households in firms with differing productivity levels. Perhaps even more surprisingly, however, is the implication that those who do not work in any firm are equally well off as those who do. That is, optimal private unemployment compensation provides full insurance against the risk of layoff.

Combining the first two first-order conditions with the third first-order condition, we also find that

$$h(1) - h(0) = e^{u+\epsilon}f'[n\psi(\epsilon)]. \tag{13.1.20}$$

Here we see that the marginal product of labor equals the goods value of the difference in utility levels between working full time and consuming the entire endowment of time as leisure. This restriction on the optimal level of employment is a straightforward modification of the standard marginal product of labor–marginal utility of leisure relationship to the case of a nondivisible allocation of time. Depending on the particular shapes of the $f(\cdot)$ and $h(\cdot)$ functions, it is possible for

$$x(\epsilon) \gtreqless \psi(\epsilon). \tag{13.1.21}$$

That is, the proportion of workers who work when employment is all or nothing can be greater than, equal to, or less than the fraction of time spent working when work hours are completely flexible. Alternatively, we cannot determine unambiguously whether the total amount of labor employed by the firm rises or falls when employment is assumed to be lumpy.

The principal contribution of the analysis of this section is that it points out the possibility of unemployment in a model in which the constrained optimal amount of labor is always employed. We also again note that the across-firm variation in wage payments is, in general, smaller than would be the case if an auction market outcome obtained. Such a reduction in the variability in measured wages is not a sign of wage "rigidity" but rather a sign of the efficient operation of a contract market that shifts risk away from risk-averse households and toward risk-neutral firms.

## A Contractual Theory of "Keynesian" Unemployment

As noted above, workers in the model of the previous section are indifferent between working and being laid off. However, some might argue that the full unemployment insurance required for this result to hold might generate incentive problems. If worker heterogeneity and worker effort in production are considered, it is in the interest of the firm to provide incentives for workers to gain reputations as more rather than less productive workers. One way to achieve such an incentive is to base layoffs on previous worker productivity and to make sure that the retained workers are always strictly better off than those workers who are laid off.

An attractive way to model these sorts of moral hazard considerations is to retain the assumption of worker homogeneity but to simply assume that the costs to the firm of providing full unemployment insurance are prohibitive. In this section, we therefore follow the original analysis of Azariadis (1975) and constrain the firm to make wage payments only to those workers who are employed; that is, we constrain the firm to set $c_0 \equiv 0$ for all $\epsilon$. In this case, the firm maximizes the Lagrangian expression

$$\mathcal{L} = E_\epsilon\{\psi(\epsilon)U[c_1(\epsilon) - h(1)] + [1 - \psi(\epsilon)]U[-h(0)]$$
$$+ \lambda[\overline{\Pi} - e^{u+\epsilon}f[n\psi(\epsilon)] + n\psi(\epsilon)c_1(\epsilon)]\}. \tag{13.1.22}$$

Differentiating the above expression with respect to $c_1$ and $\psi$, we obtain the first-order conditions

$$U'[c_1(\epsilon) - h(1)] = -n\lambda, \tag{13.1.23}$$

$$U[c_1(\epsilon) - h(1)] - U[-h(0)] = -n\lambda\{c_1 - e^{u+\epsilon}f'[n\psi(\epsilon)]\}. \tag{13.1.24}$$

Combining these expressions, we find that

$$e^{u+\epsilon}f'[n\psi(\epsilon)] = c_1(\epsilon) - \frac{U[c_1(\epsilon) - h(1)] - U[-h(0)]}{U'[c_1(\epsilon) - h(1)]}. \tag{13.1.25}$$

This equation has the interpretation of a restriction on the optimal level of employment. As such, it is the natural counterpart of a similar condition of the preceding section. However, the concavity of the utility function guarantees that

$$U'[c_1(\epsilon) - h(1)][c_1(\epsilon) - h(1) + h(0)] < U[c_1(\epsilon) - h(1)] - U[-h(0)]. \tag{13.1.26}$$

Rearranging, we find that

$$c_1(\epsilon) - \frac{U[c_1(\epsilon) - h(1)] - U[-h(0)]}{U'[c_1(\epsilon) - h(1)]} < h(1) - h(0). \tag{13.1.27}$$

Therefore, the value of $e^{u+\epsilon}f'[n\psi(\epsilon)]$ in the present example must exceed the value of the same expression in the preceding section. Since $f'' < 0$, the level of employment without private unemployment compensation must exceed the level of employment when firms are able to provide such insurance. The failure of a complete insurance market leads to a kind of overemployment result like that developed by Green and Khan (1983) in another context.

While the overemployment result discussed above is of interest in its own right, the principal result of the present analysis is that unemployment appears, ex post, to be involuntary in the sense of Keynes (1936). In particular, although all households voluntarily agree to their employment contracts in advance, those assigned to unemployment after the realization of $\epsilon$ come to regret having agreed to the contract and would prefer to work, even for compensation that is less than $c_1$. That is, the unemployed would prefer to renege on the contract and attempt to underbid the employed workers to get their jobs.

Although the unemployed would prefer to work, remember that the level of unemployment is actually too low. Employment is higher and unemployment is lower than in the case in which a complete market in insurance exists. This result comes about because the only way that risk-neutral firms can insure households against unfavorable draws of $\epsilon$ is by promising to employ some of them beyond the point of the usual marginal productivity condition. The households prefer the sure reduction in average utility levels inherent in the possibility of suboptimal employment over time over the very large risk of reduced welfare that comes about with an uninsured spell of unemployment.

Although there are a number of other areas into which the microeconomics of employment contracts has progressed, the most important results from the point of view of macroeconomics can be stated fairly succinctly. First, in the presence of employment contracts, there is no presumption that the actual wage paid to any worker need play any allocative role, and therefore the real wage need not, in general, equal the marginal product of labor. Second, wage rates across sectors are likely to be less variable than would be the case in the absence of employment contracts. Third, even though the level of employment may equal or even exceed the efficient level of employment, the appearance of involuntary unemployment is quite plausible.

## 13.2 WAGE INDEXATION AND EMPLOYMENT DETERMINATION

In this section, our attention shifts away from considerations of risk and centers instead on informational problems. In particular, we now look at employment contracts that attempt to achieve efficient employment levels in the face of several stochastic disturbances that may not be directly observable. The literature we survey here essentially ignores the considerations of risk shifting that were a key motivation for the contracts of the previous section. This oversight can only be justified by the interrelationship of two alternative possibilities. First of all, it is possible that the gains from trade in risk-bearing services are small enough to make risk shifting, a priori, an insignificant exercise. Second, it may be the case that realizations of $\epsilon$ and $u$ may not be directly observable, particularly by the workers. In this case, it will not, in general, be possible to write contracts that are directly contingent on their outcomes.

We generally follow both tacks in this section, first, by ignoring the potential for contracts to efficiently allocate risk and, second, by concentrating on difficulties in observing and/or verifying the outcomes of the disturbances and properly employing the productive efficient amount of employment services. In the most basic form of the model we consider, there is an economywide real disturbance, which properly calls for changes in the level of employment, and an economywide nominal disturbance, which should be neutral with respect to the level of employment. If employment contracts can be written that are contingent on both disturbances separately, such contracts can always replicate the auction market outcome. Alternatively, if employment contracts can only be made contingent on some observable linear combination of the disturbances, then such contracts generally provide for only partial proper responses to real disturbances and partial improper responses to nominal disturbances.

## An Auction Market Model

Continue to assume that there are a large number, call it $k$, of individual firms each producing a homogeneous, nonstorable product. The level of production at firm $i$ is given by

$$Y_i = e^{u + \epsilon_i} L_i^\alpha, \qquad 0 < \alpha < 1, \qquad i = 1, \ldots, k, \tag{13.2.1}$$

where $Y_i$ represents the level of output at firm $i$, $L_i$ represents the level of employment at firm $i$, and $u$ and $\epsilon_i$ are zero-mean, normally distributed random variables.

As in the analysis of Section 13.1, considerations of firm-specific human capital preclude the migration of workers across firms. Therefore, we again face the potential of bilateral monopoly, and so firms may need to employ explicit or implicit labor contracts. However, before we introduce such contracts, let us begin our analysis as if each firm's labor market could indeed function as an auction market.

The demand for labor at each firm, $L_i^d$, equates the local marginal product of labor with the local real wage. That is, $L_i^d$ solves

$$\frac{W_i}{P} = \alpha e^{u + \epsilon_i} (L_i^d)^{-(1-\alpha)}. \tag{13.2.2}$$

Denote $w_i \equiv \ln W_i$, $p \equiv \ln P$, $\ell_i^d \equiv \ln L_i^d$, and $\ell_i \equiv \ln L_i$. Taking logarithms of the above expression, we obtain

$$\ell_i^d = \frac{\ln \alpha}{1 - \alpha} + \frac{u + \epsilon_i}{1 - \alpha} + \frac{1}{1 - \alpha}(p - w_i). \tag{13.2.3}$$

In this section, we are less concerned about the distribution of employment across households and more concerned with the aggregate volume of employment. We therefore adopt our earlier assumption that worksharing is feasible. Furthermore, to reduce the necessary amount of notation, we normalize the number of households per firm at unity. Each household's utility function is again assumed to be of the form

$$V_i = U[c - \beta L_i^{1 + 1/\eta}], \tag{13.2.4}$$

where $L$ and $x$ are taken to be equivalent upon the assumption that $n = 1$.

Maximization of the above utility function defines a labor supply schedule of the form

$$\frac{W_i}{P} = \beta \left( 1 + \frac{1}{\eta} \right) (L_i^s)^{1/\eta}.$$ (13.2.5)

Taking logarithms of the above expression, we obtain

$$\ell_i^s = -\eta \ln \left[ \beta \left( 1 + \frac{1}{\eta} \right) \right] + \eta(w_i - p), \quad \text{write } \ell_i^s \equiv \ln L_i^s.$$ (13.2.6)

If each firm's labor market were able to operate as an auction market, then equilibrium at each firm would be characterized by

$$\ell_i^d = \ell_i^s$$ (13.2.7)

or

$$w_i - p = \frac{\ln \alpha + \eta(1 - \alpha)\ln[\beta(1 + 1/\eta)]}{1 + (1 - \alpha)\eta} + \frac{u + \epsilon_i}{1 + (1 - \alpha)\eta}.$$ (13.2.8)

Now plugging the equilibrium local real wage back into the local labor demand schedule and the resulting level of employment back into the local production function, we obtain

$$\ell_i = \frac{\eta}{1 + (1 - \alpha)\eta} \left[ \ln \alpha - \ln \left[ \beta \left( 1 + \frac{1}{\eta} \right) \right] + u + \epsilon_i \right],$$ (13.2.9)

$$y_i = \alpha^* + \frac{1 + \eta}{1 + (1 - \alpha)\eta}(u + \epsilon_i),$$ (13.2.10)

where we adopt the notation

$$\alpha^* \equiv \frac{\alpha\eta}{1 + (1 - \alpha)\eta} \left[ \ln \alpha - \ln \left[ \beta \left( 1 + \frac{1}{\eta} \right) \right] \right] \quad \text{and} \quad y_i \equiv \ln Y_i.$$ (13.2.11)

It is now convenient to define the geometric averages

$$Y \equiv \left( \prod_{i=1}^{k} Y_i \right)^{1/k}, \qquad L \equiv \left( \prod_{i=1}^{k} L_i \right)^{1/k}, \qquad W \equiv \left( \prod_{i=1}^{k} W_i \right)^{1/k}.$$

We now take the logarithm of $Y$ to obtain

$$y = \alpha^* + \frac{1 + \eta}{1 + (1 - \alpha)\eta} \left( u + \frac{1}{k} \sum_{i=1}^{k} \epsilon_i \right),$$ (13.2.12)

where $y$ denotes a logarithm measure of aggregate output, $y \equiv \ln Y$. If we again adopt the assumption that the number of firms $k$ is large enough so that the sampling mean of $\epsilon_i$ equals the expected value of $\epsilon_i$, which is equal to zero, by assumption, the above expression may be rewritten as

$$y = \alpha^* + \frac{1 + \eta}{1 + (1 - \alpha)\eta} u.$$ (13.2.13)

The intuition behind this expression is fairly straightforward. Local shocks to productivity $\epsilon_i$ average out across the economy and have therefore no effect on aggregate output.[7] Alternatively, an increase in productivity that affects all firms in the economy (i.e., an increase in $u$) increases the demand for labor at each firm. The rise in the demand for labor raises real wages and generates an increase in the equilibrium level of employment. This increase in employment combines with the increase in worker productivity to generate a more than proportionate increase in (log) aggregate output.

To complete the analysis of the macroeconomy, we need only add a monetary sector to determine the aggregate logarithm of the price level $p$. Assume that the logarithm of the supply of money is set exogenously by the monetary authority. That is, let

$$m^s = \overline{m}, \quad \text{a constant.} \tag{13.2.14}$$

Next assume that the logarithm of the demand for money is given by the simple stochastic Cambridge form

$$m^d = p + y + v, \tag{13.2.15}$$

where $v$ is a zero-mean, independent, normally distributed random variable with variance $\sigma_v^2$.[8] Prices are completely flexible, and the aggregate price level equates the supply of and demand for real money balances. We therefore obtain

$$\overline{m} = p + y + v \tag{13.2.16}$$

or

$$p = \overline{m} - \alpha^* - v - \frac{1 + \eta}{1 + (1 - \alpha)\eta}u. \tag{13.2.17}$$

Note that money is completely neutral in this model. The equilibrium real wage and employment levels are determined independently of the aggregate price level, and the aggregate price level is simply directly proportional to the level of the nominal money supply and inversely proportional to the value of the money demand shock $v$. Alternatively, an increase in productivity, or a favorable supply shock (an increase in $u$), unambiguously lowers the aggregate price level. This result was previewed in Chapter 5. The increase in output that accompanies the increase in $u$ raises the demand for real money balances. However, since the nominal supply of money is fixed at $m = \overline{m}$, the aggregate price level must fall to keep the supply of and demand for real money balances equal to one another.

---

[7]By analogous reasoning, local disturbances do not affect the aggregate level of employment $\ell \equiv \ln L$ and the aggregate nominal wage rate $w \equiv \ln W$. Therefore, without loss of generality and to avoid some cumbersome notation, we consistently deal directly with the aggregate magnitudes $\ell$ and $w$ rather than making specific reference to the local magnitudes $\ell_i$ and $w_i$.

[8]The way the model is set up, the random variable $v$ must be interpreted as a positive shock to the demand for real money balances. However, since we assume throughout that the money market equilibrium condition is continually satisfied, the random variable $v$ may also be given an interpretation as an inverse money supply shock. Therefore, the inverse of the coefficients on $v$ in the equilibrium conditions of the models we study give the sign and magnitude of the effects of money supply shocks. However, the effects of money supply shocks are not the central focus of the present chapter, and so we do not define a separate symbol to denote such potential money supply shocks.

Decentralized wage setting by Walrasian auctioneers precludes the need for information about $u$ and $v$ in enforcing labor contracts or in formulating an appropriate monetary policy. However, consider the following signal extraction problem. Suppose that we know the values of $\overline{m}$ and $\alpha^*$ and can observe the value of $p$. How would we construct an optimal estimate of the money demand shock $v$?

With the information structure set out in this way, agents are able to observe a signal $z$ given by

$$z \equiv \alpha^* - \overline{m} - p = v + \frac{1 + \eta}{1 + (1 - \alpha)\eta} u. \tag{13.2.18}$$

From our analysis of Chapter 10, we therefore construct an optimal estimate of $v$ given by

$$E(v|p) = \theta z, \quad \text{where } \theta \equiv \frac{\sigma_v^2}{\sigma_v^2 + \left[\dfrac{1 + \eta}{1 + (1 - \alpha)\eta}\right]^2 \sigma_u^2}. \tag{13.2.19}$$

The value of $\theta$ as constructed above proves useful in later analysis.

## A Fully Contingent Employment Contract

Let us now assume that the relationship between workers and firms in a segmented labor market precludes the functioning of local Walrasian auctioneers. Alternatively, the existence of the bilateral monopoly problem and the existence of negotiation costs requires an ex ante agreement about wages and employment levels. One common explicit contract form that we observe in environments like this one is a contract in which workers agree in advance on a wage level, which may be contingent on the level of prices and other local or aggregate economic conditions. Once such contingencies are realized, the firm then has the prerogative of choosing that level of employment at this contractual wage rate that maximizes profits. Employment is therefore determined along the standard labor demand schedule at the resulting contractual wage rate.[9]

Many economists have argued that this type of contract form is likely to dominate implicit contractual relationships that efficiently shift risk. Some of the justifications offered for the likelihood of adoption of contracts, like those of this section, include the observation that even in cases in which such contracts are clearly suboptimal, an appropriate optimal risk-shifting contract is sufficiently complex and has sufficiently counterintuitive contingencies that workers are not likely to agree to them. Furthermore, such contracts often include contingencies based upon quantities, such as worker productivity, which are hard to verify and are subject to moral hazard problems.[10]

In this section, we consider a case in which there is full, ex post information available about the realizations of the random variables $u$ and $v$ affecting the macroeconomy. In this case, the type of contract described above in which employment is demand determined at

---

[9]Such contracts, while they attempt to achieve productive efficiency, completely ignore potential gains from trade in risk-bearing services. Such a feature might be incorporated into contracts of this sort by the addition of bonuses of some kind, but this consideration goes beyond the scope of the present analysis.

[10]For an expanded discussion of the types of arguments alluded to here, see Barro (1977) and Fischer (1977b).

the contractual wage is fully capable of replicating the auction market wage and employment levels. Recall that the equilibrium aggregate auction market real wage rate is given by

$$w - p = \frac{\ln \alpha + \eta(1 - \alpha)\ln[\beta(1 + 1/\eta)]}{1 + (1 - \alpha)\eta} + \frac{u}{1 + (1 - \alpha)\eta}. \tag{13.2.20}$$

With both $u$ and $v$ observable and verifiable by both workers and firms, is there a contingent nominal wage rate that guarantees the emergence of the above real wage as an equilibrium outcome? If so, then firms are sure to set output and employment levels such that

$$y = \alpha^* + \frac{1 + \eta}{1 + (1 - \alpha)\eta}u, \tag{13.2.21}$$

and so the equilibrium price level would be given by

$$p = \overline{m} - \alpha^* - v - \frac{1 + \eta}{1 + (1 - \alpha)\eta}u. \tag{13.2.22}$$

Therefore, combining equations (13.2.11), (13.2.20), and (13.2.22), we find that the appropriate aggregate contractual wage rate is given by

$$w^c = \overline{m} + \frac{(1 - \alpha\eta)\ln \alpha + \eta \ln[\beta(1 + 1/\eta)]}{1 + (1 - \alpha)\eta} - v - \frac{\eta}{1 + (1 - \alpha)\eta}u. \tag{13.2.23}$$

As long as the disturbances $u$ and $v$ are observable and verifiable, this relatively simple contract form is capable of guaranteeing an efficient allocation of time. Note that since $p$ moves one-for-one with changes in $v$, the optimal contractual wage should also move one-for-one with changes in the aggregate price level that are due to purely nominal disturbances. Alternatively, although positive values for $u$ lead to reductions in the aggregate price level and the optimal contractual wage rate, an increase in $u$ generates an even greater reduction in $p$, and so increases in $u$ generate appropriate increases in the real wage rate. The optimal contract therefore guarantees the proper increase in employment at a point on both the labor supply curve and the new, appropriately shifted labor demand curve.

A natural criticism of the above contract form is that the outcomes of $u$ and $v$ are not likely to be observable by either workers or firms. However, as demonstrated by Karni (1983), the above contract may be replicated by a contract with explicit contingencies tied to the aggregate price level $p$ and the aggregate output level $y$. In particular, suppose that the contract calls for a nominal wage rate given by

$$w^c = \gamma_0 + \gamma_1 p + \gamma_2 y. \tag{13.2.24}$$

Furthermore, continue to assume that the firms may decide on the level of employment according to their ex post labor demand schedules. The resulting equilibrium price and employment levels are then given by

$$y = \frac{\alpha \ln \alpha}{1 - \alpha} + \frac{\alpha(p - w^c)}{1 - \alpha} + \frac{u}{1 - \alpha}, \tag{13.2.25}$$

$$p = \overline{m} - y - v. \tag{13.2.26}$$

Plugging in for $w^c$ from above, we obtain

$$w - p = \frac{\gamma_0 - (1 - \gamma_1)\overline{m} + \alpha(1 - \gamma_1 + \gamma_2)\ln \alpha}{1 + \alpha(\gamma_2 - \gamma_1)}$$

$$+ \frac{1 - \gamma_1 + \gamma_2}{1 + \alpha(\gamma_2 - \gamma_1)} u + \frac{(1 - \alpha)(1 - \gamma_1)}{1 + \alpha(\gamma_2 - \gamma_1)} v. \tag{13.2.27}$$

We now find that contractual settings of

$$\gamma_0 = \frac{(1 - \alpha)\ln \alpha + \eta(1 - \alpha)\ln[\beta(1 + 1/\eta)]}{1 + \eta},$$

$$\gamma_1 = 1, \tag{13.2.28}$$

$$\gamma_2 = \frac{1}{1 + \eta}$$

result in an equilibrium real wage rate equal to the equilibrium auction market real wage rate. This alternative contract form therefore also ensures an efficient allocation of time.

Note that this contract involves a very simple one for one indexation of the nominal wage rate to the aggregate price level. This property of the optimal contract was previewed by the preceding optimal contract, which involved a one-for-one indexation of the wage rate to the term $\overline{m} - v$. We also now find an independent effect of increases in $y$ on the equilibrium contractual wage rate. This effect is the counterpart of the effect of changes in $u$ on $w^c$ from the preceding example.

## Optimal Indexation of Wages to Prices

Many might argue that attempts to index wages to levels of output are no more likely to be successful than attempts to directly index wages to the disturbance terms $u$ and $v$. The aggregate output level can only be observed and measured after employment levels have been determined. However, employment levels can only be determined after firms compute the contractual nominal wage rate and choose the proper point on their labor demand schedules. Although such simultaneity is inherently involved in the process by which the economy converges on equilibrium in the presence of Walrasian auctioneers, such a process is perhaps more difficult to justify once such a fiction is abandoned in favor of more "realistic" institutional arrangements.

It might be argued that although price data is collected and disseminated fairly quickly, data on aggregate output is collected and disseminated more slowly. Furthermore, contingencies based upon aggregate output appear less frequently in explicit contracts and may therefore be viewed as an unlikely element of implicit contracts as well. Finally, in the presence of firm-specific shocks $\epsilon_i$, aggregate output may be less informative for local conditions than the aggregate price level, and since $\epsilon_i$ is not likely to be recoverable from aggregate data, contingencies based on $y$ are likely to be less efficiency enhancing.

The optimal contract based only upon aggregate price-level contingencies for a variant of the present analysis is presented by Gray (1976). As noted in previous sections, the optimal nominal wage rate is simply the auction market real wage rate plus the aggregate price level, or

$$w = p + \frac{\ln \alpha + \eta(1 - \alpha)\ln[\beta(1 + 1/\eta)]}{1 + (1 - \alpha)\eta} + \frac{u}{1 + (1 - \alpha)\eta}. \tag{13.2.29}$$

Therefore, as long as $p$ is observable and contracts may include $p$ as a contingency, the determination of the optimal contractual wage rate involves the need to take into account the level of the aggregate productivity shock $u$. If the value of $u$ is directly observable, or if the exact value of $u$ may be inferred from observation of $p$ and $y$, then there is no problem. The employment contract is always able to call for a real wage rate equal to the auction market real wage rate.

However, in the present example, $u$ cannot be measured either directly or indirectly. Therefore, the best hope one can have for setting the real wage close to that value given above lies in the construction of an estimate of $u$ given the observation of $p$. This problem has already been referred to as the signal extraction problem in Chapter 10. However, such a problem can only be solved if the equilibrium properties of $p$ are already known. Unfortunately, in the present example, the equilibrium stochastic properties of $p$ can only be deduced after the precise form of the employment contract has been specified.

We therefore consider the alternative method of assuming that the optimal employment contract is of the form

$$w^c = \gamma_0 + \gamma_1 p. \tag{13.2.30}$$

We then choose $\gamma_0$ and $\gamma_1$ to minimize the expected squared deviation between the level of output implied by the contract and the level of output that obtains in the auction market case. We have already shown that in the auction market case, the level of output, call it $y^*$, is given by

$$y^* = \alpha^* + \frac{1 + \eta}{1 + (1 - \alpha)\eta} u. \tag{13.2.31}$$

In order to solve for the equilibrium level of output in the case of contracts of the form $w^c = \gamma_0 + \gamma_1 p$, we need to solve the system of equations

$$w = w^c = \gamma_0 + \gamma_1 p, \tag{13.2.32}$$

$$y = \alpha\ell + u, \tag{13.2.33}$$

$$\ell = \ell^d = \frac{\ln \alpha}{1 - \alpha} - \frac{w - p}{1 - \alpha} + \frac{u}{1 - \alpha}, \tag{13.2.34}$$

$$p = \overline{m} - y - v. \tag{13.2.35}$$

Combining equations (13.3.32)–(13.2.35), it is straightforward to demonstrate that the equilibrium level of output under the proposed contract is given by

$$y^c = \frac{\alpha[\ln \alpha - \gamma_0 + (1 - \gamma_1)\overline{m}]}{1 - \alpha\gamma_1} + \frac{u}{1 - \alpha\gamma_1} - \frac{\alpha(1 - \gamma_1)}{1 - \alpha\gamma_1} v. \tag{13.2.36}$$

We now seek to choose $\gamma_0$ and $\gamma_1$ to minimize

$$\mathcal{L} \equiv E\{(y^c - y^*)^2\} = \left[ \frac{\alpha[\ln \alpha - \gamma_0 - (1 - \gamma_1)\overline{m}]}{1 - \alpha\gamma_1} \right]^2$$

$$+ \left[ \frac{\alpha[\eta - \gamma_1(1 + \eta)]}{[1 + (1 - \alpha)\eta][1 - \alpha\gamma_1]} \right]^2 \sigma_u^2 + \left[ \frac{\alpha(1 - \gamma_1)}{1 - \alpha\gamma_1} \right]^2 \sigma_v^2. \tag{13.2.37}$$

Inspection of the above expression reveals that the first term may be minimized at zero by a value of $\gamma_0$ given by

$$\gamma_0^* = (1 - \gamma_1)\overline{m} + \frac{[1 - \alpha\eta(1 - \gamma_1)]\ln \alpha + \eta(1 - \alpha\gamma_1)\ln[\beta(1 + 1/\eta)]}{1 + (1 - \alpha)\eta} \tag{13.2.38}$$

for any arbitrarily selected value of $\gamma_1$. We next seek to choose the optimal value of $\gamma_1$, call it $\gamma_1^*$, to minimize

$$\mathcal{L} = \frac{\alpha^2[\eta - \gamma_1(1 + \eta)]^2}{[1 + (1 - \alpha)\eta]^2(1 - \alpha\gamma_1)^2} \sigma_u^2 + \frac{\alpha^2(1 - \gamma_1)^2}{(1 - \alpha\gamma_1)^2} \sigma_v^2. \tag{13.2.39}$$

Our earlier definition of $\theta$ allows us to make the substitution

$$\frac{\sigma_u^2}{[1 + (1 - \alpha)\eta]^2} = \frac{1 - \theta}{\theta} \frac{\sigma_v^2}{(1 + \eta)^2}. \tag{13.2.40}$$

Therefore, the above loss function may be rewritten as

$$\mathcal{L} = \frac{\alpha^2\sigma_v^2}{(1 - \alpha\gamma_1)^2} \left[ \frac{1 - \theta}{\theta(1 + \eta)^2}[\eta - \gamma_1(1 + \eta)]^2 + (1 - \gamma_1)^2 \right]. \tag{13.2.41}$$

Differentiating expression (13.2.41) with respect to $\gamma_1$ and setting the resulting expression equal to zero, we find that the optimal value of $\gamma_1$ is given by

$$\gamma_1^* = \frac{\theta + \eta}{1 + \eta} \Rightarrow w^c = \gamma_0^* + \frac{\theta + \eta}{1 + \eta}p. \tag{13.2.42}$$

Note that as long as $\theta < 1$, as is generally the case, the optimal contract calls for a less than one-for-one indexation of wages to prices. This result obtains because an increase in the price level may signal a purely nominal disturbance, which calls for a neutral, equiproportional rise in $w$, or alternatively, such a price increase may signal an adverse supply shock that appropriately calls for a reduction in the real wage rate.

Now plugging in for $\gamma_1^*$ in the expression for $\gamma_0^*$ and the other equations describing equilibrium, we obtain the following closed-form solutions for the endogenous variables:

$$y = \alpha^* + \frac{1 + \eta}{(1 + \eta) - \alpha(\eta + \theta)}u - \frac{\alpha(1 - \theta)}{(1 + \eta) - \alpha(\eta + \theta)}v, \tag{13.2.43}$$

$$p = \overline{m} - \alpha^* - \frac{1 + \eta}{(1 + \eta) - \alpha(\eta + \theta)}[u + (1 - \alpha)v], \tag{13.2.44}$$

$$w - p = \frac{\ln \alpha + \eta(1 - \alpha)\ln[\beta(1 + 1/\eta)]}{1 + (1 - \alpha)\eta}$$

$$+ \frac{1 - \theta}{(1 + \eta) - \alpha(\eta + \theta)}[u + (1 - \alpha)v]. \tag{13.2.45}$$

Note, in this case, that output continues to increase in response to favorable supply shocks (increases in $u$) but that output now falls in response to a positive money demand shock (an increase in $v$). When real money demand rises and the nominal money supply is fixed at $m = \overline{m}$, money demand–money supply equilibrium may only be maintained through a reduction in the aggregate price level $p$. However, the fall in prices, since it, in general, only partially translates into a fall in the nominal wage rate ($\gamma_1^* < 1$), results in an increase in the real wage rate. This increase in the real wage rate then results in a reduction in labor demand, employment, and output.

In order to gain some further intuition behind these results, we consider in turn two special cases: first, the case of $\sigma_u^2 = 0$, no real shocks; second, the case of $\sigma_v^2 = 0$, no nominal shocks. With $\sigma_u^2 = 0$, we find that $u \equiv 0$, $\theta = 1$, and

$$\gamma_1^* = 1 \Rightarrow w^c = \gamma_0^* + p, \tag{13.2.46}$$

$$y = y^* = \alpha^*, \qquad p = \overline{m} - \alpha^* - v. \tag{13.2.47}$$

In this case nominal shocks generate equiproportionate increases in the price level. The levels of output and employment are properly insulated from these purely nominal disturbances. Nominal wages are indexed one-for-one to changes in the aggregate price level, and so the real wage is constant.

With real disturbances but no nominal disturbances, we find that $v \equiv 0$, $\theta = 0$, and

$$\gamma_1^* = \frac{\eta}{1 + \eta} \Rightarrow w^c = \gamma_0^* + \frac{\eta}{1 + \eta}p, \tag{13.2.48}$$

$$y = y^* = \alpha^* + \frac{1 + \eta}{1 + (1 - \alpha)\eta}u, \qquad p = \overline{m} - \alpha^* - \frac{1 + \eta}{1 + (1 - \alpha)\eta}u. \tag{13.2.49}$$

We again find that the level of output is equal to the auction market level of output. However, indexation of wages to prices is less than one-for-one. In the face of a favorable productivity shock, $u > 0$, the aggregate price level falls. However, the contractual wage rate falls less than one-for-one, implying an increase in the real wage rate. Workers are happy to supply the contractually mandated increase in employment, while the outward shift in the labor demand schedule dominates the backward movement along the labor demand schedule. Therefore, output rises both due to the direct effect of the increase in $u$ and due to the appropriate increase in employment.

With $\sigma_u^2 > 0$ and $\sigma_v^2 > 0$, we get an intermediate case in which

$$\frac{\eta}{1 + \eta} < \gamma_1^* = \frac{\theta + \eta}{1 + \eta} < 1. \tag{13.2.50}$$

In these circumstances, wages are more closely indexed to prices than in the case in which $\sigma_v^2 = 0$, but there is still less than full indexation to prices as in the case in which $\sigma_u^2 = 0$. In such intermediate cases, the level of output equals the auction market level $y^*$ with probability zero. With only one feasible contingency $p$, the contract is incapable of properly responding to changes in both $u$ and $v$.

## Nonindexed Contracts and Optimal Monetary Policy

If we further assume that contracts are unable to include aggregate price-level contingencies, then such contracts obviously perform even more poorly relative to the auction market outcome $y^*$. In particular, suppose that the contractual nominal wage rate is completely fixed at $\overline{w}$. In this case, we find that

$$w = w^c = \overline{w}, \tag{13.2.51}$$

$$y = \alpha \ln \alpha + \alpha(\overline{m} - \overline{w}) + u - \alpha v, \tag{13.2.52}$$

$$p = (1 - \alpha)\overline{m} + \alpha\overline{w} - \alpha \ln \alpha - (1 - \alpha)v - u. \tag{13.2.53}$$

Clearly, it is best for the nominal wage rate $\overline{w}$ to be set such that

$$\alpha^* = \alpha \ln \alpha + \alpha(\overline{m} - \overline{w}) \tag{13.2.54}$$

or

$$\overline{w} = \overline{m} + \frac{(1 - \alpha\eta)\ln \alpha + \eta \ln[\beta(1 + 1/\eta)]}{1 + (1 - \alpha)\eta}. \tag{13.2.55}$$

However, such a contract is unable to affect the way the disturbance terms $u$ and $v$ impact upon the level of output. The effects of these disturbances on the equilibrium level of output in this model generally differ from their effects on the equilibrium level of output in the auction market model. Furthermore, the expected value of $(y - y^*)^2$ in this case exceeds the value of $(y - y^*)^2$ in the case of the optimal contingent contract $w^c = \gamma_0^* + \gamma_1^* p$.

In this case of a purely rigid nominal wage rate, it is however possible that the monetary authority might improve upon matters if the monetary authority has information about the realizations of $u$ and $v$ and if the monetary authority can act upon this information in a timely manner.

As an extreme possibility, suppose that the monetary authority is able to monitor both $u$ and $v$ and that the monetary authority is able to implement a monetary policy of the form

$$m = \overline{m} + \phi_1 u + \phi_2 v. \tag{13.2.56}$$

In this case, equilibrium in the economy is governed by

$$w = w^c = \overline{w}, \tag{13.2.57}$$

$$y = \alpha \ell + u, \tag{13.2.58}$$

$$\ell = \ell^d = \frac{\ln \alpha}{1 - \alpha} - \frac{w - p}{1 - \alpha} + \frac{u}{1 - \alpha}, \tag{13.2.59}$$

$$p = \overline{m} + \phi_1 u + \phi_2 v - y - v. \tag{13.2.60}$$

Solving, we find that

$$y = \alpha \ln \alpha + \alpha(\overline{m} - \overline{w}) + [(1 - \alpha) + \alpha(1 + \phi_1)]u - \alpha(1 - \phi_2)v \tag{13.2.61}$$

$$= \alpha^* + [(1 - \alpha) + \alpha(1 + \phi_1)]u - \alpha(1 - \phi_2)v.$$

Optimal policy in this case is always capable of achieving $y = y^*$. In particular, the monetary authority need only set

$$\phi_1^* = \frac{\eta}{1 + (1 - \alpha)\eta}, \qquad \phi_2^* = 1. \tag{13.2.62}$$

We therefore find that optimal monetary policy should attempt to offset purely nominal disturbances. In particular, a positive realization of $v$ exerts downward pressure on the aggregate price level. However, in light of such a disturbance, the monetary authority should increase the money supply in a way that exactly offsets the potential effect of $v$ on $p$. This result obtains because purely nominal disturbances do not affect the appropriate level of employment. It is therefore in the interest of the policymaker to isolate the real wage rate and hence the level of employment from such nominal disturbances. This result is analogous to that developed by Fischer (1977a). He observes, in a similar context, that monetary policy should "counteract nominal disturbances which tend to increase the price level."

We also find that the optimal monetary policy calls for an increase in the money supply in the face of a favorable real disturbance ($\phi_1^* > 0$). As we have already observed, a favorable supply shock raises the equilibrium real wage rate in the auction market economy. Therefore, if our benchmark of economic efficiency is the auction market allocation, a fixed nominal wage rate requires a reduction in the aggregate price level in order to facilitate the desired increase in the real wage rate. However, in the absence of policy, the fall in the aggregate price level is too extreme, and hence the increase in the real wage rate is excessive. Therefore, optimal monetary policy calls for an increase in the money supply to dampen the reduction in the aggregate price level that would occur in the absence of policy.

This last result is in contrast to Fischer's (1977a) prescription that optimal monetary policy "accommodate real disturbances that tend to increase the price level." Fischer would therefore argue that an increase in $u$, which lowers the aggregate price level, should call for an optimal reduction in the money supply. Alternatively, the analysis of this section calls for an increase in the money supply in light of an increase in the value of $u$. The principal difference between the present analysis and that of Fischer lies in the policymaker's objective function. Throughout the analysis, we have stressed an objective of attempting to keep the level of output as close as possible to $y^*$, the auction market level of output. However, optimal policy in Fischer's analysis minimizes the variance of output around its unconditional mean of $\alpha^*$. Therefore, Fischer's policymaker attempts to offset the effects of supply shocks on the level of output even if such effects on output and employment represent Pareto-optimal adjustments.

Fischer's policymaker minimizes a loss function given by

$$\mathcal{L} = E\{[-((1 - \alpha) + \alpha(1 + \phi_1))u + \alpha(1 - \phi_2)v]^2\} \tag{13.2.63}$$

$$= [(1 - \alpha)^2 + 2\alpha(1 - \alpha)(1 + \phi_1) + \alpha^2(1 + \phi_2)^2]\sigma_u^2 + \alpha^2(1 - \phi_2)^2\sigma_v^2.$$

Minimization of this loss function requires settings of $\phi_1$ and $\phi_2$ given by

$$\phi_1^* = -\frac{1}{\alpha}, \qquad \phi_2^* = 1. \tag{13.2.64}$$

We therefore find that the optimal response to money demand shocks is unchanged from the previous analysis. However, we also now find that policy should attempt to accentuate the tendency of favorable supply shocks to lower the aggregate price level and the tendency for adverse supply shocks to increase the aggregate price level.

## Some Concluding Remarks

This chapter has analyzed labor contracts from two entirely different perspectives. In Section 13.1, we analyzed optimal risk-shifting contracts. That analysis demonstrated that in the presence of such contracts, the real wage rate only inadvertently equals the marginal product of labor. Furthermore, we demonstrated that such contracts often call for what appears to be involuntary unemployment even though such unemployment results from Pareto-optimal employment contracts.

In the present section, Section 13.2, we examined contracts whose only purpose is to attempt to replicate the auction market employment outcome in the face of several potentially indistinguishable stochastic disturbances. Here we found that if contracts in this setting are not able to be separately contingent on all disturbances, then a transmission mechanism exists by which exogenous disturbances can push the economy away from the auction market allocation. Furthermore, we found instances in which proper conduct of monetary policy can have an effective and beneficial impact on the economy. This result is in contrast to results presented in Chapter 12 in which monetary policy is neutral at best and unambiguously harmful at worst.

Unfortunately, while the microeconomic foundations of the models of Section 13.1 are very strong, the microeconomic foundations of the models of this section are much less strong. Contract terms that specify employment is demand determined often, as Barro (1977) points out, fail to explore all possible avenues for achieving productive efficiency. This shortcoming has led many macroeconomists in the direction of models that are more in the tradition of the competitive, market-clearing paradigm, like the models we review in Chapters 14 and 15.

## REFERENCES

Azariadis, Costas, ''Implicit Contracts and Underemployment Equilibria,'' *Journal of Political Economy,* December, 1975, 1183–1202.

Azariadis, Costas, ''Escalator Clauses and the Allocation of Cyclical Risks,'' *Journal of Economic Theory,* June, 1978, 119–155.

Baily, Martin N., ''Wages and Employment Under Uncertain Demand,'' *Review of Economic Studies,* January, 1974, 37–50.

Barro, Robert J., ''Long-Term Contracting, Sticky Prices and Monetary Policy,'' *Journal of Monetary Economics,* July, 1977, 305–316.

Fischer, Stanley, ''Long-Term Contracts, Rational Expectations, and the Optimal Money Supply Rule,'' *Journal of Political Economy,* February, 1977a, 191–205.

Fischer, Stanley, ''Long-Term Contracting, Sticky Prices and Monetary Policy: A Comment,'' *Journal of Monetary Economics,* July, 1977b, 317–323.

Gordon, Donald F., "A Neo-Classical Theory of Keynesian Unemployment," *Economic Inquiry,* December, 1974, 431–459.

Gray, JoAnna A., "Wage Indexation: A Macroeconomic Approach," *Journal of Monetary Economics,* April, 1976, 221–235.

Green, Jerry, and Charles M. Khan, "Wage-Employment Contracts," *Quarterly Journal of Economics,* Supplement, 1983, 173–187.

Grossman, Herschel I., "Risk Shifting and Reliability in Labor Markets," *Scandinavian Journal of Economics,* 1977, 187–209.

Karni, Edi, "On Optimal Wage Indexation," *Journal of Political Economy,* April, 1983, 282–292.

Keynes, John M., *The General Theory of Employment, Interest, and Money,* New York, Macmillan, 1936.

Rosen, Sherwin, "Implicit Contracts: A Survey," *Journal of Economic Literature,* September, 1985, 1144–1175.

# Chapter **14**

## Equilibrium Stochastic Monetary Models

This chapter presents a review of models in which misperceptions of purely nominal disturbances lead to changes in real output and employment. Such models were introduced in Chapter 5 and were discussed in a little more detail in Chapter 7. However, such earlier discussion dealt with uncertainty in a very ad hoc manner. Misperceptions about relative prices or intertemporal terms of trade were merely postulated as a possibility. Alternatively, the analysis of this chapter derives such misperceptions as equilibrium outcomes.

Incomplete information models like those we analyze in this chapter are generally based upon the confounding of two types of uncertainty: uncertainty about local versus aggregate price-level movements and uncertainty about intertemporal relative prices. Such works are stochastic equilibrium analyses that follow in the tradition of Lucas and Rapping's (1969) model of intertemporal substitution. The classic early works in this area was due to Lucas (1972) and Barro (1976).

This chapter focuses primarily on models of the type postulated by Barro (1976, 1980).[1] Section 14.1 sets up the basic model of Barro (1980) and solves the model for the case of full contemporaneous information. Section 14.2 develops a solution strategy for models of this type and solves a particular example of such a model that is very similar to Barro (1976). Section 14.2 also discusses the effects of exogenous disturbances in this model and presents an analysis of optimal monetary policy. Section 14.3 then discusses the results of a number of extensions of the basic model and discusses empirical evidence on the validity of such models as explanations of money-income correlations.

---

[1] There is a general tendency for subsequent authors to embrace the Barro framework as opposed to the Lucas framework. This preference is probably due to the fact that Barro's log-linear structure is more amenable to further experimentation. However, McCallum (1984) develops a useful log-linear version of the original Lucas model.

The research program this chapter summarizes was launched with very high expectations. At the time of the publication of the original Lucas and Rapping (1969) paper, the commentary of Friedman (1968), and the Phelps (1970) volume, it was generally believed that models of this class represented the best hope for describing macroeconomic fluctuations in competitive, market-clearing models with rigorous microeconomic foundations.

Although these models certainly pass muster with regards to their microeconomic foundations, empirical support for these models is weak at best.[2] For this reason, these models have lost considerable support among macroeconomists. As we later point out, it is hard to believe that lack of information can be an important element in the propagation of economic disturbances in an era in which aggregate price and especially aggregate money supply data are very quickly disseminated.

However, the study of macroeconomic models based on misperceptions remains an important exercise for at least three reasons. First, such models are an important part of the heritage and history of macroeconomic thinking and research. Second, although the applicability of such models to modern, industrialized countries may be limited, their applicability to historical episodes and to current events in less developed countries may be more compelling. Third, these models provide an important reference point against which to compare the properties of other models of macroeconomic fluctuations. In particular, disappointment with the models of this chapter was an important impetus for the development of real business cycle models discussed in Chapter 15, which also attempt to model macroeconomic fluctuations with models ground in the perfectly competitive tradition.

## 14.1 EQUILIBRIUM STOCHASTIC MODELS: A GENERAL FRAMEWORK

In this section, we introduce the basic equilibrium stochastic macroeconomic model and discuss its solution in the case in which agents possess full contemporaneous information about movements in the money supply. The formal analysis in this section closely follows Barro (1980), although most of the component parts of this model have already been developed in earlier chapters.

### Goods Market Equilibrium

Goods market trade in this model takes place in informationally distinct markets, or islands. At the beginning of each period, all agents are randomly reallocated to new islands, and production and trade subsequently occur. In each market, indexed by $z$, goods supply is directly related to the local expected real rate of return $\rho_t(z)$, and demand is inversely related to the local expected real rate of return.

The inverse relationship between goods demand and the expected real rate of return was first introduced in the case of zero expected rate of inflation in Chapters 1 and 2 and subsequently generalized to nonzero expected inflation in Chapter 6. The direct relation-

---

[2]This empirical evidence is discussed in Section 14.3

ship between goods supply and the expected real rate of return was developed in Chapters 5 and 7 based upon the intertemporal substitution behavior of labor suppliers.

The intuition behind these real rate-of-return effects on goods supply and goods demand is straightforward. An increase in the real rate of return translates current work effort into expanded future consumption opportunities. The resulting increase in current work effort implies an increase in current goods supply. An increase in the real rate of return also promotes substitution of future consumption for current consumption, and so current consumption falls. Such a reduction in consumption implies a reduction in current goods demand.

We further postulate that goods supply and goods demand depend on unperceived movements in the nominal money supply. Barro (1980) demonstrates that this particular functional form captures the essential elements of typical wealth effects on consumption demand and labor supply in models of the type that we study in this chapter. We therefore assume that goods demand is directly related to unperceived money and that goods supply is inversely related to unperceived money.

The microeconomic foundations of wealth effects on consumption demand was presented in Chapter 2. An increase in wealth allows for increased consumption, both in the present and in the future. Therefore current goods demand rises. An increase in wealth also allows for a simultaneous increase in the consumption of goods and leisure. Therefore, current work effort is reduced and so current goods supply falls. In log-linear form, we posit market $z$ supply and demand functions of the form[3]

$$y_t^s(z) = k^s + \alpha_s \rho_t(z) - \beta_s(m_t - E_z m_t) + u_t^s + \epsilon_t^s(z), \tag{14.1.1}$$

$$y_t^d(z) = k^d - \alpha_d \rho_t(z) + \beta_d(m_t - E_z m_t) + u_t^d + \epsilon_t^d(z). \tag{14.1.2}$$

In this formulation, $y_t$ denotes the logarithm of output, $m_t$ denotes the logarithm of the money supply, and $\rho_t(z)$ denotes the locally anticipated real rate of return. The random variables $u_t^s$, $u_t^d$, $\epsilon_t^s(z)$, and $\epsilon_t^d(z)$ are all mutually independent, serially uncorrelated, and normally distributed with zero mean and known variances. The random variables $u_t^s$ and $u_t^d$, respectively, represent aggregate supply and aggregate demand disturbances and the random variables $\epsilon_t^s(z)$ and $\epsilon_t^d(z)$, respectively, represent local, market-specific supply and demand disturbances. The variable $E_z m_t$ denotes the expected value of the logarithm of the current aggregate money stock conditional on all information available at time $t$ in market $z$. Finally, the parameters $k^s$, $k^d$, $\alpha_s$, $\alpha_d$, $\beta_s$, and $\beta_d$ are all positive constants.

Market clearing requires that the expected rate of return in each market satisfy

$$\rho_t(z) = \frac{k}{\alpha} + \frac{\beta}{\alpha}(m_t - E_z m_t) + \frac{u_t}{\alpha} + \frac{\epsilon_t(z)}{\alpha}, \tag{14.1.3}$$

where

$$k \equiv k^d - k^s, \qquad \alpha \equiv \alpha_d - \alpha_s, \qquad \beta \equiv \beta_d - \beta_s, \tag{14.1.4}$$

$$u_t \equiv u_t^d - u_t^s, \qquad \epsilon_t(z) \equiv \epsilon_t^d(z) - \epsilon_t^s(z). \tag{14.1.5}$$

---

[3]Notation in this chapter represents a compromise between notation adopted elsewhere in the text and notation used in Barro (1976) and throughout much of the subsequent literature.

Plugging $\rho_t(z)$ back into the market $z$ supply function and collecting terms, we find that local output $y_t(z)$ is given by

$$y_t(z) = y^* + \frac{H}{\alpha}(m_t - E_z m_t) + \frac{\alpha_s}{\alpha}[u_t^d + \epsilon_t^d(z)] + \frac{\alpha_d}{\alpha}[u_t^s + \epsilon_t^s(z)], \qquad (14.1.6)$$

where we have employed the additional definitions

$$y^* \equiv \frac{\alpha_d k^s + \alpha_s k^d}{\alpha}, \qquad H \equiv \alpha_s \beta_d - \alpha_d \beta_s. \qquad (14.1.7)$$

For most of the ensuing analysis, we adopt the additional assumption that $H > 0$. That $H > 0$ is necessary and sufficient for unperceived increases in the money supply to generate increases in output and employment.

Aggregating over markets, we assume that the number of markets is large enough so that the sample means of $\epsilon_t^s(z)$ and $\epsilon_t^d(z)$ are equal to their expected values of zero. If we then define $y_t$ as the arithmetic mean of the $y_t(z)$'s, aggregate output is given by

$$y_t = y^* + \frac{H}{\alpha}(m_t - \overline{E_z m_t}) + \frac{\alpha_s}{\alpha}u_t^d + \frac{\alpha_d}{\alpha}u_t^s, \qquad (14.1.8)$$

where $\overline{E_z m_t}$ represents the average expectation of the logarithm of the money supply across markets. We therefore note that local disturbances have no aggregate effects. Aggregate output is positively related to the average extent of unperceived money and positively related to the aggregate supply and aggregate demand disturbances.

Furthermore, note that the expected real rate of return in each submarket is positively related to the local value of unperceived money and is also positively related to the aggregate and local excess-demand disturbances $u_t$ and $\epsilon_t(z)$. Finally, while the $\epsilon_t(z)$ disturbances cancel out in their effects on aggregate output, local markets with positive supply and demand shocks experience higher than average levels of production.

The current form of this model shares a number of important properties with the models of Sections 2.1 and 6.2 in the case in which actual and expected rates of inflation are equal. In particular, equilibrium in the goods market, the equilibrium levels of production, and the equilibrium expected rates of return can be solved for without reference to the markets for money or earning assets except to the extent to which such markets provide information in determining the value of $m_t - E_z m_t$.

## Money Market Equilibrium

Analysis of equilibrium in the goods markets is sufficient to obtain solutions for the local expected real rates of return and output levels as functions of unperceived money and the other stochastic disturbance terms. However, the money and earning asset markets generally are needed to solve for the equilibrium nominal goods prices and the equilibrium nominal rate of interest. Barro (1980) introduces the possibility of an economywide earning asset market into the basic model. The demand for money is assumed to take the form

$$m_t^d = p_t + \delta y_t - \gamma r_t + v_t, \qquad (14.1.9)$$

where $m_t^d$ denotes the logarithm of nominal money demand, $p_t$ denotes the logarithm of the aggregate price level, and $r_t$ denotes the nominal rate of interest. In this formulation, $v_t$ is a serially uncorrelated, zero-mean, normally distributed random variable that is independent of all other disturbance terms and $\delta$ and $\gamma$ represent positive constants. All agents have access to the money market and all agents are therefore able to observe the current, economywide nominal rate of interest $r_t$.

The logarithm of the nominal supply of money is assumed to take the form

$$m_t^s = m_{t-1} + \mu + x_t. \tag{14.1.10}$$

The constant $\mu$ denotes the unconditional average rate of growth of the nominal money supply, and $x_t$ is a serially uncorrelated, zero-mean, normally distributed random variable that is independent of all other disturbance terms. The logarithm of the nominal money supply therefore follows a random walk with drift.

Money market equilibrium is assumed to obtain at every point in time, so that

$$m_t = m_t^d = m_t^s = m_{t-1} + \mu + x_t. \tag{14.1.11}$$

Agents know the values of $\mu$ and $m_{t-1}$ at time $t$ as well as the probability distributions of all the disturbance terms. However, agents may only infer the values of $m_t$, $p_t$, and $x_t$ from the information available from the observation of $r_t$ and the local price level $p_t(z)$.

Equating money supply and money demand, we find that the equilibrium economywide nominal rate of interest must satisfy

$$r_t = \frac{1}{\gamma}\left[ p_t + \delta y^* + \frac{\delta H}{\alpha}(x_t - \overline{E_z x_t}) + \frac{\delta}{\alpha}(\alpha_s u_t^d + \alpha_d u_t^s) + v_t - m_{t-1} - \mu - x_t \right], \tag{14.1.12}$$

where we have employed the relationship

$$m_t - \overline{E_z m_t} = m_{t-1} + \mu + x_t - m_{t-1} - \mu - \overline{E_z x_t} = x_t - \overline{E_z x_t}. \tag{14.1.13}$$

That is, the only part of the current nominal money supply that may not, on average, be perceived is that component that corresponds to the unperceived value of the term $x_t$.

## Equilibrium Conditions in the Incomplete Information Case

We are now ready to sketch out the solution strategy for obtaining reduced-form equations for $p_t(z)$, $p_t$, and $r_t$. By definition, the expected real rate of return in each market must equal the economywide nominal rate of interest minus the locally perceived expected rate of inflation. The change in prices expected by a market $z$ participant is the logarithm of nominal price he or she expects to confront next period minus the current logarithm of nominal price in market $z$, $p_t(z)$. Since all agents are to be randomly distributed to new markets at the beginning of next period, the best estimate of the logarithm of local price for next period is simply the expected logarithm of aggregate price, $E_z p_{t+1}$.

We therefore require in each market $z$ that

$$r_t = p_t(z) + [E_z p_{t+1} - p_t(z)]. \tag{14.1.14}$$

Rearranging the above equation to solve for $p_t(z)$, we obtain

$$p_t(z) = p_t(z) + E_z p_{t+1} - r_t \tag{14.1.15}$$

or

$$p_t(z) = E_z p_{t+1} + \frac{k}{\alpha} + \frac{\beta}{\alpha}(x_t - E_z x_t) + \frac{u_t}{\alpha} + \frac{\epsilon_t(z)}{\alpha} - \frac{1}{\gamma} \tag{14.1.16}$$
$$\times \left[ p_t + \delta y^* + \frac{\delta H}{\alpha}(x_t - \overline{E_z x_t}) + \frac{\delta}{\alpha}(\alpha_s u_t^d + \alpha_d u_t^s) + v_t - m_{t-1} - \mu - x_t \right].$$

The above equation may be solved by the method of undetermined coefficients first introduced in Chapter 10. Let us first posit a solution for $p_t(z)$ of the form

$$p_t(z) = \pi_0 + \pi_1 m_{t-1} + \pi_2 x_t + \pi_3 v_t + \pi_4^d u_t^d + \pi_4^s u_t^s + \pi_5 \epsilon_t(z). \tag{14.1.17}$$

We may now use the above equation to generate the following expressions for $p_t$ and $E_z p_{t+1}$:

$$p_t = \pi_0 + \pi_1 m_{t-1} + \pi_2 x_t + \pi_3 v_t + \pi_4^d u_t^d + \pi_4^s u_t^s, \tag{14.1.18}$$

$$p_{t+1} = \pi_0 + \pi_1 m_t + \pi_2 x_{t+1} + \pi_3 v_{t+1} + \pi_4^d u_{t+1}^d + \pi_4^s u_{t+1}^s$$
$$= \pi_0 + \pi_1 \mu + \pi_1 m_{t-1} + \pi_1 x_t + \pi_2 x_{t+1} \tag{14.1.19}$$
$$+ \pi_3 v_{t+1} + \pi_4^d u_{t+1}^d + \pi_4^s u_{t+1}^s,$$

and so

$$E_z p_{t+1} = \pi_0 + \pi_1 \mu + \pi_1 m_{t-1} + \pi_1 E_z x_t. \tag{14.1.20}$$

The $p_t(z)$ equation may now be rewritten as

$$p_t(z) = \pi_0 \left(1 - \frac{1}{\gamma}\right) + \frac{k}{\alpha} - \frac{\delta y^*}{\gamma} + \left(\pi_1 + \frac{1}{\gamma}\right)\mu + \left[\pi_1 \left(1 - \frac{1}{\gamma}\right) + \frac{1}{\gamma}\right]m_{t-1}$$
$$+ \frac{1}{\gamma}(1 - \pi_2)x_t + \pi_1 E_z x_t + \frac{\beta}{\alpha}(x_t - E_z x_t) - \frac{\delta H}{\alpha \gamma}(x_t - \overline{E_z x_t}) - \frac{1}{\gamma}(1 + \pi_3)v_t$$
$$+ \frac{1}{\alpha}\left(1 - \frac{\alpha \pi_4^d}{\gamma} - \frac{\delta \alpha_s}{\gamma}\right)u_t^d - \frac{1}{\alpha}\left(1 + \frac{\alpha \pi_4^s}{\gamma} + \frac{\delta \alpha_d}{\gamma}\right)u_t^s + \frac{1}{\alpha}\epsilon_t(z).$$
$$\tag{14.1.21}$$

## Solution with Full Contemporaneous Information

As we demonstrate in the next section, the computation of expressions for $E_z x_t$ and $\overline{E_z x_t}$, are, in general, quite complicated procedures. However, we can get a good deal of intuition into the workings of the model by first considering the case in which $E_z x_t = \overline{E_z x_t} = x_t$. In this more simple case, the above expression simplifies to

$$p_t(z) = \pi_0 \left(1 - \frac{1}{\gamma}\right) + \frac{k}{\alpha} - \frac{\delta y^*}{\gamma} + \left(\pi_1 + \frac{1}{\gamma}\right)\mu + \left[\pi_1 \left(1 - \frac{1}{\gamma}\right) + \frac{1}{\gamma}\right]m_{t-1}$$
$$+ \left[\pi_1 + \frac{1}{\gamma}\left(1 - \pi_2\right)\right]x_t - \frac{1}{\gamma}\left(1 + \pi_3\right)v_t \tag{14.1.22}$$
$$+ \frac{1}{\alpha}\left(1 - \frac{\alpha \pi_4^d}{\gamma} - \frac{\delta \alpha_s}{\gamma}\right)u_t^d - \frac{1}{\alpha}\left(1 + \frac{\alpha \pi_4^s}{\gamma} + \frac{\delta \alpha_d}{\gamma}\right)u_t^s + \frac{1}{\alpha}\epsilon_t(z)$$

The undetermined coefficients must therefore satisfy

$$\pi_0 = \pi_0\left(1 - \frac{1}{\gamma}\right) + \frac{k}{\alpha} - \frac{\delta y^*}{\gamma} + \left(\pi_1 + \frac{1}{\gamma}\right)\mu,$$

$$\pi_1 = \pi_1\left(1 - \frac{1}{\gamma}\right) + \frac{1}{\gamma},$$

$$\pi_2 = \pi_1 + \frac{1}{\gamma}(1 - \pi_2),$$

$$\pi_3 = -\frac{1}{\gamma}(1 + \pi_3),$$  (14.1.23)

$$\pi_4^d = \frac{1}{\alpha}\left(1 - \frac{\alpha\pi_4^d}{\gamma} - \frac{\delta\alpha_s}{\gamma}\right),$$

$$\pi_4^s = -\frac{1}{\alpha}\left(1 + \frac{\alpha\pi_4^s}{\gamma} + \frac{\delta\alpha_d}{\gamma}\right),$$

$$\pi_5 = \frac{1}{\alpha}.$$

These equations may be readily solved to obtain

$$\pi_0 = \frac{k\gamma}{\alpha} - \delta y^* + (1 + \gamma)\mu,$$

$$\pi_1 = \pi_2 = 1,$$

$$\pi_3 = -\frac{1}{1 + \gamma},$$  (14.1.24)

$$\pi_4^d = \frac{\gamma - \delta\alpha_s}{\alpha(1 + \gamma)},$$

$$\pi_4^s = -\frac{\gamma + \delta\alpha_d}{\alpha(1 + \gamma)},$$

$$\pi_5 = \frac{1}{\alpha}.$$

The full information reduced-form expressions for $p_t(z)$, $E_z p_{t+1} - p_t(z)$ and $r_t$ are therefore given by

$$p_t(z) = \frac{\gamma k}{\alpha} - \delta y^* + (1 + \gamma)\mu + m_{t-1} + x_t - \frac{1}{1 + \gamma}v_t$$

$$+ \frac{\gamma - \delta\alpha_s}{\alpha(1 + \gamma)}u_t^d - \frac{\gamma + \delta\alpha_d}{\alpha(1 + \gamma)}u_t^s + \frac{\epsilon_t(z)}{\alpha},$$  (14.1.25)

$$E_z p_{t+1} - p_t(z) = \mu + \frac{1}{1 + \gamma}v_t - \frac{\gamma - \delta\alpha_s}{\alpha(1 + \gamma)}u_t^d + \frac{\gamma + \delta\alpha_d}{\alpha(1 + \gamma)}u_t^s - \frac{\epsilon_t(z)}{\alpha},$$  (14.1.26)

$$r_t = \frac{k}{\alpha} + \mu + \frac{1}{1 + \gamma} \, v_t + \frac{1 + \delta\alpha_s}{\alpha(1 + \gamma)} \, u_t^d - \frac{1 - \delta\alpha_d}{\alpha(1 + \gamma)} \, u_t^s. \qquad (14.1.27)$$

A few comments are now in order. First, note that the rate of growth of the nominal money supply $\mu$, which is neutral in its effects on the expected real rates of return and the levels of output, generates one-for-one increases in the nominal interest rate and the expected rate of inflation. Next consider permanent, unanticipated increases in the nominal money supply $x_t$. Such disturbances cause a permanent increase in the price levels $p_t(z)$. However, since the effect of increases in $x_t$ are temporary with respect to the money growth rate, there is no effect of $x_t$ on the nominal interest rate or on the expected rates of inflation.

Next consider the effects of shocks to the demand for money $v_t$. Unlike shocks to the money supply process, these shocks are assumed to be purely transitory. A temporary increase in the demand for money raises the nominal rate of interest, just as would be the case of our analyses of Chapters 2 and 6. Such a disturbance also depresses the current goods prices $p_t(z)$. However, since the shock is purely temporary, the effect of the shock on the price level is also purely temporary, and so a positive money demand shock generates an expectation of inflation. This expectation of inflation is exactly equal to the temporary rise in the nominal interest rate, so that the expected real rates of interest and the levels of output are unaffected by the money demand shock.

A richer menu of money supply and money demand shocks could easily be added to the model. In particular, both the money supply and money demand shocks could contain both temporary and permanent components. While such more general cases could generate a greater variety of time series properties for the nominal interest rate and expected inflation, all such types of shocks would be neutral with respect to the expected real rates of return and the levels of output.

Next consider shocks to aggregate demand and aggregate supply, $u_t^d$ and $u_t^s$. As we previously demonstrated, positive shocks to aggregate demand raise both the current expected real rates of return and the current levels of output. Positive shocks to aggregate supply lower the current expected real rates of return and raise the current levels of output. However, since both shocks are assumed to be purely transitory in nature, neither shock has any effect on $E_z p_{t+1}$. Therefore, the effect of either shock on the expected rate of inflation must be equal and opposite to its effect on the current aggregate price level $p_t$.

Let us next consider in a little more detail the effects of aggregate demand shocks. As noted above, for $u_t^d > 0$, the current aggregate level of output rises. Furthermore, we also note that this disturbance also unambiguously raises the nominal rate of interest. However, with increases in both $y_t$ and $r_t$, the net effect on money demand is ambiguous. Therefore, holding constant the money supply and money demand shocks, a positive value for $u_t^d$ may either raise or lower the aggregate price level $p_t$ depending on the relative elasticities of money demand with respect to income $\delta$ and with respect to the nominal rate of interest $\gamma$.

Favorable aggregate supply shocks, $u_t^s > 0$, raise current aggregate output $y_t$ and lower the current expected real rates of interest $\rho_t(z)$. Furthermore, a favorable aggregate supply shock unambiguously lowers the current aggregate price level $p_t$. Since the supply shock is assumed to be purely transitory, the fall in prices generates the expectation of inflation. Therefore, with expected real rates of interest falling and with the expected rates of inflation rising, the net effect on the nominal rate of interest is theoretically ambiguous.

However, as long as $\alpha_d\delta < 1$, positive aggregate supply shocks unambiguously lower both the nominal rate of interest and the expected real rates of interest.

Finally, consider the effects of purely local supply and demand shocks $\epsilon_t^s$ and $\epsilon_t^d$. Such disturbances affect the local nominal price $p_t(z)$, the local level of output $y_t(z)$, and the locally expected rate of inflation $E_z p_{t+1} - p_t(z)$. However, such shocks have no effects on any aggregate variables including the economywide nominal rate of interest. Since agents at each location observe different local prices $p_t(z)$, agents have differing, although rational, expected rates of inflation. Such differences in expected inflation rates are required, however, to reconcile differences in local expected real rates of interest with a common economywide nominal rate of interest.

## 14.2 THE ENDOGENOUS INFORMATION CASE

In solving the model of the previous section, we made use of the assumption that $E_z x_t = x_t$. While this assumption greatly simplifies the calculation of reduced-form equations for the endogenous variables, such full information is not likely to be available to economic agents except under some very special sets of assumptions. Furthermore, the principal aim of stochastic equilibrium models like the ones we study in this chapter is to explain a channel of influence for monetary shocks to affect the allocation of resources. Therefore, because all monetary shocks are neutral in the case of full information, the assumption of full information is not a particularly interesting one in the context of such models.

In this section, we first sketch out a solution procedure for solving models like that of Section 14.1 under the more general case of incomplete information. We then derive a closed-form solution to a very simple case in which information is still incomplete but in which the form of the incompleteness is particularly simple.

### A General Solution Strategy

In the most general case of the previous section, we posited a local price equation of the form

$$p_t(z) = \pi_0 + \pi_1 m_{t-1} + \pi_2 x_t + \pi_3 v_t + \pi_4^d u_t^d + \pi_4^s u_t^s + \pi_5 \epsilon_t(z). \tag{14.2.1}$$

Once the undetermined coefficients in the above expression are known, market $z$ agents are able to construct a local informational signal of the form

$$l_t(z) = p_t(z) - \pi_0 - \pi_1 m_{t-1} = \pi_2 x_t + \pi_3 v_t + \pi_4^d u_t^d + \pi_4^s u_t^s + \pi_5 \epsilon_t(z). \tag{14.2.2}$$

In similar fashion, we can also posit a trial solution for the nominal interest rate process of the form

$$r_t = c_0 + c_1 m_{t-1} + c_2 x_t + c_3 v_t + c_4^d u_t^d + c_4^s u_t^s. \tag{14.2.3}$$

The principal difference between the nominal interest rate process and the local price process is that the local process includes a local disturbance term of the form $\pi_5 \epsilon_t(z)$ while the (aggregate) nominal interest rate process does not. In the case of full information, the $c_i$ coefficients were given by

$$c_0 = \frac{k}{\alpha} + \mu,$$

$$c_1 = c_2 = 0,$$

$$c_3 = \frac{1}{1 + \gamma}, \tag{14.2.4}$$

$$c_4^d = \frac{1}{\alpha} \frac{1 + \delta\alpha_s}{1 + \gamma},$$

$$c_4^s = -\frac{1}{\alpha} \frac{1 - \delta\alpha_d}{1 + \gamma}.$$

In the more general, incomplete information case, the solution for the $c_i$'s is more complex, but it is still conceptually straightforward. Once the $c_i$'s have been solved for, agents are able to form the aggregate or global signal:

$$g_t = r_t - c_0 - c_1 m_{t-1} = c_2 x_t + c_3 v_t + c_4^d u_t^d + c_4^s u_t^s. \tag{14.2.5}$$

Agents therefore have access to two bits of information, $l_t(z)$ and $g_t$, in addition to their knowledge of the $\pi_i$ and the $c_i$ coefficients and the stochastic structure of the economy. Given this information, it is now a relatively straightforward (although admittedly somewhat tedious) application of the signal extraction problem of Chapter 10 to construct an optimal estimate of the current disturbance $E_z x_t$ of the form

$$E_z x_t = \theta_0 + \theta_l l_t(z) + \theta_g g_t, \tag{14.2.6}$$

where the $\theta_i$ solve

$$\begin{bmatrix} 0 \\ E x_t l_t \\ E x_t g_t \end{bmatrix} = \begin{bmatrix} 1 & 0 & 0 \\ 0 & E(l_t^2) & E(l_t g_t) \\ 0 & E(l_t g_t) & E(g_t^2) \end{bmatrix} \begin{bmatrix} \theta_0 \\ \theta_l \\ \theta_g \end{bmatrix}. \tag{14.2.7}$$

While it is straightforward to show that $\theta_0 = 0$, calculation of $\theta_l$ and $\theta_g$ can only yield expressions for $\theta_l$ and $\theta_g$ that are complicated functions of the $\pi_i$ and $c_i$ coefficients and the variances of the underlying disturbances. However, in principle, the rational forecast of $x_t$ for agents in market $z$ can now be expressed as

$$E_z x_t = (\theta_l \pi_2 + \theta_g c_2) x_t + (\theta_l \pi_3 + \theta_g c_3) v_t \\ + (\theta_l \pi_4^d + \theta_g c_4^d) u_t^d + (\theta_l \pi_4^s + \theta_g c_4^s) u_t^s + \theta_l \pi_5 \epsilon_t(z). \tag{14.2.8}$$

It is also readily apparent at this point that the average expectation $\overline{E_z x_t}$ is simply equal to the above expression evaluated at $\epsilon_t(z) = 0$.

We may now plug the expressions for $E_z x_t$ and $\overline{E_z x_t}$ back into the original expressions for $p_t(z)$ and $r_t$ and complete the method of undetermined coefficients. This procedure provides a set of equations in the $\pi_i$ and $c_i$ coefficients that are in principle sufficient to solve for all of the undetermined coefficients of the model.[4]

---

[4]For more details on this procedure, the interested reader is referred to Barro (1980) and King (1981, 1982, 1983). It is, however, important to note that this procedure often fails to provide unique solutions for the $\pi_i$'s.

## A Simple Monetary Misinformation Model

In order to get a flavor for the solution strategy in models of this kind and to formally prove some very basic results, let us now consider the case in which money is the only store of value. That is, we now consider the solution of the model in the absence of an economywide bond market. Although this case is somewhat less "realistic," it nevertheless is capable of generating some of the more important implications of this type of model, and the solution in this case is drastically simpler than the solution of the model of the previous section.

The formal analysis of this case follows closely that of Barro (1976). We retain most of the structure of the basic model of Section 14.1. The only notational change is that we suppress the roles of $k$ and $\mu$. Although $\mu$ can be shown to generate nonneutralities in the present model, such nonneutralities only result from the artificial elimination of a market in nominal bonds. As in our earlier analysis, the local expected real interest rate and output level are given by

$$\rho_t(z) = \frac{\beta}{\alpha}(m_t - E_z m_t) + \frac{u_t}{\alpha} + \frac{\epsilon_t(z)}{\alpha}, \tag{14.2.9}$$

$$y_t(z) = \frac{H}{\alpha}(m_t - E_z m_t) + \frac{\alpha_s}{\alpha}[u_t^d + \epsilon_t^d(z)] + \frac{\alpha_d}{\alpha}[u_t^s + \epsilon_t^s(z)]. \tag{14.2.10}$$

We also continue to assume that

$$m_t = m_{t-1} + x_t. \tag{14.2.11}$$

With no alternative store of value, the expected real rate of return is simply equal to the expected real return on money, which in turn is equal to minus the expected rate of inflation. We therefore require that

$$\rho_t(z) = -[E_z p_{t+1} - p_t(z)]. \tag{14.2.12}$$

We again adopt a trial solution of the form[5]

$$p_t(z) = \pi_1 m_{t-1} + \pi_2 x_t + \pi_3 u_t + \pi_4 \epsilon_t(z). \tag{14.2.13}$$

The expected future price level is therefore given by

$$E_z p_{t+1} = \pi_1 m_{t-1} + \pi_1 E_z x_t. \tag{14.2.14}$$

Recalling that we still have $m_t - E_z m_t = x_t - E_z x_t$, the equilibrium condition for $p_t(z)$ is now given by

$$p_t(z) = \pi_1 m_{t-1} + \left(\pi_1 - \frac{\beta}{\alpha}\right)E_z x_t + \frac{\beta}{\alpha} x_t + \frac{u_t}{\alpha} + \frac{\epsilon_t(z)}{\alpha}. \tag{14.2.15}$$

In the present example, the only bit of contemporaneous information agents have

---

[5] In this particular case, the equilibrium value for the constant term $\pi_0$ would be indeterminant without some additional structure like a demand-for-money function. We also find that the terms $u_t^d$ and $u_t^s$ now enter the local price function with equal and opposite coefficients. We therefore no longer need to postulate separate values for $\pi_4^d$ and $\pi_4^s$.

access to is the value of the local goods price $p_t(z)$. With this bit of information, agents are able to construct the signal

$$s_t(z) = \alpha \left[ p_t(z) - \pi_1 m_{t-1} - \left( \pi_1 - \frac{\beta}{\alpha} \right) E_z x_t \right] = \beta x_t + u_t + \epsilon_t(z). \qquad (14.2.16)$$

From this signal, it is a straightforward signal extraction problem to construct the optimal estimate

$$E_z x_t = \frac{\theta}{\beta} [\beta x_t + u_t + \epsilon_t(z)], \qquad (14.2.17)$$

where

$$\theta \equiv \frac{\beta^2 \sigma_x^2}{\beta^2 \sigma_x^2 + \sigma_u^2 + \sigma_\epsilon^2}, \qquad (14.2.18)$$

and where the terms $\sigma_x^2$, $\sigma_u^2$, and $\sigma_\epsilon^2$, respectively, represent the variances of $x_t$, $u_t$, and $\epsilon_t(z)$.

Now plugging in for $E_z x_t$ in the above equilibrium condition, we obtain, after rearranging terms,

$$p_t(z) = \pi_1 m_{t-1} + \left[ \frac{\beta}{\alpha} + \left( \pi_1 - \frac{\beta}{\alpha} \right)\theta \right] x_t + \left[ \frac{1}{\alpha} + \left( \pi_1 - \frac{\beta}{\alpha} \right) \frac{\theta}{\beta} \right] [u_t + \epsilon_t(z)].$$
$$(14.2.19)$$

We therefore require

$$\pi_1 = 1,$$

$$\pi_2 = \left[ \frac{\beta}{\alpha} + \left( \pi_1 - \frac{\beta}{\alpha} \right)\theta \right], \qquad (14.2.20)$$

$$\pi_3 = \pi_4 = \left[ \frac{1}{\alpha} + \left( \pi_1 - \frac{\beta}{\alpha} \right) \frac{\theta}{\beta} \right].$$

Upon rearranging terms, we find that

$$\pi_2 = \theta + \frac{\beta}{\alpha} (1 - \theta),$$
$$(14.2.21)$$
$$\pi_3 = \pi_4 = \frac{1}{\beta}\pi_2 = \frac{\theta}{\beta} + \frac{1 - \theta}{\alpha}.$$

The equilibrium price process is therefore given by

$$p_t(z) = m_{t-1} + \left[ \theta + \frac{\beta}{\alpha} (1 - \theta) \right] x_t + \left( \frac{\theta}{\beta} + \frac{1 - \theta}{\alpha} \right) [u_t + \epsilon_t(z)]$$
$$(14.2.22)$$
$$= m_{t-1} + \left( \frac{\theta}{\beta} + \frac{1 - \theta}{\alpha} \right) [\beta x_t + u_t + \epsilon_t(z)].$$

More importantly, however, we also know from the construction of $E_z x_t$ that

$$x_t - E_z x_t = (1 - \theta)x_t - \frac{\theta}{\beta} [u_t + \epsilon_t(z)]. \tag{14.2.23}$$

Now plugging into the original equilibrium conditions for $\rho_t(z)$ and $y_t(z)$, we find that

$$\rho_t(z) = \frac{1 - \theta}{\alpha} [\beta x_t + u_t + \epsilon_t(z)], \tag{14.2.24}$$

$$y_t(z) = \frac{H}{\alpha} (1 - \theta)x_t + \frac{1}{\alpha\beta} [(1 - \theta)\alpha_s\beta_d + \beta_s(\alpha_s + \theta\alpha_d)][u_t^d + \epsilon_t^d(z)]$$

$$+ \frac{1}{\alpha\beta} [(1 - \theta)\alpha_d\beta_s + \beta_d(\alpha_d + \theta\alpha_s)][u_t^s + \epsilon_t^s(z)]. \tag{14.2.25}$$

Therefore, in the absence of full information, monetary shocks do affect both the expected real rate of return and the level of output. In the full information case, $x_t$ shocks are correctly perceived, and because such shocks only affect the real economy through the term $x_t - E_z x_t$, such shocks are completely neutral in that case. In the present case, however, positive shocks to $m_t$ are partially inferred to be $u_t$ and $\epsilon_t(z)$ shocks and are only partially perceived to be the monetary shocks that they in fact are. Therefore, the term $m_t - E_z m_t = x_t - E_z x_t = (1 - \theta)x_t$ is positive and output and the expected real rates of return rise relative to what they would have been otherwise.

From the above equation in $y_t(z)$, we see that the elasticity of output with respect to monetary shocks is equal to $(H/\alpha)(1 - \theta)$. From the definition of $\theta$, we know that

$$1 - \theta = \frac{\sigma_u^2 + \sigma_\epsilon^2}{\beta^2\sigma_x^2 + \sigma_u^2 + \sigma_\epsilon^2}. \tag{14.2.26}$$

We therefore note that the elasticity of output with respect to monetary shocks falls as the variance of monetary shocks $\sigma_x^2$ rises. Lucas (1973) also derives this result in a somewhat different model and presents some cross-country evidence supporting this hypothesis. We shall see, however, that insulation from monetary shocks comes, in this model, at a cost of worsened resource allocation.

The lack of full information also results in distortions in the effects of real shocks. To see this more clearly, consider the difference between the level of output in the present case and the level of output that results in the full information case. Full information output, denoted by $\hat{y}(z)$, is that level of output that obtains when $E_z x_t = x_t$. Plugging in above, we note that

$$\hat{y}_t(z) = \frac{1}{\alpha}[\alpha_s[u_t^d + \epsilon_t^d(z)] + \alpha_d[u_t^s + \epsilon_t^s(z)]]. \tag{14.2.27}$$

The excess of output over full information output $y_t(z) - \hat{y}_t(z)$ is, after collecting terms, given by

$$y_t(z) - \hat{y}_t(z) = \frac{H}{\alpha} (1 - \theta)x_t - \frac{H\theta}{\alpha\beta}[u_t + \epsilon_t(z)]. \tag{14.2.28}$$

This expression confirms our earlier result that positive monetary shocks ($x_t > 0$) generate output levels that are "too high." Furthermore, we find that while positive local and aggregate demand shocks ($u_t^d + \epsilon_t^d(z) > 0$) generate increases in output, such shocks lower output relative to full information output. To understand this result, note that positive shocks to demand raise nominal prices $p_t(z)$. Some rearranging of our earlier expressions for $E_z x_t$ also allows derivation of

$$E_z x_t = \frac{\theta}{\pi_2}(p_t(z) - m_{t-1}). \tag{14.2.29}$$

Therefore, an increase in the local nominal price is always perceived, in part, as a positive monetary shock. However, if there is, in fact, no current monetary shock, then $m_t - E_z m_t$ falls, and so there is an offsetting tendency for output to fall. Therefore, the output increase in response to increases in demand is insufficiently small.

We also now note that while positive local and aggregate supply shocks ($u_t^s + \epsilon_t^s(z) > 0$) generate increases in output, such shocks, which correspond to negative values of $u_t + \epsilon_t(z)$, also raise output relative to its full information level. Favorable supply shocks generate reductions in nominal prices $p_t(z)$, and so such shocks are therefore partially perceived as negative monetary shocks. However, if $x_t = 0$, $m_t - E_z m_t$ rises, and so there is a tendency for output to respond more elastically to supply shocks than in the case of full information.

## Optimal Monetary Policy

We first discussed optimal monetary policy in flexible-price, stochastic macroeconomic models in Chapter 12. In that setting, we demonstrated that any change in the deterministic component of the money supply process had no effect on the stochastic properties of the output process. Changes in the deterministic component of the money supply process are limited in the present analysis to changes in $\mu$, the expected rate of growth of the nominal money supply. In the full information case of Section 14.1, changes in $\mu$ affect the nominal interest rate and the expected rates of inflation but are neutral with respect to the levels of output and the expected real rates of interest.

Although we formally suppress the rate of growth of the nominal money supply in the analysis of Section 14.2, the original Barro (1976) analysis demonstrates that changes in $\mu$ have the potential for changing the output and expected real interest rate processes. However, such an effect only operates by changing the expected real rate of return to holding money in a setting in which there is no alternative store of value whose rate of return can include an equilibrium inflation premium. Such effects are not likely to be of importance except in economies with artificially controlled capital markets.

A more interesting question to ask of models like the ones that we analyze in this chapter is that of the optimal variance of the money supply process, $\sigma_x^2$. Suppose that the monetary authority is considering further randomization of the process of money growth. Clearly such a change affects the value of $\theta$, and so such a change has definite allocative effects. However, are there circumstances in which these effects might be beneficial? In previous chapters, we sometimes consider a monetary policy objective that seeks to minimize the variance of output around its unconditional mean, although we also generally concluded that the rationale for this sort of objective function is rather weak. In the present context, this type of policy objective might seek to minimize the variance of output in a representative market $z$. Such a policy would seek to minimize

$$
\mathcal{L}_y = \left(\frac{H}{\alpha}\right)^2 (1 - \theta)^2 \sigma_x^2
$$

$$
+ \left(\frac{1}{\alpha\beta}\right)^2 [(1 - \theta)\alpha_s\beta_d + \beta_s(\alpha_s + \theta\alpha_d)]^2 \{E(u_t^d)^2 + E[\epsilon_t^d(z)]^2\} \tag{14.2.30}
$$

$$
+ \left(\frac{1}{\alpha\beta}\right)^2 [(1 - \theta)\alpha_d\beta_s + \beta_d(\alpha_d + \theta\alpha_s)]^2 \{E(u_t^s)^2 + E[\epsilon_t^s(z)]^2\}.
$$

To gain insight into this problem, let us first consider how the first term in the above expression, the direct contribution of $\sigma_x^2$ to $\mathcal{L}_y$, varies with changes in $\sigma_x{}^2$. We may rewrite the first term of the above expression as

$$
\left(\frac{H}{\alpha}\right)^2 (1 - \theta)^2 \sigma_x^2 = \left(\frac{H}{\alpha}\right)^2 \frac{\sigma_u^2 + \sigma_\epsilon^2}{\beta^2\sigma_x^2 + \sigma_u^2 + \sigma_\epsilon^2} \sigma_x^2. \tag{14.2.31}
$$

This expression is equal to zero, both at $\sigma_x^2 = 0$ and as $\sigma_x^2 \to +\infty$. Therefore, the output process can be completely neutralized from monetary shocks either by eliminating such shocks entirely or by expanding such shocks without limit. As $\sigma_x^2$ approaches plus infinity, $\theta$ approaches unity and monetary (and all other shocks) are ignored by goods suppliers and goods demanders. All changes in nominal prices are perceived as monetary in origin, and therefore, all allocative functioning of the price process vanishes. Alternatively, at values of $\sigma_x^2$ on the interval $(0, +\infty)$, $\mathcal{L}_y$ is strictly positive.

Let us next consider how the entire expression for $\mathcal{L}_y$ varies with changes in $\sigma_x^2$. As a prelude, we adopt the following additional notation:

$$
\sigma_d^2 \equiv E(u_t^d)^2 + E[\epsilon_t^d(z)]^2, \tag{14.2.32}
$$

$$
\sigma_s^2 \equiv E(u_t^s)^2 + E[\epsilon_t^s(z)]^2, \tag{14.2.33}
$$

$$
q \equiv \frac{\sigma_d^2}{\sigma_u^2 + \sigma_\epsilon^2} \quad \text{and} \quad 1 - q \equiv \frac{\sigma_s^2}{\sigma_u^2 + \sigma_\epsilon^2}, \tag{14.2.34}
$$

where

$$
\sigma_u^2 = E(u_t^d)^2 + E(u_t^s)^2 \quad \text{and} \quad \sigma_\epsilon^2 = E[\epsilon_t^d(z)]^2 + E[\epsilon_t^s(z)]^2. \tag{14.2.35}
$$

We may now differentiate the above expression for $\mathcal{L}_y$ with respect to $\sigma_x^2$. After some straightforward algebraic manipulation, we can show that

$$
\frac{d\mathcal{L}_y}{d\sigma_x^2} = \frac{2H}{\alpha}(1 - \theta)^2 \left[(1 - q)\beta_d - q\beta_s - \frac{H}{2\alpha}\right]. \tag{14.2.36}
$$

Note that the sign of $d\mathcal{L}_y/d\sigma_x^2$ is independent of the size of $\theta$. Therefore, if we seek to minimize $\mathcal{L}_y$ with respect to $\sigma_x^2$, we must either find that we should set $\sigma_x^2 = 0$ or that we should set $\sigma_x^2 = +\infty$. If there are only demand shocks ($\sigma_s^2 = 0$), then unlimited monetary variance is always optimal. Alternatively, if there are only supply shocks ($\sigma_d^2 = 0$) or if both types of shocks are present ($0 < q < 1$), then the optimal policy depends on the absolute values of $q$, $H$, $\beta_s$, $\beta_d$, and $\alpha$.

The results derived above should help to cast further skepticism on the wisdom of policies that blindly seek to minimize the unconditional variance of output. Such policies often require that the monetary authority produce sufficient chaos so that agents ignore allocative signals. As we pointed out in earlier chapters, a more easily defensible policy objective is to seek to minimize the variance of output around its full information level.

In the present model, such a policy would seek to minimize

$$\mathscr{L}_{(y-\hat{y})} = \left(\frac{H}{\alpha}\right)^2 \left[(1 - \theta)^2 \sigma_x^2 + \frac{\theta^2}{\beta^2}(\sigma_u^2 + \sigma_\epsilon^2)\right]. \tag{14.2.37}$$

Clearly, this loss function can only be set to zero by choosing $\sigma_x^2 = 0$, which also implies that $\theta = 0$. Furthermore, it is straightforward to demonstrate that the above loss function is monotonic in $\sigma_x^2$ so that a policy of minimization of the variance of money growth is preferable even when it is infeasible to set $\sigma_x^2 = 0$ precisely.

Barro (1976) also experiments with some feedback policies similar to those introduced in Chapter 12. However, such policies fail to affect the output or expected real interest rate processes unless the monetary authority possesses superior information. However, such a result is not surprising in view of our results of Chapter 12 and the observation that monetary policy can only be effective in the present model to the extent that it can alter $m_t - E_z m_t$. Furthermore, Barro demonstrates that while policy may be effective when the monetary authority possesses superior information about $u_t$ and/or $\epsilon_t(z)$, such a policy is never strictly preferred to the monetary authority simply announcing the information that it possesses.

## 14.3 A REVIEW OF MORE RECENT DEVELOPMENTS

This section discusses the literature in the area from a more general perspective than that of the specific models analyzed in Sections 14.1 and 14.2. In particular, we first review some of the results of models similar to Barro's (1980) model with incomplete information. Such works focus on the effects of differing information structures on the results obtained in the more simple models. This section also discusses empirical work inspired by stochastic monetary models and considers the question of whether such models present attractive and realistic explanations of business cycle behavior in actual economies.

### Extensions of the Basic Model

In Section 14.2, we sidestepped formal analysis of Barro's (1980) model for the case of imperfect contemporaneous information. In this paper, Barro specifically analyzes the general model of Section 14.1, with aggregate supply and aggregate demand variances set equal to zero. In that analysis, most of the results of Barro (1976) are reconfirmed, but several additional insights are also generated.

From the standpoint of the individual economic agent, the principal novelty of the addition of an economywide bond market is the addition of a second source of information about monetary shocks. Now agents form their expectations $E_z m_t$ based on observation of both the local price level $p_t(z)$ and the economywide nominal interest rate $r_t$. For a plausible set of assumptions about the relative sizes of key parameters, Barro finds that price increases still signal unanticipated monetary expansions, while increases in the nominal interest rate can provide inference of monetary expansions or monetary contractions.

Monetary shocks are still likely to generate increases in output and expected real interest rates, just as in the basic model. Barro also finds that monetary shocks are likely to lower the nominal interest rate. To reconcile these opposing movements in nominal and real rates of interest, the expected rate of inflation must fall. Barro argues that such a response of expected inflation comes about through increases in both $p_t(z)$ and $E_z p_{t+1}$, with the increase in $p_t(z)$ being larger in absolute value. Finally, to accommodate a fall in the nominal rate of interest along with an increase in output, the average price level must rise less than in proportion to the increase in the money supply so that real balances fall.

Barro also finds support for the result that increased monetary variability lowers the responsiveness of the real economy to a monetary shock of given magnitude. However, Barro can only infer this result from a comparison of cases in which $\sigma_x^2 = 0$ and $\sigma_x^2 = +\infty$. Barro cannot demonstrate a monotonic relationship between the output responsiveness to money shocks and the variance of money shocks.

One key advantage to the extended model is that it allows an analysis of the effects of shocks to money demand. However, here Barro finds the somewhat paradoxical result that upward shifts in the money demand function ($v_t > 0$) result in increases in output. Positive values for $v_t$ generate reductions in prices, just as would be the case in standard models. However, the fall in $p_t(z)$ is taken as an indicator that $m_t$ is negative. Therefore, if $x_t$ equals its mean of zero, $x_t - E_z x_t$ is positive, and this result provides an explanation for the increase in output. Barro also finds that the nominal interest rate is likely to rise and that this additional bit of information may reduce the absolute value of $m_t - E_z m_t = x_t - E_z x_t$, but such an effect is unlikely to result in a change in the sign of this expression.

King (1983) further analyzes the basic Barro (1980) framework and provides some additional results and insights. One important confirmation in this work is King's numerical simulations, which show that the responsiveness of output to monetary shocks declines monotonically with increased monetary variability over a wide range of parameter values. King also shows that the existence of an economywide bond market generally reduces the forecast variance of $m_t$. This effect also tends to reduce the sensitivity of output to monetary shocks.

King (1982, 1983) also investigates a number of potential channels for the effectiveness of feedback monetary policies in economies with aggregate information signals. In such models, feedback policies, since they are based upon bits of information already included in agents' information sets, can have no direct effect on $m_t$ that will not already be incorporated in $E_z m_t$. However, such feedback policies may be effective by exerting a change in the way agents process the contemporaneous information they receive.

An economywide bond market provides agents with a noisy signal about the average value of $E_z p_{t+1}$. However, in computing $E_z p_{t+1}$ in the presence of feedback, agents are forced to make estimates of the present shocks which policy will respond to in the next period. King demonstrates conditions under which the appropriate feedback parameters allow this process to enable agents to become fully informed about the current monetary shock. In this case, all monetary shocks are fully perceived, and so such monetary shocks are neutral.

Unfortunately, the practical applicability of these policy implications is likely to be quite limited. First of all, as we later point out, empirical support for the underlying model is not very strong. Second, even if these models provide the correct explanation of macroeconomic fluctuations, the actual implementation of optimal policy in them is most complex. A careful reading of the King papers shows that optimal policy rules in these models may not square well with economic intuition, and their solution generally requires a considerable amount of numerical calculations even if the policymaker is certain that he or she has exactly the correct model. Furthermore, we have very little information about how sensitive these optimal policy rules are to apparently minor model misspecifications.

Finally, King (1981) explores another potentially important source of information about monetary shocks. In the case of the contemporary U.S. economy and in many other countries, agents have access to published estimates of almost contemporaneous values of the monetary aggregates. Surely, maximizing agents are likely to use such estimates in forming their expectations of the current wealth variable. King demonstrates that possession of such information does indeed affect the properties of equilibrium stochastic monetary models. One key prediction of the theory is that output movements should be uncorrelated with announced money supply estimates. Alternatively, the difference between the actual money supply and the announced money supply should be correlated with output movements.

## Empirical Issues

The most appropriate way to estimate and test equilibrium stochastic monetary models is to jointly estimate the individual structural equations and test for the validity of the cross-equation restrictions predicted by the theory. Unfortunately, such ambitious test procedures rarely yield conclusive results.

An alternative procedure is based on the observation that one unanimous prediction of all models of this class is that fully anticipated money should be completely neutral with respect to output movements. For the models we study in this chapter, this result is equivalent to the absence of an $m_{t-1}$ term in any of the output equations.

Barro (1977, 1978) and Barro and Rush (1980) conduct tests of this key neutrality hypothesis. The basic testing strategy proceeds as follows. First an estimation equation for the money supply is fitted over the entire sample period. Then the estimates of this equation for each time period form a series on expected money, and the residuals from this equation are identified as a series on unexpected money. Finally, some measure of aggregate economic activity like real output or the unemployment rate is separately regressed on anticipated and unanticipated money. If equilibrium theory is correct, unanticipated money may explain movements in economic activity, but anticipated money should not. The Barro and Barro and Rush results are largely consistent with the equilibrium approach.

Mishkin (1982) argues that Barro's two-step approach produces invalid test statistics. Mishkin's joint estimation of an output equation and a money equation leads to a rejection of the hypothesis that only unanticipated money matters. Since the validity of this hypothesis is a necessary, although not sufficient, condition for acceptance of the equilibrium monetary model, such evidence is particularly damaging for the validity of this modeling approach.

Even more damaging to the equilibrium approach is evidence presented by Boschen and Grossman (1982). As noted above, results of King (1981) suggest that monetary announcements should be neutral with respect to economic activity. However, Boschen and Grossman find that perceived monetary shocks, as captured by the information contained in money supply announcements, are not neutral with respect to real output. Furthermore, Boschen and Grossman fail to find evidence that subsequent revisions in money supply data, which are in principle an excellent proxy for misperceived money, have no explanatory power with respect to aggregate fluctuations.

The most widely accepted verdict on the empirical validity of misinformation models of the transmission of macroeconomic disturbances is in the negative. A further implication of a lack of empirical support for these models is that their generally negative implications about the role of activist policy would also be invalid. However, the potential lack of validity of these policy ineffectiveness results does not, in and of itself, provide support for policy activism. Such support can only be provided as the result of an alternative model that can be empirically validated. In any event, the paucity of empirical support for misinformation models has led equilibrium macroeconomic theorists in the direction of real as opposed to monetary sources of business cycle fluctuations. Such real business cycle models are the subject of the following chapter.

# REFERENCES

Barro, Robert J., "Rational Expectations and the Role of Monetary Policy," *Journal of Monetary Economics,* January, 1976, 1–32.

Barro, Robert J., "Unanticipated Money Growth and Output in the United States," *American Economic Review,* March, 1977, 101–115.

Barro, Robert J., "Unanticipated Money, Output, and the Price Level in the United States," *Journal of Political Economy,* August, 1978, 549–580.

Barro, Robert J., "A Capital Market in an Equilibrium Business Cycle Model," *Econometrica,* September, 1980, 1393–1417.

Barro, Robert J., and Mark Rush, "Unanticipated Money and Economic Activity," in Stanley Fischer, ed., *Rational Expectations and Economic Policy,* Chicago, University of Chicago Press, 1980.

Boschen, John F., and Herschel I. Grossman, "Tests of Equilibrium Macroeconomics Using Contemporaneous Monetary Data," *Journal of Monetary Economics,* November, 1982, 309–333.

Friedman, Milton, "The Role of Monetary Policy," *American Economic Review,* March, 1968, 1–17.

King, Robert G., "Monetary Information and Monetary Neutrality," *Journal of Monetary Economics,* March, 1981, 195–206.

King, Robert G., "Monetary Policy and the Informational Content of Prices," *Journal of Political Economy,* April, 1982, 247–279.

King, Robert G., "Interest Rates, Aggregate Information, and Monetary Policy," *Journal of Monetary Economics,* August, 1983, 199–234.

Lucas, Robert E., Jr., ''Expectations and the Neutrality of Money,'' *Journal of Economic Theory,* April, 1972, 103–124.

Lucas, Robert E., Jr., ''Some International Evidence on Output-Inflation Tradeoffs,'' *American Economic Review,* June, 1973, 326–334.

Lucas, Robert E., Jr., and Leonard A. Rapping, ''Real Wages, Employment, and Inflation,'' *Journal of Political Economy,* September/October, 1969, 721–754.

McCallum, Bennett T., ''A Linearized Version of Lucas' Neutrality Model,'' *Canadian Journal of Economics,* February, 1984, 138–145.

Mishkin, Frederic S., ''Does Anticipated Policy Matter?: An Econometric Investigation,'' *Journal of Political Economy,* February, 1982, 22–51.

Phelps, Edmund S., ed., *Microeconomic Foundations of Employment and Inflation Theory,* New York, Norton, 1970.

# Chapter **15**

## Real Business Cycle Models

Perhaps the most consistent characteristic of the time series properties of aggregate measures of economic activity is the tendency for such measures to exhibit significant positive serial correlation through time. Traditional, Keynesian-style macroeconomic models explain such persistence by appealing to sticky prices and short-run quantity adjustment mechanisms. In part, such explanations were offered because many economists believed that equilibrium theories of persistence could not be constructed. However, failure to adequately motivate the behavior of wage- and price-setting agents in such models has been an important aspect of their greatly reduced popularity. Although Taylor (1980) demonstrates that fairly short-lived but overlapping labor contracts can give rise to persistence, such models are still subject to Barro's (1977) critique for their apparently suboptimal employment contingencies.

Early equilibrium models of macroeconomic fluctuations like that of Section 5.2 invoke expectational errors as the principal source of output movements. To explain persistent movements in output and employment, such models may therefore require persistence in expectational errors. However, such persistent expectational errors are inconsistent with the assumption of rational expectations, and such mechanisms are therefore not very persuasive.

Equilibrium theorists have therefore directed their energies in other directions. Sargent (1987b, Ch. 18) emphasizes the role of employment adjustment costs. However, such costs are hard to measure, and such models are therefore hard to empirically refute. Blinder and Fischer (1981) emphasize the role of inventory dynamics. In their model, perceived favorable movements in relative prices lead to increases in output and reductions in stocks of inventories. Even if such relative price movements prove to be illusory, subsequent output remains high as inventories are built back up to their preferred levels. Topel (1982) and Eichenbaum (1984) find relatively favorable evidence regarding the role of movements in inventories in the propagation of economic disturbances. However, while such inventory dynamics may be an important channel for the propagation of disturbances, such movements are not likely candidates as the source of such disturbances.

A tradition, which includes the pioneering work of Lucas (1975), relates serial correlation in output to movements over time in the stock of capital. In such models, periods of high output are also periods of high investment. But high current investment leads to a persistently larger stock of productive capital. In the original Lucas setup, the propagation mechanism by which such persistent expansions originate has its roots in monetary misperceptions of the sort analyzed in Chapters 5 and 14.

Real business cycle theory continues in the tradition of explaining persistence in output movements by appealing to above-average rates of investment. However, instead of linking such episodes to monetary shocks, real business cycle theory presents explanations of output fluctuations that are completely independent of the monetary process. In such models, output fluctuations originate in shocks to current productivity.

Real business cycle theory's emphasis on productivity shocks as a source of real output fluctuations does not, in and of itself, differentiate the theory from the nominal contracting models of Section 13.2. Such models also included the possibility of real productivity shocks as a potential source of output fluctuations. However, in the basic real business cycle model, productivity shocks are the only source of real output fluctuations, whereas in nominal contracting theory, real output fluctuations arise from difficulties in distinguishing between productivity shocks and purely nominal disturbances. A further distinguishing feature of real business cycle models is that in such models the propagation mechanism for disturbances is due to the technology of the investment process rather than any form of potentially ad hoc nominal rigidities.

Although real business cycle theory provides a very clever means of accounting for typical time series properties of macroeconomic variables over the course of typical business cycles, many macroeconomists find a literal interpretation of such models very hard to swallow. In order for the basic real business cycle model to be correct, it is necessary to postulate what many believe are unrealistically large stochastic movements in productivity. Furthermore, it is necessary to believe that neither anticipated nor unanticipated movements in the money supply are capable of generating movements in aggregate output but rather that any correlation between money and output is due to a reverse causation running from movements in real output to movements in money. For these reasons, real business cycle proponents have yet to make a compelling case for their arguments.

Section 15.1. presents the basic real business cycle model of Long and Plosser (1983). Section 15.2 then shows how this model can account, not only for persistence in measures of aggregate output, but also for comovement of output across sectors even in the face of white-noise productivity shocks. Section 15.3 then discusses some alternative formulations of real business cycle theory and evaluates evidence on the usefulness of such models for explaining actual business cycle episodes.

## 15.1 A ROBINSON CRUSOE ECONOMY

This section poses and solves the intertemporal optimization problem for a simple version of the production model of Long and Plosser (1983). In this basic model, the representative agent chooses levels of consumption, saving, leisure, and produced inputs into the production process. The solution to the representative agent's problem can, in theory, be supported by a general equilibrium set of prices. The properties of the resulting general equilibrium allocations can then be compared to the behavior of quantities in actual market economies.

## Representative Agent Tastes and the Productive Technology

The representative agent derives utility from the consumption of two produced goods[1] and leisure. Agents expect to live forever and seek to maximize the expected value of

$$U = \sum_{t=0}^{\infty} \beta^t \left( \theta_0 \ln Z_t + \theta_1 \ln C_{1t} + \theta_2 \ln C_{2t} \right), \tag{15.1.1}$$

where  $\beta$ = constant discount factor
$Z_t$ = period $t$ leisure
$C_{it}$ = period $t$ consumption of commodity $i$
$\theta_i$ = constant taste parameters

The representative agent is endowed with $H$ units of time in each period that may be allocated to leisure or allocated to the production of each of two consumption goods. Time allocation must therefore satisfy

$$H = Z_t + L_{1t} + L_{2t}, \tag{15.1.2}$$

where $L_{it}$ denotes the input of current labor toward the production of the $i$th good.

At the beginning of period $t$, the representative agent reaps the harvest of production started in the previous period, period $t - 1$. Denote the levels of production of goods 1 and 2 available at the start of period $t$ by $Y_{1t}$ and $Y_{2t}$, respectively. Produced output may either be consumed or used as inputs for future production. The representative agent is therefore constrained by

$$Y_{1t} = C_{1t} + X_{11t} + X_{21t}, \tag{15.1.3}$$

$$Y_{2t} = C_{2t} + X_{12t} + X_{22t}, \tag{15.1.4}$$

where $X_{ijt}$ denotes the input of good $j$ into production of good $i$ in period $t$.

Current inputs of labor, $L_{it}$, and commodities, $X_{ijt}$, are transformed into produced outputs that are available at the start of the next period, period $t + 1$. Assume that production is governed by the Cobb-Douglas production functions

$$Y_{1t+1} = \lambda_{1t+1} L_{1t}^{b_1} X_{11t}^{a_{11}} X_{12t}^{a_{12}}, \tag{15.1.5}$$

$$Y_{2t+1} = \lambda_{2t+1} L_{2t}^{b_2} X_{21t}^{a_{21}} X_{22t}^{a_{22}}, \tag{15.1.6}$$

where $a_{ij}$ and $b_i$ are constant, positive production parameters and $\lambda_{it+1}$ represent stochastic productivity shocks. In this simple example, we assume that $\lambda_{it}$ are independent and

---

[1]Generalization to $n$ goods is straightforward. Analysis of the $n$-good case is provided in the original Long and Plosser (1983) paper.

serially uncorrelated. We further assume that

$$u_{it} \equiv \ln \lambda_{it}, \qquad E(u_{it}) = 0, \qquad i = 1, 2, \qquad t = 0, \ldots . \tag{15.1.7}$$

An important feature of this technology is that both commodities can be used as inputs in the production of either commodity. In particular, for $a_{ij} > 0$, $i, j = 1, 2$, both inputs are essential to the production of both outputs. This feature of the production technology accounts for the positive correlation of sectoral outputs, which is an important feature of models of this type.

The production technology specified above is also formally similar to the types of technologies adopted in models of economic growth like those studied in Chapter 8. In such models, output that is not consumed is used to augment the stock of productive capital. However, in the present model, such capital is assumed to fully depreciate in a single time period.

## Representative Agent Optimization

We are now ready to state and solve the representative agent's maximization problem. The representative agent seeks to maximize

$$U = E\left[ \sum_{t=0}^{\infty} \beta^t \left( \theta_0 \ln Z_t + \theta_1 \ln C_{1t} + \theta_2 \ln C_{2t} \right) \right] \tag{15.1.8}$$

subject to

$$Y_{1t+1} = \lambda_{1t+1} L_{1t}^{b_1} X_{11t}^{a_{11}} X_{12t}^{a_{12}}, \tag{15.1.9}$$

$$Y_{2t+1} = \lambda_{2t+1} L_{2t}^{b_2} X_{21t}^{a_{21}} X_{22t}^{a_{22}}, \tag{15.1.10}$$

$$Y_{1t} = C_{1t} + X_{11t} + X_{21t}, \tag{15.1.11}$$

$$Y_{2t} = C_{2t} + X_{12t} + X_{22t}, \tag{15.1.12}$$

$$H = Z_t + L_{1t} + L_{2t}. \tag{15.1.13}$$

A standard solution strategy for the above problem is to define an appropriate Lagrangian expression and to maximize this Lagrangian with respect to $Z_t$, $C_{it}$, $i = 1, 2$, $t = 0, \ldots .$ However, the dimensionality of such a solution strategy renders such methodology rather cumbersome. Dynamic programming provides an alternate, iterative solution strategy. This solution strategy is based upon the Bellman (1957) equation or value function[2]

$$
\begin{aligned}
V(Y_{1t}, Y_{2t}) \\
= \max[\theta_0 \ln Z_t + \theta_1 \ln C_{1t} + \theta_2 \ln C_{2t} + \beta E_t V(Y_{1t+1}, Y_{2t+1})].
\end{aligned}
\tag{15.1.14}
$$

The solution strategy now takes account of the property of this problem that the maximum expected value of the value function at time $t$ depends only on the state vari-

---

[2] In the general case, $V$ includes $\lambda_{1t+1}$, $\lambda_{2t+1}$ as arguments. However, such terms are not present in the case of serially uncorrelated $\lambda_{it}$'s.

ables $Y_{1t}$ and $Y_{2t}$. The simplified objective function may now be maximized over the much smaller control set $Z_t$, $L_{1t}$, $L_{2t}$, $C_{1t}$, $C_{2t}$, $X_{11t}$, $X_{12t}$, $X_{21t}$, $X_{22t}$.[3]

While the dynamic programming approach is helpful in reducing the dimensionality of the problem, this technique does not provide a general method of deriving the functional form of the value function $V$. Such a function must generally be found by trial and error. In the present example, a valid value function is given by

$$V(Y_{1t}, Y_{2t}) = K + \gamma_1 \ln Y_{1t} + \gamma_2 \ln Y_{2t}. \tag{15.1.15}$$

That this value function is in fact the correct one becomes apparent later on in the derivation of the solution.

Plugging in for $Y_{1t+1}$ and $Y_{2t+1}$ in the value function, the maximization problem may be rewritten as

$$
\begin{aligned}
V(Y_{1t}, Y_{2t}) = \max\{&\theta_0 \ln Z_t + \theta_1 \ln C_{1t} + \theta_2 \ln C_{2t} + \beta \\
&\times E_t[K + \gamma_1(\ln \lambda_{1t+1} + b_1 \ln L_{1t} + a_{11} \ln X_{11t} + a_{12} \ln X_{12t}) \\
&+ \gamma_2(\ln \lambda_{2t+1} + b_2 \ln L_{2t} + a_{21} \ln X_{21t} + a_{22} \ln X_{22t})]\}.
\end{aligned}
\tag{15.1.16}
$$

Noting that $E_t(\ln \lambda_{1t+1}) = E_t(\ln \lambda_{2t+1}) = 0$, we define the Lagrangian

$$
\begin{aligned}
\mathcal{L} = &\theta_0 \ln Z_t + \theta_1 \ln C_{1t} + \theta_2 \ln C_{2t} + \beta K \\
&+ \beta\gamma_1(b_1 \ln L_{1t} + a_{11} \ln X_{11t} + a_{12} \ln X_{12t}) \\
&+ \beta\gamma_2(b_2 \ln L_{2t} + a_{21} \ln X_{21t} + a_{22} \ln X_{22t}) \\
&+ \mu_0(H - Z_t - L_{1t} - L_{2t}) + \mu_1(Y_{1t} - C_{1t} - X_{11t} - X_{21t}) \\
&+ \mu_2(Y_{2t} - C_{2t} - X_{12t} - X_{22t}).
\end{aligned}
\tag{15.1.17}
$$

We now seek to maximize this Lagrangian expression with respect to $Z_t$, $L_{it}$, $C_{it}$, $X_{ijt}$, $\mu_k$ for $i, j = 1, 2$, $k = 0, 1, 2$. First-order conditions are given by

$$\frac{\partial \mathcal{L}}{\partial Z_t} = \frac{\theta_0}{Z_t} - \mu_0 = 0, \tag{15.1.18}$$

$$\frac{\partial \mathcal{L}}{\partial L_{1t}} = \frac{\beta\gamma_1 b_1}{L_{it}} - \mu_0 = 0, \tag{15.1.19}$$

$$\frac{\partial \mathcal{L}}{\partial L_{2t}} = \frac{\beta\gamma_2 b_2}{L_{2t}} - \mu_0 = 0, \tag{15.1.20}$$

$$\frac{\partial \mathcal{L}}{\partial C_{1t}} = \frac{\theta_1}{C_{1t}} - \mu_1 = 0, \tag{15.1.21}$$

$$\frac{\partial \mathcal{L}}{\partial X_{11t}} = \frac{\beta\gamma_1 a_{11}}{X_{11t}} - \mu_1 = 0, \tag{15.1.22}$$

$$\frac{\partial \mathcal{L}}{\partial X_{21t}} = \frac{\beta\gamma_2 a_{21}}{X_{21t}} - \mu_1 = 0, \tag{15.1.23}$$

---

[3]For more on this solution strategy, see Sargent (1987a).

$$\frac{\partial \mathcal{L}}{\partial C_{2t}} = \frac{\theta_2}{C_{2t}} - \mu_2 = 0, \tag{15.1.24}$$

$$\frac{\partial \mathcal{L}}{\partial X_{12t}} = \frac{\beta \gamma_1 a_{12}}{X_{12t}} - \mu_2 = 0, \tag{15.1.25}$$

$$\frac{\partial \mathcal{L}}{\partial X_{22t}} = \frac{\beta \gamma_2 a_{22}}{X_{22t}} - \mu_2 = 0, \tag{15.1.26}$$

$$\frac{\partial \mathcal{L}}{\partial \mu_0} = H - Z_t - L_{1t} - L_{2t} = 0, \tag{15.1.27}$$

$$\frac{\partial \mathcal{L}}{\partial \mu_1} = Y_{1t} - C_{1t} - X_{11t} - X_{21t} = 0, \tag{15.1.28}$$

$$\frac{\partial \mathcal{L}}{\partial \mu_2} = Y_{2t} - C_{2t} - X_{12t} - X_{22t} = 0. \tag{15.1.29}$$

## Optimal Quantities and Equilibrium Prices

Combining the first three first-order conditions with the budget constraint on total hours, we find that

$$L_{1t} = \frac{\beta \gamma_1 b_1}{\theta_0 + \beta \gamma_1 b_1 + \beta \gamma_2 b_2} H, \tag{15.1.30}$$

$$L_{2t} = \frac{\beta \gamma_2 b_2}{\theta_0 + \beta \gamma_1 b_1 + \beta \gamma_2 b_2} H, \tag{15.1.31}$$

$$Z_t = \frac{\theta_0}{\theta_0 + \beta \gamma_1 b_1 + \beta \gamma_2 b_2} H. \tag{15.1.32}$$

In this simple example of the Long and Plosser model, note that total labor input and labor inputs in each sector are all constant. In particular, these employment levels are not related to the levels of output $Y_{1t}$ and $Y_{2t}$ or to the size of the productivity shocks. Clearly, these implications of the theory do not square well with experience. However, we have already demonstrated in Chapter 5 that more general forms of the utility function are capable of generating equilibrium employment levels that vary either directly or inversely with the level of productivity even in a static, one-good framework.

We next combine the first-order conditions in $\mu_1$ with the budget constraint on $Y_{1t}$ to obtain

$$C_{1t} = \frac{\theta_1}{\theta_1 + \beta \gamma_1 a_{11} + \beta \gamma_2 a_{21}} Y_{1t}, \tag{15.1.33}$$

$$X_{11t} = \frac{\beta \gamma_1 a_{11}}{\theta_1 + \beta \gamma_1 a_{11} + \beta \gamma_2 a_{21}} Y_{1t}, \tag{15.1.34}$$

$$X_{21t} = \frac{\beta\gamma_2 a_{21}}{\theta_1 + \beta\gamma_1 a_{11} + \beta\gamma_2 a_{21}} Y_{1t}. \qquad (15.1.35)$$

Analogously, we combine the first-order conditions in $\mu_2$ with the budget constraint on $Y_{2t}$ to obtain

$$C_{2t} = \frac{\theta_2}{\theta_2 + \beta\gamma_1 a_{12} + \beta\gamma_2 a_{22}} Y_{2t}, \qquad (15.1.36)$$

$$X_{12t} = \frac{\beta\gamma_1 a_{12}}{\theta_2 + \beta\gamma_1 a_{12} + \beta\gamma_2 a_{22}} Y_{2t}, \qquad (15.1.37)$$

$$X_{22t} = \frac{\beta\gamma_2 a_{22}}{\theta_2 + \beta\gamma_1 a_{12} + \beta\gamma_2 a_{22}} Y_{2t}. \qquad (15.1.38)$$

Production of good 1 is therefore divided in fixed proportions between consumption of good 1, input of good 1 in the production of good 1, and input of good 1 in the production of good 2. Similarly, production of good 2 is divided in fixed proportions between consumption of good 2, input of good 2 in the production of good 1, and input of good 2 in the production of good 1.

Although the simple, chosen forms of the utility and production functions lead to simple fixed proportion allocations of current production, these simple forms still contain the seeds of the serial correlation and intersectoral correlation properties of the model. Higher than normal output of either good in the present period is always partially allocated toward future production of both goods.

We earlier pointed out that the representative agent's optimal allocations could be supported by a general equilibrium wage-price vector. Such equilibrium prices are given by the relevant marginal rates of substitution in the representative agent's utility function. Suppose we assign the role of numeraire to good 1. The equilibrium relative price of good 2 is then given by

$$\frac{P_{2t}}{P_{1t}} = \frac{\partial V/\partial Y_{2t}}{\partial V/\partial Y_{1t}} = \frac{\gamma_2 Y_{1t}}{\gamma_1 Y_{2t}}. \qquad (15.1.39)$$

The relative price of good 2 is therefore inversely related to the supply of good 2 and directly related to the supply of good 1.

Of greater interest are the properties of the real wage rate $W_t/P_{1t}$. The equilibrium real wage rate is given by

$$\frac{W_t}{P_{1t}} = \frac{\partial V/\partial Z_t}{\partial V/\partial Y_{1t}} = \frac{(\theta_0 + \beta\gamma_1 b_1 + \beta\gamma_2 b_2)Y_{1t}}{\gamma_1 H}. \qquad (15.1.40)$$

The real wage rate (expressed in units of the numeraire) is therefore directly related to the level of output of the numeraire good. Real wages move procyclically in this model. Recall that in Chapter 5 we noted that an important deficiency of intertemporal substitution models of employment and output determination is their tendency to predict countercyclical real wage rates. In such models, the only types of disturbances that result in procyclical real wage rates are productivity shocks. It is therefore not surprising that a model such as the present one that is built entirely around productivity shocks should exhibit procyclical real wage rates.

## The Equilibrium Value Function

Before proceeding with our macroeconomic analysis, it is useful at this point to double check that the form of the $V(\cdot)$ function we postulated above is in fact correct. In this endeavor, it is first useful to adopt the following shorthand notation for the coefficients of the equations derived from the first-order conditions above:

$$Z_t = k_{00}H, \qquad L_{1t} = k_{10}H, \qquad L_{2t} = k_{20}H, \tag{15.1.41}$$

$$C_{1t} = k_{01}Y_{1t}, \qquad X_{11t} = k_{11}Y_{1t}, \qquad X_{21t} = k_{21}Y_{1t}, \tag{15.1.42}$$

$$C_{2t} = k_{02}Y_{2t}, \qquad X_{12t} = k_{12}Y_{2t}, \qquad X_{22t} = k_{22}Y_{2t}. \tag{15.1.43}$$

We next plug the optimal values of the choice variables into the original statement of the objective function to obtain

$$
\begin{aligned}
V(Y_{1t}, Y_{2t}) = {} & \theta_0 \ln(k_{00}H) + \theta_1 \ln(k_{01}) + \theta_1 \ln(Y_{1t}) + \theta_2 \ln(k_{02}) + \theta_2 \ln(Y_{2t}) + \beta \\
& \times E_t\{K + \gamma_1[\ln(\lambda_{1t+1}) + b_1 \ln(k_{10}H) + a_{11} \ln(k_{11}) \\
& + a_{11} \ln(Y_{1t}) + a_{12} \ln(k_{12}) + a_{12} \ln(Y_{2t})] \\
& + \gamma_2[\ln(\lambda_{2t+1}) + b_2 \ln(k_{20}H) + a_{21} \ln(k_{21}) \\
& + a_{21} \ln(Y_{1t}) + a_{22} \ln(k_{22}) + a_{22} \ln(Y_{2t})]\}.
\end{aligned}
\tag{15.1.44}
$$

Noting that $E_t(\lambda_{1t+1}) = E_t(\lambda_{2t+1}) = 0$ and collecting terms, we find that

$$
\begin{aligned}
V(Y_{1t}, Y_{2t}) = {} & \theta_0 \ln(k_{00}H) + \theta_1 \ln(k_{01}) + \theta_2 \ln(k_{02}) \\
& + \beta K + \beta\gamma_1 b_1 \ln(k_{10}H) + \beta\gamma_2 b_2 \ln(k_{20}H) + \beta\gamma_1 a_{11} \ln(k_{11}) \\
& + \beta\gamma_1 a_{12} \ln(k_{12}) + \beta\gamma_2 a_{21} \ln(k_{21}) + \beta\gamma_2 a_{22} \ln(k_{22}) \\
& + [\theta_1 + \beta(\gamma_1 a_{11} + \gamma_2 a_{21})] \ln(Y_{1t}) \\
& + [\theta_2 + \beta(\gamma_1 a_{12} + \gamma_2 a_{22})] \ln(Y_{2t}).
\end{aligned}
\tag{15.1.45}
$$

Matching coefficients, we find that a correct form of the $V(\cdot)$ function has the coefficients

$$
\begin{aligned}
K = {} & \frac{1}{1 - \beta}\{\theta_0 \ln(k_{00}H) + \theta_1 \ln(k_{01}) + \theta_2 \ln(k_{02}) + \beta\gamma_1 b_1 \ln(k_{10}) \\
& + \beta\gamma_2 b_2 \ln(k_{20}) + (\theta_0 + \beta\gamma_1 b_1 + \beta\gamma_2 b_2) \ln(H) + \beta[\gamma_1 a_{11} \ln(k_{11}) \\
& + \gamma_1 a_{12} \ln(k_{12}) + \gamma_2 a_{21} \ln(k_{21}) + \gamma_2 a_{22} \ln(k_{22})]\},
\end{aligned}
\tag{15.1.46}
$$

$$\gamma_1 = \theta_1 + \beta(\gamma_1 a_{11} + \gamma_2 a_{21}), \qquad \gamma_2 = \theta_2 + \beta(\gamma_1 a_{12} + \gamma_2 a_{22}). \tag{15.1.47}$$

We have therefore affirmed the original postulated form of the $V(\cdot)$ function as correct.

## 15.2 TIME SERIES BEHAVIOR OF AGGREGATE OUTPUT

A principal motivation behind construction of real business cycle models is the hope that such models mimic the serial correlation properties of actual market economies. We are therefore most interested in the time series behavior of the output processes of the model of the previous section.

## The Output Processes

Recall the original specifications of the production functions:

$$Y_{1t+1} = \lambda_{1t+1} L_{1t}^{b_1} X_{11t}^{a_{11}} X_{12t}^{a_{12}}, \tag{15.2.1}$$

$$Y_{2t+1} = \lambda_{2t+1} L_{2t}^{b_2} X_{21t}^{a_{21}} X_{22t}^{a_{22}}. \tag{15.2.2}$$

Since the output processes are log linear in form, it is useful to define

$$y_{it} \equiv \ln(Y_{it}), \tag{15.2.3}$$

$$x_{ijt} \equiv \ln(X_{ijt}). \tag{15.2.4}$$

It is also useful to recall that we have already adopted the convention that $u_{it} \equiv \ln(\lambda_{it})$. We earlier stated the assumption that

$$E(u_{it}u_{js}) = 0 \quad \text{for } i \neq j, \ t \neq s. \tag{15.2.5}$$

In discussing the time series properties of the model, we adopt the additional assumption that

$$E(\boldsymbol{u}_t\boldsymbol{u}_t') = \boldsymbol{I}, \tag{15.2.6}$$

where $\boldsymbol{u}_t'$ is the transpose of the vector,

$$\boldsymbol{u}_t = \begin{bmatrix} u_{1t} \\ u_{2t} \end{bmatrix}, \tag{15.2.7}$$

and $\boldsymbol{I}$ represents the two-dimensional identity matrix.

The production function may now be written as

$$y_{1t+1} = a_{11}x_{11t} + a_{12}x_{12t} + u_{1t+1}, \tag{15.2.8}$$

$$y_{2t+1} = a_{21}x_{21t} + a_{22}x_{22t} + u_{2t+1}. \tag{15.2.9}$$

However, in the previous section, we demonstrated that the solution of the representative agent's maximization problem implied the linear relationships

$$X_{ijt} = k_{ij}Y_{jt} \quad \text{or} \quad x_{ijt} = \ln(k_{ij}) + y_{jt}. \tag{15.2.10}$$

Plugging in above, we obtain

$$\begin{bmatrix} y_{1t+1} \\ y_{2t+1} \end{bmatrix} = \begin{bmatrix} k_1 \\ k_2 \end{bmatrix} + \begin{bmatrix} a_{11} & a_{12} \\ a_{21} & a_{22} \end{bmatrix} \begin{bmatrix} y_{1t} \\ y_{2t} \end{bmatrix} + \begin{bmatrix} u_{1t+1} \\ u_{2t+1} \end{bmatrix}, \tag{15.2.11}$$

where

$$k_1 = a_{11} \ln(k_{11}) + a_{12} \ln(k_{12}), \tag{15.2.12}$$

$$k_2 = a_{21} \ln(k_{21}) + a_{22} \ln(k_{22}). \tag{15.2.13}$$

We therefore see that the output levels $y_{it}$ can be expressed in an autoregressive representative with the stochastic term given by the logarithms of the productivity shocks.

## Time Series Properties of the Output Processes

There are a number of alternative ways that the above autoregressive expression for the output process may be written, which give additional insight into the properties of the Long and Plosser model. First, let us define

$$\hat{y}_{t+1} \equiv y_{t+1} - (I - A)^{-1}k, \tag{15.2.14}$$

where

$$A \equiv \begin{bmatrix} a_{11} & a_{12} \\ a_{21} & a_{22} \end{bmatrix}, \qquad k \equiv \begin{bmatrix} k_1 \\ k_2 \end{bmatrix}. \tag{15.2.15}$$

Plugging into the above expression for $y_{t+1}$, we find that

$$\hat{y}_{t+1} = A\hat{y}_t + u_{t+1}. \tag{15.2.16}$$

In this example, individual sector outputs have constant unconditional means given by $(I - A)^{-1}k$. The vector $\hat{y}_{t+1}$ therefore represents deviations of $y_{it+1}$ from these unconditional means. Individual time series representations for $\hat{y}_{1t}$ and $\hat{y}_{2t}$ may now be obtained as follows. Let $L$ denote the lag operator

$$Lz_t \equiv z_{t-1}. \tag{15.2.17}$$

The relationship $L\hat{y}_{t+1} = \hat{y}_t$ allows us to rewrite the above equation as

$$\hat{y}_{t+1} = AL\hat{y}_{t+1} + u_{t+1} \tag{15.2.18}$$

or

$$(I - AL)\hat{y}_{t+1} = u_{t+1} \tag{15.2.19}$$

or

$$\begin{bmatrix} 1 - a_{11}L & -a_{12} \\ -a_{21} & 1 - a_{22}L \end{bmatrix} \cdot \begin{bmatrix} \hat{y}_{1t+1} \\ \hat{y}_{2t+1} \end{bmatrix} = \begin{bmatrix} u_{1t+1} \\ u_{2t+1} \end{bmatrix}. \tag{15.2.20}$$

This system may be solved to yield the processes

$$\hat{y}_{1t+1} = (a_{11} + a_{22})\hat{y}_{1t} + (a_{11}a_{22} - a_{12}a_{21})\hat{y}_{1t-1} + u_{1t+1} - a_{22}u_{1t} - a_{12}u_{2t}, \tag{15.2.21}$$

$$\hat{y}_{2t+1} = (a_{11} + a_{22})\hat{y}_{2t} + (a_{11}a_{22} - a_{12}a_{21})\hat{y}_{2t-1} + u_{2t+1} - a_{22}u_{2t} - a_{12}u_{1t}. \tag{15.2.22}$$

Even with a form of the model in which there are only two sectors, output in each sector may be cyclical in the sense that a single, nonzero realization of $u_{it}$ may induce dampened oscillatory response in that sector. With many more sectors, a considerable variety of impulse responses becomes possible.

Successive lagged substitutions of the autoregressive representation for $\hat{y}_{t+1}$ into itself yields the moving average representation[4]

$$\hat{y}_{t+1} = Iu_{t+1} + Au_t + A^2u_{t-1} + A^3u_{t-2} + \ldots. \tag{15.2.23}$$

---

[4]The following is only valid if the characteristic roots of $A$ lie within the unit circle.

Lagging the above process by $j$, we may calculate the expectation

$$
\begin{aligned}
E(\hat{y}_t \hat{y}'_{t-j}) &= E[(I u_t + A u_{t-1} + \ldots)(I u_{t-j} + A u_{t-j-1} + \ldots)] \\
&= A^j E[u_{t-j} u'_{t-j} + (A u_{t-j-1})(A u_{t-j-1})' + \ldots] \\
&= A^j E[u_{t-j} u'_{t-j} + A u_{t-j-1} u'_{t-j-1} A' + \ldots].
\end{aligned}
\tag{15.2.24}
$$

However, since $E(u_{t-j} u'_{t-j}) \equiv I \sigma^2$, the above expression may be rewritten as

$$
E(\hat{y}_t \hat{y}'_{t-j}) = A^j (I + AA' + (AA')^2 + \ldots) \sigma^2
\tag{15.2.25}
$$

or

$$
E(\hat{y}_t \hat{y}'_{t-j}) = A^j \Gamma_0 \sigma^2,
\tag{15.2.26}
$$

where

$$
\Gamma_0 \equiv I + AA' + (AA')^2 + \ldots.
\tag{15.2.27}
$$

Recall that the elements of $A$ are equal to the (nonlabor) input shares of the original Cobb-Douglas production functions. Therefore, as long as the technology is governed by constant returns to scale, a finite matrix $\Gamma_0$ always exists. The matrix $A$ and the matrix $\Gamma_0$, which is formed from $A$, summarize the autocorrelation properties of the output processes. In general, individual sectoral outputs and representative measures of aggregate output all exhibit positive serial correlation. Furthermore, the off-diagonal elements of $\Gamma_0$ give the contemporaneous cross-sectional correlations of the outputs in sectors 1 and 2. Many candidate $A$ matrices imply positive contemporaneous correlation between the outputs in the two sectors.

The most preferred way to proceed with an analysis of this kind of model is to formally test the model against data drawn from market economies. The appropriate strategy would include estimation of the entire model and tests of all the cross-equation restrictions imposed by the forms of the utility and production functions. Unfortunately, such tests, when they imply acceptance of the theory, generally are of low power. Alternatively, rejections of the theory can occur if any of the many special assumptions of the model are violated.

Long and Plosser pursue an alternate research strategy that purports to demonstrate the realism of their model. The elements of the matrix $A$ may be interpreted as elements of an input-output matrix. Long and Plosser consider a six-sector model of the U.S. economy based on such an input-output matrix for the six chosen sectors. The model is then simulated with a white-noise stochastic input process whose variance is chosen to generate realistic output processes for the six sectors. That such simulations are capable of capturing the general flavor of U.S. business cycle behavior is then viewed as evidence of the usefulness of the model. The authors find that the realism of their simulations is particularly noteworthy given the very simple and very restrictive nature of the assumptions of their model.

## 15.3 A REVIEW OF MORE RECENT DEVELOPMENTS

The previous two sections present, in some significant detail, the basic real business cycle model of Long and Plosser (1983). This section first outlines the complementary analysis of Kydland and Prescott (1982) and then discusses some further, more recent theoretical advances in the area. This section also examines some of the available empirical evidence relating to the question of whether real business cycle models offer an attractive alternative to more conventional explanations of business cycle phenomena.

## Extensions of the Basic Model

The principal other seminal work in the real business cycle literature is that of Kydland and Prescott (1982).[5] Like the analysis of Long and Plosser (1983), the source of output fluctuations in the Kydland and Prescott model is also found in productivity shocks. However, while the two models share a number of similarities, there are also some significant differences.

Like the Long and Plosser model, the Kydland and Prescott model provides an explanation for serial correlation in output movements. In the Kydland and Prescott model, serial correlation is induced in part by serial correlation in the productivity shocks and in part by the assumption of a time-to-build investment technology. In the time-to-build framework, capital expenditure projects initiated in period $t$ make no contribution to productive capacity until $J > 0$ periods later in period $t + J$. This setup is in contrast to the Long and Plosser framework in which intermediate inputs add to production after just a single period of time.

Kydland and Prescott's time-to-build technology is able to provide an explanation for the much greater volatility of investment expenditures relative to consumption expenditures that is a generally recognized stylized fact of business cycle analysis. Conformity of the model to this particular feature of actual business cycle experience is more difficult to address in the Long and Plosser model, which blurs the distinction between capital goods and intermediate factors of production. Kydland and Prescott compare their time-to-build technology with the alternative of capital stock adjustment costs as a means of explaining persistence. Kydland and Prescott find that capital stock adjustment costs of a magnitude necessary to explain persistence tend to significantly dampen the volatility of investment to unrealistically low levels. Alternatively, the time-to-build technology contains no particularly strong disincentive for investment variability while retaining the property of persistent deviations of output from trend.

Another principal novelty of the Kydland and Prescott analysis is its treatment of preferences for leisure. In Chapter 5, we noted that models based upon intertemporal substitution had a hard time explaining the coincident comovement of output, consumption, and employment. Intertemporal substitution models tend to predict a negative contemporaneous correlation between consumption and employment while the stylized facts suggest otherwise. The basic form of the Long and Plosser model is silent on this issue because it predicts a constant level of employment.

In the Kydland and Prescott model, preferences are not of the time-separable form. Alternatively, low levels of leisure in the present period reduce the marginal utility of leisure in future periods for a given level of future work effort. This type of preference technology provides a vehicle through which agents may "save up" leisure. This additional margin of intertemporal substitution possibilities is consistent with an increased willingness for workers to supply more labor when productive opportunities improve.

---

[5]Prescott (1986) contains a more recent overview of the real business cycle literature as viewed from the Kydland and Prescott (1982) perspective.

Kydland and Prescott follow a similar strategy to that of Long and Plosser for empirical verification of their model. Kydland and Prescott adopt "reasonable" magnitudes for some of the parameters of their model and then estimate some remaining free parameters from actual, recent U.S. business cycle experience. The authors then chose an exogenously determined value for the variance of their unobservable productivity shock in the hopes that the resulting numerical model can explain the actual business cycle behavior of key aggregate magnitudes.

Kydland and Prescott find that their model fits the data well and that this fit is generally robust to changes in some of their key assumptions. However, as pointed out by McCallum (1986, p. 400), "if someone believes that the variance of actual technology shocks is only (say) one tenth as large as the value implied by the Kydland-Prescott model, he will find nothing in the Kydland-Prescott results that would require him to alter his belief." Kydland and Prescott are therefore silent on the issue of whether there are other disturbances or other propagation mechanisms that might explain the record as well or better then their own model. Indeed, Kydland and Prescott (1982, p. 1360) specifically choose not to test their model against a less restrictive autoregressive model since "this most likely would have resulted in (their) model being rejected, given the measurement problems and the abstract nature of (their) model."

Both the Long and Plosser model and the Kydland and Prescott model are specifically designed to exclude any role for money. This strategy is pursued in a desire to demonstrate that models can be built that provide reasonable explanations of business cycle properties without a reliance upon any particular nonneutral role for money. Real business cycle models are, in fact, perhaps most useful in demonstrating that money is not an indispensible ingredient in realistic business cycle models.

However, the absence of money from these models leaves them silent on the stylized fact of business cycle behavior that measures of money and economic activity are, almost uniformly, positively correlated. This issue is addressed in an important paper by King and Plosser (1984). King and Plosser add monetary, or financial, services as an additional, produced intermediate input in a setup that is similar to the Long and Plosser model discussed in Sections 15.1 and 15.2. King and Plosser further argue that such financial services lead to increased production in other sectors of the economy and that measures of inside money are likely to be positively correlated with the level of monetary, or financial, services.

The King and Plosser analysis demonstrates that if there is comovement among output levels across sectors in the economy, then the level of transaction services should be positively correlated with real output. If, additionally, inside money is positively correlated with the level of transaction services, then the model provides the desired link between real output and real measures of inside money.

The King and Plosser model has the following empirical implications. If the monetary authority does not respond to changes in the level of real economic activity, then the level of outside money should be uncorrelated with business cycle fluctuations in aggregate output. However, given a noncyclical path of outside money, real business cycle phenomena should impart a positive correlation between measures of inside money and measures of real output. King and Plosser present empirical evidence in favor of these hypotheses.

One major difficulty with the empirical evidence presented by King and Plosser is that their assumption that the monetary authority exogenously determines the size of the monetary base, without reference to economic conditions, is not formally tested. This omission is particularly troublesome for analysis of recent U.S. experience given the strong presumption that the Federal Reserve System allows the monetary base to vary considerably in response to movements in short-term interest rates. Furthermore, while the King and Plosser analysis is able to present suggestive evidence in favor of the real business cycle model, their analysis does not constitute a formal test of the model versus an alternative hypothesis.

## Empirical Issues

Much of the empirical work relating to the issue of assessing the plausibility of real business cycle models focuses on the issue of whether money affects real variables or not. Although a channel of causation from money to real income has long been almost universally accepted by macroeconomists, this view has recently come under considerable challenge. Resulting doubt about the role of money in explaining business cycle phenomena has therefore been an important factor in the growing respectability of the real business cycle view.

The most carefully articulated tests of the hypothesis that money affects real output are those presented by Sims (1972, 1980a). Sims finds strong evidence of comovement between money and output as well as evidence that money shocks "cause" output movements in the sense that the monetary shocks predate the related output movements. However, Sims's tests of this relationship are undertaken in vector autoregressive models that exclude interest rate movements. Further research by Sims (1980b) as well as more recent work by Litterman and Weiss (1985) cast significant doubt on the original Sims view of the pattern of money-income causality. Both Sims (1980b) and Litterman and Weiss (1985) find that when interest rate movements are added to the vector autoregressions, money no longer plays a significant causal role on output. In particular, interest rate movements precede related movements in both money and output. That innovations in the money supply process might not induce real output movements would be damaging to both the labor contracts models and the equilibrium stochastic monetary models of output and employment determination.

Virtually all of the recent evidence that points in the direction of monetary neutrality is derived in the context of unrestricted vector autoregression analysis. However, as Cooley and LeRoy (1985) point out, this type of inference is not generally valid. In particular, Cooley and LeRoy demonstrate that absent a correctly specified structural model, it is not possible to properly test for economic exogeneity of output with respect to movements in the money supply. Furthermore, without a specific model, it is not even possible to identify what one means by an exogenous money supply shock.

A related problem with the interpretation that money shocks may be neutral is the implicit assumption, in most empirical studies, that such monetary shocks are, in fact, exogenous. As McCallum (1983) points out, if the monetary authority is responding to interest rate movements, then simple examination of vector autoregressions containing money and interest rates may be misleading. Alternatively, it is possible that real interest rates may be purely exogenous with respect to the money supply process as would be the case in real business cycle models. The appearance of a reverse causation from real output to money is then possible if money demand reacts to expected future output movements in the face of current interest rate movements. In such a scenario, a current increase in real interest rates might induce an expected future decline in output. Such an anticipated fall in output might reduce expected future money demand, leading to higher expected future prices, increased current expected inflation, and higher current nominal interest rates.

Even if the assumption of exogenous nominal money is correct, a real business cycle interpretation of the evidence may not be compelling. A recent paper by Bernanke (1986) using a slightly different decomposition of residuals still finds that interest rate shocks are much more closely correlated with future output shocks than are monetary shocks. However, Bernanke cannot completely reject any role for monetary shocks in explaining such future output movements.

Additional support for the real business cycle view of aggregate fluctuations is provided by Nelson and Plosser (1982) and by Stulz and Wasserfallen (1985). The basic argument here is that traditional methods of decomposing economic time series into cyclical and trend components are seriously flawed. In particular, such methods greatly overestimate the cyclical component. If, as these authors contend, the cyclical component of output is very small, monetary shocks are likely to be empirically unimportant if such shocks are understood as affecting at most the cyclical component of output. However, as pointed out by McCallum (1986), the Nelson and Plosser and Stulz and Wasserfallen arguments rely on their contention that what they identify as the trend component of output follows a random walk. If, as McCallum suggests, the trend component of output is closely approximated by but not identically equal to a random walk, then arguments about the relative importance of the cyclical component of output may not be justified.

Further evidence on the issue of whether or not innovations in output have permanent effects is presented by Campbell and Mankiw (1987) and Cochrane (1988). Campbell and Mankiw conclude their output shocks have permanent effects. Alternatively, Cochrane finds little long-term persistence in real output series. However, the empirical resolution of this issue is not a sufficient test of real business cycle models against a diffuse set of alternative models. First of all, real business cycle models can be constructed to mimic either stationary or nonstationary output series. Second, it is not necessarily the case that Keynesian-style macroeconomic models imply that output shocks have purely transient effects. For example, Blanchard and Summers (1986) discuss a number of Keynesian-style ''hysteresis'' models in which macroeconomic disturbances such as aggregate demand shocks generate permanent changes in real output.

Although some empirical evidence favors the real business cycle view, there remains a considerable amount of skepticism on the part of macroeconomists about the validity of such theories. In part, such skepticism comes from a reluctance to accept the evidence that monetary shocks may not explain output movements very well. However, even if the validity of such evidence about the role of monetary shocks is accepted as valid, such evidence does not necessarily constitute grounds for acceptance of the real business cycle models. Just because output movements may not be well explained by monetary shocks does not mean that such output movements are necessarily due to inherently unobservable productivity shocks. Clearly, more research in this important area is warranted.

## Some Concluding Remarks

This chapter provides a relatively careful study of the real business cycle model of Long and Plosser (1983). In this model, material inputs into the production of current output are predetermined. The technology by which these inputs are transformed into current output levels is then subject to exogenous current period productivity shocks. Subsequent to the realization of these shocks, current period output must be allocated between current period consumption levels and inputs into next period's production processes. In general, periods of high productivity generate higher than normal levels both of current consumption and of material inputs into future production. It is through this smoothing of the returns-to-productivity shocks that links levels of production through time and leads to positive serial correlation in output levels.

It should be remembered that the basic Long and Plosser model has the property that aggregate and sector-specific employment levels are constant through time. Intuitively, intertemporal income and substitution effects exactly cancel out. While this property of the Long and Plosser model is not a general characteristic of all real business cycle models, it does nevertheless raise concerns about real business cycle models' ability to explain employment and unemployment fluctuations. Another important criticism of the basic Long and Plosser model is the complete absence of money from the analysis. This feature of the Long and Plosser model leaves one with the impression that real business cycle models have no room for the possibility of effects of either anticipated or unanticipated money supply movements. While models of this type may admit a role for money, a generally accepted integration of nonneutral money into real business cycle models remains an unfinished part of this general research agenda.

A driving force in the development of real business cycle models is an attempt to provide a model grounded in the competitive equilibrium tradition that closely mimics the behavior of actual economic performance. This project is ultimately motivated by a desire to provide an explanation for macroeconomic fluctuations that is consistent with maximizing behavior. However, such competitive equilibrium models are not the only sorts of models that are consistent with maximizing behavior. In Chapter 16, we examine recent advances in Keynesian macroeconomics that attempt to reconcile actual or apparent price and wage stickyness with the maximizing behavior of private agents.

# REFERENCES

Barro, Robert J., "Long-Term Contracts, Sticky Prices, and Monetary Policy," *Journal of Monetary Economics,* July, 1977, 305–316.

Bellman, Richard, *Dynamic Programming,* Princeton, NJ, Princeton University Press, 1957.

Bernanke, Ben S., "Alternative Explanations of the Money-Income Correlation," *Carnegie-Rochester Conference Series on Public Policy,* Amsterdam, North Holland, Autumn, 1986, 49–100.

Blanchard, Olivier J., and Lawrence H. Summers, "Hysteresis and the European Unemployment Problem," *NBER Macroeconomics Annual,* 1986, 15–78.

Blinder, Alan S., and Stanley Fischer, "Inventories, Rational Expectations, and the Business Cycle," *Journal of Monetary Economics,* November, 1981, 277–304.

Campbell, John Y., and N. Gregory Mankiw, "Are Output Fluctuations Transitory?," *Quarterly Journal of Economics,* November, 1987, 857–880.

Cochrane, John H., "How Big Is the Random Walk in GNP?" *Journal of Political Economy,* October, 1988, 893–920.

Cooley, Thomas F., and Stephen F. LeRoy, "Atheoretical Macroeconometrics: A Critique," *Journal of Monetary Economics,* November, 1985, 283–308.

Eichenbaum, Martin S., "Rational Expectations and the Smoothing Properties of Inventories of Finished Goods," *Journal of Monetary Economics,* July, 1984, 71–96.

King, Robert G., and Charles I. Plosser, "Money, Credit, and Prices in a Real Business Cycle," *American Economic Review,* June, 1984, 363–380.

Kydland, Finn E., and Edward C. Prescott, "Time to Build and Aggregate Fluctuations," *Econometrica,* November, 1982, 1345–1370.

Litterman, Robert B., and Laurence Weiss, "Money, Real Interest Rates, and Output: A Reinterpretation of Postwar U.S. Data," *Econometrica,* January, 1985, 129–156.

Long, John B., and Charles I. Plosser, "Real Business Cycles," *Journal of Political Economy,* February, 1983, 39–69.

Lucas, Robert E., Jr., "An Equilibrium Model of the Business Cycle," *Journal of Political Economy,* December, 1975, 1113–1144.

McCallum, Bennett T., "A Reconsideration of Sims' Evidence Concerning Monetarism," *Economic Letters,* 1983, 167–171.

McCallum, Bennett T., "On 'Real' and 'Sticky-Price' Theories of the Business Cycle," *Journal of Money, Credit, and Banking,* November, 1986, 397–414.

Nelson, Charles R., and Charles I. Plosser, "Trends and Random Walks in Macroeconomic Time Series," *Journal of Monetary Economics,* September, 1982, 139–162.

Prescott, Edward C., "Theory Ahead of Business Cycle Measurement," *Carnegie-Rochester Conference Series on Public Policy,* Amsterdam, North Holland, Autumn, 1986, 11–44.

Sargent, Thomas J., *Dynamic Macroeconomic Theory,* Cambridge, MA, Harvard University Press, 1987a.

Sargent, Thomas J., *Macroeconomic Theory,* 2nd. ed., Orlando, FL, Academic, 1987b.

Sims, Christopher, "Money, Income, and Causality," *American Economic Review,* September, 1972, 540–555.

Sims, Christopher, "Macroeconomics and Reality," *Econometrica,* January, 1980a, 1–48.

Sims, Christopher, "Comparison of Interwar and Postwar Business Cycles: Monetarism Reconsidered," *American Economic Review,* May, 1980b, 250–257.

Stulz, Rene M., and Walter Wasserfallen, "Macroeconomic Time-Series, Business Cycles, and Macroeconomic Policies," *Carnegie-Rochester Conference Series on Public Policy,* Amsterdam, North Holland, Spring, 1985, 9–54.

Taylor, John B., "Aggregate Dynamics and Staggered Contracts," *Journal of Political Economy,* February, 1980, 1–23.

Topel, Robert H., "Inventories, Layoffs, and the Short-Run Demand for Labor," *American Economic Review,* September, 1982, 769–787.

# Chapter 16

## New Keynesian Macroeconomic Models

From its inception, Keynesian macroeconomics has rejected many of the specific assumptions and much of the general modeling strategy of classical economic theory. In particular, Keynes simply asserted the importance of characteristics like money illusion and wage stickyness, which were thought to be in direct conflict with classical microeconomic analysis. Moreover, the Keynesian tradition has been built upon the notion that such market failures and evidence of irrational behavior were so obviously important for the study of the behavior of aggregate economic outcomes that the use of such assumptions as maintained hypotheses was a legitimate modeling strategy.

However, as has been clear throughout the earlier chapters of this text, recent thinking among macroeconomists has favored macroeconomic models with sound microeconomic foundations. The bulk of the early work in this area has been provided by new classical writers like Robert Barro, Robert Lucas, and Thomas Sargent. More recently, the growing literature on real business cycle models has been very much within the classical microeconomic tradition.

The level of sophistication of these modern classical approaches to macroeconomic analysis has left many observers with the impression that most Keynesian macroeconomic analysis is inconsistent with the usual economic methodology of maximizing behavior on the part of economic agents. In response to such criticism, a significant body of recent research has been devoted to demonstrating that most Keynesian-style results are in fact compatible with more standard microeconomic modeling techniques.

Modern Keynesian intuition would suggest at least three characteristics that a model should possess to be a realistic candidate for describing actual economic events. First, a model should be consistent with the existence of involuntary unemployment. Second, a model should be consistent with the notion that increases in aggregate output are almost always welfare improving. Finally, a realistic model should permit nominal disturbances such as monetary shocks to generate changes in real economic activity.

This chapter surveys two specific branches of the rapidly growing field of new Keynesian macroeconomic analysis. Section 16.1 reviews efficiency wage models of employment and output determination. Models of this class explore the possibility that levels of worker effort may be positively affected by changes in real wage rates paid by firms. Efficiency wage models of this sort are capable of explaining real wage rigidity and the emergence of involuntary unemployment as an equilibrium outcome.

Although efficiency wage considerations are capable of explaining real wage rigidity, such models are not consistent with the types of nominal rigidities discussed in Chapters 5 and 13. Furthermore, efficiency wage considerations are neither a necessary nor a sufficient condition for monetary nonneutralities. Section 16.2 explores macroeconomic models that attempt to rationalize such nominal rigidities as consistent with maximizing behavior.

The microeconomic foundations of new Keynesian sticky-price macroeconomic models are based upon the following general set of assumptions. First, nominal rigidities in product markets are more likely to affect the allocation of resources than nominal rigidities in labor markets because wages rates paid in labor markets may simply reflect installment payments on long-term relationships. Second, in order for sticky prices to emerge as maximizing behavior, individual firm profit functions must be continuous in the price the firm charges. This consideration makes monopolistically competitive models most useful for macroeconomic analysis. Third, since the type of costs that most observers attribute to price changing are likely to be small relative to the costs of aggregate economic contractions, it must be the case that small price-setting costs faced by individual price setters have greatly amplified aggregate effects.

The model of Section 16.2 is based upon these three key presumptions. Such a model is shown to be capable of supporting sticky-price equilibria in which aggregate employment and output are significantly different than flexible price levels. Furthermore, the model of Section 16.2 is consistent with the property that higher aggregate output is associated with increased welfare and the potential for monetary policy to affect the allocation of resources.

## 16.1 EFFICIENCY WAGE MODELS OF UNEMPLOYMENT

A commonly agreed-upon stylized fact in macroeconomics is the existence, at least in some times and at some locations, of involuntary unemployment. Such involuntary unemployment is said to exist when unemployed individuals stand ready and willing to work at less than the prevailing real wage rate. These unemployed individuals are, nevertheless, unable to underbid existing workers in order to obtain employment.

In Chapter 5, we studied a model in which a sticky nominal wage rate could account for the persistence of involuntary unemployment. However, the sticky-wage model is subject to the criticism that the wage-setting agent is never explicitly identified nor is any sound justification provided for why the wage-setting agent fails to quickly lower wages in response to an excess supply of labor.

In Chapter 13, we examined models of wage and employment determination based upon the existence of implicit or explicit labor contracts. Microeconomic models of labor contracts explain the appearance of involuntary unemployment as an ex post regret of the outcome of a risk-shifting arrangement that was willingly entered into ex ante by both the worker and the firm. In such models, unemployment is not, strictly speaking, involuntary in nature. Alternatively, macroeconomic models of labor contracts assume that contracting costs preclude the writing of contracts that call for the ex post efficient level of employment. Employment in such models is left at the discretion of firms that may demand a quantity of labor that is less than the quantity supplied at the contractually specified wage rate.

However, neither labor-contracting model offers a completely satisfying account of involuntary unemployment. The microeconomic contracting literature is forced to rely on differences in tastes for risk bearing between workers and firms. Many students of labor markets are not convinced that such risk preferences are strong enough to account for the extent and persistence of what they would characterize as involuntary unemployment. Furthermore, many would argue that most of what is characterized as involuntary unemployment represents departures from efficient employment of labor services rather than an efficient solution to the allocation of risk. Alternatively, the macroeconomic literature on labor contracts is forced to rely on hard-to-identify contracting costs that somehow prevent workers and firms from exhausting all mutually advantageous transactions.

The efficiency wage hypothesis offers an attractive alternative to sticky nominal wage rate models and implicit contract models as a rationale for the existence of involuntary unemployment.[1] Efficiency wage models rely upon the possibility that worker productivity may be directly linked to the real wage rate paid by the firm. If such a link between productivity and wages exists, it may be in firms' interests to pay a real wage rate that exceeds the level consistent with market clearing in the labor market. Even though a pool of unemployed workers may be available for firms at less than the current real wage rate, a cut in real wages may cost the firm more in lost productivity than it gains in a lower average wage bill. In such a framework, the appearance of an excess supply of labor may be entirely consistent with the maximizing behavior of both workers and firms and also consistent with full exhaustion of all gains from trade in the labor market.

## A Formal Model of Efficiency Wages

The basic efficiency wage model is presented succinctly by Yellen (1984). Suppose that the representative firm produces output with labor as the only variable factor of production. Assume that production is governed by

$$Y = af(L), \qquad f' > 0, \qquad f'' < 0, \tag{16.1.1}$$

where $Y$ denotes output, $L$ denotes labor services, and $a$ denotes a potential exogenous shock to productivity.

Instead of the usual assumption that $L$ represents the number of workers employed or the number of man-hours worked by the firm's work force, we now identify $L$ as the number of efficiency units of labor. Efficiency units are equal to the size of the work force

---

[1]A good introduction to this theory is provided by Yellen (1984). Katz (1986) provides a more extensive review of the literature.

$N$ times the level of worker "effort" $e$. The identifying characteristic of efficiency wage theory is the assumption that effort $e$ is an increasing function of the real wage rate $w$.

Real firm profits, denoted by $\Pi/P$, are given in this model by

$$\frac{\Pi}{P} = af[e(w)N] - wN. \tag{16.1.2}$$

Now suppose that labor is supplied inelastically at $N = \overline{N}$. If worker effort were independent of the real wage rate, then equilibrium in the labor market would require that the real wage rate equal the marginal productivity of an additional worker. In particular, we would find

$$w = af'(\overline{e}N)\overline{e}, \tag{16.1.3}$$

where $\overline{e}$ represents the fixed level of worker effort. The equilibrium wage rate $w^*$ would equate labor supply and labor demand at $N = \overline{N}$, and there would be no involuntary unemployment. Furthermore, the equilibrium real wage rate

$$w^* = af'(\overline{e}\overline{N})\overline{e} \tag{16.1.4}$$

would be monotonically increasing in the exogenous productivity parameter $a$.

As noted above, efficiency wage theory adopts the alternative assumption that worker effort $e$ is rising in the real wage rate. With this alternative assumption, the representative firm chooses both $w$ and $N$ to maximize real profits. That is, the representative firm's maximization problem is given by

$$\max_{w,N} \frac{\Pi}{P} = af[e(w)N] - wN. \tag{16.1.5}$$

First-order conditions for this maximization problem are given by

$$\frac{\partial(\Pi/P)}{\partial N} = af'e - w = 0, \tag{16.1.6}$$

$$\frac{\partial(\Pi/P)}{\partial w} = (af'e' - 1)N = 0. \tag{16.1.7}$$

Equation (16.1.6) is the standard equality between the real wage rate and the marginal product of labor. Equation (16.1.7) requires the firm to minimize labor costs per efficiency unit. Combining equations (16.1.6) and (16.1.7), and rearranging, we obtain

$$\frac{w}{e}\frac{\partial e}{\partial w} = 1. \tag{16.1.8}$$

That is, the efficiency wage is the wage rate that equates the elasticity of effort with respect to the real wage rate with unity. If this real wage rate exceeds the competitive market-clearing real wage rate $w^*$, then employment is less than $\overline{N}$ and involuntary unemployment exists in equilibrium. Those potential workers who are not employed would be willing to work at a lower real wage rate, and yet these potential workers cannot find employment.

A key implication of the efficiency wage model is the prediction that the real wage rate is independent of the productivity shock $a$. Furthermore, the real wage rate is also independent of any demand side disturbances that could easily be incorporated into the formal model. Efficiency wage models therefore provide a formal rationale for real wage rate rigidity. Second, while the equilibrium wage rate is independent of the productivity shock $a$, the level of employment is not. Favorable supply shocks lead in this model to increases in employment with no change in the real wage rate. This model is therefore immune to the objection often raised by critics of both sticky nominal wage rate models and imperfect information models that such models often predict a countercyclical real wage rate, a prediction uniformly rejected by empirical studies.

A slight variation of the basic efficiency wage model is its application to the case of dual labor markets. The dual labor market model includes a primary sector in which efficiency wage considerations are important and a secondary sector in which wages and employment are determined in the more traditional competitive manner. In the dual labor market model, higher wages are paid to the otherwise identical workers in the primary sector as compared with the wages paid those workers employed in the secondary sector. Jobs are rationed in the primary sector with all those workers failing to gain employment in the primary sector relegated to employment in the lower paying secondary sector or as unemployed workers waiting for jobs to become available in the primary sector. A distinguishing characteristic of both the basic efficiency wage model and its dual labor market counterpart is that otherwise identical individuals experience potentially large differences in utility levels. In the basic model, unemployed workers experience a marginal utility of leisure that may be substantially less than the real wage rate received by employed workers. In the dual labor market version of the efficiency wage model, otherwise identical workers may receive significantly different real wage rates in equilibrium.

## Some Alternative Rationales for Efficiency Wages

The key assumption in efficiency wage models is the direct link between the real wage rate a worker receives and his or her level of "effort" on the job. This indispensible part of the theory can be rationalized in a number of different though not mutually exclusive ways.

Perhaps the most concrete link between productivity and wages is that hypothesized by Leibenstein (1957). With wage rates close to the substance level, an increase in the real wage rate allows for improved worker nutrition and increased physical strength. A healthier work force therefore produces more output per unit of time spent working.

An alternative rationale for the real wage–effort relationship is provided by Shapiro and Stiglitz (1984). In this model, worker effort can only be monitored at some significant cost to the firm. Therefore, it may be possible for workers to "shirk" on the job and avoid detection for some time. In the purely competitive model, workers who are caught shirking, although they may be fired from their jobs, can immediately regain employment at another firm at the same wage rate. Therefore, there is no incentive not to shirk and all workers shirk in equilibrium. Alternatively, firms that pay a real wage rate above the competitive level have an effective punishment mechanism for workers caught shirking. Fired individuals may only be able to get work in the competitive sector at a much lower wage rate. This incentive structure may lead to an equilibrium in which workers at high-wage firms put in greater average effort than workers at low-wage firms.

Alternatively, Salop (1979) considers the possibility that firms that experience lower employee turnover may have higher levels of worker productivity. Such economies in production may come about because more senior workers may be more productive and because the firm may be forced to bear some of the resulting costs of experienced worker turnover. In such a model higher real wage rates reduce the quit rate faced by the firm, and therefore a higher wage may reduce turnover and increase average productivity.

Weiss (1980) presents a model of adverse selection in hiring that also provides a rationale for efficiency wages. In this scenario, firms are unable to measure, ex ante, the productivity of heterogeneous workers. However, if workers are aware of their own productivity, acceptance wages will, on average, be positively correlated with worker ability. Therefore a higher wage rate may result in a more productive work force.

Akerlof (1982) provides a motivation for efficiency wages that is more closely identified as sociological in its articulation. In models of this type workers and firms engage in an exchange of gifts. The firm voluntarily gives the workers a wage that exceeds the competitive wage, and the worker gives the firm a work effort that significantly exceeds some minimum standard. In such models, a wage exceeding the competitive level is required to maintain the gift exchange equilibrium, and the resulting increase in worker productivity is enforced through "work norms" and peer pressure. Interestingly, Akerlof demonstrates that some optimal outcomes that are feasible by means of a gift exchange could not be supported by a purely market mechanism.

While all of these rationales for a positively sloped efforts function have some appeal, they are all subject to varying degrees of criticism. The purely biological model of worker effort is clearly applicable only to the least developed of market economies. Problems of shirking, inefficiently high turnover, and adverse selection in hiring all have a natural alternative solution in which the firm requires new hires to post performance bonds. In the event that the worker shirks, quits prematurely, or is later found to be less productive than he or she claimed, the performance bond would be forfeited to the firm. In the case of sociological explanations of worker productivity, although such models have some intuitive appeal, it is difficult to quantify the intangible factors involved in the gift exchange relationship, and such explanations are difficult to set up as potentially refutable hypotheses.

Perhaps the most powerful of these objections to the efficiency wage model is the possibility that performance bonds may render the efficiency wage solution suboptimal. The underlying tension in efficiency wage models is the property of such models that the wage rate paid performs two functions: allocating scarce labor resources and solving a particular form of market failure. Such potential market failures are clearly better solved by the use of an independent mechanism, and performance bonds are the obvious candidate. However, it may be the case that imperfections in capital markets make it difficult for workers to post such bonds. Furthermore, there is a moral hazard problem that arises because firms may be tempted to make false claims against the bonds. While the possibility of deferred compensation for workers may partially solve some of these difficulties with performance bonding, it may well be the case that some combination of performance bonds and efficiency wages may prove optimal in many labor market relationships.

## A Critical Assessment of Efficiency Wage Models

While efficiency wage models provide neat explanations of involuntary unemployment and real wage rigidity, such models are hard to empirically verify. Direct tests of efficiency wage theory against specific alternatives are not immediately obvious. However, one robust implication of efficiency wage theory is the possibility that otherwise identical workers may persistently receive different levels of compensation.

Katz (1986) uses this particular property of efficiency wage models as a means of providing some indirect evidence on the usefulness of the models. In particular, Katz looks for wage differentials across industries and across occupations to see if such differentials persist after correcting for other individual specific characteristics. Because Katz fails to find competitive explanations for the remaining, relatively large wage differentials that persist, he interprets his results as favorable to the efficiency wage hypothesis.

Despite such suggestive results, the usefulness of efficiency wage explanations of labor market phenomena remains to be proven. It may be the case that existing empirical studies on wage differentials have failed to adequately capture individual differences in training and skills. Alternatively, it may be the case that more sophisticated competitive explanations for any remaining differentials simply remain undiscovered. In any event, more careful and innovative empirical work is required before a full evaluation of efficiency wage models is completed.

However, no matter how useful efficiency wage explanations may be for understanding some particular characteristics of labor markets, the usefulness of such theories for providing explanations of macroeconomic phenomena would still be quite limited. First of all, efficiency wage theory, while potentially capable of explaining real wage rigidity, is incapable of explaining the sort of nominal wage rigidities necessary to support traditional Keynesian models of nominal wage rigidity. Furthermore, efficiency wage theories have little to say about how wages and employment vary through time and across space. There is, for example, no particular reason to suppose that efficiency wage effects are likely to be more or less important in economic expansions as opposed to economic contractions.

Although efficiency wage theory cannot provide new candidate explanations for sources of aggregate fluctuations, such theories may turn out to be a quite useful part of the mechanism by which such fluctuations are propagated. One recurring objection to many business cycle models is that they imply implausibly large labor supply elasticities. However, efficiency wage models have the characteristic that movements in employment are mainly driven by labor demand considerations rather than labor supply considerations. Efficiency wage aspects are therefore often included in more completely specified new Keynesian models of employment and output determination like that of Akerlof and Yellen (1985).

# 16.2 MONOPOLISTICALLY COMPETITIVE MACROMODELS WITH "MENU" COSTS

In the previous section, we analyzed efficiency wage models of employment and output determination. Such models are interesting because they provide plausible explanations of involuntary unemployment and a relatively rigid relative wage structure. However, such models primarily address the issue of real wage rigidity. In particular, such models are neither a necessary nor a sufficient condition for the existence of nominal rigidities and a potential link between real variables such as employment and output and nominal variables like the nominal money supply.

Furthermore, even to the extent that efficiency wage models or other models of the labor market may point to short-run rigidities in nominal wage rates, such labor market rigidities may not be that important a source of macroeconomic fluctuations. As pointed out in Chapter 13, the employer-employee relationship may be inherently long-lived in nature, and the nominal or real wage rate at any point in time may not serve an important allocative role.

Such difficulties with purely labor market foundations of Keynesian macroeconomic models have prompted renewed interest in possible rationales for nominal rigidities in product markets. In particular, Cecchetti (1986) finds considerable evidence of nominal rigidities in the newsstand price of magazines, a market in which changes in real prices are almost certain to have allocative effects. Furthermore, Blanchard (in press) points to empirical evidence that nominal prices may be more sticky than nominal wages.

This section presents the basic microeconomic foundations of rigid product price models. Such models are more carefully specified versions of the analysis of Chapter 3. In order to provide rigorous microeconomic foundations for rigid nominal goods prices, several general modeling properties appear to be required. First, the perfectly competitive paradigm of the frictionless Walrasian auctioneer would need to be replaced by a structure that provides specific identities for price-setting agents. New Keynesian macroeconomic models generally rely on a monopolistically competitive market structure in which each firm has the ability to set its own price over a broad range without facing either zero or infinite demand for its product.

Second, the price-setting agent must face specific costs of changing nominal (as opposed to real) prices. Such costs, often identified as "menu" costs, could include the costs of printing new price lists or menus. Alternatively, Rotemberg (1982) emphasizes the possibility that firms that change their nominal prices frequently may be viewed as erratic, and such behavior may result in reduced sales.

Unfortunately, such specific price-setting costs are very hard to pin down and they are certainly not likely, in the aggregate, to be of a size comparable to the kinds of costs most traditional Keynesian macroeconomists attribute to business cycle fluctuations. A third requirement of a consistent Keynesian scenario would therefore be the property that even small price-setting costs might lead to much larger sized fluctuations in employment and output. Such a link is provided by Akerlof and Yellen's (1985) analysis, which demonstrates that second-order departures from the frictionless actions of individual economic agents can lead to first-order departures from aggregate equilibrium outcomes.

## A Monopolistically Competitive Macroeconomic Model

This section provides a formal analysis of a monopolistically competitive macroeconomic model along the lines of Rotemberg (1987). The economy is composed of $J$ firms each of which produces a differentiated product with labor as the only variable input into the production process. The economy is also composed of a large number of households whose behavior may be captured by the actions of a representative household that behaves atomistically in the labor and product markets.

In order to highlight the major novelties of monopolistically competitive macroeconomic models, we concentrate our analysis primarily on a single period of time. Such a focus abstracts from considerations of intertemporal substitution in labor supply, investment, and life-cycle consumption-saving behavior. We further assume that the representative household chooses consumption levels and labor supply to maximize a utility function of the form

$$V = \frac{1}{\beta}\left[\frac{1}{J}\sum_{i=1}^{J}(JC_i)^{\theta}\right]^{\beta/\theta} - L, \qquad 0 < \beta < 1, \qquad 0 < \theta < 1, \tag{16.2.1}$$

where $\beta$ and $\theta$ are constants, $C_i$ represents consumption of the $i$th good, and $L$ represents labor supply. The representative household chooses consumption and labor supply subject to an income constraint given by

$$\sum_{i=1}^{J} P_iC_i = WL + \sum_{i=1}^{J} \Pi_i, \tag{16.2.2}$$

where $P_i$ denotes the price of good $i$, $W$ represents the nominal wage rate, and $\Pi_i$ denotes the nominal profits of firm $i$, which are distributed to the representative household.

In addition to its choice of consumption levels and labor supply, the representative household also chooses optimal holdings of real money balances. Such choices could be directly incorporated into the rest of the maximization problem by assuming that real money balances enter the representative household's utility function. Alternatively, we simply specify a demand-for-money function of the form

$$M^d = PY, \tag{16.2.3}$$

where

$$P \equiv \left[\frac{1}{J}\sum_{i=1}^{J}(P_i)^{-\theta/(1-\theta)}\right]^{-(1-\theta)/\theta}, \tag{16.2.4}$$

a price index, and

$$Y \equiv \frac{1}{P}\sum_{i=1}^{J} P_iC_i = \frac{WL}{P} + \frac{1}{P}\sum_{i=1}^{J} \Pi_i, \tag{16.2.5}$$

aggregate real income. We further assume that the money market clears continuously, and so

$$M = M^d = PY \rightarrow \frac{M}{P} = Y. \tag{16.2.6}$$

The representative household maximizes the Lagrangian expression

$$\mathcal{L} = \frac{1}{\beta}\left[\frac{1}{J}\sum_{i=1}^{J}(JC_i)^{\theta}\right]^{\beta/\theta} - L + \lambda\left[WL + \sum_{i=1}^{J}\Pi_i - \sum_{i=1}^{J}P_iC_i\right]. \tag{16.2.7}$$

First-order conditions for this maximization problem are given by

$$\frac{\partial \mathcal{L}}{\partial C_i} = \left[\frac{1}{J} \sum_{i=1}^{J} (JC_i)^\theta\right]^{\beta/\theta - 1} (JC_i)^{-(1-\theta)} - \lambda P_i = 0, \qquad i = 1, \cdots, J, \qquad (16.2.8)$$

$$\frac{\partial \mathcal{L}}{\partial L} = -1 + \lambda W = 0. \qquad (16.2.9)$$

The first-order condition for optimal labor supply implies that $\lambda = 1/W$. Plugging this last first-order condition into the first $J$ first-order conditions, summing over $J$, and rearranging, we obtain

$$\frac{1}{J} \sum_{i=1}^{J} (JC_i)^\theta = W^{\theta/(1-\theta)} \left[\frac{1}{J} \sum_{i=1}^{J} (JC_i)^\theta\right]^{(\beta-\theta)/(1-\theta)} \left[\frac{1}{J} \sum_{i=1}^{J} (P_i)^{-\theta/(1-\theta)}\right]. \qquad (16.2.10)$$

Now recalling the definition of the aggregate price level $P$ above, we can rearrange the above expression as

$$\frac{1}{J} \sum_{i=1}^{J} (JC_i)^\theta = \left(\frac{W}{P}\right)^{\theta/(1-\beta)}. \qquad (16.2.11)$$

The original $J$ first-order conditions may also be written as

$$JC_i = \left(\frac{W}{P_i}\right)^{\theta/(1-\beta)} \left[\frac{1}{J} \sum_{i=1}^{J} (JC_i)^\theta\right]^{(\beta-\theta)/\theta(1-\theta)}. \qquad (16.2.12)$$

Now plugging in for $(1/J) \sum_{i=1}^{J} (JC_i)^\theta$ from above, we obtain

$$(JC_i)^\theta = \left(\frac{P_i}{P}\right)^{-\theta/(1-\theta)} \left(\frac{W}{P_i}\right)^{\theta/(1-\beta)}. \qquad (16.2.13)$$

We have therefore demonstrated that the demand for good $i$ is inversely related to the relative price of good $i$, $P_i/P$, and directly related to the real wage rate expressed in units of good $i$, $W/P_i$.

The sum of the first $j$ of original first-order conditions may also be written as

$$\left[\frac{1}{J} \sum_{i=1}^{J} (JC_i)^\theta\right]^{\beta/\theta} = \frac{1}{W} \sum_{i=1}^{J} P_i C_i = \frac{P}{W} Y. \qquad (16.2.14)$$

Now plugging in $(1/J) \sum_{i=1}^{J} (JC_i)^\theta = (W/P)^{\theta/(1-\beta)}$, we obtain:

$$\left(\frac{W}{P}\right)^{\theta/(1-\beta)} = \frac{P}{W} Y. \qquad (16.2.15)$$

Throughout the analysis, we assume that the technology is linear, and so we are assured that $Y_i = L_i$, and in the aggregate, $Y = L$. We may therefore invert the above expression to obtain the semireduced-form labor supply schedule

$$L^s = \left(\frac{W}{P}\right)^{1/(1-\beta)}. \tag{16.2.16}$$

We therefore find that labor supply is increasing in the real wage rate $W/P$.

The individual demand functions for goods were given above as

$$JC_i = \left(\frac{P_i}{P}\right)^{-1/(1-\theta)}\left(\frac{W}{P}\right)^{1/(1-\beta)}. \tag{16.2.17}$$

However, since the labor and money markets are assumed to clear, we know that $L = (W/P)^{1/(1-\beta)} = Y = M/P$. We may therefore relate the goods demand functions to the level of real money balance as

$$JC_i = \left(\frac{P_i}{P}\right)^{-1/(1-\theta)}\frac{M}{P}. \tag{16.2.18}$$

The demand for good $i$ is inversely related to the relative price of good $i$ and directly related to the level of real money balances $M/P$.

We next turn our attention to the behavior of the $J$ firms. As noted above, the technology is linear so that $Y_i = L_i$ for all $J$ firms. Since all firms face an identical problem, we consider the decision process for an arbitrarily selected firm $i$. Firm $i$'s problem is given by

$$\max_{P_i, Y_i, L_i, D_i} \Pi_i = P_i Y_i - WL_i - cD_i \tag{16.2.19}$$

subject to

$$Y_i = L_i, \tag{16.2.20}$$

$$Y_i = C_i = \frac{1}{J}\left(\frac{P_i}{P}\right)^{-1/(1-\theta)}\frac{M}{P}, \tag{16.2.21}$$

where $\Pi_i$ denotes firm $i$ profits, $P_i$ is the price charged by firm $i$, $L_i$ is the amount of labor services employed by firm $i$, $c$ is the menu cost of changing prices, and $D_i$ is a binary decision variable that takes the value $D_i = 0$ if firm $i$ sets $P_i = P^0$ and $D_i = 1$ if firm $i$ sets $P_i \neq P^0$. Throughout the analysis $P^0$ denotes the uniform base period price that the firms may charge without incurring a menu cost.

## Frictionless Equilibrium

In order to get some intuition into the workings of this model, we first analyze the case of $c = 0$. That is, we temporarily ignore the complications introduced by the existence of menu costs. Plugging the constraints into the profit function, the maximization problem is given by

$$\max_{P_i} (J\Pi_i) = (P_i - W)\left(\frac{P_i}{P}\right)^{-1/(1-\theta)}\frac{M}{P}. \tag{16.2.22}$$

Differentiating with respect to $P_i$ and rearranging, we obtain the first-order condition

$$P_i^* = \frac{W}{\theta}, \tag{16.2.23}$$

where $P_i^*$ denotes the optimal firm $i$ price level in the case of zero price-changing costs. We therefore find that the optimal firm $i$ price is increasing in the nominal wage rate. Furthermore, since $0 < \theta < 1$, an increase in the nominal wage rate results in a greater than one-for-one increase in firm $i$'s optimal price level. Plugging the above expression for the optimal price back into the demand and profit functions, we find that

$$JY_i^* = \theta^{-1/(1-\theta)} \left( \frac{W}{P} \right)^{-1/(1-\theta)} \frac{M}{P}, \tag{16.2.24}$$

$$\frac{J\Pi_i^*}{P} = \theta^{-1/(1-\theta)} \frac{1-\theta}{\theta} \left( \frac{W}{P} \right)^{-\theta/(1-\theta)} \frac{M}{P}. \tag{16.2.25}$$

The case in which $c = 0$ is a useful benchmark against which to compare situations in which the existence of menu costs may lead to sticky-price equilibria. Particular interest centers on the equilibrium real wage rate $(W/P)^*$, equilibrium aggregate employment $L^* = \Sigma_{i=1}^{J} L_i^*$, and equilibrium aggregate output $Y^* = \Sigma_{i=1}^{J} Y_i^* = L^*$. In order to characterize economywide equilibrium, we first note that since each of the $J$ firms faces an identical problem, equilibrium requires that $P_i^* = P_j^*$, $i \neq j$. We therefore find that

$$P^* = P_i^* = \left[ \frac{1}{J} \sum_{i=1}^{J} (P_i^*)^{-\theta/(1-\theta)} \right]^{-(1-\theta)/\theta} \tag{16.2.26}$$

or

$$P^* = \frac{W}{\theta}. \tag{16.2.27}$$

We may now equate the expressions for labor supply and labor demand to obtain

$$\theta = L^{(1-\beta)} \tag{16.2.28}$$

Since the equilibrium levels of employment, output, and the real money supply are all equal, we obtain

$$L^* = Y^* = \left( \frac{M}{P} \right)^* = \theta^{1/(1-\beta)}. \tag{16.2.29}$$

Furthermore, we note that since employment lies along the labor demand curve in equilibrium, it must be the case that

$$\left( \frac{W}{P} \right)^* = \theta. \tag{16.2.30}$$

Another useful benchmark case is that in which $\theta = 1$. This case corresponds to a situation in which the representative household views all $J$ goods as perfect substitutes. Such a case forces firms to act as perfect competitors. In this case we find that

$$L^* = Y^* = \left(\frac{M}{P}\right)^* = \left(\frac{W}{P}\right)^* = 1. \tag{16.2.31}$$

Cases in which $\theta < 1$ involve levels of output and employment that are strictly less than the perfectly competitive level. Furthermore, we find that the real wage rate is also less than that which would prevail if the output market were competitive. However, these results should not be surprising. Microeconomic theory tells us that monopolistic behavior tends to reduce equilibrium output levels.

It is also informative to note that the representative household's level of utility in the no-menu-cost equilibrium is given by

$$V(Y^*) = \frac{(Y^*)^\beta}{\beta} - Y^* = \frac{\theta^{\beta/(1-\beta)}}{\beta} - \theta^{1/(1-\beta)}. \tag{16.2.32}$$

We can also see how the representative household utility level is related to aggregate output by calculating

$$\frac{dV}{dY} = Y^{-(1-\beta)} - 1. \tag{16.2.33}$$

In the neighborhood of equilibrium, we find that

$$\frac{dV}{dY}\bigg|_{Y=Y^*} = \theta^{-1} - 1 = \frac{1-\theta}{\theta} > 0 \tag{16.2.34}$$

as long as $\theta < 1$. We therefore note that the monopolistically competitive equilibrium level of output is too low. Higher output would make the representative household better off. It is also of interest to note that the Pareto-optimal level of output is given by $Y = 1$. Not surprisingly, the perfectly competitive level of output is also Pareto optimal.

## Firm Behavior with Nonzero Menu Costs

The price-changing technology introduced in the previous section is lump sum in nature. That is, any nonzero price change incurs a fixed cost $c$ independent of the size of the price change. This type of price-changing cost is therefore most literally identified as a menu cost. For this type of price-changing technology, the firm must compare the maximum profit level associated with a price change with the profit level that is realized if the firm sets $P_i = P^0$.

Primary interest in models of this type centers on the question of whether sticky-price equilibria may exist. In particular, we ask whether it is optimal for firm $i$ to maintain a price level of $P_i = P^0$ if all other firms similarly set $P_j = P^0, j \neq i$. If this is the case, then we have established a fixed-price Nash equilibrium.

Let us denote by $\Pi_i^0$ the profit level earned by firm $i$ when it charges $P_i = P^0$ and all other firms also charge $P^0$. Let us denote by $\Pi_i^1$ the before price-changing cost profit level earned by firm $i$ when firm $i$ makes the optimal change in its price to price level $P^1$ when all other firms maintain their price level at $P^0$. Firm $i$ should therefore refrain from making the price change whenever

$$\Delta \equiv J\Pi_i^1 - J\Pi_i^0 < c. \tag{16.2.35}$$

The profit function for firm $i$ when all other firms charge $P^0$ is given by

$$J\Pi_i(P_i) = (P_i - W)\left(\frac{P_i}{P^0}\right)^{-1/(1-\theta)}\frac{M}{P}. \tag{16.2.36}$$

Now recall that with $J$ large and all other firms charging $P^0$, we get $P = P^0$ independent of $P_i$. Let us also now recall that labor market equilibrium requires that $W = \theta P$. Finally, recall that the flexible-price equilibrium price level $P*$ is defined by $M = P*\theta^{1/(1-\beta)}$. The profit function for firm $i$ may therefore be rewritten as

$$J\Pi_i(P_i) = \theta^{1/(1-\beta)}\frac{P*}{P^0}\left(\frac{P_i}{P^0}\right)^{-1/(1-\theta)}(P_i - \theta P^0). \tag{16.2.37}$$

It is now useful to expand the above expression for $\Delta$ as a function of the exogenous "original" price level $P^0$ in a Taylor series around the point $P^0 = P*$. This exercise allows us to approximate the advantage to changing prices as a function of the difference between the frictionless equilibrium price level $P*$ and the base price $P^0$. The appropriate Taylor series expansion is given by

$$\Delta(P^0) \simeq \Delta(P*) + \frac{d\Delta}{dP^0}\bigg|_{P^0=P*}(P^0 - P*) + \frac{1}{2}\frac{d^2\Delta}{d(P^0)^2}\bigg|_{P^0=P*}(P^0 - P*)^2. \tag{16.2.38}$$

In calculating the above derivatives, it is useful to write $d\Delta/dP^0$ as

$$\frac{d\Delta}{dP^0} = \frac{d(J\Pi_i^1)}{dP^0} - \frac{d(J\Pi_i^0)}{dP^0} = \frac{\partial(J\Pi_i^1)}{\partial P_i}\frac{dP_i}{dP^0} + \frac{\partial(J\Pi_i^1)}{\partial P^0} - \frac{\partial(J\Pi_i^0)}{\partial P^0}. \tag{16.2.39}$$

By the envelope theorem and as a result of the fact that $P^1$ is selected to maximize $\Pi_i^1$, the first term in the above expression is identically equal to zero. It is now relatively straightforward to perform the steps involved in computing the Taylor series expression. We now find that

$$\frac{\Delta}{P*} \simeq \theta^{1/(1-\beta)}\frac{1-(1-\theta)^2}{2(1-\theta)}\frac{(P^0-P*)^2}{(P*)^2}. \tag{16.2.40}$$

The important characteristic of the above expression is that it includes only terms of order 2 (and greater than 2 in the exact expression) in the difference $P^0 - P*$. To see if a fixed-price level $P^0$ is a Nash equilibrium, we now need only compare $\Delta$ with the price-changing cost $c$. If $\Delta < c$, then not changing prices is optimal for all firms. Furthermore, since $\Delta$ is proportional to $(P^0 - P*)^2$, very small menu costs may still be compatible with $c > \Delta$.

We have now demonstrated that price-changing costs of order of magnitude $(P^0 - P*)^2$ can generate a fixed-price equilibrium. However, are such fixed-price equilibria associated with significant changes in aggregate output relative to $Y*$, the flexible-price equilibrium level of output? Furthermore, are such fixed-price equilibria capable of generating first-order welfare losses with respect to the flexible-price equilibrium? It turns out that the answers to both of these questions are in the affirmative.

As a prelude to computing the fixed-price equilibrium level of output $Y^0$, we note that output levels $Y_i = C_i$ always lie on the demand curves

$$JC_i = \left(\frac{P_i}{P}\right)^{1/(1-\theta)} \frac{M}{P}. \tag{16.2.41}$$

But in any uniform price equilibrium, $P_i = P^*$ for all $i$. Furthermore, the flexible-price equilibrium price level $P^*$ solves $M = P^*\theta^{1/(1-\beta)}$. Aggregating over firms, we therefore obtain

$$Y^0 = \theta^{1/(1-\beta)} \frac{P^*}{P^0}, \tag{16.2.42}$$

where $Y^0$ denotes the level of output in the fixed-price equilibrium. The difference between the fixed-price equilibrium level of output and the flexible-price equilibrium level of output is therefore given by

$$Y^0 - Y^* = \frac{\theta^{1/(1-\beta)}}{P^0}(P^* - P^0). \tag{16.2.43}$$

We also noted above that the equilibrium level of representative household utility is equal to

$$V = \frac{1}{\beta}Y^\beta - Y. \tag{16.2.44}$$

The difference between the level of utility in the fixed-price equilibrium and flexible-price equilibrium is therefore appropriately equal to

$$V^0 - V^* \simeq \left.\frac{\partial V}{\partial Y}\right|_{Y=Y^*} (Y^0 - Y^*) \tag{16.2.45}$$

or

$$V^0 - V^* \simeq \frac{1-\theta}{\theta} \frac{\theta^{1/(1-\beta)}}{P^0}(P^* - P^0). \tag{16.2.46}$$

We have therefore confirmed our earlier assertion that changes in output levels and utility levels due to price inflexibility are *first* order in the term $P^* - P^0$ while the underlying price-changing costs need only be *second* order in the term $P^* - P^0$. Therefore, price-changing costs that, in the aggregate, may appear trivial in nature may lead to significant deviations of the economy away from the flexible-price equilibrium.

It is also interesting to note a basic asymmetry in the results depending on whether $P^0 \gtrless P^*$. Although relatively small deviations of $P^*$ away from $P^0$ can lead to fixed-price equilibria in which $Y \neq Y^*$, such fixed-price outcomes in which $P^* > P^0$ are unambiguously welfare improving relative to $P^* = P^0$, while outcomes in which $P^* < P^0$ are unambiguously welfare reducing relative to $P^* = P^0$. We therefore see that "inflationary" shocks that increase the equilibrium aggregate price level may, if prices are sticky, result in an improvement in economic conditions. Alternatively, "deflationary" shocks, which reduce the equilibrium aggregate price level, may, if prices are sticky, result in a worsening of economic conditions.

This asymmetry in the effects of changes in $P^*$ relative to $P^0$ square very nicely with several traditional Keynesian intuitions. First, there is the Keynesian notion that downwardly rigid prices are more of a concern than upwardly rigid prices. Alternatively, economists with a more classical perspective might tend to view either type of rigidity as equally troublesome. Second, Keynesian economists typically favor social welfare functions that are monotonically increasing in real output. Alternatively, new classical macroeconomists often view economic expansions as indicative of an underconsumption of leisure.

## Policy Implications of New Keynesian Macroeconomic Models

Results of the previous section could be interpreted as suggestive of a role for an activist monetary policy. If shocks that generate increases in $P^*$ relative to $P^0$ can lead to increases in output relative to $Y^*$ and if such increases in output are welfare enhancing, then it would appear that an inflationary bias in the conduct of monetary policy might be optimal. However, while it is true that the comparative statics effect of an increase in $M$ in the model of this section may be an unambiguous increase in representative household utility, such a comparative statics exercise should be interpreted with great caution.

The model presented above is a highly stylized, static model that attempts to capture some of the properties of economies with small menu costs. However, analysis of alternative monetary regimes properly calls for a fully specified dynamic stochastic model. Unfortunately, the development of such models is still in its infancy. Rotemberg (1987) reviews some attempts at dynamic generalizations of the simple model developed in this section and finds that the case for monetary nonneutralities is much weaker than casual extrapolations from a purely static model might suggest. A higher rate of inflation combined with an unchanging structure of price-changing costs would likely lead to a dynamic equilibrium in which prices are changed more frequently. While such a change in the frequency of price changing may or may not move the economy closer to $Y^*$, it is very unlikely that such a policy change would be capable of generating a permanently higher average level of output.

Furthermore, as pointed out by Ball and Romer (1987), use of monetary policy is probably not the most effective way of trying to push output up to the Pareto-optimal level. Presumably, a policy of output subsidies could be utilized to solve the problem of underproduction inherent in the monopolistically competitive market structure. Ball and Romer also go on to examine the question of the likely efficacy of a monetary policy that attempts to offset fluctuations in output relative to its average level. However, while Ball and Romer find that such policy may be successful, they also find that the gains to such an optimal policy are only of the same order of magnitude as the price-changing costs that are the original source of such output fluctuation. Since most students of this type of analysis concede that such costs are likely to be small, the benefits to such policy activism, even when optimally implemented, are therefore also likely to be somewhat small.

## A Critical Assessment of New Keynesian Macroeconomic Models

Although a very considerable body of theoretical literature has developed that explores the possibility of strengthening the microeconomic foundations of Keynesian macroeconomics, to date there has been considerably less effort put forth in testing these models. As is often the case, a primary problem centers on the design of a test or series of tests that would discriminate between new Keynesian models and their leading competitors.

One particularly troublesome aspect for the empirical verification of these models is that many versions of them are characterized by multiple equilibria. As one example of this problem, consider the model analyzed in this section. While we demonstrated the possibility of the existence of an equilibrium in which no firm changes its price, this equilibrium need not be unique.

The construction of a fixed-price Nash equilibrium proceeded along the following lines. We analyzed the incentives faced by a single firm under the assumption that no other firm changes its price. If, under those circumstances, the firm under consideration also keeps its price constant, then a fixed-price equilibrium must exist. However, it is possible in the same circumstances that it is optimal for one single firm to change its price to $P*$ if all other firms do. In such a circumstance, a flexible-price equilibrium is also a Nash equilibrium. Alternatively, equilibria may exist in which some fraction of firms change their price while the remainder do not. Rotemberg (1987) surveys a growing body of literature on the possibility of multiple equilibria in new Keynesian macroeconomic models.

Unfortunately, when multiple equilibria exist, it is often not possible to determine which of the equilibria the economy will settle upon. Furthermore, it is often not possible to rule out cases in which the economy jumps back and forth from one equilibrium to another. In such circumstances almost anything becomes possible, and it is therefore difficult to enumerate sets of events that would refute the models in question.

Although it has been difficult to marshall very strong evidence in favor of new Keynesian explanations of aggregate macroeconomic events, Ball, Mankiw, and Romer (1988) provide some very clever indirect tests of these models by focusing on a specific set of the models' implications. If price-changing costs are specifically of the menu variety, then the frequency of price changes should rise in equilibrium with the average rate of inflation. At higher inflation rates, specific values of nominal prices become obsolete faster, and menu costs therefore become a less significant deterrent to frequent price changes. One particular implication of this analysis is that while new Keynesian models predict effects of nominal aggregate demand on levels of real output, such effects should diminish in magnitude as, at higher inflation rates, price changing becomes more frequent.

Ball, Mankiw, and Romer design tests that are a slight variant of the tests of new classical macroeconomic models conducted by Lucas (1973). In the original Lucas study, Lucas found that more variable rates of inflation were associated with a weaker effect of inflation rate surprises on the level of aggregate output. Such evidence was consistent with the new classical hypothesis that greater variability in the aggregate price level would lead agents to interpret most individual price changes as reflecting changes in aggregate prices rather than changes in relative prices. Such perceived changes in aggregate prices should not induce changes in the supplies of labor services or goods. Alternatively, the new Keynesian models suggest that it is higher average rates of inflation rather than more variable rates of inflation that should lead to a diminished output response to aggregate demand disturbances. Ball, Mankiw, and Romer are therefore able to exploit these differing hypotheses in the form of a test of the new Keynesian models against the new classical models. Ball, Mankiw, and Romer's results are favorable for the new Keynesian perspective.

However, an unfortunate fact of life for this type of empirical work is the generally very strong correlation between levels of inflation rates and inflation rate variability. Therefore, the results of tests such as those of Ball, Mankiw, and Romer tend to be very sensitive to the particular specification chosen and the particular set of data employed. Furthermore, such tests, while they may be able to discriminate in favor of either the new classical or the new Keynesian approach, unfortunately have very little to say about the merits of new Keynesian models relative to the merits of other alternative models such as real business cycles models.

Most proponents of real business cycle models are convinced by the empirical evidence cited in Chapter 15 that neither anticipated nor unanticipated money has any effect on aggregate output. While it may be possible to construct a new Keynesian model that is consistent with complete monetary neutrality, it is an almost universal characteristic of new Keynesian models that monetary shocks should have a pronounced direct effect on the level of aggregate economic activity. Therefore, studies supporting monetary neutrality would have to be interpreted as evidence against new Keynesian macroeconomic models.

As a reading of the last several chapters would suggest, macroeconomics is currently in a state of flux in which no one viewpoint or modeling strategy appears to have a clear upper hand. However, if there is a unifying theme among the alternative approaches, it would center on the analytical technologies employed. It therefore seems likely that most forthcoming research will continue in the formulation of model economies that are built upon the foundations of maximizing behavior on the part of economic agents. The "conventional" macroeconomic model of the future will therefore likely be the one whose microeconomic foundations and whose predictions about the behavior of aggregate economic variables most closely mimics the behavior of actual economies.

# REFERENCES

Akerlof, George A., "Labor Contracts as a Partial Gift Exchange," *Quarterly Journal of Economics,* November, 1982, 543–569.

Akerlof, George A., and Janet L. Yellen, "A Near-Rational Model of the Business Cycle, With Price and Wage Inertia," *Quarterly Journal of Economics,* Supplement, 1985, 823–838.

Ball, Laurence, and David Romer, "Are Prices Too Sticky?" mimeo, New York University, 1987.

Ball, Laurence, N. Gregory Mankiw, and David Romer, "The New Keynesian Economics and the Output-Inflation Tradeoff," *Brookings Papers on Economic Activity,* vol. 1, 1988, 1–65.

Blanchard, Olivier, J., "Empirical Structural Evidence on Wages, Prices, and Employment in the United States," *American Economic Review,* in press.

Cecchetti, Stephen, "The Frequency of Price Adjustments: A Study of the Newsstand Price of Magazines," *Journal of Econometrics,* April, 1986, 255–274.

Katz, Lawrence F., "Efficiency Wage Theories: A Partial Evaluation," *NBER Macroeconomics Annual,* 1986, 235–276.

Leibenstein, Harvey, "The Theory of Underdevelopment in Densely Populated Backward Areas," in Harvey Leibenstein, ed., *Economic Backwardness and Economic Growth,* New York, Wiley, 1957.

Lucas, Robert E., Jr., ''Some International Evidence on Output-Inflation Tradeoffs,'' *American Economic Review,* June, 1973, 226–234.

Rotemberg, Julio J., ''Sticky Prices in the United States,'' *Journal of Political Economy,* December, 1982, 1187–1211.

Rotemberg, Julio J., ''The New Keynesian Microfoundations,'' *NBER Macroeconomics Annual,* 1987, 69–104.

Salop, Steven C., ''A Model of the Natural Rate of Unemployment,'' *American Economic Review,* March, 1979, 117–125.

Shapiro, Carl, and Joseph E. Stiglitz, ''Equilibrium Employment as a Worker Discipline Device,'' *American Economic Review,* June, 1984, 433–444.

Weiss, Andrew, ''Job Queues and Layoffs in Labor Markets with Flexible Wages,'' *Journal of Political Economy,* June, 1980, 526–538.

Yellen, Janet L., ''Efficiency Wage Models of Unemployment,'' *American Economic Review,* May, 1984, 200–205.

# Index

ISBN 0-06-044324-3

90000

9 780060 443245